A

# Genealogical Memoir

OF THE

# LO-LATHROP FAMILY

.IN THIS COUNTRY,

## EMBRACING THE DESCENDANTS,

AS FAR AS KNOWN,

OF

The Rev. JOHN LOTHROPP, OF SCITUATE AND BARNSTABLE, MASS., AND MARK LOTHROP, OF SALEM AND BRIDGEWATER, MASS.

AND

THE FIRST GENERATION OF DESCENDANTS OF OTHER NAMES.

BY THE

REV. E. B. HUNTINGTON, A.M.

MRS. JULIA M. HUNTINGTON,
RIDGEFIELD, CONN.
1884.

The Collegiate Church of St. Martin—Lowthorpe Parish.

# NOTE.

The Rev. Mr. Huntington's Genealogy of the Lothrop-Lathrop Family was substantially ready for the press in 1872–1873, the materials having been collected long before. The panic of 1873 and his untimely death in 1877 caused delays in the publication. The manuscript needed revision, there were corrections and additions to be made. Had the author lived, it is hardly possible there should have been no mistakes in such a work, and with him passed away all knowledge of many of the references and authorities which he used, and some of the errors were thus placed beyond correction.

In August, 1883, a friend, though overladen with business cares, kindly offered to see the work through the press, but without being able to give it any thorough editorial revision. Much new material has been added, a voluminous correspondence has been entered into, many corrections, made necessary by an illegible manuscript and other causes, have been made, and the publication has thus been unavoidably delayed until now.

Many acknowledgments should be made for kindly aid given by those who were interested in the work. To name them all would be impossible, to omit any would be invidious, and only the general thanks of a grateful heart can now be tendered.

RIDGEFIELD, CONN.,                     JULIA M. HUNTINGTON.
    JULY 15, 1884.

# ENGRAVINGS.

# I.

## THE ENGLISH LOWTHROPS.

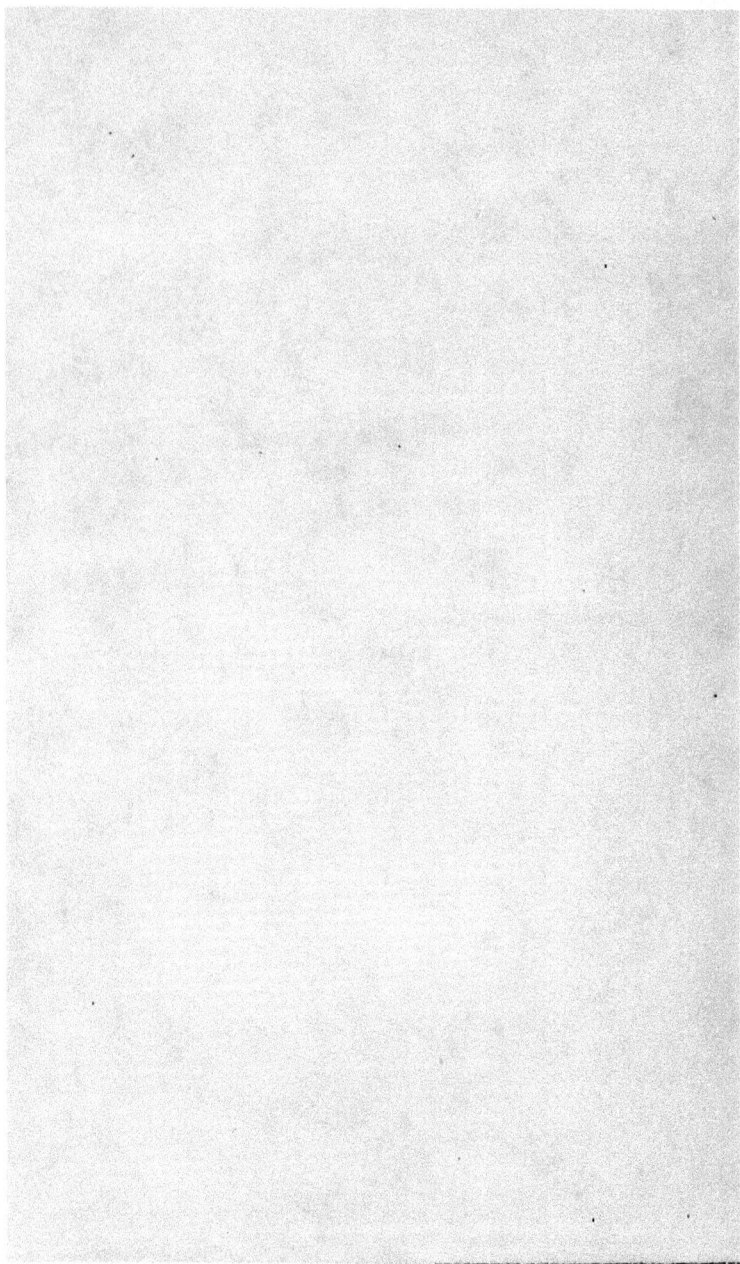

# LOWTHORPE.

LOWTHORPE is a small parish in the wapentake of Dickering, in the East Riding of York, four and a half miles northeast from Great Driffield, having about 150 inhabitants. It is a perpetual curacy in the archdeaconry of York. This parish gave name to the family of Lowthrop, Lothrop, or Lathrop. The church, which was dedicated to St. Martin, and had for one of its chaplains, in the reign of Richard the Second, Robert de Louthorp, is now partly ruinated, the tower and chancel being almost entirely overgrown with ivy. It was a collegiate church from 1333, and from the st) f its architecture, must have been built about the time of Edward III.

There has been no institution to it since 1579. The church consists of a nave, chancel, and tower at the west end; the latter is finished with brick and clumsy pinnacles. It was formerly a very ha.dsome structure, the windows being lofty, of three lights, with trefoil heads, and three quarterfoils in the sweep of the arch. The portion of the church now used for divine service is the nave, the chancel having been desecrated for a considerable period. In this part of the church are two large ash trees and some curious monuments, one of which is a brass tablet rendered illegible through the weather. Affixed .o the north side of the nave is the following historical tablet in bad repair:

"The collegiate church of Lowthorpe was an ancient rectory, dedicated to St. Martin.

"A.D. 1333 it was endowed by Sir John de Haslerton, who founded in it six perpetual chantries.

"A.D. 1364, Sir Thomas de Haslerton added another chantry for the souls of himself and Alice, his wife. He endowed the church with the manor of Lawthorpe and the mansion house.

"A.D. 1776, the inhabitants of the township of Lowthrope repaired the roof of the church.

"A.D. 1777, the church was paved, and the chancel contracted and painted by Sir William St. Quintin, Bart., lord of the manor and patron of the living, descended from the family of the Haslertons."

Dugdale, in his Monasticon, Vol. VI, Part 3, 1474, gives these additional particulars of its endowment: "Here was a collegiate body or large chantrey, consisting of a Rector, six chaplains, and three clerks, founded in this church in the beginning of the reign of King Edward the Third by Sir John Haserlerton, patron, who got the archbishop to appropriate the parochial tithes for their maintenance."

In 1869 the south side of the chancel was entirely rebuilt, leaving, however, the tower and chancel as they have stood for many generations. The church is a perpetual curacy, and the present Patron is William Thomas, St. Quinton, Esq.

## (1.) LOWTHORPE LOTHROPS.

The following are such notices of the Lowthorpes of this parish and its near vicinity as I could glean during my English search:

1216. WALTER DE LOWTHORPE, elected sheriff for Yorkshire.

1292. WALTER DE LOWTHORPE is summoned to answer to the king, Edward I, for attempting to regulate the "assize of beer" on all of his tenants in Lowthorpe and other places without a license from the king. He stoutly defended himself, insisting upon his unquestioned right "anent custom thro his ancestors without interruption, beyond the memory of man."

1287. ROBERT and RICHARD LOWTHORP, of Whepsted, Thingoe hundred, Suffolk, were licensed May 6th, 16th Edward I (1287) by the crown at the gate of St. Edmunds to give to the Abbot in Mortmain eighty-seven acres of land, five acres of meadow and twelve acres of wood, in Whepsted, for the support of certain chaplains celebrating daily in the Chapel of St. John. The above lands they had purchased of Peter de Bradfeld and his wife Agnes, and of William Mitchell.                          *Gage's Suffolk*, p. 397.

1317. ROBERT DE LOUTHORP is presented by the Abbey of St. Edmunds to the rectorship of Horningsheath.                          *Ibid.*, 523.

1392. At the death of ROBERT LOWTHROP an inquisition was held regarding certain tenements in Beverley which he had given to the Church of St. John in that town, the revenues from which were to be appropriated for masses by the chaplains there, for the repose of his soul.

1450. ROBERT LOWTHORPE, of Bridlington, receives 20s., by will, from William Sywardley, Esq., of Sywardley, April 9, 1450.   *Surtees Soc., Vol. 2.*

1474. Aug. 3, ROBERT LOWTHORP, of Bridlington, makes his will, which was proved at York on the 3d of the following November. He gives his landed estate to his relatives at Lowthorpe and Cherry Burton. The will gives us the name of his wife, Catherine ———, who was also his executrix. This will is printed as illustrating the position and character of the man, and as no children are named, as suggesting that he left no other family than his wife. This is also noteworthy as being the earliest will now preserved in the registry at York of any person of the name Lowthorp.

It is written in the abbreviated Latin peculiar to that period. The following is the translation:

"In the name of God, Amen, the third day of the month of August, fourteen hundred and seventy-four. I Robert Lowthorpe, of Bridlington, being of sound mind and memory make my testament in this manner.

"In the first place, I give my soul to God Omnipotent, and to the blessed Mary, and to all his saints, and my body to be buried in the church of the blessed Mary of Bridlington.

"Also, I give my best animal for my mortuary.

"Also, I give to the light of St. John of Bridlington one silver gilt zone with eighty pearls and ten silver gilt pendants, after the death of Catherine my wife.

"Also, I give to every Priest present at my funeral on the first, sixpence, and on the seventh day, fourpence.

" Also, I give to every Chaplain present the first and the seventh day, twelve-pence.

" Also, I give for wax to be placed about my body, the first day and the seventh, four pounds.

" Also, I give to the fabric of the church of St. Peter of New York, twelve-pence.

" Also, I give to the fabric of St. Mary of Bridlington, three shillings and fourpence.

" Also, I give to the parish altar of Bridlington one burde cloth (gold tissue), and one towell and twill.

" Also, I give to the high altar of Lowthorp one burde cloth and one towell and twill.

" Also, I give to the guild of the Holy Trinity of Bridlington three and four-pence.

" Also, I give to the guild of St. Mary of Bridlington, twenty pence.

" Also, I give to the Friars' Preachers of Kingston-upon-Hull, twenty pence.

" I give the residue of all my goods not above bequeathed, to Catherine, my wife, whom I make my executrix, to order and dispose thereof to the health of my soul, as may seem best to her.

" In witness whereof, I have placed my seal, these being witnesses: Anthony Kirby, Parish Chaplain; John Chapman, Richard Glover, Chaplain; William Hedon, John Brigham, John Somerby, William Edwards, John Sutton, and others.

" The present testament was proved the third day of the month of November, in the year of our Lord aforesaid, and administration, committed to Katherine, widow and executrix in the same will."

In addition to the foregoing records of the English Lowthrops, by the kind-ness of Col. J. L. Chester of London, who has been so successful in his anti-quarian researches for so many years among the English church and civil records, I am able to supply the following list. These records may be of future use in completing the genealogy of that branch of the English Lothrops from which the American family of the name is derived.

From Col. Chester's Oxford Matriculations the following two records are taken.

LATHORPPE, CHRISTOPHER. June 19, 1607, at Baliol College, his father being a plebeian, and he 16 years of age.

LOWTHORPPE, JOHN, Oct. 15. 1602, at Christ Church College, his father being a plebeian of York, and he 16 years of age.

It is probably the second of these two matriculations, which led to the mis-take so often repeated in print, regarding the graduation of Rev. John, the American pioneer, from Christ Church College, Oxford. The following are from Col. Chester's parish register notes, and the several parishes are succes-sively indicated.

### MUMSBY, Lincolnshire.

LATHROP, ROBERT. son of Robert and Mary, baptized Oct. 7, 1655.

LATHROP, GERVICE, son of Robert and Mary, baptized Nov. 9, 1664

LATHROP, MARY, wife of Mr. Robert, buried Feb. 20, 1685.

LATHROP, ROBERT, Gent., buried Nov. 19, 1688.

### LONDON.

LATHROPE, MRS., of Swan's Yard, buried in St. Leonard's, Shoreditch, Sept. 16, 1665.

### MARTON, Lincolnshire.

LATHROP, MR. ROBERT, buried Sept. 12, 1670.

### CHELSEA, London.

LATHROP, MR. ROBERT, buried in the church Sept. 14, 1719.

HALSTEAD, MARY HENRIETTA, grandchild of Mr. Lowthorp, buried Apr. 2, 1721,

LOWTHORP, REV. MR. JOHN, buried in the church Sept. 5, 1724.

LOWTHORP, FRANCIS, Gent., buried Jan. 29. 1726-7.

LOWTHORP, MRS. ELIZABETH, buried Aug. 15, 1739.

LOWTHORP, MRS. MARY, buried Dec. 1, 1739.

LATHORPE, SAMUEL, chirurgeon of the ship Swanne, makes his will Sept. 22, 1636. The will is found in Book Lee, of the London Will Office, page 95, and furnishes the following list of legatees:

MARGERY LATHORPE, his mother, at Bardnay, Lincolnshire.

SUSANNAH LATHORPE, his sister, at Bardnay.

ALICE LATHORPE, sister, at Bardnay.

Francis, son of Thomas Morley of Jathnell, Lincolnshire, and three other of the oldest children of Thomas Morley.

The poor of the parish of Bardnay.

Elizabeth Johnson, his sister-in-law.

Katherine Harryson, his sister-in-law.

Margaret, daughter of Elizabeth Johnson.

Mrs. Jeremy Sambroke of St. Stephens. Coleman's street, London.

Thomas Clark, his friend, and his wife Elizabeth.

John Prowd, comdr. and John Wilson, purser, of ship Swanne.

THOMAS LATHROPE, his brother, of Yorks, merchant, to be his residuary legatee.

From Bigland's Gloucestershire, the following records are taken:

LATHROPP, RICHARD, Gent., died Sept. 19, 1741, aged 39 years, in the parish of Clifton, in the hundred of Barton Regis.

LATHROPP, HANNAH, wife of the above Richard, died Jan. 4, 1789, aged 72.

LATHROPP, ROBERT, their son, died young.

From Nichols' Leicester, p. 145:

LOWTHROP, JOHN, M.A., F.R.S., rector at Franland Hundred, Coston Church in 1686, at the Revolution, being a non-conformist he vacated his office.

LOWTHROP, JOHN, is reported in Nichols' Leicester, p. 420, as of St. John's College, Cambridge, and as degraded from the ministry in 1690, for his letters to the bishop of Sarum. He afterwards became librarian to the duke of Chandos. The same record reports his death at "Canons," the duke's seat, Sept. 2, 1724, and his burial Sept. 5th, in Chelsea. (See Chester's list, above.)

Manning & Bray's Surrey, Vol. 1, 144:

John Lowthorpe, instituted Vicar of Woking, Aug. 31, 1411.

The following names are found on subsidy rolls for the places and dates reported:

Lowthrope, Robert of Hornsay, 1558.

Lowthroppe, John of Hessell Co., Kingston-upon-Hull, 1579.

Lowthropp, Roger of Kingston-upon-Hull, 1579.

The following marriage is reported in Burke's History of the Commoners, Edition of 1836:

Lathrop, Robert, Gent., of Shrewsbury, married Susannah, daughter of Richard Scott and Susanna Gardner. This Richard Scott was born in 1648 and married in 1670.

## (II.) ROBERT LOWTHORP OF LOWTHORPE.

1. Robert, whose wife was Isabell ——. He resided at the time of his death at his manorial seat of Pockthorpe, in the parish of Nafferton, Dickering wapentake, East Riding of York. His will, dated Sept. 4, 1538, was proved Nov. 9, 1539. An inquisition, post-mortem, was held Nov. 6, 1539, to determine what lands he held of the crown, and in the returns it is stated that he died Aug. 12, 1539, possessed of lands in Lowthorpe and adjoining villages, and that Christopher Lowthorpe was his son and heir, then aged eight years and more.

2. Christopher, born about 1530, and married Elizabeth ——. His residence was in Lowthorp, where his will was made July 23, 1569. The will was proved June 17, 1570. In it he makes bequests to his eldest son Marmaduke of his mansion house with two closes thereto belonging, and one-half an oxgang of land, and to his younger son Christopher, one oxgang of land in Lowthorpe. His wife, Elizabeth, was to improve the mansion house, three closes, and one and a half oxgangs of land, until the sons should come of age. The will also provided that Christopher should give to his sister Elizabeth five marks out of "wools-croft" when she is of age. It also gives to John Brearwood, his brother-in-law, lands and tenements in Scarborough.

3. Isabell.

## 2. CHRISTOPHER.

4. Marmaduke, who married Margary ——. He was buried, March 13, 1609-10. His will had been made on the seventh of the same month, and proved on the tenth of the following October. In his will he names his wife Margery, his sons Christopher, Robert, and Francis, and his daughters Elizabeth, Alice, and Margaret, all of them being minors.

5. Christopher, baptized May 27, 1561.

6. Robert, baptized March 25, 1565, and buried Aug. 3, 1568.

7. Elizabeth, who is named in her father's will, was baptized May 11, 1568.

### 4. MARMADUKE.

8. ELIZABETH, baptized Feb. 28, 1593-4.

9. ANNE, baptized Oct. 22, 1595, and buried Jan. 12, 1602-3.

10. MARMADUKE, baptized Oct. 3, 1597.

11. ALICE, baptized Jan. 26, 1600-1.

12. FRANCIS, baptized May 20, 1603, and married Bridget ——. He was chosen church warden in the parish in 1627, and buried Oct. 1, 1633, leaving an only daughter.

13. CHRISTOPHER, baptized May 26, 1605, and married Anne ——. His residence was at Fortin, North Riding of York, where his will bears date Aug. 22, 1655, and was proved in 1661.

14. MARGARET, baptized Sept. 2, 1607.

15. ROBERT, baptized Nov. 19, 1609, and married, July 18, 1637, Margaret, daughter of Richard Foxe, curate of Lowthorpe. He was buried Aug. 26, 1648.

### 12. FRANCIS.

16. MARGARET, baptized Oct. 28, 1632.

### 13. CHRISTOPHER.

17. MARMADUKE.

18. JOHN.

19. CHRISTOPHER.

20. ELIZABETH.

21. ALICE.

### 15. ROBERT.

22. CHRISTOPHER, baptized Nov. 11, 1638.

23. ANNE, baptized Sept. 26, 1641.

24. DOROTHY, baptized April 23, 1643.

25. BRIDGET, baptized Oct. 12, 1645.

26. ROBERT, baptized June 4, 1648.

According to Mr. Somerby's testimony, the above record furnishes the last entry of the Lowthropp name in the parish register of Lowthorpe.

### (III.) STAFFORDSHIRE LATHROPPS.

MICHAEL LAYTHORPE, of Staffordshire, was from the Lowthorp family of Lowthorp, and was settled in Staffordshire early in the sixteenth century. He had died before 1560. His pedigree is preserved in three Harleian MSS., No. 1,173, No. 1,439, and No. 6,104. The first MSS. reports the visitation made in 1583, by Robert Glover, Somerset Heralds Marshal, to William Flower; the second reports the visitation in 1614, by Richard St. George, Esq.; and the third the visitation of 1663, reviewed in 1664 by William Dugdale. From these sources and from the will office in London, the following pedigree has been compiled:

### MICHAEL LATHROPP.

2. JOHN LATHROPP, his son and heir, married Alice, daughter of Robert Lilly of Torksey, Lincoln County. He is reported as living in Torksey "in ye Priory neere Lincoln."

3. THOMAS LATHROPP de Bramshall, of Leighe (Lee), Staffordshire, married Mary, daughter of Robert Salte, of Yoxall and of Ganch, his wife, daughter of John St. Andrew, of Gotham County, of Nottingham. The will of this Thomas is dated at Leighe, als Lee, May 21, 1614. In it he first provides that his body is to be buried in the church of Leighe. He makes a bequest to his wife Mary, conditioned by her marrying; to Ralphe, his third son, a minor; to Nicholas, his eldest son; to Humphrey, his second son; to his sister, Jane Whitcomb; to his brother, Robert Lowthroppe; to his cousin, George Henshowe; to his godsons, Henry Hill and Nicholas Wright; to Parnel Sherret, mayd; to two children of Catherine Shipton; to Mr. Edward Holbeighe, Lincolnshire; to Alice Swanns, late Alice Miluehouse, "in receipt of my part of X trees which my cosen Salte had of Lawrence Miluehouse"; to poor people of Roxall; to John Jackson and to Francis Rate, the last two to distribute his gift to the poor of Roxall.

4. ROBERT.

### 3. THOMAS. Lee.

5. NICHOLAS, born in 1582, and married.

6. HUMPHREY.

7. RALPH.

8. JANE, who married Francis Whitcomb of Berwick, in the County of Salop.

### 5. NICHOLAS.

9. SAMUEL, who was living in 1664. His wife's name is not given in the pedigree.

### 9. SAMUEL.

10. ELIZABETH.

11. JANE.

12. MARY.

The MSS., 6,104, which gives the latest generations of this family, supplies the following blazon for the Arms: Quarterly, g sa. An eagle displayed. Ar. crest a cornish chough proper.

### MICHAEL OF STAFFORDSHIRE.

From three different manuscripts the following three pedigrees were copied. I print the three with all the variations and contradictions, showing some of the difficulties attending the construction of family pedigrees, even with the aid of a College of Heraldry.

Our first MSS., No. 1173, page 105, contains the report of the visitation of Staffordshire, 1583, "maid by Robart Glover als (alias) Somersett Herauld Marshall to Will^{s} Flower, als Norroy King at Armes, Anno Dom. 1583." A later hand had added to the same report whatever bears later date than 1583, and had affixed "—1614" to the former date.

2

```
                    Michell    —
                    Lathorpe.
              ┌─────────┴──────────┐
          John Lathrope of — Alise da. of
          Torkesey in Comd.   Robert of Torkesley.
          Lincolne.
          ┌─────────┴─────────┐
       Thomas Lathrope — Mary da. of
       of Leigh in Comd.   Robert of porall
       Stafford.            & South.
   ┌──────────┬────────────┼───────────────────┐
Nicholas    Humphrey     Raffe.      Jane uxor ffrancis
Lathrope    21                       Whitecombe of Bar-
34 years                             wicke in Comd. Stafford.
old 1614.
```

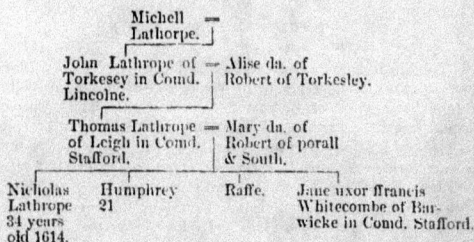

The pedigree of Michael Lathropp, Staffordshire, a branch of the family of Lowthorpe of Lowthorpe, Yorkshire, collated from the following Harleian MSS. in the British Museum:

    I.  The MSS. No. 1173—Visitation of 1583, by Robert Glover, Somerset Herald's Marshall to Wm. Flower.

    II.  The MSS. No. 1439—Visitation of 1614, by Richard St. George, Esq., Norroy.

    III.  The MSS. No. 6104—Visitation of 1663, reviewed 1664, by William Dugdale.

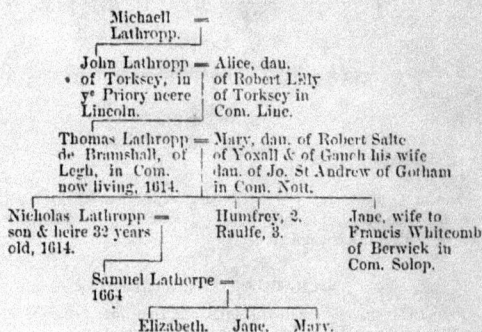

```
                    Michaell    —
                    Lathropp.
              ┌─────────┴──────────┐
          John Lathropp — Alice, dau.
        • of Torksey, in   of Robert Lilly
          yᵉ Priory neere   of Torksey in
          Lincoln.          Com. Linc.
          ┌─────────┴─────────┐
       Thomas Lathropp — Mary, dau. of Robert Salte
       de Bramshall, of   of Yoxall & of Gauch his wife
       Legh, in Com.      dau. of Jo. St Andrew of Gotham
       now living, 1614.  in Com. Nott.
   ┌──────────────┬────────────────┬──────────────────┐
Nicholas Lathropp —     Humfrey, 2.        Jane, wife to
son & heire 32 years    Raulfe, 3.         Francis Whitcomb
old, 1614.                                 of Berwick in
   │                                       Com. Solop.
Samuel Lathorpe —
1664
   ┌──────────┬─────────┐
Elizabeth.  Jane.    Mary.
```

Quarterly.  g  sa. an eagle displayed ar.
crest a cornish chough proper.

The same pedigree is thus reported in Harleian MSS. No. 1439, visitation of 1614, "made by Richard St. George, Esq. als Norroy Knight at Arms in Anno Domini 1614":

Michaell =
Lathropp.

John Lathropp = Alice, dau.
of Torksey in | of Robert Lilly
Com. Linc. | of Torksey in
Com. Linc.

Thomas Lathropp = Mary, dau. of Robert Salte
of Legh in Com. | of Yoxall, & of Ganch his wife
Staff, now living | dau. of Jo. St Andrew of Gotham
1614. | in Com. Nott.

Nicholas Lathropp,      Humfrey, 2.      Jane, wife to
sonne & heir 32 yrs     Raulfe, 3.       Francis Whitcomb
old, 1614.                               of Berewick in Com.
                                         Solop.

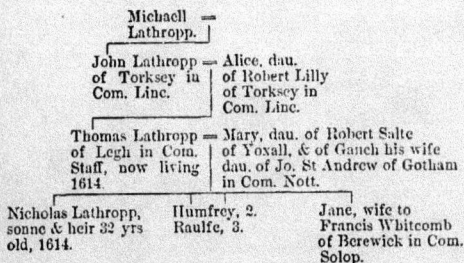

In the visitation of Staffordshire, in 1663, by Wm. Dugdale, which was reviewed in 1664, we have reported in Harl. MSS. 6104 the same pedigree again, but beginning one, and ending two generations later.

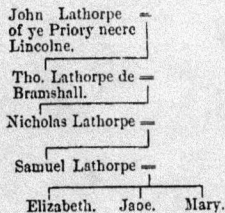

John Lathorpe =
of ye Priory neere
Lincolne.

Tho. Lathorpe de =
Bramshall.

Nicholas Lathorpe =

Samuel Lathorpe =

Elizabeth.      Jaoe.      Mary.

Quarterly. g sa. an eagle displayed ar.
crest a cornish chough proper.

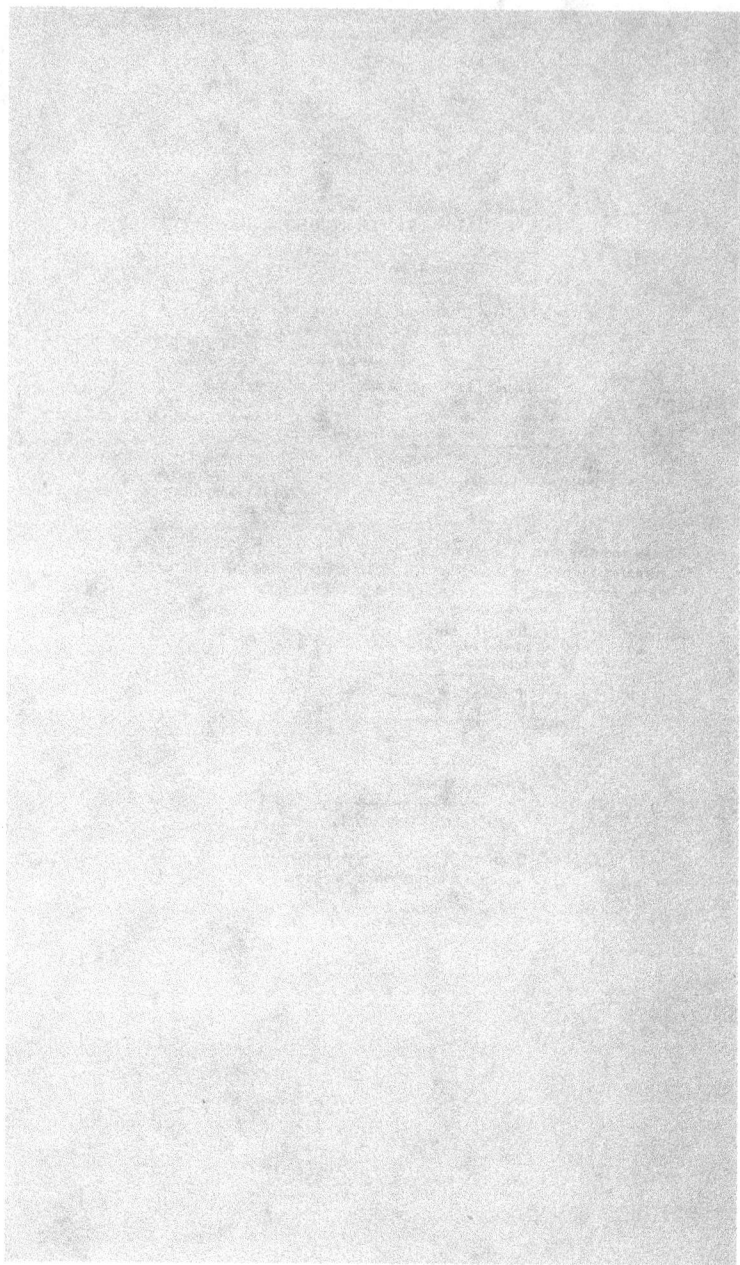

## II.

## JOHN LOWTHROPPE OF LOWTHORPE.

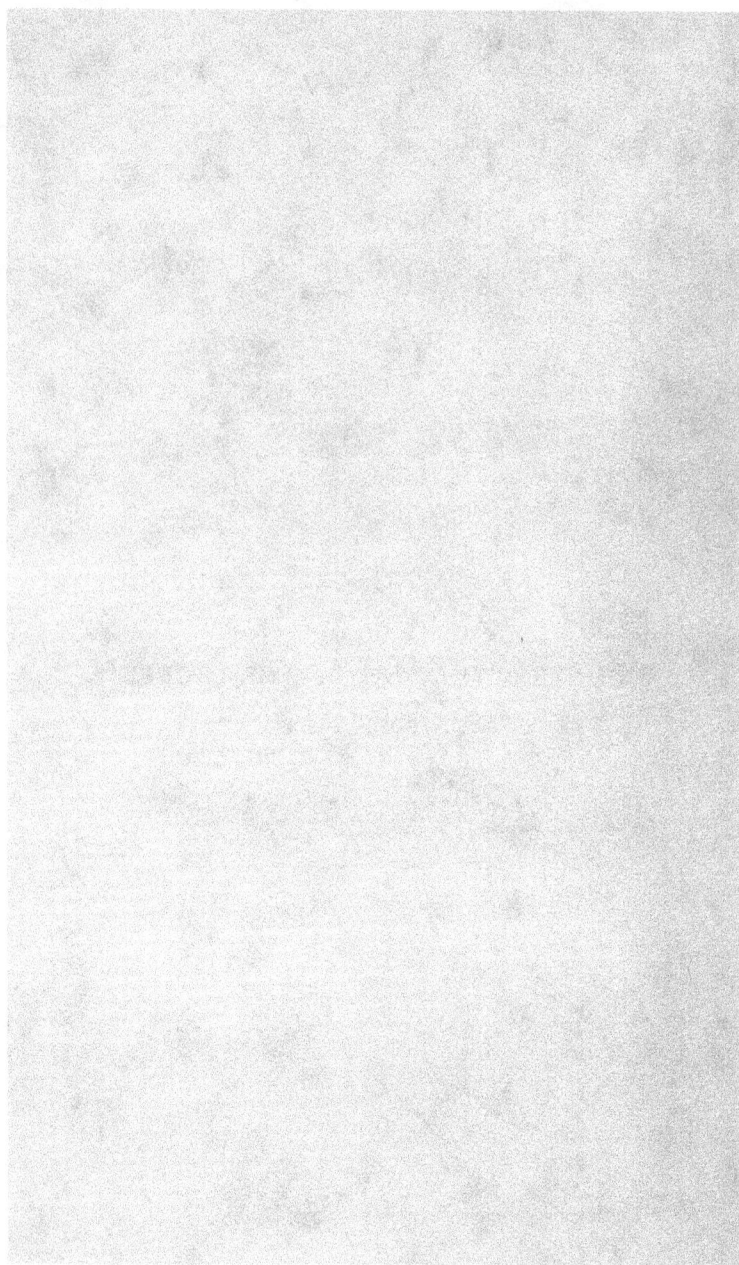

## JOHN LOWTHROPPE OF LOWTHORPE.

Our pedigree of that branch of the old Lowthorpe family which had its earliest known English seat in Lowthorpe, wapentake of Dickering, East Riding of Yorkshire, must begin in JOHN LOWTHROPPE, gr.-grandfather, to Rev. John Lothropp, the American pioneer. Early in the sixteenth century he was living in Cherry Burton, a parish about four miles from Lowthorpe. He was, though belonging to a junior branch of the family, a gentleman of quite extensive landed estates both in Cherry Burton and in various other parts of the county. In the 37th year of Henry VIII (1545), he appears on a Yorkshire subsidy roll, assessed twice as much as any other inhabitant of the parish. Of his parentage and of the names of his brothers and sisters, if he had any, we shall probably be unable to find the record, the early parish registers having disappeared. No record of baptisms before 1597, none of burials before 1561, and none of marriages before 1562, now remain.

This John Lowthroppe left the son ROBERT whose record we are able to give, and also three daughters whose families are mentioned, though their own names are not designated in the will of the son. Whether there were still other children we may never be able to learn.

### 1. JOHN. Cherry Burton.

2. ROBERT succeeded to the estates of his father in Cherry Burton, and during his lifetime made considerable additions to them. He had married Ellen ———, who survived him fourteen years, and at her death left a will, which supplies for us the names of some of her descendants which, but for this will, might not have reached us. The names preserved to us in this will are the eldest son Thomas, and his children Robert, Elizabeth, and Isabell, and Robert's wife, Alice Clarke; her son Lawrence, and his wife Elizabeth and their children, Edward and Agnes; her daughter Margaret, the wife of Robert Hodgeson, and her own sister Margaret. Her sons were the executors of her will.

Mr. Robert Lothrope died in 1558. His will, bearing date, North Burton (Sheributon), July 16, 1558, was proved at York, Oct. 20, 1558, and makes the following bequests. It will be seen that the later will of his widow, as reported above, confirms the list of his children as given in the will below. This will is thus fully reported as best setting before us the condition and social position of this representative of the Lothrop family more than three centuries ago.

### 2. WILL OF ROBERT LOWTHROPPE OF CHERRY BURTON.

1. To ye blessed sacrament of ye altar for forgotten tythes, v s.
   To poor people at his burial, 4 marks, by executors.

3. To ye church of "Sheriburton," 6s. 8d.

4. To son JOHN all lands and tenements in So. Dalton and all freehold lands and titles; the lands in Burton purchased of Richard Feole and Marmaduke Whytinge; and in default of issue from him, the reversion of the foregoing to be unto son Lawrence and his heirs.

5. To son THOMAS all lands and their appurtenances in Walkinton.

6. To daughter Margaret a messuage in Beverlaie, in the Tenore of Christopher More. If she fail of issue this also to go to son Lawrence.

7. To wife ELLEN, during widowhood, and then to son Thomas all leases and terms of years of his two "fermolds" in Burton and Rainthorpe. If she should marry or die the leases to remain in Thomas and his executors and heirs. The said Ellen and Thomas are to succor "with meat and drink and house room" in said "fermold" in Burton all the rest of the children to their several marriages.

8. To daughter Margaret, 40 marks.

9. To son JOHN, a gray stoned horse.

10. To son Thomas, an ambling gelding, dapple gray.

11. To son Lawrence, a bright bay gelding.

12. To daughter Margaret, a branded fleet cow, in consideration of one I sold which my father gave to her. Also a lead, a table, two chairs, two trestles and a forme with a great                with eaves, two basings, two lavers, two candlesticks, twelve pieces of pewther, and "ye best (beast), yt came from Beverlaie."

13. To "everie of my godchildren, 4d."

14. To "everie of my sister's children, 8d."

15. To my three sisters, everie of them, 6s. 8d.

16. To John Swinburne, John Pickering, William Fisher, Robert Barnes, Gawin and Hewe Mason—my servants, every of them, halfe a quarter of barlye (two bushels).

17. To Catherine Shadlock, maid servant, half a quarter of barley and a bushel of wheat.

18. Elizabeth Thornton and Isabell Coke, maid servants, either of them a mett (two bushels) of barley.

19. To ye township of So. Burton, 6s. 8d.

20. To children of William Burne, every of them, 8d.

21. To William and John, sons of Henry Sowersby, 7d. each.

22. To Alison Simson and Henry Bynks, 4d.

23. To Robert Binks, 4d.

24. To every of my three sons a bound waine and gear.

25. To Richard Eshton, a quarter of barley.

26. To Robert Hoyeson, Robert Wilson, William Burne, Robert Patenson, and John Patenson, 20d.

27. To Thomas Jervis, 6s. 8d.

28. To Mr. John Eglesfield, Esq., supervisor of this will, 20s.

29. To son Thomas, two draughts nante—a hawked and browne—and fourtie (40) weathers such as he will choose.

30. To son John, a cow "such as daughter Margaret will appoint," and a couple "stotes goying at Harswell such as he choose."

31. To son Lawrence, two stotes.

32. To daughter Margaret, two whies goying at Harswell.

33. "To yᵉ Prests," 20d.

34. To yᵉ Clerk, 12d.

35. To William Burne, "my buckskin doublet."

36. To Robert Johnson, "my vilett jacket."

37. To Simon Naves, "my second best vilett jacket."

38. To son Thomas, a "jack" (coat of mail), "bill" (battle ax), steel cap, and pair of splents.

39. To wife Ellen, son John, son Thomas, son Lawrence, and daughter Margaret, the rest of the estate, and all of them are appointed executors.

## ROBERT. Cherry Burton.

3. THOMAS, born in Cherry Burton and married (1) Elizabeth (widow) Clark, who was buried in Etton., July 29, 1574. He married (2) Mary, who was buried in Etton, Jan. 6, 1588; and (3) Jane, who after his death became the wife of —— Coppendale.

He removed to Etton, Harthill wapentake, East Riding, Yorkshire, about 1576, and here he died in 1606, having made his will Oct. 5, 1606, which was proved in the following January. The several legacies specified in this will are printed in full. It will be noticed that neither of the sons who were educated is named in the will.

### WILL OF THOMAS OF CHERRY BURTON.

1. Jaine, my wieff, lease for 12 yr. for ed. of my younge children whom I give unto her with these legacies.

2. Richard my soone, if he die, then to my sonne Mark, and if he be not of age XXI, my sonne to be a tutor unto him.

3. Jane my wieff and Lawrence my sonne, lease of Westwood, leas in territories of Scarbrough.

4. Robart—three kye gatts in Etton.

5. Markes, Lawrence, Joseph, and Bartholomew—moiety of lease of Etton pke or Calfe pke.

6. Bartholomew, pte Freehold lande called temple wood.

7. Robart—best horse.

8. Isabel Burne, my daught', one cowe.

9. Katherine Aket, my daught', one cowe.

10. Wm. Wykam, Thos. Wykam, and Jayne Wykam, children to my daughter Andrie Wykam, one cowe among them.

11. Robert—my best, bound wayne.

12. Robert, all my freehold land in So. Dalton and Walkinton.

13. Jane, Anne, Isabell, and Elizabeth Akeit, daughters of Wm. Akeit, my son-in-lawe each of them, one ewe.

14. Poore of Etton, vjˢ—viijᵈ.

15. The rest to Jane, my wief, Richard, Lawrence, Marks, Joseph, Bartholo-

3

mew, my sons, and Margaret, Luce, and Jane Lowthorp, my daughters whom I make executors.

Witness.  Thos. Cardener, Alexander Lyon, Henry Fenby.

Proved, Jan. 13, 1606-07.

4.  JOHN, whose lands in South Dalton on his decease, having no children, came to his elder brother Thomas.

5.  LAWRENCE.  The will of his mother (1572) makes bequests to his wife Elizabeth and to his two children, Edward and Agnes.

6.  MARGARET, who according to her mother's will (1572) was the wife of Robert Hodgeson.  The will also gives the names of three of her daughters—Elline, Jane, and Elizabeth.

## 3.  THOMAS.          Etton, Yorkshire.

7.  ROBERT, born in Cherry Burton, married, Jan. 27, 1607-8, Ann Pattison. He received from his father's will both lands and tenements in South Dalton and Walkington, the first in the wapentake of Harthill, and the second in that of Howdenshire, both in the East Riding of Yorkshire.

8.  CATHERINE, married June 12, 1607, William Akett, of Leckonfield, Harthill wapentake, East Riding of Yorkshire, who is named in the will of her brother Thomas, then rector of Dengie, Essex.  In her father's will her children are named: Jane, Anne, Isabell, and Elizabeth Akeit.

9.  AWDREY, who is reputed in her father's will as the wife of a Wickham. Her children are named in the will as: William, Thomas, and Jayne, and the family name is spelled Wykam.

10.  ELIZABETH, married, Feb. 19, 1587-8, Thomas Rowood.

11.  ANNE, baptized at Etton, Feb. 13, 1568-9, and died young.

12.  ISABELL, baptized at Etton, July 3, 1570.

13.  MARTIN, baptized at Etton, Oct. 21, 1572, and buried, Nov. 12, 1572.

14.  ANDREW, baptized at Etton, April 23, 1574.

### 2d Wife's.

15.  ANNE, baptized at Etton, July 29, 1576.

16.  MARY, who is named in her brother Thomas' will, Oct. 20, 1628, as the wife of John Gallant.

17.  THOMAS, baptized in Etton, Oct. 14, 1582, and was admitted to Queen's College, Cambridge, under George Mountaine as his tutor, June 30, 1601, and took his Bachelor's degree in 1604.  He married Elizabeth ———, and in his will, which bears date Oct. 20, 1628, and which was proved in Consistory Court, London, May 6, 1629, he names as legatees his wife Elizabeth, and makes the following bequests: to eldest daughter Anne, when she shall come of age; to second daughter Jane, his Wilkes estate, Tillingham, Essex Co.; to his third daughter Elizabeth, lands in Allhorne, Essex Co.; to his youngest daughter Mary, the Yates gap land and Meale Field, Southminster, Essex; to his brothers John and William; to William Akett, of Leckenfield, his brother-in-law; to his sister Mary, wife of John Gallant, and to several servants.

18. JOHN, baptized in Etton, Dec. 20, 1584, and became the pioneer and founder of the LOTHROP-LATHROP family in America. His record and that of his descendants immediately follow this record of the English Lowthrops.

19. WILLIAM, baptized May 24, 1587, and is named in his brother Thomas' will, Oct. 20, 1628.

### 3d Wife's.

20. MARGARET, baptized in Etton, Feb. 13, 1590–1.

21. ISABELL, baptized in Etton, Sept. 29, 1592.

22. LUCY, baptized in Etton, Jan. 4, 1593–4, and married, June 16, 1613, Ralph Cawnsby.

23. RICHARD, baptized in Etton, Oct. 12, 1595, and married Dorothy Lowdon. He settled in Cherry Burton, where his will was made Feb. 8, 1640–1, and where his wife died in 1613. He left two sons, Thomas of Cherry Burton, and Richard of North Cave, near Cherry Burton, who died unmarried in 1659; and a Mary, a posthumous daughter. In his will, dated Feb. 8, 1640–1, and proved June, 1641, he remembers the poor of Cherry Burton, of Bishops Burton, of Etton, and of Leconfield; the Church of Cherry Burton; his eldest son Thomas, when of age; his unborn child, if it reaches majority; his wife Dorothy; his mother, Jane Coppendale; his younger son Richard, his brother Joseph, and his son Thomas; his brother Bartholomew; his sister Mary Garwood and her daughter Elizabeth, and to John, son of William Lowthrop.

The will of Dorothy Lowthrop, widow of this Richard, dated May 15, 1641, and proved May 9, 1645, names as legatees, son Thomas, son Richard, daughter Mary, mother Jane Brown, mother Jane Coppendale or dayk, brothers, sister Lowson, brother Lawrence Lowthrop and his children, and his brother Bartholomew Lowthrop.

24. MARK, baptized in Etton, Sept. 27, 1597. Mr. Somerby in his work prepared for Mr. Motley, before mentioned, says of this Mark: "He was among the settlers of West Bridgewater in Massachusetts, where he died about the year 1686. His children were Elizabeth, Mark, Samuel, and Edward," etc.

It would have greatly simplified my record of the American Lo-Lathrops if I had not soon found another record for this Mark. His will was brought to light in London just in season to save the perpetuation of the error in our American record.

Before his death he had removed to North Cave, near Cherry Burton, in Harthill wapentake, Hunsley Beacon, Yorkshire, when he probably had never married. His will bears date, North Cave, January, 1659–60, and was admitted to probate in London April 17, 1660. He names as his only legatees, his brother Bartholomew, brother William, Margaret Bateman, sister Lucy, and sister Jane. He also made his brother Bartholomew his executor and residuary legatee.

Of course the above will disproves of the supposition which for years misled my search, that this Mark Lothrop was the pioneer who settled in Bridgewater, Mass., and whose descendants I have not been able to connect with the family of the Rev. John.

25. LAWRENCE, baptized in Etton, Aug. 29, 1599, and is mentioned in the will of his nephew Richard, 1659, as the father of three children. He was, in 1641, one of the witnesses to his brother Richard's will.

26. JANE, baptized in Etton, March 14, 1600-1.

27. JOSEPH, baptized in Etton, Dec. 31, 1602. He and his son Thomas are mentioned in the will of his nephew Richard.

28. BARTHOLOMEW, baptized in Etton, March 1, 1604-5, and named in the wills of his brother Richard, 1641, and nephew Richard, 1659.

Of the places named in these wills and pedigrees, all are very near to Lowthorpe, Bridlington, and Napperton being in the same wapentake; Cherry Burton, North Cave, So. Dalton, and Etton in Harthill wapentake, Walkinton in Howdenshire wapentake.

III.

REV. JOHN – THE PIONEER.

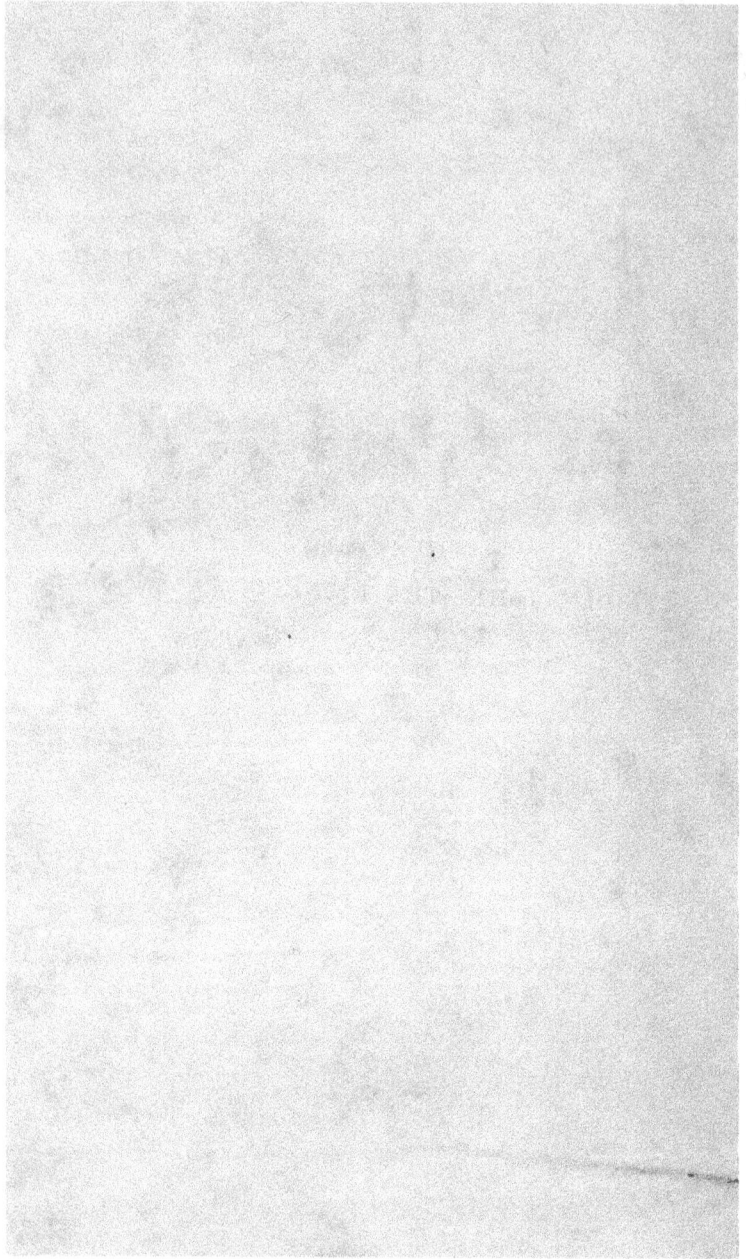

## REV. JOHN, THE PIONEER.

JOHN LOTHROPP, for this is the form in which he wrote his name, deserves, in this work, a much more complete biography than our sources of information will furnish. Of printed materials towards such a biography, we have but very few, and these very meager. Neal's "History of the Puritans"; Gov. Winthrop's "Journal"; Morton's "New England Memorial"; a "Biographical Sketch" written by Rev. John Lathrop, D.D., of Boston, for his kinsman of the Lathrop blood, Rev. Abiel Holmes, D.D., of Charlestown; and that brief but just sketch in Dr. Sprague's "Annals of the American Pulpit," and Mr. Otis' quite exhaustive collections printed in the Yarmouth paper, will exhaust the list. A few gleanings from English records, before his inmigration to America, and a few from American records after that date, must complete the story as we are now able to tell it.

Baptized, as our English record shows, in Etton, Yorkshire, Dec. 20. 1584, he was educated, not in Oxford as Dr. Lathrop's sketch supposes, but in Queen's College, Cambridge, where he was matriculated in 1601, graduated B.A. in 1605, and M.A. in 1609.

Authentic records next locate him in Egerton, 48 miles southeast from London, in the Lower Half hundred of Calehill, Lathe of Scray, County of Kent, as curate of the parish church there. To this living he was admitted about 1611 by the Dean and Chapter of St. Paul. Our baptismal records, already given, show that he was there in the fall of 1614, and last report his family there in the fall of 1619. It was probably his first and only parish charge as a minister of the English Church. That he was an acceptable minister we have no reason to doubt. The church in which he officiated was an ancient structure, standing on the summit of a rounded hill, and could be seen from a great distance. The site was very beautiful; the church itself, dedicated to St. James, consisted of two aisles and a chancel. At the west end rose its square tower with a beacon turret, altogether constituting a feature which gives a charm to so many a pleasant English landscape.

Here Mr. Lothropp labored faithfully as long as his judgment could approve the ritual and government of the Church. But when he could no longer do this, we find him conscientiously renouncing his orders and asserting the right of still fulfilling a ministry to which his heart and his conscience had called him.

Accordingly, in 1623 his decision is made. He bids adieu to the church of his youth, and with no misgivings, now in the fullness of his early manhood, subscribes with a firm hand to the doctrines, and espouses with a courageous heart the cause of the Independents. Henceforth his lot is with conventicle men in his mother land, and with the exiled founders of a great nation in a new world. We will not stop to justify his renunciation, nor his espousal.

the story we are to tell fails of doing this, any other proof we could summon would equally fail.

The date of his leaving Egerton is 1623, and the next year he is called to succeed the Rev. Henry Jacob, an independent minister who, having been for eight years the pastor of the First Independent Church in London, resigned his place to remove to Virginia. This church, at that date, was situated on Union St., Southwark, and from the burial lot attached to it, was still later known as the Deadman's Place. Not a vestige now remains above ground to show the locality. One single stone, still buried, or which certainly was lying buried July 20, 1872, when I visited the spot, beneath the rubbish and earth in the rear yard of —— Barclay & Perkins great brewery will yet testify for that old house. At that date the congregation of dissenters to which he ministered had no place of public worship, their worship itself being illegal. Only such as could meet the obloquy and risk the danger of worshiping God in violation of human statute, were likely to be found in that secret gathering. Yet in goodly numbers, in such places in Southwark as they could stealthily occupy, they held together and were comforted and instructed by the minister of their choice. For not less than eight years they so worshiped. No threats of vengeance deterred, and no vigilance of officious ministers of the violated law detected them. More watchful grew the minions of Laud. Keen-scented Church hounds traversed all the narrow ways of the city whose most secret nooks could by any possibility admit even a small company of the outlaws. One of the wiliest of these pursuivants of the bishop, Tomlinson by name, tracked Mr. Lothropp and his followers to their retreat. They had met for worship as had been their wont, little thinking that it would be their last gathering with their beloved minister. How far they had gone in their service we shall probably never know. What words of cheer they had spoken or heard we may not repeat. Their private sanctuary, a room in the house of Mr. Humphrey Barnet, a brewer's clerk in Black Friars, is suddenly invaded. Tomlinson and his ruffian band, with a show of power above their resistance, sieze forty-two of their number, allowing only eighteen of them to escape, and make that 22d day of April, 1632, forever memorable to those suffering Christians, by handing them over in fetters to the executioners of a law which was made for godly men to break. In the old Clink prison, in Newgate, and in the Gatehouse, all made for felons, these men, "of whom the world was not worthy," lingered for months. In the spring of 1634, all but Mr. Lothropp were released on bail. He, their leader, the chief offender, was deemed too dangerous to be set at liberty. Like the gifted Hooker, it was felt that his words and his example had "already more impeached the peace of our Church," than the church could bear. "His genius will still haunte all the pulpits in ye country, when any of his scolers may be admitted to preach."

And so his prison doors swung to again and seemed to leave him no hope of release or escape.

During these months a fatal sickness was preying upon his wife, and bringing her fast toward her end. The "New England's Memorial," by Nathaniel Morton, published in 1669, and then near enough the date of the incidents given, to be a credible witness, gives us these touching incidents of that imprisonment: "His wife fell sick, of which sickness she died. He procured liberty of the bishop to visit his wife before her death, and commended her to God by prayer, who soon gave up the ghost. At his return to prison, his poor children, being many, repaired to the bishop at Lambeth, and made known unto him their miserable condition, by reason of their good father's being continued in close durance, who commiserated their condition so far as to grant him liberty, who soon after came over into New England."

The State Papers in the New Record Office, Fetter Lane, London, have preserved some of the Star Chamber records of those days during which Mr. Lothropp was thus imprisoned. The following copies from these records will tell their own story:

"June 12, 1634. John Lathrop of Lambeth Marsh. Bond to be certified, and he attached if he appear not on next court day.

"June 19. Bond ordered to be certified and to be attached for non-appearance.

"Oct. 9. John Lathrop and Samuel Eaton, to be attached for non-appearance.

"1634-5, Feb. 19. John Lathrop and Sam. Eaton for contempt in not appearing to answer touching their keeping conventicles, their bonds ordered to be certified and they attached and committed.

"1634, Apr. 24. John Lathrop enlarged on bond to appear in Trinity term, and not to be present at any private conventicles."

This last record was probably the order of the court which opened the way for the escape of Mr. Lathrop to America. At any rate the year had not ended before the following record showed him to be a freeman in a land in which he rejoiced to find

> A Church without a bishop
> And a State without a king.

The record is found on page 71 of Gov. Winthrop's Journal, under date of Sept. 18, 1634:

"The Griffin and another ship now arriving with about 200 passengers. Mr. Lathrop and Mr. Sims, two godly ministers coming in the same ship."

The next page of the journal has this item, which shows how tender the conscience of Mr. Lothropp was on a question of Christian propriety.

"Mr. Lathrop had been pastor of a private congregation in London, and for the same, kept long time in prison, upon refusal of the oath, ex-officio, being in Boston upon a sacrament day, after the sermon, desired leave of the congregation to be present at the administration, but said that he durst not desire to partake in it, because he was not then in order, being dismissed from his former congregation, and he thought it not fit to be suddenly admitted into any other, for example sake, and because of the deceitfulness of man's heart."

On reaching Boston with that portion of his London flock who had accompanied him, he found already the preparations begun to welcome him to a new home in Scituate. At least nine pioneers had built their houses in that new settlement, and to it, with such of his people as were ready to accompany him, he repaired Sept. 27, 1634. Sometime near the end of September he makes

4

an entry in the private journal to preserve the names of those pioneers who had so prepared the way before him. Their names, Hatherly, Cudworth, Gillson, Anniball, Rowiyes, Turner, Cobbes, Hewes, and Foster, show them to have been mainly London and Kent men; and would suggest that they had known of Mr. Lothropp's previous career and had called him to come among them as their minister. A letter, written in December by one of them, James Cudworth, to the Rev. Dr. John Stoughton, of St. Mary's Church, Alderman-bury, London, confirms this supposition. In referring to the unsettled plantations near Boston, of which he names three, Duxbury, Scituate, and Bear Cove, he then speaks of the second:

"Oures, Cittewate, to whom the Lord has bine verey gracious, & his p'vidence has bine Admoralely sene oure beyenge to bringe vs oure Pastor, whome wee so longe expected—M' Lathorpe, who the Lord has brought to vs in safety, whome wee finde to bee a holy, Reuerat & heuenly minded man."

This shows that in some sort the new home and field of ministerial labor had been already prepared for Mr. Lothroppe at Scituate. Of his cordial welcome to it, we have this pleasant testimony from the pen of Mr. Otis.

"The kindly reception which was extended to him, and the cordial welcomes with which he was greeted, were most gratifying to his feelings, and he resolved that Scituate should be his future home—the fold into which he would gather together the estrays of his scattered flocks. His grateful heart believed that the hand of God had opened this door for him,—had at last given him a resting-place from his toils. Here, protected by law, he could build up church institutions, and here he and his family could dwell together in peace, surrounded by the loving friends of his youth. Willing hands quickly built a house for his family, of "meane" proportions, and of "meaner" architecture, yet it was a shelter from the storm—a place that he could call his own—a blessing from 'Him who had not where to lay His head.'"

Of the house which is thus characterized as of "meane proportions," Mr. Otis gives this description:

"The walls were made of poles filled between with stones and clay, the roof thatched, the chimney to the mantel of rough stone, and above of cob-work, the windows of oiled paper, and the floors of hand-sawed planks."

The following record, preserved for us in the handwriting of the Scituate pioneer, is perhaps the only record extant regarding his call and settlement in the ministry at Scituate:

"Jann: 19, 1634, att my house, uppon w'h day I was chosen Pastour and invested into office."

Whatever the service of investiture may have been, there can hardly be room for doubt that it was as simple and unpretending as the times and the people calling for it compelled. Previously to this date the services had been held in Mr. James Cudworth's house; and afterwards, for some time, we find the congregation worshiping in private dwellings.

But of the beginning of his work in Scituate we have fortunately a record preserved in the copy made by the Rev. Dr. Stiles, President of Yale College in 1769, from the original in the handwriting of Mr. Lothropp himself. The following extract from this copy, which was printed in the Historical and Genealogical Register for July, 1855, is worthy of preservation in this sketch:

" Touching the congregation (& church) of Christ collected att Scituate. The 28 of September, 1634, being the Lord's day, I came to Scituate the night before & on the Lord's day spent my first Labours, Forenoon & Afternoon.

" Upon the 23 of Novemb. 1634 o' Breathren of Situate that were members at Plimouth were dismissed from their membershipp, in case they joyned in a body att Situate.

" Upon January 8, 1634 (O. S.) Wee had a day of humilation & and then att night joyned in covenaɴ ᵗ togeather. So many of us as had beene in Cove‑nuunt before."

Then follow the names of eight brethren and the wives of four of them, and the eleventh, "myselfe," shows that this pioneer minister at Scituate counted himself as one of the infant church, which he was called to serve.

That Mr. Lathrop was still a widower at this date is probable from the man‑ner in which his own record is made. But that he soon married again is shown by the records of his church, made by himself in 1635. Record No. 25 gives us this knowledge: "My wife and Brother Foxwell's wife joyned having their dismission from elsewhere, June 14, 1635." Who this second wife was we shall not probably be able ᵗ ʾcarn, save that her Christian name was Anna. That she was the mother of all of his children born in this coun‑try is doubtless true. Mr. Otis supposes her to have been the daughter of William Hammond of Watertown, and says that she was a widow. He also gives the date of her marriage Feb. 17, 1687‑8, which, as Mr. Lathrop had been dead over thirty years, could not have been. He also says that she died Feb. 25, 1687‑8. which is possible.

The settlement at Scituate was increased by a large addition in the summer of 1635, mainly by a new immigration from Kent. The worship of the people had thus far been held in the house of Mr. Cudworth. On Monday, Jan. 29, 1635, a meeting was held in Mr. Lothropp's house, a meeting for humiliation and prayer. In that private dwelling, by the votes of the brethren assembled, Mr. Lothropp was formally chosen the minister of the place, and by the laying on of their hands he was, as he fully believed, in true Apostolic manner once more inducted into the pastoral office.

Down to Nov. 11, 1638, Mr. Lothropp had entered on this record sixty‑two names, and among them from his own family circle the following:

No. 36 and 37. Isaac Robinson & My Sonn Fuller joyned having their Letters dismissive from the church at Plimouth unto us Novemb. 7, 1636.

No. 51. My Sonn Thomas Lothropp joyned May 4, 1637.

No. 60 & 61. My Brother Robert Linnell & his wife having a letter of dis‑mission from the church in London joyned to us, Septemb. 16, 1638.

The records made by Mr. Lothropp, from which we have now copied, are a good witness to us of what we shall have occasion to note hereafter, his unusually methodical and efficient business habits. They have been deemed of such importance as to have been copied not less than five times, at least all of them which survived the wear of that first century of change. Taken to

Connecticut by the Rev. Elijah Lothrop of Gilead, No. 295, and falling into
the hands of the Rev. Dr. Ezra Stiles of Yale College, in 1769, he made a
copy of them, which are now among his manuscript papers in Yale Library.
The Rev. Mr. Carleton, of Barnstable, copied Dr. Stiles's copy, and from this
copy, collated with another, made by the Rev. Jonathan Russell, Mr. Otis
prepared the copy of the "Scituate and Barnstable Church Records," which
was printed in Vols. IX and X of the New England Historical and Genealogical Register.

On his consenting to settle in Scituate, the court granted him a farm, which
their committee laid out, according to Mr. Deane, on the southeast side of
Coleman's hill. It was "nigh the first Herring brook when it approaches
nearest to the Sand hills; bounded by Josiah Chickett's land west, by John
Hewes' land & the high way south, & by Humphrey Turner's east." He was
also assigned shares in the New Harbor Marshes between his house and the
North river.

Though welcomed to this field by some who must have known him in England, and who probably had been his parishioners there, we learn from Mr.
Deane that his ministry in Scituate "was not prosecuted with great success
or in much peace." The principal reason assigned for his early removal to
Barnstable has been the difference between himself and some of his people on
the question of baptism. While this or some other cause of alienation in the
church is most apparent in the records which he left, another ground of dis-
satisfaction at Scituate, is the only one formally named in the letters which
follow, and which are here introduced for the two-fold purpose of explaining
the removal which so soon followed the settlement, and also to preserve the
only authentic document from his pen—excepting the church records—now
known to the author to exist. That copies of his "Queries respecting Baptism" were printed in London, a few years after his removal to Barnstable, we
know from "Hamburg's Independents," in which he refers to them. Yet
probably no copy of the issue can now be recovered; certainly none is indexed
among the Lothrop collections in the British Museum, and no antiquary of
whom I enquired in England had ever seen it.

The letters which now follow were found among Mr. Winslow's papers, and
were published in the first volume, second series of the Massachusetts Historical
Collections:

*"Situate, February* 18, 1638.

*"To the right worthy and much-reverenced, Mr. Prince, governor—Grace, mercy
and peace be forever multiplied.*

"Sundry circumstances of importance concurring towards the present state
of myself and the people in covenant with me, presse me yett againe to sett
pen to paper, to the end that the busyness in hand might with greater expedition be pressed forward, if it may be: not willing to leave any lawful means
unattempted, that we are able to judge, to be the means of God, that soe we
might have the more comfort to rest in the issue that God himselfe shall give
in the use of his own means. Yett I would be loth to be too much pressing
herein, least the more haste on our part should occasion the less speed, or

overspurring, when by reason of abundance of freeness, there needs none at all, I should dishearten, and so procure some unwillingness. But considering your godly wisdome in discerning our condition and presuming of your love unfeigned to us-ward, which cannot but effect a readiness on your part, in passing by and covering of our infirmitye, I am much emboldened, with all due reverence and respect, both to your place and person, to re-salute you.

"The truth is, many greviances attend mee, from the which I would be freed, or att least have them mitigated, if the Lord see it good. Yett would I raither with patience leave them, than to grieve or sadd any heart, whose heart ought not to be grieved by me, much lesse yours; whom I honour and regard with my soule, as I do that worthy instrument of God's honour, together with your-selfe, Mr. Bradford, because I am confident you make the advanceing of God's honour your chiefest ho ur. And the raither I would not bee any meanes to grieve you, inasmuch as I conceive you want not meanes otherwise of grief enough. But that I be not too tedious, and consequently too grievous. The principal occasion of my present writing is this: Your worthy selfe, together with the rest joyned and assisting in government with you, much reverenced and esteemed of us, having gratiously and freely uppon our earnest and humble suites, granted and conferred a place for the transplanting of us, to the end God might have the more glorye and wee more comfort: both which wee have solidd grounds to induce us to believe, will be effected: For the which free and most loveing grant, we both are and ever remain to bee, by the grace of the highest, abundantly thankeful. Now here lyes the stone that some of the breathren here stumble att; which happely is but imaginarye, and not reall, and then there will be no need of remoreall. And that is this, some of them have certaine jelousies and fears, that there is some privie underminceing and secrett plotting by some there, with some here, to hinder the seasonable successe of the work in hand, to witt of our removeall, by procuring a procrastination, in some kinde of project, to have the tyme deferred, that the convenienceye of the tyme of removeing beeing wore out before we can have free and cleare passage to remove, that soe wee might not remove att all. But what some one particular happely with you, with some amongst us here, may attempt in this kinde for private and personal ends, I neither know, nor care, nor fear, foras-much as I am fully perswaded that your endeared selfe, and Mr. Bradford, with the rest in general, to whom power in this behalfe belongeth, are sincerelye and firmelye for us, to expeditt and compleate the busyness as soon as may be, so that our travells and paines, our costs and charge, shall not be lost and in vaine herein, nor our hopes frustrated. Now the trueth is, I have been the more willing to endite and present these few lines, pa tly to wipe away any rumour that might bee any wayes raised upp of distrustfullness on our partes, especially, to clear my own innocenceye of having any suspition herein; as alsoe to signifye since the place hath been granted and confirmed unto us; some of the breathren have sold their houses and lands here, and have put themselves out of all. And others have put out their improved grounds to the half increase thereof, upon their undoubted expectation forthwith as it were to begin to build and plant in the new plantation. Wherein if they should be disappointed, it would be a means to cast them into some great extremitye.

Wherefore lett me intreate and beseech you in the bowells of the Lord, without any offence, both in this respect, as also for other reasons of greater importance, which I will forbear to specifye; To do this further great curtesey for us, to make composition with the Indians for the place, and priviledges thereof in our behalfe, with that speed you cann; and wee will freely give satisfaction to them, and strive to bee the more enlarged in thankefulnesse to you. I verily thinke wee shall never have any rest in our spiritts, to rest or stay here; and I suppose you thinke little  *  *  *  *  otherwise, and am therefore the more confident that you will not neglect any opportunitye, that might make for our expedition herein. I and some of the breathren have intreated our brother John Coake, who is with you, and of you, a member of your congregation, to bee the best furtherance in such occasions, as either doe or may concerne us, as possibly hee may or cann, who hath alsoe promised unto us his best service herein. Thus wishing and praying for your greatest prosperitye every wayes, I humbly take my leave.

"Remaining to be at your command and service in the Lord.

"JOHN LOTHROPP.

"From *Scituate*, *Feb.* 18, 1638.                          [Superscribed thus.]

"*To the right worthy and much-honored Governor Prince, att his home in Plimouth.*

"*Give these I pray.*"

### SECOND LETTER.

"*To the right worthy and much-honoured Mr. Prince, our endearoured governor of Plymouth,—Grace, mercy, and peace be multiplyed.*

· My dear and pretious,

"Esteemed with the highest esteeme and respect, above every other particular in these territoryes; being now in the roome of God, and by him that is the God of gods, deputed as a god on earth unto us, in respect of princely function and calling. Unto whom wee ingeniously confesse all condigne and humble service from us to bee most due. And if we knowe our hearts, you have our hearts, and our best wishes for you. As Peter said in another case, doe wee in this particular say, it is good for us to be heere: (wee mean under this septer and government) under which wee can bee best content to live and dye. And if it bee possible we would have nothing for to separate us from you, unless it be death. Our souls (I speak in regard of many of us) are firmaly lincked unto your worthy self, and unto many, the Lord's worthyes with you. Wee shall ever account your advancement ours. And I hope through grace, both by prayer and practice, wee shall endeavour to our best abilitye, to advance both the throne of our civill dignitye, and the kingly throne of Christ, in the severall administrations thereof in the midst of you. Hereunto (the truth is) we can have no primer obligation, than the straite and stronge tyes of the gospell. 'If we had no more, this would alwayes bee enough to binde us close in discharge of all willing and faithful duetye both unto you and likewise unto all the Lord's annointed ones with you. But seeing over and above, out of your gratious dispositions (through the grace and mercy of the Highest) you are pleased to sett your faces of favour more towards us, (though a poor and contemptable people) than towards any other particular people whatsoever, that is a people distinct from yourselves. As wee have had good and cleare experience hereof before, and that from tyme to tyme; soe wee now againe in the renewed commiseration towards us, as most affectionate nurseing fathers, being exceeding willing and readye to gratifye us, even to our best content, in the point of removall: Wee being incapacitated thereunto, and that in divers weighty considerations, some, if not all of which, are well known bothe to yourselfe, and to others with you. Now your love being to us transcendent, passing the love you have shewn to any without you, wee can soe much the more, as indebted unto our good God in praises, soe unto yourselves in services. We will ever sett downe in humble thankfullness in the perpetual memory of your exceeding kindnesse. Now we stand stedfast in our resolution to remove our tents and pitch elsewhere, if wee cann see Jehovah going before us. And in very deed, in our removeing, wee would have our principal ende, God's own glorye, our Sion's better peace and prosperitye, and the sweet and happie regiment of the Prince of our salvation more jointly imbraced, and more fully exalted. And if externall comfortable conveniences as an overplus, shall bee cast in, according to the free promi.. of the Lord, wee trust then, as wee shall receive more complete comfort from him, soe he shall receive more complete honour by us: for which purpose we humbly crave, as the fervencye of your devotions, soe the constancye of your wonted christian endeavours. And being fully perswaded of your best assistance herein, as well in the one as in the other, wee will labour to wait at the throne of grace, expecting that issue that the Lord shall deeme best.

"In the intrim, with abundance of humble and unfeigned thankes on every hand on our parts remembered, wee take our leave, remaining, obliged forever unto you, in all duety and service.

"JOHN LOTHROPP.

"From *Scituate*, the 28 of this 7th mouth, [*September*] 1638."

N. B. Three names are subscribed beneath the name of Mr. Lothropp, which are not perfectly legible: the first appears to be *Anthony Aniball;* the second, —— Cobb; the third, —— Robinson; to which are added the words, "In behalf of the church." [Superscribed thus:]

"*To the right worthy and much-reverenced Mr. Prince, Governor at Plimouth.*"

Leaving the foregoing letters to explain as they may the reasons for a removal, we find the following statement of Mr. Otis as to its date: "Mr. Lothropp and the large company arrived in Barnstable, Oct. 11, 1639, O. S., bringing with them the crops which they had raised in Scituate. Pressed as they must have been with the preparations needed for wintering comfortably in their new home, they did not forget that the main object of their pilgrimage from the mother land, was the service and glory of God. With no house of worship yet built, they meet and worship in the rude pioneer house of one of their number," poor Mr. Hull. Ten days after their arrival they gave a whole day to fasting, humiliation, and prayer, whose object was "For the grace of God to settle us here in church estate and to unite us together in holy walking, and make us faithful in keeping covenant with God and one another."

Eleven days later, on the eleventh of December, they set apart another day for religious worship, this time for the worship of thanksgiving. "The day was very cold, and after the close of the public service they divided into three companies to feast together, some at Mr. Hull's, some at Mr. Mayo's, and some at brother Lumberd, Senior's."

What sort of thanksgiving service they had under the lead of Mr. Lothropp, appears from the records of the Scituate church, in reporting the first Thanksgiving in the new town, Dec. 22, 1636, the record covering not only the religious offering of the public service, but also the festive and social offerings in their several homes, afterward. It is here quoted as setting before us, clearly, a practical estimate of the pioneer minister and his people:

"Beginning some half an hour before nine, and continued until after twelve o'clocke, ye day being very cold, beginning with a short prayer, then a psalm sung, then more large in prayer, after that another psalm, and the WORD taught, after that prayer, and then a psalm. Then making merry to the creatures, the poorer sort being invited by the virtue."

On coming to Barnstable, he built, according to Mr. Otis, a small house where Eldridge's hotel now stands. Mr. Palfrey tells us that "Four acres for a house lot had been assigned to Mr. Lothrop, soon after his arrival, on the east side that inclosure which probably had been used for interments from the first settlement." But the first home of the new pastor was both too small and uncomfortable. His second was a more substantial building, and made ready for occupancy about 1644. That it was built of solid and enduring material is well attested in the simple fact that its frame still stands. Mr. Otis thus testifies concerning it: "The house has undergone many transformations, but the original remains. It is now one of the prettiest buildings in the village, and is occupied for a parsonage and a public library."

It was with no ordinary emotions that I called to see that house in which the last years of the worthy pioneer of a large proportion of our Lothrop and Lathrop race in this country had closed his mortal life. Though more than 229 years have passed away since its frame was built, here is still somewhat that left us, as a hint at least of the work and worth of the day of Puritan beginnings here. Its foundation builders were no mere fancy men, were in no sense fast men—they were content by humble, hard toil to work God's best materials into most enduring forms, on which the coming generations could build in all time to come the worthiest monuments of these stout-hearted, truth-loving pioneers.

Mr. Otis, who has written more upon the American life of our pioneer than any other writer, and who being on the ground where he spent the last years of his ministerial life and thoroughly familiar with all the records of the church and town, and perhaps had facilities for forming an estimate of his character and influence which no other man has used to the same extent, has at several points in his weekly articles on "John Lothropp and his descendants," given glimpses of the man which we can do no better than to preserve.

In No. 230 of his articles, he says: "John Lothrop and his followers were held by the people to be martyrs in the cause of Independency. No persecutions, no severity that their enemies could inflict, caused him, or one of his followers to waver. They submitted without a murmur to loss of property, to imprisonment in loathsome jails, and to be separated for two years from their families and friends, rather than subscribe to the forms of worship that Charles and his bigoted prelates endeavored to force on their consciences."

In No. 243, he says of him and his sons: "Mr. Lothrop was as distinguished for his worldly wisdom as for his piety. He was a good business man, and so were all of his sons. Wherever one of the family pitched his tent, that spot soon became a center of business, and land in its vicinity appreciated in value. It is the men that make a place, and to Mr. Lothrop's in early times, Barnstable was more indebted than to any other family."

From No. 231, we take the following: "Whatever exceptions we may take to Mr. Lothrop's theological opinions, all must admit that he was a good and true man, an independent thinker, and a man who held opinions in advance of his times. Even in Massachusetts, a half century has not elapsed since his opinions on religious toleration have been adopted by the legislature."

Mr. Lothrop fearlessly proclaimed in Old and in New England the great truth that man is not responsible to his fellow man in matters of faith and conscience. Differences of opinion he tolerated. During the fourteen years that he was pastor of the Barnstable church, such was his influence over the people that the power of the civil magistrate was not needed to restrain crime. No pastor was ever more beloved by his people, none ever had a greater influence for good. * * * * To become a member of his church, no applicant was compelled to sign a creed or confession of faith. He retained his freedom. He professed his faith in God, and promised that it should be his constant endeavor to keep His commandments, to live a pure life, and to walk in love with the brethren."

Mr. Morton, who "thought meet in his Memorial to nominate some of the Specialest" of the worthy ministers whom God had sent into New England, names as the fourth on his list "Mr. John Laythorp, sometimes preacher of Gods word in Egerton," and elsewhere in the Memorial he testifies to his former fidelity in London, in witnessing against the errors of the times. Still again he says of him: "He was a man of humble and broken heart spirit, lively in dispensation of the Word of God, studious of peace, furnished with godly contentment, willing to spend and be spent for the cause of the church of Christ."

Mr. Lothropp died in Barnstable, Nov. 8, 1653, the last entry on his church records in his own hand having been made June 15, 1653.

A will was made by him which he failed of signing, though it was, without objection, admitted to probate. Letters of administration were however granted March 7, 1653–4 to "Mrs. Laythorpe," and Mr. Thomas Prence was "appointed and requested by the court to take oath unto the estate at home." The following is a memoranda of the will as left by Mr. Lothropp:

"To my wife my new dwelling house. To my oldest son Thomas, the house in which I first lived in Barnstable. To my son John in England, and Benja min here, each a cow and £5. Daughter Jane and Barbara have had their portions already. To the rest of the children, both mine and my wife's, each a cow. To each child one book, to be chosen according to their ages. The rest of my library to be sold to any honest man who can tell how to use it, and the proceeds to be divided," etc.

The inventory estimates the rest of the Library to be worth £5.

SECOND GENERATION.

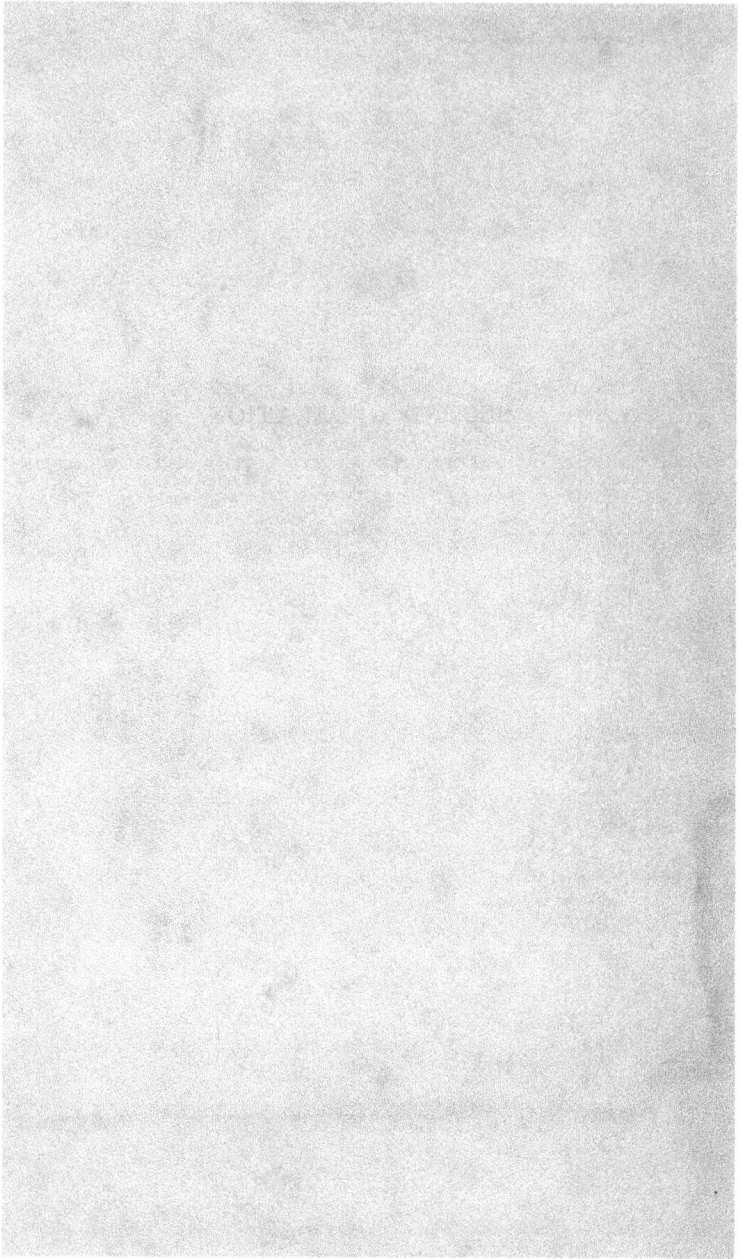

# SECOND GENERATION.

## REV. JOHN.

2. JANE, born in England and baptized in her father's church in Egerton, County of Kent, Sept. 29, 1614. She came with her father to America in 1634, and was married in Scituate, April 8, 1635, "y⁴ 4th day of the weeke," by Capt. Miles Standish, of Plymouth, to Samuel Fuller. This marriage was solemnized at the house of Mr. James Cudworth. Mr. Fuller was a son of Edward Fuller and his wife Ann, who had come over in the Mayflower with his parents, and who, as Savage informs us, "outlived the hardships" of that immigration. Both the father and mother died the first winter, and Samuel was left in the care of his uncle Samuel, who had also come over in the Mayflower, and who proved to be one of the most valuable members of that primitive community, and memorable as the first physician who came to New England to settle. He died Oct. 31, 1683, one of the last survivors of the Mayflower. They had nine children:

Hannah Fuller, who married, Jan. 1, 1658, Nicholas Bonham.

Samuel Fuller, "sonn of my sonn Samuel Fuller," baptized Feb. 11, 1637-8, and married Anna, daughter of Capt. Matthew Fuller.

Elizabeth Fuller, married —— Taylor.

Sarah Fuller, born in Scituate and baptized in Barnstable, Aug. 1, 1641, and died young.

Mary Fuller, born in Barnstable, and baptized June 16, 1644, and married Nov. 18, 1674, Joseph Williams, son of John of Haverhill, who was born April 18, 1647.

Thomas Fuller, born May 18, 1650.

Sarah Fuller, born Dec. 14, 1654, and married —— Crow.

John Fuller.

A child, born Feb. 8, 1658, and died 15 days later, as Savage has it, "one of the latest Mayflowers."

3. ANNE, baptized in Egerton, England, May 12, 1616, and buried April 30, 1617.

4. JOHN, baptized in Egerton, England, Feb. 22, 1617-18. This child probably died before the family came to America; certainly before the birth of the second John in 1644-5.

5. BARBARA, baptized in Egerton, England, Oct. 31, 1619, and married, July 19, 1638, John Emerson. Her father's record of this marriage is: "My sonn Emmersonn & and my daughter Barbarah marryed at Duxberry by Captain Standige."

That they settled at least for a time in Scituate is shown in this record in Mr. Lothropp's own hand: "One Linkes slaine by a bow of a tree in y⁴ cutting down of the tree, March 6, and buryed in the way by John Emmersonn's house near Goodman Stockbridge, March 10, 1637."

Mr. Savage supposes this John Emerson may have been of Ipswich, Massachusetts, and that John, who came over in the ship Abigail, 1635. He is entered on the ship list as a baker, age 20, and as Mr. Coffin supposed, the son also of a John Emerson.

6. THOMAS, born in England, and probably in Egerton, about 1621, as we infer from his own deposition, taken April 4, 1701, in which he states that he is "about 80 years of age." The will of his father designates him as his eldest son, which is proof that the John who was baptized in 1617-18 was not living. The probability is that his birth succeeded the withdrawal of his father from the curacy of the parish church in Egerton, Kent, where the older children were recorded. At least this is certain, that the baptism of his older sister is the last baptism at Egerton found on the copy of the baptisms which the father made.

At the age of about thirteen he came with his father to Scituate, at which place we find this first record regarding him in this country: "My sonn Thomas Lothropp joined May 4, 1637."

This was his admission to the church in Scituate, from which he removed with his father to Barnstable, in 1639, where he soon gained distinction among the pioneers of the new town.

The second record we find is in Barnstable, as follows: "My sonn Thomas and brother Larnett's daughter, widow Ewer, were married in the Bay (Boston) Dec. 11, 1639." The "daughter" above referred to, was Sarah, daughter of William Larned, and widow of Thomas Ewer.

Elizabeth, a daughter of this Sarah Ewer by her former husband, was baptized April 9, 1641, and was married, as we learn from a third record from the same hand as the above, to Thomas Blossom, June 18, 1645, "at my sonn Thomas his house," the Thomas Blossom above having been born in Leyden about 1620.

In 1641 Thomas Lothrop is reported as land surveyor at Barnstable, and in 1643 as one liable to bear arms.

He became quite a large landholder and an enterprising business man. He was enrolled as freeman June 3, 1656. He served the town in several offices, indicating his standing as in honor among his fellow townsmen. His death took place in 1707.

.7. SAMUEL, born in England, and came with his father to Scituate in 1634, thence to Barnstable, where he married, Nov. 28, 1644, Elizabeth Scudder, who had been dismissed from the church in Boston Nov. 10, 1644, to remove her church relation to that in Barnstable. She is reported in Savage as a sister to that John Scudder who was in Barnstable in 1640. He had made the acquaintance of Miss Scudder in Boston, where he commenced his business life as house builder, afterwards combining with this extensive farming operations. Their marriage was recorded by his father on the Barnstable Church Register as follows: "My sonn Samuel & Elizabeth Scudder marryed at my house by Mr. Freeman, Nov. 28, 1644."

They settled in Barnstable, where his house stood next that of John Scudder.

He is reported, in 1643, as one of the five Lothrops at Barnstable liable to bear arms.

In 1648 he removed to New London, Connecticut, then called Pequot. We now find Mr. Lothrop mentioned in two letters from Governor Winthrop to his son John, Jr., at Pequot. In one of these, bearing date Aug. 14, 1648, on the subject of obtaining a minister for the settlement, he writes: "Your neighbour Lothrop came not at me (as I expected) to advise about it," etc.

His house lot in the new plantation was the third in order from that of John Winthrop, Jr., Esq., and his name is one of the first eighteen to whom were assigned lands on the east side of the "great river" of Pequot, and for these the lots were drawn on the 17th and 31st of January, 1648-9.

Almost at once Mr. Lothrop is assigned by his new townsmen to places of responsibility and honor. The General Court of the State, May, 1649, organized a local court at Pequot, having for its judges John Winthrop, Esq., Samuel Lothrop, and Thomas Minor, giving them power to sit in the trial of all causes between the inhabitants in which the differences were under forty shillings.

In 1650 he appears with fifteen other townsmen in town meeting "to arrange a system of co-operation with Mr. Winthrop in establishing a mill to grind corn."

He received a large grant of land, also, on the west side of the Pequot river north of the settlement. It was about five miles up the river at a place called Namussuck. A farm of 260 acres at this place remained in the family until 1735, when it was sold by his grandson Nathaniel, after settling all claims, for 2,300 pounds.

His "cattle marks" were recorded before 1650. When, in 1657, Uncas, routed by the Narragansetts, had been chased into the fort at the head of the Nahantick and was there besieged, Lieut. James Avery, Mr. Brewster, Samuel Lothrop and others, well armed, succeeded in throwing themselves into the fort and aided in the defence.

He sold his town homestead in 1661 to the Rev. Gershom Bulkley. This house stood beyond the bridge over the mill brook, on east side of highway toward Mohegan, "probably where now (1852) stands the Hallam House."

In 1679 is recorded a contract of Mr. Lothrop for building the Second Church in New London.

He removed to Norwich in 1668. Miss Caulkins in history of Norwich says, "after the first thirty-eight proprietors the next inhabitants who came in as grantees of the town are John Elderkin and Samuel Lothrop." A house lot was first granted to John Elderkin, who, finding it too far from his business, had it conveyed to Samuel Lothrop.

Mr. Lothrop appears to have erected a house on the town street before 1670, which from that time became his home. The house built by Dr. Daniel Lathrop, his great-grandson, about 1745, probably stands upon the same site—now Mrs. Gilman's.

The house lot of about seven acres on which he settled, covered mainly that hill side enclosed by the streets and lanes, as now, which lies south of the present residence of Daniel W. Coit, Esq., and extending down to the present

Main street. He added during his life time successive tracts of land amounting to about four hundred acres.

The town records of that time are very imperfect, but we find Samuel Lothrop recorded as "Constable" in 1673 and 1682, and as "Townsman" in 1685—dignified local offices in those days.

After the death of his first wife, of which no record is preserved, he married in 1690, in Plymouth, Mass., a maiden lady, Abigail, the daughter of Deacon John Doane of Plymouth. She was born January 29, 1632, and lived until 1734, Mr. Lothrop having died February 29, 1700. The following notice of the second Mrs. Lothrop is found in Miss Caulkins' history of Norwich: "On her hundreth birthday a large audience assembled at her house, and a sermon was preached by the pastor of the church. At this time she retained in a great degree the intelligence and vivacity of her earlier years. At the time of her decease the descendants of her husband amounted to 365."

Mr. Lathrop left a nuncupative will, proved in 1701.

8. JOSEPH, born in England, probably in Lambeth, London, in 1624. He probably also came over to America with his father in 1634. The first record known to the author regarding him in this country is that of his marriage—the last Lothropp marriage recorded by his father in the registers of the Barnstable church:

"Joseph Lotbropp and Mary Ansell marryed alsoe by him (Brother Thomas Hinckley) Dec. 11, 1650." He settled and lived in Barnstable, where his name on the local records show him to have been an enterprising and honored man. He was a deputy for the town in the general court of the State for fifteen years, and for twenty-one years served as one of the selectmen of the town. On the organization of the county he was appointed the register of the probate court, and recorded in 1606 the first deed put on record in the county. The court had appointed him in 1653 to keep the ordinary of the town. He was admitted freeman, June 8, 1655. In 1664 we find him an acting constable, and in 1667 a receive. of excise. That he was also in the military line is shown in the titles of lieutenant and captain which successively mark his name.

Mr. Freeman, in his history of Cape Cod County, speaks of him as a "conspicuous member of the Council of War in 1676." He also reports Lieut. Joseph Laythorpe and his brother Barnabas Laythorpe as commissioned to hold select courts in Barnstable in 1679; and names both of these brothers among the agents for the settlement of Sippecan.

His standing is still further shown in a letter from Capt. William Basset written from Casco, in September, 1689, to Gov. Thomas Hinckley, reporting his skirmishes with the Eastern Indians. At the close of this report the captain presents his own and his lieutenants service to the Governor, Esq. Lothrop, and Mr. Russill. We know enough of that day to be assured that none but a prominent and public man would be thus complimented.

Mr. Lothrop probably had no collegiate education, yet he must have been a well educated man—probably with a legal education. His will bears date Oct. 9, 1700, and was proved Apr. 9, 1702, between which dates his death, of which no record is preserved, must have occurred.

He names in his will as heirs, his four sons, Samuel, Barnabas, Hope, to whom he left the homestead, and Thomas; and his two daughters, Mary Denes and Elizabeth Fuller.

In the inventory of his estate are reported 27 volumes of law books, and 43 volumes of classics and sermon books, the inventory amounting to £8216. One other item of the inventory—"three negroes,"—shows that it belonged to an age past now beyond recall.

9. BENJAMIN, born in England, and brought over in 1634, to Boston. He married in Barnstable, Martha ——, and settled in Charlestown, Mass., where he was a man of note, holding the office of first selectman in 1683.

Goodwife Martha Lathrop was admitted to the church in Charlestown in the year 1660.

1ST CHILD
SEC. WIFE

10. BARNABAS, "Bernabus, son of John Lothropp," as his father wrote it in the baptismal record, baptized at Scituate, Mass., June 6, 1636, and married (1) Dec. 1, 1658, Susanna Clark, daughter of Thomas and Susanna (Ring) Clarke of Plymouth, granddaughter of the born a Clarke who was the mate of the Mayflower. She died, as her headstone shows, Sept. 28, 1697, aet. 55. (2) Wid. Abigail Dodson, who died Dec. 21, 1715, aet. 72. The church records report that she was "dismissed from the 1st church in Boston, and removed here, Feb. 23, 1706-7." She died, so the church records show, in Boston, Dec. 21, 1715, at 72 years of age. He was also a noted man. He became the first judge of probate in Barnstable on the organization of the court, having his brother Joseph, as clerk. Was Deputy from 1675 to 1682. Judge of Common Pleas 1692, and the same year appointed counsellor with Governor Hinckley, Governor Bradford, and John Walley, to represent New Plymouth at Boston, under the new charter. Died Oct. 26, 1715. On his headstone his title is Esq. The inscriptions on these three stones in the old burying lot near the county jail in Barnstable are as distinct as when first cut. In his will, dated June 8, 1713, and probated Nov. 27, 1715, he names the following legatees, with the relationship indicated: his wife Abigail; his only son Barnabus; his grandson Barnabus, the "only son of my son John, deceased"; grandson John, son of "my son Nathaniel, deceased"; his brother John and two sisters, Abigail Clark and Bathshewa Marsh; his daughter-in-law, Elizabeth Crocker; his grandson, Joseph Lewis, son of Ebenezer Lewis; and "my seven children now remaining; my kinswoman Bethya Hinckley, now dwelling with me, my six daughters, Abigail Sturgis, Susanna Shurtlef, Bathshewa Freeman, Anna Lewis, Sarah Skeffe, and Thankful Hedge; and Bethya Claghorn "who is my daughter-in-law."

11. "A child born in Scituate, July 30, 1638, and died the same day."

12. ABIGAIL, baptized in Barnstable, Nov. 2, 1639, O. S., "the first record since our coming to Barnstable, Oct. 11, 1539." She married Oct. 7, 1657, James, son of Thomas Clark and Susanna, daughter of widow Susanna Ring. They settled in Plymouth, to which place the father had come in the ship Ann, in 1623.

13. BATHSHA, as spelled in the records made by her father, baptized in Barnstable, Feb. 27, 1641, and married Alexander Marsh. She was probably his second wife. They lived in Braintree, Mass., where his will was made Mar. 19, 1697, and he died March 7, 1698. His will calls his wife Bathsheba,

6

whose death, Jan. 8, 1723, age, 82, is certified by her gravestone in the Dorchester burying lot. Their children were:

John Marsh, a minor at the date of his father's will, 1697.

Rachel Marsh.

Phebe Marsh.

Ann Marsh, who became the wife of Samuel French, of Braintree, Mass., and had a family of 8 children: Samuel, born Nov. 17, 1680; Samuel the second, Hannah, Mary, Alexander, Josiah, Nathaniel, and Benjamin.

His widow's will, whose former husband is said to have been John Fuller, bears date Oct. 7, 1738, and is recorded in Book V, p. 362. It was proved Oct. 19, 1738, and names as legatees: son Benjamin; the heirs of son John Fuller, deceased; grandson John Lothrop; daughter Reliance Prince; daughter Bashua Webb, and daughter Phebe Thacher. Executor, son-in-law, Elisha Thacher.

Hannah was the second wife of Dr. John, son of Matthew Fuller, and by him had a daughter Bethia, Dec., 1687; John, born Oct., 1689, and Reliance Sept. 8, 1691. These names will make the names in the will intelligible.

14. JOHN, born in Barnstable, Mass., Feb. 9, 1644, and married Jan. 3, 1671-2, at Plymouth, Mass., Mary, probably daughter of James and Mary (Tilson) Cobb of Scituate, where she was born Dec. 3, 1653. His name on the marriage record is Laythrope, and she is called Mary Colsgain. He married (2) Dec. 9, 1695, Hannah, widow of Dr. John Fuller. He died Sept. (18) 27, 1727, at 11 o'clock A. M., and is recorded as 85 years old, on the Barnstable church records.

On Mr. Otis' authority we know that he was a man of note among the seafaring men of the coast in that early day, sailing as captain in command of his own vessel. On the New Haven, Conn., records is found this evidence of his seamanship.

"These certify I received on board of yᵉ Swan, John Lothrop, Mr., 8 bbls. pork, 28 bush. wheat of Sam'l Hemingway of New Haven, for use of Capt. Elisha Hutchinson of Boston, and doe promis to deliver yᵉ same on paying freight 3s. d. per bbl. and 6d. bush. Apr. 1, 1691.          Jo. LOTHROP."

His will, Book IV, p. 407, dated Mar. 9, 1726-7, and probated Feb. 9, 1727-8, names as his legatees his wife Hannah; son John's son Joseph; the children of his daughter Mary Howland, and those of his daughter Elizabeth Lewis; and his sons, Barnabas and Benjamin. His son Barnabas and his wife Hannah are executors.

15. —— "a man childe of John Lothropp dying immediately after it was borne, buryed Jann. 25, 1649."

John Lothrop, 1672, at Swansey, was admitted an inhabitant of the second rank. If this is the person so admitted, he probably did not remain there long, since his children are all recorded in Barnstable.

THIRD GENERATION.

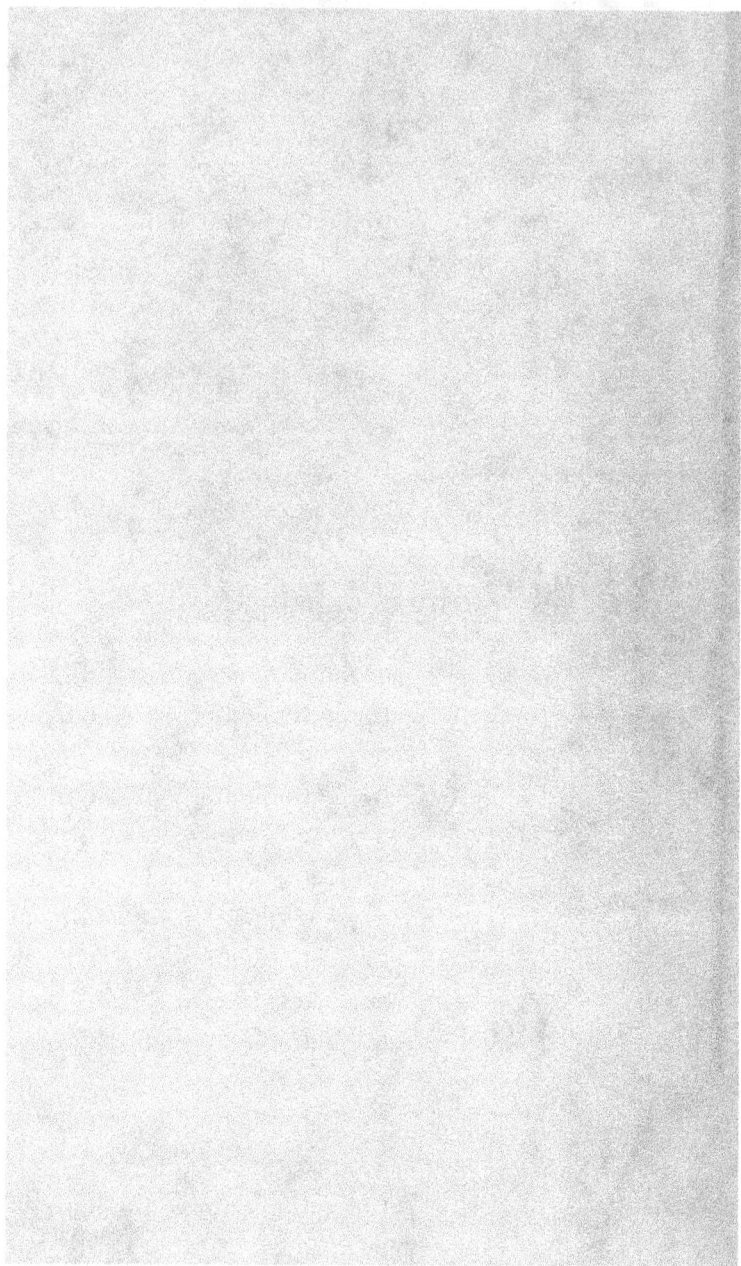

16. MARY, born Oct. 4, 1640, and married as his second wife, in Barnstable, Dec., 1656, John Stearns of Billerica, Mass. He died March 5, 1668-9, and she married May 6, 1669, Capt. William French of Billerica. Capt. French died Nov. 20, 1681, aged 78. She married for her third husband, in 1684, Isaac Mixer, Jr., of Watertown, and she was his third wife. She was living in 1735 "very aged." John Stearns was the eldest son and third child of Isaac and Mary Stearns of Watertown. This Isaac came to America with his wife and three children, as Bond supposes, in the same ship with Gov. Winthrop in 1630, and settled in Watertown where five more children were added to his family, and where he died in 1670. The children of Mary Lothrop, by her first husband, were: Isaac Stearns, born April 17, 1658, and died Oct. 9, 1659; Samuel Stearns, born Sept. 3, 1659; Isaac Stearns, born Dec. 21, 1661; Nathaniel Stearns, born Nov. 30, 1663; Thomas Stearns, born Dec. 6, 1665. Her children by her second husband were: Mary French, born April 30, 1670, who married Nathaniel Dunkler of Watertown and had three children, Hezekiah, Nathaniel, and Damaris; Sarah French, born Oct. 29, 1671, and married Joseph Crosby of Billerica, and had ten children; David, William, Thomas, Robert, Sarah, Rachel, Mary, Prudence, Deborah, and Hannah; Abigail French, born April 14, 1673, and died April 13, 1674; Hannah French, born 1676, and married John Child.

17. HANNAH, baptized in Barnstable, Oct. 18, 1642.

18. THOMAS, baptized July 7, 1644, and was living in 1697.

19. MELETIAH, baptized Nov. 22, 1646, married May 20, 1667, Sarah Farrar, daughter of Thomas and Elizabeth (Hood) Farrar of Lynn, Mass. He died Feb. 6, 1712, and his widow, May 28, 1712, aged 64 years. His will, dated Oct. 29, 1711, and probated Feb. 25, 1711-12, names as legatees his wife Sarah, "his" grandson Melatiah, son of my son Isaac; granddaughter of Jedidah, "my five children, Isaac, Shubal, Tabitha, Dimock, Elizabeth Lothrop," and Sarah Troop and sons Joseph and Thomas.

20. BETHIAH, born July 23, 1649, and married in July, 1668, John Hinckley, probably a son of Samuel Hinckley. They settled in Barnstable where she died, July 10, 1694, and he, Dec. 7, 1709. Their children were: Sarah Hinckley, born in the end of May, 1669, and married John Crocker; Samuel Hinckley, born Feb. 2, 1670-1. He settled in Stonington, Ct., and was living in 1710; Bethia Hinckley, born latter end of March, 1672, and died April 12, 1715; Hannah Hinckley, born middle of May, 1673, and married June 2, 1708, Benjamin Lewis; Jonathan Hinckley, born Feb. 15, 1677; Ichabod Hinckley, born Aug. 28, 1680; Gershom Hinckley, born April 2, 1682. In the settlement of the estate and in the mother's will, the following children

are also named: Mary Hinckley; Abigail Hinckley; Mercy Hinckley, who in her will names also a brother, Job Hinckley.

## 7. SAMUEL.      Norwich, Conn.

21. JOHN, baptized in Boston, Dec. 7, 1645, married Dec. 15, 1669, Ruth Royce, daughter of Robert. He and his sister Elizabeth were married at the same time by Commissioner Daniel Wetherell, and the record appears among the other records of the Commissioner's Court. The next year we find him called to Wallingford, as the following vote on record shows:

"Sept. 10, 1677. Vote to send for Jo. Lothrop to come and conclude arrangements for building the mill."

By some marvel of dispatch which we could hardly look for in those early days, within three days' time he had already entered on the work of building the mill. The only explanation of it seems to have been in the pressing necessities of the new town, which would not allow them to wait even for the usual settlement of the terms on which the mill should be built, as the following record will suggest:

"Sept. 13, 1667. Vote that if Jo. Lothrop go on with all speed and complete his mill which he hath begun—leaving all agreement to a convenient time—the town grants him his 30 acres."

That grant covered the site of the mill. To it were added two other grants, one of 44 acres "peculiar" to it, and one of 40 acres upland. The town also remits his tax for building the mill.

In 1681, the entire control of the mill was put into his hands. His heirs sold the property in 1704, but to this day the meadow is called the "Lotrop Lot." He died, as the Wallingford records show, Aug. 25, 1688, Æt. 44. Ruth, his widow, in Feb. 19, 1689-90, drew lot No. 4, in the distribution of that date. The inventory of his estate was presented to probate May 18, 169-, and is recorded in Book No. 2, of the New Haven probate records, and in it he is named "John Lothrop, late of Wallingford."

22. ELIZABETH, born in March, 1648, and married Dec. 15, 1665, Isaac, son of Robert Royce of New London, and settled in Wallingford. After his death she married Joseph Thompson of Wallingford, who was a collector of taxes there as late as 1681, and had six children: Elizabeth, Samuel, James, Phebe, Hannah, and Keziah. Joseph Thompson, who married Hannah Clark, Feb. 1, 1709-10; John Thompson, born Feb. 1, 1685, and married June 23, 1710, Sarah Culver. They had six children: Abel, Abel 2d, Anna, Marsh, Sarah, and John. Hannah Thompson, born April 16, 1687.

23. SAMUEL, born in March, 1650, married Hannah Adgate, Nov., 1675, who died Sept. 18, 1695. He then married, Dec. 30, 1697, Mary Edgerton of Norwich. They settled in Norwich where she died Jan. 31, 1727-8, and he Dec. 9, 1732. His rank among the citizens of Norwich is shown in the enrollment of 1730, where his name stands next to the two Deacons Huntington, their names following those of the three ministers, Lord, Willes, and Kirtland. He was a member of the First Church in Norwich.

24. SARAH, born in October, 1655, and married as his second wife, April 21,

1681, Nathaniel, son of Nathaniel Royce of Wallingford, where they settled, and where he died Nov. 11, 1706. He was a carpenter and joiner and blacksmith, and died Feb. 8, 1736, having had four wives. His children by Sarah Lothrop were:

  1. Sarah Royce, born in Wallingford, April, 1683.

  2. Hester Royce, born in Wallingford, Sept. 10, 1685, and died Oct. 14, 1703.

  3. Lois Royce, born in Wallingford, July 29, 1687, and married Samuel Hall.

  4. Elizabeth Royce, born in Wallingford, Dec. 28, 1689.

  25. MARTHA, born in January, 1657, and married, in 1677, John, son of John Moss, the immigrant of this name, at New Haven, and who became so prominent in the new town of Wallingford. He occupied for his homestead the lot on which the elegant home of Moses Y. Beach stood in 1873, and there the elder Moss died at the age of 103 years in 1707. The son died March 31, 1717, and she Sept. 21, 1719. Their children were:

  1. Mary Moss, born in Wallingford, Jan. 7, 1677.

  2. Esther Moss, born in Wallingford, Jan. 5, 1678.

  3. Samuel Moss, born Nov. 18, 1680, and married Dec. 15, 1703, Susannah, daughter of —— Hall. He became a prominent man of his town, and a deacon in the church. They had nine children: Theophilus, Martha, Susannah, Samuel, Esther, Isaac, Sarah, Isaiah, and Bethiah.

  4. John Moss, born Nov. 10, 1682, and married Feb. 25, 1708, Elizabeth Hall. Children: Hannah, Elizabeth, Samuel, Joseph, Mary, John, Levi, Eunice, and Thankful.

  5. Martha Moss, born Dec. 22, 1684.

  6. Solomon Moss, born July 9, 1690, and married Jan. 28, 1714, (1) Ruth Peck, and (2) Sarah ——. By his first wife he had nine children, and by his second three: Martha, Susannah, Daniel, Abigail, Solomon, Ruth, Martha, Abigail, Lois, Jonathan, and Sarah.

  7. Isaac Moss, born July 6, 1692, and married May 2, 1717, Hannah Royce. Their children were: Herman, Hannah, Orzell, Jesse, Elihu, and Mehetable.

  8. Mary Moss, born July 23, 1694, and married June 28, 1714, Solomon Munson, and had three children: Martha, Samuel, and Elizabeth. Afterward he married June 14, 1733, Sarah Peck, by whom he also had three.

  9. Israel Moss, born Dec. 31, 1696, and married Lydia ——, and had seven children: Nathaniel, Isaiah, Lydia, Sarah, Kiriah, Asahel, and Keziah.

  10. Benjamin Moss, born Feb. 10, 1702, and married Abigail ——, and had eight children: Abigail, Benjamin, Barnabas, Timothy, Abigail, Joseph, Martha, and Eunice.

  26. ISRAEL, born in October, 1659, and married April 8, 1686, Rebecca Bliss, daughter of Thomas and Elizabeth —— Bliss, who went from Saybrook to Norwich. Her grandfather was Thomas Bliss, Sen., of Hartford. They settled in Norwich.

  His rank among his townsmen in 1730, when all the freemen were enrolled, was next to his brother Samuel. He was a man of worldly thrift, and had a family of enterprising sons, who are said to have planted themselves on seven hills within the old nine-miles square of Norwich. He died March 28, 1733, and she Aug. 22, 1737. His headstone in old Norwich Town burial ground is the oldest one now there with an inscription on it. It gives us this tribute to his worth: "Here lies buried ye body of Mr. Israel Lothrup, ye Husband of Mrs. Rebekah Lothrup, who lived a life of exemplary piety & left ye Earth for Heaven Mar. ye 28, 1733, in ye 73d year of his age."

—27. JOSEPH, born in October, 1661, and married (1) April 8, 1686, Mary Scudder, who died Sept. 18, 1695. He married (2) Feb. 2, 1696-7, Elizabeth "Waterhouse," daughter of Isaac and Sarah Watrous. She was born March 22, 1661, and died Nov. 29, 1726. He married (3) Nov. 22, 1727, Mrs. Martha Perkins, widow of Dea. Joseph Perkins of Newent, now Lisbon, then a part of Norwich. He was a member of the First Church. He died in Norwich, July 5, 1746, and to his death record is added "born 1661."

28. ABIGAIL, born in May, 1665, and married Dec. 9, 1686. John, son of Christopher and Ruth (Rockwell) Huntington. See Huntington family for their numerous descendants. They had nine children: Abigail Huntington, born Feb. 19, 1687; married James Calkins; John Huntington, born April 20, 1688, and died in 1690. John Huntington, born July 4, 1691, and married Thankful Warner, of Windham, Ct., and settled in Tolland; Hannah Huntington, March 25, 1693-4, and married Joseph Rockwell, of Windsor; Martha Huntington, born Dec. 9, 1696, and married Noah Grant, of Tolland, and became the ancestress of President Ulysses S. Grant.

29. ANNE, born in August, 1667, and married William, third son of William and Sarah (Calkins) Hough, of New London. He was born Oct. 13, 1657, and died April 22, 1705, and she, in Norwich, Nov. 19, 1745. William Hough, Sen., was the son of Edward Hough, of Westchester, County of Chester, England. He came to Gloucester, Mass., when he married Oct. 28, 1645, Sarah, daughter of Hugh Calkins, the pioneer.

## S. JOSEPH.    Barnstable, Mass.

"Still born maide child," buried.

30. A CHILD, b. Nov. 19, 1651, and buried same day.

31. JOSEPH, born Dec. 5, 1652, and died at 24 years of age, Oct., 1676.

32. MARY, born March 22, 1654, and married Jan. 16, 1674. Edward Crowell, a grandson, probably, of John Crow of Charlestown, 1635, as the name was changed, according to Savage, in that generation. At the date of her father's will she was the wife of a Mr. Denes. The death of her first husband was probably not recorded. Her children, as recorded, are: Mary Crowell, born March 16, 1674; a child, born March 14, 1676, and died March 19, 1676; Yelverton Crowell, born Feb. 17, ——; Joseph Crowell, born March 1, ——; Benjamin Crowell, born April 14, ——; Bathshua Crowell, born June 26,——; and died in the spring of 1684; Edward Crowell, born June 6, 1685.

33. BENJAMIN, born July 25, 1657. No children recorded.

34. ELIZABETH, born Sept. 18, 1659, and married Dec. 29, 1680, Thomas Fuller. Their children, as reported by Otis, were: Hannah, born Nov. 17, 1681; Joseph, born July 12, 1683; Mary, born Aug. 6, 1685; Benjamin, born Aug. 6, 1690; Elizabeth, born Sept. 3, 1692; Samuel, born April 12, 1694; Abigail, born Jan. 9, 1695-6.

35. JOHN, born Nov. 28, 1661, and died Dec. 30, 1663.

36. SAMUEL, born March 17, 1663–4; married July 1, 1686, Hannah, born Oct. 10, 1665, daughter of John and Mary (Bodfish) Crocker, who died Oct. 11, 1738. His will, dated Oct. 18, 1728, names as legatees his sons Benjamin, Joseph, and Samuel, his daughters Hannah and Abigail, who were to have a room in his house till their marriage, and his daughter Mary Davis, and Benjamin Lothrop, Esq.

37. JOHN, born Aug. 7, 1666. This name is not in the father's will in 1700.

38. BARNABAS, born Feb. 24, 1668–9.

39. HOPE, born July 15, 1671, married Nov. 15, 1696, Elizabeth Lathrop, who was born in Barnstable, Nov. 15, 1677, a daughter of Melatiah Lothrop, No. 19. They settled first in Barnstable where he is enrolled among the townsmen in 1695, and where the oldest of their children were born. He subsequently removed to Falmouth, Mass., and still later to Connecticut. He purchased 150 acres of land in Tolland, in 1726, of Daniel Eaton. The deed identifies him as from Falmouth in the county of Barnstable, in his Majesty's province of Massachusetts Bay. Waldo, in his *Tolland*, reports the tradition that he was brother instead of father to John, also then resident in Tolland. How early he removed with his family, if indeed as a family they ever came to Connecticut, we have no date to show. The tradition is that they resided for years in Hartford, and also that for a time at least they lived in Sharon, Conn. He died Oct. 2' 1736, and she died Feb. 21, 1763.

40. THOMAS, born Jan. 6, 1673–4, and married, April 23, 1697, Experience, daughter of James Gorham and Hannah Huckings. She was born July 28, 1678, and died Dec. 23, 1733. They lived in Barnstable, where his name on the records indicate him as a thrifty and honored citizen. His will, Book IX. p. 300, dated May 24, 1751, and probated Aug. 3, 1757, names as legatees: daughter, Rebecca Lothrop; daughter, Mehetabel Davis; daughter, Mary Taylor; daughter, Lydia Bacon; daughter, Elizabeth Bartlett; grandson, Thomas Lothrop, son of Thomas, deceased; heirs of son Ansel, deceased; heirs of son James, deceased; and son Seth Lothrop. Sole executor, son Seth. He died July 3, 1757.

41. HANNAH, born Jan. 23, 1675–6, and died Feb. 1, 1680–1.

## 9. BENJAMIN. Charlestown, Mass.

42. MARTHA, born Nov. 3, 1652, and baptized by Rev. Thomas Shepard, 1st church, in 1660, and married, Dec. 2, 1669, John Goodwin of Charlestown. They lived in Charlestown until after the birth of their fourth child, then removed to Boston. They were living here when the dismal reign of witchcraft began, and four of their children became helpless victims of the costly delusion. Mr. Goodwin died in Boston, Jan. 21, 1712, aged 65 years, and was buried according to Drake's *Boston* on Copp's Hill. His widow married John Pearson, in 1714, and died Sept. 26, 1728, and was buried by the side of her first husband. Their family consisted of eight and perhaps more children: Nathaniel Goodwin, born in 1672, and settled in Middletown, Conn.; Martha Goodwin, born in 1674 and baptized with her brother, Mar. 26, 1676;

7

she married Ebenezer Clough, and their daughter Martha was the wife of Elias Parkman; John Goodwin, born Sept. 23, 1677, and married Mary Hopkins; Mercy Goodwin, born Apr. 17, 1681; Benjamin Goodwin, born in Boston, 1683, and married Francis White, who, after his death, became the wife of Maj. John Bowles; Hannah Goodwin, born in Boston in 1687, and married William Parkman; Elizabeth Goodwin, born in Boston in 1694, and married Joseph White.

43. HANNAH, born Sept. 15, 1655, and baptized same date with her sister Martha, and married Aug. 21, 1679, Henry, son, probably, of Jeremy and Mary Swain of Charlestown.

44. BENJAMIN, baptized with the two older children, Aug. 5, 1660. He probably married in 1689, Abigail, daughter of Richard and Elizabeth (Tuthill) Edwards of Hartford, Conn. He died in 1690, without issue, and his widow married in 1697, Capt. Thomas Stoughton of East Windsor. Richard Edwards was the only child of William Edwards the pioneer of this name in Hartford, Conn., and his wife Agnes Spencer.

45. MARY, baptized June 9, 1661, and married, May 21, 1679, William Brown. She was his second wife, the first being Mary Goodwin. Mrs. Mary Brown died Dec. 23, 1713, and Mr. Brown, Oct. 19, 1724, aged 78.

46. SARAH, born Apr. 10, 1664, and baptized on the 17th, and died while yet a child.

47. ELIZABETH, baptized May 21, 1665.

48. REBECCA (kah, so recorded, 1872, p. 49), born Nov. 14, 1666, and baptized on the 18th.

49. MERCY (see record as above, p. 52), born Dec. 17, 1670, and baptized the next day.

50. JOHN (record, p. 54), born July 15, 1672, baptized on the 21st and died young.

### 10. HON. BARNABAS. Barnstable, Mass.

51. JOHN, born Oct. 7, 1659, and died in April, 1666.

52. ABIGAIL, born Dec. 18, 1660, and married, in 1680, Thomas Sturges. They lived in Yarmouth, Mass. Their children on record were: A daughter, born in 1681; Judy Sturges, born in 1683; Edward Sturges, born Dec. 10, 1684; Thomas Sturges, born Apr. 4, 1686; Hannah Sturges, born Sept. 18, 1687; John Sturges, born Dec. 2, 1690; Elizabeth Sturges, born Dec. 25, 1692; Abigail Sturges, born Oct. 28, 1694; Thankful Sturges, born Mar. 18, 1697; Jacob Sturges, born Jan. 14, 1700; A son, born in 1702. Besides the above were four other children who died in infancy.

53. BARNABAS, born Mar. 22, 1662–3, and married Nov. 14, 1687, Elizabeth Hedge. They settled in Barnstable, where we find his name as one of the townsmen in 1689. His will, dated Oct. 10, 1732, was proved Nov. 29, 1732, his death having occurred Oct. 11, 1732. In his will he makes bequests to his wife, Elizabeth, son "Kimbel," and daughters Elizabeth, Susannah, Sarah, Mercy, and Thankful.

54. SUSANNAH, born Feb. 28, 1664–5, and married, Oct., 1683, William Shurtleff, son of William and Elizabeth (Lettice) Shurtleff of Plymouth and

Marsfield. They settled in Plymouth, where he was a prominent man. He
served as a selectman and was a representative to the State Assembly, and
active in other offices of honor and trust. He was especially prominent as a
military man among the pioneers. His remains were interred on Cole's Hill,
the first burying lot of the Plymouth pilgrims, and his headstone bears this
inscription: "Here lyes y[e] body of Capt. William Shurtleff who Dec[d] Feb[ry]
The 4[th], 1729-30, in The 72[d] year of his age." His wife had died Aug. 9, 1726.
She was ancestress to the late eminent antiquary, Dr. Nathaniel B. Shurtleff
of Boston. Their children all born in Plymouth were: Jabez Shurtleff, born
Apr. 22, 1684; Thomas Shurtleff, born Mar. 16, 1687; Jacob Shurtleff, baptized
Aug. 11, 1688; William Shurtleff, baptized Apr. 4, 1689, graduated at Harvard
in 1707, and ordained a Congregational minister in New Castle, N. H., and
later installed over the church in Portsmouth, N. H. Susannah Shurtleff,
baptized in 1691, and married, Dec. 29, 1709, Josiah, son of Dea. Elkanah and
Elizabeth (Cole) Cushman. Their daughter Susannah Cushman married Benjamin Shurtleff, and was the great grandmother of Dr. N. B. Shurtleff above
mentioned. John Shurtleff, born in June, 1693; Barnabas Shurtleff, born Mar.
19, 1696; Ichabod Shurtleff, born Nov. 8, 1697; Elizabeth Shurtleff, born Mar.
28, 1699; Mary Shurtleff, born Dec. 2., 1700; Sarah Shurtleff, born June 8, 1702;
Samuel Shurtleff, Abigail Shurtleff, Nathaniel Shurtleff, born Dec. 2, 1707.

55. JOHN, born in 1667 and married Elizabeth Green of Charlestown. He
died Oct. 23, 1695, and his widow married, Dec. 23, 1701, Thomas Crocker.
She died Aug. 1, 1753, aged 89 years.

56. NATHANIEL, born Nov. 23, 1669, and married Bethia ——. He died in
1700, and his widow married Nov. 6, 1701, Robert Claghorn, by whom she had
four children.

57. BATHSHUA, born Aug. 10, 1673, and married Freeman.

58. ANNA, born in Barnstable Aug. 10, 1673, and married, in April, 1691,
Ebenezer Lewes. The children recorded to them in Barnstable were: Sarah
Lewes, born Jan. 13, 1691-2; Susannah Lewes, born Apr. 17, 1694; James
Lewes, born Aug. 4, 1696; Ebenezer Lewes, born May 9, 1699; Hannah Lewes,
born Feb. 14, 1701; Lothrop Lewes, born June 13, 1702, and married, July 26,
1727, Sarah Wakeman of Fairfield, where their children are recorded—Ebenezer, Jonathan, Sturgess, Sarah, and Deborah; George Lewes, born Apr. 5,
1704; Nathaniel Lewes, born June 12, 1707-8; John Lewes, born July 15, 1709;
David and Abigail "gemini," born Nov. 8, 1711.

59. THOMAS, born Mar. 7, 1674-5, and died Oct. 13, 1675. Reg. viii., 271.

60. MERCY, born June 27, 1676, and died July 3, 1677.

61. SARAH, who married —— Skeff.

62. THANKFUL, baptized Sept. 19, 1683, and married, Jan. 25, 1699-1700,
John Hedge.

63. JAMES, baptized Mar. 30, 1684, and died young.

64. SAMUEL, baptized June 16, 1685, and died young.

## 14. CAPT. JOHN.  Barnstable, Mass.

65. JOHN, born Aug. 5, 1673, and married Esther ——, and lived in Boston
where the children were born. He was a seafaring man. He died in Boston.

His will, which designates him as "Mariner of Boston," names as legatees his wife Esther, who, with Jonathan Loring, was executor of his will; son Joseph, but "if he dye" his portion to be given to Rev. Benjamin Wadsworth, minister of the 1st church, and to the first church for the benefit of the poor, and his brother Barnabas and his sisters Mary, Martha, Elizabeth, Hannah, Abigail, and Experience. He died in 1716.

66. MARY, born Oct. 27, 1675, and married, Sept. 8, 1697, James Howland.

67. MARTHA, born Nov. 11, 1677.

68. ELIZABETH, born Sept. 16, 1679, and married, Nov., 1698, James, son of James and Sarah (Lane) Lewes of Barnstable. The children recorded to them were: Mary Lewes, born Aug. 16, 1700; Elizabeth Lewes, born May 8, 1702; James Lewes, born July 9, 1704; Barnabas Lewes, born Mar. 17, 1706; Solomon Lewes, born June 26, 1708.

69. JAMES, born July 3, 1681, baptized Mar. 30, 1684, and died young.

70. HANNAH, born in Barnstable, May 13, 1682-3, and married, Dec. 25, 1707, John, born Dec. 20, 1677, son of Sergeant James and Sarah (Lewes) Cobb of Barnstable. They lived in Barnstable where their children were born. She died April 3, 1747. Ephraim Cobb, born Dec. 5, 1707; John Cobb, born July 1, 1711, and died Mar. 1, 1713; John Cobb, born Oct. 2, 1719, and died in 1736.

71. JONATHAN, born Nov. 14, 1684, bap. Jan. 28, 1685, and died young.

72. BARNABAS, born Oct. 22, 1686, married, Feb. 20, 1706, Bethia Fuller, who died Oct. 26, 1714, aged about 28 years. He married (2), Dec. 25, 1718, Hannah Chipman. In his will, dated Apr. 3, 1756, and proved May 4, 1756, he names as his legatees: his wife Hannah, and his three sons, John, Jonathan, and Barnabas. His wife Hannah was made his executrix. Her will was dated May 26, 1763, and proved July 1, 1763, and names as legatees, her daughter-in-law Thankful Lothrop; her three granddaughters Hannah, Mary, and Rebecca Lothrop; and her two sons, Jonathan and Barnabas. Her sole executor, her son Barnabas.

73. ABIGAIL, born Apr. 23, and baptized May 12, 1689.

74. EXPERIENCE, born Jan. 7, 1691-2, and baptized Jan. 29, 1692.

75. BATHSHUA, born Dec. 19, 1696, and baptized Dec. 27th with the name Barshua. That she married a Webb is made known by her mother's will in 1738.

76. PHEBE, born in September, 1701, and married Elisha Thacher.

77. BENJAMIN, born Apr. 8, 1704, and married (1), Dec. 22, 1727, Experience, daughter of Thomas Howland of Plymouth, Mass. She was born Nov., 1705, and died Sept. 5, 1748. Her headstone stands still on Burial Hill in Plymouth. He married, for his second wife, widow Mary Hedge, whose maiden name was Hullet. She died June 3, 1795, aged 75. At the time of his second marriage he is styled Capt. B. Lothrop of Kingston. Letters of administration on his estate were granted Oct. 1, 1787, in which he is designated as gentleman, and late of Kingstown. A dower was granted to his widow Mary.

# FOURTH GENERATION.

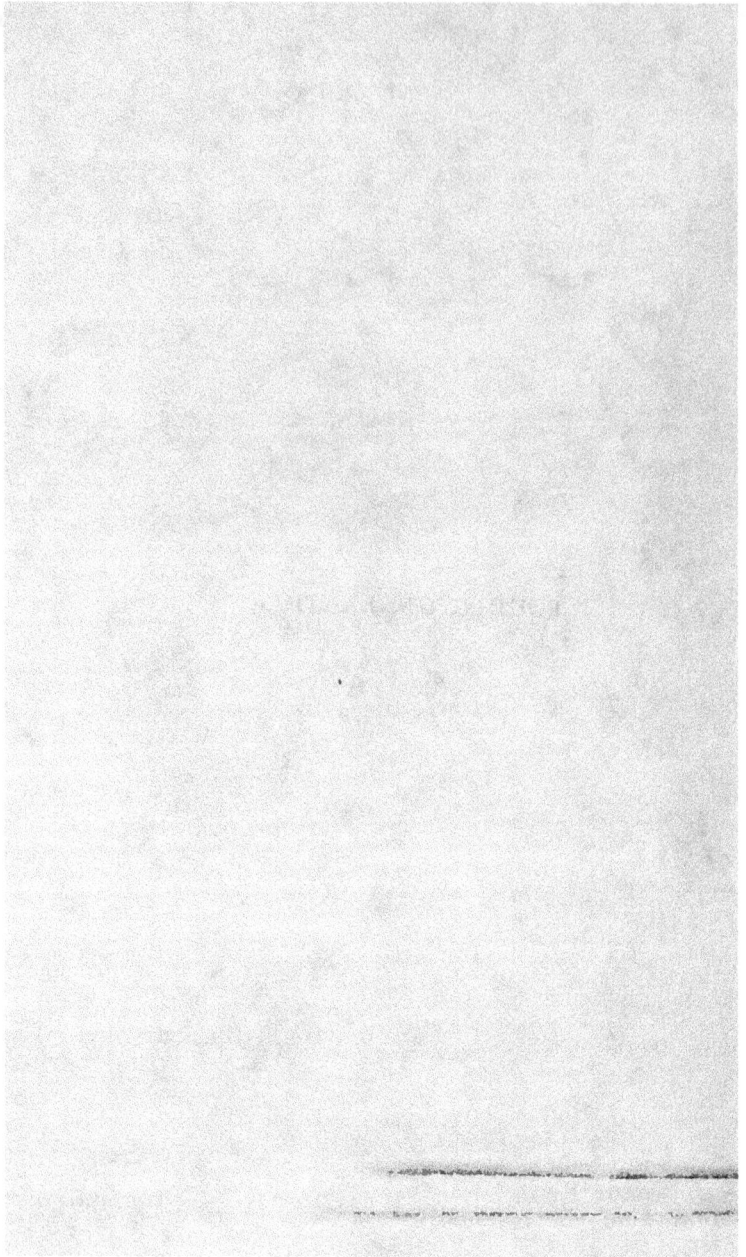

78. THOMAS, born Aug. 22, 1668.  In 1711, he was living and reported to be 43 years old.

79. TABITHA, born April 3, 1671, and married, May 4, 1699, as his second wife, Shubael, son of Shubael and Joanna (Bursley) Dimmock, who was born in Barnstable, in Feb., 1663.  Their children were: Samuel Dimmock, born May 7, 1702, Joanna Dimmock, born Dec. 24, 1708, and died soon; Mehetable Dimmock, born June 20, 1711.

80. ISAAC, born June 23, 1673, and married Elizabeth, daughter of Mr. Jonathan Barnes of Plymouth, who was born Aug. 16, 1677.  He settled in Plymouth, where he became one of the first of the citizens in the oldest of New England towns.  He filled acceptably every town office which he held, and represented the town in the General Court of the State.  He died Sept. 7, 1743, and his widow Oct. 19, 1757.  His will, dated Feb. 17, 1742, and witnessed by James Warner, John and Geo. Watson, and Edward Winslow, had his son Isaac as sole executor.  Its bequests were to wife Elizabeth, of his personal estate, £500; son Melatiah, the John Holme's land; "yet if he contend in law that I owe him for his liveing with me," nothing; daughter Elizabeth Bartlett, £1,000, besides what he had already given her; son Isaac, the house I now live in; grandsons Isaac, Nathaniel, Thomas, and Caleb, when 21 years old  granddaughter Elizabeth Bartlett, when 18 years old.  His invente  proved, .a April, 1744, amounted to £1,741, 16s. 8d.  The celebrated farm, "Playne Dealing," occupied by Governor Prince in 1666, was bought by him in 1711, and is still in possession of his descendants, and is now known as "Lothrop Farm."

81. JOSEPH, born Dec. 15, 1675, and married, Jan. 14, 1695, Abigail, the sixth child of Richard and Mehitable (Dimmock) Childs, born June 16, 1672.  He always lived in Barnstable, and occupied the house in which his great grandfather had last lived and died.  He was also a man of note.

His will, Book VIII, pp. 33 and 51, bears date Feb. 10, 1747, and was probated March 26, 1748.  Its legatees are: wife Abigail, to whom he gave all his slaves, with directions to free a male slave at her decease; granddaughters Abigail Russel, Rebecca Russel, and Martha Russel, and grandsons John Russel, and Jonathan Russel.  Sole executor, his grandson, John Russel.  His widow's will, Book IX, p. 52, dated June 25, 1748, and probated July 3, 1753, names as legatees: granddaughters Abigail, Martha, and Rebecca Russel, and great grandchild Lothrop Russel, afterwards called John Russell.  The property to her granddaughters included the money for which her negro woman Billah should be sold for, she however having the right of choosing her own master.  Sole executor, Joseph Blish, Jr., kinsman.

82. ELIZABETH, born Nov. 23, 1677, and married, Dec. 17, 1696, Hope Lothrop, No. 39.

83. ICHABOD, born June 20, 1680, and had probably died before his father's will was made, Oct. 29, 1711, as he alone of the children is not named.

84. SHUBAEL (Shobal), born April 20, 1682, and is named in his father's will in 1711.

85. SARAH, born March 5, 1683-4, and married (1), Sept. 18, 1702, Joseph, born in Barnstable, Oct. 6, 1682, son of Thomas and Hannah (Chipman) Huckins, and (2), Oct. 14, 1708, John Troop.

## 21. JOHN.                           Wallingford, Conn.

86. SAMUEL, born, probably, in Norwich. His location in the family is indicated by the following testimony of his uncles, on record in Wallingford, in the year 1728:

"Israel Lothrop, æt. 69, & Joseph Lothrop, æt. 67, both of Norwich, sayeth that Samuel Lothrop, of Wallingford, was the first child & eldest son of our eldest brother, John Lothrop, and Ruth, his wife."

He married Ruth ———, who died June 8, 1738. That he succeeded his father as proprietor of the grist mill is abundantly shown in the town records. Under date of Yalesville, July 22, 1695, we have this record:

"If Samuel Lothrop grinds every man's corn well he may keep the mill two months longer, but he will be turned out on complaint of the committee forthwith."

. The next year we find his name, among other petitioners to the town, in opposition to certain oppressive taxes with which they were threatened. In 1701 he is reported on the grand list at £36, which was considerably above the average of the list. The will of this Samuel is dated Feb. 26, 1744, and in it he is defined as "of Wallingford." Only two legatees are named—his wife, Lydia, to whom he gives one-half of his farm and house, and his "Sabbath-day house at town until my daughter Ruth come of age:" and Ruth, who is said to be "my only child." The inventory of the estate, as exhibited by the executors, Capt. Ezekiel Royce and Lieut. Joseph Royce, amounted to £1,504, 16s. 1d., and in it was a "great bible," 40 shillings.

87. RUTH, born, probably, in Norwich, as her birth is not recorded in Wallingford, and married, March 17, 1697-8, Samuel Post, son of John Post and Hester Hyde, of Norwich. He was born in Norwich, March 8, 1668, and died April 25, 1735, and she Aug. 10, 1750. Their children, all born in Norwich, were: Samuel Post, born Dec. 22, 1698. and married, Jan. 11, 1733, Sarah Griswold, of Guilford, by whom he had six children—Samuel, Samuel 2d, Sarah, Anne, Ruth, and Dorcas. John Post, born July 30, 1700, and died Aug. 26, 1718; Nathaniel Post, born Sept. 6, 1702, and married (1), Abigail Birchard, and (2), Experience Griswold. Their children were: Jabez, John, Jabez 2d, and Abigail. Jabez Post, born Dec. 5, 1704, and died March 6, 1725; Esther Post, born Dec. 18, 1706, and married, May 14, 1743, Thomas Edgecomb, by whom she had one son, Stephen; Stephen Post, born April 5, 1709, and died, unmarried, April 14, 1735; Ruth Post, born Oct. 15, 1711, and married, Nov. 25, 1731, Joseph, son of Thomas and Hannah (Backus) Bingham. They removed from Norwich to Charlestown, Mass., and thence to Bennington, Vt.

Their children were: Joseph, Stephen, Jeremiah, Calvin, Ruth, Mary, Eunice, Esther, Lois, and Lucretia.

88. ELIZABETH, born probably in Wallingford, Conn., certainly recorded there, April 15, 1678.

89. JOHN, born, and recorded in Wallingford, May 19, 1680, and married (1), Abiah ———, before 1710; married (2), in Norwich, Feb. 14, 1721, Lydia Palmeter. These two marriages have seemed to be justified, the husband having removed from Wallingford to Norwich about the time when the birth of his daughter Abiah was entered on the record in 1728. Reported on the grand list of Wallingford, in 1701, at £18. His will, dated at Norwich, Aug. 4, 1753, names as legatees, his wife Lydia, his sons Barnabas and John, and his daughter Bethia.

90. BETHIA, born in Wallingford, Dec. 27, 1682, and died Dec. 8, 1716. Letters of administration were granted by the Court of Probate at New Haven, Jan. 17, 1716–17, to her brother Samuel Lothrop, Esq. She is designated as "late of Wallingford."

91. BARNABAS, born in Wallingford, June 14, 1684.

92. HANNAH, born in Wallingford, Jan. 30, 1686.

## 23. SAMUEL. Norwich, Conn.

93. HANNAH, born in Norwich, Jan. 6, 1677, and married, June 30, 1698, Jabez, son of Jacob Perkins of Ipswich, Mass. He and his brother Joseph had purchased, in 1695, a large tract of land in that part of Norwich which is now Lisbon. On which, after his marriage, he settled. He became one of the wealthiest and most honored citiz s of Norwich. He was admitted inhabitant in due form in 1701, and died there Jan. 15, 1741–2. She was an excellent Christian woman, and died April 14, 1721, after which he married, for his second wife, Charity Leonard. His children by his first wife were: Jabez Perkins, born June 3, 1699, and married Rebecca Leonard, by whom he had eleven children—Jedidiah, a daughter, a son, Jabez, married Ann Lathrop, Elkanah, Rebecca, Samuel, Hannah, Charity, Charity 2d, and Samuel 2d; Hannah Perkins, born July 7, 1701, married Joshua Huntington, son of General Jabez, and for whose descendants see Huntington Family Memoir; Elizabeth Perkins, born in October, 1703; Mary Perkins; Jacob Perkins, born May 22, 1705, married Jemima Leonard of Taunton, Mass., and had thirteen children—Jacob, Jemima, Simeon, Jabez, Hezekiah, Ebenezer, Daniel, Elkanah, Zebulon, Zephaniah, Lucy, Judith, and Mary; Lucy Perkins, born July 12, 1709; Judith Perkins, born March 2, 1714.

94. ELIZABETH, born Nov. 1, 1679, and married, as his first wife, Nov. 5, 1701, John, born in March, 1670, second son of Thomas Waterman, the pioneer of this name in Norwich, and his wife Miriam, daughter of Lieut. Thomas Tracy. She died Oct. 5, 1708, and her husband married again, Sept. 27, 1709, Mrs. Judith Woodward, and again, April 16, 1721, Elizabeth Basset. Miss Caulkins says that by his first wife he had a family of six or seven sons and two daughters. The only children of this Elizabeth of which I have found

8

any records, are: Elizabeth Waterman, born Oct. 5, 1702; a child, unnamed, born June 22, 1704; John Waterman, born June 8, 1706, and died April 23, 1730; Hannah Waterman, born Sept. 28, 1708, died Aug. 15, 1758.

95. THOMAS, born Aug. 25, 1681, and married, Feb. 24, 1708–9, Lydia, daughter of Joshua and Mehetable (Smith) Abel of Norwich. She died March 22, 1752. He became a thriving man, having a good record as a Christian citizen. Letters of administration on his estate were taken out Oct. 22, 1774, by his brother Joshua and Joseph Coit. The inventory of his estate £4452, 9s. 10d. That of Mrs. Lothrop was £5852, 6s. 10d.

96. MARGARET, born Oct. 1, 1683, and died April 1, 1696.

97. SAMUEL, born Jan. 6, 1685, and married, July 24, 1715, Deborah Crow. Their names are both on the roll of the First Church in 1717. In the probate records he bears the title of Esquire. His will bears date Oct. 30, 1754, when he is said to be of "Newent," and the legatees are his wife, son Ezra, son Elisha, and daughter Deborah Avery. The same parties are mentioned in the distribution. He died Nov. 7, 1754.

98. SIMON, born May 3, 1689, and married, (1) Mary Lothrop, No. 105, daughter of Israel Lothrop and Rebecca Bliss. (2) March 24, 1714, Martha Lothrop, No. 106. Their names were both entered on the roll of the First Church of Norwich in 1721. Mr. Lothrop soon exhibited his large business talent, attaining early to the first rank among his townsmen. His name early appears as one of the pioneers in occupying and improving the locality which was soon to become the site of the City of Norwich. In 1721 a square of 20 feet is granted him, with two of the Huntingtons and Daniel Tracy, on the west side of Rocky Point, on which to lay the foundations of their business prosperity. In 1724 the town vote him liberty " to build a wharf at the Landing place at his own charge, provided it shall be free to all mortals." Ten years later the town give him the special right of building a warehouse on the hillside opposite his dwelling house, 30 feet by 40, to hold for his personal use during the town's pleasure. In addition to his prominence as an enterprising business man, he became still better known as a military officer. The history of Norwich, by Miss Caulkins, says of him: " Col. Simon Lothrop was a man of more than ordinary renown. He commanded one of the Connecticut regiments in the successful expeditions against Annapolis and Louisburg, and was valued for his judgment in council as well as for his gallant bearing in the field. At one period he was left for a considerable time in the chief command of the fortress at Cape Breton." He had entered the service as Lieut.-Col. commanding the Connecticut regiment for the above expedition, and received the commission of Colonel Oct. 29, 1745.

Mr. Lothrop was several times a representative from Norwich in the General Assembly of the State. He was often under appointments from the Assembly on important commissions, relating alike to the interests of business and religion. Of his home-life we have these touches in the history before quoted: "He was an upright man, zealous in religion, faithful in training up his family, and much respected and esteemed for his abilities and social virtues." Of both his military popularity and his business thrift we have preserved for us the following hearty tribute in the spirit of the times which produced it:

> "Col. Lotrop he came on,
>   As bold as Alexander;
> He wa'n't afraid, nor yet ashamed
>   To be the chief commander.
>
> Col. Lotrop was the man,
>   His soldiers loved him dearly;
> And with his sword and cannon great,
>   He helped them late and early.
>
> Col. Lotrop, staunch and true,
>   Was never known to baulk it;
> And when he was engaged in trade,
>   He always filled his pocket."

His will is dated April 2, 1772, and names as his legatees, wife Martha; son Elijah; son Rufus; daughter Martha Devotion of Windham; daughter Mary Bingham, to whom were given the land and buildings bought of Col. John Dyer in Canterbury; Eunice Huntington; Lucy Fitch; granddaughter Hannah Truman; grandson David Nevins; and granddaughter Eunice Carew, and her husband, Ebenezer Carew.

In the distribution of widow Martha Lathrop's estate, April 20, 1776, the legatees named are: Elijah ʳ d Rufus Lathrop; Eunice Huntington; Mary Bingham; Hannah Truman; and grandson Simon Fitch.

His death occurred Jan. 25, 1774, and that of ⸱is widow Oct. 16, 1775. Their remains lie interred side by side in the Norwich Town burying ground.

99. NATHANIEL, born July 15, 1693, and married, April 25, 1717, Ann, daughter of Joseph and Elizabeth (Huntington) Backus, who was born in Norwich, Jan. 27, 1695, and died Aug. 24, 1761. He settled first on the Namussuck farm, which his great-grandfather had owned in New London, but in 1735 sold that farm and removed to Norwich. He was, with his older brother the Colonel, in the Louisburg expedition, having been commissioned lieutenant Dec. 12, 1745. He died in Norwich, as his gravestone attests, March 20, 1774.

## 26. ISRAEL. Norwich, Conn.

100. ISRAEL, born in Norwich, Feb. 1, 1687, and married, June 20, 1710, Mary Fellows. Her name appears on the roll of the West Farms Church as early as 1721. After her death he married (2), June 9, 1747, Mrs. Sarah Tuttle. He settled on the eastern declivity of Blue Hill, in the southwest part of the present town of Franklin, Conn. He was considerably in official life, both military and civil, and was an active man in promoting all the interests of society. His will, bearing date March 22, 1758, named as legatees, his wife Sarah; his deceased son Israel's three daughters, Ann, Lois, and Ednah; his daughter Mary Birchard; daughter Catharine Hackly; youngest daughter, Prudence; and his sons, Jedidiah, Simeon, and Ezekiel.

101. WILLIAM, born in Norwich, Sept. 20, 1688, and married Dec. 18, 1712, Sarah, daughter of Dea. Simon and Lydia (Gager) Huntington, [See Huntington Family.] They settled on Plain Hills, in the north part of Norwich. He was

a farmer, and his record was that of an enterprising business man, and a good citizen. In religion he was an earnest and zealous disciple, scarcely satisfied with what he looked upon as too rigid and formal, the modes adopted in the established Congregational Church, with which he united in 1732—his wife having been a member from 1717. After her death, which occurred April 20, 1730, he married (2), August 5, 1731, Mary Kelly, who, the same year united with the First Church of Norwich. It was during her lifetime that the great outbreak occurred from the Separatists, and both she and her husband were among the leaders in that disturbing movement. Both of them were warned to appear before the church August 28, 1745, and answer for their presumption in joining with others to "set up" a separate meeting. Mr. Lothrop assigned five reasons for his separation, viz.: 1. "The minister (Rev. Dr. Lord), denying the power of godliness, though not in word, yet in practice. 2. Insisting on imprudencies, and not speaking up for that which is good. 3. Not praying for their meeting (the Separatist) and not giving thanks for the late glorious work (that which attended the preaching of Mr. Whitfield). 4. Not a friend to lowly preaching and preachers, particularly not letting Mr. Jewett preach once, and once forbidding Mr. Crosswell. (These were both separate and revival preachers, and therefore obnoxious to the standing order). 5. Not having the sacrament for six months in the most glorious part of the late times; and often enough since the church is in difficulty, and oftener now than ever."

Mrs. Lothrop assigned these reasons for her withdrawal: 1. "As to communion in the church at the sacrament, I did not commune because I was in the dark, and thought I was not fit. 2. Another reason, because I was not edified. 3. Because the power of godliness, it seems to me is denied here, and is elsewhere. 4. By covenant I am not held here any longer than I am edified."

Mrs. Lothrop died in Norwich, April 19, 1760, and he married (3), May 20, 1761, Phebe French. He died Sept. 27, 1778, as his gravestone, still standing quite by itself on the south side of the old part of the Norwich Town cemetery, testifies. His will, dated Oct. 25, 1771, names as legatees, his wife Phebe; son Andrew; grand'laughter Sarah, only surviving child of son Ezra; Jeremiah, Eunice, and William, children of son Jeremiah, deceased; son Ebenezer; son Jonathan; son John, and son Zachariah.

In the distribution of the estate, Nov. 21, 1778, the following parties are named: Phebe, widow; Capt. Andrew; granddaughter Sarah Barret, wife of Ezekiel Barret, and only daughter of Ezra, deceased, son of Wm. Lothrop; Jeremiah, grandson; Eunice Elderkin, only daughter of Jeremiah, deceased, and wife of Rodolphus Elderkin; William, grandson and youngest son of Jeremiah; Capt. Ebenezer, second surviving son; Jonathan, third surviving son; John, fourth surviving son, and Zachariah, youngest son.

102. JOHN, born in Norwich, Oct. 2, 1690, and married, April 7, 1713, Elizabeth, daughter of Joshua and Mehetable (Smith) Abel of Norwich. They settled on Meeting-House Hill, West Farms parish of Norwich, now Franklin. He and his wife united with the church in West Farms, in 1720. He was prominent in the church and town. Dr. Woodward, in his excellent record of

the town, gives this testimony: Clergymen and distinguished individuals from abroad were often his guests during their temporary sojourn in the place.

Letters of administration on his estate were given to his widow Elizabeth, May 5, 1752. In the division of the estate, Nov. 14, 1752, the heirs named are: the widow and the children, Zebulon, John, second, Azubah, Bethia, Elizabeth, Rebecca, Ann, and Rhoda.

103. SAMUEL, born in Norwich, July 12, 1692, and married, June 26, 1712, Elizabeth Waterman.

104. REBECCA, born April 20, 1695, and married, Feb. 21, 1715–16, Hon. Isaac, son of Dea. Christopher and Sarah (Adgate) Huntington.

105. MARY, born Nov. 15, 1696, and married Simon Lathrop, No. 98. She must have died soon after her marriage, as the following record shows:

106. MARTHA, born Nov. 15, 1696, and married, March 24, 1714, after the death of her sister Mary, Simon Lothrop, No. 98.

107. BENJAMIN, born July 31, 1699, married, Nov. 13, 1718, Martha Adgate, who died March 26, 1735–40. He married (2), June 15, 1741, Mary (Worthington) Jones, widow of Daniel Jones, of Colchester, and daughter of William Worthington, of Colchester, and his wife, Mrs. Mehitable Morton, a daughter of Isaac Graves, of Hatfield, Mass. She died in Norwich, Aug. 4, 1770, aged 68 years. His will is dated Feb. 11, 1774. He united with the church in West Farms parish of Norwich in 1740, and his second wife in 1748.

108. EBENEZER, born in Norwich, Feb. 7, 1702–3, and married, May 13, 1735, Lydia, daughter of Thomas and Lydia (Tracy) Leffingwell, of Norwich, where she was born July 28, 1706. He was a man of note in town, both in civil and military affairs, and was known b° t by his military title of captain. He died Jan. 28, 1781, and the only portio.. of the sandstone inscription now visible on the gravestone of his wife is "——dia consort ·f Cap—— Lothrop." In the distribution of his estate, in 17⁻8, the following legatees are named and defined: eldest son, Ebenezer, of Windham; second son, Zephaniah; third son, Jedidiah; daughter, Mrs. Sybel Tracy; daughter, Zipporah Huntington; daughter, Mrs. Lydia Lathrop; daughter, Zerviah Lathrop; daughter, Anna Perkins; and the heirs of daughter, Mrs. Sarah Coit.

109. JABEZ, born Jan. 11, 1706–7, and married (1), Nov. 28, 1728, Elizabeth Burnham, who died April 14, 1730. He married (2), May 30, 1734, Delight Otis, who died Oct. 15, 1747. He married (3), Lydia Lothrop, widow of Dr. Joseph Wetherell, on whose estate she had been appointed administratrix, June 16, 1748. He died Feb. 11, 1796.

## 27. JOSEPH.

110. BARNABAS, born Feb. 4, 1686, and married, Jan. 12, 1709–10, Abigail Abell, and died May 25, 1710, in Norwich. She then married, Feb. 4, 1717–18, Christopher, son of Dea. Christopher and Sarah (Adgate) Huntington. [See Huntington Family.]

111. JOSEPH, born Sept. 18, 1688, in Norwich, and married, April 13, 1735, Mary Hartshorn. She united with the church in Franklin, then West Farms parish of Norwich, in 1737. The inventory of his "estate in Norwich and

Waterbury" bears date March 1, 1757. The distribution was made Nov. 6, 1758, to his widow and four children, designated as "eldest son," "2d son," "youngest son," and only daughter.

112. ABIGAIL, born Sept. 16, 1693, and married Jacob Hazen, who died Dec. 22, 1755. The children recorded to them: Howlet Hazen, born Sept. 13, 172-, and died Feb. 19, 1721-2; Abigail Hazen, born July 22, 1722; Howlet Hazen, born March 19, 1723-4; Temperance Hazen, born Aug. 26, 1727; Jacob Hazen, born last day of November, 1729; Mary Hazen, born March 22, 1732, and died Dec. 7, 1732.

113. MEHETABLE, born Nov. 2, 1697, and married (1), William Bushnell, of Norwich, where four children are recorded to them: William, born Dec. 2, 1716; Mehetable, born Feb. 17, 1717-18, and died Dec. 12, 1718; Samuel, born Nov. 1, 1719; Benjamin, born Dec. 16, 1722. She married (2), Oct. 3, 1722, Captain Thomas Stoughton, Jun., of East Windsor. He was the oldest son of Captain Thomas Stoughton, Sen., of East Windsor, and his second wife, Abigail, the widow of Benjamin Lathrop, and daughter of Richard and Elizabeth (Tuthill) Edwards, of Hartford. He was born April 9, 1698, and died Jan. 14, 1748, and she Jan. 19, 1781-2. . They were settled. in East Windsor, where the children recorded to them were: Thomas Stoughton, born Sept. 29, 1723; Mehitable Stoughton, born April 18, 1725, and died Feb. 5, 1744; Leviah Stoughton, born May 26, 1729; Elizabeth Stoughton, born Jan. 13, 1731.

114. SAMUEL, born May 23, 1699.

115. ELIZABETH, born Jan. 17, 1700-1.

116. SARAH, born Oct. 18, 1702.

117. TEMPERANCE, born Oct. 6, 1704.

118. SOLOMON, born in Norwich, Dec. 13, 1706. and married, Feb. 6, 1728-9, Mrs. Martha, widow of Thomas Todd, of Rowley, Mass., and daughter of Dea. Joseph and Martha (Morgan) Perkins, of Lisbon, Conn., where she was born Aug. 28, 1705. He settled in Norwich. His son, the Rev. Dr. Joseph Lathrop, of West Springfield, in his own autobiography, thus speaks of him, not from his own personal recollections. of course, but from some of the father's papers which had fallen in his hands:

"From memoirs which he left, and from letters which he wrote to his particular friends, and which I have seen, I have formed an opinion of him, as a person of early and eminent piety, of good natural talents, and of more than a common education for that day. This idea has been confirmed by information from some of his contemporaries. In his writings I have seen very serious and grateful acknowledgments of the wonderful preservation of his life in a moment of imminent danger when he was a youth."

After his death, which occurred May 10, 1733, his widow married, May 29, 1739, Matthew Loomis, of Bolton, Conn. Their children were: Matthew Loomis, Levi Loomis, Mary Loomis; Andrew, born March 14, 1746-7, and married, Dec. 22, 1768, Beulah, daughter of Dea. David and Thankful (Loomis) Strong, of Bolton; Jerusha Loomis; Mabel Loomis.

119. RUTH, born Dec. 11, 1709.

120. ESTHER, born Nov. 17, 1712.

121. ZERUIAH, born April 9, 1718, and married, in 1739, William, son of Lieut. James Bradford, of Canterbury, Conn. She died soon after the birth of her only child, Zerviah Bradford, born in Canterbury in 1740.

## 36. SAMUEL.

122. MARY, born Oct. 19, 1688, and had married Daniel Davis, before the will of her father in 1728. She is named in her father's will, and in those of her sister Hannah in 1751, and her sister Abigail in 1757, and in that of her brother Joseph.

123. HANNAH, born Nov. 11, 1690, and died unmarried in 1751. Her will, dated June 25, 1751, and proved Sept. 3, 1751, is recorded in Probate Records at Barnstable, Book VIII, p. 468. It names as legatees: Sister Mary Davis, of Connecticut; brother Benjamin Lothrop; sister Abigail Lothrop; brother Samuel Lothrop; grandson Prince Lothrop, son of Samuel; nephew Joseph Lothrop, son of brother Joseph, deceased; executor, brother Benjamin Lothrop.

124. ABIGAIL, born Oct. 10, 1693, and died unmarried. Her will, dated May 18, 1757, and proved June 18, 1757, is recorded in Book IX, p. 286. It names as legatees, brother Samuel; kinsman Joseph Lothrop; sister Mary Davis; kinsman Nathan Foster; kinsman Benjamin Lothrop; and kinsman David Lothrop; executors, Isaac Jones and Joseph Lothrop.

125. BENJAMIN, born April 16, 1696, and married, April 30, 1730, Experience, daughter of John Benseley, born Nov. 30, 1706. He was a carpenter, and inherited his father-in-law's estate. His will, dated Nov. 9, 1752, and proved Feb. 6, 1755, names as his legatees his sons Benjamin and Joseph, and his daughter Mary Lothrop; executors, William and Benjamin Crocker.

126. JOSEPH, born Nov. 10, 1698, and married, in 1725, Rebecca Palmer. They lived in Barn able, where his will was made. It was dated Feb. 4, 1731-2, and proved Aug. 30, 1732. The legatees are his wife, Rebecca; brother Benjamin; brother Samuel; and sisters Hannah, Abigail, and Mary Davis. His wife, Rebecca, was sole executrix. Book V, p. 126.

127. SAMUEL, born April 28, 1700, and married Experience.

## 39. HOPE. Barnstable, Mass.

128. BENJAMIN, born in Barnstable, Oct. 18, 1697, and married, May 26, 1720, Mercy, daughter of Dea. John and Anna (Annable) Baker, of Windham, who was born Aug. 18, 1699. This Dea. John Baker was son of Samuel Baker, of Hull, who married Fear, daughter of Isaac, the son of Rev. John Robinson, of Leyden. Samuel Baker was son of Rev. Nicholas Baker, of Hingham, Eng., who was born about 1611, and was ordained third minister of Scituate in 1660, having been a graduate of St. John's College, Cambridge, England, in 1631. As the first five of his children are recorded in Barnstable, he probably was settled there until he purchased, Aug. 26, 1731, his home lot in Windham, Conn., some three months after the birth of his fifth child. The lot which he then bought, No. 3, was the original Cates' homestead, the most prominent lot of the new settlement at Windham. The price, for those

times, was very great, £500, indicating Mr. Lothrop to be a man of means.
From the first he took an influential place among the citizens of Windham.
He united with the Congregational church at Windham in 1734, his wife having joined by letter in 1732. He died in Windham, June 16, 1758, and his
widow June 16, 1777.

129. JOHN, born in Barnstable, Oct. 3, 1699, and purchased 120 acres of land
in Tolland, Conn., June 4, 1726, and in the deed is said to be "now a resident
in Tolland." He had come, so Waldo says, from Falmouth, Barnstable
County, Mass. He stood among the first men in Tolland, as is evident from
the offices he held, as selectman for five years, as justice of the peace and as
representative of the town in the State Legislature for five sessions—1748-1751.
He was also town clerk in 1722. He died Oct. 17, 1752, and following this is
the strangely incomplete record, "Mrs. Ann Lathrop died." Though imperfect, it preserves for us at least the Christian name of John Lathrop's wife.

130. REBECCA, born Nov. 25, 1701.

131. SARAH, born Dec. 31, 1703; died in 1734.

132. EBENEZER, born May 1, 1706; died, Sept., 1752.

133. ICHABOD, born June 20, 1708, and published Sept. 17, and married,
Nov. 9, 1732, Abigail, daughter of Dea. John and Anna Annable Baker, who
was born Feb. 1, 1713, a younger sister of his brother Benjamin's wife. He
settled in Tolland, Conn., where he died Oct., 1752.

134. SOLOMON, born Sept. 10, 1710. He went to Tolland with his father,
where he married Susannah ——, and where two children were born to them.
He died in Tolland, March 5, 1738. (Feb. 28, Record).

135. ELIZABETH, born Jan. 20, 1712, and married, Dec. 5, 1734, Peletiah, son
of Deacon Francis West, a Tolland pioneer. The children recorded to them
in Tolland were: Elizabeth West, born Sept. 17, 1735; Susannah West, born
Mar. 23, 1737; Eleazor West, born Nov. 9, 1738, and married, Dec. 6, 1761,
Olive Redington. The children reported in Waldo's *Tolland* are Charles and
Thankful.

135. HANNAH WEST, born Mar. 28, 1741; Zerviah West, born Aug. 2, 1743;
Eunice West, born Apr. 30, 1745; Elijah West, born March 7, 1747; Daniel
West, born July 22, 1749; Prudence West, born June 1, 1751; Mary West,
born June 28, 1753.

136. MELATIAH, born Feb. 20, 1714, married, probably in Tolland where
the record was made, Nov. 15, 1738, Mercy Hatch, daughter of Joseph Hatch,
one of the pioneers of Tolland, where she was born, Aug. 23, 1717. A record
made by her son Josiah states that "this family," that of his father Melatiah,
"commenced in Connecticut, whence they removed in 1755 into Duchess
county, N. Y., then town of Dover, where they were chiefly brought up."
He died Sept. 5, 1787, and his wife, whose name in the record of her son is
Marah, was born Aug. 6, 1718, and died in Columbia Co., N. Y., Oct. 16, 1788.

137. MARY, born June 29, 1716, and married, June 23, 1740, Walter Henderson of Windsor, who died Jan. 6, 1746, aged 39. Their children, as recorded
in Windsor were: William Henderson, born Sept. 30, 1744; Mary Henderson,
born May 17, 1743.

138. JOSEPH, born Sept. 12, 1720, and married, probably in Tolland, where the marriage was recorded, June 17, 1741, Prudence, daughter of Samuel and Sarah (Delano) West, who was born in Tolland, Sept. 5, 1726. He settled in Tolland, where he was a man respected alike for his good business tact and for his piety. He was selectman from 1764, to 1773, the last year being first selectman. He was also deacon in the Congregational Church of Tolland. He died in May, 1788.

139. HANNAH, born Nov. 19, 1722.

## 40. THOMAS. Barnstable, Mass.

140. A SON, born Jan. 10, 1697-8, and died the third of the next month.

141. DEBORAH, born Apr. 21, 1699.

142. MARY, born Apr. 4, 1701, married —— Taylor.

143. JAMES, born Aug. 9, 1703, and married, Jan. 20, 1732, Patience Coleman, and settled in Barnstable. He was drowned at sea in April, 1718, and his widow died in January, 1787, as her gravestone testifies, in her 80th year.

144. THOMAS, born July 8, 1705, married, June 3, 1736, Deborah Loring of Hingham. Appointed administrator on estate of his brother Joseph, late of Boston, Mass., May 2, 1737. He died soon after his marriage. Otis thinks that he married, Sept. 16, 1736, Mary Parker, and lived in Barnstable.

145. ANSEL, born in July, 1707, married, Jan. 8, 1737, Mary Thomas. He was a mariner, and died before Sept. 27, 1750, in Plymouth, at which date letters of administration were granted to " Mary," widow of Ancil Lothrop.

146. JOSEPH, born Dec. 8, 1709, and married, in 1758, Deborah Perkins, of Plymouth. The Inventory of his estate amounted to £311, 3s. 6d., proved May 4, 1764, by his widow " Deborah," makes him a cordwainer.

147. SETH, born . Mar., 1712, and married (1), Aug. 11, 1737, Mary Fuller of Barnstable; and (2) Mary Fuller of Sandwich. His children were all by his first wife. His second wife lived to be 95 years old, and died in Barnstable, Jan. 19, 1809. Her m   .ory still survives in the sweet fragrance of her gentle and loving life. His will, dated June 9, 1798, was proved Oct. 29, 1798, and is recorded in Book XXVII, page 270. It names as legatees, three sons, Nathaniel, John, and Benjamin; and his two daughters, Thankful, wife of Sturgess Howes, and Mary, wife of Edward Childs. Its executors were his sons John and Benjamin.

148. JOHN, baptized June 27, 1725.

149. LYDIA, baptized June 27, 1725, and married, Jan. 17, 1734, Ebenezer Bacon.

150. ELIZABETH, baptized June 27, 1725, and married, Aug. 24, 1738, Thomas Witherell of Scituate.

151. MEHITABLE, baptized June 27, 1725, married, Aug. 2, 1729, Daniel Davis, and died Nov. 19, 1761.

152. REBECCA, baptized June 27, 1725, married, May 16, 1734, as his second wife, Joseph Hatch of Tolland, Conn. His first wife was the mother of four children: Amy, Joseph, Mercy, and Jonathan. Mr. Hatch was probably son of Ichabod Hatch of Falmouth, Mass. He was a prominent pioneer in the

9

settlement of Tolland, Conn. He was the first tavern keeper, and the first military officer in Tolland—being commissioned captain in 1725. His descendants are still living in Tolland. By Rebecca Lothrop he had four children: Lemuel Hatch, born Feb. 29, 1735; Rebecca Hatch, born June 8, 1737, and died Sept. 14, 1739; Ebenezer Hatch, born Apr. 21, 1740; Timothy Hatch, born Aug. 14, 1741.

153. ANSEL, born July 25, 1725, and married.

### 53. BARNABAS, JUN.     Barnstable, Mass.

154. MERCY, born Mar. 1, 1689, and died July 30, 1741. She died single. Her will, dated Dec. 9, 1740, and probated Aug. 12, 1741, recorded Book VI, p. 36, names as legatees, mother Elizabeth Lothrop; sister Thankful Lothrop; and nephew Barnabas Howes. Executrix, Sister Thankful Lothrop.

155. ELIZABETH, born Sept. 15, 1690, and married, Dec. 14, 1711, Henry March. She died Feb. 14, 1768, and, as her brother Kembel's will shows, they had at least one son: Nathaniel Marsh.

156. BARNABAS, born Nov. 10, 1692, and died Apr. 6, 1693.

157. NATHANIEL, born Feb. 23, 1693-4. The probate records, Book IV, page 108, show that letters of administration on his estate were granted at Barnstable, Mar. 28, 1723, to Barnabas Lothrop. He probably died unmarried.

158. LEMUEL, born Dec. 26, 1695.

159. BARNABAS, born Feb. 8, 1697-8, and died 1734.

160. SUSANNAH, born Oct. 8, 1699, and married, Nov. 12, 1730, John Sturgis.

161. THANKFUL, born Sept. 24, 1701, and died unmarried, soon after her sister's will was made, in 1741.

162. SARAH, born Apr. 22, 1703, and married Jeremiah Howes. That they had a son Barnabas Howes is shown in the will of her sister Mercy.

163. MARY, born July 15, 1705, and died, as her gravestone shows, June 1, 1722, aged 16 years, 11 months, and 16 days.

164. KEMBEL, born June 21, 1708. His will, dated Mar. 4, 1733, and probated July 6, 1734, Book V, page 179, calls him a felt maker, and would show that he had no family. Its legacies are made to his mother Elizabeth, his sisters, Elizabeth Marsh, Susanna Sturgis, Sarah Howes, Marcy, and Thankful; and to "Nathaniel, sister Elizabeth's son," a silver-hilted sword, which was my grandfather Lothrop's. He died Mar. 29, 1734, as his gravestone in the jail hill burying ground in Barnstable shows.

### 55. JOHN.     Barnstable, Mass.

165. BARNABAS, born in Barnstable, Nov. 23, 1694, and died, as his headstone in the burying ground on jail hill in Barnstable shows, Dec. 11, 1714, aged 20 years and two months.

166. ELIZABETH, born in Barnstable, Sept. 3, 1692, and died Nov., 1694, as her headstone shows, and her name is spelled Lathrop. These two stones, of hard fine slate, have still their inscriptions as distinct as when first cut.

## 56. NATHÁNIEL.          Barnstable, Mass.

167. JOHN, born Oct. 28, 1696, and baptized Apr. 21, 1700. He married (1), Hannah Hadaway, who died Aug. 2, 1741. He married (2), Thankful Sanders of Wareham, to which town they removed in 1752.

168. "HANNA," baptized in Barnstable, Apr. 21, 1700.

## 65. JOHN.          Boston, Mass.

169. JOSEPH, born probably in Boston, and was living at the date of his father's will in 1727. He was probably young, as the legacy, in case he should die, was elsewhere appropriated.

## 72. BARNABAS.          Barnstable, Mass.

170. JOHN, born Aug. 25, 1709, and was living when his father's will was made in 1756.

171. HANNAH, born July 6, 1712.

172. JONATHAN, born Sept. 28, 1719, and died Dec. 9, 1784. He married (1), Dec. 12, 1751, Mary Thacher, who died May 11, 1761. Married (2), June 27, 1762, Eunice Cobb, and lived in Hyannis.

173. BARNABAS, born June 29, 1721, and married, Feb. 3, 1743. N. S., Mrs. Thankful Gorham. He settled in Barnstable, and was there living when his father's will was made in 1756.

174. SAMUEL, born Oct. 5, 1728.

175. MARY, born Mar. 12, 1747.

## 77. CAPT. BENJAMIN.          Kingston.

176. HANNAH, born July 6, 1729, and died May 25, 1736.

177. JOHN, born June 7, 1731, and died June 30, 1761, unmarried.

178. BENJAMIN, born Oct. 10, 1733, was a mariner and had died before June 22, 1757, when letters of administration were granted to John Lothrop on his estate. He is called "mariner," and in the account rendered Dec. 31, 1754, mention is made of an old "scooner" in the hands of Benjamin Lothrop of Kingston.

179. THOMAS, born Oct. 11, 1735, and died June, 1736.

180. THOMAS, born Apr. 29, 1737, and died Sept. 18, 1737.

181. JOSEPH, born Feb. 2, 1741.

182. THOMAS HOWLAND, born Feb. 6, 1743.

FIFTH GENERATION.

183. A DAUGHTER, born in Plymouth, Oct. 28, 1699, and died Nov. 19, 1699.

184. MELATIAH, born in Plymouth, June 29, 1701. He is named as legatee in his grandfather's will, Oct. 29, 1711, and died, single, July 6, 1771. His nephew Isaac was appointed administrator on his estate on the 20th of the same month, and for bondsmen two of his nephews, Nathaniel and Thomas — the bond being £1,000. The inventory of the estate, rendered Aug. 13, 1771, was £987, 15s. 6d.

185. ELIZABETH, born in Plymouth, Apr. 15, 1705, and married Samuel Bartlett, Esq., of Plymouth. She died Nov. 17, 1745, and he married Elizabeth Wetherell, and had by her three children: two Samuels and an Elizabeth.

The children of the first wife were: Lothrop Bartlett, born Aug. 16, 1723, and died Sept. 20, 1723; a daughter, still-born, Oct. 10, 1724; Elizabeth Bartlett, born Aug. 25, 1725, and died Sept. 30, 1730; Margaret Bartlett, born Apr. 22, 1728, and died Apr. 25, 1728; Hannah Bartlett, born Aug. 15, 1731, and died Apr. 21, 1732; Margaret Bartlett, born Apr. 15, 1737, and died Dec. 31, 1739; Elizabeth Bartlett, wh  was living Feb. 17, 1742, when her grandfather's will was made, and at that date not eighteen years of age.

186. ISAAC, born in Plymouth, Feb. 13, 1707, and graduated at Harvard College in 1726. He married (1) Hannah, daughter of Edmund Freeman, Esq., of Harwich. She died Dec. 11, 1730, at the age of 30 years. He married (2) Priscilla, daughter of Caleb Thomas of Duxbury, and widow of John Watson, Esq., of Plymouth, who had died Sept. 9, 1731. After his death she married the Rev. Noah Hobart of Fairfield, Connecticut, to whom she had been affianced before her marriage to Mr. Watson. The story of her successive marriages is told very pleasantly by the Rev. John L. Watson, D.D., of Orange, N. J., in the New England Historical and Genealogical Register for January, 1873. She died in Plymouth, to which place she had returned from Fairfield after the death of her third husband, June 23, 1796, in the 90th year of her age — her last years having been spent in the house in which she had lived with her second hu  and. By her first husband she had two sons: William and Elkanah Watson. The children whom she bore to Mr. Lothrop will be fully reported in their place in the next generation. She had no children by the third marriage.

Mr. Lothrop always lived in Plymouth, and soon became one of the best known and most honored citizens in the Colony. The following testimonial from Thatcher's " Plymouth" expresses the public sense of their great loss at his death:

"Died in this town greatly lamented, Isaac Lothrop, Esq., at the age of 43. He was one of the Justices of the Court of Common Pleas, and his death occasioned a general gloom in the town and throughout the county. At the opening of the next Court, May 15, Nicholas Seaver, Esq., Chief Justice, and Peter Oliver, Esq., one of the Justices of the said Court, both expressed from the bench the grief and sorrow with which the Court and Bar were affected by the melancholy event, and observed that Colonel Lothrop was held in profound regard as a Judge, and was greatly respected for his moral and Christian virtues. He possessed a large estate, and transacted extensive business in the mercantile line, in which he sustained an honorable and upright character. Few men have been more affectionately beloved, nor any whose death could diffuse more heartfelt sorrow among the poor, and in every social circle."

His gravestone on Burial Hill bears this testimony:

"This stone is erected to the memory of that unbiassed judge, faithful officer, sincere friend and honest man, Colonel Isaac Lothrop, who resigned his life on the 26th day of April, 1750, in the 43d year of his age."

Letters of administration were granted, May 21, 1750, to his widow Priscilla. In the inventory, proved Nov. 2, 1751, is an item of land in Connecticut, and another of two pews, one of which was in the third or north parish of the town, for his widow and children. The inventory was a large one for the day, £23,803, 6s. 3d.

In Pilgrims Hall, at Plymouth, may yet be seen the commission, given in 1732, by Jonathan Belcher, Esq., Gov. of Massachusetts, to this Isaac Lothrop.

### 81. HON. JOSEPH.     Barnstable, Mass.

187. MEHITABEL, born Oct. 22, 1701, and married, Apr. 12, 1722, Dr. John Russel, and died in 1747. They had five children, all born in Barnstable, and named in the following order in their grandfather's will: Abigail Russel, Rebecca Russel, Martha Russel, John Russel, Jonathan Russel.

### 86. SAMUEL.     Wallingford, Ct.

188. BARNABAS, born probably in Wallingford, May 6, 1705. That he died before 1744 is reasonably certain from the will of his father at that date, which calls Ruth his only child.

189. RUTH, born probably in Wallingford, Mar. 15, 17—. The following probate records reveal new family relations: On the first Monday of April, 1752, Enas Tuttle, jun., of New Haven, administrator on estate of Ruth Lothrop, "heiress of Samuel Lothrop," exhibits the inventory of her estate, amounting to £2,459, 8s. 6d. This Mr. Tuttle had been appointed administrator in March of that year, "in right of his wife Martha, who was Martha Brocket, half-sister to the deceased." On "Sept. 3, 1775, John Post of Norwich, in behalf of Nathan Post and Joseph Bingham, in the right of his wife Ruth, all of Norwich, which said Nathan is son, and said Ruth daughter, to Ruth Post late of Norwich, which Ruth Post was Ruth Lothrop, sister to Samuel Lothrop, the father of Ruth Lothrop, a minor of Wallingford, deceased."

## 89. JOHN. Windsor and Norwich, Conn.

190. "ABIAH, born in Windsor, May 10, 1710, and here (Norwich) entered December, 1728, at the desire of her father, John Lothrop."

191. "BATTUYAH" (Bethia), born in Norwich, Feb. 17, 1723, and was a member of the present Franklin Church in 1711.

192. BARNABAS, born in Norwich, Mar. 27, 1727, and married, in Norwich, Oct. 26, 1748, Elizabeth Roath, who died Dec. 7, 1749. He married (2), May 10, 1750, Hannah Bellows, whose death was not on the records. He married (3), Apr. 29, 1752, Dorcas Andrews. These three marriages are together on the Norwich records, and as no children are recorded to either marriage there probably were none. He died before Dec. 11, 1753, when his widow took out letters of administration on his estate.

193. JOHN, born in Norwich, Feb. 17, 1728-9, and married, July 15, 1752, Sarah, daughter of Simon Peck of Uxbridge, Mass. She was born Oct. 24, 1735. They settled in Bethel, Vt. For his children's records I have been largely indebted to his grandchildren.

## 95. THOMAS.

194. DANIEL, born in Norwich, May 1, 1712, so the Norwich records state. He graduated at Yale College in 1733, with the degree A. M. in course. After his graduation he went to England, and as Dr. Ezra Stiles's manuscript records show us, studied "chirurgery" in St. Thomas's Hospital in 1737. He returned to his native town, where he became prominent, if not first, among the business men of the town. As importer of drugs he and his brother Joshua built up a wide reputation and large estates for their day.

He married, Dec. 13, 1744, Mrs. Jerusha, daughter of Gov. Joseph Talcott, who was born in Hartford, May 3, 1717. In the language of Mrs. Sigourney, she was "a lady of noble bearing, cultivated intellect, and eminent piety. Though far advanced in years, when I first beheld her, time had not impaired either her physical or mental system. Her tall, majestic form was unbowed, her step elastic, and her heart in ardent, healthful action. My early life retains no more cherished or indelible picture than her beautiful age. Dr. Lathrop was one of the most liberal of the sons of Norwich in devising for the prosperity of the church and the improvement of the town. His own mansion was a model of elegance beyond anything which had before been built.

His will, dated Sept. 9, 1776, names as legatees: His wife; son Joshua; Mrs. Abigail Wadsworth; Mr. Daniel Huntington, of Woodbury, son of my deceased friend; Ezekiel Huntley and Lydia Howard, £25; Daniel Lathrop Coit; Daniel Lathrop, son Broth. Joshua; Yale College, £500; First Society of Norwich, £500; Norwich School, £500.

He died Jan. 9, 1782, and his widow, Sept. 14, 1805, at eighty-nine years.

Jerusha's will, Dec. 9, '99.—Brother Mathew Talcott; grandchildren of brother Samuel Talcott; three children of Sister Hooker, viz.: James, Horace, and Eunice Ellery; William, grandson of Brother Samuel Talcott, silver tankard; Eunice and Elizabeth, daughters of Sister Wadsworth, deceased, silver porringer; Esther Russel, wife of Thaddeus Learned; Daniel L. Coit,

10

silver butter cups; Thomas Coit, son of Brother Thomas Coit; heirs of Joshua Coit; children of Elizabeth Leffingwell, deceased; Thomas Lathrop, Daniel Lathrop, and Lydia Austin, children of Brother Joshua; Daniel, son of Brother Joshua, Jerusha, daughter of Thomas; Hannah Huntington, grand-daughter of Brother Joseph Coit, deceased; Ezekiel Huntley; First Society.

195. LYDIA, born in Norwich, April 10, 1718, and married, as his second wife, Jan. 1, 1739-40, Joseph, son of John and Mehetabel (Chandler) Coit. They settled in New London, where he was a ship-master and engaged in commercial pursuits, until the period of the Revolution, when he removed to Norwich, where he died, April 27, 1787, and she, Jan. 10, 1794. They were both noted for their uniform and cheerful piety. Of their descendants, a fuller list will be found in the Coit Family. Their children, all born in New London, were:

i. Lydia Coit, born June 17, 1741, and married, Aug. 28, 1764, William Hubbard, of Boston.

ii. Elizabeth Coit, born April 5, 1743, and married, Aug. 28, 1764, Col. Christopher Leffingwell, for whose eminence among the citizens of Norwich, and for whose numerous descendants, see Leffingwell Family.

iii. Lucy Coit, born July 2, 1746, and married, Nov. 26, 1766, Gen. Andrew, son of Gen. Jabez and Elizabeth (Backus) Huntington, of Norwich. For their family record in full, see Huntington Family.

iv. Lucretia Coit, born April 13, 1748, and died unmarried.

v. Joseph Coit, born Sept. 23, 1750, and married, Feb. 10, 1773, Elizabeth Palmes, of Preston. He settled in Hartford, in the drug business. He died on a visit to Norwich, Dec. 18, 1779, leaving two children; and his widow married Capt. William Coit, and became stepmother to a large family of children. She died Aug. 29, 1803.

vi. Thomas Coit, born July 17, 1752, and married, (1), April, 1778, Frances Mary Baker, who died Oct. 13th of the same year, aged twenty-one. He married, (2) October, 1782, Sarah Chester, of Wethersfield, who died Dec. 6, 1834.

vii. Daniel Lathrop Coit, born Sept. 20, 1754, and married, Nov. 23, 1786, Elizabeth, daughter of Capt. Ephraim and Lydia (Huntington) Bill. They settled in Norwich, where he had served his apprenticeship in the drug business with his uncles, Lathrop. Of his large success in business, and of the eminent social position of his children, we have a pleasant record in the Coit Family. Their oldest son, Daniel Wadsworth Coit, is still lingering among us — a much-beloved resident of his native town. Three of the daughters became the wives of Prof. James L. Kingsley, of Yale College; of Peletiah Perit, the eminent merchant of New York, and of the late William C. Gilman of Norwich. Mr. Coit died, Nov. 27, 1833, and his widow, in New York, Mar. 8, 1846.

viii. Jerusha Coit, born June 21, 1756, and died, single, Sept. 19, 1776.

ix. Joshua Coit, born Oct. 7, 1758, graduated at Harvard in 1776, and became a lawyer. He married, Jan. 2, 1785, Ann Boradill, daughter of Nicholas and Elizabeth Hallam, of New London. They settled in New London. He soon became popular in his profession, and was called to serve his town and State in civil life. As the representative of the town in the State Legislature, he was repeatedly Clerk and Speaker of that body. He was also chosen Representative from his Congressional District in 1793, and continued to serve until his death, which occurred Sept. 5, 1798. His widow survived him forty-six years, and died Mar. 22, 1814, aged eighty years.

196. JOSHUA, born in Norwich, May 8, 1723, and graduated at Yale College in 1743. He became eminent among the business men of his native town. His brother Daniel and himself are reported in the sketch of Dr. Woodward as having been "successively the most celebrated druggists of their day in Connecticut. Importing medicines directly from Europe, they not only supplied a wide area of country about home, but also received orders from New York."

He married, May 21, 1748, Hannah, daughter of David and Rachel (Schellinx) Gardiner. Her paternal grandparents were John and Sarah (Coit) Gardiner, great-grandparents, David and Mary (Herningman) Gardiner, and her great, great-grandparents, the pioneers of Gardiner's Island, Lion and Mary (Williamson) Gardiner. She died, July 24, 1750. He married, (2,) Nov. 5, 1761, Mercy, daughter of Rev. Nathaniel Eells, of Stonington.

The following tribute, from Mrs. Sigourney's *Past Meridian*, is well worth a place in this family memorial:

"Among childhood's unfading sketches of my native place, is the figure of a beautiful old man of eighty-four, Dr. Joshua Lathrop, who, until the brief illness that preceded dissolution, took daily equestrian excursions, withheld only by very inclement weather. Methinks I clearly see him now; his small, well-knit, perfectly upright form, mounted upon his noble, lustrous black horse, readily urged to an easy canter, his servant a little in the rear. I see the large, fair, white wig, with its depth of curls, the swarthy cocked hat, the rich buckles at knee and shoe, and the nicely plaited ruffles, over hand and bosom, that in those days designated the gentleman of the old school. Repeated rides in that varied and romantic region, were so full of suggestive thought to his religious mind, that he was led to construct a good little book, in dialogue form, on the works of nature and nature's God, entitled, 'The Father and the Son,' which we younglings received with great gratitude from its kind-hearted author. His quick, elastic step in walking, his agility in mounting his steed, as well as his calm and happy temperament, were remarkable, and a model for younger men."

His will, dated May 29, 1795, names as legatees his wife, "Mercy, son Thomas, daughter Lydia Austin, friends and neices Abigail Gardiner, Hannah Thomas, Mehetabel Carew, and Sally Eells, living with me."

His death occurred Oct. 29, 1807, and that of his widow, July 7, 1833, at ninety-one years of age.

The Norwich History, page 520, which has preserved so much of the past of that delightful town, adds this touch to the picture sketched by Mrs. Sigourney of this eminent son of Norwich:

"He was the last in Norwich of the ancient race of gentlemen that wore a white wig. This, with the three cornered hat, the glittering buckles at his knee and in his shoes, the spotless ruffles in his bosom, and the gold-headed cane, made him an object of admiring wonder to young eyes."

The *Panoplist* has also preserved for us a very pleasant memorial of this worthy patriarch of the family, from the sermon preached by his pastor, Rev. Dr. Strong. Vol. iii, p. 575.

## 97. SAMUEL.

197. Deborah, born Jan. 9, 1716–17, and married, Sept. 21, 1738, Rev. Ephraim, son of Rev. John and Ruth (Little) Avery, of Truro, Mass. He was born April 22, 1713, and graduated at Harvard in 1731. He was ordained first pastor of the Congregational Church in Brooklyn, Conn., in 1735. He remained pastor of the church until his death, Oct. 20, 1754.

After his death his widow married John Gardiner, fifth proprietor of Gardiner's Island, and after his death she married, (3.) June 3, 1767, Col. (afterwards Gen.) Israel Putnam, of historic fame, and died at his headquarters, Highlands, N. Y., in 1777. He died in Brooklyn, May 17, 1790. He was great-grandson of that John Putnam who came from Bucks Co. in England, to Salem, Mass., in 1641, whose oldest son Thomas married Ann Holyoke, and had son Joseph, the father of Gen. Israel, by his wife Elizabeth, daughter of Israel Porter. For the ancestry of Mr. Gardiner, see next preceding sketch.

   i.   John, born July 14, 1739, graduated from Yale College, 1761; married, June 26, 1769, Ruth, (born May 5, 1741,) daughter of Jebriel and Kesia Smith, of Huntington, Long Island, New York. He died Aug. 20, 1779. His wife died Oct. 4, 1779.

   ii.   Ephraim, born April 13, 1741, graduated from Yale College, 1761; was Episcopal Minister of the Church in Rye, New York, in 1735. Married, Hanna ———. He died 1777.

   iii.   Samuel, born April 13, 1741, twin brother of Ephraim. He died young.

   iv.   Samuel, born Nov. 7, 1742.

   v.   Elisha, born Dec. 3, 1744, died Jan. 4, 1782.

   vi.   Elizabeth, born Dec. 5, 1746. Married Rev. Aaron Putnam, Brooklyn, Conn. She died Dec. 7, 1835.

   vii.   Septimius, born July 21, 1749, died Oct. 10, 1754.

   viii.   Deborah, born July 5, 1751, married, March 4, 1773, Dr. Joseph Baker, (born Dec. 15, 1748,) son of Samuel and Prudence Baker. She died Feb. 13, 1777.

   ix.   Ruth, born Jan. 13, 1754, probably married ——— Williams.

198. Ezra, born Dec. 4, 1718, and married, in Newent, Norwich, Jan. 20, 1742–3, Charity, daughter probably of Jabez Perkins, by his second wife, Charity Leonard. He died Nov. 9, 1760. The inventory of his estate, admitted to probate Dec. 10, 1760, styles him Lieutenant Ezra Lothrop.

199. Samuel 3d, born Jan. 1, 1720–21, married, Feb. 10, 1742–3, Elizabeth Bishop. In his will, dated Jan. 30, 1750–1, he is said to be of New Concord Society, now Bozrah, Conn., and his legatees named are: wife Elizabeth, son Elisha, and son Samuel. The distribution of the estate, made Mar. 8, 1765, names as the legatees, Elizabeth, wife of Wm. Witter, Esq., eldest son Samuel, son Thomas, son Simeon, son John, and daughters, Susannah and Elizabeth.

He died Aug. 20, 1754, and, as we infer from the will, his widow married William Witter. She lived, according to the testimony of her granddaughter Mrs. Farnham, No. 839, to be 105 years old.

200. ELISHA, born Dec. 29, 1723, and married, May 28, 1745, Abigail Avery. They lived in that part of Norwich which is now Lisbon, where his will, dated June 19, 1788, gives him the title Esq., and names as heirs: son Septimius, son Elisha, daughters Deborah and Mary, and granddaughter Amy Bishop.

201. ELIZABETH, born Jan., 1725-6, and died Oct. 30, 1726.

202. HANNAH, born June 15, 1728, and died Jan. 8, 1731-2.

## 98. SIMON.

203. MARTHA, born Mar. 7, 1715-16, and married, (1.) in 1738, Rev. Ebenezer Devotion, son of Rev. Ebenezer and Hannah (Buck) Devotion of Suffield, where he was born, May 18, 1714. He graduated at Yale in 1732, and was ordained as pastor of the Congregational Church in Scotland, Windham Co., Conn., Oct. 22, 1735. He remained there, a very acceptable preacher and pastor, until his death, July 16, 1771. She married, (2.) as his second wife, Rev. Dr. Coggswell, the successor of her first husband in the pastorate of the Scotland church.

Of the children by her first husband:

i. Ebenezer Devotion became a prominent man as farmer and merchant in Scotland.

ii. Martha Devotion married, Apr. 17, 1761, the Hon. Samuel Huntington, signer of the Declaration of Independence. See Huntington Family.

iii. Hannah Devotion married, in 1764, the Rev. Dr. Joseph, brother of Gov. Huntington, who had married her sister Martha. See also Huntington Family.

204. SIMON, born June 18, 1718, and died, as the Norwich records report, "in St. Eustatia, about 8 or 9 July, 1740."

205. ELIJAH, born in Norwich, Sept. 4, 1720, and married, Jan. 23, 1745-6, Susanna, daughter of Richard and Elizabeth (Lynde) Lord, of Lyme, Conn., where she was born, Jan. 10, 1724. They lived in Norwich, where he soon took rank among the most enterprising business men of the town. He and his wife were interred in the Chelsea burying-lot. Their grandson John, in 1835, set new stones to their graves, to preserve the records on the older and ruder stones. They give us the date of his death, Mar. 13, 1814, aged 93 years, and her's, Feb. 3, 1808, aged 83 years.

206. HANNAH, born July 1, 1722, and married, probably a Truman.

207. EUNICE, born Apr. 14, 1725, and married Nov. 17, 1746, Jonathan Huntington. For their record see Huntington Family.

208. MARY, born July 1, 1729, and married David Nevins of Norwich. They settled in Canterbury, where she united with the Congregational Church in 1752. They had a family of five children:

i. David Nevins, born in Canterbury, Sept. 12, 1747, and who became a prominent man. He was especially noted for his patriotism during the Revolution. He died in New York, Jan. 21, 1838, having had a family of twelve children.

    ii.   Samuel Nevins, who died unmarried.

    iii.  Betsey Nevins, who died single.

    iv.  Mary Nevins, who became the wife of Nathan Lord of Lisbon.

    v.   Martha Nevins, who married Capt. James Hyde of Norwich.

After the death of Mr. Nevins in 1757, she married, (2,) ———— Bingham, by whom she had at least one daughter, Aurelia Bingham, who became the wife of ———— Tappan.

209. RUFUS, born Oct. 29, 1731, and married, (1,) Hannah ————, who died Apr. 18, 1785, aged 46. He married, (2,) Zerviah ————, who united with the First Church in Norwich in 1788, and died Jan. 4, 1795, aged 57. He died Aug. 18, 1805. He and both of his wives were interred in the Norwich Town burying-lot. They probably had no children. The estate which he left and the local records indicate him as an active and successful business man.

His will, bearing date Feb. 16, 1797, names as legatees his nephew Rufus Lathrop Choat; the First Church; the Town; his nephews, David and Samuel Nevins; his niece and nephew, Mary and Nathan Lord; Martha, wife of Capt. James Hyde; Aurelia Tappan, daughter of sister Mary Bingham; nephew Daniel Huntington, son of sister Eunice; niece Lucy Hyde; and Hannah Turner, the wife of Dr. John Turner, and daughter of his sister, Eunice Huntington.

In the division of the estate, June 6, 1807, are named Elijah Lathrop; the heirs of Martha Devotion; Mrs. Hannah Truman; Mrs. Mary Bingham; Mr. Simon Fitch; the heirs of Eunice Huntington; Miss Lucretia Huntington; and Rufus L. Choat.

The next year receipts are recorded from the following heirs: Lucretia Huntington, Rufus L. Choat, Elijah Lathrop, Daniel Huntington, Lucy Hyde, Hannah Truman, John and Hannah Turner, Simon Fitch, Mary and Nathan Lord, Martha Hyde, Hannah Teal, Ebenezer Devotion and Mary Bynam, and the Town receipts for a legacy of $104.42.

210. ELIZABETH, born Aug. 23, 1733, and died, as her headstone in the Norwich town cemetery reports, "of consumption, Mar. 6, 1763."

211. LUCY, born Sept. 1, 1735, and married, May 8, 1758, Ichabod Fitch. They had one son, who is reported on the Norwich records:

    Simon Fitch, born Dec. 18, 1758.

## 99. NATHANIEL.       Norwich, Conn.

212. ASA, who died Nov. 10, 1761.

213. NATHANIEL, who married Margaret. He died Jan. 8, 1757.

214. ZEBADIAH, born in Norwich in 1725 and married Clorinda, daughter of Rev. Simon Backus of Wethersfield, and his wife Eunice, daughter of the Rev. Dr. Timothy Edwards of East Windsor. She was born in Newington, Conn., Oct. 31, 1730, and died in Norwich, Oct. 25, 1803. He died Nov. 14, 1793.

215. AZARIAH, born in 1728, and married, Dec. 20, 1764, Abigail, daughter of Hon. Isaac and Rebecca (Lothrop) Huntington. They both joined the First Church of their native town in 1773. He was one of the solid and enterprising

men of the town, both in the church and in civil life. He died, Feb. 25, 1810, and his widow, March 9, 1820, aged 80. The inventory of his estate in 1817 was admitted at ———.

216. ANNA, not Annie, as Goodwin reports it, born, so the Norwich records, Aug. 13, 1735, and married, as his second wife, July 24, 1757, Col. William Bradford, son of Lieut. Charles and Elizabeth (Bradford) Whiting, of Canaan, N. Y. This Elizabeth Bradford was daughter of Samuel and Hannah (Rogers) Bradford of Duxbury, Mass., and her mother, Hannah Rogers, was daughter of John Rogers and Elizabeth Paybodie, a granddaughter of John Alden and Priscilla Mullens of the Mayflower. Col. and Judge Whiting, born April 15, 1731, was a man much honored, both in military and civil life. He died, in Canaan, Oct. 13, 1796, and his widow, Jan. 20, 1815. They had a family of eleven children, for whom and their children see Goodwin's Notes.

217. CHLOE, born Aug. 30, 1737, and died Oct. 23, 1746.

218. LUCY, died Apr. 7, 1747.

### 100. ISRAEL, JUN.

219. ISRAEL, 3d, born Mar. 19, 1710-11, and married Oct. 5, 1737, Edmah Mozeley, and settled in Norwich. He was deceased at the date of his father's will, Mar. 22, 1758.

220. EPHRAIM, born Jan. 23, 1713-14, died June 17, 1742. He united with the church in West Farms Parish, Norwich, in 1741.

221. MARY, born Sept. 3, 1715, married ——— Birchard.

222. JEDIDIAH, born Jan. 4, 1718, and married, (1,) Sept. 27, 1742, Abigail, daughter of Daniel and Abigail (Wattles) Hyde, who was born in Norwich Oct. 2, 1723, and died Oct. 1, 1751. He married, (2,) May 18, 1752, Jemima, daughter of John and Jane (Hyde) Birchard who was born Feb. 13, 1729, and died in Bozrah, Sept. 1, 1789. At what time the family settled in Bozrah does not appear. He was a man held in honor, both in civil and in military life. His will, dated at Bozrah, Oct. 11, 1790, as that of Captain Jedidiah Lathrop, names as legatees, his sons, Jedidiah, Ephraim, Uriah, Zephaniah, and Israel; and his daughters, Mary West, Abigail Fish, Phebe Gardner, Olive Stark, and Jemima Gardner. His death occurred June 9, 1792.

223. CATHERINE, born Aug. 11, 1720, and married ——— John Hackley of Lebanon. They had at least one son. Andrew Hackley, born in Lebanon 1755, and married in 1780, Hannah, daughter of Zebulon and Lydia (Bourn) Metcalf.

224. SIMEON, born Jan. 15, 1722-3, and married, Jan. 11, 1749, Hannah, daughter of Benjamin and Lydia (Hazen) Abel of Norwich. They settled in Bozrah, where he was a deacon in the Congregational Church. His wife died Sept. 17, 1802. In his will, dated Bozrah, Feb. 17, 1804, he names as his legatees: his grandsons Giles and Simon Lathrop, sons of his son Simeon; granddaughter Hannah; sons Roger, Oliver, and Zabdiel; daughter Hannah, wife of Christopher Calkins; daughter Eunice, wife of Stephen Woodworth; daughter Lydia, wife of John Fish, and Sarah Lathrop.

225. EZEKIEL, born Sept. 5, 1724, and married, Oct. 18, 1753, Abigail

Lyon, who died Feb. 14, 1806, aged 86. His inventory was proved, Mar. 15, 1771, amounting to £554, 9s. 3d.

226. PRUDENCE, born Mar. 16, 1747-8, and called in her father's will, his "youngest daughter."

#### 101. WILLIAM.

227. WILLIAM, JUN., born June 15, 1715, and married May 13, 1745. Dorcas, daughter of Hon. Isaac and Rebecca (Lathrop) Huntington of Norwich. He was born in Norwich, Feb. 23, 1721-5. Her gravestone stands alone in the southwest corner of the East Chelsea lot, and gives the date of her death July 11, 1801. His death is recorded next to his marriage, as occurring July 15, 1770. His remains lie a few feet north of his father's in the Norwich Town Cemetery. Probably they had no children.

228. JOSHUA, born June 6, 1717, and died Dec. 16, 1717.

229. EZRA, born May 18, 1719, and married, Feb. 25, 1746, Esther Clark. They lived in Norwich. He died Sept. 15, 1753, and letters of administration were taken out by his widow Esther, Nov. 6, 1753. After his death she married Jabez son of Nathan and Elizabeth (Tracy) Backus, by whom her oldest son was Oliver Backus, born Jan. 18, 1755. (Hyde, 154.)

230. JEREMIAH, born Feb. 11, 1721, and married Dec. 9, 1746, Lydia Armstrong. Letters of administration were taken out by his widow, after his death; and on her death letters were taken out Mar. 1, 1757, by her brother, Joseph Armstrong. The legatees named are Jeremiah, eldest son; William the second and youngest; and Eunice the only daughter. He died, Sept. 27, 1753, and she, Sept. 20, 1755.

231. JAMES, born May 3, 1724, and died Dec. 29, 1726.

232. ANDREW, born Apr. 20, 1728, and married, (1,) Oct. 15, 1755, Deborah Woodworth who died, Oct. 18, 1760, aged 27 years. He married, (2,) Sept. 14, 1763, Abigail Fish. His will dated Bozrah, July 1, 1795, names as his legatees, his wife; his son Andrew; his daughter Abigail Wattles; his daughter Deborah Lathrop; and his daughter Martha. He died, so the Bozrah records testify, July 9, 1803, and his widow, Jan. 12, 1812, at 79 years of age. Appointed guardian to Sarah, daughter of brother Ez.

233. EBENEZER, JUN., born June 20, 1732, and married May 11, 1758, Phebe Ayres. Was named in her father's will, 1771.

234. JONATHAN, born June 22, 1734, married, Mar. 16, 1758, Theoda Woodworth of Norwich. In 1771 he was appointed guardian to Eunice, daughter of his brother Jeremiah. His will dated Apr. 11, 1817, gives daughter Betty $1,800; son Daniel $2,200; son Roger $2,200; son Jesse $2,200; daughter Lucy McCall $1,100, and son Ezra $2,200. He died where Seymour More now lives, Dec. 14, 1817, and his wife Dec. 22, 1816, at 80 years of age, as their gravestones show.

235. JOHN, born in Norwich May 6, 1739, and graduated at Princeton, N. J., in 1763. He studied theology and was ordained pastor of the Old North Church, Boston, May 18, 1768. He was twice married, (1,) Jan. 30, 1771, to Mary, daughter of John Wheatley, who died Sept. 24, 1778, aged 35 years; and (2) at Wells, Me., Sept. 14, 1780, to Mrs. Elizabeth, widow of —— Sayer, and

daughter of Rev. Samuel Checkley, sen., of the New South Church, Boston. She died, Jan. 28, 1809, aged 58 years. See 2d Church, Boston, p. 125, *et seq;* see Sprague Unit. Pul.; see 2d Ch., Boston. An engraving by Edwin of Philadelphia, from a sketch of his face by Henry Williams, was executed in 1812, for the November number of the *Polyanthus,* at the expense of its proprietor, Mr. Joseph T. Buckingham. A second was engraved by ——

236. ZACHARIAH, born March 25, 1742, and married, April 24, 1768, Mrs. Mehitable Cleveland. The following certificate, it is hoped, will settle most solidly the marriage bond of this married couple:

"NEW LONDON COUNTY: ss. NORWICH, April 24, 1768.
Personally appeared Mr. Zachariah Lothrop and Mrs. Mehitable Cleveland, both of Norwich, and were joined together in marriage according to law.
*Coram* BEN. HUNTINGTON, *Justice."*

He died Dec. 26, 1817, and she, Sept. 15, 1825. He was appointed by the Court of Probate April 17, 1771, guardian to William Lathrop, Jr., son to his brother Jeremiah, deceased.

### 102. JOHN. Norwich, Conn.

237. ZEBULON, born in Norwich, Jan. 10, 1717, and married, Sept. 4, 1740, Lois, daughter of Dr. Theophilus and Elizabeth (Hyde) Rogers of Norwich, where she was born July 22, 1721. They lived and died in Norwich. She died Sept. 21, 1777, and he, Jan. 13, 1781, and were both interred in the Franklin cemetery.

238. AZUBAH, born in Norwich, March 3, 1718-19, and died April 23, 1719.

239. AZUBAH, 2d, born in Norwich, June 18, 1720, and married as his second wife, Dec. 2, 1755, (when she for honor was called Mrs.,) Mr. Abijah Fitch. The only child recorded to them is: John Fitch, born Feb. 8, 1758, and died Aug. 15, 1759. By a former wife, Ann Wallbridge, he had four children: John, who died young; Hannah; Jerusha; and Abijah.

240. BETHIA, born in Bozrah, July 26, 1722, and married, in 1743, Joseph Sanford. She united with the West Farms parish church in Norwich, in 1748, and died in 1808.

241. ELIZABETH, born in Norwich, May 26, 1726, and married, in 1743, John Packer. Franklin Church Records.

242. REBECCA, born in Norwich, Dec. 15, 1728, and married Abial Squire, and lived in Lebanon, where two children were recorded to them: Rhoda Squire, born July 7, 1754; Abial Squire, born March 2, 1758.

243. SARAH, born in Norwich, Sept. 23, 1731, and died April 17, 1744.

244. ANNA, born in Norwich, March 23, 1734, and married, Nov. 17, 1754, Elijah, son of Benjamin and Lydia (Hazen) Abel of Norwich. She died Dec. 15, 1761. Their children, all born in Norwich, were: Elijah Abel, born Oct. 18, 1755; Abel Abel, born Sept. 14, 1757; Jabez Abel, born Oct. 17, 1759; Aimey Abel, born April 3, 1762; Eunice Abel, born March 7, 1764.

245. RHODA, born in Norwich, June 2, 1740, and married, May 28, 1760, Eli, son of Capt. Matthew and Elizabeth (Huntington) Hyde. They settled in

11

Franklin, Conn., where he died Oct. 6, 1815, and she, Feb. 10, 1821. For their descendants, see Hyde Family. Their children, all born in Norwich, were:

i.  Uri Hyde, born March 4, 1763, and died, unmarried, in 1832, in Franklin.

ii.  Christopher Hyde, born Nov. 14, 1767, was married three times and had eight children.

iii.  Eli Hyde, born Jan. 20, 1778, married Sarah, daughter of Samuel Nott, D.D., of Franklin. He was a Presbyterian clergyman, and had a family of eight children.

iv.  Octavia Hyde, born March 24, 1761, and died Oct. 24, 1789.

v.  Anne Hyde, born April 7, 1765, and married, Jan. 26, 1803, Elijah Clark Hyde.

vi.  Rhoda Hyde, born April 30, 1770, and married Jesse Lathrop, No. 518.

vii.  Lydia Hyde, born Jan. 20, 1772, and died in Franklin, single, Dec. 16, 1802.

viii.  Lovice C. Hyde, born Dec. 26, 1773, and married Milton, only child of Abner and Temperance (Wales) Hyde.

ix.  Elizabeth Hyde, born Feb. 25, 1776, and married, Feb. 25, 1798, Jabez Fitch, son of Prosper and Eliza (Lord) Rudd.

x.  Clarissa Hyde, born April, 1780, and married, June 3, 1798, Simeon, son of Simeon and Elizabeth (Waterman) Backus.

246. JOHN, born in Norwich, and married Lydia, daughter of Jabez and Lydia (Abel) Hyde of Franklin, Conn., where she was born Jan. 6, 1744. He lived in Franklin, where his will was dated, June 10, 1803. In it he gives his entire estate to his wife, and on her death it is to be divided between her brother Joseph Hyde and John Lathrop of the County of Tolland, a son of Zebulon Lathrop, formerly of Lebanon. He died in Franklin, Oct. 8, 1803, and his widow, July 15, 1822. They had no children. Her name is on the Franklin church records as having united with it in 1799. His cane is now in the possession of Mr. Charles Lathrop of Tolland.

247. AZEL. This name is entered here after the most careful balancing of hints, and names, as the most probable place for it, though neither the Norwich nor Franklin records report it. Of course we have no birth or baptismal date. But we know that he married Elizabeth, daughter of Phineas and Anne (Rogers) Hyde of Franklin, where she was born April 11, 1755. After his death she married Ezra Huntington, and died in Ashford, Conn., in 1835.

### 103. SAMUEL.                                          Bozrah, Conn.

#### [Franklin Church Records.]

248. ELISHA, born July 13, 1713, and married, Jan. 31, 1732, Margaret Sluman, who died Oct. 10, 1742. He married Jan. 23, 1743, Hannah, daughter of Capt. John and Hannah (Denison) Hough, who was born in New London. They settled in Bozrah, but removed to Lebanon, N. H. He was a military man and was much honored by his fellow townsmen, both in Bozrah and in

Lebanon. He was killed by the falling of a tree in Lebanon, N. H., July 2, 1787, and his widow died in Hanover, N. H., Jan. 16, 1807.

249. SAMUEL, born Jan. 12, 1717, and married, according to the Franklin church records, in 1735, Charity Sluman.

### 107. BENJAMIN.                    Norwich, Conn.

[This family were all recorded in Norwich.]

250. LUCY, born Sept. 20, 1719, and married, Dec. 25, 1740, Josiah, son of Josiah and Rebecca Loomis of Windsor. This second Josiah was son of Samuel Rockwell who married Mary Norton: and Samuel was the son of the pioneer Deacon William Rockwell of Windsor. They settled in Norwich, where he died, Aug. 25, 1795, and she, Nov. 7, 1800. They had two children: Lucy Rockwell, born May 18, 1748, and married Jacob McCall; Josiah Rockwell, born May 18, 1743, and married Lydia Marsh.

251. BENJAMIN, born March 25, 1721, and married Elizabeth, daughter of Daniel and Abigail (Waters) Hyde. They settled in Franklin, Conn., where he united with the church in 1741. He married (2) Huldah ———. He died June 23, 1768, having made his will May 4, 1768.

252. CYPRIAN, born June 2, 1722, and married Mary Stark, who was born in Lebanon, Conn., and died there, Oct. 8, 1813, aged 87. For record of his descendants I am mainly indebted to Mrs. Almira M. Swift of Colchester, mentioned in father's will, 1774. He died, as Mrs. Otis' record shows, Oct. 6, 1785.

253. MATTHEW, born May 23, 1725, and died Dec. 2, 1782.

254. GIDEON, born April 2, 1727, and died Dec. 5, 1732.

255. MARY, born March 22, 1729, and died Nov. 5, 1736.

256. ARUNAH, born March 22, 1732, and died Dec. 9, 1732.

257. RHODA, born Oct. 23, 1734, and died Aug. 25, 1735.

258. ARUNAH, 2d, born Dec. 1, 1735, and married (1), Martha ———, and (2d), Sarah ———. He died June 22, 1817, and wife Sarah, April 11, 1815.

259. MARY, 2d, born Nov. 13, 1737, and died April 14, 1737.

260. ABIGAIL, a child of the second wife, who is named in the father's will in 1774.

### 108. CAPT. EBENEZER.

261. SYBELL, born in Norwich, Oct. 13, 1726, and married, May 17, 1752, Samuel, son of Daniel and Abigail (Letlingwell) Tracy of Norwich. He was born in Norwich April 23, 1723, a graduate of Yale College in 1744. They settled in Norwich where they had,

    i.   Daniel Tracy, born Jan. 8, 1751, and died Jan. 27, 1753.

    ii.  Sybel Tracy, born Aug. 2, 1753.

    iii.  Lydia Tracy, born Sept. 6, 1755.

    iv.  Daniel Tracy, born in 1758, and married, Nov. 15, 1782, Mrs. Lucretia Hubbard.

    v.   Zebadiah Tracy, born April 26, 1760.

    vi. Ebenezer Tracy, born Nov. 11, 1762.

    vii. Abigail Tracy, born Jan. 18, 1765.

    viii. Thomas Tracy, born Dec. 23, 1767.

  262. LYDEA, born in Norwich, Oct. 14, 1728, and died July 7, 1738.

  263. ANNE, born in Norwich, Feb. 15, 1730-31, and married, as we infer from the distribution of her father's estate, a Mr. Perkins. By a mistake Chancellor Walworth, in his Hyde Family, married this Anne to Elijah Abel. For that Anna, see No. 244.

  264. ZIPPORAH, born in Norwich, May 11, 1733, and married, as his second wife, Jan. 24, 1759, Rev. Simon, son of Dea. Ebenezer and Sarah (Leflingwell) Huntington of Norwich. They had four sons: Roger, Daniel, Ebenezer, and Erastus. For their numerous descendants see the Huntington Family Memoir.

  265. SARAH, born in Norwich, Oct. 2, 1735, and married, as his first wife, Mar. 21, 1759, William, son of Col. Samuel and Sarah (Spaulding) Coit. He was born Feb. 13, 1735, became a ship-master and merchant in Norwich, and died there Nov. 16, 1821. She died Feb. 21, 1780. They had a family of nine children, and they and their children are numerously represented among the first families of Norwich, for a fuller list of whom than is here given, see Coit Family.

    i. Abigail Coit, born Jan. 26, 1760, married Gen. Joseph Williams, and had ten children. Among them were the wives of Hon. Erastus Huntington, son of Zipporah, No. 264; Russel Hubbard; and both wives of Dr. Wm. P. Eaton.

    ii. William Coit, born Apr. 27, 1761, and died Apr. 24, 1785.

    iii. Elisha Coit, born Dec. 22, 1762, and married Rebecca S. Manwaring. He was long honored as a Christian merchant in New York city.

    iv. Sarah Coit, born Feb. 11, 1765, and married Benjamin Coit, and had eight children.

    v. Lydia Coit, born Sept. 4, 1766, and married Thomas Fanning.

    vi. Daniel Coit, born Apr. 7, 1768, and died, aged 22 years.

    vii. Levi Coit, born Apr. 24, 1770, and married Lydia Howland.

    viii. Eliza Coit, born Jan. 11, 1772, married Dr. Dwight Ripley. She was his second wife, and had a family of twelve children, one of whom was the wife of Gov. Wm. A. Buckingham. A son, Judge Geo. B. Ripley, married Hannah Gardiner, No. 817.

    ix. Lucy Coit, born Sept. 9, 1773, and died May 1, 1844, unmarried.

  266. ZERVIAH, born in Norwich, May 6, 1738, and died unmarried.

  267. LYDIA, born in Norwich, July 4, 1740, married ——— Lathrop.

  268. EBENEZER 3d, born Mar. 30, 1743, married, Dec. 8, 1768, Deborah Lathrop. They settled in Windham, and removed in 1795 to Canajoharie, N. Y. He died in Norway, N. Y., in 1804, and her death is reported in Munsel's "Annals of Albany," Mar. 29, 1814, aged 67.

  269. ZEPHANIAH, born Mar. 26, 1746, and married, Jan. 19, 1769, Hannah Lathrop, No. 420. They settled on the farm which had been his father's, or a part of it. From the distribution of his estate, Apr. 22, 1817, we learn the names of the following legatees: his widow Hannah, who was to have the

"Mansion house" and five acres, beginning at guide-post at the corner of the road from Lathrop's bridge to the court house, and the road from said bridge landing; Asher Lathrop; the heirs of Mrs. Hannah Pitcher, wife of Elijah; Mrs. Sally Justin, wife of Ira; and Mrs. Anna Smith, wife of Elisha.

He died Oct. 25, 1815, as his gravestone, now standing in the new part of Norwich Town cemetery, shows.

270. JEDIDIAH, born in Norwich, Apr. 17, 1748, and married (1), Oct. 20, 1772, Civil, daughter of John Perkins by his second wife, Lydia, daughter of Solomon Tracy. She died June 19, 1797, aged 46. He married (2), Feb. 15, 1807, Anne Eames. He died June 19, 1817, and was interred in the Norwich Town cemetery. His will, dated Feb. 13, 1817, names as legatees: his wife Anna; son Ebenezer; daughter Lydia, wife of Alexander Gordon; and the heirs of his daughter Civil, late wife of Caleb Worden.

## 109. JABEZ.

271. ELIZABETH, born Mar. 28, 1730.

272. JABEZ, born May 11, 1736, and died Jan. 8, 1737.

273. REBECCA, born June 10, 1738.

274. ISAAC, born Feb. 2, 1740, and married, Dec. 20, 1764, Lucy Pike. On the distribution of his estate, Dec. 7, 1778, the following parties are named as heirs: his widow; Isaac, his only son; his eldest daughter, Lucy; his second daughter, Molly; and Lydia, his youngest daughter.

275. HEZEKIAH, born Aug. 16, 1742.

276. DELIGHT, born May 7, 1744.

277. DAVID, born Aug. 9, 1746, and died Apr. 27, 1747.

## 110. BARNABAS.

278. ABIGAIL, born Jan. 1, 1710-11.

## 111. JOSEPH.

279. JONATHAN JOHN SCUDDER, designated in distribution of his father's estate, Nov. 6, 1758, the "eldest son." He married, July 27, 1763, Mrs. Priscilla Wood, and the Norwich records report his death, Mar. 20, 1780.

280. BARNABAS, born in Norwich, Apr. 19, 1738, and married, July 7, 1757, Sarah Davis. This member of the family, after long research, I was able to identify from the very clear statements, made separately, but in perfect agreement, by his grandson Daniel, and his granddaughter Mrs. Lamson.

He became a Baptist preacher, and after a somewhat roving life, died in New Milford, Conn. In the distribution of his father's estate, in 1758, he is designated as the second son.

281. JOSEPH, born June 9, 1740, and had died probably before the father's estate was settled in 1758.

282. ZEBADIAH, called in his father's distribution, youngest son. This is probably the Zebediah who is reported, on the Franklin Church records, as dying in 1782.

283. MARY, who is named the only daughter, in the distribution of the father's estate.

### 118. SOLOMON. Norwich, Conn.

284. MARTHA, born in Norwich, Dec. 1, 1729, and died July 15, 1733.

285. JOSEPH, born in Norwich, Oct. 20, 1731, and married, May 16, 1759, Elizabeth Dwight.

[The following memoir was furnished by the Rev. Geo. F. Cushman, D.D. of New York city.]

Few of the descendants of Lathrop, the pioneer, have reached greater distinction, or conferred more luster upon the name, than the Rev. Joseph Lathrop, D.D., for sixty-five years the pastor of the Congregational Church in West Springfield, Mass. As a husband, father, and citizen; as a scholar and divine, a thinker and writer; as a wise counselor and friend; as a faithful shepherd, he was honored alike in life and in death. He was beloved and revered by his contemporaries, and at the centennial of his ordination, late generations strove to pay to his memory the deserved tribute of praise. His fame has gained rather than lost by the lapse of time. Even in his life-time it had crossed the seas; it was bounded by no sectarian lines. He was a Congregational minister, in the days when it meant more than it does now, but an eminent Episcopal clergyman could say, "The best works in my library are those of the Rev. Dr. Joseph Lathrop." He was a distinguished light to those without as well as within his own fold. His influence in the valley of the Connecticut was almost without limit. He was ranked with the most distinguished of the New England divines. He was a man of the ripest intellect, of the deepest piety, and now, five generations since his birth, his name is lovingly recalled, and, like the alabaster box of ointment exceeding precious, its fragrance fills the land, so true is it that

> "The sweet remembrance of the just
> Shall flourish when he sleeps in dust."

Joseph Lathrop was born in Norwich, Connecticut, October 20, 1731. His father was a man of good repute for his piety and talent, and possessed such advantages of education as the times afforded, but died while his son was still in infancy. Left to the care of his mother, she was equal to the responsibility, and she not only instilled into her son those principles of piety which characterized his after life, but she taught him the rudiments of learning. At sixteen he had determined, at any cost of his little patrimony, to obtain a collegiate education, and he was prepared for college by the Rev. Mr. White of Bolton. He entered Yale College in 1750, and was graduated in 1754. Though his mind was already made up to enter the Congregational ministry, after his graduation he became a teacher in Springfield, Mass., mean while pursuing his theological studies. In 1756 he applied for admission to the ministry, and the same year was called to the charge of the Congregational Church in West Springfield. He accepted the call, entered at once upon his duties, and three years later, 1759, he married Miss Elizabeth Dwight, with whom he lived for more than sixty years, and who survived him.

Mr. Lathrop was found admirably qualified for his duties as a minister, and his parish grew and prospered under his care. He was faithful and pains-taking, a diligent preacher, his face was familiar in the houses of his flock, and he was an illustration of the truth that "a house-going parson makes a church-going people." In the pulpit he taught his congregation what they were to believe and do; in his daily walk and conversation he was an example to his flock, giving now a friendly warning and now a word of praise, and happy was the child upon whose head in earnest blessing the hand of Parson Lathrop was laid. He was in every way identified with his people, he made their interests his own. He was a student of books, but he was no less a student of men, and as he went from house to house he conned the most important lessons of wisdom, to be reproduced afterwards in his sermons. Day by day he thus strengthened the bonds that united him to his charge; the people trusted to his wisdom, and he was strengthened by their love. But notwithstanding, the sky was sometimes overcast, and the waters were troubled. Evil came from without. There was at one time some fear of the spread of Baptist principles; at another a roving imposter who proved to be a wolf in sheep's clothing, like Alexander the coppersmith, threatened to do much harm in Mr. Lathrop's hitherto united fold. He was prepared for the emergency and contended earnestly for the faith once delivered to the Saints. With great plainness he instructed his people in what he believed to be the truth, and the "tyranny was soon overpast." The sermons he delivered upon the latter occasion, were masterpieces of controversy, and general in their application, and at the instance of his people they were published, and soon went through some twelve editions, so great was the demand for them. Under the title of "Wolves in Sheep's Clothing" they were reprinted in Edinburgh, Scotland, and now, after nearly a hundred years they may be read with pleasure and profit. In our age there would seem to be something of severity even in the title page, but Mr. Lathrop could not be indifferent to the truth, and as a faithful shepherd it was his duty to protect his flock; he was no hireling, to flee at the approach of danger. This was afterwards well illustrated during, and at the close of the war of the Revolution. The continental currency was so depreciated as to become almost worthless; the people were poor and suffered great privations. These sufferings Mr. Lathrop willingly shared. At times he was reduced to great straits for want of money; his small salary was irregularly paid and a large sum in arrears accummulated. These arrears Mr. Lathrop voluntarily forgave; when the clouds began to disappear he could not endure to see the parish struggling under the burden of a debt to himself. St. Paul was a tent-maker and labored with his own hands, and Mr. Lathrop did not think it misbecame him to eke out his salary by personal labor upon his little farm. He had taken his parish, as was common in those days, for better or for worse, and he cheerfully shared their ill as well as their good fortune. In their prosperity, the people had willingly offered themselves for him, and when need was, he was as ready to endure for them, and so while he followed the plow or swung the scythe, he reaped lessons of spiritual husbandry. No honors, no offers of emolument could tempt him away. His fame extended far beyond the parochial bounds. In 1791, Yale College conferred upon him the honorary degree of Doctor in Divinity, as did Harvard University in 1811. In 1792, he was elected a Fellow of the American Academy of Arts and Science, and in 1793 he was appointed a Professor in Divinity in Yale College. Yale was his Alma Mater; the position was one congenial to his tastes. Students in Divinity had come to him in his quiet parish, at least a score, and among them Dr. Appleton, the late President of Bowdoin College; he would have the advantages afforded by the companionship of scholars and by the college library; his salary would be doubled, and there would be a hope that he might make some provision against the infirmities of age. But none of these things moved him. Great as the temptation was, he resisted it, and said to his people, "I shall not go; the Lord do so to me and more also, if aught but death part me and thee."

The life of Dr. Lathrop was thence forward not more eventful than would be the life of most ministers of equal distinction in a country parish. His people appreciated the man and the sacrifices he had made for them; they were enriched by his growing fame. They built him a new barn, it was followed by a new meeting-house. When councils were called in neighboring parishes, Dr. Lathrop was a foremost man among them; he was often selected to preach occasional sermons, and, as far away as Boston was, his services were brought into use there. He was the exemplar of an industrious man. He was in no sense a sensational preacher, they are the product of our times, but he improved all occasions, he found

> "Tongues in trees, books in the running brooks,
> Sermons in stones, and good in every thing."

Tradition relates, it seems incredible, that he wrote above five thousand sermons in the course of his long ministry. Many of them were published in pamphlet form, and passed through several editions. Six volumes of his sermons were issued during his lifetime, and after his death a seventh volume with an autobiography was published and several of these volumes came to a second edition. He was also the author of a volume of miscellany, consisting of political, moral, and entertaining papers. For a further account of the publications of Dr. Lathrop, with lists of many of his sermons, and the occasions and reasons of their being printed, we refer to his Autobiography, and to the Memoirs of him in Sprague's "Annals of the Christian Pulpit." Very few of our American divines have written so many sermons or written them so well, and fewer still have left behind them so many published volumes. To publish a volume of sermons is easy: the sermons of Dr. Lathrop have the honor not only of being published, but of being read, and they survive to our own day as a monument of his learning and piety.

Dr. Lathrop's ministry was continued through many years, and his eye was not dim and his natural force was not abated. At the age of eighty he preached a sermon in review of his long ministry, as he did five years later at the close of its sixtieth year. This was in 1816. Two years later, growing infirmities, he was now eighty-eight, compelled him to ask for an assistant or colleague, and he was fortunate enough in securing one like-minded with himself in the Rev. William B. Sprague, D.D., afterwards the distinguished author of the "Annals of the American Pulpit." Dr. Lathrop still sometimes assisted in the services of God's house, but the work of his life was done. Like Samuel, the venerable man had anointed his successor; like Simeon, he was now ready to sing the *Nunc dimittis*. On the last day of 1820, full of honors and of years, he entered into the rest that remains for the Israel of God, and heard the "well done" of the Master whom he had served. His death, though not unexpected, was a cause of sorrow, not only to his people, but wherever he was known. Every thing was done to pay honor to his lifeless remains. Multitudes gathered to his burial, his young colleague delivered a memorial discourse, and in the Town House Cemetery, all that was mortal of that man of God, Dr. Joseph Lathrop, awaits the resurrection of the just. Thirty-six years later the centennial of his ordination was celebrated in the parish in which he lived and died, and the numbers present, of his kinsmen and of the friends of the church, showed in what loving remembrance he was still held. The Rev. Dr. Sprague of Albany, the colleague of 1820, delivered a glowing memorial discourse of the venerable Father in God; tributes were paid to him in many other addresses, and the proceedings were published in a pamphlet of more than a hundred pages. In 1874, occurred the centennial of West Springfield. The historical address was by Dr. Thomas E. Vermilye, the proceedings make a pamphlet of one hundred and forty-five pages, and large portions of the space are given to Dr. Lathrop. It is not too much to say that he was the central figure in the history of that town, and to his teachings it owes much of its deserved fame.

But we must draw this imperfect sketch of a remarkable man to a close. We have already exceeded our limits and have been tempted to forget that we were preparing a genealogy and not writing a life. Those who desire further information are referred to Dr. Lathrop's Autobiography, to Sprague's "Annals of the American Pulpit," to the Encyclopædias and to the Centennial Pamphlets. They will there find abundant proof that we have not overrated the worth of Dr. Lathrop. He was a man of large intellect, a deep and original thinker, a ready writer, an impressive preacher, a faithful pastor, with a heart full of all virtues, of manners devout and dignified, and yet agreeable, a man who would have made his mark in any age and in any country, and in a family of the notable sons of the Pioneers, it is easy to regard him as *facile princeps*.

## 125. BENJAMIN. Barnstable, Mass.

286. MARY, born April 30, 1731, and married, May 31, 1753. Nathan Foster.

287. BENJAMIN, born July 1, 1741, and became insane. Nathan Foster was appointed his guardian, Oct. 26, 1765.

288. JOSEPH, who is named in his father's will in 1752, and who died while yet young.

## 126. JOSEPH. Barnstable, Mass.

289. REBECCA, baptized July 20, 1729, and died young.

290. JOSEPH, baptized May 13, 1732, after the father's death. He is named in his aunt Hannah's will, June 25, 1731.

## 127. SAMUEL. Barnstable, Mass.

291. PRINCE, named in his aunt Hannah's will, June 25, 1731, as son of Samuel—and probably by mistake designated as grandson. He married, Oct. 23, 1762, Martha Basset of Barnstable, where the marriage is recorded.

12

### 128. BENJAMIN.                    Windham, Conn.

292. A son, born Aug. 20, 1721, and died in thirteen days.

293. A daughter, born April 8, 1723, and probably died unnamed.

294. Nathaniel, born April 8, 1723, and died Oct. 26, 1725.

295. Elijah, born Nov. 18, 1724, and married Nov. 15, 1753, Silence, daughter of Zephaniah and Hannah (King) Leonard of Taunton. She was born Apr. 27, 1731. They were married by Rev. John Wales of Paynham, Mass. He was a graduate of Yale in 1749 and became a minister of the Congregational denomination and settled in Gilead society in Hebron, Conn., in April, 1752, where he continued to labor successfully until his death, Aug. 3, 1797. His wife died Oct. 15, 1799. We are indebted to him for preserving for us so much of the Scituate and Barnstable Church record as have reached our times. In 1769, the Rev. Ezra Stiles, D.D., afterwards president of Yale College, on a visit at his house, with his own hand, copied about 30 pages of the record which Rev. John Lothrop of Barnstable had kept while pastor at Scituate and Barnstable. This copy of Dr. Stiles has been several times copied, and in 1855-6 was printed in the New England Historical and Genealogical Register, and has been of great service to many Antiquarians and Genealogists. It is to be hoped that the balance of those old records may some day be recovered. Mr. Lothrop was active among the ministers of the State in all the work of caring for the churches, being often reported in the exercises of the Association to which he belonged, and of councils of which he was a member. His name, which in the beginning of his ministry was spelled Lothrop, in 1756 as member of the "Presbytry," there assembled in Kensington to ordain Mr. Samuel Clark, he is enrolled Latrop of Gilead; and in 1762 the same man as Elijah Lathrop was Scribe of the Association Meeting at Stepney.

296. Rev. Benjamin, born in Barnstable, Mar. 27, 1726, and married in Windham, July 8, 1751, Sybil, daughter of John and Sybil (Whiting) Backus who was born in Windham, Mar. 1, 1728-9. Her mother, Sybil Whiting was daughter of Rev. Samuel Whiting of Windham, and her father was son of John Backus, the pioneer of this name in Windham, and Mary Bingham. Mary Bingham was the daughter of Dea. Thomas Bingham also a Windham pioneer. Mr. Lathrop became a prominent man in Windham. He became also a preacher of the Baptist denomination after having been for years a member of the Congregational church. He died in Windham, July 16, 1804; his widow surviving him until the June of 1822. His gravestone bears this inscription: "Dedicated to the memory of Elder Benjamin Lathrop, who after faithfully discharging his duty as a minister of the gospel of Christ, worn out with bodily infirmities, calmly resigned his breath on the 16th of July, 1804, in the 79th year of his age." Of his character and that of his family we find this affectionate tribute in the Personal Memoirs of the late Joseph T. Buckingham of Boston. "My mother was offered an asylum in the house and family of a Mr. Lathrop, an offer that was gladly accepted. Here she remained several years, earning something by needle-work, but charged nothing for food or house room beyond what assistance she might be able to render to the family. I feel it a pleasure as well as a duty to pay a

tribute of respect and gratitude to this gentleman and christian, and his family. BENJAMIN LATHROP was a plain honest farmer and a blacksmith,—a man of powerful intellect, and much given to theological controversy. Some years before my remembrance he had seceded from the Congregational church, and held separate religious services with a small party of friends,—sometimes alternately at the dwelling house of each, and sometimes in a school-house. This society, to which Mr. Lathrop constantly preached on Sundays, while during the rest of the week he labored on his farm or at the anvil and forge, were called Separatists, and the term was considered as a by-word and reproach. In process of time they adopted the distinguishing tenets of the Baptists, and Mr. Lathrop was ordained by ministers of that denomination from other towns, over the little flock to which he was attached. The ordination services were performed under the shade of a large and beautiful oak, in a pasture near his dwelling. An intimacy had for several years subsisted between the family of this worthy gentleman and my elder brothers. His children were near the same age. He and his wife had frequently visited my mother in her days of sickness, poverty, and affliction. He was not in affluent circumstances, and was dependent entirely on the product of his farm and an occasional job of work at his anvil for a living : for it was a fundamental principle on which he and his associates had separated from their fellow worshipers at the church that a preacher of the gospel should not preach for hire, and that all taxes for the support of preaching were illegal and unchristian. Yet my mother kept her room and sat at his table gratuitously; and her children, whenever they visited her, were welcomed with cheerfulness and affection. Mr. Lathrop and his wife were to her as brother and sister, friend and physician. They have long since gone to receive their reward, where I trust the widow's thanksgiving and the orphan's gratitude will be accepted and acknowledged as testimonials of their obedience to the precepts of Him who has invited those that feed the hungry, visit the sick, and receive the stranger to their dwelling to sit at his right hand and partake of the glories of his kingdom." In a letter to the Author in 1859, Mr. Buckingham also thus testifies to his regard for this benefactor of his boyhood. "If age and physical infirmity did not forbid I would not hesitate to make a journey to Stamford to tell a grand-daughter of Benjamin Lathrop how much I revere that name.

297. ELIZABETH, baptized in Barnstable, Nov. 24, 1727, and died May 18, 1730.

298. MERCY, born in Barnstable, Aug. 26, 1729, and died Oct. 1, 1802. Married Carey.

299. ELIZABETH, born in Barnstable, Mar. 9, 1731, and married Joshua Ripley of Windham. Their ninth child: Erastus Ripley, born in Windham Jan. 17, 1770, and graduated at Yale College in 1795. He became a preacher and was settled in Meriden, Conn., in 1803, and dismissed in 1822. After a brief settlement in Montville he returned to Meriden, where he died Nov. 17, 1843.

300. ANNA, born in Windham and there recorded, Feb. 15, 1733, died Aug. 29, 1774. Letters of administration on her estate were granted under date of Jan. 6, 1776, to her brother Benjamin, which make her heirs to have been: her

brothers Benjamin, Elijah, and John; Mercy Carey, Elizabeth Ripley, Lydia Gilbert; Sarah Frink; and Benjamin and Lebbeus sons of her deceased brother Nathaniel.

301. NATHANIEL, born Dec. 29, 1734, and married Anna Fitch. He died in Canterbury, where he was a land-holder, Apr. 30, 1762. His widow was admitted to the Canterbury church the same year. She afterwards married Jonathan Haskell, and by him she had two children, Sally, and Jonathan who became a Baptist minister. They settled in Wyoming.

302. ABNER, born Mar. 22, 1737, and died Aug. 5, 1741.

303. JOHN, born Apr. 4, 1738, graduated at Yale College, 1762, and settled in New Haven where he was married by Rev. Samuel Bird, Oct. 31, 1764, to Mary, daughter of Mr. Timothy and Jane (Harris) Jones of that city, born Dec. 12, 1743. That he was a man of note as well as education is evident from the records of the city. He was prominent during the Revolutionary period for the promptness and efficiency with which he acted in the American cause. We find him reported as one of the New Haven Committee, Nov. 6, 1775, " to call together suspected persons to be examined." He died in 1789. Pierpont Edwards and Eunice Lothrop were appointed administrators on the estate of John Lothrop late of New Haven, deceased, Aug. 3, 1790. Thomas Howe and David Austin, Esq., Committee on Estate of John Lothrop, exhibit inventory Sept. 3, 1790, and the court allow to the widow £24, 7s. 9d. The inventory specifies ten acres of land in the southwest part of Cheshire, and four other lots of land in New Haven and West Haven. On the 2d of May, 1794, Pierpont Edwards, Esq., presents an addition to the inventory of a right in the western lands which was ordered sold, for £71, 17s. 2d. for the benefit of creditors.

304. SOLOMON, born Feb. 23, 1739–40, and died Sept. 1, 1740.

305. LYDIA, born Aug. 15, 1742, and married ―――― Gilbert of Hebron.

306. SARAH, born Jan. 23, 1745, and married ―――― Frink. Children: Sally Frink, Lucius Frink who married a Backus, Alfred Frink who married a Page, George Frink.

## 129. JOHN.                                    Tolland, Conn.

307. DAVID, born Oct. 1723, and married July 28, 1747, Clarinda Delano. He died Oct. 2, 1787. As their dates are all on the Tolland records he probably lived and died there.

308. JONATHAN, born Sept. 18, 1727, and married Dec. 20, 1755, Rachel Ladd.

309. ANNA, born Mar. 10, 1730.

310. JOHN, born May 6, 1732, and married Dec. 10, 1754, Lucy Gray of Coventry. He died, as his grandson Rowland's record says, Mar. 24, 1812, " in the 80th year of his age, born in May." Lucy his wife died Dec. 25, 1807, in the 67th year of her age.

311. THATCHER, born Jan. 26, 1734, and married, Nov. 10, 1755, Submit Loomis, daughter of Moses and Elizabeth (Bidwell) Loomis of Windsor, who died Aug. 22, 1794, aged 59. He died Dec. 30, 1806. He is reported in the

Windsor History as having succeeded Timothy Skinner, of Wapping, as sexton in Wapping parish in Windsor, and who died in 1777. A letter from him to his children in Longmeadow, has preserved the names of his four sons.

312. LYDIA, born June 21, 1736.

313. ELIZABETH, born Apr. 22, 1740, and married, Feb. 24, 1763, Col. Solomon, son of Joshua and Milicent Wills, who was born Oct. 14, 1731. He early enlisted in the Revolutionary service and rose to the rank of Colonel. After the war he was in the public Civil service for the rest of his life. He served his townsmen in many offices with great fidelity and acceptance, was associate judge of Tolland County for seven years and a member of the State Legislature for twenty-three sessions. He died Dec. 10, 1807. Their children, as reported in Waldo, were: Azariah Wills, born May 30, 1772, and settled in Franklin, N. Y.; Solomon Wills, born Jan. 10, 1775, and settled in Pennsylvania; Wareham Wills, born July 27, 1780, and settled in Pennsylvania; Roxalana Wills, born Dec. 3, 1763, and became the first wife of Col. Eliakim, youngest son of Col. Samuel and Sarah (White) Chapman, and died Nov. 24, 1780; Nancy Wills, born Sept. 3, 1765, and became the second wife of Col. E. Chapman, as above; Elizabeth Wills, born Nov. 30, 1767, and married Capt. Ashbel Steele; Melicent Wills, born Sept. 12, 1769, and married Col. Elijah Smith.

## 133. ICHABOD. Tolland, Conn.

314. ABIGAIL, born Oct. 15, 1733, and married, Nov. 26, 1754, as his second wife, Samuel, son of Dea. Francis West of Tolland, the father of her sister Sarah's husband, by his first wife, Sarah Delano. She had by him two children: Ann West, born Sept. 12, 1756; Ruth West, born Dec. 21, 1759.

315. SARAH, born Mar. 20, 1735, and died June 6, 1739.

316. HOPE, born July 6, 1737, and married, May 3, 1760, Hannah Hubbard, of Tolland. He settled in Tolland and was a prominent citizen of the town. He represented the town four times in the State Legislature. During the Revolutionary period he was an active partisan for the war, and rendered efficient service on the committees of the town. Witness the following extract from the acknowledgment made to Tolland by the Boston citizens through their committee, Henry Hill, under date of Boston, Oct. 24, 1774.

"Gentlemen, this is to acknowledge the receipt of your kind and generous donation by the hand of our worthy friend, Mr. Hope Lathrop, which shall be applied to the relief of our poor sufferers by means of the cruel and oppressive port bills."

Mr. Lathrop had served also in the campaign of 1758, being a private in the Company of Capt. Samuel Chapman at that date. He died in Tolland, Nov. 8, 1792.

317. SARAH, born Jan. 22, 1740, and married, Mar. 25, 1756, Samuel West, Jun., son of Samuel and Sarah Delano West. The children born to them in Tolland, were: Sarah West, born Nov. 19, 1757; Tryphena West, born Jan. 21, 1760; Ichabod West, born June 7, 1762; Stephen West, born Feb. 15, 1765; Frederick West, born Apr. 2, 1767; Grace West, born Sept. 26, 1769; Prudence West, born Feb. 23, 1772.

318. ANNA LO., born Apr. 5, 1742, of Coventry, Conn., and married, Nov. 5, 1761, Jacob, son of Thomas and Sarah (Miller) White, who was born in Andover, Conn., Jan. 20, 1736. He settled in Torrington, Conn., where he died in 1788, and she died in Burke, Vt., Oct. 22, 1822. Children: Dan White, born Sept. 22, 1762, and married Rowena Wilson. He was the pioneer in settling in Burke, Vt. Thomas White, born Nov. 28, 1764, and married Jedidah, daughter of Ashbel and Patience Baldwin, of Goshen, Conn. They settled in Torrington, and had three children; Jacob White, born Aug. 28, 1768, married, and had four sons; Lucinda White, born Sept. 19, 1771, and died in Burke, Vt.; Anna White, born May 8, 1774, and married (1) Juber Beardsley, and (2) John Vanduree; Elam White, born Apr. 14, 1778, and married (1) Wealthy, daughter of Amasa Coe, and (2) Esther ——. By his first wife he had eight children, and by his second, one.

319. SOLOMON, born May 24, 1746, and married, Nov. 26, 1767, Elizabeth ——, who was born Nov. 5, 1750, as her own family bible attests, and died in the triumphs of Christian faith, Apr. 19, 1774. He died in Albany, June 6, 1785.

320. MARY, born Sept. 14, 1748.

## 134. SOLOMON.  Tolland, Conn.

321. MERCY, born Oct. 1, 1736.
322. SUSANNA, born Apr. 2, 1738.

## 136. MELATIAH.

323. DEBORAH, born Aug. 11, 1739, and married —— Gray, and died in Dutchess Co., N. Y., June 13, 1770.

324. LUCY, born Sept. 9, 1740, married —— St. John, and lived in Western N. Y., near Chenango Valley, died June 18, 1805.

325. JEDIVIAH, born Feb. 19, 1742, married —— Barnabas, and died in Dutchess Co., N. Y., Mar. 13, 1770.

326. SIMON, born Jan. 1, 1744, married Hannah Davis, and died Dec. 27, 1820, in Ontario Co., N. Y. His widow died in 1823.

327. EUNICE, born Nov. 14, 1745, married —— Nash, died Jan. 25, 1802, in Chenango Co., N. Y. Two sons in New York city.

328. WALTER, born Jan. 24, 1747, died Jan. 25, 1823, Dutchess Co., N. Y.

329. MARY, born Sept. 13, 1748, married —— Weston, died Mar. 17, 1780, in Columbia Co., N. Y. One son, who was a prominent man, Hon. Roswell Weston, of Sandy Hill, N. Y.

330. MELATIAH, born Dec. 12, 1749, died June 17, 1826, in Saratoga County, N. Y.

331. EZRA, born Aug. 19, 1751, the family bible of the late Judge D. N., of Carbendale, has this birth in Kent, Ct., in 1750. Married 1779(?) Miriam, daughter of "old Dea. Thurston" whose fame for piety was in all the churches, died Feb. 12, 1825, in Ontario Co., N. Y.

332. JERUSHA, born Sept. 28, 1753, married —— Stillwell, and died Sept. 15, 1769, in Dutchess Co., N. Y.

333. ICHABOD, born May 25, 1755, went early to the Huron river region in Ohio, and died Apr. 15, 1813.

334. JOSIAH, born in Amenia, Dutchess Co., N. Y., May 29, (Aug. according to his own record) 1757, married Rachel Perry, born July 15, 1762, and settled in Sherburne, Chenango Co., N. Y., in 1793. Last of his father's family, he died Mar. 7, 1854, aged 96 years, 6 months.

335. EBENEZER, born July 24, 1759, married Ruth Bettis, who was born Apr. 1, 1767, and died Nov. 15, 1835, of Madison Co., N. Y. He died Aug. 23, 1826, in Madison Co., N. Y.

336. JOHN, born Mar. 1, 1762, married Jan. 19, 1794, Prudence, daughter of Eleazer and Thankful (Lothrop) Hutch, No. 337, born June 8, 1776, (*Tolland* 91.) A farmer in Sherburne, Chenango Co., died July 17, 1825, and she died Dec., 1841.

337. ELIZABETH, born Mar. 1, 1762, married —— Hubbard, and died Aug. 12, 1794, in White Hall, Wash. Co.

338. ELEAZER, born Mar. 26, 1766, (21, Josiah's Record,) married Eunice (Hollister) Nichols, died in Brockport, Monroe Co., N. Y., Dec. 24, 1842.

### · 138. JOSEPH. Tolland, Conn.

339. THANKFUL, born in Tolland, Oct. 21, 1746, and married, Dec. 31, 1767, Eleazer Hatch, of Tolland, where they settled. The children reported to them in Waldo's *Tolland*, are: Semantha Hatch, born Nov. 22, 1768; Morana Hatch, born June 1, 1770; Zadoc Hatch, born Jan. 6, 1772, married, June 13, 1793, Caroline Holbrook, and had a family of nine children; Nathaniel Hatch, Jan. 19, 1774, and died Aug. 6, 1803; Prudence Hatch, born June 8, 1776; Grace Hatch, born Apr. 3, 1778, and died Oct. 22, 1850; Jeduthan Hatch, born Dec. 20, 1780; Leetana Hatch, born Apr. 15, 1785.

340. PRUDENCE, born Aug. 16, 1749, and married, Mar. 22, 1770, Solomon, son of Solomon and Abigail (Strong) West, of Lebanon, who was born Aug. 23, 1744. She died Nov. 30, 1771. They had one child: Solomon West, born July 26, 1771, and died Aug. 21, 1771.

341. NATHANIEL, born Aug. 16, 1752, and died Apr. 28, 1771.

342. REBECCA, born Aug. 28, 1760.

### 143. JAMES. Barnstable, Mass.

343. DEBORAH, born Apr. 15, 1733, and married a Turner of Plymouth, where they now have descendants.

344. MARY, born April 6, 1735, and married, Dec. 5, 1749, Joseph Thoms.

345. JAMES, born March 25, 1737, and married, in 1765, Rebecca Paine.

346. MARTHA, baptized June 21, 1741, and married, April 20, 1761, Samuel Baker.

347. EBENEZER, born May 15, 1743, married Elizabeth, daughter of James Davis. She was born March 25, 1748, and died Dec. 18, 1828. He died in Barnstable, Jan. 27, 1814.

General Ebenezer Lothrop, though a man of large prominence in the community in which he lived and died, left but few records behind him, but among them is the record of his baptism, the very day of his birth, which would indicate that, like so many of the Lothrops, he came of God-fearing parents. His education, as the word is commonly used, was confined to such advantages as were afforded by the village school. These advantages were greatly improved by his natural force and ability, and by the acute observation which characterized him; and it may well be said that his books were men. He secured universal respect among his fellow citizens, who often looked to him for counsel and guidance.

He was all his life, and until his sudden death in 1844, a worker in iron, and especially the iron that was used in ship-building, agricultural implements, etc., and he brought up several of his sons to his own calling. At his place of business he was brought in contact with the prominent men of the day, who marked his energy and worth. While still a youth, he was fired with military ardor, and volunteered in the colonial service for duty in Nova Scotia. It was in this service, that on the weary marches he was often relieved of his pack by a Marshpee Indian, who in after years was a frequent visitor at the home of the General, and was always gladly welcomed by the family.

When the time came that tried men's souls, and the mutterings of the coming war of the Revolution were heard, he proved himself an ardent lover of his country, and was ready to make any sacrifice for her good. While in the service, his family, as well as himself, endured many privations and hardships.

In November, 1775, he was First-Lieutenant of a company commanded by Captain James Davis, and during the whole period of the struggle, his time and means were devoted to the cause. He served chiefly as coast guard, but he was often called into the Continental service for duty outside the State, in Rhode Island and elsewhere. In June, 1776, with General Joseph Otis and other citizens of Barnstable, thirteen in all, he signed a patriotic protest. The regiment in which he served was in the brigade of General Otis. In 1796, Mr. Lothrop was himself commissioned as Lieutenant-Colonel of the regiment by Governor Samuel Adams, and the next year was made, by Governor Increase Sumner, Brigadier-General. The regiment was the First Regiment of the Third Brigade of the Fifth Division of the Militia of Massachusetts, and it should be noted that Nathaniel Lothrop was, during the war, a Captain in the same regiment. As a soldier, General Lothrop was a stern disciplinarian. On one occasion, when a man of wealth and position came to the mustering ground in his carriage, and remained in it, showing no disposition to take his place in the ranks, a file of men, by General Lothrop's orders, took the man from his carriage, and marched him at a double quick to the place assigned him. The patriotic fire of General Lothrop did not die with him, but survived in two of his sons, one of whom became a Captain in the war of 1812.

From 1807 to 1809, General Lothrop was a Representative in the Great and General Court of Massachusetts. His wife, Elizabeth, a daughter of Captain James Davis, (in whose company General Lothrop served,) who survived him, is well remembered as a woman of great energy of character, and as well fitted by her natural abilities to be a brave man's counsellor and friend. General Lothrop, who in person was tall and slender, and of a florid complexion, was widely respected in life, and honored in death. He was a man of ability and integrity, and one of those patriotic sires who left to his descendants something better than houses and lands, the precious legacy of an unstained name.

348. DAVID, baptized Oct. 7, 1744, and married, probably, July 12, 1770, Bathsheba, daughter of John May, Jun., of Plymouth,

## 144. THOMAS LO. Barnstable, Mass.

349. THOMAS, born in 1738. His father having died when he was quite young, he was taken into the family of Dea. John Jacob, of Cohasset, by whom he was educated, and of whom he became the principal heir. He married Ruth Nichols, of Cohasset, where he settled. He became a man of note, and was equally serviceable to his townsmen and county in civil and military life. He attained a Colonel's rank in the State militia. He died Sept. 4, 1813; his widow in 1818.

## 145. ANSEL LO. Plymouth, Mass.

350. JOSEPH, born July 22, 1737, and died Oct. 6, 1738.

351. MARY, born Oct. 1, 1739, "daughter of Ansell, Mariner." Chose, Sept. 16, 1756, Ebenezer Spooner, gentleman, as her guardian. She died single, about 1792.

352. BETTY, born Aug. 14, 1741, had Ebenezer Spooner appointed her guardian by Judge John Cushing, Sept. 16, 1756.

353. ANSELL, born Mar. 16, 1742-3, had guardian appointed as above.

354. JOSEPH, born Sept. 20, 1745, and died Nov. 18, 1746.

355. WILLIAM, born April 15, 1748.

356. LYDIA, born July 12, 1750. Her guardian, Ebenezer Spooner, was appointed at the same time as for her sister and brother above. She married, April 15, 1770, see Fairfield records, William, son of Mr. Samuel Beadle, of Great Bursted, in Essex County, Eng. They have one child recorded to them in Fairfield :

Ansell Beadle, born Feb. 2, 1771.

## 146. JOSEPH LO.

357. REBECCA, born Dec. 20, 1758, who was probably dead when her father's estate was settled, as her name does not appear in the settlement.

358. DEBORAH, born ——, 1760.

359. TEMPERANCE, born after the death of her father, June 17, 1761.

## 147. SETH LO. Barnstable, Mass.

360. NATHANIEL, born Dec. 27, 1739, and married twice. The name of his first wife I have not found. His second, as his will shows, was Mehetabel ——. His death had occurred before May 12, 1817, when his will, which bears date Mar. 19, 1807, was proved. It is on record at Barnstable, Book xxxiii, p. 19. Names as legatees: Wife Mehetabel, my second wife ; son Thomas, by my first wife ; and daughter Susannah, now wife of Ebenezer Cobb, Jun. Executor, Eleazer Cobb, Jun., son-in-law,

13

361. JOSEPH, born May 1, 1742, and probably died before his father's will was made.

362. THANKFUL, born Aug. 2, 1741, and died in infancy.

363. JOHN, born April 5, 1745, and married Mary, No. 384, sister of Capt. Isaac Lothrop, of Barnstable, who lived to be 91 or 92 years old. He died Mar. 25, 1822, and she, June 19, 1840.

364. THANKFUL, born Feb. 18, 1746-7, and married Sturgis Howes, as we learn from her father's will.

365. MARY, born Mar. 24, 1748-9, and married Edward Childs, and had no children.

366. BENJAMIN, baptized July 1, 1753. He was living at the date of his father's will in 1798, and had no family.

367. SETH, born Dec., 1756, and probably died, without issue, before his father's will was made.

368. THOMAS, born July 4, 1758, and probably was not living when his father's will was made.

### 167. JOHN LO.          Barnstable, Mass.

[This family are all recorded in Barnstable.]

369. HANNAH, born April 18, 1725.

370. MARY, born June 20, 1730.

371. NATHANIEL, born Sept. 22, 1732.

372. JOSEPH, born July 10, 1735, and died Aug. 2, 1741.

373. LOT, born Nov. 17, 1737.

374. BARNABAS, Oct. 17, 1740.

375. BETHIA, baptized Oct. 6, 1745.

376. ABIGAIL, baptized April 12, 1752.

### 172. JONATHAN LO.

377. JOSEPH, born Oct. 9, 1752, O. S.

378. REBECCA, born Oct. 29, 1755, N. S., and is named in her grandmother Hannah Lothrop's will, in 1763.

379. MERCY, born July 10, 1758.

380. THOMAS, born April 9, 1763.

381. JONATHAN, born Feb. 13, 1766.

382. DAVID, born June 20, 1770, married Sarah ——.

His will, dated June 11, 1844, and proved Mar. 12, 1850, names as his legatees his wife Sarah, and his three children, John, Asa, and Rebecca. Executor, wife Sarah.

### 173. GEN. BARNABAS LO.          Barnstable, Mass.

383. HANNAH, born on Monday, Mar. 4, 1745.

384. MARY, born Thursday, Mar. 12, 1747, and married John Lothrop, No. 363.

385. BARNABAS, born Friday, Jan. 27, 1749.

386. ABIGAIL, born Sunday, Apr. 8, 1752, and married Eliezer, son of Thomas and Lydia (Harlow) Ewer of Plymouth. He was a tanner and shoe-

.

maker and lived in Plymouth. The children were: Isaac Ewer, Barnabas Ewer, Ansel Ewer, Abigail Ewer.

387. ISAAC, born Thursday, Feb. 8, 1754, N. S., and died in infancy.

388. JOHN, born Nov. 23, 1755, and married Deborah Crocker of Hyannis, Mass., where he settled. She died in 1807, and he, Mar. 27, 1830.

389. ISAAC, 2d, born Sept. 6, 1758, and married, (1) Betsey Scudder, who died July 25, 1795, and (2) in 1796, Mary Crocker, who died Aug. 23, 1845. He was a blacksmith and lived in Barnstable, as his great grandson's letter shows, and died there Mar. 11, 1835.

390. DEBORAH, baptized Dec. 30, 1759, and married Josiah Davis, Nov. 13, 1788.

391. BENJAMIN, born Apr. 4, 1762 and died Mar. 21, 1822, probably single. At his death record in Barnstable he is designated as brother to the John Lothrop above.

392. RACHEL, born May 5, 1765, and died unmarried.

SIXTH GENERATION.

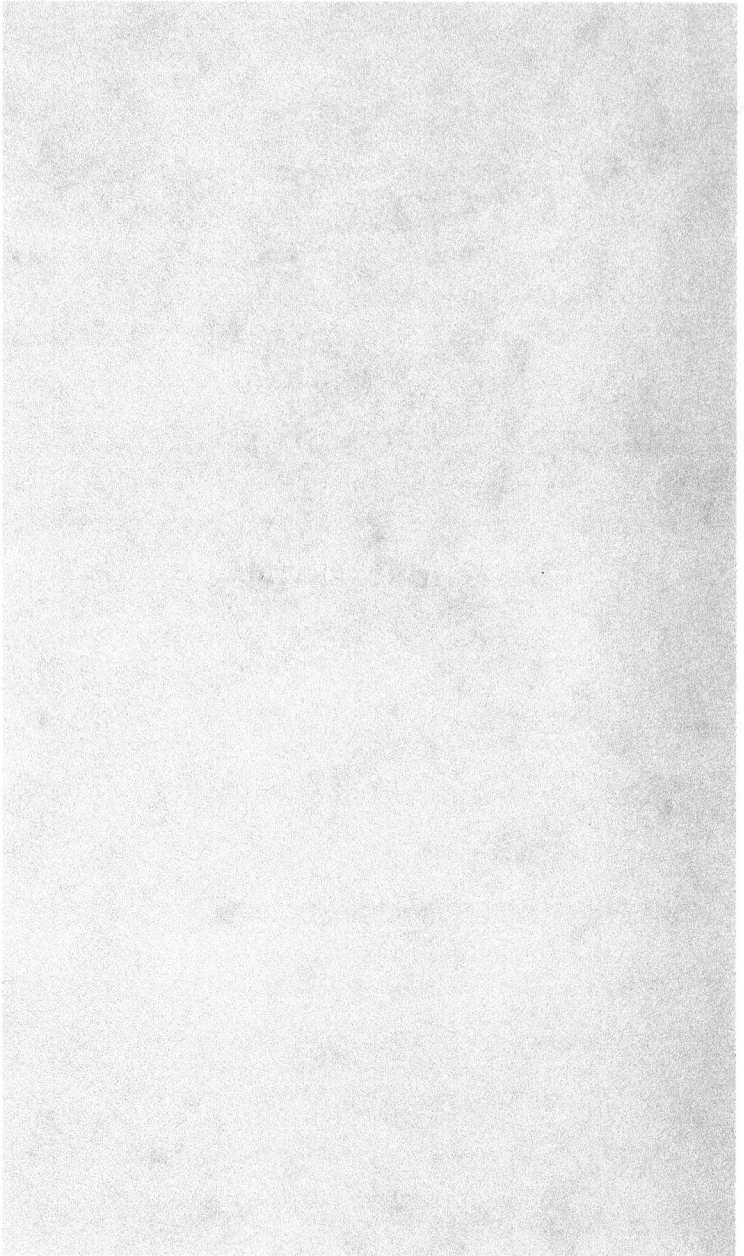

393. FREEMAN, born in Plymouth, Dec. 7, 1730, and died Jan. 9, 1731.

394. ISAAC, born in Plymouth, Dec. 11, 1735-6, O. S. He probably never married, as no record of any family remains to him. He became early a prominent man among his townsmen. He evidently took more than an ordinary interest in all that pertained to the early history of New England, in whose oldest town he had his birth, and spent his life. It was doubtless this interest which made him the register of probate for the county from 1778 for the rest of his life. He was a representative to the Provincial Congress in 1774 and '75. To him, probably more than to any other person, we are indebted for the organization of the Old Colony Club, Jan. 16, 1769. The seven names subscribing at that date the original constitution of that club, were: Isaac Lothrop, Pelham Winslow, Thomas Lothrop, John Thomas, Edward Winslow, Jr., John Watson, and Elkanah Cushman; of whom four, either by name or marriage, belong to the Lothrop family. Of them Isaac Lothrop was chosen their president: Thomas Lothrop, his younger brother, their secretary; and Elkanah Cushman, who had married Mary Lathrop, their steward. All honor to these seven sons of Plymouth for that first commemoration of Forefathers' day. It was the same interest in the early history of New England which made him one of the incorporators, in 1794, of the Massachusetts Historical Society. His will bears date July 4, 1808, and the inventory of his estate was witnessed in court the next year. The legatees named in the will are: Harriet, wife of Chandler Robbins, and Caleb Lothrop, "children of my brother Thomas"; his brother, Nathaniel Lothrop; and his sister, Priscilla Burr.

395. NATHANIEL, born in Plymouth, Nov. 26, 1737; graduated at Harvard in 1756, at the head of his class; and devoted his long and useful life to the study and practice of medicine. He married (1) Helen Hobart, daughter of Rev. Noah Hobart of Fairfield, Conn. She was born in Fairfield, Oct. 26, 1741, and died in Plymouth, June 1, 1780. He married (2), May 30, 1802, Lucy Hammett of Plymouth. She died April 17, 1824, and he died Oct. 20, 1828. He had no children. He lived, though greatly beloved and honored, even beyond his desire for life. His will bears date Feb. 19, 1828, and is notable for the number of its bequests, and for their distribution outside of the Lothrop name. The names are appended, and their connection will be easily inferred from the intermarriages found in this branch of the family: Barnabas Hedge, $1,500, in trust for Priscilla Lothrop Buckley, wife of John Bulkley of New York; Pilgrim Society, $500, towards completing Pilgrim Hall; Eunice D. Hedge, wife of Barnabas; Isaac Lothrop Hedge; Thomas

Hedge; Ellen Hobart Hedge; each of the daughters of Barnabas and Eunice D. Hedge; Nathaniel Lothrop Hedge; Betsey Dunham, widow; Isabella and John B. Thomas; ———, wife of William Simmons; Eliza, wife of Isaac Goodwin; Lucy Lothrop Goodwin; Lucy Hammett West, daughter of Dr. Samuel; four daughters of Gershom Burr; and Charles William Capers, son of my niece Abigail Capers, deceased.

396. Thomas, born in Plymouth, Feb. 10, 1739, and married, Jan. 31, 1773, Lydia, daughter of Nathaniel Goodwin.

397. Caleb, born in Plymouth, Nov. 25, 1742, and died in Martinique, May 28, 1766, probably unmarried.

398. Priscilla, born in Plymouth, Aug. 1, 1747, and married, in 1767, Hon. Gershom, son of Thaddeus and Abigail (Sturges) Burr of Fairfield, Conn., where he was born, June 10, 1744, and died May 12, 1774. She died in 1810. They had one son, Gershom Burr, who married (1), Sept. 10, 1789, Susannah Young, and (2), Oct. 13, 1801, Elizabeth, daughter of Rev. Andrew Elliot. He lived in Fairfield, where he had seven children: Thaddeus, Susanna, Isaac Lothrop, Andrew Elliot, Jonathan Sturgis, Priscilla Lothrop, and Susanna Young.

### 193. JOHN.      Bethel, Vt.

399. John, who is reported as having married and lived in Bethel, Vt.

400. Sarah, who married (1) a Hickson, and (2) a Wolcott, and lived in or near Bethel, Vt.

401. Bethiah, who married Moses Smith, and had a family of several children.

402. Lois, who married Elijah Smith, brother of Moses, and also lived in Bethel.

403. Lucy married Joshua Putnam, and had at least one daughter, Lois Putnam.

404. Daniel, born March 3, 1768, and married in Bethel, Lucy Smith, sister of Moses and Elijah, and removed from Windsor, Vt., in 1811, to Granby, Mass. He afterwards went to Dover, Me., where he died, March 3, 1841. His widow, who was born in 1773, died in Watertown, Conn., at his son Albert's, Nov. 14, 1859.

405. Simon, married Polly Backman, and went to the West.

406. Annis, of whom I learned nothing but the name.

407. Moses.

408. Asa.

### 194. DANIEL.      Norwich, Conn.

409. Daniel, born Feb. 2, 1745-6.

410. James, born April 28, 1748.

411. Joseph, born Dec. 26, 1749.

The three children above mentioned probably died young. The only memorial of them is the single stone which marks each of their graves next south of their parents, with only the three christian names upon it.

412. Joshua, born very likely in England, as the name is not on the Norwich records. Yet he is named in his father's will, in 1776. He probably died young, as no further record is found of him.

### 196. JOSHUA LO-LA. Norwich, Conn.

413. THOMAS, born in Norwich, Sept. 11, 1762, and married in Boston, Oct. 9, 1783, Lydia, daughter of William and Lydia (Colt) Hubbard, who was born in Boston July 5, 1765. She was granddaughter of his Aunt Lydia, and died Dec. 26, 1790, leaving two children. He married (2), Sept. 21, 1791, Hannah, daughter of Capt. Ephraim and Lydia (Huntington) Bill of Norwich, where she was born, Sept. 21, 1769. He always lived in Norwich, and well sustained the social position to which he was born. · He was especially held in remembrance as one who used his large wealth generously for the deserving poor; and as exhibiting to his generation a noble specimen of the old-time gentleman. His will bears date July 16, 1810, and his death, according to his headstone in the cemetery, occurred Dec. 28, 1817. His widow survived him almost a half century, and died at the age of ninety-two, Jan. 28, 1862.

414. LYDIA, born in Norwich, Oct. 10, 1764, and married, June 5, 1783, Rev. David, son of David Austin of New Haven, where he was born, March 19, 1759. He graduated at Yale in 1779, and was licensed to preach in 1780 by the New Haven East Association. His marriage was recorded in Norwich, June 10, 1802, from a certificate signed by Joseph Strong, clerk and minister of the First Society of Norwich. Mr. Austin was at once a very popular preacher. After spending some years abroad he returned and preached with very great acceptance for some time in the Second Church of Norwich. He was ordained pastor of the Presbyterian church of Elizabeth, N. J. He entered on his work with great enthusiasm, and as preacher and writer, and especially as a student of prophecy, he soon overtasked his vigorous intellect and became possessed of a delusion which for years he could not shake off. Removing to Norwich where his wife's father had made provision, in 1807, for his support, he was after a few years brought out of the delusion by the patient and skillful care of his wife, and at length began to supply the pulpit in Bozrah, in which service he continued as long as he lived. The writer remembers him as the first minister of his boyhood. Of large muscular frame and polished manners, he was the idol of the youth of his congregation. His wife died in Norwich Oct. 25, 1818, and he, Feb. 5, 1831.

415. DANIEL, born April 3, 1766, and died June 29, 1766.

416. DANIEL, born in Norwich, Oct. 13, 1769, and graduated at Yale in 1787, and took his master's degree in course. He married, Aug. 14, 1793, Elizabeth Tracy Turner, born May 15, 1771, daughter of Dr. Philip and Lucy (Tracy) Turner of Norwich. He settled in Norwich, and was engaged in the drug business, mainly as a general agent abroad.

He died July 13, 1825, and his widow, Oct. 10, 1850.

417. JOSHUA, who probably died young.

### 198. EZRA LO. Norwich, Conn.

418. EZRA, born Jan. 24, 1743-4, and is reported as having been a sea captain.

419. JEDIDIAH, born in Newent, Jan. 29, 1745-6, and married, Oct. 29, 1767, Sarah Tracy, born in Newent, Jan. 25, 1747, daughter of Dea. Andrew and

14

Ruth Tracy. He was a saddler and harness-maker. They went to Brooklyn, Pa., about 1818, and resided there many years, but both died at about the same time, at the residence of their daughter, Mrs. Ross, on the Wyalusing Creek, Pa.; he in December, 1879, and his wife soon after, aged eighty-two.

420. HANNAH, born Sept. 25, 1748, and married Zephaniah Lathrop, No. 269.

421. CHARITY, born April 7, 1752, and is reported as having married a. Lathrop.

422. ELKANAH, born Nov. 9, 1754, and according to the recollections of Mrs. Bibbins, he was a Baptist minister, and lived in Canada.

423. SAMUEL, born Aug. 9, 1760, and like his oldest brother was a sea faring man.

## 199. SAMUEL. Norwich, Conn.

424. REV. SAMUEL, born Nov. 30, 1743, and married, Dec. 3, 1761. Lois, No. 547, daughter of Zebulon and Lois (Rogers) Lathrop, of Norwich, West Farms, where she was born April 22, 1742. He married (2) in Plymouth, Mass., Nov. 24, 1763, Sally Oakman, who was born in Plymouth in 1741. He first settled in Norwich, but removed to Wells, Vt.

He was a preacher of the Baptist denomination, and to the last wore the old style cocked hat and knee buckles. His death occurred at sixty-two years of age, as his daughter, Mrs. Farnham, testifies ; and his wife's at eighty-four, in the year 1825.

425. THOMAS, born May 13, 1745, and married, Dec. 19, 1771, Wealthy Ann, daughter of Col. John and Abigail (Dyer) Cobb, who was born in Canterbury, Conn., Oct. 18, 1755. He was educated with reference to the ministry, but became a school teacher, first in his native State, and afterwards in Vermont, into the southern part of which State he removed soon after the Revolutionary war. He subsequently settled in Burlington, Vt., where he also followed teaching, and where he had a good reputation in his profession. He there died Mar. 20, 1826, and his widow, Sept. 22, 1827.

426. SIMEON, born Feb. 11, 1746-7, and married, April 13, 1760, Esther Branch of Lisbon, who was born in 1746, and died Jan. 3, 1820. They lived in Lisbon, where he died Dec. 30, 1826.

427. JOHN, born May 25, 1749, and had a family, though the name of his wife I have been unable to find.

428. SUSANNA, born Oct. 21, 1751.

429. ZACHARIAS, born Jan. 19, 1751, and died April 15, 1758.

430. ELIZABETH, born Jan. 19, 1754.

## 200. ELISHA.

431. ELISHA, born July 28, 1745, and married (1), Lydia Kirkland, who died Jan. 22, 1774, aged twenty-six years, and (2), Mrs. Lydia Huntington, who died Jan. 7, 1816, aged seventy-five.

He died at Demerara, Sept. 23, 1790, as his gravestone testifies. The head-stones of himself, both wives, and his daughter Sarah, are in the East Chelsea lot.

His will, dated Jan. 8, 1790, in the Colony of Essiquibo and Demerara, declares him a citizen of Norwich ; and names as his legatees : His sister-in-law, Anna Vera Kirtland ; his wife Lydia ; and his children, Lydia, James, and Sarah, all of Norwich.

432. DEBORAH, born June 22, 1741.

433. ANNA, born June 5, 1749.

434. SOLOMON, born Nov. 5, 1751, and died Oct. 24, 1754.

435. MARY, born Mar. 17, 1755.

436. SEPTIMIUS, born in 1756. Married (1). ———— Adams ; (2), Elizabeth Perkins. He died Oct. 12, 1819, aged sixty-three years ; as his gravestone shows. His widow married a Dr. Rose.

His will, bearing date June 23, 1819, names as his legatees : His wife Betsey, and six children of Lucy L. Kimball : Septimius, Solomon, Wealthy A. Manning, Abigail A. Latham, Harry B., Nelson P., and John E.

## 205. ELIJAH. Norwich, Conn.

437. ELIJAH. born in Norwich. Oct. 20, 1747, and married April 27, 1774, Dorcas Kibbe, of Enfield, Conn., and settled in Norwich.

438. HANNAH, born in Norwich, Sept. 5, 1749, and married Benadam, son of William and Martha (Wheeler) Williams, who was born Mar. 21, 1747.

439. ANNA, born in Norwich, July 13, 1751.

440. EUNICE, born in Norwich, Sept. 13, 1753. Married, Dec. 18, 1772, Rev. Thomas Brockway of Columbia, Conn., who was born in Lyme, Conn., in 1744, and graduated at Yale in 1768.

    i.  Diodate Brockway, born in Columbia, Dec. 26, 1776, and graduated at Yale in 1797, and settled as pastor in Ellington, where he married Moranda Hall, Oct. 29, 1779, by whom he had seven children.

    ii.  John Hall Brockway, son of Rev. Diodate, graduated at Yale in 1820, and was a prominent citizen of the State, which he represented in the National Congress from 1839 to 1843.

    iii.  Maria Brockway, born July 23, 1796, and married Silas Gates Strong, son of Dea. Ezra and Nancy (Gates) Strong, of Hanover, N. Y.

441. JERUSHA, born in Norwich, Feb. 7, 1756.

442. NANCY, born in Norwich, ————, ————, and married, Judge Nathaniel Niles, a son of Judge Samuel Niles of South Kingston, R. I., where he was born April 3, 1741. This name is not on the Norwich records.

443. SIMON, born in Norwich, Feb. 24, 1760, and married, Dec. 19, 1782, Mary, daughter of Prosper and Keturah (Cheeseboro) Wetmore of Norwich, where she was born, March 16, 1761, and where she died, Nov. 29, 1802. He married (2) ? Amelia, daughter of ———— Green, and widow of ———— Davis.

444. LYNDE, born in 1762, as we learn from his gravestone in the Chelsea burying-ground, and married in Norwich, Oct. 9, 1783. Abigail, daughter of Elijah and Abigail Adyas, who died Jan. 4, 1788, aged twenty-seven years. He married (2), May 4, 1795, Polly, daughter of ———— Hommedieu, father of William and Giles. He died, Feb. 5, 1827, and was buried in the East Chelsea lot.

445. GURDON, born in Norwich, Sept. 10, 1763, and married, Dec. 22, 1796, Jemima Pember.

### 213. NATHANIEL.        Norwich, Conn.

446. Burrel, born April 5, 1749, and died, as his gravestone in the Norwich Town Cemetery shows, Aug. 4, 1773. I have found no other record of this name.

447. Hannah, born Feb. 10, 1750-1.

448. Asa, born Nov. 16, 1755, and married, Sept. 3, 1780, Elizabeth Lord, who was born in 1757. He died in Norwich, March 26, 1835, and his wife, Aug. 23, 1805, as their gravestones in the Norwich Town Cemetery show.

### 214. ZEBADIAH.        Norwich, Conn.

449. Joseph, born in 1755, and died at West Point in 1778.

450. Zebadiah, born in 1758, and married, Dec. 11, 1783, Sarah Starr, daughter of William Starr of Middletown, where they settled. She was born May 1, 1759, and died in June, 1849. He died in Middletown, in January, 1804.

451. Simon Backus, born in 1760, and married, March 1, 1792, Molly Culver. He died Dec. 14, 1805.

452. Asa, born ——, and married, ——, daughter of Ebenezer Jones, of Norwich. He died in Norwich Oct. 29, 1808; and she in St. Mary, Georgia. No children.

453. Eunice, born ——, and died unmarried in New Canaan, N. Y., in 1820.

454. Nathaniel, born in 1768, and died in Stockbridge, Mass., 1848.

### 215. AZARIAH.        Franklin, Conn.

455. Gurdon, born in Norwich Dec. 6, 1767, and graduated at Yale in 1787. He became a physician and married Lucy, daughter of Dr. John Turner. They had two children.

456. Charles, born in Norwich, Jan. 11, 1770, graduated at Yale in 1788, and became a lawyer. He married, Joanna, daughter of Col. Christopher and Elizabeth (Coit) Leffingwell. He died Jan. 17, 1831. She died in New York at the house of Rev. William A. Hallock, May 15, 1854, aged 79.

457. Nabby, born in Norwich, Mar. 24, 1772, and married Feb. 5, 1793, Wm. B., son of Col. Wm. Bradford and Annie (Lathrop) Whiting of Albany. She died, as her gravestone in the Norwich Town lot testifies, Aug. 25, 1805, at 33 years of age, and he died Jan. 26, 1840. Children: William Whiting, who married Mary Pearce. Charlotte Whiting, who married L. Winchester. Edward Whiting, who died in Montreal. Mary S. Whiting.

458. Charlotte, born in Norwich, Apr. 16, 1774, and died Nov. 3, 1777.

459. Burrel, born in Norwich, May 25, 1776. He went early to the South, and married in Savannah, Ga., Dec. 25, 1808, Mary Rosalie A., daughter of George and Mary Boulineau, a French lady, and a native of the West Indies. After her death he married (2), in Savannah, Nov. 19, 1840, Mary

H., widow of William F. Simpson, Esq. Mr. Lathrop was an Elder in the Presbyterian Church in Savannah, and is remembered as a devotedly Christian citizen.

460. GERARD, born in Norwich, Aug. 19, 1778, married Mary Ely, Nov. 15, 1809, eldest child of Rev. Zebulon Ely of Lebanon, Conn., born in Lebanon Aug. 30, 1784. United with the Lebanon Church 1809.

461. CHARLOTTE, born in Norwich in Feb. 21, 1781, married Dec. 19, 1802, as his first wife, Charles Phelps, son of Judge Andrew Huntington of Norwich, Conn. He was a prominent business man both in Norwich and New York, where he died Sept. 28, 1850. She died Jan. 8, 1805.

462. AUGUSTUS, born in Norwich, Feb. 11, 1785; married Polly Gale, (Nov. 14, Mrs. as. Rec.), May 28, 1809. She was born July 21, 1785. He died Oct. 7, 1819, and his widow, July 4, 1839, aged 54.

## 219. ISRAEL, 3d.        Norwich, Conn.

463. ANN, born Sept. 11, 1738.

464. LOIS, born Mar. 22, 1740.

465. EDNAH, born Apr. 3, 1742.

## 222. CAPTAIN JEDIDIAH.      Bozrah, Conn.

466. ISRAEL, born Apr. 30, 1743, and died Oct. 2, 1760.

467. MARY, born Apr. 23, 1745, and married, Oct. 31, 1765, Captain Elia West, son of Nathan and Mary (Hinckley) West. They settled in Bozrah, where he was a prominent citizen.

468. JEDIDIAH, born Feb. 9, 1746-7, and married (1), Dec. 18, 1769, Amy Gardner, daughter of Jonathan Gardner, and his wife Mary, who was a daughter of Sampson Houghton of Montville. They sell, Jan. 21, 1783, land to their father Jonathan Gardner of Norwich, in Montville, and are said then to be of Colchester.

469. EPHRAIM, born July 22, 1749, and died, as we learn from the Franklin Church records, in 1798, aged 50 years, probably without having married.

470. DANIEL HYDE, born Sept. 14, 1751, and died Sept. 23, 1751.

471. DANIEL, born July 31, 1753, and died Nov. 4, 1773.

472. URIAH, born May 12, 1755, and lived near Pittsfield. He died in December, 1828, as a letter from his brother Zephaniah, No. 474, dated Jan. 10, 1829, to *his* son Zephaniah, Jun., No. 957, testifies.

473. ABIGAIL, born Feb. 24, 1757, and married Joseph Fish, and settled in Pittstown, N. Y.

474. ZEPHANIAH, born in Bozrah, Mar. 9, 1760, and married Jan. 29, 1784, Rachel, born Feb. 24, 1764, daughter of Zebedee and Esther (Hough) Wood of Hawley, Mass., to which place he had gone from Bozrah in 1780. He was toward the close of the Revolutionary war in the army. From the first he was a leading man among the settlers of the town, holding for many years the first offices in the town. He was also deacon of the Congregational Church. He was one of the old type of strict Calvinists, and one of the best type of

the early New England puritan characters. He died in Hawley, May 21, 1837, and his widow, Sept. 23, 1841.

475. PHEBE, born July 1, 1762, and married, Dec. 13, 1780, John Gardner of Bozrah. Their children, all born in Bozrah, were: John Gardner, born May 7, 1783, and married Violate, daughter of William and Sybil (Lathrop) Crocker. Rebecca Gardner, born May 31, 1785. James Gardner, born June 27, 1788. Jemima Gardner, born July 22, 1791. Jedidiah Lathrop Gardner, born Sept. 4, 1793. Phebe Gardner, born July 9, 1801. Uriah Gardner, born Nov. 18, 1805.

476. OLIVE, July 13, 1764, and married in 1786, Joshua, son of Abial and Chloe (Hinckley) Stark of Lebanon, Conn. They settled in Bozrah in 1791. He was quite a prominent citizen of the town, and was several times its representative in the State legislature. She died July 7, 1825, and he married Ruth Yeomans, the widow of James Stark of East Haddam, and removed to Canajoharie, N. Y., where he died Mar. 29, 1839. His children, all by his first wife [see Hyde, 718].

477. JEMIMA, born Dec. 31, 1767, and married, Oct. 28, 1789, Lemuel, son of Jonathan and Abiah (Fitch) Gardner of Bozrah, where he was born July 10, 1763. They lived successively in Bozrah, Norwich, and Montville, where he died July 10, 1839, and she Mar. 11, 1850. Their children were: Lorinda Gardner, born in Bozrah, Jan. 15, 1790, and married in 1810, Levi Whaley of Montville. They had eight children: Levi Gardner, Charles Lathrop, David Chauncey, Theodore Dwight, Mary Anne, Jane, Maria, Sara' Ann, and who married Marvin Leffingwell of Montville, and Lorinda. Of their families the children are given in the Hyde Family. Almira Gardner, born May 27, 1792 [Hyde, p. 254]. Sidney Gardner, born in Bozrah Apr. 17, 1795, and married June 23, 1823, Maria, daughter of Thomas Fanning of Norwich. They had four children, Sidney Alfred, Sarah Ann, Frederick Lester, and Charles Henry. Amelia Gardner, born in Bozrah, June 6, 1799, and married in November, 1840, Rev. Christopher Leffingwell, a Baptist Minister of "Leffingwell Town." Sarah Gardner, born in Norwich, May 28, 1806, and died single, Oct. 15, 1821. John F. Gardner, born in Norwich, Nov. 5, 1808, and married, Feb. 25, 1829, Martha Crary of Preston. They had three children: Henry, Albert, and Mary Helen.

478. ISRAEL, born Nov. 18, 1770, and married (1), Nov. 18, 1794, Deborah Lathrop, daughter of Capt. Andrew, No. 503. He married (2), about 1802, Martha White of Otsego county, N. Y.

## 224. DEACON SIMEON. Bozrah, Conn.

479. HANNAH, born in Norwich Aug. 20, 1749, and married, July 9, 1769, Christopher Calkins.

480. EUNICE, born in Norwich Aug. 17, 1751, and married, Oct. 29, 1772, Stephen Woodworth of Bozrah.

481. SIMEON, born in Norwich Aug. 4, 1753, and married, Dec. 9, 1781, Elizabeth Calkins of Bozrah, where he settled. He died in 1786, and his widow married Jesse Abel, Esq., of Bozrah, son of Samuel and Elizabeth

(Sluman) Abel, by whom she had six other children. She died Aug. 2, 1826. In the distribution of his estate, July 4, 1786, he is called Simeon, Jun., and the following parties are his heirs: His widow, his eldest son Giles, second son Simeon, and Hannah his youngest child.

482. ROGER, born in Norwich Dec. 3, 1734. In the distribution of his estate, Oct. 23, 1816, he having died single, his heirs were: His eldest sister, Hannah Calkins; sister Eunice Woodworth; the heirs of his eldest brother Simeon; his second brother Oliver and his fourth heir; Lydia Fish, his third sister; Sarah Lathrop, fourth sister; Zebediah, third brother and seventh heir; and Andrew, his fourth brother and eighth heir.

483. OLIVER, born in Norwich Sept. 9, 1756, and married, Dec. 13, 1781, Eunice, daughter of Capt. David and Desire (Clark) Hough of Bozrah. They settled in Hartland, Vt.

484. LYDIA, born in Norwich Sept. 2, 1758, and married, April 2, 1798, John Fish of Bozrah. Their children, all born in Bozrah, were:. Simeon Fish, born Feb. 1, 1787; John Fish, born Sept. 25, 1788; Miller Fish, born June 5, 1791; Electa Fish, born April 23, 1793; Lydia Fish, born Aug. 6, 1796; Margaret Fish, born Nov. 17, 1799.

485. SARAH, born in Norwich Sept. 22, 1760. She never married, and was living in Bozrah when her father's will was made, in 1804.

486. ZABDIEL, born in Norwich Nov. 30, 1762, and married (1), Sept. 22, 1783, Margaret Tracy of Norwich, who died Oct. 4, 1783. He married (2), June 16, 1785, —— Harris of Lebanon. They lived in Bozrah, moved to Susquehanna, Penn., after 1795, as he was then rated on the tax-list with ten other Lathrop tax-payers. Asa, Walter, and Ezekiel, moved with him.

487. ANDREW, born Oct. 26, 1764, and married (?) (1), Jan. 22, 1789, Lucretia Smith of Franklin, who died in Bozrah Oct. 9, 1801. He married (2), May 30, 1802, Zerviah Polley. She died about 1840, and he April 21, 1843.

## 225. EZEKIEL. Pennsylvania.

488. NEHEMIAH, born Aug. 3, 1754.

489. ASA, born Feb. 2, 1756, and married Allis Fox. He was living in Bozrah in 1792, as the will of his brother James shows, and as late as 1795, as the tax-list of that year shows.

490. EZEKIEL, born Nov. 16, 1757, married, —— Crocker. He was in Bozrah in 1795, as the tax-list of that year shows.

491. JAMES, born May 16, 1761, married in June, 1787, Lucy, widow of Dr. Kilbourn and daughter of —— Whiting. They settled on Blue Hill in the southwest part of Franklin, Conn. His will, dated Franklin, May 18, 1792, names as legatees, his wife Lucy, his mother, and his two children—Lois and James. He also appoints his brother Asa of Bozrah his executor. His death the Franklin church records report in 1793.

492. SYBIL, born April 11, 1762. Married, 1787, Capt. William Crocker. They settled in Bozrah, where they both died. Their children were: Sophia, who married Cyrus Stewart; Ezekiel Lathrop Crocker, who went south, and died there; George W. Crocker; William Crocker; Abby, who married Dyer Harris.

## 229. EZRA. Norwich, Conn.

493. OLIVER, born in Norwich, June 14, 1747, and died Feb. 1, 1750-51.

494. SARAH, born in Norwich, April 18, 1751, and married a son of Capt. Ebenezer and Esther Baldwin, and as such receipts for her part of her father's estate. She is mentioned in her grandfather's will, Oct. 25, 1771, as the only surviving child of his son Ezra.

495. EZRA, born in Norwich, Sept. 16, 1753, and died Oct. 30, 1770.

## 230. JEREMIAH.

496. JEREMIAH, born in Norwich, Feb. 14, 1747-8, married, Aug. 30, 1770, Lydia Mix. They lived in Norwich, where their gravestones, in the town cemetery, report his death Dec. 30, 1816, and hers, March 24, 1819. All of this family had legacies from their grandfather's will, 1771.

497. EUNICE, born in Norwich, May 8, 1751, and married Rodolphus Elderkin. In 1771, April 17, her uncle Jonathan was appointed her guardian.

498. WILLIAM, born in Norwich, Sept. 9, 1753. In 1771 the Court of Probate appointed his uncle Zachariah his guardian. He married Cynthia Elderkin, sister of Rodolphus, who married Eunice, his sister, and resided successively in Norwich, in Canandaigua, N. Y., and in Otsego, N. Y., where he died July 29, 1832, and his widow, Jan. 10, 1847, aged about ninety.

## 232. CAPTAIN ANDREW. Bozrah, Conn.

499. JESSE, born June 22, 1760, and died Jan. 9, 1761.

500. ABIGAIL, born Aug. 9, 1761, and married (1), —— Wattles, and by him had three children: Andrew, Eunice, and Abigail. She married (2), —— Tucker, and lived and died in Broome, Schoharie County, N. Y.

501. DEBORAH, born June 10, 1766, and died Nov. 6, 1766.

502. EUNICE, born June 24, 1768.

503. DEBORAH, born March 23, 1770, and married Israel Lathrop. No. 478.

504. ANDREW, 3d, (Capt.) born April 4, 1772, and married in Bozrah, June 1, 1797, Sybil Downer of Bozrah, who was born in that town June 15, 1773. He died in Blenheim, Schoharie County, N. Y., Oct. 20, 1833, and his widow in New York City, Feb. 22, 1862.

505. MARTHA, born June 24, 1771, and was probably never married. She is mentioned in her father's will in 1795.

506. WEALTHY, born March 27, 1778.

## 233. EBENEZER, JUN.

507. JAMES, born April 14, 1759.

508. MARY, born March 11, 1761, died (?) Feb. 26, 1789.

509. LUCRETIA, born April 11, 1763.

510. ESTHER, born Jan. 28, 1765.

511. PHEBE, born March 5, 1767.

512. ELIZABETH, born Dec. 20, 1768.

513. SETH, born March 17, 1771.

514. JOHN, born June 10, 1773.

## 231. JONATHAN.

Norwich, Conn.

515. ELIZABETH, "Betty," born in Norwich Feb. 2, 1759. She died single in Norwich.

516. DARIUS, born in Norwich July 14, 1760, and married Nov. 23, 1786. Lydia McCall of Lebanon. He died Sept. 15, 1827, and she, March 22, 1814; so their gravestones in Norwich Town cemetery testify.

Darius' distribution: Mary Lathrop of Columbia, County of Tolland; Daniel and Sophia Morse of Norwich; Chester and Mira Bell of Lebanon; Seymour and Elizabeth Morse, and John B. Lathrop.

517. ROGER, born in Norwich Nov. 9, 1762, and married Alice Armstrong. He died in Andover, Ct., July 20, 1830, where he and two of his children were buried.

518. JESSE, born in Norwich May 5, 1765, and married, April 15, 1797, Rhoda, daughter of Eli and Rhoda (Lathrop) Hyde of Norwich. They lived in Franklin, where he died Aug. 11, 1845, and his wife in 1864, aged ninety-three years. They had both united with the Franklin Church in 1814.

519. LUCY, born in Norwich Feb. 28, 1767, and married Dyer McCall.

520. EZRA, born in Norwich Dec. 9, 1770, and married in Bozrah, Dec. 19, 1796, Rebecca, daughter of Elijah and Lydia (Baldwin) Huntington. They settled on a portion of the old Huntington farm in the southwest part of the town, where the family always lived. She died, May 25, 1812, and he married (2), June 22, 1815, Mary Pierce of Plainfield, who died in Bozrah, March 8, 1863, aged eighty years. He died July 18, 1840, and his headstone bears the fitting inscription : "An honest man's the noblest work of God."

## 235. JOHN, D.D.

Boston, Mass.

521. JOHN, born in Boston Jan. 13, 1772, and graduated at Harvard in 1780. He married (1), April 25, 1792, Ann, eldest daughter of Joseph and Ann (Dawes) Pierce, who died Oct. 10, 1800. He married (2), in Calcutta, Hindostan, about 1801, Jane Thompson (of Scotch descent), and (3), also in Calcutta, about 1808, Grace Elleanor Harrison, a stepdaughter of William Bell. He wrote for the *Polyanthus*, a series of papers under the title of the "Moral Censor," and a "Course of Lectures on Natural Philosophy," which were held in high regard by the proprietor, the late Joseph T. Buckingham of Boston.

522. JANE TYLER, born in Boston Dec. 18, 1772, and died Oct. 12, 1774.

523. WILLIAM, born in Boston Dec. 25, 1773, and died Nov. 8, 1774.

524. JANE, born in Boston Dec. 26, 1774, and died Oct. 20, 1775.

525. MARY, born in Boston Nov. 13, 1775, and died Nov. 21, 1775.

526. JANE TYLER, born Feb. 5, 1777, and married, May 24, 1821, Caleb Loring of Boston. She died Feb. 2, 1846, leaving no children.

527. ELIZABETH, born in Boston May 18, 1782, and died in 1832, having never married.

528. SAMUEL CHICKLEY, born in Boston Aug. 16, 1783. He never married, and his death occurred about 1823.

529. ANN, born in Boston Aug. 21, 1784, and died Sept. 23, 1785.

530. ANN, born in Boston Nov. 11, 1785, and married, Nov. 1, 1807, Thomas.

15

son of ——— Motley of Boston. She died in April, 1861, and he, March 7, 1865. Their children were :

    i.    Thomas, married Maria B. Davis.
    ii.   John Lothrop, married Mary Elizabeth Benjamin.
    iii.  Edward, married Ellen Rodman.
    iv.  Emma, married Samuel William Rodman.
    v..  Preble, died unmarried.
    vi.  Anna Lothrop, married Alfred Rodman.

Of these children, John Lothrop Motley, born April 15, 1814, in Massachusetts, graduated at Harvard in 1831. He completed his studies on the Continent. Returning to America he read law, but soon afterward devoted his attention to literature. He was Secretary of Legation to St. Petersburg in 1840, and, having decided to write a history of Holland, passed several years in Holland and Germany preparing himself for that work.

The first of his series of histories was entitled " *The Rise of the Dutch Republic*," and was published in three volumes in London, in 1856. It is a work of rare merit, and has been successful from the day of publication.

This was followed in 1860 — '67 by " *The History of the United Netherlands.*" This was followed by " *The Life of John Barneveld*" in 1874, which was more of a history than a biography, and was really an introduction to what he purposed to make his greatest work — " *The Thirty Years War*," which, however, Mr. Motley did not live to write.

In 1861 Mr. Motley was sent as Minister Plenipotentiary to Vienna, and in 1869 as Minister to England.

His wife died in 1874, and he May 30, 1877, and was buried in Kensal Green Cemetery, near London.

*The Edinburg Review*, in reviewing his " *United Netherlands*," gives us this estimate of his character as a historian : " Mr. Motley combines as a historian two qualifications seldom found united. To great capacity for historical research he adds much power of pictorial representation."

The following tribute is from the *Westminster Review* : " We lay down the first two volumes of this noble work (The United Netherlands) with a high appreciation of Dr. Motley's great and varied abilities. For diligence in research, for sound and extensive knowledge, for vigorous language and for living dramatic representation he is entitled to hold a foremost place among the first historians of our age."

In 1860 he received the degree of D. C. L. from the University of Oxford, and that of LL. D. from Harvard. He also received the degree of LL. D. from the University of Cambridge, England.

## 236.  ZACHARIAH.    Norwich, Conn.

531.  SOLOMON, born Sept. 12, 1769.  I have learned nothing more of him than that he was named in his father's will in 1818.

532.  GEORGE, born Oct. 1, 1770.  Married and settled in Bethany, N. Y. Named in his father's will in 1818.  He died in 1849.

533. POLLY, born March 24, 1772, and married (1), Hezekiah Allen, who was living at the date of her father's will in 1818. (2), —— Smith.

534. GURDON, born Nov. 24, 1773, and married (1796, Franklin Church record) Jemima Pember. They removed to Warren, Herkimer County, N. Y. He died Sept. 15, 1820. She died Jan. 20, 1846.

535. SALLY, born June 19, 1775, and married Solomon Williams. (Called Sally Lathrop in her father's will in 1818.) She died Sept. 10, 1825.

536. PHEBE, born Dec. 13, 1776, and married Abel Bliss of Wilbraham.

537. FANNY, born Oct. 15, 1778, and married Josiah Cleveland of Norwich.

538. STEPHEN SEWELL, born Dec. 31, 1780, and died April 25, 1782.

539. NANCY, born Oct. 31, 1782, and married George Marshal Hyde, son of Capt. James and Martha (Nevius) Hyde, and born in Norwich, Feb. 6, 1782. They settled in Tolland, Ct. One child, Caroline, who became the wife of Rev. Mr. Brown, a Baptist clergyman, and had one son, George Hyde Brown.

540. BILLE, born Sept. 21, 1784, and married Phebe French. Called William in his father's will, but recorded as above.

541. HENRY, born Sept. 23, 1786, and married Linda Rindge, May 30, 1814. Son Charles in Bethany.

542. ROSWELL, born July 6, 1788. Died single Oct. 13, 1802.

543. CHARLES, born April 22, 1790. Died single May 1, 1826.

## 237. ZEBULON. Norwich, Conn.

544. ZEBULON, born in Norwich, Nov. 29, 1744, and married Alice Edgerton, who died in Lebanon, Conn., Feb. 3, 1794, aged 49. He removed to Tolland, where he purchased a farm of Samuel Tilden in the southeast part of Tolland, Mar. 26, 1800. He died in Tolland, Mar. 29, 1814.

545. URIAH, born in Norwich, Apr. 30, 1750, and married, Dec. 30, 1784, Lois Hinckley, and settled in Bozrah.

546. ELIZABETH, born in 1753, and died in Coventry, Conn., Dec. 4, 1806, as Veranas' record shows.

547. LOIS, born in Norwich, Apr. 22, 1742, and married, Dec. 31, 1761, Samuel Lathrop, No. 424. They lived in Lebanon, where she died, July 18, 1813. I find a record of one child, Eunice, born June 4, 1763.

## 247. AZEL. Franklin, Conn.

548. DANIEL, who is reported as having gone west early.

549. AZEL, who married, Aug. 13, 1798, Amphila, daughter of Capt. Josiah and Lucretia (Hyde) Buel of Lebanon, where she was born, July 29, 1782. She was living in Utica, aged 93 years, in 1872. He died, according to his son's statement, in 1819, in Lyme, Conn.

550. DAVID, removed west early.

551. JOHN, of whom I have learned nothing but the name.

552. ERASTUS, born in Norwich, May 18, 1784, and was married in New London, June 1, 1807, by Rev. Thomas West, to Sarah Bailey, who was born, Jan. 13, 1790. He died July 30, 1851, in Hartford, and she in Illinois, July 6, 1856.

553. HORACE, born in 1793, and married Betsey Hartshorn. He was a carpenter and removed from Connecticut in 1819. He died Feb. 14, 1859, and his widow, June 12, 1861.

## 218. CAPT. ELISHA.     Lebanon, N. H.

554. ELIAS, born Oct. 28, 1732, and married, Jan. 28, 1762, Hannah Gurdon, who was born, Dec. 3, 1742, and died Dec. 9, '88. They settled in Canaan, N. H., where she died. The Montville land records report Elias and Hannah Lathrop of Norwich, June 14, 1783, as selling a tract of land in Montville, which belonged to our honored father, Joseph Gurdon, to which sale Elias Lathrop, Jr., was witness. After the death of his wife he went to Virshire, Vt., with one of his sons, and died there, Aug. 8, 1802. He is reported as having at one time been engaged in the African slave trade, and that as part penalty for the work he was doing, he was poisoned by the natives. We are indebted to his family bible, where records were made by his own hand, for the complete list of his family.

555. ELIJAH, born Apr. 8, 1735, and died Nov. 7, 1742.

556. LEBBEUS, born in Norwich, Jan. 3, 1739, and married ——. He lived and died in Bozrah, leaving at least two children. Letters of administration were granted to Elijah Huntington of Bozrah, Dec. 1, 1794, in which he is said to have been late of Bozrah, and to have died intestate. In the distribution of the estate, Dec. 5, 1795, the only heirs mentioned are his widow; "Polly, eldest heir," and Lebbeus. The Christian name of his widow is not given.

557. THADDEUS, born in Norwich, Feb. 8, 1742, and married Anne Gurdon, sister of Hannah, wife of his brother Elias. They settled in Canaan, N. H., where she died, Apr. 21, 1781. They sell land in New London "North Parish" to Sherwood Fitch, and again Oct. 6th of the same year, as the Montville records show. He died at Chelsea, Vt.

558. ELIJAH, born in Norwich, Oct. 20, 1743, and married, Apr. 10, 1763, Elizabeth Elderkin, at Horton, Nova Scotia. She was born Oct. 30, 1740. They settled in Lebanon, N. H, where she died Feb. 17, 1812, and he married (2), Mar. 4, 1813, Rhoda Gill. He died Dec. 2, 1822.

559. ELIZABETH, born in Norwich, Nov. 20, 1744, and married John, son of Solomon and Zermah (Wickwere) Hamilton, who was born Apr. 6, 1740, and lived in Norwich. After her death her husband removed to Lebanon, N. H. They had two children, John and Jonathan.

560. HANNAH, born in Norwich, Mar. 22, 1747, and married, Feb. 18, 1773, Lemuel, son of Capt. David and Desire (Clark) Hough of Norwich. They settled in Lebanon, N. H. They had nine children.

561. GEORGE, born in Norwich, Jan. 21, 1749.

562. SLUMAN, born Sept. 25, 1750, and married, Jan. 18, 1785, Katherine Avery of Lisbon. They lived in Lebanon, N. H., where he died, Dec. 4, 1834, and his widow, Mar. 17, 1846, at 84 years of age.

563. JOSHUA, born in Norwich, Apr. 30, 1752, and died Oct. 20, 1752.

564. JOSHUA, 2D, born in Norwich, Oct. 1, 1753. He had a family in Chelsea, Vt.

565. AZARIAH, born in 1754, and married Mercy Bennet, who was born in 1752. He is reported a son of Capt. Elisha of Lebanon, Vt., and as having removed from Massachusetts to New York, near Utica, quite early in life. A Revolutionary soldier, and was a prisoner. He died at Chittinango Ripps, Sullivan, Madison Co., N. Y.

565-1. DENISON, born in Norwich, July 21, 1755.

566. SAMUEL, born in Norwich, Nov. 22, 1756, and married, May 15, 1786, Lois, daughter of Theophilus and Lois (Gifford) Huntington. They lived in Lebanon, N. H., where he died Jan. 12, 1821, and she Apr. 4, 1840. In 1774, he volunteered his service in the cause of the American Colonies against England, and was in the Bunker Hill engagement, and was among the wounded on that memorable 17th June. He afterwards purchased a tract of land in Lebanon, N. H., on which he settled in his rude shanty until such time as he could build the frame house, in which he lived the rest of his life. He was in business a very energetic man, and for years was quite successful. His wife was a most excellent Christian woman.

567. MARGARET, born in Norwich, July 2, 1758, and died July 13, 1759.

568. ELISHA, born in Norwich, Apr. 15, 1760.

569. WILLIAM, born in Norwich, June 4, 1763, and married Feb. 8, 1790, Lydia, daughter of Benjamin and Ann (Waterman) Harris, who was born in Norwich in 1768. He became a physician and settled in Washington, N. Y., where both of them died in April, 1812.

570. SARAH, born in Norwich, Apr. 27, 1765, and married (1), Oliver Adams, a physician of Plainfield, N. H., (2), David Morse of Sharon, Vt. They lived first in Plattsburg, N. Y., and afterwards in Johnstown, N. Y., where they died.

571. ANNA, born in Norwich, Jan. 27, 1766, and died Jan. 29, 1766. A child, unnamed, which died in infancy.

### 2 19. SAMUEL.

572. DAVID.

### 251. BENJAMIN.

573. MATTHEW, who had died when his father's will was made, May 4, 1768.

574. WALTER, who married May 13, 1779, Esther Fox, is mentioned in grandfather's will, 1774, as having the "English goods" for his portion.

575. ASA, married Sept. 17, 1782, Alice Fox of Bozrah, where he settled.

576. LUCY, born, as recorded in Norwich, Mar. 17, 1766.

### 252. CYPRIAN. Stafford, Vt.

577. RHODA, born Nov. 9, 1747, and married Allen Wightman. They lived near Skaneateles, in Onondaga County, N. Y. She died in 1835, aged 88.

578. MARY, born June 11, 1750, and died single, June 16, 1813.

579. JAMES, born July 11, 1752, and married Jan. 21, 1779, Mary Stark, and settled somewhere in the valley of the Hudson.

580. CHARLES, born Mar. 17, 1755, and married (1), Jan. 20, 1779, Lucy Stark, who died Apr. 11, 1790. He married (2), July 2, 1791, Lucy Williams, who died Sept. 1, 1843, aged 84 (94) years. He died Sept. 11, 1849.

581. AMY or Almy born July 6, 1757, and married Dyer Hull.

582. ABIAL, born May 16, 1760, and married in 1789, Lucy Randall, who was born in Connecticut, July 29, 1760. He settled in western New York in 1818, near the village of Leroy where he died Dec. 28, 1847, at the residence of his son-in-law, Erastus Bailey. His life was uneventful, yet filled up with faithful work, and with acts of genuine benevolence. Its beginning was in the days which called for self-denying patriotism; and he entered with youthful interest into such service as he could render. His father and two older brothers having been called into military service on the opening of the Revolutionary war, he supplied as he best could their places in the family at home. And to his latest days he did not forget his toils or cease to know the devotion of those who thus bore the burden of the trying days. He was blessed all through life with the vigor and health which come from regular habits both in work and in living. He retained his faculties to the last, and then as peacefully as he had lived, in the closing words of his obituary, " he took his departure," like one who lays him down to quiet sleep, " the wheels of life seeming to pause from too long use, rather than from decay."

583. ADGATE LATHROP, born Aug. 29, 1764, and married (1). Anne House, and (2), Jan. 26, 1799, Martha, daughter of Joseph Morse. He was early a carpenter and joiner, and located on the Montague farm. In 1816 he removed to Stafford, and died there Apr. 10, 1840, and his widow, who was born Mar. 9, 1771, died in Genesee, N. Y., in 1850, from a fall which dislocated her neck. He died in April, 1840.

584. JERUSHA, born Jan. 25, 1767, and married Col. Jehiel Johnson. They settled in Bozrah, where he died Jan. 28, 1825, aged 62 years. She died Jan. 22, 1832. They had no children of their own, but adopted for a son, the late Col. Jehiel Johnson of Bozrah, a nephew of the senior colonel; and for a daughter, Jerusha Whiting, daughter of Mrs. Johnson's sister Anne. These adopted children became, as the next record will show, husband and wife.

585. ANNE, born in Lebanon Mar. 26, 1769, and married in the same town Apr. 6, 1797, William, son of Col. Caleb and Lois (Lyon) Whiting, who was born in Bozrah, in 1770. They settled in Bozrah, where she died Oct. 25, 1822, and he, Jan. 28, 1848. Col. Caleb Whiting was born in 1729, and was son of William of Norwich, born in 1701, who was son of Rev. Samuel of Windham, born in 1670, the son of John, the pioneer of Salem, Mass., 1635. The children of Anne and William Whiting all born in Bozrah, were:

 i. Nathan Whiting, born Mar. 31, 1798, and married Lydia Lathrop Waterman of Bozrah. He died in Montville Oct. 25, 1871, and his wife is also dead.

 ii. Seth Whiting, born Oct. 26, 1799, and married May 17, 1828, Mary M., daughter of John and Mary (Cheney) Downer of Bozrah, where she was born Mar. 15, 1801, and died Feb. 28, 1855. He afterward married a Mrs. Post, and they were, in 1873, living in Bozrah.

 iii. Jerusha Whiting, born Nov. 8, 1802, and married, Jan. 1, 1826, Col.

Jehiel, son of Isaac and Phebe (Birchard) Johnson, who was born in Bozrah Mar. 19, 1802, and died July 29, 1861.

iv. Mary, born May 22, 1804, and married William Smith of Bozrah, who died May 3, 1833. She died May 22, 1835.

v. Cyprian Lathrop Whiting, born June 16, 1807, and married in Montgomery County, N. Y., Sept. 13, 1831, Jerusha Lathrop Johnson, sister of Col. Jehiel, who was born in Bozrah Dec. 16, 1812. He died in Waukau, Wis., Apr. 29, 1869.

## 258. ARUNAH. (ARANNAH.) Oxford, N. Y.

586. BENJAMIN, born in Norwich, Conn., April 1, 1769, and married, in Sunderland, N. Y., Sept. 27, 1795, Caroline C. Brownson, who died April 29, 1829, aged fifty-one years. He died in Sunderland, N. Y., July 4, 1822.

587. HUBBEL, born Feb. 26 [Jan. 29], 1779, and married, March 27, 1802, Laura, daughter of Col. Eli Brownson, who was an officer in the battle at Bennington. She was born, May 30, 1785, and died Jan. 13, 1841. He died March 19, 1842.

588. SIMON, born —— ——, and married in December, 1818, Jerusha Newcomb. He died in St. Charles, Ill.

589. CHAUNCY, who lived and died in Ohio.

590. LUCINDA, who married (1), a Mr. Enos, of Oxford, N. Y., and (2), Rufus Sheldon, of Sennett, N. Y., where she died. Her daughter is Mrs. Wm. Hager, Victory, Cayuga Co., N. Y., granddaughter Mrs. Grove Bradley, Weedsport, N. Y.

591. SALLY.

592. PHEBE.

593. LUCY, who married, Jan. 4, 1801, Edward King, in Norwich, N. Y. She died Oct. 4, 1825. They had seven children: Lucinda King, married Lucas Bradley, of Racine, Wis.; Louisa King, married Austin H. Lathrop, No. 1211; Laura King, died single; Rufus King; Edward King, lived in Racine and had two sons and one daughter; Isaac King, who had one son and one daughter; William King, who had two sons and two daughters.

594. A CHILD that died in Franklin, 1787.

## 268. EBENEZER. Windham, Conn.

595. GURDON, born in Norwich, May 23, 1770, and there recorded. He married, Jan. 7, 1795, Elizabeth Rudd, who was daughter of Deacon Jonathan and Mary (Tracy) Rudd of Windham, where she was born, March 13, 1772. They settled in Canajoharie, N. Y., where he was in the grocery business. Thence they went successively to Fairfield, Albany, Auburn, and Weedsport, where she died Sept. 19, 1831, and he, Sept. 1, 1832.

596. ERASTUS, born in Windham, Conn., Scotland parish, May 23, 1772, and married (1), in Cherry Valley, N. Y., in 1801, Judith, daughter of Griffin Crafts, who died Jan. 17, 1813. He married (2), Mrs. Lucy Morse Johnson. He was a practical surveyor, and a school and music teacher. Soon after his marriage he located himself as pioneer in the County of Jefferson, N. Y., where he built the "Lathrop Mills," laying thus the foundations of the new town of

Rutland. There, for twenty years, he exercised his inventive faculty and mechanical ingenuity. Among his inventions was a roof dam and a screw-wheel, requiring but a small fall of water. He died while engaged in selling the patent for this invention at Greenfield, Hancock County, Indiana, Oct. 16, 1830.

597. ANNE, born Oct. 14, 1774, and married, Oct. 29, 1796, Jonathan, son of Eliphalet Huntington of Windham, Conn. See Huntington family.

598. OLIVER, born in Windham, Conn., May 8, 1776, and married in January, 1808, Eliza Johnson. After her death he married (2), Eliza Graham, who after his death married Jonathan Huntington. He was a physician, and stood high in his profession.

599. ABIGAIL, born May 5, 1780, and married in October, 1799, Sheldon Mallory. Their children were : Joel Mallory of Troy; Ebenezer L. Mallory of Troy; Ann Eliza Mallory of Troy; Chas. F. Mallory of Romeo, Mich.; Emeline Mallory, married Bates, and settled in Wisconsin.

600. ELISHA, born April 10, 1784, and married in January, 1819, Sarah Hastings.

601. NATHANIEL.

### 269. ZEPHANIAH.

602. ASHER, born July 11, 1769–70, and married, Sept. 25, 1791, Temperance Tillotson.

603. HANNAH, born Sept. 22, 1772, and married Elijah Pitcher. He died before his father's will.

604. SARAH, born Nov. 11, 1783, and married Ira Justin.

605. ANNA, born Aug. 22, 1786, and married Elisha Smith.

606. LEVI, born Aug. 28, 1788, and died Jan. 6, 1872, according to his grave-stone, near his father's, in the Norwich Town cemetery.

### 270. JEDIDIAH.

607. LYDIA, born Jan. 4, 1774, and married Alexander Gordon.

608. ROSWELL, born July 26, 1776, and died April 15, 1783.

609. EBENEZER, born March 11, 1781.

610. CIVIL, born Sept. 9, 1783, and married Caleb Worden. She had died before her father's will, Feb. 13, 1817.

### 271. ISAAC.                    Norwich, Conn.

611. ISAAC, born Oct. 1, 1765, and named in his father's will as an only son.

612. LUCY, born July 24, 1767 ; called in her father's will his oldest daughter.

613. JABEZ, born Feb. 7, 1769, and had died before his father's will was made, Dec. 7, 1778.

614. MOLLY, called in her father's will the second daughter.

615. LYDIA, called in her father's will the youngest daughter.

## 279. JONATHAN, J. S.

[These four children are recorded in Norwich :]

616. John, born May 11, 1761.

617. Thriphena, born Dec. 31, 1766.

618. Mary, born April 18, 1769.

619. Anson, born Sept. 21, 1771.

## 280. BARNABAS. New Milford, Conn.

620. Joseph, born Nov. 20, 1758, and had, as his nephew Daniel thinks, a large family.

621. Daniel, born in Norwich, Oct. 23, 1760, and died July 23, 1761.

622. Sarah, born Oct. 20, 1762.

623. Daniel, born in Norwich, Nov. 18, 1765 ; the record in a family Bible, now in the possession of his nephew John's family, being : " Sixty-nine years old, Nov. 18, 1834." He married (1), Grace Loveredge, who was born in 1768, and (2), Esther Gaylor. He moved to New Milford in 1796, and died there in 1861, " in the ninety-seventh year of his age."

624. Rufus, who married Debby Ackly, went a short distance west of the Catskill Mountains, where he became a successful farmer. He died in South Cairo, N. Y.

625. Anne, was reported as the youngest of the family.

## 285. REV. JOSEPH, D.D. West Springfield, Mass.

626. Solomon, born March 27, 1760, and died April 27, 1787. (Memoir xxxv.)

627. Seth, born in West Springfield, Aug. (April, his own,) 11, 1762. He became a physician and settled in his native town. He married, Aug. 29, 1787, Anne, daughter and fifth child of Abiel and Abigail (Fenton) Abbot of Hampton, Conn., who was born Sept. 18, 1765. He died Feb. 26, 1831. She died in Armada, Mich., Sept. 13, 1846.

628. Joseph, born in West Springfield, Feb. 18, 1765, and as we learn from his father's autobiography, died from the rattles, Oct. 19, 1767.

629. Joseph, born in West Springfield, Mass., Dec. 24, 1766, and married, Sept. 9, 1790, Rowena, daughter of Col. Levi and Jerusha (Clark) Wells of Colchester, Conn. He settled in Wilbraham, where he became a prominent citizen. He represented the town in the State Legislature. He died Dec. 11, 1831, and his widow, Sept. 28, 1843.

630. Samuel, born Dec. 24, 1766, and died Oct. 19, 1767.

631. Samuel, born in West Springfield, May 1, 1772, and married, Nov. 4, 1797, Mary, daughter of William and Sarah (Miles) McCrackan, who was born Oct. 1, 1778. Mr. Wm. McCrackan was born in Glenluce, Scotland, in January, 1736, and his wife, Sarah Miles, in Wallingford, in May, 1748. He graduated at Yale College in 1792, and became a lawyer. He soon attained eminence in his profession, and was honored with important official trusts. He was for ten years a member of the Massachusetts Senate, of which also he

16

was for two years, 1829 and 1830, the president. He also represented the State in the Congress of the United States for four successive Congresses, 1818-26. He died in West Springfield, July 11, 1846, and his wife, Nov. 22, 1855.

632. DWIGHT, born in West Springfield, April 9, 1780. He became a merchant and settled in New York City. He married, Feb. 16, 1806, Lora, daughter of Jere and Elizabeth (Brewster) Stebbins of Windham, who was born March 1, 1782. He died Nov. 12, 1818, in West Springfield, and his widow in Northampton, Oct. 17, 1860, and was buried beside her husband in West Springfield.

### 295. REV. ELIJAH.          Gilead, Conn.

633. MARY, born Dec. 31, 1754, and married (1), Aug. 10, 1780, Col. Thos. Brown of Coventry, and (2), May 9, 1805, John, son of John and Gerusha (Stoughton) Staniford. She died Oct. 9, 1813, and he married, Jan. 21, 1816, Lydia Bingham of Windham, Conn. Col. Thomas Brown was born April 23, 1733, and died Nov. 8, 1803.

634. HANNAH, born Jan. 18, 1756, and died Nov. 20, 1756.

635. SILENCE, born May 12, 1757, married, Oct., 1781, Seth King.

636. HANNAH, born May 9, 1759, married, Feb., 1776, Daniel Wells.

637. ANNA, born Sept. 14, 1760, married, June, 1778, Gardner Gilbert.

638. ABIGAIL, born July 21, 1762, married, Oct., 1784, Paul Pitkin.

639. "ELIZABETH SEPTIMA," baptized April 1, 1763, married, Nov., 1787, Samuel Kellogg. They had one child, Elizabeth Septima.

640. LOUISA OCTAVA, born March 28, 1766, married, Dec., 1788, Levi Loomis. Had one child, Laura Loomis.

641. ELIJAH LEONARD, born March 1, 1768, married in May, 1794, Elizabeth Hubbard, who was born June 20, 1776. A lawyer; studied with Sylvester Gilbert of Hebron and Enoch Perkins of Hartford. In 1806 removed to Castleton, Vt.; twenty years later he removed to Central New York, and died in Auburn, May 10, 1841. His wife died, Oct. 5, 1850, at her daughter's, Mrs. Doane, Battle Creek, Mich., where she was buried.

642. LUCY NONA, born Feb. 24, 1770, married, April 7, 1789, Chauncey Langdon.

643. LAURA DECIMA, born Oct. 18, 1774, and died Dec. 7, 1789.

### 296. REV. BENJAMIN.          Windham, Conn.

644. ROSWELL, born in Windham Feb. 22, 1752, and married, Oct. 22, 1772, Sarah, daughter of Samuel and Abigail (Bingham) Badger, who was born in Windham, Nov. 28, 1753. He resided in Hartford and Springfield, where he died July 25, 1806. His widow died July 19, 1847.

645. ELIZABETH, born in Ashford, Feb. 11, 1754, and married William Jones of New Haven, where they settled. They had at least one daughter, Anna Jones, who married Solomon, son of Solomon and Anna (Denison) Huntington, and settled in Mexico, N. Y. For their numerous descendants see Huntington Family Memoir.

646. LEBBEUS, born Dec. 27, 1755, and died July 10, 1761.

647. ABNER, born Feb. 18, 1758, and married, Oct. 1, 1796, Betsey, daughter of Elisha and Jerusha (Webb) Abbe of Windham, where she was born Dec. 13, 1775. He was a sea captain and made several voyages to the East. His last voyage was to China. He died Aug. 25, 1798.

648. SINDEL, born March 1, 1761, and died Aug. 2, 1764.

649. LORAIN, born Aug. 21, 1763, and died Sept. 13, 1765.

650. WEALTHY, born July 29, 1766, and married, as his second wife, Jabez Hazen. They settled in Lisle, N. Y., and had children: Luke Hazen, Hart Hazen, Lucretia Hazen, John Hazen, Phebe Hazen.

651. JOHN, born Aug. 10, 1768, and married, Aug. 18, 1794, Sarah, daughter of Dr. Samuel and Sarah (Marsh) Lee of Windham, where she was born June 29, 1771. He was a skillful architect and engineer, and became a contractor for building heavy bridges. The causeway and bridge east of Hartford was quite a feat of his engineering skill for the day in which they were built. He was also engaged at Columbia, Penn., building a bridge over the Susquebanna in 1813. Another heavy work, for the time, was a bridge at Stratford over the Housatonic. His family always resided in Windham, where his wife died Dec. 21, 1822, and he, July 1, 1824.

652. SYBIL, born in Windham, July 17, 1771, and married Eliphalet Young of Mansfield, Conn. She died in Coventry Oct. 20, 1812. Mr. Young, in 1814, removed to Tolland, Conn., where he resided until his death, Jan. 17, 1844. Their children, so far as reported, were:

i. Edwin Young, born in 1798, in Mansfield, and married (1), Mary Chapman of Tolland, and (2), Jemima Curtis(?) of Philadelphia. He was for twenty-five years the efficient superintendent of the House of Refuge for Boys in Philadelphia, where he died in the spring of 1870. Manufacturer of cane-seat chair-bottoms.

ii. Julia Young, born in Windham, Conn., May 14, 1800, and married, in Tolland, Oct. 21, 1824, Ira K. Marvin. She died Feb. 24, 1875. They have had eight children as follows : Jane Maria, born Jan. 11, 1826, married Wm. Butler of Rockville, Conn.; Julia Ann, born Jan. 23, 1828, married (1), E. H. Cole, graduate Wesleyan University, and (2), G. U. Bartholomew of Bristol, Conn.; Sybil Lathrop, born July 16, 1830, married Enos B. Cole; Harriet, born in Sept. 1832, died in two months; Edwin Eliphalet, born Oct. 8, 1833, married Cynthia P., daughter of Hon. Loren P. Waldo, living in Hartford ; Lucy Catherine, born March 11, 1837, married Joseph P. Root of Tolland ; Clara Hilbourne, born Sept. 10, 1840, married Charles A. Hawkins of the Tolland County Bank; Samuel Harvey, born May 8, 1845, married Angie Bartholomew, living in Urbana, Ohio.

iii. Benjamin Lathrop Young, born in Mansfield, Feb. 10, 1803, and married, Oct. 18, 1829, Betsey Fergerson, daughter of Daniel Fergerson of Tolland. He died at the age of sixty-nine. Their children were: Henry, Edwin, Mary, Julia, Charles; Samuel Young, born in Coventry in 1811, and died at about fourteen months.

### 301. NATHANIEL.                    Canterbury, Conn.

653. BENJAMIN.

654. LEBBEUS, born in Canterbury, Oct. 23, 1761, and was taken by his step-father with his mother to Wyoming, where they were living at the time of the massacre. He enlisted, but being unequal to the campaign was compelled to return; Mr. Haskell, his stepfather, and almost the entire command falling victims to the Indians. At the end of the hostilities he found himself in charge of his mother's family, and began farming in Brookfield, N. Y. At twenty-one years of age he united with the Baptist Church in Brookfield, and at twenty-six began to preach. He married (1), Oct. 15, 1781, Mary Dobson from Brookfield, N. Y., who died Aug. 12, 1793, leaving no children. He married (2), Harriet, daughter of Henry Wisner of Phillipsburg, N. Y. He became soon somewhat prominent among the Baptist clergy. In 1819 we find him presiding at a council held in Stamford, Conn., for considering the local trouble existing with the Reverend Elders Ferris and Webb. The same year he was settled in Samptown, N. J., where he was a successful and esteemed pastor until 1841. He was a good man, who is still remembered for his great native ability with but little of the culture which the schools gave, but with ability occasionally to move an audience by the earnest eloquence of his fervent piety and strong, sober reasoning. He was a strong Calvinist and an uncompromising defender of the literal truth of the Bible. His personality was marked in all he did even to the eccentricities which he could not conceal.

### 303. JOHN.                    New Haven, Conn.

655. FANNY, born in New Haven, and there recorded, July 24, 1765.

656. MARY, born in New Haven, March 25, 1767, according to the New Haven records, and married, May 29, 1799, the Hon. George, son of Moses and Abigail Metcalf Bliss of Springfield, Mass. She died May 1, 1805, leaving no children.

657. JOHN HOSMER, born in New Haven, May 20, 1769, and graduated at Yale in 1787. He pursued the study of law in New Haven and Hartford, and was admitted to the bar in Connecticut. He married, Feb. 1, 1797, Jerusha, daughter of Rev. Samuel and Jerusha (Bingham) Kirkland. He removed to Georgia, where he was successful in accumulating a fortune, and returned north and settled in Utica, N. Y.

658. HENRY, who was half-brother to John H.

### 307. DAVID.                    Tolland, Conn.

659. SAMUEL, born Nov. 7, 1748, and died July 11, 1751.

660. HANNAH, born April 9, 1750.

661. SAMUEL, born April 15, 1752, and died Oct. 16, 1760.

### 308. JONATHAN.                    Tolland, Conn.

662. RACHEL, born and recorded in Tolland, Oct. 22, 1751.

### 310. JOHN.

662-1. DESIRE, born and died Nov. 11, 1755.

662-2. ANNE, born Oct. 19, 1756, baptized on the 24th of the same month, and died on the 23d of the next month. These two records are taken from the autograph family register made by the father, and now in Thomas C. Lathrop's hands at Stafford Springs.

663. LUSCALLA, born Nov. 23, 1757, and married Jan. 14, 1779, Eliab Ladd, son of Jonathan, jun., and Anne (Tyler) Ladd, who was born in Tolland, Apr. 21, 1754. She died Nov. 30, 1827. The children recorded to them in Tolland were: Joseph Ladd, born Oct. 22, 1779, and died in infancy. Luther Ladd, born Dec. 20, 1780, and died in infancy. Ariel Ladd, born Feb. 9, 1783. Stephen Ladd, born Nov. 8, 1784. Sura Ladd, born Oct. 30, 1786, and died May 22, 1816. Roxy Ladd, born Sept. 8, 1788, and died in infancy. Roxy Ladd, born Jan. 29, 1790, and died in infancy. Presinda Ladd, born Sept. 9, 1791.

664. PRESINDA, born Jan. 30, 1761, and married, Feb. 13, 1783, William, son of John and Mehitabel (Steele) Huntington of Tolland. They settled in Watertown, N. Y., where they had a family of eight children. She died Mar. 20, 1810. For their record, and that of their descendants, see Huntington Family Memoir.

665. JOHN, born Apr. 24, 1763, and was killed Dec. 10, 1780, as this record in the clerk's office of Tolland testifies: "John, the son of John Lathrop and Lucy his wife, departed this life December 10, 1780, by the sword of the enemy at Horseneck." And Mr. Waldo in his *Tolland* adds: "He was under eighteen years of age, and was struck dead by a blow on the head with a sabre, by a dragoon. Col. Solomon Williams, to whose wife Mr. Lathrop was nephew, assisted in wrapping him in his blanket and laying him in the grave of a soldier." His father's record says that he died on the Sabbath.

666. ELIZABETH, born in Tolland in 1765, the father's record says on Friday, and married, Aug. 17, 1785, Andrew, son of James and Abigail (Huntington) Steele of Tolland, where he was born Dec. 25, 1763. He died in Brookfield, Vt., Feb. 18, 1811, and she died Sept. 16, 1837. Their children were: Benoni Steele, born Dec. 22, 1785, and died Jan. 5, 1786. Aaron Steele, born in Randolph, Vt., Feb. 28, 1787, and married (1), Martha Gaylord, and (2), Sarah Leonard. They lived in Chicopee, Mass. Polly Steele, born Apr. 5, 1791, and married Oct. 16, 1811, Elisha Allis, jun. Andrew Steele, jun., born June 6, 1793, and married Nancy Ann Starks of Haverhill, N. H. He died in 1835. Danforth Steele, born Apr. 19, 1797, and married in 1820, Lydia Abel of Williamstown, Vt., and died in 1830, having had three children, Henry, Leonard, and Andrew. Lana Steele, born June 20, 1799, and married in 1820, Charles Preston. She died Nov. 6, 1834. Elizabeth Steele, born July 8, 1801, and married Nov. 18, 1819, Zelotis Bigelow, jun.; Lucy Gray Steele, born July 27, 1803, and married in 1826, Joseph Bean.

667. ELVIRA, born June 13, 1768, and died Sept. 14, 1844 (Dec. 5, 1836, Family Record).

668. ROWLAND, born Mar. 10, 1771, and married, Jan. 1, 1799, Hannah

Crafts of Tolland, who died Oct. 15, 1820, in the 44th year of her age. He
married (2), Feb. 28, 1821, Hannah, daughter of Thomas Cleaveland of Hartland, Vt. She died Feb. 4, 1868, at her son's, Thomas C., in the 73d year of her
age. The Hon. Loren P. Waldo, in his History of Tolland, gives us this estimate
of Mr. Lathrop. He "possessed more than ordinary abilities. When young,
he passed for what in those days was called a wild young man, but his wild-
ness ended with youth and he early became a very steady man and a most
exemplary Christian. He was a member of the Methodist denomination and
was a local preacher. His public performances were creditable for fervency,
candor, and sincerity. He had a good knowledge of human nature, and had
a shrewdness peculiar to himself in his remarks upon almost every topic. Mr.
Lathrop was proverbial for integrity and uprightness in all his dealings, and
constant and true in his friendships. He was highly esteemed by his acquaintance, and never seemed to be more happy than when he was doing them some
good. He was twice elected to the General Assembly, but never appeared to
be over-anxious for political preferment. The influence of his example was
most salutary, and a recollection of his guilelessness and simplicity will cause
his memory to be long respected. He died Sept. 14, 1844." The records of
the family which he made are now in his son's hands.

669. LUCY, born Nov. 1, 1774, married —— Rawdon. Children: Eliakim,
Ralph, Freeman, Lathrop, and one daughter.

670. JONATHAN, born Feb. 17, 1776, and died May 13, 1776.

671. MOLLY, born Sept. 12, 1779, married (1), —— Woodward, of Tolland;
(2), —— Torrey, of Vt.

### 311.  THATCHER.                    East Windsor, Conn.

671-1. BETTY LATHROP married George Buckland, East Hartford. Children: Chester Buckland, Asenath Buckland, Norman Buckland, Willard
Buckland, Walter Buckland, Anna Buckland, Cyrus Buckland.

672. LYDIA, born Sept. 2, 1756, and died Mar. 10, 1772.

673. LUTHER, born in "Tolland or Coventry" Oct. 5, 1766, and married
Mar. 24, 1795, in Wilmington, Vt., Lucy Hartwell, who was born June 6,
1766. He settled in Wilmington, Vt., where he died Mar. 10, 1831.

674. DAVID, born Apr. 26, 1758, married in 1785, Anna Chipman, and lived
in East Windsor till he removed to Longmeadow in 1804. Eight children:
died Mar. 19, 1817, aged 59. Anna, the wife, died May 14, 1845, aged 84
(gravestone).

675. ——.

676. LORING, born Apr. 3, 1770, married May 4, 1800, Miriam Foster of
Windsor, daughter of Pelatiah, and born June 12, 1773. His headstone shows
that he died Jan. 7, 1847, aged 77; she died Feb 17, 1845, aged 72. They
removed to East Longmeadow. Five children, all dead.

677. VALLELEY, so reported in Stiles' Windsor, born in East Windsor, and
married Elizur Atkins, and died, aged 22 years, Oct., 1794, leaving one child.
Freeman Atkins, who died Nov. 5, 1798, aged 5.

678. LURA, born 1762. She married a Mr. Hall. Her headstone in the
cemetery at East Longmeadow gives the date of her death, Nov. 16, 1815, and
her age, 83 years. Her children were: Clarissa Hall, who married David

White; Sophia Hall, who married Cornelius Wolcott; Lura Hall, who married Elam Kellogg; George Clark Hall, who married Lucy Lathrop; Eunice Hall, who married Moses Kibbe; Minerva Hall, who married Joseph Sweetland; Laura Hall, who married —— Gabriel.

679. SUBMIT, born 1765, and married Ephraim Hunn, who died June 15, 1862, aged 96. She died Sept. 19, 1818, aged 83. Their children were: David Lathrop Hunn, Ephraim Hunn, Submit Hunn, Roxa Hunn, Cindonia Hunn, Sophronia Hunn, Erastus Hunn, Polly Hunn.

## 316. HOPE.

680. REBECCA, born Oct. 1760, and married Dec. 16, 1779, Eleazer Steele, jun., son of Eleazer and Ruth (Chapman) Steele, who was born Aug. 20, 1753. She died Mar. 3, 1806, and he June 24, 1809. Children: a son, born Mar. 8, 1781, and died Mar. 29, 1781; Joel Steele, born Aug. 14, 1782, who became a Methodist preacher and married (1), Jerusha Higgins, and (2), Abigail Stratford, and had a family of eleven children; Eleazer Steele, born Aug. 22, 1784; Jedothan Steele, born Feb. 25, 1787; Ralph Steele, born May 8, 1789; Ruth Steele, born Jan, 4, 1792; Minerva Steele, Sept. 10, 1794, and married Jarvis Crandall and died Feb. 25, 1831; Marilla Steele, born Jan. 16, 1797, and died June 19, 1798; Sandford Steele, born Feb. 27, 1799, and married Caroline E., daughter of Rev. Henry P. Sumner of Hebron, Conn., and had ten children; George Steele, born Nov. 4, 1801, and married Betsy Minerva Nash of Hebron, Conn., and had seven children; Sarah Steele, born Apr. 25, 1805.

681. EDNA, born Feb. 15, 1763, and married as his third wife, Dec. 23, 1784, Ebenezer, son of Ephraim, jun., and Esther (Ladd) Grant of Tolland. Their children, recorded are: Juliana Grant, born Nov. 16, 1784; Phebe Grant, born Aug. 5, 1787; Harry Grant, born July 2, 1789; Edna Grant, born Aug. 1, 1791; Ebenezer Grant, born June 16, 1793; Oliver Grant, born Jan. 31, 1795.

682. SARAH, born July 4, 1765.

683. ICHABOD, born June 30, 1767, and married Dec. 25, 1789, Eunice, daughter of John and Sarah (Cobb) Steele, who was born in Tolland, Mar. 19, 1767.

684. HANNAH, born July 12, 1768.

*2d wife.*

685. HORACE born Apr. 25, 1775.

686. GRACE, born Feb. 21, 1776.

687. SOLOMON, born Apr. 21, 1779.

688. GRANT, born Jan. 25, 1782, and married Sybil —— ^BLISS^. His death is recorded in Tolland, Mar. 21, 1823. ^B. 7 JAN 1791^

689. SOPHIA, born July 2, 1785.

690. AZEL, born Jan. 28, 1788.

691. LAURA, born Nov. 19, 1790.

## 319. SOLOMON.                    Tolland, Conn.

692. ELIZABETH, born Dec. 4, 1770, and married Mar. 8, 1792, Stephen, son of Ichabod and Mercy (Hatch) Griggs of Tolland, where the following

children are recorded to them: Harriett Griggs, born Dec. 27, 1792; Chauncey Griggs, born Apr. 10, 1796; Ralph Griggs, born Jan. 31, 1798; Solomon Lathrop Griggs, born Apr. 7, 1800; Austin Griggs, born July 26, 1805; Leverett Griggs, born Nov. 6, 1808, graduated at Yale in 1829, and was tutor in his Alma Mater in 1832 and 1833, D.D., 1868 Sec.  Licensed to preach in 1833, by New Haven West Association.

693.  RALPH RUDOLPHUS, born Mar. 25, 1769.

694.  ABIGAIL, born Nov. 16, 1772.

### 326.  SIMON. Ontario Co., N. Y.

695.  ISAAC, born in New Canaan, N. Y., about 1766, and married Lois Sawyer.  They had five sons and four daughters.

696.  SOLOMON, born in New Canaan, N. Y., in 1768, and married Clarissa Dunwell, and lived in Michigan in 1830.  They had five sons and six daughters.

697.  DEBORAH, born about 1770, and married Daniel Mason of Norwich, Conn.  They settled in Hartford, N. Y., where he was a prominent citizen. She died in 1817.  They have at least two sons : Daniel Mason ; David Mason, who died at Binghamton, N. Y.

698.  PHEBE, born about 1773, and married Reuben Davis in Lima, N. Y., and had one daughter, married a Parker and lived in Michigan.

699.  PHILANDER, born in September, 1775, and married in Franklin, Conn., in 1798, Elizabeth, daughter of Capt. David Mason.  He settled in Lima, N. Y., and moved to Ohio in 1834.  He died in Delaware County, Ohio, Nov. 20, 1842, and his widow in Columbus, Ohio, May 1, 1850.  He was a farmer, and held in deserved repute for his sterling integrity: and his wife is remembered as a woman of personal culture and worth.

700.  ARMON, born in 1777, and married in Canaan, Thirza Johnson.  They settled in Pittsford, N. Y., but removed in 1818 to Sangamon County, Ill., and had a large family.

701.  IRENE, born in 1782-3, and married in Lima, N. Y., William Frost. She died in Geneva, N. Y., in 1828, and the family removed to Michigan. They had the following children : Caroline Frost ; Mary Frost ; Hannah Frost ; Irene Elizabeth Frost, born in Richmond, N. Y., Oct. 10, 1815, and married George Saunders, son of Nathan and Julia (Strong) Green, and settled in Des Moines, Iowa, they had seven children, of whom three sons, Wm. B. Green, George Wesley Green, and Charles W. Green were soldiers in the Union Army during the late war of the rebellion ; Bradley Frost.

702.  MARTIN DAVIS, born about 1780, and married, 1814, Rebecca Wright, a Quakeress.  He was physician in Waynesville, Ohio, and won a good reputation.  He died in 1824, and his widow, who was a lady of intellectual culture and refinement, in 1872.

703.  LORRAIN, born May 25, 1786, and married Isaac Fitch.  They lived in Lima, N. Y.  They had nine children.  Of Mrs. Fitch, the biographer of her son, that eminent Christian philanthropist and teacher, James Mason Fitch, says:  "His mother was a woman of strong native sense, remarkable faith, and devoted piety.  She died in 1854, at the age of sixty-seven, having lived

to see all of her family converted, her husband included, and all but two asleep in Jesus." Their children were : Louisa Fitch ; Albert Fitch ; Martin Fitch ; James Mason Fitch, born in Lima, N. Y., Dec. 31, 18x5, of whom a pleasant biographical sketch is found in the Congregational Quarterly for April, 1868, with a steel-plate engraving. Theodore Fitch ; Fayette Fitch ; John Fitch ; Maria Fitch, married Rev. Mr. Torrey, a Presbyterian minister.

704. COLBY, born in 1789, and married in Lima, in 1811. Edith Perry. After her death he married Polly Perry. He settled in northern Ohio.

### 330. MELATIAH. Sullivan, N. Y.

704-1. ABRAM, born Jan. 6, 1778, in Chatham, Columbia County, N. Y., and married, in 1804, Sarah Carpenter, at Balston Springs, Saratoga County, N. Y. In 1806 he removed to a two-hundred-acre tract which he had bought in the forest then covering the present town of Sullivan, Madison County, N. Y., and began pioneer life in earnest. Here he lived for fifty-eight years, and did his part in clearing up the wilderness, and founding and sustaining the institutions of Christian civilization. He was a pillar in the Methodist Church, and his house was a preaching station of the heroic "circuit-riders." Abram Lathrop, in the spring of 1863, went to live with his daughter, Mrs. George Pack, in Michigan. At her home he died Dec. 18, 1866, and his excellent wife did not long survive him.

704-2. WILLIS.

704-3. MELATIAH, a subaltern company officer in the war of 1812, and died in the service at New York.

704-4. SARAH, married Abraham Raymond.

704-5. POLLY, married Nathan Calkins, in Saratoga County, N. Y.

704-6. RACHEL, married ―――― Burgess.

704-7. LYDIA, married Samuel Gregory ; died in 1854, in Jefferson County, N. Y.

### 331. EZRA.

705. SALMON, born in New Concord, Columbia County, N. Y., Jan. 5, 1781, and married, Aug. 28, 1805, Aurelia Noble, eldest daughter of John and Lydia Noble, who was born in Benson, Vt., July 18, 1790, and died in Carbondale, Penn., April 13, 1872.

The following obituary is from the Carbondale (Pennsylvania) *Advance:* The passing away of the oldest resident of our town, at the advanced age of nearly ninety years, and of one whose life for so many years had been identified with its welfare and progress, seems to demand something more than the simple announcement of his decease. Mr. Salmon Lathrop, the subject of this sketch, who died in this city on the morning of Wednesday, November 4, 1868, was born on the 5th of January, 1781, in Columbia County, in the State of New York. At an early period in his life he removed with his father's family to the town of Sherburne, Chenango County, New York, then a comparatively wild and unknown region of country. Here his youth was spent on his father's farm, clearing away the wilderness and developing the resources of that now most beautiful and productive region of the Empire

17

State. With slight advantages of education, as may well be presumed, it was a matter of no little difficulty to procure the knowledge which his mind thirsted for, yet he succeeded in fitting himself for a school teacher, which business he followed for some years in the winter months.

In the summer of 1805 he was married to Aurelia Noble, with whom he lived most happily for nearly sixty-four years. The responsibilities of a family now led him to seek a wider field for his enterprise ; and a few years later, when the great mind of that eminent man, DeWitt Clinton, had planned and finally succeeded in putting under way that gigantic work now known as the Erie Canal, he undertook the building of many miles of that famous work. He continued in this line of business at intervals for many years, having built large portions of the Pennsylvania Canal, Chenango Canal, New York and Erie Railroad, and other public works.

Removing to Carbondale in 1827, at the request of the Messrs. Wurts, who were then laying the foundation of what has since become the extensively ramified works of the Delaware and Hudson Canal Company, he commenced the development of the then unknown and slightly valued resources of the Lackawanna coal region. Under his supervision the first steps were taken towards laying bare the vast and unexplored coal fields which now so much contribute to the wealth of the country, and give employment to myriads of people. With a few others who had been attracted to the place by the reported discoveric of coal, he commenced the laying out and building up of the town, which has since become a city of 10,000 inhabitants, and the seat of one of the most extensive coal operations in the United States.

The first frame building erected in the place was built by him as an addition to the log structure (now destroyed) known for so many years as the "log tavern." Soon after he commenced the erection of the store and dwelling combined, on what is known as the "Richmond corner," and of the large frame hotel known as the "Mansion House," of which latter place he was for so long a time the host.

Through preëminently a man of active life, and more than usually ambitious to succeed in worldly enterprises, he did not neglect the cultivation of the heart and mind ; and for a good part of his life he was a most earnest and devoted Christian. Indeed, as he grew older in years he grew riper for Heaven ; and to those with whom he came in daily association his example and deportment were a precious earnest of his simple and Christ-like devotion to the Master's work. Though his general character is sufficiently described by the term "Christian," yet he had certain traits, for which he was more particularly remarkable. Not that they form any basis for undue exultation or boasting, but they so strongly marked the man that they should be mentioned in detail to leave upon record the truth, and as an incentive to the youth of the land who aim at a higher excellence in life.

He was a man of unusual simplicity and tenderness of heart. His ear was ever open to the cry of distress, and while possessed of means he was ready to aid the deserving and to sympathize with the comfortless. To the benevolent operations of the church he was a bountiful contributor, and his heart was particularly wrapped up in the anticipated conversion of the heathen world to the light and liberty of the gospel of Christ.

He was a man of the strictest integrity. Through a most intimate acquaintance, extending over a period of more than forty years, the writer of this sketch has never known him to swerve from the path of rectitude in his business relations. Though engaged in the most active business of life, and handling large sums of money, he was never known to wrong a fellow-being, even the most humble and unprotected, of a penny. Frequently suffering himself from the dishonesty of others, and finally losing by this means all his worldly possessions, not a single stain of dishonesty was upon his character.

He was a man of extreme modesty. Never fond of display, though a man of strong prejudices, and of a mind unusually faithful to its convictions, he was not forward or obnoxious in the presentation of his views—either religious or political—and he preferred both in church and State rather to follow than to lead. This disposition led him to decline office when tendered, and frequently to acquiesce, for the sake of peace, in measures not exactly in accordance with his better judgment. But he never shrank from the discharge of known duty. However it may have conflicted with his natural retiring disposition, it was but necessary for him to see his path clear and he was sure to walk in it.

He was a man of untiring industry. It is no figure of speech to say that he was never idle. Every moment of the time usually devoted to business, found him usefully occupied, and his ambition to labor with his hands never flagged, even up to a short period prior to his decease. In fine, in all the characters he bore, he proved himself faithful and diligent. As a husband he was affectionate and considerate, never for a moment wavering in fidelity and devotion to the wife of his choice; as a father, though stern and uncompromising in his demands for implicit obedience, he was kind and forgiving; and it was the pride of his heart to see his children grow up to be respected as men and women, and to make, without exception, the choice of the same God, who, for so many generations, had been worshiped by his ancestry. As a citizen, his heart and life were devoted to the interests of the government. His love of country was unbounded; and during the late rebellion, by his words and acts of patriotism, he contributed not a little to incite the youth of his acquaintance to buckle on their armor for the defense of their native land. As a friend, he was constant and warm-hearted, though from his unobtrusiveness the circle of his intimate acquaintances was not largely extended.

His death was calm and peaceful — even triumphant. The approach of the "King of Terrors" did not cause him dismay or grief. His "house was in order," and he had the near presence of the Saviour who had in His own person conquered the "last enemy." His wish that his surviving children, three in number, should be near him in his last sickness, was gratified; and his dying pillow was smoothed in a great measure by the abundance of their filial sympathy and affection. Nine of his seventeen grandchildren were also gathered around his bed of death, who ministered with tender love to his necessities; all receiving his parting blessing, and cherishing up in their hearts the memory of his precious example.

May we not say in conclusion, in view of the long and useful life and happy death of this aged pilgrim, in the words of the text chosen by his dear widow for the funeral discourse, "Precious in the sight of the Lord is the death of his saints."                                                                        C. E. L.

706. CURTIS, who at one time lived in Lockport, N. Y.

707. BETSEY, who married Stephen Northrop, Genesee, N. Y., buried most of her children.  Rev. Ira Scott, pres. and Ezra now living.

708. ELEAZER, born in Sherburne, N. Y.  Educated at Hamilton College, and was tutor there.  Graduated from Theo. Sem., Andover, Mass., in 1820. He married Eliza Maria Lathrop (No. 1391), Nov. 10, 1823, and died in Port Gibson, Miss., Feb. 1, 1832.  He was a member of the Senior class in the Andover Theological Seminary in 1820, and was reported as then from Homer, N. Y.

709. LUCY, married ―― Clark, and died leaving a family near Tecumseh, Mich.

710. POLLY, married Levi Lee; child: J. L. Lee.

711. JUNIUS, went to Missouri.

712. JASON, born in Sherburne, Mar. 4, 1800, and married at Perry, N. Y., Sept. 15, 1831, Fanny A., daughter of Dr. Otis Higgins of Perry.

713. WALTER, near Tecumseh, Mich.

714. SOPHRONIA, who died at the age of ten.

715. HARRIET (a name given by Prof. Alvan Lathrop).

### 334.  JOSIAH LO.          Sherburne, N. Y. in 1793.

716. ZILPHA, born in Chatham, Columbia Co., Apr. 9, 1785, and married ―― Brown, and died in Sherburne, Aug. 24, 1805.

717. LEWIS, born in Chatham, Nov. 30, 1786, and married Marilla Marsh, who was born in Rocky Hill, Conn., Nov. 24, 1793.  He settled in Sherburne, where he died Aug. 20, 1853, and his wife Dec. 28, 1856.

718. CLARISSA, born in Chatham, Dec. 24, 1788, and married ―― Curtiss, ――.  She died in Sherburne, Dec. 1863 [?]

719. JOHN, born in Chatham, Feb. 1, 1791, and died in Sherburne, in December, 1808.

720. ERASTUS, born in Chatham, Feb. 13, 1793, died in Oshkosh, Wis., May 5, 1862.

721. ROSWELL, born in Sherburne, Chenango Co., N. Y., Sept. 11, 1795, and died Mar. 20, 1796.

722. WELTHY, born in Sherburne, Sept. 25, 1798, and died Sept. 3, 1802.

### 335.  EBENEZER.          Peterboro'.

723. JOSEPH B., born Aug. 1, 1787.  A lawyer, Sandy Hill, N. Y., died in Buffalo, 1857.

724. JOHN H., born Nov. 14, 1789, and married (1), May 5, 1813, Susan Furman, who was born June 28, 1789.  He married (2), Nov. 24, 1853, Lucretia Smith, who was born Apr. 25, 1810, died Sept. 13, 1856.

725. MARY, born Mar. 10, 1792, married ―― Palmer, died Aug. 19, 1825.

726. JULIA, born June 24, 1795, still living.
727. ABIGAIL, born July 12, 1797, and died Apr. 12, 1828.
728. CELINA D., born Sept. 7, 1799, and died Oct. 30, 1817.
729. SOPHIA, born May 25, 1802, and died Feb. 28, 1818.
730. ANSON, born Dec. 13, 1803, and died 1870.
731. DEBORAH M., born Dec. 1, 1805.
732. RUTH ANN, born Apr. 9, 1807, and died Sept., 1832.

## 336. JOHN. Sherburne, N. Y.

733. MYRA, born Mar. 3, 1793, and died Apr. 3, 1796.
734. MARCIA, born Jan. 6, 1797, and died Sept. 22, 1801.
735. JOHN HIRAM, born in Sherburne, New York, January 22, 1799; graduated at Yale College in 1819; studied law as a science and was admitted to the bar, but became a teacher by profession. After teaching at various points in New England, he was called to Hamilton College in 1829, as Professor of Mathematics and Natural Philosophy. August 15, 1833, he married Frances E. Lothrop, daughter of John Hosmer and Jerusha (Kirkland) Lothrop, of Utica, New York. In 1835 he was advanced to the Maynard Professorship of Law, Civil Polity, and Political Economy in Hamilton College. In 1840 he was elected first President of the University of the State of Missouri, and, accepting the trust, devoted more than eight of the best years of his life to organizing and building up a broad and liberal system of collegiate education in the then far west. In the year 1845, the degree of Doctor of Laws was conferred upon him by Hamilton College. In the autumn of 1849, he accepted the Chancellorship of Wisconsin State University at Madison, to which he had been elected the previous spring. Here his skill and experience as an organizer of a State educational system were brought to bear upon much the same condition of things that he had found in Missouri eight or nine years before, and the highest measure of success crowned his efforts. After nearly ten years residence in Madison, amid the pleasantest social relations, he was induced to accept the twice offered Presidency of Indiana State University, a well established institution, though under temporary embarrassments, which his administration hoped to relieve. After a year devoted to this end, he felt strongly inclined to lay aside the cares of administration with which he had been burdened so many years, and accept a professorship in the Missouri University, a retreat in the growing shade of the tree planted and watered by his own hand in time gone by. He returned to Columbia in 1860, as Professor of English Literature in the University, but the complications of the civil war soon brought his administrative power again into requisition, and after preserving the continuity of the institution for four years as Chairman of the Faculty, he was, in 1865, officially confirmed President for the second time.

Under the new and promising conditions of peace in Missouri, he matured plans in accordance with his cherished idea for making the University such in the fullest sense, by the establishment of schools for the various professions and arts in connection with the academic department. He put on foot efforts for securing the agricultural college fund to the University, and everything seemed to point to a great step forward in the history of the institution. Suddenly he was stricken down by an acute attack of typhoid fever, and died in the midst of his labors, in the full vigor of his mind, on the 2d of August, 1866. He rests in the cemetery at Columbia, and a spire of Massachusetts granite records the leading events of his useful and beneficent life.

He possessed a clear, logical mind, capable of broad generalization and disciplined by years of critical study. His humor was refined and graceful; his sarcasm keen and delicate, and his diction finished and elegant. He was an extensive writer, communicating with the public in lectures, pamphlets, addresses, and the daily press, upon a variety of subjects for which his varied learning and sound philosophy especially fitted him. Education, finance, free trade, internal improvements, agriculture, besides the philosophies of his class lecture-room, were some of the matters of general importance that engaged his able pen from time to time. He carried on a large literary and social correspondence, and his letters might be taken as models of their kind. During his long and varied professional life, he filled every chair of instruction common to the universities of the day, showing a rare extent and versatility of learning. His favorite department was the philosophy of morals. His lectures on ethics were an original and forcible development of the subject,—combining and harmonizing the advanced views of modern thinkers with th fundamental truths and faith of Christianity. It is to be regretted that in the busy routine of his life he failed to carry out his intention of editing, in book form, his system of ethics, and other valuable matter, to which he had given much thought and research. He held many advanced views, some of which are already sanctioned by the logic of events. Early in life he took the then startling position that there was no necessary connection between the professions of teaching and theology; that either the one or the other should absorb the entire energies of the man, as in law or medicine. And the growing distinctness of the profession of the "educator" proves this view of the case to have come into general recognition. He was of the opinion that no restriction should be put upon the education or vocation of woman,—and his belief that the higher institutions of learning would be thrown open to all who could pass the necessary examinations successfully is sustained by present facts. Socially, it is perhaps not too much to say of him that he was "*facile princeps.*" Universally affable and approachable to all classes of society, with fine conversational powers united to a dignified and courtly address, he left an uneffaceable impress upon all communities with which he was associated. Though naturally of a delicate constitution, by the same conscientious observance of the laws of health which he gave to all law, human and divine, in his perfectly regulated life, he rarely lost a day from illness,—and at sixty-seven years of age no symptom of old age had diminished his power of endurance or limited his usefulness—only a few days before his sudden prostration by the acute disease that so soon proved fatal, he writes playfully to his old friend, Gerrit Smith: "Age is ripening you and me; decay we don't admit. We will continue to sow seed-thoughts while we may; the harvest is by and by."

The character of one so modest in asserting his own claims and so unselfish in his labors for the general good as he, usually meets its fullest and most thorough appreciation among those who knew it least,—and to those who enjoyed personal friendship with him, and to his army of students scattered all over this and into other countries, who held him, almost without exception, in respect and love amounting to veneration, he was "the noblest Roman of them all;" and in the tender relations of family, he was the beloved husband and father, the guide, philosopher, and friend. His religion was that of humanity, of charity, with a faith in the benevolent government of the universe by a Supreme Power, and a hope of immortality of progression and development beyond the grave. He had no sectarian bias, though an unfailing attendant upon church service, contributing to all churches alike. Late in life he was confirmed in the Episcopal Church, having long had a preference for its mode of worship. The exalted Christian philosophy which had regulated his life sustained him in the hour of death.

In an address delivered upon his installation as Chancellor of Wisconsin University,—he gives his conception of the ideal professor,—a description that might well be applied to his own character,—and in that we find a fitting answer to what was once said by some baffled inquirer, that it was impossible to find out his politics or religion. He was, to use his own words in closing his tribute to the ideal educator, "too intensely American to be partisan, too profoundly Christian to be sectarian."

His widow is still living.

736. MILES, born Nov. 11, 1800, and died unmarried Mar. 18, 1826.

737. MARCUS, born May 2, 1802, and married in Sherburne, Jan. 31, 1827, Amanda H., daughter of Moses and Diantha Hopkins.

738. MYRA, born Aug. 6, 1804, and has never married.

739. MARCIA, born Aug. 31, 1806, and died Mar. 5, 1808.

740. CHARLES H., born March 18, 1811, and married Jan. 20, 1842, Louisa, daughter of William and Lois Newton of Sherburne, N. Y. He died Mar. 17, 1865.

### 238. ELEAZER. Sherburne, N. Y.

741. ALVAN, born in Sherburne, N. Y., Jan. 6, 1800, and married in Pittsfield, Mass., Apr. 12, 1830, Caroline E., daughter of Phinehas Allen of Pittsfield, where she was born May 14, 1809. She died in Poughkeepsie, N. Y., Feb. 27, 1845, leaving behind her the legacy of a very precious memory. He died April 12, 1872, having been killed at a railroad crossing in Rochester where he resided. "He was a man earnestly engaged in the cause of religion," and had been attending an evening service at the Presbyterian Chapel when the fatal casualty occurred.

742. DIANTHA, born ——, 1802, and married, Aug. 18, 1824, Judge Josiah, son of Josiah and Mary (Birchard) Tracy of Honesdale, Pa., who was born Oct. 1, 1796. They settled in Painesville, Ohio, where he was a merchant. In 1832 they removed to Vermilion, Ohio, and thence in 1835 to Huron, Ohio, where she died, Apr. 23, 1840. He removed to Mansfield, Ohio, where he died Jan. 11, 1857. He was a prominent man and much in public life—having been Mayor of Huron, a State Senator, and a Judge of the County Court. They had seven children: Lathrop J. Tracy, born in Painesville May 26, 1825. Eunice

M. Tracy, born Apr. 4, 1829, and died next year.  Frederick E. Tracy, born
May 6, 1831, married Amos Lord of Honesdale, and settled in Zanesville,
Ohio.  Ruth M. Tracy, born in Huron. Apr. 6, 1833, and died next year.
Sarah P. Tracy, born in Huron, June 13, 1835, and died in 1839.  Mary D.
Tracy, born in Huron, Jan. 12, 1839, and died single in 1837.  Frances Tracy,
born Apr. 10, 1840, and died in infancy.

743.  ELEAZER HOLLISTER, born in Sherburne, N. Y., Jan. 24, 1809.  The
first twenty years of his life was spent with his father upon the farm and in
acquiring—at the village school—the foundations of a good education; then
being anxious to enter college he went to Amherst, Mass., and studied for one
year with a private teacher.  He was called home by the death of his mother,
and thinking it his duty to remain at home with his father he abandoned study
and turned his attention to mercantile pursuits.

In the spring of 1834 he was married to Mary Angeline, daughter of Levi
and Tryphena (Foster) Ray of Norwich, N. Y., and soon after settled in
Brockport, N. Y., as a merchant.

He was a man of unblemished character—scrupulously honest in all his
dealings—sympathetic and kind to the poor and beloved and respected by all.
For many years he was the superintendent of the Sabbath School in the Presbyterian Church, and when about forty years of age was elected a Ruling Elder,
which office he filled with acceptance till ill health compelled him to relin-
quish the active duties of life.

He died at Brockport, August 30, 1854, in the joyous hope of a blessed
immortality through Jesus Christ.  His widow married (2), Rev. Dr. Wm. A.
Hallock of New York.  See No. 914.

### 347. GEN. EBENEZER.                Barnstable, Mass.

744.  DESIRE, born in Barnstable, Dec. 2, 1769, and married, Jan. 17, 1793,
Josiah Hinckley, son of Jabez and Deborah (Wing), died Mar. 4, 1856, in
Barnstable: 2 children, (1) Betsey, born Oct. 19, 1793, died Nov. 27, 1793; (2)
Josiah, Jr., born October 24, 1794, and married, July 9, 1815, Mercy C.,
daughter Jos. and Mercy (Davis) Easterbrooke of Barnstable.

745.  ROBERT, born in Barnstable, Oct. 6, 1771, and married, Dec. 8, 1793,
Susanna Allyn, who was born July 25, 1770, and died Oct. 18, 1853.
They lived in Barnstable, where he died Sept. 28, 1840, they had four
daughters and one son, the Rev. Davis Lothrop, now living (1883) in Harwich.

746.  THOMAS, born in Barnstable, Aug. 6, 1774, and married, 1797, Betsey
Mosher of Gorham, Me.  He served his apprenticeship with his father, and
removed to ——, Me.  He died in Liverpool, N. S., Dec. 21, 1820.  His wife
was born Mar. 11, 1780, and died Feb. 2, 1849.  They had a family of five
children, of whom the late Deacon Ansel Lothrop of Boston was one.

747.  EBENEZER, JR., born Mar. 22, 1778, and married, Jan. 20, 1799,
Temperance Lewis.  He died Oct. 21, 1825, at 47 years of age.  She died Nov.
11, 1837, aged 57.  He was a very successful business man, his calling being
that of a house carpenter.  He was a Captain of militia during the war of
1812, and a very worthy man and useful citizen.  Their children, all born in

Barnstable, were: Thomas, born Feb. 26, 1800, settled in Provincetown, and died about two years ago leaving a family—two of his sons are practitioners of medicine in Buffalo, N. Y., one of them being lecturer in the Medical College there; Mehitable, born Jan. 19, 1802, married Leander Stafford; Eliza Davis, born Mar. 13, 1804, married Stephen Smith, and lived in Boston; Adeline, born May 26, 1806, married Ebenezer Sturgis Smith, agent for underwriters. Their residence was in Provincetown; Temperance, born Aug. 14, 1809, died Dec. 27, 1809; Temperance, born Jan. 6, 1811, died July 14, 1811; John Lewis, born Aug. 27, 1813, married Sarah N. Nickerson of Provincetown, and died about two years ago in Somerville, near Boston. He was a successful and highly respected physician; Temperance Lewis, born July 27, 1815, married David Porter Howes. They reside in Dennis. Mr. Howes has been, until quite recently, an Inspector of the customs in Boston; a son, born in 1817, died in infancy; Lucy Jane, born June 8, 1819, married Artemas Paine of Provincetown, and live there.

748. Ansel, (baptized Anselm,) born in Barnstable, Sept. 2, 1780, and married Lois Whittier, who was born in Readfield, Me., Dec. 2, 1785, and died in Belfast, Me., Feb. 19, 1839 or 1840. He served his apprenticeship with his father, and early went into Maine. He died in Searsmont, Me., in Dec. 1834. His daughter Elizabeth is the wife of Doctor Ludwig of Portland, Me.

749. Charles, born ——, married Fanny Baxter of Barnstable, Aug. 29, 1813. He was Captain of an infantry company in the war of 1812, acted as Aid to Gen. Dearborn, and died in New York city. His widow married Dr. Smith of the United States Navy.

750. David, born in Barnstable, and married, in 1812, Clarissa Hovey. He served his apprenticeship with his father, and with his brothers Thomas and Ansel went to Maine early in life.

### 348. DAVID. Plymouth, Mass.

751. A daughter, born and died in Dec., 1771.
752. Bathsheba, born in Plymouth, Aug. 6, 1773.

### 349. COL. THOMAS. Cohasset, Mass.

753. Susan(Nah?), born in Hingham, Dec. 25, 1759, and married, in Cohasset, Oct. 12, 1777, Haugh Oakes. They settled in Cohasset, where he died in the spring of 1824, and his widow in 1834. Their descendants have been numerous:

i. Deborah Oakes, born Mar. 17, 1778, married for her 2d husband, Sept. 15, 1801, Daniel Pratt, who died Aug. 20, 1854. She died July 15, 1856. Children: Susan Pratt, born June, 1803, in Springfield, Vermont married John Miller; Thomas M. Pratt, married Catharine Burke. Live in Kansas; Mary R. Pratt, married Norman K. Whitney; Elizabeth H. Pratt, born Sept. 15, 1817, married George I. Nash; Daniel B. Pratt, born Aug 9, 1820, married Rosanna Ellis. Reside in Irving, Barre Co., Mich.

18

ii. Lucretia Oakes, born in Cohasset, April, 1781, and married, in 1800, Job Pratt of Cohasset. She died July 7, 1832, and he Jan. 7, 1853. Their children are: James Pratt, born at Cohasset, Jan. 9, 1802, married Betsey Willcutt of Cohasset, in 1824, died at sea about 1843; Sarah Pratt, born in Cohasset, Dec. 31, 1807, married Thomas J. Brown, Feb. 24, 1828. She died July 24, 1838; Job Pratt, born in Cohassett, May 14, 1819, married Susan Nichols of Cohasset, July 2, 1845; George Pratt, born in Cohasset, May 14, 1804; George Pratt, 2d, born in Cohasset, Aug. 5, 1812, married, June 12, 1838, Elizabeth B. Wilson, residence Griggsville, Ill.; Thomas Pratt, born in Cohasset, April 7, 1822, married Sarah P. N. Tover of Cohasset, Oct. 22, 1850.

iii. Susannah Oakes, born in Cohasset, in May, 1784, and died in infancy.

iv. Theodosia Oakes, born in Cohasset, in September, 1787, and died in infancy.

v. Ruth Lothrop Oakes, born in Cohasset, May 10, 1790, and married, Feb. 12, 1815, Caleb Bailey, a farmer of Cohasset. He died June 11, 1850, and she died Nov. 8, 1870. Their children: Martha Bailey, born in Cohasset, Feb. 3, 1816; Mary O. Bailey, born in Cohasset, Nov. 11, 1817, died Feb. 19, 1837; Elizabeth P. Bailey, born in Cohasset, Jan. 9, 1820, died May 13, 1821; Ruth L. Bailey, born in Cohasset, Apr. 19, 1822; Lucretia O. Bailey, born in Cohasset, June 29, 1824; Susannah O. Bailey, born in Cohasset, Mar. 2, 1827; Elizabeth Bailey, born in Cohasset, July 20, 1829; Caleb F. Bailey, born in Cohasset, Nov. 6, 1831, died May 30, 1838.

vi. Susannah Oakes, born at Cohasset, Jan. 14, 1793, married, Jan. 1, 1812, Elijah Whitney of Springfield, Vt. She died July 25, 1854. Their children: Lucretia Oakes Whitney, born Nov. 3, 1815, married, Mar. 6, 1840, James Lovell of Chester, Vt.; Theodosia Helen Whitney, born Mar. 20, 1819, died Feb. 12, 1826; James Whitney, born July 1, 1823, married, Jan., 1854, Martha Damon of Springfield, Vt., where they now reside; Theodosia Maria Whitney, born Jan. 1, 1826; Mary Jane Whitney, born June 13, 1830, died Oct. 18, 1832; Julia Ann Whitney, born June 8, 1833, died June 22, 1835.

vii. Theodosia Oakes, born in Cohasset, Jan. 14, 1796, and married, July 13, 1818, Wm. H. Stoddard, a s. ip carpenter of Cohasset. He died Nov. 26, 1867, and she died May 14, 1872. Their children were: Hannah Stoddard, born in Cohasset, Feb. 7, 1819, married Edward F. Tilden of Marshfield, Mass., Nov. 25, 1841; Mary E. Stoddard, born in Cohasset, Oct. 23, 1823; Caroline A. Stoddard, born in Cohasset, May 11, 1832, died Oct. 20, 1833; Susan Caroline Stoddard, born in Cohasset, June 20, 1839, died Feb. 25, 1865; Lincoln Stoddard, born in Cohasset, Feb. 21, 1821; married Elizabeth Towle of Cohasset, June, 1844; Theodosia O. Stoddard, born in Cohasset, Mar. 4, 1827, died Aug. 23, 1828; Theodosia O. Stoddard, born in Cohasset, Jan. 3, 1830, married Franklin Hardwick, Quincy, Mass., Jan. 3, 1850; James C. Stoddard, born in Cohasset, Feb. 14, 1836, married J. Frances Vining of South Weymouth, Apr. 3, 1862.

viii. Mary Oakes, born at Cohasset, June 23, 1800, married, June 6, 1824, James Lovell of Springfield, Vt. She died at Chester, Vt., July 29, 1839.

Children: James Lovell, Jr., M.D., born July 18, 1826, married, Sept. 5, 1857, Vesta M. Wilkeson of Townshend, Vt., where she died on the same day; Bezaleel Wood Lovell, born Nov. 18, 1829, married, May, 1866, Mary Sessions of Arkwright Summit, New York.

754. DEBORAH, born Nov. 14, 1761, and married, Jan. 31, 1779, Seth Briggs of Cohasset. They settled in Cohasset, where they had three children. She died May 1, 1848. Warren Briggs, who died in Cohasset, in May, 1796, aged twelve years; Thomas Briggs, who died unmarried, Oct. 16, 1839; Rachel Briggs, who married in November, 1803, Adna Bates of Cohasset. They settled in Boston, where he died, Feb. 9, 1831, aged 50, and she, June 10, 1857, aged 75. Their children were, all born in Boston: Thomas L. Bates, born 1804, died in Arkansas, 1854, aged 50; Rachel Bates, born Mar., 1807, died in Boston, July 8, 1857, aged 50; Caroline C. Bates, born June, 1809, married in Boston, 1831; Adna Bates, born Aug. 17, 1812; John W. Bates, born ——; Susan A. Bates, born Dec. 3, 1818, married Dec. 4, 1843; Clarissa Bates, born 1821, died 1831; Thomas L., married Abigail Ames Beard of Littleton, about 1829, who died about 1839, married again in the west about 1852.

755. JOHN JACOB, born in Hingham, Nov. 12, 1763, and married Bethia Tower of Cohasset. He was a sea-faring man. He was appointed administrator on his father's estate, Dec. 6, 1814, the widow having declined serving, Oct. 5, 1813.

756. SARAH, born Sept. 9, 1765, married (1), Apr. 19, 1784, Thomas Bates of Cohasset, married (2), Dea. David Beal of Cohasset. Children: Hannah Bates, born July 7, 1785; John Bates, born July 14, 1787, died Jan., 1827; Mercy Bates, born Apr. 22, 1789, died Aug., 1865; Sarah Bates, born Aug. 2, 1793, died, 1846; Polly Bates, born Aug. 3, 1797, died ——; Thomas Bates, born July 16, 1800, died 1803; Maria L. Bates, born Dec. 17, 1802, died Sept., 1865.

757. RUTH, born in Hingham, Aug. 17, 1767. Married Gershom Pratt, May 31, 1789. She died March 7, 1842. Their children were : Elizabeth Pratt, born in Cohasset, June 10, 1790; Clara Pratt, born in Cohasset, April 3, 1792; Caleb L. Pratt, born in Cohasset, April 16, 1794; Levi Pratt, born in Cohasset, Aug. 25, 1798; James Pratt, born in Cohasset, April 15, 1800; John Pratt, born in Cohasset, July 13, 1801; Clara S. Pratt, born in Cohasset, Jan. 15, 1805; Ruth N. Pratt, born in Cohasset, July 4, 1807.

758. THOMAS, born July 15, 1769, and died Oct. 7, 1778.

759. ANSELM, born in Cohasset, Dec. 2, 1771, and married (1), Oct. 22, 1794, Eunice Burr of Cohasset. He married (2), Jan. 7, 1810, Priscilla Lincoln of Cohasset, who died Feb. 18, 1846. He was a master mariner and farmer, and died in Cambridge, Mass., May 27, 1853.

760. CALEB, born in Cohasset, May 3, 1774, and never married. He was a mariner, and was lost at sea in 1800.

761. PETER, born in Cohasset, April 3, 1776, and married, in 1798, Betsey Tower of Cohasset, who died April 2, 1859. He was engaged in the mackerel fishery, and was also a merchant and farmer. During the war of 1812 he held a captain's commission in the State Militia. He was also considerably occupied

with several civil offices to which he had been called by his townsmen. He died Dec. 27, 1848.

762. CLARA, born in Cohasset, April 10, 1779, and died May 17, 1779.

763. CLARA, born in Cohasset, June 17, 1780, and married, in 1800, Ezekiel Pratt, M.D., of Cohasset. She died Feb. 12, 1808, and he, Oct. 9, 1860.  Dr. Pratt was a graduate of Harvard, and spent his long and honored life in the practice of medicine in Cohasset. They had three children: Jane Pratt, born Oct. 26, 1801, and married, in Boston, Oct. 19, 1823, Ephraim Nute of New Hampshire. They had one child, Clara L., who lived only about a year. Mrs. Nute died May 19, 1860, and her husband in 1871. Ezekiel Pratt, born April 5, 1805, and died in 1809 ; Nichols Pratt, born Feb. 10, 1808, and married, Dec. 23, 1835, Ruth, daughter of Henry Snow of Cohasset. They had five children :  Clara J., born July 30, 1836, and died May 2, 1838 ; Henry F., born Aug. 12, 1838, and married, Jan. 26, 1871, Ella Savin of Boston, where their child, Ruth S., was born in 1872 ; Nichols, born Sept. 23, 1840, and married, Nov. 8, 1866, Abbie Veazie of Belfast, Me., and have two children, Willie and Ralph H.; Mary Jane, born Nov. 6, 1842, and married, Feb. 26, 1860, Elisha Burr of Hingham, and has five children : Frank N., born April 14, 1861 ; Elisha, born July 27, 1864 ; Mary F., born July 29, 1865 ; Ella, born Jan. 15, 1871 ; Fanny, born in 1872 ; John P. P., born July 17, 1875.

764. ELIZABETH, born in Cohasset, April 1, 1782, and died Sept. 8, 1782.

### 360.  NATHANIEL.        Barnstable, Mass.

765. THOMAS, born Feb. 2, 1767, and was the son of his father's first wife.

766. SUSANNAH, born Nov. 17, 1776, and married Eleazer Cobb, Jun., as her father's will shows.

### 363.  JOHN.

767. SETH, born in Boston, Mass., in 1778, and married Nancy, daughter of Eben White, who was born in 1779, and died in 1853.  He was a builder in Boston, where he died Dec. 14, 1826.  He had a son Eben W.

768. RUTH, born July 12, 1780, and married Collins Hawes of Dennis.

769. ANSEL, born June 25, 1782, and married Deborah Nye of Sandwich. His will, dated March 5, 1857, was proved May 15, 1857, and names as legatees: Wife Deborah ; granddaughter Abby N. Holbrook : grandsons Benjamin and Ansel Lothrop ; and two daughters, Mercy V. Chase and Mary Webster. Executor, son-in-law, Oliver L. Chase.  He died March 28, 1857.

770. ABIGAIL, married June 19, 1796, Dea. Ebenezer Crocker, and went West.

771. MARY, born Aug. 10, 1785, married Jeremiah Crowell of Dennis.

772. HANNAH, born May 26, 1788, and married Isaac Ewer of Oysterville, and died without children.

### 382.  DAVID.        Yarmouth, Mass.

773. JOHN, born in Yarmouth, Aug. 8, 1794, and married, Jan. 5, 1817, Maria, daughter of Alexander Baxter of Yarmouth. He was a sea-faring man, and settled in Hyannis, where he died Jan. 14, 1866, and his wife, March 25,

1862. His will was dated the day before his death, and proved Sept. 11, 1866. Besides his children he names as legatees the children of his daughter Lydia.

774. REBECCA, born in Yarmouth, Oct. 8, 1795, where she still lives unmarried. She was one of her father's legatees in 1844.

775. EUNICE, born July 11, 1797, and married Joseph Linnel of Yarmouth, where they settled permanently, and where she died in 1820. They had two children : Dorcas Smith Linnel, born June 10, 1818 ; Joseph Linnel, who was born in 1821.

776. SALLY, born Oct. 17, 1799, and married Capt. Ira Baxter of Yarmouth. Their children were : Daniel Baxter, Bethia Baxter, Alexander Baxter, Hersilia Baxter, Martha Baxter, Ira Baxter.

777. ASA, born Nov. 27, 1804, and married in New Bedford, where he is engaged in the shoe trade.

### 388. CAPT. JOHN LO, JUN. Hyannis, Mass.

778. MEHETABLE CROCKER, born in Barnstable, Jan. 25, 1798, where she also died about 1830 unmarried.

779. DEBORAH, born in Barnstable, Nov. 1, 1800, where she died March 16, 1865, unmarried.

780. JOHN, born in Barnstable, according to his own testimony, Jan. 14, 1802, (Jan. 12, 1803, according to town records), and married, March 1, 1826, Hannah Coleman, daughter of Joseph and Zerviah Basset of Barnstable, where she was born March 11, 1801. He has lived in Barnstable, and in 1873 was in charge of the lighthouse at Hyannis. He has long gone by the name of "Pilot John."

### 389. ISAAC. Barnstable, Mass.

781. JAMES SCUDDER, born in Barnstable, Aug. 28, 1780, and married Hitty, daughter of Joseph and Experience (Davis) Annable of Barnstable, where she was born, March 14, 1779. He settled in his native town as a blacksmith, and was highly respected as a worthy citizen. His wife died May 15, 1843; and he Feb. 10, 1863.

782. BARNABAS, born March 10, 1782, and died in October, 1806, at sea, having never married.

783. JOSIAH, born March 11, 1785, and married Chloe Crocker. He settled in Barnstable and was a shoemaker. He died in a fit, Aug. 20, 1852. His widow died in New Bedford, in 1862, aged seventy-four.

784. SALLY, born Nov. 10, 1788, married, June 8, 1809, Allen Hinckley of Barnstable, by whom she had two sons, and where she died in April, 1815. Henry Hinckley, born May 5, 1810, who has a family ; Barnabas Lothrop Hinckley, born Oct. 27, 1812, and had a family.

785. BETSEY, born March 14, 1791, and died single, Nov. 8, 1864.

786. DEBORAH, born August 20, 1793, and married, March 22, 1813, Joseph Bursley of Barnstable, by whom she had twelve children, all born in Barnstable. She died March 10, 1840. Sally L. Bursley, born Feb. 28, 1815, and died in September, 1870 ; Henry Bursley, born June 8, 1817 ; Abby Bursley,

born June 6, 1820 ; Elizabeth Bursley, born Oct. 6, 1821, and died June 5, 1863 ; Louisa Bursley, born Aug. 12, 1823 ; Joseph Bursley, born Dec. 1, 1824, and died Aug. 11, 1825 ; Joseph and Deborah Bursley, born June 20, 1826 ; James Bursley, born Jan. 20, 1829 ; Mary Caroline Bursley, born Sept. 24, 1831, and died June 16, 1858 ; Hannah H. Bursley, born Sept. 25, 1834, and died Dec. 11, 1845 ; Gilbert E. Bursley, born April 0, 1837.

787. HANNAH, born May 12, 1795, and married, Jan. 28, 1817, Allen Hinckley, husband of her deceased sister Sally. They had four children, and she died June 1, 1874. Frederick Hinckley, born Nov. 3, 1820, and now a Unitarian minister in Washington, D. C.; infant, born Oct. 8, and died Oct. 18, 1821 ; Charles Dudley Hinckley, born Feb. 24, 1824, and died Sept. 4, 1825 ; Sarah Hannah Hinckley, born July 1, 1836, and died March 31, 1842.

788. CAROLINE, born July 21, 1805, and married, March 28, 1841, Wm. J. Titcomb of Barnstable.

789. MARY C., born Dec. 2, 1800, and married, in June, 1842. Joseph Bursley, husband of her deceased half-sister Deborah. She died Aug. 24, 1873.

790. HENRY, born in 1802, and died at sea in 1818.

791. THANKFUL G., born Feb. 29, 1804, and married, in Dec., 1828, Thomas, son of Thomas and Mary (Hinckley) Stetson. His ancestors, according to the Stetson family, were : Thomas, Anthony, Robert, and Joseph, who was the eldest son of " Cornet " Robert Stetson, the pioneer of this name at Scituate.

792. JOSEPH C., born May 3, 1798, and married Ruth Finney. He died Feb. 10, 1843.

793. ISAAC, born in Barnstable, Nov. 22, 1808, and married (1), Jan. 31, 1833, Frances Symmes, who was born Dec. 11, 1810, and died Sept. 22, 1843. He married (2), Aug. 1, 1844, Angelina Phipps, who was born Nov. 17, 1815. He was a hatter in Boston, and died in Charlestown Oct. 26, 1852.

### 391. BENJAMIN, JUN. Barnstable.

794. WILLIAM, born March 30, 1791.

795. REBECCA, born April 9, 1793, and died July 12, 1817.

796. ISAAC, born April 4, 1798.

797. MARY DAVIS, born Feb. 27, 1801.

798. EDWARD BANGS, born Aug. 7, 1803.

SEVENTH GENERATION.

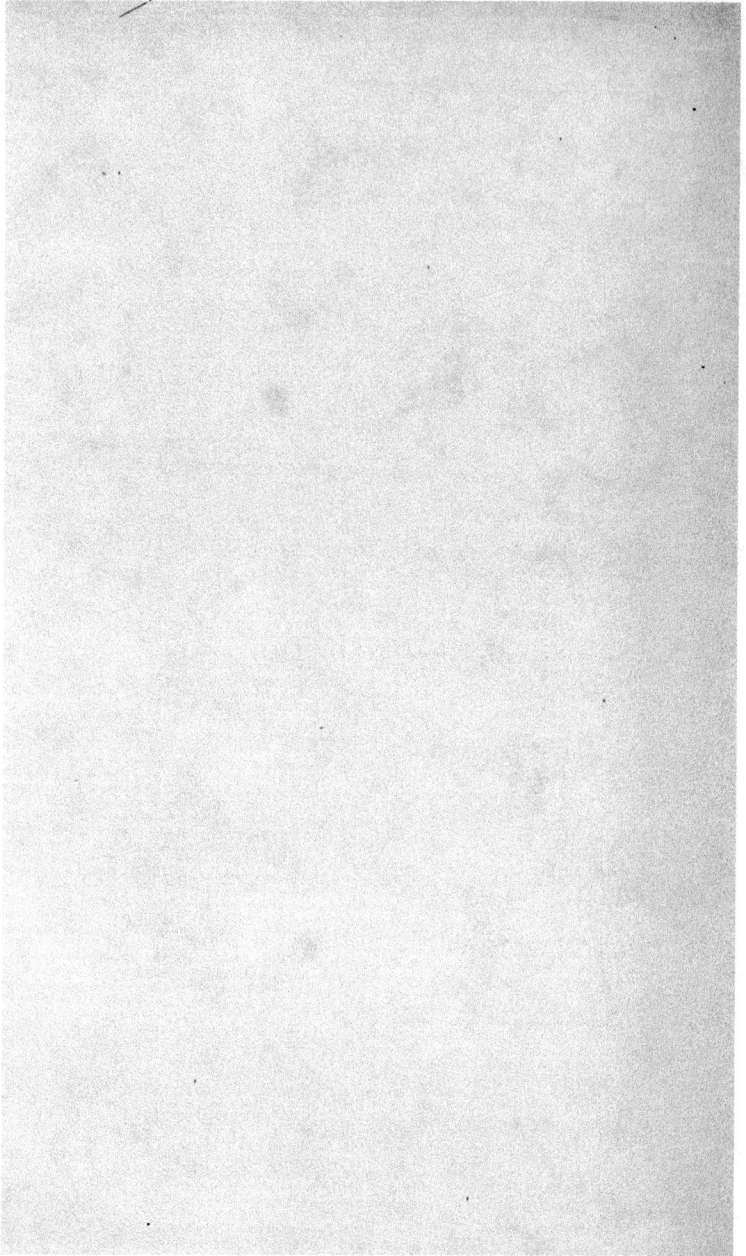

## 396. THOMAS.

800. HARRIET, born ——, married Chandler Robbins.
801. CALEB.

### 404. DANIEL.    Granby, Mass.

802. ERASTUS, born Sept. 2, 1793, in Granby, Mass., married Rebecca Maine Ward, daughter of Nehemiah and Harriet (Packard) Ward of Wilbraham, where she was born March 22, 1793, and settled in Woodbury, Ct.

803. SMITH, born in Granby, 1796, married Sally Ward, sister of Rebecca and three years younger. He is now (1873) in New Rutland, Ill. She died in Windsor Locks.

804. LUCY, born Aug. 24, 1798, and married Alva Bartlett. They settled in Dover, Me. Their children have been :
  i.    Eliza P. Bartlett, born 1818.
  ii.   Henry D. Bartlett, born 1820.
  iii.  Daniel Bartlett, born 1822.
  iv.   Aaron Bartlett, born 1825.
  v.    Erastus Bartlett, born 1827.
  vi.   Sabra A. Bartlett, born 1831, and died in 1849.
  vii.  Alphonso Bartlett, born 1832.
  viii. Laurinda Bartlett, born 1840.
  ix.   Albert Bartlett, born 1843, and died at six years.

805. PERMELIA, born Aug. 25, 1800, married Samuel Lambert, in Dover, Me., where she is now living, having lost her husband.

806. DANIEL, JUN., married Eliza Hinckley, in Westford, Ct. Children in Vineland, N. J.

807. SABRY, born May 24, 1806, married Sumner Ward of Dover, Me. Their children have been: Sarah Ward; Josiah Ward; Luther Ward, in Tornica, Ill.; Lucy Ward ; Sumner Ward ; Rosilla Ward, married ——, now in Vermillion, Ill.; Alfred Ward ; Eddy Ward.

808. ALBERT, born Windsor, Vt., March 18, 1810, married, Nov. 6, 1831, in Dover, Vt., Sarah Stratford Samson, daughter of William and Sarah Clark Samson, who was born Dec. 26, 1809, in Bridgewater. Twin with Alfred.

809. ALFRED, born in Windsor, Vt., March 18, 1810, and married, Aug. 21, 1831, Deborah A. Robinson, daughter of Rev. Nathaniel ——, in Dover, Me., and lives in New Rutland, Ill. Their children are: Lewis, a Baptist minister since 1828 ; John Stillman, a lawyer in Ottoway.

810. JOHN, born July 14, 1814, married (1). Sally Robinson, (sister above,) of Tonica, Ill., and (2), Melissa Howard. Children: Eliza Ellen, married Wm. Smith, and has a family; Coydon, died young.

19

### 113. THOMAS.      Norwich, Conn.

811. Joshua, born July 25, 1787, and married in Norwich, Sept. 20, 1809, Rebecca Hunt Perit, daughter of John Perit. She was born in Scotland, Conn., July 25, 1789, and died in Leroy, N. Y., Sept. 12, 1862. He died in Leroy, Aug. 30, 1856, where he had been a merchant.

812. Jerusha, born in Norwich, Feb. 8, 1789, married. Sept. 6, 1809, Pelatiah Perit. She died Oct. 18, 1821, and her remains were taken to the family lot in Norwich for interment.

813. Lydia Austin, born Sept. 21, 1792, and married, as his second wife, May 7, 1816, Aaron Porter, son of Rev. Aaron and Abiah (Hyde) Cleveland, an importer of Boston. His first wife had been Abby Saulsbury of Boston, and his third wife was Mary Huntington, daughter of Rev. Dr. Joseph and Mary Huntington Strong of Norwich. He was a man of extensive business. By her he had one son.

814. Mary, born in Norwich, Oct. 14, 1795, and died when attending school at Bethlehem, Pa., July 31, 1809.

815. Emily, born July 30, 1798, and married, June 1, 1819, George Lathrop Perkins of Norwich City. He has been for years the treasurer of the Norwich & Worcester Railroad. Their children have been : Mary Lathrop Perkins, born in Norwich, Aug. 30, 1820, and died March 14, 1842: George Perit Perkins, born in Norwich, Oct. 14, 1822, and died Aug 10, 1829 ; Thomas Hezekiah Perkins, born in Norwich, Aug. 14, 1834, and married, July 14, 1862, Elizabeth S. Lusk ; Emily Newton Perkins, born Oct. 11, 1836.

816. William, born in Norwich, June 1, 1801, and married Jerusha Gilchrist. He died Sept. 13, 1825. His three children's gravestones stand next to the table of his parents in the Norwich Town cemetery.

817. Hannah Gardner, born in Norwich, March 9, 1806, and married, Oct. 19, 1825, George Burbank Ripley, son of Dwight Ripley of Norwich, who was born in Norwich, 1801. See class 1822. Children : William Lathrop Ripley, born April 30, 1827 ; Dwight Ripley, born June 8, 1829 ; Hannah Lathrop Ripley, born Nov. 14, 1830 ; Harriet Ripley, born Sept. 6, 1832 ; James Dickinson Ripley, born Nov. 14, 1837 ; George Colt Ripley, born Aug. 24, 1839 ; Emily Lathrop Ripley, born June 15, 1841.

### 116. DANIEL.      Norwich, Conn.

818. Jane Eliza, born in Norwich, July 26, 1795, and married Jonathan G. W. Trumbull, son of David and Sarah (Backus) Trumbull and grandson of first governor Trumbull of Connecticut. He was a graduate of Yale, and became a lawyer.

819. Frank Turner, born Aug. 9, 1798. He never married. He died in Norwich May 13, 1832.

820. Ann Matilda, born March 10, 1800, and died in Norwich Oct. 14, 1839.

821. Cornelia Sophia, born in Norwich, July 30, 1804, and married George G. Willes. They had one son, William Henry Willes. She died June 20, 1849, as her gravestone testifies.

### 319. JEDIDIAH.

822. JEDIDIAH, born Aug. 16, 1768, in Windham, Scotland, married Mary, daughter of Thomas Caldwell, Nov. 21, 1793, and lived in Guilford, Conn., many years. She died May 24, 1831, in her sixty-fifth year. He died in Norwich, Jan. 30, 1859, and was interred in Guilford.

823. SARAH, born Jan. 8, 1771, in Newent, and married in Lisbon, Sept., 1797, Benj. Austin of Preston. She died in 1846, aged seventy-six. They had three children: William, Susan, and Jedidiah Austin.

824. ANDREW, born Feb. 10, 1773, died, and was buried in Lisbon.

825. CHARITY, born in Newent, March 23, 1774, and married in September, 1796, Freeman Tracy of Lisbon. They had one son, Albert Lathrop Tracy, born Jan. 23, 1801. She died in Lisbon, Jan. 26, 1801.

826. JUDITH, born in Newent, Feb. 28, 1777, and married, March 11, 1800, Edward Paine of Canterbury, a Methodist minister. They had one son, Edw. Lathrop, born May 29, 1801. She died June 5, 1801.

827. RUBY, born in Newent, Feb. 28, (Aug.?) 1779, and married, Dec. 24, 1800, Russel Green. They had several children in Rochester, N. Y. She died Sept. 16, 1812, in Plainfield, N. H.

828. ANDREW, born May 25, 1780, and married, about 1812, Abigail Durphey of Providence, who went South and died Dec. 7, 1819, in the parish of St. Helena, La. He married and had two children, certainly.

829. CHARLOTTE, born May 13, 1782, married, Feb. 17, 1802, Edward Paine, husband of Judith, who was drowned in the Susquehannah. She then married Jesse Ross, who lived for years on the Wyalusing Creek, Pa. After his death she lived with her sister's son, Edward Lathrop.

830. CLARISSA, born Sept. 26, 1784, and married Joel Philo, and settled in Stafford, N. Y., and had a large family.

831. ALICE, born in Lisbon, May 8, 1791, and married, Sept. 20, 1814, Rev. Elisha Bibbins, a Methodist preacher, and is now living with her son, J. S. Bibbins, in Newark, Ill. She has been a member of the Methodist Episcopal Church sixty-five years. Mr. Bibbins was born in Hamden, N. Y., July 16, 1790, and after successfully laboring in the ministry for years, went into Illinois, in 1840, and was in 1843 sent to the State legislature. On a visit to Scranton, Pa., for the purpose of meeting his old friends and recruiting his health, died very suddenly while sitting in his chair. Their children are all members of the Methodist Church, and are as follows : Edward Paine Bibbius, born May 16, 1815, and is a farmer ; Joseph Slocum Bibbins, born Nov. 1, 1821, in Newark, Kendall County, Ill.; Robert Kendall Bibbins, born Apr. 21, 1823, and is a Methodist preacher ; Andrew Tracy Lothrop Bibbins, born Aug. 13, 1826, and died in infancy; Tracy Lothrop Bibbins, born Aug. 13, 1829, and is a dealer in real estate.

### 324. REV. SAMUEL. Wells, Vt.

832. EUNICE, born in Norwich, June 4, 1763.

833. ZACHARIAH, ——, married Charlotte Button and settled in Wells, Vt. He and his wife died the same day, and were buried in one grave, in Wells.

834. SAMUEL, born in Newent, Mar. 11, 1771, and married in Cambridge, N. Y., Sept. 10, 1797, Rachel Colvin, who was born in Shaftesbury, Vt., Oct. 25, 1777, died 1820, in Auburn, N. Y.

835. EZRIAH, who was married and had at least one daughter.

836. ROBERT, born ——, married —— Colvin, sister of his brother Samuel's wife.

833². ELIZABETH, born ——, married —— Francis of Hamburg, N. Y.

837. DEBORAH, born in Wells, Vt., ——, married Capt. Ebenezer Johnson. They removed to Cazenovia, N. Y., in 1794, and thence, about 1820, to Buffalo.

838. SARAH, born in Wells, Nov. 22, 1774, and married John Green of Wells. They went to Canada and have had a large family. She died in Bushford, Canada West, now Ontario, Jan. 1, 1873, aged 98 y, 1 m, 22 d.

839. ANNA, born in Wells, in 1782, and went with her sister Deborah, on her marriage to Capt. Johnson, to Cazenovia. There she married, in 1798, Elisha Farnham, and there they lived. Mr. Farnham was Colonel of a regiment in command at Sackett's Harbor in 1812. He was one of the presidential electors who chose President Monroe; and was a man often called upon to fill important local offices, by his townsmen. They had eight children.

840. BERTHA, born ——, married Dr. Hotchkiss. They had two daughters, Mrs. Hosford of Poultney, Vt.; and Mrs. Tryon also of Poultney. She died 1801.

### 425. THOMAS.　　　Pawlet, Vt.

841. ABIGAL, born Dec. 10, 1772, and married Daniel Francis. Children: Rev. Daniel Dyer Francis, Hartford; Hezekiah; Hiram.

842. WEALTHY ANN, born Dec. 8, 1774, married Rev. Elisha Andrews. Children: Betsy; Wealthy Ann; Sarah; Elisha; Thustron; Thomas; Erastus; Heman; Stephen Pearl.

843. THOMAS, JR., born May, 1778, and was killed by a cart Apr. 4, 1797.

844. SEPTIMIUS, born Sept. 10, 1780, married Abigail Drury, in Vt., a Free Will Baptist.

845. GIDEON CONN, born Oct. 14, 1782, in Pawlet, Vt., and married Catherine Sproat of Middleboro', Mass. He settled as a tanner, in Burlington, Vt., where he died, 1855, and she in 1857.

846. STEPHEN PEARL, born in Pawlet, Vt., Oct. 14, 1782, and married, Sept. 9, 1810, Sarah Smith, born in Richmond, Mass., May 23, 1791. He died in Middlebury, Vt., Mar. 16, 1837, and she, May 3, 1865, in Delanco, N. S., and was interred in Middlebury, Vt.

847. SALLY, born May 17, 1784, married Wm. Burrit, in Vergennes, Vt., had four daughters.

848. BETSEY, born Mar. 23, 1787, married Chester Root; had Abigail.

849. POLLY, born July 10, 1789, married Chester Root, in Palmyra. Two sons, Thomas Lathrop Root, Hiram Francis Root.

850. NANCY, born Nov. 23, 1791, married Chauncey Johnson, in Burlington, Vt. Children: Wealthy Ann; Maria.

851. JOHN, born Oct. 10, 1794, and married, Mar. 15, 1821, Margaret Fuller.

### 426. SIMEON.

Lisbon, Conn.

852. ALICE, born in Lisbon, Dec. 20, 1770.

853. DANIEL, born in Lisbon, Mar. 18, 1773. Two children, died Cazenovia.

854. REBECCA, born Aug. 18, 1775, married, Nov. 10, 1799 (Lisbon Records,) Russel, son of Peleg Rose of Groton, settled in Lisbon, died Oct. 13, 1845. Children: Elijah Rose, born Feb. 10, 1801, married Lydia Brown, had two sons, lived in Hanover, Lisbon; Charles Rose, born July 3, 1802, married Emeline Hyde: Duane Rose, born July 12, 1804, matried Maria Clark, eight children; Simeon Lathrop Rose, born Feb. 4, 1808, married Frances Merritt of Lisbon, and lives in Baltimore, and has two children; Eliza Ann, born Dec. 26, 1810, married April 18, 1835, Stephen, son of Aaron and Griselle Hawley, and lived in Bridgeport, she has no children. He died Nov. 4, 1861. Rebecca Lathrop Rose, born Sept. 16, 1814, married Sanford Bromley of Lisbon, and has two children, Geo. Gurdon and Eliza Frances.

855. SUSAN, born Dec. 9, 1777, married —— Prentiss, died Apr. 18, 1849, six children.

856. MARY POLLY, born May 25, 1780, married Tim Baldwin, Canterbury, six children, died Sept. 18, 1852.

857. ELISHA, born in Norwich, Jan. 1, 1782, and married Sept. 13, 1807, Sally, daughter of Asa and Mary K. Palmer, who was born June 27, 1786, settled in Bridgeport. He died Feb. 9, 1864, and she, May 7, 1866.

858. SIMON, born May 19, 1787, married Jan. 9, 1814, Lydia Bottom (Lisbon Records), of Lisbon, five children, died Jan. 31, 1849.

859. APPLETON, born July 31, 1789, died unmarried, in Lisbon, Sept. 4, 1859.

860. HENRY, born Feb. 3, 1792, married Mary Palmer, Apr. 10, 1816, of Lisbon. She died June 9, 1872.

861. SALLY, born Feb. 3, 1792, married Chester F. Butts of Canterbury, three children. Iowa.

### 427. JOHN.

862. EBENEZER.

863. ——.

864. CALEB.

865. JOSEPH.

### 431. ELISHA, JR.

Demerara.

866. LYDIA, born May 9, 1770, and recorded in Norwich, married Backus, Killingly. See will below.

867. HENRY.

868. JAMES, born in Norwich, June 22, 1777.

869. HENRY "the second," born May 29, 1782, and died Aug. 9, 1788.

870. SARAH, born July 25, 1784. Her Will: Oct. 21, 1833—Sister Lydia Backus, of Killingly; Miss L y Coit; Am. B. C. F. M.; Am. Home Miss. Soc.; * * * * * Sabbath School, second church; Abby Cranston; Mrs. Dorothy Williams; Horace Colton; Harriet Colton; Mary Ann Colton; Mrs. Eliza, wife of Dwight Riply; Eliza Buckington; Jas. Riply; Martha Boigs, and Eliza; Mrs. John Fauing; and residue to second church.

## 436. SEPTIMUS. Lisbon, Conn.

871. WEALTHY, born ——, married ——, Ralph Manning of Windham. They settled in Schoharie County, N. Y., five children.

872. LUCY, ——, married Elisha Kimball of Preston; eight children.

873. SEPTIMUS, born Aug. 3, 1784, and married, in Providence, R. I., May 1, 1811, Judith Greenleaf, Salisbury.

874. SOLOMON, born Aug. 3, 1781, married Asenath Partridge of Griswold; three children.

875. HENRY BISHOP, born Nov. 17, 1794, in Lisbon, and married, Mar. 22, 1818, Sarah Preston, who was born in Franklin, Conn., Jan. 28, 1798, and died Apr. 5, 1847. They have lived in Albany.

876. ABIGAIL ADAMS, ——, married (1), Latham, and (2), E. P. Potter; two children.

877. NELSON PERKINS, ——, died in Albany.

878. JOHN ELISHA, Dec. 31, 1802, and married in Schenectady, Mary M., widow of John Wilkie, daughter of Archibald Currey; was living Sept. 8, 1864. No children.

## 437. ELIJAH. Norwich, Conn.

879. ELIJAH, born in Norwich, Oct. 28, 1777.

880. CHARLES, born in Norwich, Mar. 8, 1786.

881. NANCY, died in Norwich, as her gravestone testifies, Jan. 16, 1790, at two years of age.

882. NANCY, born in Norwich, Dec. 10, 1790.

## 443. SIMON. Norwich, Conn.

883. GURDON, born in Norwich, July 2, 1784, and died Dec. 7, 1786 ; his gravestone standing next to his mother's.

884. GURDON 2d, born in Norwich, May 30, 1786, and married in Charleston, S. C., Mary Keyes, an English lady. He lived and died in Charleston.

885. JAMES, born in Norwich. Aug. 22, 1788, (the rest of this family are recorded in Norwich.) He married Freelove, daughter of Capt. Simeon and Freelove (Chester) Huntington of Norwich. They settled in New York City, where she died. He was lost at sea.

886. SIMON, born Aug. 4, 1791 ; he died on his first voyage as sailor on board Capt. Walter Lester's ship, and was buried in New Orleans.

887. EDWARD, born Feb. 18, 1795, and married (1), Sophia Griswold of Norwich, who died Nov. 2, 1823. He married (2), Mary Clark of Franklin. He was a tanner and currier, and died Oct. 9, 1864.

888. BETSEY, born Apr. 4, 1797, and married (1), Oct. 20, 1816, Augustine Rogers, and (2), Nov. 6, 1836, as his second wife, Roger Bailey of Lebanon, who died Jan. 12, 1860. Her children were :

    i.    Mary Augustine Rogers, born Oct. 20, 1823, who died Aug. 4, 1852.

    ii.    Daniel Huntington Rogers.

    iii.    Thomas F. Rogers, born Apr. 10, 1821, now in South Coventry, whither he removed his church connection from the Congregational Church in Lebanon in 1872. He married Harriet Hinckley Wetmore, Nov. 28, 1844.

    iv.    Ella Augusta Rogers, removed to South Coventry in 1872.

889. GEORGE HENRY, born in Norwich, Nov. 13, 1799, and married in Marlborough, Dec. 29, 1850, Delia Ann. daughter of Sylvester Dunham, who was born Feb. 20, 1817. He spent his early years in the family of Jesse Lathrop of Franklin. On his marriage he settled in Lebanon, where he is a farmer. He and his wife united with the First Congregational Church in Lebanon in 1857 by letter, he from Franklin and she from the Methodist church in Willimantic.

890. MARY ANN, born Nov. 3, and died July 24, 1803.

891. MARY ANN, born May 27, 1806, and married, Nov. 26, 1829, Daniel Lathrop Huntington. (See Huntington Memoir.)

#### 441. LYNDE.

892. JOHN, born in Norwich, June 25, 1786, and married (1), Oct. 18, 1813, Nancy Moore, who died Aug. 7, 1825, aged 30 years, 8 months, and 23 days. He married (2), May 29, 1825, Eunice Bacon. He died in Albany, May 10, 1841.

893. GROVER L'HOMMEDIEU, born June 18, 1796. He never married, and lived in Essex, where he died.

894. ABBY ADGATE, born in Norwich, Mar. 19, 1798, and died in Norwich.

#### 448. ASA. Norwich. Conn.

895. LUCY LORD, born in Norwich, Jan. 3, 1782, and is now, (1872,) living in Norwich Town in the family of her nephew, Wm. B. Lathrop. She never married.

896. BETSEY, born in Norwich, Aug. 12, 1784, and died, single, in the same place, Mar. 9, 1870.

897. PEGGY FULLER, born in Norwich, Jan. 28, 1786.

898. NABBY LORD, born in Norwich, May 28, 1788.

899. ELEAZER LORD, born in Norwich, Mar. 20, 1792, and married, Dec. 28, 1820, Jerusha Thomas of Norwich, who was born in Norwich, Apr. 7, 1795, and died Feb. 27, 1871.

900. WILLIAM BALDWIN, born in Norwich, Sept. 1, 1793, and died on the 13th of the same month.

901. BURREL, born in Norwich, Feb. 5, 1795.

902. WILLIAM BALDWIN, born in Norwich, Apr. 7, 1798, and died Aug. 6, 1798.

#### 450. ZEBEDIAH. Middletown, Conn.

903. LUCRETIA, born in Middletown, Jan. 15, 1785, and married Nehemiah Rogers. Children : A daughter, married ——— ; a daughter, married ——— ; Clorinda Rogers, married F. Nichols, 814 Lexington Avenue.

904. SALLA, born in Middletown, Mar. 2, 1787, and died young.

905. CLORINDA BACKUS, born in Middletown, Sept. 10, 1790, and married.

906. JOSEPH BACKUS, born in Middletown, July 10, 1793, and died young.

907. JOSEPH EDWARDS, born in Norwich, Conn., February, 1796, and married, Nov. 6, 1825, Lucy Kelly, who was born in Middletown, Conn., Jan. 8, 1798. He has resided many years in Middletown, where he had a boys' private school, and where he is now, (1873,) living.

908. Sarah Starr, born in Middletown, Dec. 6, 1797, and married Selah Short. They lived in ——. Children :

i.  Theodore Lathrop Short, born Nov. 1, 1823, and died July 17, 1843, while a teller in the Middletown bank.

ii.  Frederick Henry Short, born Sept. 2, 1825, and now, (1873,) secretary and treasurer of the Cincinnati, Hamilton & Dayton Railroad Company, having his office in Cincinnati.

### 455. GURDON.

909. John, born ——. He was a merchant in Savannah, Ga. He never married.

910. Abby Maria, born ——, married Capt. Edward Whiting, of Norwich.

### 456. DEA. CHARLES.        Norwich, Conn.

911. Charles Christopher, born in Norwich, in 1794 ; was a member of the Senior Class in Yale College when he died, Dec. 3, 1814. His classmates erected a monument to his memory, on the College lot in the New Haven Cemetery, bearing this tribute .o his character and promise : " Lathrop as a son and brother was dutiful and affectionate, as a friend and companion faithful and kind, and as a student diligent and successful, as a member of the Church of Christ irreproachable in his life and conversation."

912. Harriet Wadsworth, born in Norwich, Apr. 9, 1796, and early resolved to devote her life to missionary work. She married in Norwich, Jan. 11, 1819, Rev. Miron Winslow, then under appointment to Ceylon. He had been a merchant at Bean Hill in Norwich, where he had iearned of her zeal in promoting the interests of religion at home, and when the time came for him to enter on his missionary work, he could find none better fitted to accompany him. She gave herself, with no reserve, to her missionary work. From the time of sailing from Boston June 8, 1819, to the date of her death, at Oodooville, Ceylon, Jan. 14, 1833, there was for her no respite from the service which she had given herself. Her love for her work, and her zeal in t' vice, are the most characteristic features of those busy years.

The story of this devotion was well told by her husband, who, better than anybody else, knew how deep and true it had been. Her memoir will always be prized as one of our most instructive Christian biographies.

After her death Mr. Winslow married again, in 1835, Mrs. Catherine (Waterbury) Carman, by whom he had one daughter, Catherine Waterbury, who died in infancy. He married, for his third wife, in 1838, Anne Spiers, an English lady of Madras, and had by her two children, Miron Winslow, Jun., and Archibald Spiers Winslow.

He married for his fourth wife in 1845, Mrs. Mary W. (Billings) Dwight, widow of Rev. R. O. Dwight; and for his fifth wife, in 1857, Ellen Augusta Reed of Boston, Mass. His own death occurred at Capetown, Cape of Good Hope, Oct. 22, 1864.

Rev. Mr. Winslow, D.D., LL.D., was born Dec. 11, 1789, in Williston, Vt., and was son of Nathaniel and Anna (Kellogg) Winslow, whose ancestors were Nathaniel, Kenelm, Nathaniel, and Kenelm of Marshfield, Mass., who was son of Edward Winslow of Droitwich, England. Two of his brothers, Gordon and Hubbard, were also Doctors of Divinity and eminent men. (See Historical and Genealogical Reg., July, 1865, p. 272.)

His children by his first wife were all born in Ceylon : Charles Lathrop Winslow, born Jan. 12, 1821, and died May 24, 1832. His memoir is published by the American Tract Society, and is a pleasant tribute to the youthful promise and piety of the missionary son ; Harriet Maria Winslow, born Feb. 28, 1822, and died in November, 1825 ; Joanna Winslow, born Feb. 5, 1825, and married (1), Rev. Mr. Clark, and (2), George S. King ; George Morton Winslow, born May 12, 1827, and died Aug. 15, 1828 ; Harriet Lathrop Winslow, born Apr. 19, 1829, and married Rev. John W. Dulles. They went in 1848 as missionaries to Madras, where she died Sept. 1, 1861 ; Eliza Coit Winslow, born Jan. 4, 1831, and married Henry M. Leavitt. She died Aug. 11, 1861.

913. DANIEL WHITING, born in Norwich, Conn., June 17, 1798. He united with the First Congregational church in Norwich, in 1814, and soon became a teacher and a student of theology in New Jersey. At the request of the Connecticut Missionary Society he was ordained to the work of the ministry, by the Presbytery of New Jersey, at Bloomfield, in 1823, and entered into the service of the Missionary Society. He married in Brooklyn, N. Y., June 8, 1824, Abby W., daughter of Nathaniel and Elizabeth (Coit) Howland, of Brooklyn. They settled in Elyria, Ohio, where he gathered the first Presbyterian church of the place, and where he was installed by the Presbytery of Portage, in November, 1824, its first pastor. Here he remained in the work to which he had been ordained, until his health necessitated a respite. An interruption of six years followed, during which he was engaged in literary pursuits. He was the second time installed as pastor, by the Presbytery of Elyria, at Wellington, Ohio. During the interim of his pastorates, his time had been devoted as an agent of the American Home Missionary Society, in looking after the interests of the churches in the vicinity of his home; and, in 1848, he resigned his second pastorate, and removed his family to New Haven, where they have since that date resided. He has since his ordination adhered to the Presbyterian form of church government "not as the only admissible one, but as being in his view quite as Scriptural as any other." Since October, 1870, he has been the stated preacher of the Temple street Congregational church, New Haven.

The following tribute to his memory is from the *Journal and Courier*, New Haven, Conn., Friday, April 20, 1883: Rev. Daniel W. Lathrop, who died in Jackson, Michigan, March 27, and whose remains were deposited in his burial lot in Grove street cemetery on Wednesday, accompanied to their final resting place by his only remaining son, George H. Lathrop of Jackson, his son-in-law, Mr. James H. Dunham of New York, and other members of their families, together with friends of New Haven, was for twenty-four years a

20

resident of our city. Although, from failure of his voice, unable to speak from the pulpit except occasionally, he was still actively engaged in earnest Christian work, and will be well remembered by many of our citizens. He came here to reside after having spent a quarter of a century in useful service on the "Western Reserve" in Ohio, most of the time in Elyria, in which place he was the first pastor of the Presbyterian church, which he himself helped to organize. The Sabbath following his decease that church in Elyria held a memorial service, the pulpit being draped in mourning and bearing upon it beautiful emblems, one of which was a sheaf of wheat fully ripe. A lady present on that occasion writes: "It was a lovely commemoration of a lovely Christian. The congregation was large and after the service many stopped to give their personal recollections. It was like children speaking of a father." Mr. Lathrop was a man strong in his convictions, always standing up boldly for what he considered to be right, and in those early days he was a firm friend of the anti-slavery movement, and an earnest worker in the temperance cause. Still, when in controversy he disagreed with others, he would often win his bitterest opponents to himself, if not to his cause by his kind words and noble bearing toward them. About ten years ago, and soon after the death of his beloved wife, with whom he had lived nearly fifty years, and whose useful life cannot be forgotten by her many friends in New Haven, he went to reside with his only daughter, Mrs. Harriet L. Dunham of New York, since which time he has lived either in New York, or with his son at the west, surrounded by loving children, grandchil'ren and great grandchildren who tenderly revere his memory. Although in his eighty-fifth year, unbowed by age, the wonderful beauty of his personal appearance was unimpaired. His death was like a transition; he passed in a moment from the home circle on earth to the larger company of loved ones gone before, and to the presence of the Lord and Saviour whose service on earth had been his highest joy. "Blessed are the dead who die in the Lord."

914. FANNY LEFFINGWELL, born in Norwich, Apr. 9, 1800, and united with the First Congregational church of Norwich, in 1814. She married, Sept. 1, 1829, Rev. William A. Hallock, D.D., son of Rev. Moses Hallock of Plainfield, Mass. They settled in New York city, where for forty years he was the efficient and honored secretary of the American Tract Society, and where he is still living. He was born June 2, 1794. His ancestors were: Rev. Moses, William, Noah, Peter, William, and Peter, "the pilgrim from England, who landed at Hallock's Neck, Southhold, L. I., 1640." The Hallock family has numbered many prominent names. And she was every way worthy of this connection, and, indeed, she was scarcely less honored for her zeal and efficient devotion to the Tract enterprise, than her husband. For thirty-six years she was the secretary of the female branch of the New York city Tract Society. On the occasion of her death, which occurred in New York city, Mar. 10, 1867, the board of managers of the society she had so acceptably served, paid this spontaneous tribute to her worth: "For thirty-six years the secretary of this society, she has been untiring in her labors in its behalf, and by her meek and quiet spirit has so won the hearts of all associated with her, that they feel to-day sorely afflicted." Their children all born in New York have been:

Martha Hallock, born July 25, 1831, and died in infancy; William A. Hallock, born July 2, 1833, and died in infancy; Harriet Joanna Hallock, born Feb. 8, 1835, and married, Oct. 20, 1859, Rufus Park of New York. They have three children: Frances Elizabeth Hallock, born Jan. 8. 1837, and married, Sept. 29, 1859, John E. Johnson, and has four children; Charlotte Huntington Lathrop Hallock, born Aug. 13, 1842, and died in infancy; Jeremiah Hallock, born Oct. 25, 1844, and died in infancy.

915. CHRISTOPHER LEFFINGWELL LATHROP, born in Norwich, Aug. 1, 1804, and united with the First Congregational church in 1821. He married, in March, 1832, Philura Leffingwell, daughter of Elijah Huntington of Bozrah, and his wife Lucretia Leffingwell, No. 1303. They settled in Cleveland, Ohio, where the family have continued to reside. Their children, born in Cleveland, were:

    i.    Samuel Hutchins Lathrop, born July 22, 1834.

    ii.    Elizabeth Hutchins Lathrop, born Feb. 8, 1836, and married, in 1860, William M., son of Rev. Joseph Merriam of Randolph, Ohio. He died of consumption, Nov. 5, 1867, leaving two children (1203), William Lathrop. Merriam, born in 1862; and (1204), Fanny Hallock Merriam, born in 1865.

    iii.    Charles Lathrop, born June 1, 1839, and died at the age of fifteen months.

    iv.    Christopher Leffingwell Lathrop, born Feb. 24, 1841, and died the next month.

Mrs. Philura L. H. Lathrop died in Cleveland, Aug. 13, 1843, deeply lamented as a woman of rare good sense and devoted piety. Mr. Lathrop married again, in Willoughby, Ohio, Mar. 4, 1845, Desire Branch Cushman, daughter of Dea. Charles Cushman of Bennington, Vt. He is now (1873) residing in Cleveland.

916. CHARLOTTE HUNTINGTON, born in New London, Conn., May 13, 1811. She united with the First Congregational church in Norwich, in 1827. She married, in 1836, Rev. Henry Cherry, then under appointment as missionary of the A. B. C. F. M. They sailed from Boston, Nov. 23, 1836, for Madras in the Madura Mission. She died of consumption in Ceylon, Nov. 4, 1837, and her grave is with those of two of her sisters in the Mission cemetery at Oodooville.

917. ELIZABETH COIT, born in New London, Apr. 16, 1813. She united with First Congregational church of Norwich, in 1828, and was married in the Center church, New Haven, by Leonard Bacon, D.D., Sept. 18, 1831, to Rev. Samuel, son of Samuel and Lois (Whitehead) Hutchins, Esq., of New York city, where he was born, Sept. 15, 1806. He graduated at Union College, in 1828, and studied theology. In July, 1833, they sailed for Ceylon under appointment as missionaries of the American board. There they remained devoted to missionary work for eleven years, when the failure of his health compelled their return to this country. They are now (1873) in Newark, N. J. Their children, ten in number, have been:

    i.    Mary Joanna Hutchins, born at Oodooville, Ceylon, Oct. 16, 1835.

    ii.    Charlotte Lothrop Hutchins, born at Batticotta, Ceylon, Feb. 26, 1837.

iii. Frances Elizabeth Hutchins, born at Chavagachevey, Ceylon, Dec. 26, 1837, and died Dec. 31, 1837.

iv. John Perry Hutchins, born at Manepy, Ceylon, June 15, 1840, and died in Madras, in December, 1841.

v. George Long Hutchins, born at Clapham Park, London, Eng., Mar. 13, 1844.

vi. Frances Hallock Hutchins, born in New Haven, Conn., July 22, 1847.

vii. Elizabeth Nichols Hutchins, born in Brookfield, Mass., Jan. 18, 1850.

viii. Charles Winslow Leffingwell Hutchins, born in New Haven, Conn., Aug. 21, 1852.

ix. Walter Whiting Hutchins, born in New Haven, Jan. 27, 1855.

x. Cornelia Vermilye Hutchins, born in Newark, N. J., Aug. 26, 1857.

918. HARRIET JOANNA, born in New London, Sept. 13, 1816, and united with the First Congregational Church in Norwich in 1828. She married Rev. John McCurly (Strong) Perry, son of Rev. David L. and Anna S. (Strong) Perry of Sharon, Conn., and grandson of Rev. David and Jerusha Lord Perry of Richmond, Mass. The parents of Rev. David were Joshua Perry and Mary, daughter of Thomas Leavenworth. They were appointed by the American Board, Missionaries to Ceylon; and embarked for their destined field May 16, 1835. They had but just entered on their field of usefulness when they were suddenly called away. Mr. Perry had but just completed his report of the mission for the year, when he was seized with the cholera which terminated so prematurely a life so full of promise, Saturday, Mar, 10, 1838. He had no sooner fallen than his wife felt the pangs of the same relentless disease, and on the evening of the Tuesday following, Mar 13, 1838, she too "fell asleep," breathing forth even in the intervals of intense suffering, "Sweet peace, sweet peace." They left a single daughter: Harriet Joanna Perry, born in Ceylon, Nov. 14, 1837. In 1842, she was brought to the United States and became the adopted daughter of Peletiah Perit, Esq., of New Haven.

## 459. BURREL. Savannah, Ga.

919. GEORGE AUGUSTUS, born in Savannah, Ga., Dec. 6, 1809, and married in Charleston, S. C., Nov. 15, 1832, Sarah Elizabeth Guy of Charleston, S. C. They settled in Savannah where he died about the year 1838.

920. EDWARD, born in Savannah, Mar. 12, 1814, and married (1), in Charleston, S. C., May 7, 1841, Jane Elizabeth, daughter of the Hon. Judge Samuel Davis of Thompson, Conn. She died, and he married (2), in New York City, May 25, 1854, Emily Elizabeth, daughter of Garret Noel Blucker, Esq. He received his primary education in Savannah, and uniting with the church at the age of fourteen his mind was directed to the work of the Christian ministry, and when about eighteen years old he commenced his studies with reference to that work at what was then known as the Furman Institution, Sumter District, South Carolina. He graduated at Madison University, and after finishing his studies in the theological department returned to Savannah and was ordained Feb. 14, 1841. He was at that time assistant of Rev.

Richard Fuller, D.D., now (1875) of Baltimore, Md., but then pastor of the Baptist Church in Beaufort, South Carolina. In 1844, Jan. 1, he assumed the pastoral charge of the Tabernacle Baptist Church, New York City, which position he continued to hold until Oct. 1, 1865. His health at this time being much impaired, he resigned this charge and removed to Stamford, Conn., at the invitation of his friend Mr. J. B. Hoyt, and in Feb., 1866, commenced his ministry as pastor of the Stamford ' .ptist Church. His contributions to the press have been mainly sermons and occasional articles for periodicals. The degree of D.D. was conferred upon him in 1855 by the University of Rochester.

921. MARY ELIZA, born in Savannah, Feb. 3, 1816, and died Sept. 26, 1820.

922. LOUISA, born in Savannah, Oct. 23, 1819, and died in Charleston, S. C., Oct. 16, 1821.

923. JOSEPH JAHAN, born in Savannah, Apr. 14, 1821, and married (1), Dec. 8, 1842, Mary Josephine, daughter of Wm. A. Simpson, of Savannah, where she was born May 1, 1822. He married (2), Nov. 17, 1865, Sarah Jane Thompson of Augusta, Ga., daughter of Wm. and Hannah Thompson of Augusta. They settled in Augusta.

924. MARY AMELIA, born in Cha.. 'on, S. C., Oct. 12, 1823, and married Feb. 15, 1844, Charles E. Mustin of Augusta, Ga. She died in Augusta, June 14, 1862. They had ten children, all born in Augusta:

    i.    Margaret Adelaide Mustin, born Nov. 24, 1844.
    ii.    Julia Alice Mustin, born July 11, 1846.
    iii.    Charles Edwin Mustin, born May 20, 1848, and died Apr. 4, 1850.
    iv.    Georgia Mustin, born Dec. 22, 1850.
    v.    Joseph Henry Mustin, born May 23, 1852, and died Feb. 16, 1853.
    vi.    Charles Edwin Mustin, born Jan. 8, 1854.
    vii.    Cecilia Mustin, born Oct. 12, 1855, and died Nov. 6, 1857.
    viii.    Alfred Mann Mustin, born Feb. 19, 1858, and died Aug. 14, 1870.
    ix.    Amelia Mustin, born May 6, 1860, and died June 21, 1860.
    x.    Fanny Amelia Mustin, born Sept. 7, 1861.

925. HENRY, born in Savannah, Aug. 1, 1825, and married July 5, 1859, Zeelia Wade of Natchez, Miss., where they settled.

926. CECILIA, born in Savannah, Nov. 29, 1827.

927. GEORGIANA R., born in Savannah, Apr. 26, 1830, and married Feb. 21, 1850, John B. Hogg of Savannah, Ga. They had ten children, all born in Savannah: Ida Hogg, born Mar. 19, 1852; Agness Ellis, born Jan. 5, 1854. Henry Howard, born Nov. 21, 1855; Mary Schoolcraft, born Jan. 18, 1858. William Carr, born Aug. 1, 1860; Amelia Adelaide, born Sept. 21, 1862, and died May 25, 1863; Fannie Brunner, born May 21, 1864; Edward Lathrop, born Apr. 2, 1867; George Wylly, born Sept. 21, 1869, and died July 5, 1870; Georgian Cecilia, born Nov. 1, 1871.

928. SARAH CHARLOTTE, born in Savannah, Sept. 13, 1845, married Feb. 28, 1871, Benjamine George of Savannah, Ga., where they reside (1875). They have one child: Joseph Lathrop George, born in Savannah, June 23, 1872.

## 460. GERARD.

929. ABIGAIL HUNTINGTON, born in Norwich, Sept. 10, 1810, and married Donald McKenzie, who died at sea, leaving two children: Mary Ely McKenzie, who died unmarried; Gerard Lathrop McKenzie, who married Emily Gray and has two sons, Charles Gray and Gerard Lathrop.

930. WILLIAM GERARD, born in Norwich, Oct. 29, 1812, and married in New York City, Nov. 15, 1837, Charlotte B., daughter of Nathan and Maria (Miller) Jennings of Windham, where she was born July 4, 1818. He was a merchant in New York City from 1835 to 1840, engaged in trade with China; and for more than thirty years agent and manager of the Boonton Iron Works, (nails,) Boonton, N. J., where he died March 2, 1882.

931. MILLS ELY, born in Norwich, Sept. 3, 1814, and began preparing for the ministry, but was disabled by an accident. He is now living (1873) with his brother, William G.

932. MARY CORNELIA, born May 10, 1820; married March 31, 1840, J. D. Vermilye, Esq., president Merchants' Bank, New York City.

933. CHARLES CHRISTOPHER, born in New York, March 3, 1817, and married March 1856, Mary Augusta Andrus of Newark, N. J.

934. CHARLOTTE ELIZA, born in New York City, Nov. 10, 1822.

935. EZRA STILES ELY, died in infancy.

## 462. AUGUSTUS.          Norwich, Conn.

936. AZARIAH, born May 7, 1810, married, Sept. 11, 1836, Jane, daughter of Nathan and Ruby (Baldwin) Fish, who died Oct. 21, 1842, and had one child born in 1830. He married (2), June 8, 1845, Lucy Fish, sister of his first wife. He died in Willimantic, Sept. 18, 1862, where his widow lived in 1872.

937. AUGUSTUS FREDERICK, born Oct. 15, 1811, and died Nov. 7, 1828, aged seventeen years.

938. JOHN, born June 3, 1813, and married, July 27, 1846, Laura E. Tilton. He died Apr. 23, 1849, leaving no children.

939. MARY EDGERTON, born Dec. 19, 1814, and married, May 28, 1855, Lyman Baker, and resides in New London, Conn. They had one child.

940. NABBY WHITING, born Dec. 19, 1814. Died single in Norwich, Sept. 22, 1861. In the record of her death she is called Abby.

941. JAMES STEDMAN, born July 21, 1816, and married, June 22, 1845, Juliette Stanley of Meriden.

942. SARAH GALE, born April 2, 1818, and married, June 22, 1845, Charles Champlin. Child: Sarah Bliss Champlin. She died in New London, Nov. 24, 1849.

943. CHARLOTTE AUGUSTA, born Feb. 23, 1820, married, Dec. 13, 1843, Henry W. Morgan. Children: Mary A. Morgan, born Apr. 15, 1845; Sarah Lathrop, born Dec. 17, 1850, now (1873) in New London.

## 468. JEDIDIAH.

944. WILLIAM, born in Norwich, Sept. 3, 1771, and died Jan. 16, 1772.

945. WILLIAM, born in Norwich, Sept. 11, 1773.

946. NANCY, born in Norwich, Sept. 24, 1775, and died June 25, 1789.

947. ARIEL, born in Colchester, Conn., Nov. 27, 1777, (Nov. 18, 1778, so son Andrew,) and married, Jan. 11, 1799, in Starke, Herkimer County, N. Y., Mary, daughter of Isaac and Sally Anderson. She was born Oct. 20, 1780, died in Starke, Apr. 22, 1834. He died Aug. 11, 1856.

948. MARY, born in Colchester, Conn., July 26, 1780, and married in Starke, N. Y., John Perry of Johnston, Montgomery County, N. Y. Child: Hon. Eli Perry.

949. DYER, born in Colchester, Apr. 20 1783, and died Apr. 23, 1783.

950. AMEY, born in Colchester, Apr. . ., 1783.

951. DYER, born Bozrah, Conn., May 4, 1788, and married, May 16, 1824, in Albany, Jane Ann. daughter of Daniel and Elizabeth Shields. He died Apr. 18, 1855, and his wife, Sept. 3, 1882.

Dyer Lathrop was an old and esteemed citizen of Albany, N. Y., and was known by every one in that city, and respected as universally as he was known. He removed from Herkimer County to Albany in 1811, and commenced his life there as a merchant, remaining in business until his death, in 1855. He was of the "Old School" of men, decided in every feeling, of uncompromising integrity, and great industry. Endowed with the solid sense and virtues of the olden time, he pursue' the "even tenor of his way," and after a successful career through life, die' an honored man. He was benevolent of heart and the appeal of honest charity was never made to him in vain. He was one of the incorporators of the Albany Hospital, and one of the founders of that Heaven-born institution, the Asylum for Orphan and Destitute Children, and from the time of its organization, 1829, to the time of his death was one of its main supporters. He was its treasurer for nearly twenty-four years, and to his exertions and those of two or three other philanthropists, was the asylum indebted for its very existence. In the hour of trial, when it seemed inevitable, that it could not be sustained, their individual means were freely given for the noble object, and thus the storm was weathered.

At a meeting of the Directors of the Albany Orphan Asylum, held April 19, 1855, the president announced the death of Mr. Dyer Lathrop, their late treasurer, and it was resolved as the sense of the Board,

"That, in the death of Mr. Lathrop, the community has lost one of its best citizens, and the Board a most valuable officer. Not often have we known so unassuming a manner united with such benevolence of heart, and such energy of action. For twenty-four years he has watched over the interests of our institution with the fidelity of a parent. With no reward but an approving conscience, he has not only during this long period been the faithful guardian of its finances, but in its many and often protracted embarrassments, when other means have failed, his credit has always been our reliance, till the exigency has been passed. It is the sentiment of every member of this Board, that a good man has gone from us, and that the orphan has lost a friend, whose place will not be easy to supply," etc., etc., etc.

> "So fades the summer cloud away,
> So sinks the gale when storms are o'er,
> So gently shuts the eye of day,
> So dies the wave along the shore."

"By order of the President, JAMES D. WASSON."

"Mrs. Lathrop had been for fifty years a member of the Baptist Church, and He in whom she had believed was a comfort and solace in her long illness, and around her are the everlasting arms.

"It was fitting at the last, when earthly scenes were fading from her vision, that her eyes should be lighted up with the beautiful vision of another world, that her long and toilsome journey of life should end upon a peaceful Sabbath afternoon, and that the music of the children from the neighboring church, whence sweet strains had often come to her with soothing power, should in its flight to Heaven pass this way, and bear on its wings her released soul to the home and bosom of God. Her long life of earthly usefulness and noble example is over. Like a shock of corn, fully ripe, she has been gathered to the fathers—not lost, only departed, for

> "There is no death! What seems so is transition.
> This life of mortal breath
> Is but a suburb of the life elysian,
> Whose portal we call death.

"And I heard a voice from Heaven, saying unto me, write, Blessed are the dead which die in the Lord from henceforth; yea, saith the Spirit, that they may rest from their labors, and their works do follow them."

952. NANCY, born in Norwich, Conn., Nov. 13, 1792.

### 474. ZEPHANIAH.          Hawley, Mass.

[This family were all born in Hawley, Mass.]

953. SIBBEL, born Feb. 21, 1785, and married John Tobey of Hawley. They had seven children, two living: Samuel, of Gainesville, Mich.; J. W., of Neenah, Wis.

954. ARABELLA, born Sept. 25, 1786, married Joseph Hubbard of Buckland, Mass., where they had five children. She died in Buckland, April 2, 1838. Children: Caroline Hodge Hubbard, who died in North Adams; Arabella Hubbard, who married a Townsly, and lived in Milwaukee, Wis.; William Hubbard, died; Edwin Hubbard, in Missouri; Joseph Hubbard, in the West.

955. DANIEL, born Aug. 8, 1788, and died in Hawley, Oct. 12, 1794.

956. SAMUEL, born Aug. 17, 1790, and died in Hawley, Oct. 9, 1794.

957. ZEPHANIAH, JUN., born Dec. 23, 1792, and married, in Hawley, Mass., Mar. 11, 1819, Tryphena Field, daughter of Capt. Elijah and Tryphena (Cooley) Field of Hawley, where she was born May 28, 1797. They settled at Oriskany Falls, N. Y. She died in Iowa City, Iowa, Sept. 12, 1842.

958. GEORGE HOUGH, born in Hawley, Mar. 5, 1795, and married, in September, 1822, Polly, daughter of James and Asenath (Strong) Claghorn, who was born in Williamsburg, Mar. 9, 1797, and died at Saginaw, Mich., in September, 1868. He was a farmer and a prominent citizen of Hawley, Mass., where he was Selectman and Town Clerk, and also thrice a representative of the town in the State legislature. He was a man of very general intelligence. His reading was extensive, and his knowledge of history and current literature was exceedingly exact and extensive. He died in Hawley, Sept. 8, 1862.

959. THOMAS WOOD, born Jan. 9, 1797, died in Madison, N. Y., June 20, 1843.

960. ESTHER WOOD, born Jan. 8, 1799, and married Simon Crittenden, who was born in 1797, and died Jan. 1, 1867. She died July 1, 1850. They had six children:

    i.  George D. Crittenden, who was born in Hawley, Aug. 30, 1827, married in North Adams, Mass., Sept. 6, 1853, Luclia E. Dane, and has a family of six children, living at Shelburne Falls: Hattie Evelyn, born Sept. 6, 1859; Cara Eugenia, born May 29, 1863; Philena Hume, born May 16, 1865; Alice Gertrude    a Nov. 19, 1866; Lottie Rosabell, born Nov. 8, 1868; and Esther Marion, born Nov. 20, 1870.

    ii.  Lucretia Crittenden, born Sept. 18, 1829, and married, Nov. 1, 1855, William Basset of Ashfield, who died Nov. 9, 1869.

    iii.  Olive F. Crittenden, born June 6, 1831, and married, Nov. 1, 1854, Calvin Cooley of Hawley. They have seven children: Charles S., born Apr. 29, 1856; Abbot L., born Feb. 20, 1858; Edwin W., born June 16, 1859; Olive A., born Dec. 31, 1861; Clara L., born Aug. 29, 1863; Abbie R., born Aug. 15, 1865; and Julia C., born Mar. 2, 1873.

    iv.  Caroline H. Crittenden, born Feb. 20, 1833, and married, June 20, 1866, Almon Howes of Ashfield.

    v.  Rebecca S. Crit nden, born Mar. 5, 1835.

    vi.  Charles Crittenden, born Jan. 1, 1837, and married, June 22, 1870, Julia Hall of Hawley.

961. MYRON, born Jan. 30, 1801, and married (1), ———; and (2), Eleanor Pierce; died in Western Virginia.

962. JEDEDIAH, born Feb. 15, 1804, settled in Virginia. On the opening of the Civil War he removed to Southern Illinois, and next to Tamaroa, Ill. He died Apr. 11, 1874.

963. EDWIN, born Aug. 7, 1807, and died in Hawley, Dec. 18, 1829.

964. EPHRAIM, born Jan. 8, 1811, and died Oct. 2, 1811.

## 478. ISRAEL.          Otsego, N. Y.

965. EUNICE, born ———, lived with her Uncle Andrew after her mother's death, and married Levi Sage of Green Co., N. Y. Children: Austin Sage, who lives (1873) in Cairo, Green Co., N. Y. She then married Rev. William Lull, a Methodist preacher, and had three children, two girls and a son, Delos Lull, also a Methodist preacher, living at Newburg, N. Y.; Melissa Lull, married ——— Phelps of Grand Rapids, Mich.

966. AUSTIN, died young.

967. ELIZA, married James H. Flagg of Morris, N. Y.

968. AUSTIN, born Aug. 19, 1805, in Otsego Co., N. Y., and married, Nov. 5, 1832, Amy Walker, only daughter of Daniel Walker of Lawson, Tioga Co., Pa., who died Mar. 19, 1850. He married (2), Frances Elizabeth Davenport, July 26, 1855, who died in Elkland, Pa., Nov. 9, 1856. He married (3), Feb. 3, 1857, Caroline Van Vuox, in Occola, Pa. He settled in Lawrenceville, Tioga Co., Pa. In 1831, he was in the lumber trade, and is now living there, 1874.

21

969. DELOS, born in 1803, graduated at Union College in 1832, an excellent scholar. Settled in Buffalo in the law profession, where he took a high stand; died in Albany, 1835, of brain fever.

970. MATILDA, married Norman Newel.

### 481. SIMEON.                     Bozrah, Conn.

971. GILES, born in Norwich, in September, 1782. He lived in Bozrah, where he died unmarried.

972. SIMON, born in Norwich, Dec. 30, 1783, and never married. He died in Bozrah.

973. HANNAH, born in Norwich, Nov. 29, 1785. She married, Nov. 25, 1810, Dea. Jabez Backus, and settled in Bozrah, where their first six children were born. They then removed to Lebanon, and afterwards to Bolton. He died in New Haven, Conn., Aug. 17, 1854.

### 483. OLIVER.                     Sharon, Vt.

974. OLIVER, born in Bozrah, Conn., married Betsey Brown of Strafford, Vt., married, went west, and died in Batavia, leaving two daughters.

975. RODERICK D., born in Lebanon, N. H., May 24, 1795, and married Elizabeth Burbank. They lived in Sharon, Vt., where he died in 1851, leaving no children. His widow is now, 1873, living in Newport, N. H.

976. AURELIA, married Capt. Ashley of Hartland, Vt. No children.

977. DESIRE, married Judge Josiah Dana of Chelsea, Vt. No children.

978. AMANDA, married Hon. Geo. E. Wales, an attorney-at-law. He was six years in the Legislature of Vermont, and two years Speaker of the House of Representatives. He also represented the State in the U. S. Congress for two terms, from 1825 to 1829, and from 1843 to 1848 was Judge of Probate for Hartford County. Daughter, Mrs. Perley C. Jones of Chelsea, Vt.

979. ELIZABETH, married Warham Morse, a merchant of Lebanon, N. H., where they lived. They had at least one son: Anthony H. Morse, who died in New Haven, Conn. Mrs. Morse died in Lebanon, N. H., in 1867.

980. HARRIET, married John Barter, and settled in Lebanon, N. H., as a merchant, where he died. She married (2), Dr. Thos. Winslow of Chelsea, Vt., who died. She died at Derby Line, in 1862. By her first husband she had two sons, both of whom are dead.

### 486. ZABDIEL.                     Bozrah, Conn.

981. ALFRED, born in Bozrah, Nov. 5, 1786.

982. CAROLINE, born Sept. 2, 1788.

983. ZABDIEL, born in Bozrah, June 2, 1791.

984. ASA.

985. WALTER.

986. EZEKIEL.

### 487. ANDREW. Bozrah, Conn.

987. DICE, born in Bozrah, Dec. 3, 1789, married Jared Farnum of Hanover, Feb. 19, 1817, where two children are recorded: Erastus Lathrop Farnum, born Dec. 1, 1817, and died Mar. 29, 1819; Jared Farnum, born Oct. 21, 1835; Lucretia Farnum, who married George Lawton, and died about 1853.

988. PHILENA, born in Bozrah, Apr. 10, 1791.

989. SIMEON, born in Bozrah, Nov. 25, 1792, and married, Mar. 7, 1815, Abigail, daughter of William Ryder, and settled on Blue Hill in Bozrah, where she died Aug. 29, 1817. He then married, Dec. 20, 1820, Phebe, daughter of Wm. S. Peckham, of Franklin, where she was born in 1800. She died Aug. 11, 1847, and he is still living (1873) on the old homestead on Blue Hill, in the northwest part of Bozrah.

990. APANIE, born in Bozrah, July 25, 1794, and married as his second wife, Joseph S. Ford of Bozrah. Children: Jerusha F.; Jane; and Lucy.

991. AZARIAH, born in Bozrah, Feb. 25, 1796, and married, Dec. 2, 1824, Talitha, daughter of Elisha and Nancy (Rudd) Huntington of Norwich, where she was born, Feb. 13, 1794. They lived in Franklin and Bozrah, and then removed to Vernon, Conn.

992. LUCY, born Mar. 8, 1798, died when about twenty years of age.

993. EUNICE, born June 14, 1799, married Elisha, son of Wm. S. Peckham, and lives in Pembroke, N. Y.

### 489. ASA.

994. ABIGAIL, born in 1782, and died Mar. 30, 1789, and was buried in the Bozrah Cemetery.

### 490. EZEKIEL.

995. JAMES, had two children, Jonathan and Dice.

### 491. JAMES. Blue Hill, (Bozrah,) Conn.

996. LOIS, born Nov. 27, 1787, married Jabez Scott. Lived and died in Blue Hill, Bozrah. They had three daughters: Aveline Scott, married Charles West in Hartford, and died, leaving one son; Lois, married Abery Strickland, in New London, living there. Children: Eveline, died married; Frank Abbina, died unmarried; Charles.

997. JAMES, born in Franklin, Feb. 27, 1790, and married in March, 1808, Clarissa, daughter of Elderkin and Emma (Lathrop) Spicer of Bozrah, where she was born Sept. 8, 1792, and died Oct. 15, 1877, in Franklin.

### 496. JEREMIAH.

998. LYDIA, born Aug. 4, 1771, married Lemuel Kingsley. Children: Eliza White Kingsley, born June 18, 1802, single, died Jan. 27, 1866; Wm. Lathrop Kingsley, born Apr. 20, 1805; Melissa Kingsley, born June 19, 1807.

999. ERASTUS, born Apr. 7, 1773, and married in Franklin, Dec. 25, 1800, Lucy Smith, and moved to Hinsdale, N. H. Children: Alice and Fanny.

· 1000. ANNE, born June 19, 1776, married, 1799, (so Franklin Church records,) James Gordon of Lisbon. She had died before 1819, as her heirs are mentioned in the distribution of her father's estate, in that year. In her mother's will, dated Aug. 24, 1818, three of her children are named: Esther, Delano, and Albert.

1001. OLIVER, born Nov. 29, 1777, married, and had a family living in Vermont.

1002. HAZEL, born May 24, 1781, and married, in Norwich, Aug. 3, 1806, Abigail Kirkland. He settled in Rome, N. Y., soon after his marriage, and died in Rome, Dec. 5, 1810.

1003. JARVIS, born Dec. 26, 1783, and married Hannah Lester. They lived in Norwich. He died July 25, 1855, and his wife, Mar. 10, 1859, aged seventy-eight years. Buried in Yantic Cemetery.

1004. EUNICE, born Dec. 26, 1783, married (1), Jonathan Reynolds; (2), Asa Lee of Lebanon. She is one of the legatees named Aug. 24, 1818, in her mother's will.

1005. LURA, born·Feb. 10, 1787, married Samuel A. Andrus. In the distribution of her father's estate she is called Philura.

1006. HANNAH, born Sept. 16, 1789, and died Feb. 13, 1802, as her gravestone next to her father's in the Norwich Town Cemetery asserts.

## 498. WILLIAM,. Canandaigua, N. Y.

1007. HARRIET, born in Norwich, Sept. 27, 1780, and married Dudley Loomis. They settled in Moravia, Cayuga County, N. Y., where she died in March, 1865. His death, at the age of ninety years, occurred Dec. 31, 1869. They had at least the following children: Thomas; William Loomis, who lives in Ann Arbor, Mich.; John Loomis, who lives in Tiffin, O.; Betsey.

1008. ALFRED, born in Norwich, Dec. 17, 1782, and married, Mar. 6, 1814, Mrs. Margaret (Parsons) Hubbard, widow of Stephen Hubbard of Middletown, daughter of Gen. Samuel H. Parsons of Middletown. He was a lawyer by profession, and settled first in Champion, and then in Carthage, N. Y., where she died Apr. 26, 1853, and he died May 20, 1865.

1009. WILLIAM, born in Canandaigua, N. Y., Apr. 4, 1785, and married Philena, daughter of James Blackman, and settled as a physician in Gilbertsville, N. Y., where he died Oct. 30, 1845, his wife having died Jan. 26, 1845. He studied medicine with Dr. Richardson of Burlington.

1010. JAMES ELDERKIN, born in Canandaigua, N. Y., Sept. 2, 1787, and married Esther Willis. He died Jan. 25, 1870.

1011. CYNTHIA, born Jan. 3, 1790, and never married. She died Aug. 21, 1855.

1012. GEORGE CLINTON, born Aug. 21, 1792, and married Betsey Jewel. He died in Moravia, N. Y., May 1, 1843, and his wife is also dead. They had no children.

1013. FAYETTE, born July 28, 1795, and married, in Richmond, Va., Nov. 23, 1832, Maria, daughter of Chatley and Nancy Crew of New Kent, Va. He died in Richmond, Va., May 20, 1851, where he had been a merchant in the dry goods business, and where his widow and only child still reside (1879).

1014. SOPHIA, born Apr. 5, 1798, and married Charles Chapin, and lived in Auburn, N. Y., where he died, Feb. 17, 1831, aged thirty-six years. She had died Apr. 18, 1830, leaving no children.

1015. JOHN, born June 11, 1801, and died June 26, 1801.

### 504. ANDREW. Blenheim, N. Y.

1016. WILLIAM, born Mar. 10, 1798, married June 4, 1823, Elizabeth Welles, was born in Middletown, Conn, in October, 1799. He died in Albany, N. Y., Dec. 2, 1839, and his wife is now (1873) living.

1017. GUY, born June 4, 1800, and died June 23, 1800.

1018. GAD, born June 4, 1800, and died June 20, 1800.

1019. SOPHRONIA, born July 6, 1802, and married, Sept. 20, 1825, Mathew Boughton. They had one son, George R. Boughton, who has a family.

1020. CALVIN, born in Bozrah, Mar. 15, 1804, married in Jackson, Mich., Feb. 20, 1825, Harriet, daughter of Joseph and Susan Desilva, who was born in Broome, N. Y., Mar. 29, 1806. Removed to California in 1849 and returned in 1856.

1021. LATHROP ELDERKIN, born in Otsego County, N. Y., Dec. 18, 1805, and married, in Newark, N. J., Dec. 18, 1833, Hetty Francisco, who was born in, Bloomfield, N. J., Mar. 29, 1805. He, with his brother Calvin, went to California in 1849, and has not been heard from since, though no pains have been spared to find him (1873).

1022. RICHARD DOWNER, born in Broome, Schoharie County, N. Y., July 4, 1808, married, May 29, 1834, Jane Starkweather, who died in New York, December, 1862. He married (2), Annie Davis. He was of the firm of Lathrop & Luddington. He died Feb. 14, 1873, in New York, leaving one son.

1023. ELIZA DOWNER, born in Broome, Feb. 3, 1810, and married, Feb. 4, 1829, Allen, son of Samuel and Mary Brand of Conesville, Schoharie County, where he was born, Dec. 2, 1805, and where they now (1873) live. Children:

 i. Richard L. Brand, born in April, 1830, and married.
 ii. Amelia Brand, born in 1830, and married Peter Layman, and lives at Conesville.
 iii. Sophronia Sybil Brand, born in 1834, and died in 1835.
 iv. Samuel Nelson Brand, born in 1836, and now lives at the West, and has a family.
 v. Jane Lathrop Brand, born in 1836, and is living single in Michigan.
 vi. Andrew Lathrop Brand, born in 1841, and is married.
 vii. Ellen Brand, born in 1843, and lives single with parents.
 viii. Alice Brand, born in 1845, is married and lives at Conesville.
 ix. Mary Eliza Brand, born in February, 1848, and is married.

### 516. DARIUS.

1024. SOPHIA, born Sept. 15, 1788, and married in Norwich, Nov. 26, 1817, Daniel, son of John Morse of Norwich. She died Aug. 26, 1854. No children.

1025. MIRA, born Jan. 23, 1792, and married, Mar. 24, 1813, Chester, son of Abiel Bill of Lebanon, where he was born in 1788. She died in Norwich, Dec. 13, 1863, and he, Aug. 29, 1867. One child, Orin Hart Bill, born June 23, 1815, and died Sept. 5, 1840.

1026. ELIZABETH, born Feb. 11, 1797, in Norwich, and married, Nov. 21, 1825, Seymour Morse of Plain Hills, Norwich. Child: Lydia Elizabeth Morse, born Jan. 19, 1827, and married, Oct. 4, 1848, Stephen N. Yerrington of Norwich.

1027. JOHN BACKUS, born July 25, 1800, and married, Nov. 27, 1823, Harriet M. Lester, daughter of William and Elizabeth (Burgess) Lester of Norwich. She was born Aug. 24, 1800. She united with the Canterbury Church by letter at the same time her parents did, and died Sept. 11, 1854, in Lisbon.

### 517. ROGER.        South Coventry, Conn.

1028. FRANCIS, born and recorded in South Coventry, Conn., Jan. 24, 1800, and married, Nov. 7, 1825, Clarissa, daughter of Elias and Hannah (Thompson) Janes of Pittsfield, who was born June 9, 1804.

1029. JOEL, born Nov. 7, 1802, and married Ann Parish.

1030. ALBERT, born Mar. 29, 1805, and died Jan. 5, 1808.

1031. LUCY, born Oct. 9, 1808, and married.

1032. MARY, born July 26, 1812, and died Aug. 9, 1814.

1033. MARY, born Jan 14, 1815, and married Charles Woodworth. They are settled in Rockville, Conn.

### 518. JESSE.        Franklin, Conn.

1034. ABEL, born in Franklin, Aug. 4, 1801, and died Nov. 10, 1802.

1035. DUDLEY, born in Franklin, Aug. 8, 1803, and died unmarried in the same town, Oct. 18, 1851.

1036. AMANDA, born in Franklin, Dec. 21, 1798, and united with the Franklin Church in 1821.

1037. ELIZABETH, born in Franklin, Apr. 21, 1800, united with the Franklin Church in 1821, and called Betsey on the records.

1038. SARAH HYDE, born in Franklin, Oct. 9, 1807, and united with the Franklin Church in 1831

1039. LYDIA, born in Franklin, Mar. 17, 1812, and united with the Franklin Church in 1831.

### 520. EZRA.        Bozrah, Conn.

1040. A SON, born in Bozrah, Nov. 27, 1797, and died same day.

1041. MARY, born in Bozrah, June 7, 1801, and died, (so gravestone,) May 17, 1802.

1042. MARY, 2d, born in Bozrah, June 21, 1803, and married.

1043. EUNICE, born in Bozrah, Oct. 5, 1806, and married John Kelly, and (2), —— Carrington.

1044. JANE ELEANOR, born in Bozrah, July 29, 1809, and died Jan. 11, 1810, as her gravestone in the Norwich Town Cemetery shows.

1045. REBECCA JANE, born in Bozrah, Dec. 17, 1811. She early became a decided Christian and devoted herself to the missionary life. In 1840 she became a missionary of the American Board and reached Columbo from Boston in the *Black Warrior* on the 31st December, and Jafna on Jan. 27, 1841. Here she was married to Rev. H. M. Cherry, the former husband of ——, and proceeded with him to their station at Sivagunga, near Madura, where her labors began in February, twenty-seven miles away from any other missionary or white person, they gave themselves to the work of winning the heathen. On the 27th of February she and her husband constituted two of the little church of nine members which they there organized. Mrs. Cherry was in charge of a girl's school, and it was prosperous even beyond their hopes. She died Jan. 19, 1844, of cholera at Sivagunga.

1046. JOHN LESTER, born in Norwich, Apr. 14, 1816. He has always remained on the old Huntington homestead, where he has been an ingenious and successful farmer. He married, Apr. 20, 1842, Mary A., daughter of Russel and Mary C. (Hurlbut) Harris of Bozrah, where she was born, June 25, 1818.

1047. JONATHAN GEORGE, born in Bozrah, Oct. 13, 1817, and married.

## 521. JOHN. Calcutta, Asia.

1048. ISAAC PIERCE, born Sept. 5, 1793, and died Sept. 9, 1802.

1049. ANNA MATILDA, born Jan. 2, 1795, and died Jan. 4, 1795.

1050. JOHN PIERCE, born Apr. 8, 1796, and married in Demerara, Maria Margaretta, daughter of Thomas C. and Frances Hungerford (Griffin) Long. He was educated, and was ordained deacon in the Episcopal Church in Boston in 1837, and priest, Mar. 15, 1839, in Burlington, N. J. He died in Philadelphia, Pa., Dec. 30, 1843, at which date he was chaplain in the United States Navy, and attached to the steamer *Princeton*.

1051. ANNA MATILDA, born Oct. 28, 1798, and died Sept. 28, 1800.

1052. JANE ANN.

1053. MARY ANN, who died unmarried.

1054. ANNA SABINA JACOBI, born Mar. 18, 1809, and died unmarried.

1055. ELIZABETH CHECKLEY, died unmarried.

1056. GRACE ELLEN. After the death of her father she and her mother returned to Calcutta, and she married, there, Captain Rickett. They have descendants now living in England.

## 532. GEORGE. Bethany, N. Y.

1057. CORNELIA, married —— Sterling in Illinois, and had three daughters.

1058. PORTER, born Aug. 28, 1802, and married (1), Ruth Sprague of Bethany; (2), Emily Thayer of Concord, Mich. He resided in Concord, Mich., until 1817, when he removed to Lansing, Mich., where he died, July 5, 1849.

1059. GEORGE CLEVELAND, married Mary Hall, who lived near Mason, Mich. They had several children.

1060. POLLY, married Champlin Havens of Lansing, Mich., and had two sons and two daughters.

1061. ORRIN, married Mary Ann Nichols. No children. Lived in Darien, Genesee Co., N. Y.

1062. LUMAN, married Julia Wheeler, and died in 1872.

1063. HOMER, married Olive Putnam of Batavia, N. Y.

1064. MIRANDA, living with Mrs. Sterling, oldest sister.

1065. FRANKLIN, of great promise, killed by the bursting of a cylinder of buzz saws about 1848.

### 531. GURDON.

1066. SEWELL STEPHEN, born Aug. 6, 1797, in Norwich, and married Betsey Backus, widow of Simon Backus of Norwich. He died in Pennsylvania Apr. 20, 1860 or 1861.

1067. LYDIA, born Sept. 24, 1799, in Warren, and married Walter Giddings of Norwich. They had two children: John Westley Giddings and Francis Giddings. She died May 7, 1867.

1068. LAURA MEHETABLE, born in Warren, Feb. 17, 1802, and married Willis Bronson. They had one daughter, Grisella. They lived in Waverly, N. Y.

1069. MARY PEMBER, born Oct. 31, 1805, married Wm. L. Kingsley and live (1873) on Plain Hill in Norwich. They have had four children: Cornelia Jane, George May, Cornelius Lathrop, and Jane Melissa.

1070. JOSIAH CLEVELAND, born Sept. 19, 1809, married Sophia Crouch of New York.

1071. LUCY EDGERTON, born July 31, 1813, married Geo. Bull of Newark. Children: Matilda, Margaret, Gurdon, Nathan, Mary, William, Lydia, Walter, Hattie, Harvey, and Lucy.

1072. FAYETTE ADDISON, born Apr. 17, 1815, in Norwich.

1073. GURDON, born Dec. 12, 1819, married Jan. 1832, Jane Howell of Mystic. He lived in New York City, and died Nov. 5, 1857. His widow married John Helfridge.

### 541. HENRY.

1074. HENRY UTLEY, born Feb. 27, 1815.

1075. WILLIAM PORTER, born Feb. 27, 1817.

1076. CHARLES, born in Bethany.

### 544. ZEBULON.          Tolland, Conn.

1077. ASA, died in 1780.

1078. JOHN, born in 1771, and married Polly Kinney. He died Mar. 17, 1837.

1079. URIAH, born in 1774, and married Betsey Hartshorn of Lebanon (married Betsey P. Edgerton, 1798,—Franklin Records), died at Whitesboro, N. Y., Apr. 17, 1814, aged 40.

1080. VARANUS, born ——; married in Franklin in 1797, Lucy, daughter of Hezekiah Edgerton of Tolland, who was born July 8, 1779, and died June 14, 1854. He removed from Lebanon, Conn., early in this century to Hyde

Park, Vt., and still later to Cambridge, Vt. To his record, written at about 80 years of age, we are indebted for the means of identifying several of the Lathrops in this branch of the family.

1081. WILLIAM, born in 1779, and married Mar. 22, 1803, Amelia, daughter of Captain Ammi and Esther (Chapman) Paulk of Tolland, who was born Dec. 24, 1782, and died Oct. 28, 1810. He lived in Tolla... where he died June 14, 1807.

1082. SARAH, born in Lebanon, Conn., Dec. 1, 1782, and married May 7, 1801, Capt. Daniel, son of Daniel and Mary (Cobb) Edgerton, who was born in Tolland, Sept. 11, 1778, and who became a prominent citizen. Their children were: Marvin Edgerton, born Jan. 11, 1802; Linus Edgerton, born Oct. 4, 1803; Erastus Edgerton, born June 23, 1806; Betsey Edgerton, born Sept. 30, 1808; Phebe Edgerton, born Oct. 23, 1810.

1083. ANNA, born in Lebanon, Conn., June 24, 1785, and married Mar. 23, 1803, Reuben, a younger brother of her sister Sarah's husband who was born in Tolland, June 13, 1780. The children recorded to them are: Austin Edgerton, born Mar. 26, 1805; Eliza Ann Edgerton, born Sept. 3, 1807; William L. Edgerton, born Aug. 30, 1810; Daniel Edgerton, born Sept. 26, 1813; Reuben Edgerton, born Oct. 17, 1816; Lucius Edgerton, born Apr. 19, 1820; Marvin Edgerton, born Dec. 4, 1828, and died Dec. 5, 1839.

## 545. URIAH. Bozrah, Conn.

1084. CHARLES, born in Bozrah, Sept. 22, 1785.
1085. SOPHIA, born in Bozrah, June 19, 1787..
1086. CLARISSA, born in Bozrah, June 6, 1789.
1087. LOIS, born in Bozrah, May 10, 1791.

## 549. AZEL. Utica, N. Y.

1088. HYDE.
1089. LUCRETIA, married John Latham, and died soon after.
1090. ELIZABETH HYDE, married —— Bramble, and had three sons. Lived in Prattstown, Steuben Co., N. Y.
1091. ANNE.
1092. LUCY, of Lebanon, married, Jan. 31, 1828, Jedediah Williams of Norwich. Children: Charles; and three daughters.
1093. CYNTHIA, married Benj. Kingsley, and had two sons and one daughter.
1094. AZEL J., born Nov. 30, 1813, and married, Nov. 29, 1838, Margaretta Hamilton Arthur, who died Nov. 18, 1869.
1095. JULIA, married Thos. L. Kingsley of Utica. Children: Thos ; Chas.; Lewis; Albert; May; Lizzie; Addie; and Grace.
1096. GIDEON.

## 552. ERASTUS. Hartford, Conn.

[This family were all born in Ashford, Conn.]

1097. GORDON, born in June, 1808, and was drowned, July 7, 1810.
1098. WILLIAM, born Feb. 1, 1810, and died in Illinois, in 1872.

22

1099. JULIA B., born Dec. 2, 1812, and was married in Ashford, Oct. 29, 1832, by Rev. Philo Judson, to William H. Durer. No children. She died in Vermont, June 7, 1870.

1100. SARAH, born Dec. 2, 1814, and died in Hartford, Conn., Oct. 26, 1851.

1101. JOHN W., born Jan. 9, 1816, and was married by Rev. R. G. Dennis, at Somers, Conn., Aug. 1, 1839, to Elizabeth C. Kibbe of Springfield.

1102. HARRIET M., born Mar. 13, 1818, and was married in Hartford, by Rev. Dr. Bushnell, May 3, 1837, to Joseph T. Smith.

1103. ELIZA J., born Apr. 1, 1820.

1104. MARY J., born Sept. 23, 1822, and was married in Hartford, June 10, 1846, by Rev. Dr. Patton, to George W. Moseley.

1105. CAROLINE, born Nov. 27, 1824, and was married in Hartford, Mar. 27, 1844, by J. N. Sprague, to Abner Parsons, who died. She married (2), Oct. 10, 1851, C. R. Post, in Hartford.

1106. EMELINE, born May 26, 1832, and was married in Hartford, by Rev. Dr. Patton, in July, 1851, to Henry M. Wickham.

### 553. HORACE.          Mansfield, Conn.

1107. ALBERT, born in Mansfield, Jan. 24, 1815, and married, Sept. 2, 1840, Elizabeth Carmichael, who died Aug. 7, 1849. He married (2), Dec. 18, 1850, widow Isabelle C. Close, half sister to his first wife. He is a carpenter, and is living now (1873) in Syracuse.

1108. MARIA, born in Mansfield, Conn.

1109. HORACE, JR.

1110. ERASTUS.

1111. DENISON.

1112. CATHERINE, married —— Keyes.

1113. MELANCTHON.

1114. EZRA.

1115. BETSY, married —— Gleason.

1116. JOHN.

1117. JACKSON.

### 554. ELIAS.          Chelsea, Vt.

1118. ELIAS, JR., born in Conn., Feb. 18, 1763, and married, Jan. 12, 1797, Dorcas Bohonon. He was engaged as a teamster in the Revolutionary war, and was present at the surrender of Burgoyne. He became one of the pioneers in the settlement of Vermont. He died in Vershire, Vt., Mar. 5, 1851. Wife, cousin of Daniel Webster.

1119. RUFUS, born in Conn., Feb. 12, 1765, and married, Mar. 8, 1790, Margaret, daughter of Theophilus and Lois (Gifford) Huntington. They made their way to Chelsea, Vt., on an ox-sled, and built their log-house. There they worked and brought up their family, occupying a good position among the pioneers of the town. They owned a large farm, which he managed to work successfully. He became, also, a public man, serving the town in many ways very acceptably. He died Sept. 16, 1842, and his widow at the age of 82, Nov. 29, 1849. Mr. Lathrop was a man of great native ability, and of noble traits. He had none of the polish of the schools, but a strong, good sense, and resolute will, and was sure to carry his cause. His wife was one of those evenly balanced women, with the natural delicacy and refinement which belong to the sex, and who would have graced any circle however courtly. They constituted one of those old time couples, who seemed fitted for each other, and fitted to be the founders of a strong family.

1120. ELIZABETH, born Apr. 9, 1768, married —— Storrs of Royalton, Vt., and died soon after marriage. They had one son.

1121. GURDON, born Nov. 1, 1770, married, and settled in Swanton, Vt., and died there during the war of 1812–14.

1122. JOSEPH, born Feb. 10, 1773, and married Lydia, daughter of Lieut. Governor Paul Brigham of Norwich, Vt., who died in December, 1871, at 93 years of age. He died in 1835, in Worcester, Vt.

1123. LOIS, born Sept. 10, 1776, and married in Lebanon, N. H., Jan. 25, 1798, Oliver Stearns, who was born Feb. 5, 1776. She died in October, 1814, and her husband, Oct. 12, 1862. They had nine children:

i. Olive Stearns, born Jan. 3, 1799, and married, Sept. 17, 1823, Earl Pierce of Mansfield, Conn. Their children were: Lathop S., born in Pitcher, N. Y., became a school teacher, and peddler, and married, and had two children: Miller, born in Michigan, and died in New York; and Shepard H., born in Michigan, and is a farmer, and has had at least four children: Minerva; Delia J.; Delia; and Etta.

ii. Shepard Stearns, born Oct. 14, 1800, and married, Nov. 29, 1827, Lucy H., daughter of Jared and Mary (Hartshorn) Hyde of Franklin, Conn. He was a farmer, and teacher of music in Mansfield, Conn. They had five children: Vera Ann, born Mar. 30, 1832, who was a music teacher, having graduated at the Music Vale Seminary at Salem, Conn. She married, Mar. 31, 1857, Ephraim Rood, and had two children: Alice V., born Aug. 31, 1860; and Alfred H., born July 30, 1862, and died Dec. 21, 1865; Oliver E., born Feb. 13, 1836, enlisted in the Union Army in the recent war, and died as the result of the exposure, Sept. 22, 1864; Jared H., born May 17, 1841, was a musician in the recent war, married Ellen H. Storrs, May 28, 1868, by whom he has one child: Clara M., born May 14, 1871; Valetta Delos, born Jan. 22, 1843, married, Mar. 18, 1869, Emma J. Baldwin; Charles B., born Nov. 30, 1847.

iii. Sally Stearns, born Oct. 5, 1801, and married, July 13, 1824, John Hall, Jr. (See No. 1124).

iv. Elias L. Stearns, born Apr. 9, 1803, and died Sept. 3, 1805.

v. Nathaniel P. Stearns, born Apr. 24, 1805, and married Betsey —— of Herkimer, N. Y. They have at least one son: George W., and perhaps more.

vi. Mary E. Stearns, born Sept. 27, 1806, and married, Apr. 13, 1853, Edward Marsh, who died Jan. 22, 1860. She married, June 2, 1868, Thomas B. Tilden, who died Apr. 2, 1869. She married for her third husband, Henry Brown.

vii. Sophia Stearns, born Apr. 23, 1808, and married Eliphalet Lyman of Mansfield, Conn. She died June 25, 1863.

viii. Experience Stearns, born May 2, 1811, and married Persis Lovet of Ellington, Conn.

ix. Samuel Stearns, born in October, 1814, and married, in 1842, Mary Steele of Litchfield, Conn.

1123–1. Eunice, born Sept. 10, 1776, and married, Mar. 4, 1804, Francis, son of Joseph and Mary (King) Balcam of Mansfield, Conn. They moved to Plainfield, N. H., where she died. Children:

 i. Gorton Balcam, born Jan. 6, 1805, and settled in Binghamton, N. Y.

 ii. Julia Balcam, born 1806.

 iii. Lois, married Albert Balch.

 iv. Maria.

 v. Lodisa, married in Grantham, N. H.

 vi. John Noyes of Lebanon, N. H., and died in Lebanon. He had three children: Charles, who lived in Kentucky, and had a family; Henry, who married Mary Colburn of Lebanon, N. H.; and Julia, who married Charles Gleason, a brother of Elijah, the husband of Dyer Lathrop.

1124. Hannah, born Oct. 26, 1779, and married in Lebanon, N. H., Dec. 15, 1799, John Hall of Plasto, N. H., where he was born May 10, 1773. They settled in Thetford, Vt., where he was many years a hotel keeper. She died in Thetford, Nov. 5, 1825, and he Mar. 17, 1855. Their children, half born in Norwich, Vt., and the last four in Thetford, were:

 i. Hannah Hall, born Oct. 28, 1800, and married Curtiss Cleveland of Royalton, Vt., where he was born Jan. 21, 1796, and died Nov. 30, 1870. His wife had died Oct. 5, 1837. They had two children: a son who died young: Mary E., born Oct. 6, 1834, and married in 1860, Ezra, son of David and Hannah Day of Enfield, N. H., by whom she had Colcord C., born in Warner, N. H., Feb. 26, 1864, and Bernice L., born in Enfield, Feb. 21, 1865.

 ii. John Hall, jun., born Feb. 22, 1802, and married July 13, 1824, Sally, daughter of Oliver and Lois (Lathrop) Stearns. They had three children: Experience P., born July 27, 1825, and lived and died in Illinois; Sarah M., born Aug. 7, 1827, married Sept. 3, 1848, Christopher W. Avery, and had five children: George W., born Nov. 24, 1849; Lucy M., born Nov. 14, 1852; John F., born Aug. 14, 1854; Eugene S., born Nov. 24, 1858; and Mary E., Aug. 30, 1865; and Joseph G., born Apr. 12, 1829. Mr. Hall died in Harris, O., Dec. 1843, and Sally his wife, July 19, 1831.

 iii. Mehetabel Hall, born Jan. 3, 1804, and married Joseph S. Gould, a merchant of Newbury, Vt. Their children were: Hannah L., born Mar. 31, 1825; and Maria, born Apr. 10, 1827. Mr. Gould died May 21, 1829, and his widow married in February, 1835, Joseph Gleason of Grantham, N. H., by whom she had Mary H., born Feb. 27, 1836, and Ellen, born May 17, 1838. Mr. Gleason died in Canton, Mo., in August, 1868. Hannah L. Gould married May 8, 1844, Greenlief Cummings, a merchant in Lisbon, N. H., and had Charles E., born Feb. 28, 1847; Flora L., born Oct. 29, 1856; Karl G., born June 15, 1865, and died July 23, 1865. Mr. Cummings died Oct. 4, 1865, and his widow married Mar. 20, 1873, Seldon Cook of Springfield, Vt., who was born May 4, 1808. Maria Gould married May 8, 1844, Otis Abbee of Lisbon, N. H. They had four children, of whom the oldest was George E. Mrs.

Abbee died in Madison, Wis., Feb. 29, 1869; Mary H. Gleason married Jan. 17, 1865, in Madison, Wis., Nat. Rollin, attorney-at-law. She died in Lisbon, N. H., Nov. 16. 1871; Charles E. Cummings mc---' ' in Canterbury, N. H., June 16, 1870, Ellen Ayers, and they now live in Canton, Mo., and have a daughter Susie E., born Jan. 7, 1873; George E. Abbe married, July 11, 1872, Mary E. Hawes. He is now (1873) 1st Lieut. 24th Infantry, U.S.A., and with his command at Fort Brown, Texas. They have a daughter, born Apr. 18, 1873.

iv. Maria Hall, born Aug. 31, 1805, and married in Thetford, Vt., Nov. 23, 1828, Nathaniel White, who was born Apr. 21, 1800. He was a physician and died Sept. 12, 1863, and Mrs. White is living in Lebanon, N. H. Their children were: James, born Nov. 8, 1829, and died, Oct. 13, 1837; Ellen, born Nov. 16, 1836, married in Lebanon, N. H., Dec. 1, 1863, Joseph Stickney, and lives in Wilkesbarre, Pa.; and John, born July 20, 1853, and died Aug. 9, 1863.

v. Abigail Hall, born Jan. 17, 1807, and married Marcus Banstead of Thetford, Vt. She died Aug. 21, 1873, leaving a single daughter, living in Thetford.

vi. Charles H. Hall, born Sept. 16, 1811, married Susan Barton of Croydon, N. H., who died Dec. 24, 1851, aged 38 years, and he died Aug. 12, 1869. They had two children: Oscar and Reuel D.

vii. Eliza Hall, born Nov. 13, 1814, and married Jan. 8, 1834, Latimer S. Tyler of Thetford, where he was born Oct. 2, 1806. Their children were: Charles H., born Feb. 7, 1841, and married in Belle Plain, Iowa, in 1865, Ellen Burley, and have three children: Lottie Bell, born in Clinton, Iowa, September, 1869; Milo Eastman, born October, 1871, and John, born in Tipton, Iowa, in September, 1873; Charlotte L., born Oct. 3, 1843, and died Sept. 27, 1867; and Isabella M., born May 26, 1846, and married Feb. 27, 1873, Edwin N., son of John Williams of Elgin, Ill.

viii. Mary Hall, born Sept. 17, 1817, and died Oct. 26, 1832.

ix. David Hall, born Aug. 29, 1819, and married in Norwich, Vt., Mar. 1, 1855, Nancy D. Tallman. He is a farmer, and is living (1873) in Norwich, Vt. They have three children: Mary Emma, born May 3, 1856; John Tallman, born Mar. 5, 1861, and Lizzie O., born Dec. 31, 1864.

x. Elias Lathrop Hall, born July 11, 1822, and died June 4, 1843.

1125. BENJAMIN, born June 5, 1782, and was lost at sea in 1805, having never married.

1126. ANNA, born Oct. 17, 1784, and married in 1808, Elias Woodward, a painter in Chelsea, Vt. She died in Boston, Mass., Apr. 14, 1867, and he in Chelsea, Vt., in 1810. They had four children, all born in Chelsea:

i. Susan Bliss Woodward, born Aug. 10, 1809, and from 1852, for four teen years, was in California, going by way of Cape Horn. She is now in Charlestown, Mass., after returning from her second residence in California.

ii. Emily Gorton Woodward, born Oct. 10, 1811, and married in 1845, Nathaniel Pennock, who died in Boston several years ago, and she died in 1868. Their children were: Arthur, born in Boston, Dec. 24, 1852, and Susan Adelia, born in Boston in 1855, both of whom are now living in Somerville, Mass.

iii.  Leander Woodward, born Oct. 1813, and died in Vergennes, Vt., in 1836.

iv.  William Woodward, born in 1825, and married in Boston, in 1854, Caroline Hannah.  He died in Boston in 1866.

1127.  DYCE, born Aug. 6, 1788, and married Elijah Gleason of Grantham, N. H.  They had a number of children, of whom a daughter Marcia married Professor Bond, a music teacher of Boston.

### 556.  LEBBEUS.                                  Bozrah, Conn.

1128.  POLLY, who married Jasper Woodworth of Bozrah, as his second wife. She is not known to have had but a single son by him:  Charles Woodworth, born in Bozrah, and became a carpenter.  He removed to the West.

1129.  LEBBEUS, born in Bozrah, in 1780, and married Lucretia, daughter of William Maples.  He lived in south part of the town of Bozrah, until about 1830, when he moved into Lebanon, where he died Jan. 25, 1866.

### 557.  THADDEUS.                                  Canaan, N. H.

1130.  ELISHA, married Elizabeth Griswold of Lebanon, N. H., and settled in Chelsea, Vt., where he died.

1131.  HARRIS GORTON, born in Canaan, Vt., Apr. 30, 1781, and married in Enfield, N. H., Mar. 9, 1809, Susanna Stevens, who was born in Enfield, Feb. 21, 1783.  She died in Canaan, Jan. 22, 1852, and he in Springfield, N. H., in March, 1864.

1132.  THOMAS, went to California.  Four children: James (M.D.), Benjamin G., Thomas, and Elizabeth.

1133.  THADDEUS, married Betsey Eastman of Canaan, N. H., and moved to Strongville, O., in 1816.  Died ——.

1134.  CAROLINE, married —— Hilliard and went West.

1135.  ANNA, married —— Barker of Barre, Vt.

1136.  PAMELIA, married —— Head, son of John C. Head, Quaker Village, Hartland, Vt.

### 558.  ELIJAH.                                  Lebanon, N. H.

1137.  JAMES, born in Norwich, Apr. 22, 1764, and married in New London, Conn., Dec. 12, 1790, Parthenia Bliss.  He settled in Hartford, Conn., where he spent his life.  He and his wife were both members of the First Congregational Church, under the pastorate of the Rev. Dr. Nathan Strong.  Mrs. Lathrop was especially noted for her cheerful and beneficent piety.  She died May 3, 1813, at 45 years of age.  He died on the 20th of the same month.

1138.  POLLEY, born Apr. 21, 1766, married —— Fish.

1139.  JOHN, born June 4, 1768.  He began life by "riding post," supplying a circuit of towns with their weekly newspapers.  He became a Baptist preacher, and died in Canada.

1140.  URBAN, born Mar. 24, 1770, married and had a family.

1141.  ELIZABETH, born Mar. 23, 1772, married —— Fish.  She died Nov. 15, 1814.

1142. DENISON, born in Lebanon, N. H., Dec. 25, 1773, and married (1), Oct. 26, 1797, Anna Baker, who was born Mar. 21, 1775, and died Oct. 20, 1815; (2), Belinda Finney, Mar. 17, 1818, who was born Mar. 4, 1782, and died Apr. 26, 1829; (3), Mrs. Esther (Ferguson) Bettallack, Jan. 12, 1830, who was born Oct. 22, 1793, and died Jan. 28, 1851. He died Dec. 19 (25), 1846. He purchased July 2, 1823, a part of No. 94 of the original lots laid in the city of Buffalo; and Nov. 3, 1825, No. 201 of the original survey. He also bought, Apr. 16, 1825, Nos. 144 and 145 of the original Buffalo lots.

1143. ELIJAH, born Feb. 24, 1775, and married in 1804, Mary Porter. He lived in Lebanon, N. H., until about 1812, when he removed to Batavia, N. Y. He died in 1871; his wife was born in 1779, and died in 1846.

1144. LUCINDA, born Mar. 1, 1778, married Uriel M. Woodworth.

1145. GEORGE, born Jan. 11, 1780. He married and had a family, of which I learned the names of three from their cousin Horace.

1146. FREDERICK, born Aug. 21, 1782, and married —— Eldridge.

1147. PARTHANEY, died May 3, 1813.

## 562. SLUMAN. Lebanon, N.H.

1148. AMOS AVERY, born in Lebanon, N. H., May 4, 1787, and died Nov. 20, 1798.

1149. GEORGE HOUGH, born in Lebanon, N. H., Aug. 17, 1796, and married Feb. 6, 1821, Louis Waldo of Hartford, Vt. She lived in Lebanon, N. H where she died Nov. 25, 1859, at 63 years of age. They had two children.

1150. HANNAH NILES, born in Lebanon, N. H., Feb. 15, 1789, and married Dec. 28, 1817, Nehemiah, son of Theophilus and Lois (Gifford) Huntington. He graduated at Dartmouth College in 1803, and settled as a lawyer in Peterboro. N. Y., where he won distinction at the bar. See Huntington Family Memoir.

1151. KATHERINE, born in Lebanon, N. H., Jan. 11, 1795, and died Nov. 16, 1796.

## 565. AZARIAH. Sullivan, N. Y.

1152. AZARIAH ALLEN, born in Conn., May 5, 1780, and married 1802, Lucy Mallory in Onondaga Co., N. Y. She was born near New Haven, Conn., Aug. 20, 1781. He died in Chenango Co., N. Y., May 15, 1840, and she in Manlius, Ill., Dec. 8, 1846.

1153. ELISHA, drowned in Mississippi river. He left two daughters.

1154. ELIJAH, married Rachel Boutwell of Michigan, and had six children.

1155. SALLY, married —— Morris.

1156. POLLY, married Arnold Ellis, and settled in Sullivan, N. Y.

## 566. CAPT. SAMUEL. Lebanon, N. H.

1157. ALAMEDA, born in Lebanon, N. H., May 7, 1787, and died single, June 6, 1824, in Lebanon, N. H.

1158. LOIS, born in Lebanon, N. H., Sept. 24, 1788, and married Alpheus Cutler. They settled in Iowa and had eleven children. She is still living (1873) in Minnesota.

1159. ELISHA, born Aug. 24, 1790, and died single Apr. 28, 1837.

1160. ELVIRA, born in Lebanon, N. H., June 5, 1792. She married John Randlett and settled in Leavenworth, Ia., where she died Apr. 19, 1821. They had three children:

i. Elvira Lucretia Randlett, who was born July 1, 1816, and married Abraham Edwards, a merchant of Leavenworth, Ia., and had four children: John I.; Charles; Samuel K.; and Mary E.

ii. Samuel Lathrop Randlett, who was born Apr. 28, 1818, and married Eliza Parkinson, a planter at St. Mary's, La.

iii. Minerva Randlett, born Feb. 27, 1821, and married Adin Pushea of Lebanon, N. H. They settled in Evansville, Ia., where he was a merchant.

1161. SAMUEL, born in Lebanon, N. H., Apr. 8, 1794, and married Margaret Jackson at Leavenworth, Ia. He was a mason, and died Mar. 19, 1853, at Cannelton, Ind. They had five daughters.

1162. WILLIAM, born in Lebanon, N. H., Apr. 15, 1796.

1163. SALLY, born in Lebanon, N. H., July 21, 1798, and married, Dec. 17, 1819, Thomas, son of Thomas and Susan (Leonard) Truman of Boston, Mass., who was born Mar. 14, 1794. They settled in Lebanon, N. H., where he carried on the cabinet trade. Their children, all born in Lebanon, were:

i. Sila Green Truman, born Nov. 26, 1820, and married, July 21, 1840, Capt. George W. Jackson of Louisville, Ky., by whom she had three children. After his death she married Dr. Cornelius White, a physician of Paoli, Ia., by whom also she had three children.

ii. Jedidiah Lathrop Truman, born Jan. 7, 1823, and married Elvira Saunders of Dublin, N. H., and had by her two children. They were living (1873) in Philadelphia, Pa.

iii. Orville Truman, born Mar. 10, 1824, and married Hetty Mariner, a merchant of Louisville, Ky., where they had four children.

iv. Horace Parkhurst Truman, born Mar. 18, 1829, and married Lizzie Flanders of Lebanon, N. H. They settled in Louisville, Ky., where he was a merchant. They had three children.

1164. AVERY, born in Lebanon, N. H., Apr. 15, 1801. He never married. He died Apr. 26, 1841.

1165. MARIA JEFFERSON, born in Lebanon, N. H., May 14, 1804, and married Julius Woodford, a merchant of Leavenworth, Ia. After his death she married Dudley Woodford of Connecticut, a farmer who removed to Uniontown, Ky., where they are now, (1873,) living.

1165-I. JEDIDIAH HYDE, born in Lebanon, N. H., July 5, 1806. He married in Alexandria, Va., Sept. 26, 1843, Mariana, daughter of Daniel and Mary T. (Barbour) Bryan of Virginia.

## 569. WILLIAM. Washington, N. Y.

1166. GURDON WILLIAM, born about December, 1790, and graduated at Yale College in 1809. He became a lawyer, and settled in New York City as early as 1818. He had a very good estate, and every promise of great success in his profession. He was unfortunate in his connection as law partner with Aaron Burr. He died of cholera in New York, in 1832.

### 574. WALTER. Franklin, Conn.

1167. HANNAH, born Feb. 25, 1780, married Joshua Waldo Raynsford of Canterbury, in 1800 (so Franklin records).

1168. WEALTHY, born July 27, 1782, and died in Franklin, in 1783.

1169. BENJAMIN, born June 24, 1784.

1170. WEALTHY, 2d, born July 27, 1786.

1171. DANIEL, born Mar. 23, 1789.

1172. MARTHA, born July 4, 1792.

1173. RODNEY, born Apr. 15, 1794.

1174. ELIZABETH, born July 26, 1800, in Franklin.

### 575. ASA.

1175. ABIGAIL, born Feb. 8, 1783, and died in 1790

1176. JAMES, born June 17, 1785.

1177. SUSAN, born Nov. 7, 1787.

1178. WALTER, born May 12, 1790.

1179. ABIGAIL, 2d, born June 10, 1793.

1180. ALICE, born Jan. 2, 1795.

1181. ASA, born Mar. 2, 1799.

### 580. CHARLES. Lebanon, N. H.

1182. EUNICE, born July 18, 1779, and never married.

1183. JOSHUA, born Sept. 16, 1781, and died in March, 1785.

1184. ANDREW, born Jan. 6, 1784, and died in Lebanon, Feb. 29, 1786.

1185. LUCY, born Dec. 6, 1785, and married, Feb. 15, 1810, Veach, son of Capt. Isaiah and Abigail (Williams) Loomis of Lebanon. She died Feb. 27, 1855, and he, Apr. 30, 1867. Children:

   i.   Charles Loomis, born Dec. 6, 1810, and married (1), Wealthy Grant, and (2), Frances Clark.

   ii.  Anson Loomis, born Jan. 14, 1813, and married Emily A. Phillips.

   iii.  Adgate Loomis, born Mar. 29, 1815, and died Sept. 19, 1839.

   iv.  Eunice Loomis, born May 6, 1818, and married Edward H. Strong.

1186. CHARLES, born Mar. 9, 1788, and married, Dec. 1, 1810, Roxey, daughter of Tennant and Susanna (Tennant) Chapman of South Glastonbury, who was born Oct. 7, 1789. They settled in Lebanon, but removed after the birth of their third child to the "Banks of the Ohio." He was a surveyor for the Government, and employed in laying out roads and towns in Illinois and Missouri. Kaskaskia and Vandalia were both laid out under his direction. He died in York, Ill., July 9, 1822. Mrs. Lathrop, after his death, returned to Lebanon, and thence to Colchester, Conn., where she is still living.

1187. ANDREW, born in Lebanon, Mar. 18, 1790, and married, Sept. 13, 1815, Pamelia Randall, who was born Oct. 1, 1798. In the war of 1812 he was called out June 9th to go for the defense of New London, when threatened, and served as an officer in Capt. Archibald Tuckerman's Company for

23

thirty-five days. He spent his life on a farm in his native town, where he died Nov. 13, 1870.

1188. JAMES WILLIAMS, born Sept. 13, 1792. He became a lawyer and settled in Canton, O., where he married, Apr. 26, 1826, Mrs. Susan Richardson. He soon became prominent among the leading men of the town. He was especially interested in whatever could advance the interests of education, both in the town and State. He was also brought forward in civil life. He was at the time of his early death in Columbus, O., Jan. 31, 1828, a member of the State Legislature. He left no children.

1189. SUSANNAH, born Nov. 5, 1802, and married in Lebanon, Ct., Jan. 4, 1832, Henry Otis of Lebanon. They live (1873) in Bozrah. They have no children.

### 582.  ABIEL.                                    Leroy, N. Y.

1190. LUCY, born July 19, 1790, and married (1), William Smith; (2), William Walbridge, Kero, Winnebago County, Wis.

1191. ABIEL, JUN., born Aug. 18, 1792, and married Ordelia Beckley.

1192. WEALTHY, born June 27, 1794, and married Erastus Bailey, in Leroy, N. Y.

1193. SYLVESTER R., born Dec. 12, 1796, and married, Mar. 23, 1820, Mary Beckley, who was born Jan. 2, 1801. We are glad to report his excellent life in the true words of the local obituary which was called out by his death:

"He had strong religious tendencies from his youth, but his religion was something to be done every day, rather than something to be believed. To be an every day, practical Christian was his highest aim, will be the testimony of every one who knew him. He removed from Genesee, N. Y., to Milwaukee, Wis., in 1846, and a few months later settled in Green Lake, Wis. There, in the prime of his manhood, his active intellect and earnest devotion were largely instrumental in giving a healthy direction to the moral and political sentiment of the county. His presence and his encouraging voice could always be counted on, at every public gathering for the promotion of benevolent or reformatory objects. He never shrunk from duty, nor counted the cost of its performance. 'Do right' was his motto, in public as well as in private matters. He thus won the respect of even those who disagreed with him on public questions. At various times he filled responsible positions in his town. A tender, loving, and provident husband and father, a pure and high-minded man in every relation of life, he has given us the witness of a truly noble Christian life, full of faith and good works."

1194. AVERY, born Nov. 19, 1798, in South Warsaw, N. Y.

1195. URIAH, born Oct. 20, 1800, in Columbus, O.

1196. HORACE, born Mar. 19, 1804, in Lapier County, Mich.

### 583.  ADGATE.                                  Pittsford, Vt.

1197. JOHN, born in Pittsford, May 11, 1794, and married, Sept. 24, 1821, Martha, daughter of Edward Clifford.

1198. MARY, born in Pittsford, Feb. 9, 1796, and died in Batavia, N. Y., Sept. 1, 1819.

1199. JAMES, born in Pittsford, Oct. 1, 1798.

1200. CHARLES, born in Pittsford, Jan. 2, 1802, and died in New York. He married Mary P——.

1201. HENRY, born in Pittsford, Feb. 22, 1804, married in Leroy, N. Y.

1202. FANNY, born in Pittsford, May 9, 1806.

1203. GERMAN, born in Pittsford, May 6, 1808, and died Dec. 23, 1869, in Pennsylvania.

1204. NANCY, born in Pittsford, June 4, 1810.

1205. CAROLINE, born in Pittsford, May 18, 1813.

1206. ADELINE, born in Pittsford, May 18, 1813, twin with the above.

## 586. BENJAMIN. Sunderland, N. Y.

1207. LUCY C., born Sept. 17, 1796, and married, in Arlington, Vt., Dec. 24, 1832, William McAuley, Jun. She died in North Adams, Mass., in October, 1862. Their children were: Lucy C. McAuley; Ann Maria McAuley; William Lathrop McAuley; John Glasford McAuley.

1208. JOHN B., born Aug. 29, 1800, and married, in Sunderland, Nov. 17, 1827. Removed to Arlington, Vt., in 1829, and still (1873) resides there.

1209. CAROLINE M., born in Sunderland, May 14, 1803, and now (1873) lives unmarried in Sunderland.

## 587. HUBBEL LA. Manchester, Vt.

1210. JULIA, born Dec. 18, 1805, and died Dec. 10, 1800.

1211. AUSTIN HARMON, born Apr. 14, 1809, and married July 25, 1835, Louisa King, daughter of Edward and Lucy (Lathrop) King. See No. 593.

1212. HARRIET, born June 30, 1811, and still lives at the old homestead in Manchester, Vt.

1213. WILLIAM HENRY, born in Manchester, Vt., July 16, 1816, and married June 22, 1842, Harriet A. Monroe of Shaftesbury, Vt., who was born June 11, 1821. He removed to Racine, Wis., in 1844, and still (1873) resides there. We are indebted to him for most of the record of his father's descendants.

1214. HUBBEL, born in Manchester, Vt., Dec. 20, 1819, and married Jan. 28, 1840, Parmelia C., daughter of Abner and Clara Hill of Sunderland, Vt.

1215. ELI BROWNSON, born in Manchester, Vt., Jan. 22, 1822, and married, Sarah B. McAuley of Arlington, Vt. They live (1873) on the old homestead at Sunderland, Vt.

1216. LAURA ANN, born June 10, 1824, and married, Aug. 31, 1842, Jerome J. Hill of Sunderland, Vt.

1217. CHAUNCEY ARANNAH, born Sept. 20, 1827, and married Aug., 1849, Ellen H. Wainwright of Middlebury, Vt.

## 588. SIMON LA.

1218. JULIETTE, born Dec. 5, 1819, and married (1), Jan. 24, 1839, Dwight Bradley, and (2), Jan. 6, 1848, R. S. King of Evanston. She died Sept. 1, 1873, leaving no children.

1219. HARRIETTE, born Apr. 15, 1822, and married B. T. Hunt of St. Charles, Ill., where they still live (1875) and have three sons.

1220. JERUSHA, born Feb. 20, 1831, and married Dec. 24, 1850, Noah Barnes. They are living (1875) in Hyde Park, Ill., and have a son and daughter.

### 595. GURDON. Canajoharie, N. Y.

1221. HARVEY, born in Canajoharie, Dec. 29, 1793, and died unmarried, Aug. 28, 1828.

1222. JONATHAN RUDD, born in Canajoharie, Dec. 28, 1797, and married, Oct. 5, 1831, Laura Foster. He died in Auburn, N. Y., Apr. 6, 1852, leaving no children. He was in the grocery business as his father had been. His widow married again.

1223. MARY ANN, born in Canajoharie, Apr. 28, 1800, and married Jan. 21, 1818, in Albany, William Buttre, who was born in Scotland and came to this country in 1802. They lived for a while in Auburn, and removed then to New York City. Children:

   i.   John Chester Buttre, born June 10, 1821, married Dec. 23, 1857, Elizabeth Belcher Warren. He has become one of the most successful steel plate engravers of the day, and is in business in New York City.

   ii.   Mary Elizabeth Buttre, born July 7, 1823, and died June 15, 1827.

   iii.   Mary Anne Buttre, born June 19, 1827, and died Nov. 16, 1831.

1224. GURDON LUTHER, born in Fairfield, N. Y., July 29, 1802. He never married. He died at Rock Island, Ill., in 1840.

1225. HENRY, born in Fairfield, N. Y., Dec. 24, 1806.

1226. A SON, born in Fairfield, May 1806, and died without being named.

1227. A DAUGHTER, twin with the above, also unnamed.

1228. AMY ELIZA, born in Charleston, July 9, 1808. She married in Nashville, Tenn., June 20, 1836, Julius, son of Dr. Erastus and Anne Humphrey of Canton, Conn. They lived in Tennessee for a few years, and removed to San Francisco, Cal. They had seven children:

   i.   William Henry Humphrey, born in Nashville, Apr. 23, 1837, and died Aug. 11, 1837.

   ii.   Anne Elizabeth Humphrey, born in Nashville, June 29, 1838, and died Aug. 11, 1838.

   iii.   William Henry Humphrey, born in Nashville, Apr. 18, 1840, and died Oct. 10, 1840.

   iv.   Mary Angeline Humphrey, born in Nashville, June 21, 1841.

   v.   Laura Adeline Humphrey, born in Clarkesville, Tenn., July 26, 1843.

   vi.   Alfred Lathrop Humphrey, born in Clarkesville, Tenn., Dec. 5, 1846.

   vii.   George F. Humphrey, born in Clarkesville, Nov. 1, 1848, and died in infancy.

1229. DEBORAH, born in Charleston, Sept. 21, 1810, and married Nov. 9, 1831, Seth Clark, son of Joseph and Elizabeth (Coleman) Earl of Nantucket. They lived successively in Auburn, N. Y., Nashville, Tenn., and Ottawa, Ill., where they were living when the recent war began. He and his son Charles M. were together in business, and dealt in paint, oil, glass, etc. He volunteered his services, and as colonel of volunteers did good service. He was killed at the battle of Jackson, Miss., July 12, 1863. Children:

    i.   Charles Manton Earl, born Aug. 28, 1832, married and lives (1873) in Chicago, Ill.

    ii.   Emma Elizabeth Earl, born Mar. 27, 1835, and married Nov. 14, 1860, Philo, son of Peter N. and Mary (Wilkie) Hard, a lumber merchant of Ottawa. They have one child, Henry Earl, born Jan. 1, 1862.

    iii.   Frances, born Jan. 1, 1838, and died Aug. 19, 1839.

    iv.   Frances Maria, born Feb. 22, 1840, and now live (1873) in Cairo, Ill.

### 596. ERASTUS.                     Lathrop Mills.

1230. ERASTUS CRAFTS, born at Lathrop Mills, June 4, 1801. He married (1), Mary, daughter of Rev. Uriel Spencer of York, Lucas Co., Ohio, who died July 5, 1840, at the same time with her infant daughter. He married again, —— ——, and she died within a few months and he himself, in 1841, in York, Lucas Co., O. He was a physician and music teacher. He was a christian man and a Baptist Elder.

1231. WILLIAM CAMBELL, born at Lathrop Mills, Feb. 4, 1804, and married in Henderson, N. Y., Laura Johnson. After her death he married the second time. He resided in Liberty, Wood Co., Ohio, where he died in 1851. He was a farmer and for several years a justice of the peace.

1232. EBENEZER, born at Lathrop Mills, July 4, 1806, and married Almira K. Dodge of Canajoharie, N. Y. He was early apprenticed to the cabinet business, but not liking it betook himself to the canal, as a driver. He soon left this for teaching, and finally became a lawyer. He was for years a judge of probate. He removed to California in 1850.

1233. JULIANN, born at Lathrop Mills, Apr. 6, 1807, and died in infancy.

1234. GRIFFIN CRAFTS, born at Lathrop Mills, June 6, 1809, and married.

1235. ALFRED CRAFTS, born at Lathrop Mills, Nov. 12, 1811, and married in Meriden, Conn., May 2, 1839, Stella Desire, daughter of Phineas and Desire (Cook) Hough. She died Feb. 14, 1873.

1236. JUDITH SABRINA, born at Lathrop Mills, Jan. 12, 1813. On the death of her mother when she was but five days old, she was adopted into the family of Dr. Wm. Campbell of Cherry Valley, N. Y., whose wife was sister to her mother. Her name was by the New York legislature changed from Lathrop to Campbell, and it is under the latter name that she is known as the "Genesee Girl and her little red book," and also, as that excellent missionary woman, the wife of Dr. Asahel Grant of the Nestorian Mission, to whom she was married Apr. 6, 1835. She died Jan. 14, 1839, at Ooroomeeyah, Persia.

1237. LUCY ANN, born at Lathrop Mills, Mar. 5, 1816, and died young.

1238. HARRIET J., born in Lowville, Louis Co., N. Y.; July 30, 1817, and married in 1811, Leonard P. Rising. They had five children:

1239. MARTIN BINGHAM, born in Lowville, N. Y., Feb. 5, 1819. He is still (1873) unmarried and a farmer at Spring Valley, Minn.

1240. ALBERT, born in Henderson, Jefferson Co., N. Y., Mar. 4, 1821. He is now (1873) living in Hartland, Livingstone Co., Mich., where he is a farmer.

1241. ALVIN, twin with Albert, lived but a short time.

1242. EMORY SPRAGUE, born in Henderson, N. Y., Feb. 1, 1825, and married November, 1849, Clarissa McMillan. He is settled as a farmer and miller in Glenwood, Pope Co., Minn.

1243. LUCY, born July 1, 1828, and died at ten years of age.

1244. AN INFANT, unnamed.

1245. AN INFANT, unnamed.

### 598. OLIVER.                    Buffalo, N. Y.

1246. HENRY.

1247. ELISHA.

1248. SEPTIMIUS, born in Charleston, N. Y., Mar. 7, 1807, and married in Albany, N. Y., Apr. 20, 1833, Louise Keyes of Otsego County, residence Saratoga. He died Jan. 31, 1874, and she died at Buffalo, Oct. 16, 1865. He was for eighteen years a partner in the house of Durant, Lathrop & Co., shippers from Europe to the West, and merchants in grain. A man of great benevolence and strictest integrity. He sent to Ireland the first shipload of grain and provisions during the famine, and was charitable to self-sacrifice during his life.

1249. SAMUEL, circus clown for 30 years! "Sam Lathrop."

### 600. ELISHA.                    Evanston, Ill.

1250. REV. SAMUEL GURDON, Methodist Missionary in Dakota.

1251. JAMES.

1252. MARY, who died young.

### 602. ASHER.

1253. POLLY, born Dec. 22, 1792.

1254. LYDIA, born Mar. 18, 1794.

1255. FANNY, born Jan 9, 1796.

1256. LUCY, born Nov. 6, 1798.

1257. HARRIET, born Jan. 6, 1800.

### 623. DANIEL.                    New Milford, Conn.

1258. LYDIA, born in Colchester, Conn., Nov. 12, 1787, and married Andrew Lamson of New Milford. They had three children, all living (1873): Amos Lamson, Burritt Lamson, Frederick Lamson.

1259. DANIEL, born in Colchester, Feb. 1, 1790, and married Aug. 15, 1812, Sarah, daughter of Beecher Fisher of New Milford, where they settled. He was a cooper. Both he and his wife were living when I visited New Milford in 1873, and gave me much of the information which appears in this record of the descendants of his grandfather.

1260. AMASA, born in Colchester, Conn., Sept. 30, 1792, and married Lucinda Clark of New Milfor  settled in Roxbury, Conn., and died in 1872 possessed of some we

1261. HENRY, born in Colchester, June 4, 1794, and married Angeline Owens. He lives (1873) in Naugatuck. Has three daughters.

1262. BARNABAS, born in New Milford, Oct. 29, 1796, and married Sarah Ann Driskill of Kent, Conn. He lived and died in New Milford.

1263. SALLY, born in New Milford, Dec. 20, 1798, and married John Mann of Becket, Mass., where they have lived.

1264. ALANSON, born Mar. 22, 1802, and married in Becket, Mass., where he had lived.

1265. JOHN, born Apr. 23, 1804, and married (1), Minerva, daughter of Tracy and Polly Beeman, who was born Feb. 15, 1807, and died Nov. 17, 1831. He married (2), Joanna Cook; (3), Oct. 20, 1859, Anna Maria Way, who was born Dec. 22, 1809. He died in New Milford, July 18, 1878. His family Bible supplied many dates for this family list.

1266. ANNA, born June 2, 1806, and married James Stewart. They live in Massachusetts.

1267. LAURA, born Nov. 25, 1808, married Stephen Keeler and settled in Bridgeport, where she died.

1268. HARRIET, born Oct. 13, 1812, married Wilsey Steward, and live in Massachusetts.

1269. ABIGAIL.

1270. GEORGE, son of the second wife, born Mar. 17, 1823.

## 624.. RUFUS. So. Cairo, N. Y.

1271. BARNABAS.

1272. ALANSON, a man of some enterprise.

## 627. SETH. West Springfield, Mass.

1273. BETSEY, born in West Springfield, July 28, 1788, and married, Sept. 13, 1808, Elisha Deming, son of Jonathan and Ruth (Deming) Andrews. He was born Feb. 18, 1783, graduated at Yale in 1803, and became a Congregational minister. He was settled in Putney, Vt., for over twenty years. He afterwards lived successively in West Bloomfield, and Mendon, and Pittsford, N. Y. His voice failing he became a farmer, and in 1840 removed to Armada, Mich., where he died Jan. 12, 1852. She, who had been a true help-meet, survived him until June 5, 1859. They were blessed with an excellent family of children, who with their descendants are worthily reported in the Andrews' memorial:

i. Seth Lathrop Andrews, born June 24, 1809, and married, Nov. 11, 1836, Parnella Pierce of Woodbury. He became a physician.

ii. Anne Amelia Andrews, born Jan. 8, 1812, and married, Dec. 29, 1817, Rev. Eleazer W. True.

iii. Joseph Lathrop Andrews, born Apr. 14, 1814.

iv. Charles Andrews, born Aug. 31, 1817, and died July 9, 1818.

v. Charles Andrews, born Aug. 28, 1820, and married, Jan. 29, 1845, Charlotte Hewit, and for his second wife, an Elliot.

vi. Edmund Andrews, born Apr. 22, 1824, became a physician, and married, Apr. 13, 1853, Sarah Eliza Taylor of Detroit.

vii. George Andrews, born Dec. 28, 1826, and married, Jan. 1, 1856, Mary Lathrop. He is a lawyer, and is settled in Knoxville, Tenn.

1274. SOLOMON, born Tuesday, May 11, 1790, and married, Mar. 31, 1820, Sophia Pomeroy, who was born June 5, 1791, in New Fane, Vt., a daughter of Willard and Catherine (Smith) Pomeroy of New Fane, Vt. She died in Oakwood, Nov. 15, 1853. He graduated at Yale in 1811, and became a lawyer. In 1836 he removed from West Springfield to Oakwood, Mich. He studied law with Uncle Samuel, with whom he went into practice till 1836. Went to Armada, Mich., bought a large farm, afterwards returned to Oakwood, where he died, Dec. 11, 1872. He was one of the most active in organizing the Congregational Church, and for many years its senior deacon, and beloved by all who knew him. "His work is done and he has gone to his rest with his fathers and his fathers' God."

1275. EDWARD, born Apr. 18, 1792, and married, Oct. 15, 1815, Emma, daughter of Jonathan and Ruth (Deming) Andrews, who was born Aug. 7, 1795, in Southington, Conn. He was an enterprising and thorough farmer. Settled in Armada, Mich., in 1837. He was one of the fathers of the town, and for his genial disposition was held in great esteem. He was as marked, also, in his own family, for the gentle and loving methods of his home management. He died Sept. 11, 1863, and his widow, Mar. 21, 1871, in Richmond, Mich.

### 629. HON. JOSEPH. Wilbraham, Mass.

1276. JOSEPH, born Sept. 21, 1791, and married Jane 'Iaria Leutner, who was born Apr. 12, 1795, and died Apr. 25, 1861. He was a merchant in New York, died June 23, 1833.

1277. ROWENA, born July 8, 1793, and died Aug. 4, 1793.

1278. WELLS, born Feb. 25, 1795, and married (1), in Springfield, Nov. 12, 1816, Catherine Rhodes Bonticow, who died Dec. 24, 1832. He married (2), Sept. 12, 1836, Lydia, widow of Dr. Lewis Washburn, and daughter of Benjamin and Relief (Dunbar) Ayer of Weymouth, where she was born July 30, 1806. He died Apr. 12, 1871.

1279. PAOLI, born May 14, 1797, and married (1), in Wilbraham, Apr. 20, 1830, Abigail, daughter of Noah and Statira (Hayes) Merrick, who was born in Wilbraham, Dec. 16, 1805, and died Mar. 24, 1850. He married (2), in West Springfield, Dec. 30, 1852, Elizabeth Brewster, daughter of Dr. Reuben and Pama (Stebbins) Champion of West Springfield, where she was born Apr. 3, 1818. He became quite a successful farmer, and an intelligent and trusted authority in the specialty of stock raising. He was much in office in his town and State, having represented his townsmen three times in the legislature. But he will be best known as a leader among the agriculturists of New England. For years he was president of the old Hampshire, Franklin, and Hampden Agricultural Society, and was also one of the trustees of the New England Society. He was in private life an excellent model, and won everywhere the confidence and love of those who knew him. How strongly he had won the hearts of those who were associated with him in his loved pursuits, the following testimonials show:

"But he has left to you and to all who knew him, the memory of his distinguished usefulness, his warm affections, his unspotted integrity, his unfaltering trust in God, his hope in life, his peace in death."—CHAS. C. SEWALL.

Mr. Marshall P. Wilder testifies to his excellent service in the cause of agriculture, to his gentlemanly virtues; and to the deep sense of loss felt by all who had been associated with him in advancing the interests of farming, and especially in advocating and securing the Agricultural College of the State. In an address a short time before his death, Mr. Wilder took occasion to speak of him in the following terms: "While we drop a tear of grateful remembrance over the graves of our departed associates, we would not forget one who still lives, our worthy and esteemed friend, Paoli Lathrop, whose interest in our cause has endeared him to us from the first, though his infirmity for many years has deprived us of his presence, but who has our sincere sympathy. May the remainder of his days be as tranquil and serene as his life has been exemplary and useful." Mr. Lathrop died at So. Hadley Falls, Feb. 23, 1872.

1280. SETH, born Jan. 6, 1799, and died unmarried, Oct. 3, 1834.

1281. ROWENA, born Dec. 2, 1803, and married, Oct. 3, 1828, Dr. Edward Goodrich Ufford, who was born Nov. 7, 1801, at East Windsor, and who was son of Dea. Joel and Lucy (Stanton) Ufford. He is a physician, and is now (1873) living at South Hadley Falls. His wife died of consumption, Oct. 29, 1853. Their children were:

i. Edward Wells Ufford, born Oct. 6, 1829, and died Sept. 17, 1850.

ii. Mary Gay Ufford, born Oct. 4, 1831, and died Feb. 22, 1858. She married, June 1, 1857, Truman Dunham. Child: Mary Ufford, born Jan. 23, 1858, and died Sept. 22, 1858.

iii. Joseph Lathrop Ufford, born Aug. 13, 1833.

iv. John Armstrong Ufford, born Aug. 10, 1835, and died Oct. 2, 1854.

v. Rowena Wells Ufford, born Sept. 20, 1839, died ar. 27, 1840. } Twins.
vi. Robert Hall Ufford, born Sept. 20, 1839, died et. 11, 1839. }

vii. Elizabeth Dwight Ufford, born May 19, 1841, a married Oct. 24, 1866.

viii. Edwin, son of Asaph and Mary (Gleason) Leonard, who was born Apr. 19, 1841. They have one child: Mary Valeria, born Jan. 19, 1868.

1282. RALPH, born Oct. 12, 1805, died Dec. 7, 1805.

1283. RALPH DWIGHT, born Aug. 29, 1807, and married Amanda Carpenter, who died at Wilbraham, Oct. 5, 1839. He died Feb. 11, 1838, in So. Hadley.

### 631. HON. SAMUEL. West Springfield, Mass.

1285. MARY, born Nov. 18, 1798, and died Oct. 4, 1800,

1286. NANCY HOLMES, born Sept. 14, 1800, and married, Feb. 15, 1854, Justin, son of Justin and Abigail (Belden) Ely of West Springfield. They settled in Omaha, Neb. They had no children. She died Nov. 12, 1866, and he in West Springfield, Jan. 15, 1877, aged 63. Mr. Ely was in the sixth generation from Nathaniel Ely, emigrant of 1636.

24

1287. SAMUEL, born Aug. 27, 1802, and died Dec. 17, 1825.

1288. MARY, born Aug. 18, 1804, and married, Aug. 3, 1824, Rev. William B. Sprague, D.D., of Albany. She died in Albany, Sept. 16, 1837. Children:

    i.    William Buel Sprague, born Apr. 23, 1826.

    ii.   Mary Lothrop Sprague, born Sept. 23, 1827, and married June 15, 1865, Theodore, son of John and Abby (Spencer) Townsend of Albany.

    iii.   Samuel Lothrop Sprague, born Dec. 22, 1831, and died Feb. 25, 1833.

    iv.   John A. J. Sprague, born May 6, 1834.

1289. WILLIAM McCRACKAN, born Nov. 18, 1806, and married, Nov. 4, 1833, Charlotte Elizabeth, daughter of John H. and Charlotte (Babcock) Belcher of Boston, who died May 8, 1840. He married (2), June 5, 1849, Maria B. Lefferts of Brooklyn, N. Y., who died Sept. 1, 1852. He married (3), Oct. 15, 1856, Elizabeth Kendall, daughter of Daniel A. and Abigail (Lord) Rogers of Ipswich, Mass. Died aged 69. Practised law in New York City, and afterwards secretary of Eliot Fire insurance company.

1290. JOHN, born Mar. 6, 1809, and married in Oxford, N. Y., July 24, 1838, Elizabeth, daughter of Epaphras and Elizabeth (Baldwin) Miller, who was born Dec. 13, 1818. He took great interest in the family in whose name he felt an affectionate pride. He collected an extensive list of the descendants of the Rev. John Lothropp of Barnstable, and at great pains and expense arranged them in tree-form, of which a number of copies were printed for subscribers. The only portion of the family traced to the present generation, are the descendants of the Rev. Dr. Joseph Lathrop, the eminent preacher and pastor of West Springfield. Of these there are about 150. Of the earlier generations there are about 300. Mr. Lathrop was a graduate of Yale College, class of 1829. The Yale Obituary Record for 1871, gives this account of his professional life: "After graduation he studied law in his father's office for a year or more, but not relishing the confined life of a student, he chose the profession of a civil engineer."

1291. SARAH MILES, born Feb. 20, 1811, and married, June 2, 1831, Prof. Henry Bronson, M.D., son of Bennet and Ann (Smith) Bronson, Esq., of Waterbury. Mr. Bronson received his medical diploma from Yale College in 1827, and the degree of A.M. in 1840. His standing in scholarship and in his profession, is shown in his appointment to the professorship of medicine and therapeutics in 1842, at his Alma Mater, and in his appointment to the presidency of the Medical Association of Connecticut. In 1860 he was chosen president of the New Haven County Bank. He has published a history of Waterbury, his native town, and in 1864, he contributed a historical account of Continental currency. Their children, all born in Waterbury, Conn., are:

    i.    Samuel Lathrop Bronson, born Jan. 12, 1834, and married, Nov. 30, 1861, Fannie E., daughter of Dr. Thos. Stoddard, Seymour, Conn. They had twins, born Aug. 29, 1862, and died same day.

    ii.   George Bronson, born Sept. 27, 1836, and died Jan. 31, 1837.

    iii.   Nathan Smith Bronson, Nov. 20, 1837, in New Britain, and married, May 29, 1861, Charlotte A., daughter of Burton Pond, Torringford, Conn. Have a daughter Alice, born Aug. 23, 1862.

    iv.   Stephen Henry Bronson, born Feb. 18, 1844.

1292. ELIZABETH DWIGHT, born Mar. 3, 1813, and married, Oct. 2, 1833, Washington Romeyn, son of Wm. W. and Mary (Montgomery) Vermilye. She died in Augustine, Fla., Apr. 11, 1874. Children:

i. Mary Elizabeth Vermilye, born Nov. 17, 1834, and died Jan. 18, 1836.

ii. Washington Romeyn Vermilye, born Oct. 2, 1837, a banker with his father.

iii. Samuel Lathrop Vermilye, born July 15, 1839, and died in infancy.

iv. George Smith Vermilye, born Mar. 18, 1840, and died early.

v. Samuel Lathrop Vermilye, born July 15, 1842.

vi. Emily Augusta Vermilye, born Mar. 24, 1846, and married Elbert A. Brinckerhoff.

vii. Arthur Montgomery Vermilye, born Mar. 4, 1849, and died in March, 1853.

1293. JOSEPH, born May 22, 1815, and married, Oct. 16, 1838, Abby Alexander, daughter of Medad and Jerusha Pomeroy of Warwick, Mass., who was born Sept. 16, 1815, and died Mar. 21, 1861. He has resided for several years in St. Louis, Mo.

1294. HENRIETTA BURRITT, born Mar. 22, 1817, and married, as his second wife, May 13, 1840, Rev. William B. Sprague, D.D., of Albany, and Flushing, Long Island. For children by her sister, see No. 1288.

i. Harriet Sprague, born Oct. 16, 1841, and died Dec. 14, 1841.

ii. Fanny Elizabeth Sprague, born Feb. 3, 1843.

iii. Henrietta Dwight Sprague, born Oct. 7, 1844.

iv. Edward Everett Sprague, born Jan. 3, 1848. } Twins.
v. Cornelia Martin Sprague, born Jan. 3, 1848. }

1295. MARTHA PERKINS, born Mar. 17, 1819, and married, May 13, 1840, Rev. Artemas Augustus Wood, D.D., son of Artemas and Catherine (Drake) Wood of Leominster, Mass., where he was born June 22, 1811. He graduated at Amherst College in 1831, and in theology at Andover in 1838. He has been settled as Presbyterian minister in New York City, over the Pearl street and the Broom street churches, and also over the Presbyterian church in Geneva, N. Y. He is now settled in Lyons, N. Y. They have had five children:

i. Edward Augustus Wood, born in West Springfield, Feb. 12, 1841, and is a graduate of the New York Free Academy. He married, Dec. 12, 1867, Mary Elizabeth, daughter of Dr. Genet Conger of Geneva, where he is now (1873) settled.

ii. Joseph Lathrop Wood, born Oct. 28, 1843, and died May 20, 1845.

iii. Clara Lathrop Wood, born Apr. 15, 1846, and died June 19, 1850.

iv. William Leffert Wood, born Dec. 25, 1847, and married, July 22, 1868, in Lyons, N. Y., Frances Caroline, daughter of Walter Taylor. He is now (1873) settled as bookkeeper in Indianapolis, Ind.

v. Halsey Lathrop Wood, born in New York, Dec. 7, 1849, and graduated at Hamilton College in 1870. He is now (1873) a student of medicine.

1296. ISAAC, born Mar. 1, 1821, and died Mar. 18, 1821.

### 632. DWIGHT.

1297. FRANCIS STEBBINS, born Nov. 10, 1806, and married, July 19, 1830, Caroline M., daughter of John M. and Sarah (Taintor) Gilmour. She was born June 7, 1807.

Mr. Lathrop, at the age of twenty-one, established himself in New York as a merchant, where he was soon after joined by his brother Dwight, and the firm ranked among the most prosperous in the city. The firm dissolved in 1852, and Mr. Lathrop became president of the Union Mutual Fire Insurance Company; held the position of president of Board of Marine Underwriters; was treasurer of Chamber of Commerce, and in 1877 was appointed receiver of the New Jersey Central Railroad. He was the originator of the Board of Riparian Commissioners of New Jersey, and president up to the day of his death. In 1869 Governor Randolph appointed him an Associate Judge of the Court of Errors and Appeals of New Jersey; he was reappointed and retained the position through life, and was best known by this title. Perhaps one of the most important works of Mr. Lathrop was the building of the State Lunatic Asylum at Morris Plains, New Jersey. He was president of its Board of Commissioners, and took a deep interest and great pride in the institution. He had full charge of all the expenditures, and the result has been eminently satisfactory to the people of that State. Mr. Lathrop was highly esteemed for his ability and wisdom, as well as for his wonderful energy. He was kind-hearted, and liberal to the poor. "A firm friend and a tender father." He died Mar. 3, 1882, at Madison, N. J.

1298. DWIGHT, born Sept. 23, 1808, married in Savannah, Ga., June 9, 1831, Mary Maxwell, daughter of Edward and Catherine Ann Howley Stebbins, and grand-daughter of Richard Howley, Governor of Georgia in 1780, and member of Continental Congress.

Dwight Lathrop was a merchant, first in Savannah and afterward in New York City in partnership with his brother, F. S. Lathrop, until his death, Feb. 1, 1851. The New York *Observer* of that date thus mentions him: "By his intelligence and energy, his liberal and comprehensive views, his truthfulness and uprightness, he merited what he enjoyed — universal confidence and respect."

1299. HENRY, born in West Springfield, Sept. 8, 1811, and married in Northampton, Mass., Sept. 26, 1849, Clara, daughter of Dr. Daniel Stebbins, by his second wife, Mrs. Elizabeth Gerrish (Knapp) Long. She was born in Northampton, Jan. 19, 1823. For many years he was a prominent merchant in Savannah, Ga.

1300. JERE STEBBINS, born Jan. 26, 1817, and married in Northampton, Oct. 23, 1838, Elizabeth, daughter of Charles and Elizabeth Gerrish (Knapp) Long of Newburyport, Mass., where she was born Dec. 22, 1813. He was a merchant in Savannah, Ga., for many years. Now (1883) retired from business and living at Northampton, Mass.

### 611. ELIJAH, ESQ.

1301. A DAUGHTER, born Feb. 3, 1795, and died in three days.

1302. LEONARD ELIJAH, born Aug. 26, 1796, and graduated at Middlebury

College in 1815. He was principal of the Wilmington Academy in North Carolina from 1819 to 1823; pastor of the Presbyterian Church in that place in 1823. Settled in the Congregational Church, Salisbury, Ct., in 1824, where he officiated about thirteen years. In 1836 he was settled over the First Presbyterian Church in Auburn, N. Y., where he remained fifteen years. Commenced preaching in Sharon, Conn., in 1853, and settled July, 1854. Called to Lee, Mass., and Cazenovia, N. Y. He received the degree of D.D. from Geneva College in 1840. He died Aug. 20, 1857.

1303. MARY ELIZABETH, born Apr. 16, 1800, and married David French of Williston, Vt. She died in 1829, leaving no children.

1304. LAURA LOUISA, born Oct. 16, 1802, and married Dr. John Hanks, a physician. They had three children. She died in Rochester, Apr. 14, 1853, and was buried in Mount Hope Cemetery.

1305. SILENCE LORENZO, born Jan. 7, 1805, and married Dr. Artemas Doane, a physician, and lived many years in Newark, N. Y.; then in Battle Creek, Mich., in 1848-9. They have had five children.

1306. A SON, born Jan. 29, 1808, and lived but a few hours.

### 644. ROSWELL. Windham, Conn.

1307. BENJAMIN HARVEY, born in Windham, Dec. 20, 1773, married Betsey ——. His grave, covered with stone, is on the east end of the Windham Cemetery. Children: Mary, Sally, Sybil, Betsey, Lord.

1308. SAMUEL BADGER, born in Windham, Dec. 25, 1776, and married (1), Prudence Simons; (2), Mary Harris of Middletown; (3), Mary Tinkham. He was a builder, and lived for many years in Springfield, and died in Hartford.

1309. ELIZABETH, born in Windham, March 28, 1779, and never married.

1310. CHARLES, born in Windham, Oct. 13, 1781, and married Lucy Bartlett, who was born in Norwich, Conn., July 4, 1783. She died July 10, 1821. He died Dec. 16, 1822.

1311. DANIEL, born in Windham, Jan. 23, 1784, and died at sea.

1312. HORACE, born in Windham, Feb. 15, 1787, and married Eunice Ripley. (See Huntington Family.) He was a lawyer of Cherry Valley, and representative from Otsego, in 1828, and sheriff, Otsego, 1831.

1313. THOMAS, born in Windham, May 30, 1789, and died Jan. 21, 1805.

1314. OLIVER, born in Windham, Jan. 13, 1792, and married, Feb. 23, 1816-17, Harriet, daughter of Eleazer Carey of Windham. He died in January, 1871.

### 647. ABNER. Windham, Conn.

1315. WILLIAM ABNER, born Oct. 28, 1797, married, March 28, 1824, Jerusha, daughter of Sanford and Anne (Welch) Hibbins, who was born Apr. 1, 1797. Her father was for years deacon of the First Baptist Church of Windham. He went to Oswego, N. Y.

### 651. JOHN. Windham, Conn.

1316. LAURA, born in Windham, Feb. 8, 1795, and married Thomas, son of John and Oliver (Fitch) Welch of Windham, where he was born Apr. 14, 1795. He was for many years a deacon of the Congregational Church in

Windham, and often in periods during which the church was without a pastor, the care which came upon him was scarcely less than that of a minister. He was an excellent singer, having in early life been somewhat noted as a teacher of vocal music. Mrs. Welch was remarkable for her large stores of general intelligence. Having been for many years a professing Christian, and showing in her declining years the patient resignation and assured hope of an intelligent Christian heart, she quietly passed away, July 16, 1857, at the residence of her daughter, Mrs. Huntington, in Stamford. Deacon Welch went to Cincinnati, O., to reside with his son. He died at Ypsilanti, Mich., Sept. 4, 1869.  Children:

    i.    Julia Maria Welch, born in Pomfret, Conn., May 25, 1817, and married in Windham, Mar. 6, 1843, Rev. E. B. Huntington of Norwich.  (See Huntington Family.)

    ii.    Thomas Henry Welch, born in Windham, Sept. 5, 1823, and married Clara Rent, Jan. 7, 1849.

    iii.    Charles Erving Welch, born in Willimantic, Sept. 16, 1849.

    iv.    Eliza Lane Welch, born Aug. 6, 1851, and died Feb. 23, 1853.

    v.    Clara Ellen Welch, born July 23, 1853, and died in Cincinnati, O., Aug. 4, 1855.

    vi.    Nettie Louise Welch, born in Cincinnati, Aug. 1, 1857.

1317. LEBBEUS, born in Windham, Mar. 1, 1797, and died in the same town, June 14, 1821. The local paper of that date thus mentions the death of Capt. Lathrop: "With the sincerest grief we record the death of this amiable young man.  Mild and unassuming in his manners, firm in his friendship, he was invariably a most dutiful son and a kind and most affectionate brother. His life was spent in the strict discharge of his duty, and his reputation was without reproach or stain."

1318. LUCY, born in Windham, June 8, 1799, and married in the same place, Nov. 8, 1819, Justin, son of William and Abigail (Clark) Swift of Windham, grandson of Rowland Swift, born in Lebanon, Nov. 3, 1793. They have always lived in Windham, where Mr. Swift has been always held in very high esteem, and has served his townsmen in many positions of trust. He was a merchant, and for many years was also engaged as proprietor of the Natchaug Mills, in manufacturing.  This most estimable and worthy couple are spending the quiet evening of their lives in one of the pleasantest homes it has been the writer's good fortune to know. May their sunset be as radiant and joyful as their business years were honorable and beneficent.  Their children, all born in Windham, were:

    i.    Abby Swift, born Jan. 22, 1821, and died of scarlet fever, Sept. 14, 1835.

    ii.    William Swift, born Mar. 16, 1823, and married, May 3, 1847, Harriet G., daughter of John and Mary Gray Byrne of Windham.  They have had two children: Willie, born Mar. 17, 1848, a Lieut. in the U. S. Navy, married, Sept. 2, 1872, Grace V., daughter of Commodore Ransom, U. S. Navy; and Abby, born June 29, 1851.  Mr. Swift is a merchant in his native town. He has also been for years a judge of probate for his district.  He was choir director of the Congregational Church of Windham.

iii. Sarah Swift, born Apr. 26, 1830, and died Sept. 1, 1835.

iv. Julia Swift, born May 21, 1832.

Mrs. Lucy Lathrop Swift died Sept. 20, 1876. This most excellent woman was one of the eight children of John and Sarah Lee Lathrop of Windham. Her grandparents on her father's side were Rev. Benjamin Lathrop, so well known in his generation, as an earnest and conscientious preacher of the Baptist faith, and Sybil Backus; and this grandmother was daughter of Sybil Whiting, who was daughter to Rev. Samuel Whiting, the first, and for a quarter of a century the very acceptable pastor of Windham. Her grandparents on her mother's side were Dr. Samuel Lee and Sarah Marsh, daughter of Dr. Marsh, the elder of Norwich. Both of these physicians were eminent surgeons, and both held commissions and rendered important service in the Revolution. Her paternal ancestry ran back from Rev. Benjamin, as above, through Benjamin a sturdy pioneer quite early in the Windham settlement; Hope, a Barnstable farmer, thrifty and enterprising in early life, and later an emigrant to eastern Connecticut; and Joseph, the boy-emigrant from London, to become an honored citizen here in Barnstable, Mass., where he was to endear himself to the people for his strong sense, and his sterling social and Christian qualities; to that Rev. John Lothropp, the pioneer of this family in America. First, as a curate in the English Church; secondly, as a leader among the Independents in London, and the second pastor of the oldest Congregational Church there; and thirdly, as the faithful and laborious minister of Scituate and Barnstable, Mass., he left a record of scholarship, and piety, and practical work, for which his descendants to the latest generations may well hold him in honor.

1319. LUCRETIA, born in Windham, July 9, 1801, and married as his second wife, Mar. 6, 1825, Chester Hunt, M.D., of Windham. Dr. Hunt was son of Eldad and Huldah (Benton) Hunt of Columbia, Conn., where he was born, Feb. 24, 1789. For more than half a century he was successfully engaged in the practice of his profession in Windham, and for most of that period his practice extended very widely into the neighboring towns of Lebanon, Columbia, Coventry, Mansfield, Hampton, and Franklin. No physician of the vicinity enjoyed, more than he, the confidence of the community, or of the medical facr¹⁻ Besides his own circle of practice, he was oftener than any other physician of the neighborhood, called upon in doubtful and difficult cases, and his judgment was uniformly found to be well considered and reliable. In addition to his medical practice, Dr. Hunt performed a great amount of public service. As deputy sheriff of the county he proved a most efficient officer, and in the discharge of official and professional duties the amount of work done by him was often almost incredible. His exposures and protracted work at length told upon his strength. Disease attacked his lungs, and for several years it seemed to his friends that he could stand it but a few weeks longer at the most. Though nearly laid aside at one time for months, he had so far recovered strength as to attend to professional calls again, and was really in the harness when he at last fell. Few professional men, even, are more missed at death than he, and in few did the community ever sustain greater loss. Dr. Hunt was a lineal descendant in the fourth degree from Dea.

Jonathan and Clemence (Hosmer) Hunt of Farmington. Their son Ebenezer married Hannah, daughter of William Clark, and had a son, William, born in 1705. This William married Sarah Lyman, and had a son Eldad, born in Lebanon, in 1742. Dr. Chester Hunt was the eleventh child of this Eldad, and was the son of his second wife, Huldah Fenton. Two of his brothers were also physicians, Dr. Orrin Hunt of Bolton, Conn., and Dr. Simon Hunt of Rochester, N. Y. All of these brothers attained distinction in the profession. They all possessed sharp discernment, and a sort of intuition which grasped at once the origin and seat of disease, and gave them great promptness in their diagnosis and treatment. Dr. Chester Hunt received his diploma in medicine, in 1815, and the same year was married to Lucina Barstow of Columbia, who died in 1821, leaving one daughter, Delia Benton Hunt, born May 3, 1817, and married to James M. Hebard of Windham, Nov. 26, 1845. He married as his second wife, Lucretia Lathrop as above. The second Mrs. Hunt was one of the most queenly of women in her figure and manner. She died in Windham, Aug. 2, 1863, and he, of consumption, Aug. 20, 1869. Their children, all born in Windham, were:

i.   Sarah Louisa Hunt, born Mar. 3, 1827, and died Apr. 6, 1828.
ii.  Chester Darwin Hunt, born Aug. 11, 1829, and died Aug. 28, 1835.
iii. Elizabeth Adelaide Hunt, born Mar. 22, 1831, and died Aug. 9, 1835.
iv.  Thomas Chester Hunt, born Dec. 10, 1832, and died Jan. 23, 1844.
v.   Charles Webb Hunt, born Dec. 26, 1834, and died Feb. 7, 1835.

The only surviving child of Dr. Hunt is, therefore, Mrs. Hebard, as above, now residing in Windham, and to her we are indebted for the excellent engraving of her father which appears in this work.

1320. LYDIA, born in Windham, Aug. 8, 1803, and married, in Windham, Sept. 21, 1829, James C., son of Timothy and Julia (Elderkin) Staniford. He was born at Greenbush, N. Y., July 25, 1800. Children:

i.   John Lathrop Staniford, born in Windham, June 26, 1831. He is a jeweler, and for many years had an excellent business in Bridgeport. He returned to Windham, where he still lives. He has never married.
ii.  Henry Eckford Staniford, born in Windham, Feb. 10, 1834, and married, in Bridgeport, Conn., Dec. 6, 1866, M. Fannie, daughter of Geo. F. and Hannah M. (Graves) Tracy of Bridgeport, where they live. Children: Henry Tracy, born Mar. 1, 1869; and Agnes Lambkin, born Sept. 5, 1870; Stuart LeRoy, born Oct. 6, 1673, and died Feb. 15, 1875; Agnes Lambkin died Jan. 5, 1877.

1321. LEE, born in Windham, Jan. 20, 1806, and married, Oct. 16, 1831, Frances Roxana, daughter of Jonathan and Roxana (House) Devotion of Scotland. He always resided in his native town, and was for years connected with staging between Norwich, Conn., and Springfield, Mass. After the introduction of railroads he removed from the village of Windham to Willimantic, and was stationed there as depot master. He died in Willimantic, Dec. 18, 1863, very suddenly, and deeply regretted by the community whom he so faithfully and acceptably served. His widow still resides at Willimantic.

1322. LOUISA, born in Windham, Apr. 1, 1808, and married, May 10, 1831, Benjamin Greaves, son of Benjamin and Rebecca (Ramsdell) Greaves of Lynn,

Mass. He was settled in the shoe business in Windham, Conn., where he died of consumption, Mar. 1, 1832. After his death, Mrs. Greaves devoted herself mainly to teaching. For many years she resided at the south as teacher and matron. Her record is that of a true and faithful Christian woman She is now (1873) residing with her youngest sister, Mrs. Ramsdell, in Windham. They had but one child:

Benjamin Lathrop Greaves, born in Windham, Mar. 6, 1832, and died in New York City, Aug. 10, 1868, leaving a wife to whom he had been married but a few months. For account of the military service he rendered during the recent war, as soldier and officer. see Stamford Soldiers' Memorial.

1323. MARY ELIZABETH, born in Windham, Oct. 28, 1812, and married, Apr. 2, 1833, Thomas, son of Isaiah and Clarissa Collins Ramsdell of Mansfield, where he was born Feb. 1, 1807. He settled in Windham, where for a number of years he carried on his trade as blacksmith. Later he removed to Mansfield, and became through great success in his financial ventures one of the skillful financiers of Windham and Tolland County. In 1867 he purchased the old Stamford hotel, corner on Windham Green, and built his family residence, where he now lives. Their children:

i. Anna Elizabeth Ramsdell, born in Windham, May 18, 1834, and married, in Mansfield, Feb. 15, 1855, Richard Goodwin, son of Abram and Hester (Goodwin) Waterous of Hartford. They settled in Hartford, and he is in the hat trade. They have had four children: Richard Goodwin Waterous, born Dec. 31, 1855; Clifford Waterous, born June 27, 1858, and died Oct. 12, 1861; Annie Waterous, born May 11, 1861, and died Aug. 8, 1861; and Thomas Waterous, born Feb. 8, 1867.

ii. Mary Louisa Ramsdell, born in Mansfield, Sept. 5, 1837, and married, Dec. 16, 1863, Guilford, son of Charles and Mary (Abbe) Smith, in Windham. They are settled in South Windham. They have no children.

iii. John Lathrop Ramsdell, born in Mansfield, Nov. 18, 1844, and died Mar. 17, 1848.

#### 655. REV. LEBBEUS.

1324. MARY, born 1797, died Aug. 15, 1801, aged 4, Mount Bethel, N. Y.

1325. WM. HENRY, born Jan. 15, 1806, and died Nov. 20, 1821, Sumptown.

1326. HARRIET MARIA, married Astor Runyon. Children: Albert Lathrop, Harriet Eliza, Emma Maria, Henry Wisner.

1327. LEBBEUS WISNER, born Jan. 20, 1816, married Jane, daughter of John A. Smalley. Children: Laura Lavina, Harriet Maria.

#### 657. JOHN HOSMER. Utica, N. Y.

1328. HENRY, who died young.

1329. SAMUEL KIRKLAND, born in Utica, Oct. 13, 1804. He married (1), June 3, 1829, Mary Lyman Buckminster, daughter of Rev. Dr. Joseph and Mary (Lyman) Buckminster, of Portsmouth, N. H. She was born in 1805, and died in Boston Jan. 20, 1859. He married (2), Nov. 23, 1869, Alice Lindsey

25

Webb, daughter of Rev. Abner Webb. He was settled as the first pastor of the First Unitarian Church organized in Dover, N. H., in 1828. Here he showed himself a faithful and zealous pastor, and won for himself the reputation of an able preacher. In 1834 he had attracted the attention of the Brattle Square Church in Boston, and was soon induced to accept its pastorate. It is no slight testimonial to his power that he has for so many years occupied the pulpit of a society which had such preachers as Colman, and Cooper, and Thacher, and Buckminster, and Everett, and Palfrey. He published the following: Centennial of Independent Company of Cadets, pp 59, 1841; History of Brattle St. Church, pp. 218, 1857; Life of Rev. Samuel Kirkland.

1330. MARY ANN, born in Utica, Oct. 16, 1806, and married in the same city, June 3, 1829, Edmund Arnold Wetmore, son of Rev. Oliver and Esther (Arnold) Wetmore of Utica, N. Y. Mr. Wetmore was born in Middletown, Conn., Aug. 6, 1798. He graduated at Hamilton College in 1817 and became an eminent lawyer, and for years was law partner with Judge Hiram Denio. He subsequently became largely interested in land agencies, and in a great variety of official positions to which he was called he rendered excellent service in many ways to his fellow citizens. As Alderman and Mayor of Utica, as Treasurer of New York State Lunatic Asylum, as School Commissioner of the State, and as Trustee of Hamilton College, his Alma Mater, his labors have been invaluable. Of Mrs. Wetmore we have in the *Wetmore Family* the following: "She has largely inherited the virtues and accomplishments of her ancestry, and she has cultivated her inheritance with a diligent assiduity. During her minority she enjoyed the benefits of education and society in Cambridge, the seat of Harvard University; her uncle, John Thornton Kirkland, D.D., LL.D., being at that time president of that institution, gave her an unusual opportunity to acquire useful knowledge and accomplishments pertaining to a highly cultivated and refined society. In society she has ever been a valued member and an ornament; by her fireside have her virtues been the most conspicuous; there that which graces the family circle has always been found."

1331. CORNELIA GREEN, born at Oriskany, ———, 1808, and married Charles P. Kirkland. (Wetmore Gen., p. 419.) Of her the compiler of the Wetmore genealogy writes, while speaking of the disease, consumption, which had brought her so early in her wedded life to the grave: "the disease siezed in this instance upon one for its prey, whose personal attractions and grace of manners, whose purity of feeling, cultivated mind and happy disposition, rendered her the charm of the domestic circle, and the cherished object of affection to her friends. . . This lady possessed great benevolence of disposition, and simplicity and gentleness of feeling." Children: Julia Kirkland: Cornelia Lothrop Kirkland, born in Utica, Dec. 4, 1831, married Alex. Seward, Utica; John Lothrop Kirkland, graduated at Harvard 1849, died; John Thornton Kirkland, obituary.

1332. WM. KIRKPATRICK, born in Utica, Dec. 3, 1810, and married in New York City, Sept. 11, 1833, Sarah Eayers, daughter of Matthew L. Davis of New York City. She died Jan. 17, 1874, in New York.

1333. FRANCIS E., married John Hiram, LL.D.—See No. 735.

1334. JOHN THORNTON KIRKLAND, born in New Hartford, Oneida County, N. Y., Dec. 25, 1813. Died in Washington, Texas, Sept. 15, 1849. John Thornton Kirkland Lothrop, Commander Texas Navy. His family connections were of the most distinguished·in New York and Massachusetts. His father, John H. Lothrop, was a lawyer of distinguished eloquence at the bar of Oneida county, cotemporary with Henry R. Storrs and Samuel A. Talcott. His mother, who survives, is a daughter of the distinguished Missionary Kirkland, founder of Hamilton College, and a sister of the late president Kirkland of Harvard University.

## 668. ROWLAND. Tolland, Conn.

1335. HORACE CRAFT, born Apr. 23, 1801, and married Lorancy Hanks. They settled in Ellington. Son Edwin at Waterbury, died in Middletown 1865.

1335-1. ELVIRA, born Apr. 13, 1804, and died Jan. 26, 1805, aged 9 months.

1335-2. GARDNER, born Aug. 12, 1812, and married a Mrs. Hudson of Cincinnati. He lived and died in Cincinnati.

1336. WILLIAM, born Jan. 8, 1806, and married Jan. 1, 1828, Elizabeth Drake, who died June 30, 1830. He married (2), in 1836, Olive Chaffe of South Wilbraham. He married (3), Mary Ann Thompson of Springfield, Mass., who died Oct. 3, 1858. Now in Georgetown, Florida.

1337. JOHN, born Dec. 24, 1810, and died May 29, 1813.

1338. BENJAMIN, born June 5, 1814, married Aug. 13, 1845, Mary Jane, daughter of Ariel and Mary (Winchell) Ladd. He died at Tolland Apr. 18, 1870, and was buried in Springfield, Mass.

1339. MARY, born July 27, 1817, and married George Waterman of Providence, R. I. They had two children: George R. Waterman, born in 1841; Arthur O. Waterman, born in 1843.

1340. ROLLIN, born Dec. 19, 1821, married Caroline Lathrop, Sept. 9, 1843.

1341. THOMAS CLEVELAND, born Feb. 22, 1824, and married Sept. 7, 1851, Elizabeth Chapman of Ellington, who lived but three years after their marriage. He married (2), Sept. 12, 1864, Marietta Ballou of Tolland. They are now (1877) living in Stafford Springs. He has a ·records of this branch of the family, first begun by his grandfather John, from which some corrections can be made of the printed lists in the Tolland history.

1341-1. JOHN, born June 17, 1830, and died on the twelfth day.

## 673. LUTHER. Wilmington, Vt.

1342. A DAUGHTER, born Dec. 10, 1796, and died Dec. 20, 1796.

1343. MINERVA, born Dec. 2, 1797, died Feb. 25, 1825.

1344. ALVA, born Feb. 9, 1800, and died Feb. 26, 1800.

1345. ELIZA, born Aug. 20, 1801, and married ——, 1838, E. Shaw. No children.

1346. LUCY, born Dec. 18, 1803, and married ——, Abner Allard. They had five children:

    i.   Minervia Allard; married (1), Willis Merrill of Waterbury, and (2), ——. No children.

ii.   Albert A. Allard, married in Baltimore, and was four years in the United States service.

iii.   Edwin Allard, married a Miss Boyd, of Wilmington, Vt.  He was in the Union army from 1862 till his death in the Wilderness, killed in battle in 1864.  They had four children.

iv.   Adelaide Allard, died young.

v.   Caroline, married Z. Wheeler in Wilmington, Vt., and had four children, three of whom are now living in Whitingham, Vt.

1347. LUTHER, born May 16, 1807, and died Apr. 14, 1815.

1348. PRESCOTT, born Jan. 31, 1810, and married July 31, 1831, Mary Kellogg in Wilmington, Vt., who died.  He married (2), M. Ross.

1349. CAROLINE, born July 22, 1811, and married in 1836, Horace Rugg, after whose death she married P. J. Watson.  Her children were: Harriet A. Rugg Watson, born May 4, 1837.  She married O. H. Pierce and lives in Fitchburg, Mass.; Austin Hall Watson, born Apr. 27, 1841; Sarah Eliza Watson, born Nov. 14, 1846, and died Aug. 10, 1851; Prescott H. Lothrop Watson, born Nov. 5, 1848, married Emma Barber, and has two children.

1350. ANGELINE, born Apr. 3, 1813, and died June 25, 1819.

## 674.  DAVID.                    Longmeadow, Mass.

1351. HALSEY, born in Feb., 1790, married Mahala ———.  They settled in Penn., where he died 1873.

1352. JOSEPH, born in East Windsor, Sept. 8, 1791, and married in Somers, Conn., Jan. 16, 1817, Caroline, daughter of Frederick Kibbe.

1353. ALMIRA, born Jan. 14, 1793, married Daniel, son of Daniel and Amy Blodget Porter.  They settled in Longmeadow, where he died at the age of 53.  She is still living, (1877,) and to her the family are largely indebted for much of the records of her grandfather's descendants.  Their children were: Elvira Cynthia Porter, born Feb. 11, 1817, married Isaac P. Olmstead; Harriet Delino, born Mar. 7, 1819, married Orra K. Simons; Araminthia Amelia, born Apr. 25, 1821, married (1), Merritt Aspenwall, (2), Henry A. Fern; Sanford Lathrop, born Sept. 3, 1823, married (1), Juliette Lincoln, (2), Charlotte (Schwart) Planks; David Taylor, born Sept. 6, 1825, and died in infancy; John Clinton, born Oct. 3, 1827, married Jane More; Emeret Eliza, born July 26, 1830, married James H. Butler; David Sherman, born Aug. 5, 1833, married Elizabeth Taylor; Eugene Converse, born Dec. 13, 1837, married Susan White.

1354. ANNA, born Dec. 24, 1794, married Chauncey Buel.  They settled in Ludlow, Mass.  Their children were: Angeline Buel, who married Charles Bennet; Cordelia Buel, who married Henry Kendall; Mariam Buel, who married Austin Newell; Amanda Buel, unmarried; Lucina Buel, who married John Dunbar.

1355. NANCY, born Mar. 13, 1796, married Samuel Billings of Longmeadow, where they settled.  Their children were: Nathaniel Billings, born Feb. 20, 1814.  He married (1), Harriet Ashley, and (2), Caroline Rhodes; Asa Hamilton Billings, born March 14, 1816, and married Sarah G. Eaton; Prescott Billings, born Jan. 18, 1822, unmarried; Fanny Billings, born Feb. 12, 1825, unmarried.  Flora Billings, born Sept. 30, 1829, unmarried.

1356. FANNY, born Nov., 1799, married Penuel McClure of Hartford, Conn., where they have lived. Their children have been: Amelia McClure, who married Theodore B. Chapin; Angeline, who married Hiram Newell; Almira, who married Edgar Ellsworth; Fanny, who married James Buffington; Penuel, 1827, married Hannah ———; California; Milton, who married ———; David Lathrop, who married Lucy Uson; Joseph, who married Nelly ———; Louisa, who married ———.

1357. SALLY, born Apr. 19, 1801, married Burgess Salisbury. They have had three children: Emily Jane Salisbury, born June 1, 1834, and married Oliver Wolcott; Elizabeth Salisbury, who died unmarried; William Salisbury, who married Marietta Griffin.

1358. LUCY, born May, 1805, and married George Clark Hall. They have three children:

    i.    Harriet Sophia Hall, who married William Rogers.
    ii.    Larone Lathrop Hall, unmarried.
    iii.    George White Hall, who married Celia Hale.

### 676. LORING. Longmeadow, Mass.

1358-1. WILLIAM, born July 1, 1803, and married Louisa Taylor, who died Oct. 8, 1857, aged 45. He died Dec. 17, 1848.

1358-2. MIRIAM, born Mar. 22, 1806, and died, as her gravestone attests, Mar. 5, 1829.

1358-3. LYMAN, born Mar. 12, 1808, and died Oct. 5, 1838.

1358-4. LOMANDA, born July 11, 1812, and married Lemuel Morgan. She died Dec. 27, 1846. They had two children: Augusta Morgan; Sanford Morgan.

1358-5. LORING, JR., born Mar. 27, 1817, and married, Apr. 6, 1848, Mary Ann Holmes. He lived in Springfield, where he died Mar. 3, 1863, as the family record reports it.

### 683. ICHABOD. Tolland, Conn.

1359. JOHN S., born Sept. 23, 1790.
1360. ORRA, born Oct. 4, 1792.
1361. ELIZUR, born Feb. 19, 1796.
1362. HOPE, born Feb. 12, 1798.
1363. SANFORD, born Sept. 1, 1800.
1364. MARIA, born July 8, 1802.
1365. HIRAM, born Dec. 1, 1804.
1366. SOLOMON, born June 8, 1810.

### 688. GRANT. Tolland, Conn.

1367. EMILY S., born Feb. 25, 1807.
1368. ASAHEL A., born Dec. 27, 1810.
1369. SOLOMON B., born Apr. 20, 1812.
1370. LYDIA M., born July 29, 1815.
1371. HORACE H., born May 1, 1817.
1372. OSMAN M., born Apr. 14, 1820.

## 695. ISAAC.                              South Indiana.

1373. SILAS.
1374. JOEL.
1375. ARTEMUS.
1376. ISAAC.
1377. ICHABOD.
1378. LOIS.
1379. SALLY.

## 696. SOLOMON.                            Michigan.

1380. HOPESTILL, married.  Children: five sons, and six daughters.
1381. ELIZABETH, twin with No. 1380.
1382. HORACE, resides near Ann Arbor, Mich.

## 699. PHILANDER.

. 1383. HORACE, born in Hartford, N. Y., Jan. 20, 1800.  The following
sketch is from a very appreciative obituary notice printed in the *Ohio State
Journal*, Columbus, Nov. 8, 1849:

"He enjoyed the advantages of academical training and discipline, in the
village of Montgomery, N. Y., where he exhibited a maturity of mind beyond
his years  At the age of nineteen he left his father's house, and sought a
western home.  He manifested great energy, and decision of character, and
enterprise, in thus early casting himself forth to win his way in the world.
He first settled in Waynesville, Ohio, where he spent eleven years in the study
and practice of medicine.  He later spent two winter sessions at the University
of Pennsylvania, perfecting himself in the various branches of medicine and
surgery.  He then removed to Columbus, and settled upon the spot where he
last lived.  In 1846 he received the appointment of physician to the Ohio
penitentiary, the duties of which he discharged with great fidelity and ability
till his death.  When the cholera broke out in the penitentiary in June last,
he met the demands upon his exertions and professional skill with great
promptitude and alacrity.  At length he himself became its victim.  He fell at
the post of duty, the more honorable as it was foreseen by him as a post of
danger.  As a professional man he aimed to merit and reach a high point of
professional distinction, and so successful was he that few at his age have
excelled him in scientific and professional attainments.  His jealousy for the
honor of his profession, his impatience with medical charlatanry, his upright
professional walk, his refusal to pander to popular and vague theories, may, to
some extent, have contracted the sphere of his professional labors, but these
estimable qualities have given him a place in the affections of an enlightened
community; and his memory will long be cherished as one who was an honor
to the medical profession."  He married Jane, daughter of John and Sarah
Worrel.

1384. ELIZA MARIA, born Apr. 16, 1801, and married Rev. Eleazer Lathrop
(No. 708), Nov. 10, 1823.  They lived in Geneva, N. Y.; St. Augustine, Fla.;
Port Gibson, Miss.; and died in Lima, Livingston Co., N. Y., Dec. 29, 1832.

1385. JOHN MASON, born Sept. 3, 1804, and died Oct., 1825.

1386. MARY MASON, born Jan. 23, 1806, married Dr. Kingsley Ray, and settled in Ohio. Is living (1873) in Circleville, Ohio. Their children were: Elizabeth Lathrop Ray, born Apr. 15, 1828, married A. J. Handy, and died without children; Janetta Miller, married —— Long of New York City, and died without children; John Eleazer, born Feb., 1831, and is now living single in Meadville, Pa.; D. Brainard, a clergyman of the Episcopal Church, and now (1873) in Grace Church, Harlem, N. Y.; Legh Richmond, living in Springfield, Ohio; Louisa West, who married Rev. J. F. Ohle, rector of St. James, Lanesville, Ohio, and has a family; and Frances and Edmund Mason who died in infancy.

## 700. ARMON. Sangamon Co., Ill.

1387. TRYPHENA.

1388. TRYPHOSA.

1389. WILLIAM, and others, names not learned.

## 701. COLBY. Ohio.

1390. BETSEY.

1391. LEANDER.

1392. ORESTES.

1393. EDITHA, and others, names not learned.

## 701-1. ABRAM. Sullivan, N. Y.

1394. ORMAN CARPENTER, born June 3, 1805, in Malta, Saratoga Co., N. Y., married in 1828, Cornelia, daughter of Daniel Denton of Sullivan. She was born at Eagle Village, Onondaga Co., and was in her twentieth year at the time of her marriage. He grew up in the wilderness amid pioneer experiences, including the deprivations and hardships suffered by settlers in a new country. His devoted mother, who was always the theme of his heartiest praise, feeling a noble ambition for the education of her son, took time from the absorbing duties incident to her circumstances to teach him the rudiments of learning; and when, at the age of eight he was sent to his grandfather's in Malta for a year's schooling, he was prepared to read with the highest class in the "Columbian Orator," and in his first day at school went from the foot to the head of a long spelling class. After his return to Sullivan he occasionally attended a short winter term until he was seventeen or eighteen years of age, and then taught three terms there and at Manlius, Onondaga County. This was the extent of his school privileges, but his subsequent private studies and taste for good reading, aided by native ability and a retentive memory, gave him the equivalent of a thorough education. He remained on the homestead until 1832, when he removed, via the Erie Canal and Lake Erie, to Chautauqua County, N. Y., where he had bought a forest-covered tract of seventy acres. On this he built a log-house, and laboring with the tireless industry which characterized him through life, cleared twenty acres with his own hands. In 1836 he returned to Sullivan and took charge of the homestead and a barrel and stave factory connected with it, the latter containing the first stave machine in the State of the modern pattern, invented by his brother-in-law,

Mr. George Pack. In the same year he entered the local ministry of the Methodist Episcopal Church, of which he had become a member in 1831, and in 1840 joined the Black River Conference and was appointed to Clay, Onondaga County. From that time for twenty-six consecutive years he labored faithfully in Onondaga, Cayuga, Jefferson, Lewis, Wayne, and Oswego Counties, N. Y., on circuits of which a single one in some cases now forms five or six independent charges. He was earnest and effective in his discourses, and judicious in counsel and administration. In April, 1866, he retired from the active ministry and settled on a farm near Fulton Oswego County, where he lived to advanced age, enjoying the highest esteem of his neighbors and acquaintances for his intelligence, integrity, and agreeable, social qualities.

1396. ORILLA, married Lyman Aldrich.

1397. MINERVA.

1398. MARIA, married George Pack in 1829, and spent the later portion of her life at Lexington, Mich.

1399. MARY ANN, Atkins, Mich.

1400. ORAN. For some years a Methodist minister, and subsequently a successful business man in northern and western New York.

1401. MARCIA, married Stephen Vibbert of Sullivan, afterwards at Atkins, Mich.

1402. MELISSA, married James Hudson of Manlius, Onondaga Co., died in Michigan.

1403. OSCAR, removed to Wisconsin in 1862. Served in Union Army during the Civil War.

1404. MELINDA, married as his second wife, Stephen Vibbert.

### 705. SALMON. Carbondale, Pa.

1405. LYDIA SOPHRONIA, born in Sherburne, Chenango Co., N. Y., Feb. 4, 1809, and married, Oct. 9, 1828, David B Blanchard. They had one daughter: Helen Dwight Blanchard, born in Carbondale, Pa., Aug. 18, 1829, and married, Oct. 4, 1858, Jeremiah P. Foster of Des Moines, Iowa. She died in Equality, Ill., Nov. 8, 1838.

1406. DWIGHT NOBLE, born in Sherburne, July 28, 1811, and married, July 1, 1838, Harriet, daughter of John and Mary (Grant) Ridgeway. Judge Lathrope died very suddenly at Carbondale, Oct. 8, 1872, of paralysis; during the most of his life he was an assiduous and very successful attorney in Carbondale, but retired from active practice some years since with an ample competence, and has since been much of the time absent on travels in the west, in the south, and in Europe. Improvement in health, which had become somewhat impaired by close and unremitting application to professional business, was one of the objects sought in these travels. He seemed to have attained it in a good measure, but a silent, concealed foe has thus suddenly in an hour, almost in a moment, sapped the foundations of life, and removed an honored and beloved citizen. Mr. Lathrope's age at the time of his death was about sixty-two years.

1407. MARCIA MIRANDA, born in Sherburne, N. Y., Sept. 19, 1814, and died Feb. 6, 1819.

1408. LUCRETIA JENNETTE, born in Sherburne, Jan. 25, 1818, and married, Mar. 17, 1836, William, son of George and Abby Wurts, who was born in Montville, Morris County, N. J., Nov. 25, 1809, and died July 15, 1858. Children:

    i.   George Lathrop Wurts, born Mar. 20, 1837, at Wilkesbarre. He died Oct. 30, 1838.

    ii.   Helen Sophronia Wurts, born Aug. 12, 1839.

    iii.   Harriet Lathrop Wurts, born Feb. 8, 1842; married May 7, 1863, Rev. Franklin Chappell Jones.

    iv.   Theodore Frelinghuysen Wurts, born May 31, 1844, at Wilkesbarre; married, at Belvidere, Warren County, N. Y., Apr. 8, 1868, Anna Vanuxem, daughter of Edward and Elizabeth Kruxen Vanuxem.

    v.   Eliza Aurelia Wurts, born Oct. 25, 1846, at Wilkesbarre.

    vi.   William Alexander Wurts, born Jan. 14, 1851, at Carbondale.

    vii.   Frederick Henry Wurts, born July 13, 1853, at Carbondale.

    viii.   George Albert Wurts, born Jan. 30, 1856, at Carbondale; died May 17, 1862, at Carbondale.

1409. DUDLEY WATSON, born in Sherburne, N. Y., June 1, 1820, and died in Florida, Montgomery County, N. Y., Oct. 14, 1821.

1410. CHARLES EDWARD, born in Bloomingburg, Sullivan County, N. Y., Mar. 5, 1827, and married, at Wilkesbarre, Pa., Feb. 18, 1849, Charlotte, daughter of Jesse and Hannah Dilley. He was educated as a printer, and was editor and publisher of different newspapers for about ten years. During these years he was prosecuting the study of law, and was admitted to the Bar at Wilkesbarre, Pa., in January, 1857. Removing to Independence, Ia., he commenced the practice of law there the same year, where he remained until 1861, when he accepted a clerkship in t'e Navy Department in Washington City. In 1863 he was appointed naval storekeeper at the Washington Navy-yard, at which post he continued serving the Government until January, 1867. In the April following he was appointed superintendent of the Government Printing Office, from which post he removed in 1869 to Carbondale, where he now resides, and resumed the practice of law.

1411. FREDERICK HENRY, born in Carbondale, Oct. 13, 1833, and died Jan. 27, 1834.

### 706. CURTIS.         Lockport, N. Y.

    1412.   WILLIAM BRUFFEE, born in Homer, Nov. 15, 1816.

    1413.   SALLY SOPHRONIA, born in Homer, Feb. 14, 1817.

    1414.   LUCY CAROLINE, born in Geneseo, Oct. 16, 1819.

    1415.   FIDELIA, born in Geneseo, Oct. 20, 1821.

    1416.   JANE, born in Geneseo, June 16, 1823, died in 1858.

    1417.   LUCETTA A., born in Geneseo, May 26, 1825, died in 1826.

    1418.   AURELIA, born in Geneseo, Feb. 15, 1827, died in 1838.

    1419.   LOUSIA, born in Lockport, Nov. 12, 1828, died in 1836.

    1420.   CHILD, unnamed, born June, 1830, died same year.

    1421.   HELEN, born in Lockport, July 13, 1831, died June 1845.

    1422.   MYRON BROWN, born in Lockport, Feb. 23, 1833, died Oct. 18, 1819.

26

1423.  MIRIAM LOUISA, born in Lockport, Feb. 26, 1834, died July 4, 1834.
1424.  CHARLES ELEAZER, born in Lockport, July 16, 1835, died Oct., 1859.
1425.  HENRY DWIGHT, born in Lockport, Oct. 13, 1836.
1426.  MIRIAM THURSTON, born in Lockport, March 13, 1838, died same year.
1427.  LEWIS BACON, born in Lockport, Aug. 26, 1839, died in 1861.

### 708.  REV. ELEAZER.

1428.  ELIZABETH, born Nov. 1, 1821, and died Aug. 6, 1825.

1429.  HENRY DURANT, born Sept. 13, 1829, in Elmira, N. Y.; went in 1831 to Ohio; graduated from Kenyon College, Gambier, O., in 1853; was principal of Kenyon Grammar School.  He entered the ministry of the Episcopal Church in 1862; was Rector of St. John's, Lancaster, O., till February, 1864, and in the service of the U. S. Church Committee till June 1, 1865; Rector of St. John's, Gold Hill, Nevada, till Sept. 1, 1867; Rector of Church of the Advent, San Francisco, from 1867.  He received the degree of D.D. by Kenyon College in 1870.  He married, Sept. 4, 1855, Sarah Burrows McElroy.

### 712.  JASON.                    Perry, N. Y.

1430.  M. AMELIA, born in Albion, N. Y., Aug. 17, 1832.
1431.  HELEN A., born in Perry, Mar. 31, 1834.
1432.  ELIZA A., born in Perry, Mar. 28, 1838.
1433.  ARISTINE, born in Perry, June 28, 1857.

### 717.  LEWIS LA.                    Sherburne, N. Y.

1434.  JOHN MILTON, born in Sherburne, May 6, 1813, and died in Clinton, Madison County, May 16, 1837.

1435.  HARRIET ANN, born in Sherburne, June 21, 1815, and married Nelson Brown, who was born Apr. 12, 1812, and who died in Burlington, Otsego County, N. Y., Oct. 12, 1852.  She died at Sherburne, Nov. 14, 1845.  Their children were: John Milton Brown, born in New Berlin, Apr. 20, 1841, and died at Sherburne, Oct. 4, 1845; Ellen Lathrop Brown, born in New Berlin, Sept. 16, 1842, married, in Sherburne,  uly 21, 1869, Rev. Dwight K. Barker, who was born in Utica, N. Y , Mar. 3' 1833.  Settled in Rochester.

1436.  CORNELIA, born in Sherburne  Sept. 13, 1825, and married, in Sherburne, Sept. 1, 1846, Seneca B. Rexford, who was also born in Sherburne, Dec. 12, 1822, and died July 11, 1856.

1437.  GEORGE WATTS, born in Sherburne, Mar. 29, 1829, and married Mary E. Havely, who was born in Sherburne, Oct. 10, 1830.  They settled in Algoma, Wisconsin.

1438.  CHARLES DWIGHT, born in Sherburne, Mar. 29, 1829, and died April 12, 1829.

### 724.  JOHN H.

1439.  MARY W., born May 25, 1815.
1440.  ELIZA, born June 17, 1819.
1441.  CHARLES, born Sept. 4, 1820, and died in March, 1823.

1442. DAVID L., born Dec. 17, 1822.

1443. CAROLINE A., born Feb. 8, 1825, and married, Dec. 28, 1841, Philo Remington of the " Remington Fire Arms."  Children:

i.  Ida Remington, born Nov. 2, 1842, married, Dec. 23, 1868, W. C. Squire, General Agent E. Remington & Sons.  Children: Philo Remington Squire, born Feb. 22, 1870; Shirley Squire, born Apr. 13, 1872.

ii.  Ella Remington, born June 18, 1845, and married E. P. Greene of Amsterdam, a manufacturer.  Their children are: Frank Remington Greene, born Nov. 27, 1867; William K. Greene, born in Dec., 1869; and Harry Priest Greene, born in Nov., 1871.

1444. EBENEZER, born Feb. 1, 1828, and married, May 3, 1855, Charlotte B. Wallace.

1445. SUSAN, born Apr. 12, 1830, and died in September, 1831.

1446. JOHN, born Feb. 28, 1832.

### 735.  JOHN HIRAM, LL.D. (CHANCELLOR.)

1447. JOHN HOSMER, born June 23, 1834, and died single in April, 1857.

1448. LEOPOLD, born Aug. 8, 1835, and died single Apr. 27, 1858.

1449. JERUSHA, born May 8, 1838, and died Sept. 10, 1839.

1450. KIRKLAND, born Feb. 13, 1840, and died Dec. 24, 1840.

1451. FRANCES E., born Nov. 25, 1842, and married, Oct. 19, 1871, William Medill Smith, at Columbia, Mo.  He is a lawyer of Kansas City, Mo.  They have three children: Floy, born Mar. 2, 1876; Medill, born Sept. 16, 1879; John Lathrop, born July 2, 1882.

1452. THERESA, born Nov. 25, 1846; married Charles C. Ripley, Oct. 21, 1875.  They have one child: John Lathrop, born Feb. 27, 1881.

1453. GARDINER, born Feb. 16, 1850; married Eva Grant, Jan. 16, 1879. They have two children: Fannie, born Mar. 10, 1880; Jessie, born Mar. 31, 1881.

### 737.  MARCUS.

1454. JOHN MILES, born Nov. 22, 1828, and died July 28, 1831.

1455. CAROLINE DIANTHA, born Aug. 18, 1831.

1456. WILLIAM HOPKINS, born May 4, 1833, and married, in 1862, in Cincinnati, O., Mary A., daughter of Samuel and Mary Sargent.  He graduated at Hamilton College in 1853, and studied law.  "A man of fine talents, unquestioned ability, and was very highly esteemed and respected by all who knew him.  From a patriotic sense of duty, he entered the service as Lieutenant in the Thirty-ninth Ohio Volunteers; was soon promoted to Colonel of the One Hundred and Eleventh U. S. A., Colored Infantry," and fell while bravely defending an important post on the Northern Alabama Railroad.

The brave and gallant Colonel has fallen, but the memory of his noble deeds, his patriotism, his heroism, will be a precious heritage to those who deeply, sadly mourn his loss.

1457. JOHN CHARLES, born Jan. 11, 1836, and married, Apr. 1, 1866, Mary A., daughter of Justus H. and Mary A. Hawley.

1458. FRANCES AMANDA, born Mar. 31, 1841, and died Mar. 1, 1842.

### 740. CHARLES H.

**1459.** WILLIAM NEWTON, born Sept. 5, 1843, and died Mar. 18, 1858.

**1460.** CHARLES HENRY, born Sept. 1, 1849, and married, Jan. 5, 1871, Alice G., daughter of Russel and Cordelia Alcott of Sherburne.

**1461.** HOMER, born July 19, 1853, and died Apr. 4, 1854.

### 741. PROF. ALVAN.          Rochester, Vt.

**1462.** ALLEN KIRKLAND, born June 4, 1837, and died Mar. 5, 1841.

**1463.** CHARLOTTE EMILY, born in Poughkeepsie, Mar. 14, 1839, and married, Dec. 11, 1860, M. Byron Rich, a lawyer of Chicago, Ill., where she died Jan. 3, 1862. She was a woman of great personal excellence, and is cherished in the strongest affections of those who knew her. She left no children.

**1464.** SARAH MARIA, born Aug. 23, 1840, and married (1), Dec. 22, 1858, E. R. Woodruff, a lawyer of Chicago, Ill., who died in Tiskilua, Ill., June 3, 1863. She married (2), Jan. 9, 1866, Charles Russel Garlick of Pittsfield, Mass., who was born Sept. 1, 1836, and who was an enterprising merchant in Pittsfield. He died suddenly, Oct. 16, 1869. She married (3), May 23, 1872, in Mansfield, O., at the residence of her cousin, Lathrop D. Tracy, C. H. Nichols, M.D., of Washington City, superintendent of the Government Asylum for the Insane. She has had no children.

**1465.** CHARLES HENRY, born in Poughkeepsie, July 16, 1843, and married, in Prescott, Wis., Dec. 18, 1871, May, daughter of John and Hester Martin, who was born in Stormont, Canada, Dec. 11, 1846.

**1466.** JAMES ROOSEVELT, born in Poughkeepsie, Sept. 1, 1844, and married, in Washington City, D. C., Oct? 9, 1866, Mary Elizabeth Richardson, who was born in Richmond, Va., Dec. 25, 1845. He entered upon his duties as superintendent of Roosevelt Hospital, New York City, Nov. 1, 1883.

### 743. E. HOLLISTER.          Brockport, N.Y.

**1467.** ELLEN AMELIA, born in Sherburne Nov. 29, 1835, and married Oct., 1853, John, son of Amasa Spring of Brockport They were settled in Brockport, N. Y., in the drug business. She died ' . Brockport Jan. 26, 1862. Children: Minnie Holmes Spring, born in Br￰ ￰port Apr. 3, 1855; Edward Lathrop Spring, born in April, 1857; Gertie Spring, born Apr. 9, 1859.

**1468.** MARY CORNELIA, born in Brockport, Sept. 30, 1838, and died in the same town, Aug. 14, 1841, of scarlet fever.

**1469.** HENRY HOLLISTER, born in Brockport Dec. 15, 1842, and died in Brockport of typhoid fever, Feb. 6, 1862. He had enlisted in the United States service and had reached Washington when taken down.

**1470.** MARY ADELL, born in Brockport Mar. 22, 1846, and died in the same town May 29, 1847, of measles.

**1471.** GEORGE REXFORD, born in Brockport Oct. 19, 1848, and is now (1873) in the publishing business, New York City.

### 745. ROBERT. Barnstable, Mass.

1472. DESIRE, born in Barnstable, June 12, 1795.

1473. MARY ALLYN, born in Barnstable, July 25, 1797, and died in October, 1870.

1474. TEMPERANCE LEWIS, born in Barnstable, Aug. 15, 1800.

1475. ALLYN, born in Barnstable, Dec. 4, 1802, and died Mar. 27, 1803.

1476. DAVIS, born in Barnstable, Nov. 28, 1804. He was a Baptist Minister in West Harwich, Barnstable Co.

### 746. THOMAS. Maine.

1477. CAROLINE, born Sept. 16, 1799, and married in 1826, James Flood.

1478. EBENEZER, born Dec. 28, 1800, and died at sea about 1819.

1479. ANSEL, born Mar. 20, 1804, and married May 27, 1832, Clarissa, daughter of Bowen and Hannah Crehore of Milton, Mass. He is a master builder of Boston. No children.

1480. WILLIAM, born May 18, 1805, and died July 19, 1819.

1481. CHARLES, born Sept. 8, 1807, and died at 4 years of age.

### 747. EBENEZER.

1482. THOMAS, born Feb. 26, 1800, and married, Apr. 30, 1826, Rebecca Cook of Provincetown, Mass., where he resides.

,1483. MEHITABLE, born Jan. 29, 1802, and married, July 20, 1823, Leander Stafford of Salem, Conn. They reside in Provincetown, Mass. Children:

i. John Stafford, born May 14, 1825, and died, Mar. 10, 1826.

ii. George L. Stafford, born Sept. 30, 1827, and is now living in Boston, Mass.

iii. John A. Stafford, born in New London, Conn., June 15, 1830, and married at Williston, Vt., Nov. 6, 1854, Lucia M., daughter of Daniel and Priscilla C. Robinson of Stowe, Vt., who was born, Jan. 6, 1832. They settled in Decatur, Mich., where she died, Dec. 24, 1864. Mr. Stafford married (2), at Morrisville, Vt., May 26, 1867, Mrs. Kate F. Baker, daughter of Jared and Sabrina Camp, born at Stowe, Vt., July 23, 1836. They have resided since then in Stowe, Vt., where he is a tinsmith. Mrs. Stafford's children have been,—the first four born in Decatur, Mich., and the last three in Stowe, Vt.: George E., born Aug. 10, 1855; Charles H. A., born Nov. 6, 1859; Sarah Eloise, born Jan. 6, 1862; J. Lathrop, born Dec. 16, 1864; Frank E., born May 22, 1869; Lela M., born July 20, 1871, and died in Stowe, Aug. 3, 1872; and Winnie M., born Oct. 19, 1872.

iv. Henry H. Stafford, born Jan. 5, 1833, and married, June 2, 1856, Kate Lewis Kidder of Boston, Mass. He is settled in Marquette, Mich., where he is a dealer in drugs, medicines, and fancy goods. They have five children: Edward Orr, born Oct. 19, 1858; Walter Kidder, born Apr. 15, 1862; Charles Mason, born Aug. 25, 1864; Henry Lothrop, born Dec. 18, 1866, and Alfred Cochran, born Nov. 7, 1870.

1484. ELIZA DAVIS, born in Barnstable Mar. 13, 1804, and married in

Boston, Mass., Jan. 31, 1830, Stephen Smith, son of James and Bethiah (Rider) Smith of Barnstable, where he was born Aug. 5, 1805. Children:

    i.      Eliza Davis Smith, born at Boston, May 3, 1834, married Oct. 16, 1855, at Boston by Rev. F. D. Huntington, to John Bishop Bartlett (son of John Bartlett and Eliza Finney of Plymouth, Mass.), and has two children now living, viz.: Stephen Smith Bartlett, born at Boston, Feb. 14, 1861; Annie Lothrop Bartlett, born in Boston April 8, 1864.

    ii.      Adeline Amanda Smith, born at Boston, Sept. 23, 1837, married by Rev. George H. Hepworth at Boston, Jan. 24, 1860, to William Henry Allen, son of Silas Allen and Mary Jane Presbry, and has one child: William Lothrop Allen, born at Boston, April 2, 1862.

    iii.      Charles Lothrop Smith, born at Boston, March 14, 1842, unmarried.

    iv.      Edward Francis Smith, born at Boston Nov 22, 1846, married March 29, 1870, at Hyannis, Mass., by Rev. W. H. Evans, to Harriet Ella Baker, daughter of Joshua Baker and Harriet Hallett; no children.

1485. ADELINE, born May 26, 1806, married in Boston January 31, 1830. to Ebenezer Sturgis Smith of Barnstable, son of Amasa and Hannah Smith. He was at that time a printer, but in a few years entered the mercantile business in Provincetown, Mass., where he has since resided. Children:

    i.      Ebenezer Sturgis Smith, born in Boston June 18, 1831, died in Boston Nov. 4, 1833.

    ii.      Amasa Smith, born in Boston, Nov. 17, 1832, married in Barnstable, Mass., Nov. 27, 1855, to Cynthia Phinney Chase, daughter of Captain Oliver and Mercy Chase. Occupation of Amasa Smith, merchant—residence, Provincetown.   Fred. Walton Smith, son of Amasa and Cynthia P. C. Smith, born Nov. 23, 1857, died February 24, 1861.

    iii.      Adeline Eloise Smith, born in Provincetown, May 11, 1835, married in Provincetown, February 2, 1859, to Lysander Howard Gurney, son of Azel and Mary Gurney, of North Bridgewater, Mass.; occupation, merchant. Adeline Eloise Gurney died in Provincetown, March 20, 1862. Left no children.

    iv.      Susan Sturges Smith, born in Provincetown, January 19, 1839, married October 17, 1864, to Raymond Ellington, son of Col. Raymond and Adeline M. Ellington of Louisville, Ky. Occupation merchant—residence Provincetown.

    v.      Eliza Frances Smith, born in Provincetown, May 17, 1841, married Sept. 7, 1865, to Isaac Newton Keith, son of Isaac and Delia Baty Keith, of West Sandwich, Mass.   Occupation, car manufacturer—residence West Sandwich; Adeline Eloise Keith, daughter of Isaac N. and Eliza Frances Keith, born July 30, 1868; Ebenezer Sturges Smith Keith, born Oct. 24, 1872.

    vi.      Ebenezer Harrison Smith, son of Eben. Sturges and Adeline Smith, born in Provincetown, April 19, 1847, died Mar 22, 1849.

1486. JOHN LEWIS, born in Barnstable, Aug. 27, 1813, and married, Nov. 2, 1836, Sarah M., daughter of Jonathan Nickerson of Provincetown. He entered on the practice of medicine in Provincetown in 1835, and in 1864 removed to

Melrose, from which place he went to East Somerville, Mass., where he now (1873) resides in the practice of his profession.

1487. TEMPERANCE LEWIS, born July 27, 1815, and married in Boston, Mass., June 13, 1836, David P. Howes of Dennis, Mass. Children: George P. Howes, born Aug. 25, 1840; Eben L. Howes, born July 1, 1842; Deborah P. Howes, born June 27, 1847, and married June 1, 1870, Christopher Walter Hall. They reside in Dennis, Mass., and have one son, Christopher, born Dec. 6, 1870.

1488. LUCY JANE, born June 16, 1817, and married, Apr. 20, 1841, Artemas Paine of Provincetown, where they still live. They have no children.

### 748. ANSEL. Searsmouth, Me.

1489. DAVID WHITTIER, bo n in Nobleboro, Me., Oct. 4, 1807, and married in Belfast, Jan. 22, 1832, Mary Jane, daughter of Jonathan and Jane (Patterson) White. He settled in Belfast, Me., as a merchant, where he was held in great esteem. He served his townsmen often in offices of trust, and to their satisfaction. He was treasurer and register of deeds for the county of Waldo; was deputy collector of the port of Belfast, and was also on the Governor's council. He died in Belfast, May 29, 1849.

1490. PAMELIA BRYANT, born in Nobleboro, Me., Apr. 27, 1809, and married in Searsmouth, May 16, 1833, Ebenezer W., son of Ebenezer and Mrs. Abigail (Hoskins) Hilton. After his death she married, May 13, 1847, Daniel Putnam, a merchant of Belfast, Me., who removed to St. Paul. Children: Wilmont Wood Hilton, born in Searsmouth, Me., May 13, 1835, and is a jeweler of St. Paul; Annie Elizabeth Hilton, born in Belfast, Me., Dec. 29, 1839, and married Edward Simonton, a lawyer of St. Paul.

1491. LOIS, born in Searsmouth, Me., Mar. 5, 1811, and married Oct. 7, 1832, Robert, son of Robert and Susannah (Patterson) White. She died in Belfast, Me., June 17, 1842. He was a ship-builder. Children: Augustus Stewart White, born in Belfast, Me., Sept. 17, 1833. He is a ship master. Ansel Lothrop White, born in Belfast, Me., June 10, 1835, and married Mary Alden. He is a merchant in New York City.

1492. THOMAS WHITTIER, born in Searsmouth, Me., Oct. 31, 1813, and married June 11, 1846, Sophia M., daughter of William and Mary (Mayo) Beckett. He settled in Belfast, Me., where he is a merchant.

1493. ELIZABETH, born in Searsmouth, Me., Jan. 5, 1817, and marrried in Searsmouth, Jan. 28, 1836, Dr. Gardner, son of Jacob and Susan (Hutchins) Ludwig. They are now (1873) living in Portland, Me., where he is in the practice of medicine.

1494. ANN FRANCES, born in Searsmouth, Me., Jan. 3, 1819, and married, Dec. 2, 1841, Horatio Huntington, son of Anson and Huldah (Huntington) Johnson. He is a merchant. Children: Arabella Johnson, born in Belfast, Me., Sept. 21, 1842, and married Philo Horsey, a merchant of Belfast; Horatio Huntington Johnson, born in Belfast, Me., Jan. 30, 1845; he is a practicing physician in Belfast, Me.; Charles Edward Johnson, born in Belfast, Me., Mar. 8, 1847, and still living there in trade; Mary F. Johnson, born in Belfast, Me., Apr. 6, 1858.

1495. ANSEL, born in Searsmouth, Me., Jan. 2, 1821, and married, Apr. 7, 1845, Ruth Ann, daughter of Samuel and Betsey (Whittier) Borland in Dana-riscotta, Me. He was a merchant settled in Portland, where he died Sept. 4, 1866.

1496. BENJAMIN WHITTIER, born in Searsmouth, Me., Jan. 10, 1823, and married Frances A., daughter of Oliver and Mary (Keith) Washburn. He is a merchant and settled in Ottawa, Kansas, having removed from Rockland, Me. In Eaton's history of the town of East Thomaston, Me., B. W. Lothrop & Co. are reported as having built the Spofford block, in 1848.

1497. SUMNER PATTEE, born in Searsmouth, Me., May 16, 1826, and married Jan. 6, 1850, Ann M. Sargent, daughter of Herbert and Mary E. (Rogers) Sargent. He was in the United States Navy, and was at the time of his death an acting master. He died in Boston, Mass., June 15, 1863. "Captain Lothrop was a young man of excellent qualities, of singularly mild, gentle and winning manner, which peculiarly endeared him to his friends." "Esteemed by his superiors and comrades in his profession," "he was a true representative of the American ship-master, frank, open-hearted, generous, and endearing in his attractions."

1498. JULIA MAFFET, born in Searsmouth, Me., Sept. 10, 1828, and died in infancy.

### 750. DAVID.

1499. PAULINA, born ———; married Peter Dalton in 1835, and had six children. She died March, 1852.

1500. FANNY BAXTER, married, 1835, George Rogers, and died in 1866.

1501. JOHN HOVEY, married Ruth Ann Allen, and died in 1841.

1502. CHARLES, born April 28, 1817, and married, in 1837, Eunice Lord, and lives in Augusta, Me.

1503. MARY H., unmarried.

### 755. JOHN J.              Cohasset, Mass.

[Children named in distribution of estate in 1825.]

1504. JOHN J.

1505. DANIEL.

1506. WARREN. Lydia C., widow, administratrix on estate of, Aug. 2, 1830. Warner Lothrop of Boston, administrator on estate of Thomas, late of Cohas-set, mariner, July 12, 1821. To Jo. J. Lo., father, next of kin, distribution of $3,496.01. Peter Lo., appraiser.

1507. LOUISA.

1508. CAROLINE, chooses her mother, widow Bethiah, guardian, May 5, 1824.

1509. BETHIA, chooses her mother, widow Bethia, guardian, May 5, 1824.

### 759. ANSELM.              Cohasset, Mass.

1510. CLARA, born in Cohasset, Oct. 14, 1798, and married, Oct. 18, 1818, Caleb Nichols of Cohasset. He was a painter and farmer, and was consider-ably in public life as one of the town officials. She died Aug. 8, 1864, and he May 16, 1868. Their children were:

i.   Ennice Burr Nichols, born June 2, 1819.

ii.   Charles Nichols, born Aug. 28, 1822, and married, Dec. 2, 1862, Elizabeth A. Donnell of York, Me. They had two children: Clara Maria, and Charles Bertie. They live in Boston.

iii.   Benjamin Franklin Nichols, born Jan. 17, 1825, and died Oct. 20, 1843.

iv.   Caleb James Nichols, born Mar. 3, 1830.

v.   Maria Andrews Nichols, born July 7, 1832.

1511. JAMES B., born Aug. 17, 1809, and married (1), Aug. 15, 1824, Harriet Andrews of Walpole, who was born May 25, 1806, and died Feb. 20, 1832; (2), Apr. 20, 1834, Mehetable Hall of Barnstable, who was born in 1806. He lives in East Cambridge, Mass.

1512. ANSELM, born in Cohasset, Sept. 16, 1805, and married (1), Feb. 28, 1831, Ruth Jane Johnson, who was born in Cambridge, Mass., Feb. 1, 1811, and died Oct. 8, 1840. He married (2), May 26, 1844, Elizabeth, daughter of Hezekiah and Sarah (Lewis) Spalding, who was born in Shirley, Mass., Mar. 21, 1813. He is a mason, and has been for years an extensive builder in Boston.

1513. URIAH LINCOLN, born in Cohasset, Dec. 16, 1811, and married Eliza Knights of Cambridge, Mass., where he settled. He died Sept. 1, 1839.

1514. EUNICE BURR, born in Cohasset, June 19, 1813, and married, May 3, 1840, Capt. Henry, son of Dr. Ezekiel and Merial Pratt of Cohasset. They resided in San Francisco several years, now in Chelsea, Mass. Children:

i.   George Henry Pratt, born in Cohasset, Feb. 15, 1843, and died in June, 1846.

ii.   George Henry Pratt, born in Cohasset, Apr. 7, 1849, and married, Mar. 10, 1873, Ella Dearborn of Chelsea, Mass.

1515. ELIZABETH LINCOLN, born in Cohasset, Feb. 18, 1815, and married, May 26, 1833, William Hall, who was born Apr. 2, 1811, son of William and Weltham (Gardner) Hall of West Greenwich, R. I. Their residence is in Brookline. Their children are:

i.   Priscilla L. Hall, born Nov. 6, 1834, and died June 19, 1837.

ii.   Mary E. Hall, born Oct. 19, 1837.

iii.   Etta W. Hall, born May 18, 1840.

iv.   William H. Hall, born May 18, 1840, and died July 25, 1840.

v.   William F. Hall, born Jan. 13, 1843.

vi.   Clara P. Hall, born Oct. 22, 1845.

vii.   John H. Hall, born May 29, 1848, and died July 14, 1850.

viii.   Henry J. Hall, born Dec. 18, 1850.

ix.   J. Annie Hall, born Aug. 26, 1853.

x.   Fred G. Hall, born Feb. 6, 1856.

xi.   Nellie L. Hall, born Mar. 11, 1858.

1516. PRISCILLA LINCOLN, born in Cohasset, Feb. 18, 1815, and married, in January, 1835, John, son of Archibald and Margaret (Shaw) Murdock, who was born in Perth, Scotland. They settled in Chelsea, Mass. She died Aug. 10, 1872. Child: Elizabeth Murdock, who married Eben Hoyt of the United States Navy, and who was killed.

27

1517. GEORGE BEAL, born in Cohasset, July 21, 1816, and died Nov. 16, 1816.

1518. GEORGE BEAL, born in Cohasset, July 7, 1818, and married Eunice, daughter of John and Betsey (Brooks) Wheeler, who was born in Acton, Mass., Dec. 14, 1820. He is now living in Cambridgeport, Mass.

1519. MARCIA D., born in Cohasset, Sept. 24, 1820, and married, Jan. 2, 1842, Abraham Tower, a master mariner of Cohasset, who died June 7, 1854. They occupied the old Lathrop homestead on King street, Cohasset. Their children were:

    i.    Marcia D. Tower, born Feb. 19, 1843, and married Zaccheus L. Beal, Jr., of Cohasset. They have two children: Francis Leavitt, born Dec. 31, 1864; and Sarah Cummings Tower, born Aug. 6, 1870.

    ii.    Sarah Cummings Tower, born Oct. 1, 1844, and died Oct. 6, 1859.

    iii.    Abraham Tower, born Mar. 6, 1851.

1520. CUMMINGS LINCOLN, born in Cohasset, Nov. 24, 1822, and married, Jan. 9, 1848, Ann Brown of Charlestown, where he was a builder.

1521. RUTH NICHOLS, born in Cohasset, May 18, 1825, and married, Sept. 29, 1846, James Battles of Cohasset. He was killed Apr. 8, 1861, at Cathedral Block, Franklin street, Boston. Children:

    i.    Georgiana Battles, born July 15, 1847, and died Jan. 26, 1868.

    ii.    Mary Jane Battles, born Aug 29, 1850.

    iii.    James Franklin Battles, born Jan. 27, 1860, and died Sept. 1, 1862.

### 761. PETER.     Cohasset, Mass.

1522. CALEB, born in Cohasset, May 8, 1799, and married (1), Nov. 28, 1819, Mary Snow, daughter of Ephraim Snow of Cohasset, who died Aug. 25, 1831. He married (2), Nov. 28, 1833, Jane Snow, a sister of Mary, who died Dec. 29, 1841. He married (3), in Boston, Nov. 13, 1845, Ann Herring. He was a merchant in the mackerel fisheries of his native town, and very acceptably served his townsmen in the various offices of selectman, assessor, overseer of the poor, and town treasurer. He died in Cohasset, Dec. 30, 1862.

1523. PRISCILLA N., born in Cohasset, July 26, 1801, married, Nov. 2, 1823, James Willcutt of Cohasset. She died Aug. 3, 1845, and he Dec. 8, 1864. Their children:

    i.    Peter L. Willcutt, born in Cohasset, Jan. 17, 1824, married, Apr. 14, 1858, June M. Bedford of Boston.

    ii.    Susan L. Willcutt, born in Cohasset, Mar. 24, 1826, married, Dec. 9, 1849, Henry Collua.

    iii.    Betsey P. Willcutt, born in Cohasset, Sept. 8, 1828, married, May, 1855, Joseph L. Willcutt of Boston.

    iv.    James P. Willcutt, born in Cohasset, Mar. 14, 1831. Resides in San Francisco, Cal.

1524. MARTHA T., born in Cohasset, Apr. 26, 1803, and married, James, son of —— and Ruth (Lothrop) Pratt.

1525. SARAH Y., born in Cohasset, June 16, 1805, and married, Apr. 6, 1826, William Bates of Cohasset. She died Jan. 17, 1865. Their children:

    i.    Frederick A. Bates, born in Cohasset, Aug. 6, 1826.

    ii.    Ann Jane Bates, born in Cohasset, Nov. 25, 1828, married, Oct. 17, 1855, Frank M. Nichols, New Haven, Conn.

    iii.    Robert Bates, born in Cohasset, May 17, 1831, married, Aug. 12, 1862, Loretta H. Atwood, Nashua, N. H.

    iv.    Loring L. Bates, born in Cohasset, Sept. 9, 1835, married, Jan. 17, 1868, Eliza Bourne, Cohasset.

    v.    Bela Bates, born in Cohasset, Feb. 22, 1843.

    vi.    Caleb L. Bates, born in Cohasset, Apr. 21, 1844.

1526. MARY, born in Cohasset, June 19, 1807, and married, Oct. 17, 1833, Dr. Ezra Stephenson of Barnstable. He is now living in Hingham. Their children:

    i.    Ezra Stephenson, a graduate of Harvard College.

    ii.    William L. Stephenson, born Dec. 22, 1838.

    iii.    Penelopy C. Stephenson, born June 4, 1840, died Sept. 27, 1852.

    iv.    Ezra T. C. Stephenson, born Feb. 18, 1842.

    v.    L. T. Stephenson, born Mar. 16, 1845, married, Oct. 16, 1872, Carrie T. Burret, resides in Boston.

1527. LORING, born in Cohasset, Aug. 5, 1809, and died in the same place, Mar. 21, 1814.

1528. WILLIAM, born in Cohasset, Dec. 15, 1811, and died in Cohasset, Apr. 11, 1814.

1529. ELIZABETH, born in Cohasset, Nov. 4, 1813, and married, Nov. 26, 1840, Clark Cutting of Boston. Their children were:

    i.    Thomas S. Cutting, born in Cohasset, Oct. 25, 1841, died Aug. 30, 1842.

    ii.    Thomas S. Cutting, 2d, born in Cohasset, June 9, 1843, died Sept. 8, 1851.

    iii.    Lizzie C. Cutting, born in Cohasset, Aug. 10, 1852.

    iv.    Levi C. Cutting, born in Cohasset, May 23, 1854, lost at sea in 1870.

1530. LORING, born in Cohasset, Nov. 5, 1816, and married, Sept. 25, 1839, Amanda Sophia, daughter of Eli and Clarissa (Nichols) Forbes of Boston. She was born in Boston, May 6, 1819. He graduated in 1836, at Harvard College.

1531. REBECCA A., born in Cohasset, Aug. 22, (June 16,) 1822, and married, Nov. 1, 1843, Royal Whiton, Jr., of Hingham, Mass., who was born July 26, 1820. Their children:

    i.    Esther Cleverly Whiton, born Sept. 17, 1844, died June 22, 1853.

    ii.    Royal Whiton, born July 28, 1846.

    iii.    Thomas Larkin Turner Whiton, born Sept. 6, 1848, died June 17, 1853.

    iv.    Esther Rebecca Whiton, born Apr. 2, 1854.

    v.    Henry Jackson Whiton, born Aug. 2, 1860.

### 767. SETH. Boston, Mass.

1532. SETH W., born in Boston, in 1807, and died in Australia in 1834.

1533. JOHN, born in Boston, Feb. 11, 1806, and married, Nov. 20, 1831,

Cordelia Hemmenway, who was born in Boston, Feb. 14, 1811, and died Jan. 29, 1853. He died in Boston, Jan. 3, 1864.

1534. EBEN W., born in 1811, and married in Boston, in 1834, Margaret Pool of Boston.

1535. ELIZA W., born in 1814, and married, in 1837, Amos L. Rogers of Marshfield. He died ——

1536. CHARLES B., born in Boston, in 1817, and married, in 1842, Elizabeth B. Wheldon of Eastham.

1537. MARTHA J., born in Boston, in 1820.

### 769. ANSEL.      Barnstable, Mass.

1538. SALLY NYE, born ——, married (1), Samuel W. Holbrook, by whom she had, as her father's will shows, at least one daughter: Abby N. Holbrook, who was living in 1857.

1539. MERCY CROCKER, born ——, married Oliver L. Chase. She died Dec. 14, 1862.

1540. Benjamin, born Sept., 1809, and married Sarah H. Otis.

1541. MARY, born in 1816, and married, in 1838, Dr. J. W. Webster.

### 773. CAPTAIN JOHN LO.      Hyannis, Mass.

[This family, excepting the last three, were born in Yarmouth, Mass.]

1542. LUCY BAXTER, born Dec. 19, 1818, and married Freeman, son of Captain William L. Hallet, who was born Mar. 3, 1811. He was a sail maker and has lived in Hyannis, Mass., where they had five children, and where she died, Nov. 18, 1850.

     i.    Delaphine Sprague Hallet, born Oct. 6, 1837.

     ii.    Granville Gay Hallet, born June 29, 1839, now (1873) at 132 Water Street, New York City.

     iii.   Clarence Freeman Hallet, born July 24, 1845.

     iv.    Lot F. Hallet, born Jan. 16, 1847.

     v.    Lucy Baxter Hallet, born Jan. 13, 1852.

1543. LYDIA BAXTER, born Oct. 6, 1820, and married Arthur Goodspeed. They settled and are still living in Jersey City. They have had three children: William B. Goodspeed, Isabella Maria Goodspeed, Lydia Frances Goodspeed, mentioned in grandfather's will.

1544. SYLVESTER BAXTER, born Sept. 13, 1822, and married Jan. 9, 1849, Sarah Lewis, daughter of Capt. Lemuel Baker Simmons. They are settled in Hyannis, and he is engaged in the coast trade, and sails in command of his own vessel.

1545. ASA, born July 2, 1824, and married Abigail, daughter of Heman Chase of West Yarmouth. He removed from Hyannis to Charlestown, Mass., in 1873.

1546. JOHN ATWOOD BAXTER, born June 27, 1826, and married Augusta Cook, daughter of Rev. John Allen of Farmington, Me. They have lived in Boston.

1547. FRANKLIN BAXTER, born Dec. 12, 1828, and married Aug. 28, 1863, Cornelia, daughter of Peter Norris of Hyannis. They removed to Galveston, Texas, in 1864 or 1865.

1548. HENRY ALLEN, born June 21, 1831, and married Elizabeth, daughter of Barnabas Matthews of Yarmouth. They are living in Chelsea, Mass.

1549. MARGARET BRADFORD, born Sept. 2, 1833, and married Jason Lincoln Chase of Harwich, Mass. They settled in Hyannis, where she died Sept. 22, 1855, leaving one daughter: Nellie Maria Chase, who died in infancy.

1550. JOSHUA HOPKINS, born Nov. 6, 1835, he is now living in Redwood City, San Mateo, Cal. He is unmarried.

1551. MARIA BAXTER, born June 21, 1838, and died in Hyannis, Jan. 23, 1840.

1552. HERSELIA BAXTER, born in Hyannis, Feb. 27, 1841, and married June 1, 1869, Captain Levi Lewis, son of Lemuel B. Simmons.

1553. IRA BAXTER, born in Hyannis, Nov. 25, 1846. He is in New York City in the Firm of G. G. Hallet as above (1873).

### 777. ASA LO. New Bedford, Mass.

1554. SARAH.
1555. MARIA.
1556. DAVID.
1557. MARY.

### 780. JOHN LO. Hyannis, Mass.

1558. FREDERICK GORHAM, born in Hyannis, Apr. 16, 1832, and married Jan. 15, 1854, Isadore, daughter of William Bearce of Barnstable. They are settled in Hyannis.

1559. ALONZO FREEMAN, born in Hyannis, Aug. 28, 1836, and married, Oct. 10, 1858, Cynthia J., daughter of Joseph Lewis of Centerville.

1560. JOHN PARKER KNOX, born in Hyannis, Apr. 12, 1843, and married Oct. 22, 1867, Mattie C. Yager of Georgetown, D. C., and in the recent war he enlisted, Aug. 9, 1872, into Co. E., Mass. Volunteers, in which he served for three years, a part of the time as quartermaster. He was honorably discharged Aug. 30, 1865, since which time he has been a Clerk in the office of Second Auditor, Treasury Department, at Washington.

### 781. JAMES SCUDDER LO. Barnstable, Mass.

1561. HARRISON, born Aug. 15, 1803, and married Jan. 22, 1827, Candace Caldwell, daughter of Benjamin and Olive (Pollard) Clarke of Boston. He is a carpenter, and has for twenty-two years been engaged on the Boston & Albany railroad. He is now (1873) residing in Charlestown, Mass., where he is a prominent member of the Methodist Church.

1562. ELIZABETH, born June 9, 1805, and died single, Jan. 17, 1828.

1563. HITTY ANNABLE, born Feb. 7, 1807, and married Freeman, son of Samuel and Desire Annable of Barnstable. Their children were:

    i.   Elizabeth Lothrop Annable, born June 25, 1831, and died Sept., 1835.

    ii.  James Freeman Annable, born May 1, 1839, and died Feb. 29, 1856.

    iii.  Edward Annable, born Dec. 16, 1840, and lives unmarried in Barnstable.

    iv.  William Lewis Annable, born Feb. 28, 1843, and died in May of the same year.

    v.  Emma Annable, born July 12, 1844, and married May 16, 1865, Daniel Webster, son of Nathaniel and Rebecca (Hinckley) Percival of Barnstable, and had one child: Lizzie Percival, born Dec. 1, 1867.

    vi.  Davis Annable, born Sept. 2, 1846, and is living single (1873).

    vii.  Lizzie Annable, born July 8, 1849, and is unmarried (1873).

1564. JAMES SCUDDER, born Oct. 30, 1808, and died unmarried in New Orleans, La., Jan. 7, 1847. He was a mariner, and lost his life by a steamboat explosion.

1565. EXPERIENCE DAVIS, born June 25, 1810, and married in October, 1866, Handy Harris, M. D., of Yarmouth, Mass.

1566. ANSEL DAVIS, born May 10, 1812, and married (1), Emilie, daughter of Coleman and Martha Saunders of Chatham, Mass. She died and he married (2), Ruth, daughter of Joshua and Betsey Hinckley of Barnstable. He has been a master builder, in different parts of Massachusetts. He has also held the office of deputy sheriff of his native county. His residence is in Barnstable, his native town.

1567. JOSEPH DIMMOCK, born June 2, 1814, and died unmarried in St. Mary, La., Oct. 12, 1844, where he was a clerk.

1568. BARNABAS THOMAS, born May 22, and died July 2, 1816.

1569. HENRY, born Apr. 16, 1823, and died unmarried in Marlboro', Mass., Sept. 10, 1860, where, as printer, he was in the office of the *Marlboro Mirror*, having been for years in his earlier life engaged on the *Barnstable Patriot*.


## 783. JOSIAH.        Barnstable, Mass.

1570. BARNABAS, died Apr. 6, 1808, aged two months, as his gravestone in West Barnstable burying lot shows.

1571. SYLVANUS CROCKER LATHROP, born Feb. 21, 1809, and married (1), Mary E. Holly of Barnstable. They were married in Nantucket, and she died in Norwich, Conn. He married (2), in Norwich, Sarah, daughter of Oliver Batty of Norwich. He was engaged in block, pump, and spar-making business, and went from Norwich to Mystic Bridge. He is now living in Jersey City.

1572. JAMES HAYS, born May 1, 1814, and settled as a master mason in Hyannis, Mass.

1573. SOPHRONA, born Feb. 7, 1816, and married Captain Elbridge G. Arey of Wellfleet, Mass. He was commander of a steamship and died in 1862 of swamp fever, contracted while engaged in supplying Fort Fisher with troops for General Butler's command.

1574. ALLEN CROCKER, born Mar. 17, 1818, was drowned at sea by being caught by the harpoon line when fastened to a whale, and drawn overboard.

1575. DELIVERANCE CROCKER, born May 7, 1820.

### 793. ISAAC. Charlestown, Mass.

[All born in Charlestown.]

1576. HORATIO JENKINS, born Nov. 14, 1833, and married in Charlestown Nov. 30, 1854, Mehitable Jane, daughter of Samuel Emery of Lowell, Me. She died Oct. 10, 1868.

1577. MARTHA SYMMES, born Sept. 20, 1835, and married in Charlestown Nov. 1, 1855, Charles Emery, son of Henry and Harriett (Greenleaf) Rogers of Medford; child, Isaac Lothrop Rogers, born Nov. 16, 1858.

1578. MARY FRANCES, born Aug. 31, 1837, not married, in Boston, a teacher in Jamaica Plain.

1579. CAROLINE, born Oct. 31, 1839, and married Apr. 6, 1869, William T. W. Alpine of Lawrence, where they are settled. She had two children who died. He is superintendent in a paper mill (1873).

1580. ISAAC, born Nov. 14, 1841, and married Aug. 12, 1872, Florence H., daughter Isaac Vance and Susanna Harriet Leffer of Stockton, Cal., who died June 4, 1873, now resides in Stockton. She was born in Burlington, Iowa, March 28, 1850.

1581. FRANCES SYMMES, born Sept. 22, 1843, and married Nov. 15, 1866, Nathan F. Tufts, son of Nathan Tufts of Somerville. They live in Charlestown. Children: Fanny Lothrop Tufts, born in Somerville, Jan. 12, 1868; Mary Alice Tufts, born in Somerville, Sept. 2, 1870.

1582. ANGELINA, born May 8, 1845, and died Aug. 21, 1845.

1583. ELIZABETH RHODES, born Aug. 15, 1846, married Sept. 5, 1867, S. Holbrook Buckingham of West Dedham, Mass. Children: Elizabeth Lothrop Buckingham, born in Cambridge Oct. 4, 1868; Eliza Willet Buckingham, born in Cambridge, Feb. 10, 1870.

1584. ANGELINE PHIPPS, born July 6, 1847, and died in Barnstable, Sept. 18, 1847.

EIGHTH GENERATION.

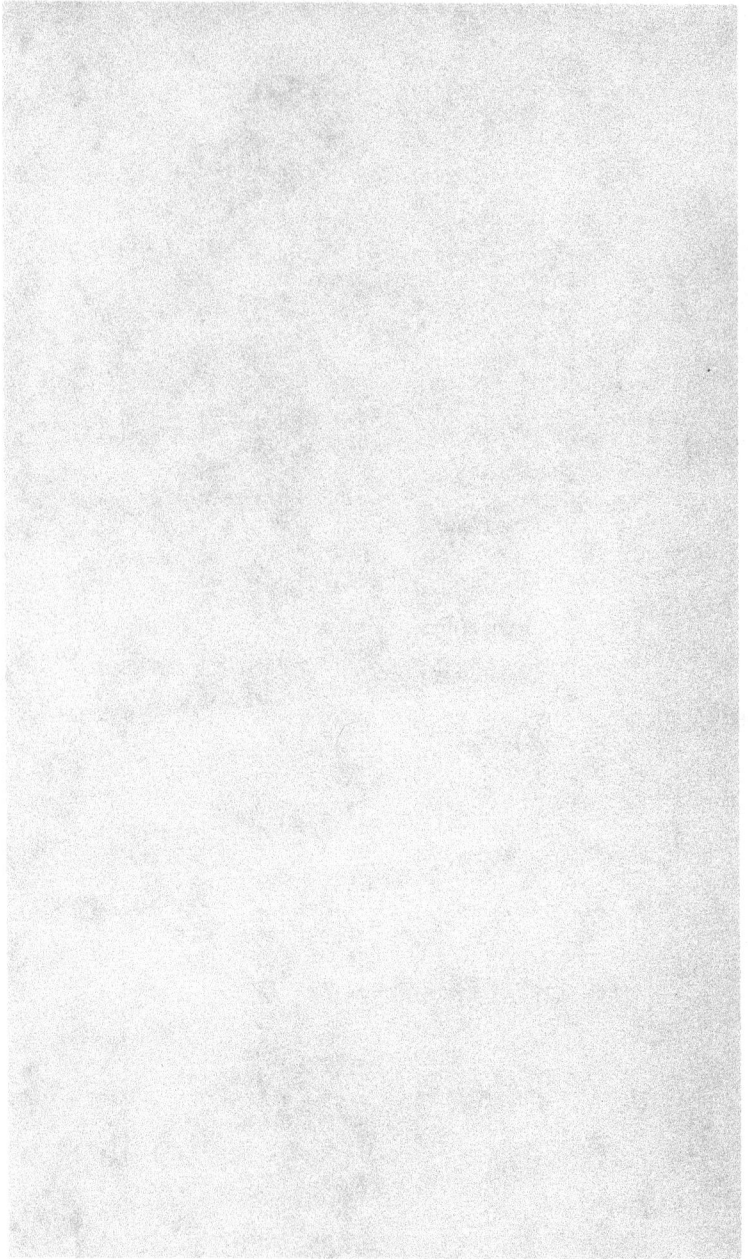

## **802.** ERASTUS.  Woodbury, Conn.

1590. CHARLES, born Sept. 18, 1818; married Susan Hutchinson, and lives in Iowa. Children: Munro, married; Lucinda Ann, married and has three children; Henry.

1591. NANCY, born March 11, 1820; married John A. Atwood, of Woodbury; only child, Lydia Ann Atwood.

1592. ERASTUS, born Jan. 3, 1822; married Semantha Clark, of Montgomery, Neb.

1593. CLARA ATWOOD, born Sept. 29, 1825; married, Oct. 8, 1846, John D. Eager, who was born May 1, 1826. Children: Fred. Cutting, born Dec. 11, 1847, in Northampton; Edwin Louis, born Oct. 12, 1853; William, born Sept. 12, 1856; George, born Mar. h 15, 1859.

1594. OLIVER HARD, born Oct. 17, 1823; married Esther Hendricks, of Springfield.

• 1595. WILLIAM, born May 4, 1827; married (1), Lucy Ward; married (2), Rosilla Ward; three children; resides in Tonica, Ill.

1596. SARAH, born Oct. 27, 1829; married George Hosmer, in the Springfield Armory, and has eight children.

1597. LUCINDA ANN, born Sept. 5, 1831, and died July 15, 1833.

1598. FRANCIS, born Oct. 26, 1833; married (1), Adeline Bartlett, and (2), Rosabel Lathrop, daughter of Rev. Alfred, of Tonica, Ill., and had three children.

1599. DANIEL, born Jan. 26, 1836, in Granby, Mass.; married Martha S., daughter of Jonathan and Melinda (Smith) Morrison, of Bernardston, Mass., who was born in Vernon, Vt.; a machinist in So. Norwalk since 1867.

## **803.** SMITH.  New Rutland, Ill.

1600. REBECCA; married —— Day, of Granby; no children.

1601. CYNTHIA; dead; married —— Whitman; one child.

1602. BETSEY; married Alpheus, son of Albert and Sarah (Samson) Lathrop, of Watertown.

## **806.** DANIEL, JUN.  Vineland, N. J.

1603. AMASA DAVIS; married —— Snell, daughter of a Baptist minister.

1604. ALTHEA BRADBURY; married Lyman, or Simonds.

1605. SUSAN JANE.

1606. ABBY MARIA.

1607. JOHN EMORY, a soldier.

1608. NANCY ELIZABETH; married twice.

1609. LUCY EMILY; married.

1610. ALBERT HENRY; married Sarah ——, of New Britain.

### 808. ALBERT. Watertown, Conn.

1611. GEORGE RICHMOND, born in Dover, Me., Sept. 4, 1833, and married Pauline Bowers, Nov., 1855. She died Sept. 14, 1856, and he married (2), Annie R. Sterling, Nov. 11, 1858.

1612. ALPHEUS DANIEL, born June 28, 1835, in Dover; married Betsey, daughter of Smith Lathrop, of Windsor Locks, Conn., March 17, 1856. He enlisted in the United States service in the recent war. Died in the Hospital, Washington, D. C., Jan. 28, 1863.

1613. CALVIN JUDSON, born in Dover, Dec. 5, 1837, and married, Nov. 11, 1858, Mary S., daughter of William Richardson, of Bridgeport. He enlisted into the United States service in the recent war; died Aug. 22, 1870.

1614. SARAH EUPHEMIA, born in Dover, Dec. 31, 1840; married George W. Holmes, of Stratford, April 22, 1864. They have two children; Wm. Frank Holmes, born Jan. 26, 1865; George Holmes, born May 5, 1867.

1615. MINNIE PAMELIA, born Jan. 17, 1845; married, Oct. 14, 1868, Odell B. Sterling, of Bridgeport, where they are now settled.

1616. CLEORA ALICE, born Jan. 21, 1847; married Charles M. Richardson, born in April, 1845, son of Henry and Verania Richardson, of Bridgeport. Divorced in 1875. Children: Arthur V., born Feb. 14, 1871; Minnie Julia, born Dec. 19, 1872; Lulu Mary, born Sept. 14, 1874.

### 809. REV. ALFRED LO. New Rutland, Ill.

1617. LEWIS C.; died in Illinois, Oct. 11, 1852.

1618. JOHN STILLMAN, born Oct. 9, 1834, and married March 14, 1858, Marcia A. Page, who died April 28, 1858. He married (2), Dec. 13, 1861, Marcia M. Mitchell. He is a lawyer, and is settled in Champaign, Ill.

1619. AUGUSTA A.

1620. ROSABELLA MARY; married Francis Lathrop, son of her uncle Erastus.

1621. ADRIANNA FRANCES.

1622. ELLA H.

1623. HOWARD A., died in Illinois Sept. 19, 1852.

### 810. JOHN.

1624. ELIZA ELLEN; married Wm. Smith.

1625. CORYDON; died young.

### 811. JOSHUA. Le Roy, N. Y.

1626. THOMAS, born in New York city, and died in infancy.

1627. MARY, born in New York city, and died in infancy.

1628. MARY, born in New York city, May 25, 1814, and married in St. Mark's Church, Le Roy, N. Y., Aug. 25, 1841, Alfred Field, son of Jacob and Eliza Bartow. Mr. Bartow is a lawyer, and is settled in Le Roy, N. Y. They have had three children.

i. Perit Lathrop Bartow, born in Le Roy, Aug. 9, 1843, and married in Dr. Adams' church, New York, Dec. 17, 1866, Mary Landir, daughter of Rev. S. H. and Abiah Cox, and had a son, Francis Shelton Bartow, born in Chicago, Ill., April 23, 1871, and died at Long Branch, N. J., July 8, 1872.

ii. Alfred Bartow, born in Le Roy, Sept. 20, 1846; is a lawyer in Chicago.

iii. Francis Shelton Bartow, born in Le Roy, Feb. 2, 1849, and married in St. Mark's Church, Le Roy, Feb. 2, 1871, Jenny Lind, adopted daughter of Chas. Kendall, Esq., and died in Washington, D.C., March 3, 1871.

1629. THOMAS PERIT, born in New York city, July 16, 1816, and married in Ravenswood, L. I., Jan. 7, 1843, Priscilla, daughter of Moses and Jemima Allen. He lived in New York city, and died July 27, 1846.

1630. LYDIA HUBBARD, born in New York city, Sept. 16, 1818, and married in St. Mark's Church, Le Roy, Jan. 9, 1850, Daniel Buell Pierson, a lumber merchant of Cincinnati, O. Their children were:

i. Joshua Lathrop Pierson, born Nov. 11, 1852.

ii. Rebecca Perit Pierson, born Dec. 12, 1855.

iii. Newbold Le Roy Pierson, born Nov. 4, 1858.

1631. REBECCA PERIT, born in New York city, Feb. 11, 1821, and married in St. Mark's Church, Le Roy, May 26, 1845, Rev. George De Normandy Gillespie, D.D., rector of St Andrew's Church, Ann Arbor, Michigan. Their children have been:

i. Joshua Lathrop Gillespie, born Dec. 9, 1849.

ii. Jane Trumbull Gillespie, born Oct. 4, 1852, and died Oct. 18, 1867.

1632. RUTH WEBSTER, born in New York city, March 21, 1823.

1633. JOSHUA, born in Le Roy, N. Y., April 7, 1825, and married in Astoria, L. I., Aug. 1, 1850, Emily R., daughter of Samuel and Margaret Blackwell, who was born in New York city, Aug. 1, 1830.

1634. JANE TRUMBULL, born in Le Roy, May 18, 1827, and died Dec. 2, 1850.

1635. JOHN PELATIAH PERIT, born in Le Roy, N. Y., Aug. 3, 1829, and married in Buffalo, N. Y., Feb. 15, 1860, Anna B., daughter of Milton and Mary Ann Noyes. He died Oct. 11, 1874.

1636. EMILY GEORGIANA, born in Le Roy, N. Y., July 31, 1831, and died in the same town, Aug. 20, 1837.

1637. FRANCIS CUMING, born in Le Roy, N. Y., April 19, 1833, and married in St. Mark's Church, Le Roy, July 10, 1861, Fanny Amelia, daughter of Fanny and Otis Comstock. He is a banker in his native town.

## 816. WILLIAM. Norwich, Conn.

1638.
1639. } THREE children, probably dying in infancy.
1640.

## 822. JEDIDIAH. Guilford, Conn.

1641. WILLIAM EDWARD, born in Guilford Aug. 31, 1794, and married April 11, 1839, Jemima Wight, of Mendon, Mass., daughter of Dr. White. He settled in Rochester in 1828, where he has resided since. He was in early life an active military man, being for a number of years a general of the 46th brigade of New York. He has been also an alderman in the city of Rochester, and the treasurer of the city. His business was the manufacture and sale of saddlery and hardware. Died in 1877, aged 83 years. He was a conspicuous mason for sixty years, and was Commander of the Great Grand Commandery of the United States.

1642. CHARLES CALDWELL, born in Guilford, Ct., Oct. 8, 1795, and married Dec. 27, 1825, Mary Adams, daughter of Dea. Russel and Ruby (Lathrop) Green, of Rochester. Died Dec. 27, 1868, in New York city.

1643. MARY CALDWELL, born in Guilford, July 2, 1798, and died in Norwich, Ct., at the residence of her brother-in-law, Wm. L'Hommedieu, Oct. 9, 1857.

1644. CORNELIA, born in Guilford, Oct. 13, 1790, and married, July 31, 1832, Wm. L'Hommedieu, of Norwich. She died Jan. 5, 1861. One daughter, Mary Caldwell L'Hommedieu, born in Norwich, Nov. 8, 1840; married Charles S. Adams, and lives in Hudson City, Jersey City Heights.

1645. RICHARD TRACY, born in Guilford, May 28, 1802, and died Nov. 8, 1812.

1646. GEORGE THOMAS, born in Guilford, Aug. 12, 1803, and died March 12, 1805.

1647. GEORGE THOMAS, 2d, born in Guilford, Sept. 21, 1805, and died of bilious fever in Georgetown, S. C., Oct. 30, 1840, and his remains were taken to Guilford for interment.

1648. HENRY PERKINS, born in Guilford, June 9, 1810, and died in New Orleans, La., Feb. 26, 1865.

### 828. ANDREW.                                       St. Helena, La.

1649. SARAH, who is reported by her grandfather in her father's marriage record.

1650. ANDREW MERCER, who was living at the father's death.

### 833. ZACHARIAH.                                     Wells, Vt.

1651. A DAUGHTER; married ――――― Potter, of Wells.

### 834. SAMUEL.                                       Auburn, N. Y.

1652. BENJAMIN COLVIN, born near Ballston Spa, Washington Co., N. Y., June 18, 1798, and married Pamelia Colburn Chapman, Sept. 18, 1832. She was daughter of Levi and Permela (Colburn) Chapman, and was born Jan. 29, 1811. He has been a merchant in Syracuse for 42 years, the oldest one now, (1873,) on the list. He studied medicine in New Haven and received his diploma, but never practiced.

1653. NARCISSA RANDOM, born in Cambridge, N. Y., April 3, 1800, and married in 1819, Joel Cody, who died in 1852 or 3. They had no children. She died at the residence of her brother Benjamin, Jan. 14, 1873.

1654. WEALTHY ANN, born in Cambridge, April 3, 1802, and married Edward Allen. She is now living in Auburn, N. Y. They have no children·

1655. SAMUEL MILTON, born in Cambridge, June 10, 1805. Married.

1656. NEAL M. DUFFIE, born in Ballston, N. Y., July 24, 1807, and married in Liverpool, N. Y., Aug. 17, 1839, Adeline E. Stilson.

### 835. EZRIAH.

1657. A DAUGHTER, who married a Mr. Pray of Panama, N. Y. He was a member of the Legislature.

### 836. ROBERT.                                  Syracuse, N. Y.

1658. MERIT, who died when about fifteen years old.

1659. GIBSON, who married, and during the War of the Rebellion enlisted into the service of the Union, and was killed in battle. He left a family.

### 844. SEPTIMIUS.

1660. BENJAMIN FRANKLIN, born ——, ——; married. He was for years proprietor of the Mansion House in Albany, and is well remembered by many friends as a most excellent host. Had two daughters.

### 845. GIDEON C.                                  Burlington, Vt.

1661. GIDEON, born in Stockbridge, Vt., April 1, 1805, and married, in Albany, N. Y., Feb. 14, 1837, Elizabeth, daughter of Robert Dunlop, who had come from Scotland, and settled in Albany. They lived a few years in Burlington, Vt., after their marriage, and then removed to Albany. He was a pioneer in the great steamboat enterprise in this country, and was a deservedly popular captain, both on Lake Champlain and on the Hudson. He will especially long be remembered as the courteous and efficient captain of the *North America*, running between New York and Albany. He removed to Stockport, Columbia County, N. Y., where he still resides (1873).

In 1832, he was in command of the *Phœnix* on Lake Champlain, between Whitehall and St. Johns, in Canada, and the first case of the cholera in this part of the country, appeared on his boat. Such was the terror of the announcement that everybody fled from the boat excepting the physician who had been called and the captain. These two men alone stayed with the victim till his death, and with such help as they could get, buried him on an island near the wharf.

### 846. STEPHEN PEARL.                                  Middlebury, Vt.

1662. FLORELLA G., born in Burlington, Vt., July 31, 1813, and married A. E. Frink, in Rutland, Vt.

1663. STEPHEN PEARL, JR., born in Shelburne, Vt., Sept. 20, 1816, and married in Andover, Vt., Mar. 20, 1844, Lucy Gibson Warner, who was born in Andover, Vt., Dec. 15, 1823, and died in Middlebury, Jan. 3, 1848. Married (2), Martha Hemingway Clements, April 9, 1849, daughter of Rev. John C. Clements of Woodstock, Vt. He died Dec. 25, 1854.

He graduated at Middlebury College, Vt., in 1829, and received the degree of M.D. in 1843. His taste leading him to the study of the physical sciences, he soon left the practice of medicine and engaged in the prosecution of scientific engagements in his native State. In 1849, being chosen Professor of Physical and Natural Science in Beloit College, Wis., he removed to Beloit, and at the time of his death was connected with the State University at Madison as Professor of Chemistry and Natural Philosophy. "Dr. Lathrop was an accurate and distinguished scholar, a successful instructor, and a faithful Christian man."

1664. CHARLES COAN, born in Shelburne, Vt., Feb. 27, 1818, and married, Oct. 3, 1841, Harriet Elizabeth Nichols, who was born in Middlebury, Vt., Nov. 21, 1819, daughter of David Nichols of Middlebury. We find him in boyhood, like so many of our better New England youth, securing his education by strenuous personal efforts, and giving up his intention of a professional career only upon the entreaties of his friends, who found that his health was already impaired by his labors and severe application. The succeeding years find him an honored citizen of Florida and Louisiana, whither he had gone in the pursuit of health and business. Enlisting heartily in every work for the public good,—political, sanitary, reformatory, and religious,—we find him spoken of as "a leading and influential member of the Legislature of Louisiana, and various other representative positions before the civil war, and in character, remarkable for benevolence and open-handed generosity. It has been his habit during his residence in New Orleans to visit often the prisons and hospitals for the purpose of scattering knowledge and administering consolation to the afflicted. His readiness of speech, quickness of perception, open, frank, and fascinating manners attract popular confidence and attention. He is prompt and off-hand in his dealings, kind and courteous in his demeanor, shrewd and practical in his ideas. Indeed he is a fair type of that large and most useful class of our population, who bring to our sunny clime, those hardy virtues which the Pilgrims of Plymouth have bequeathed to their descendants, and before whom all the obstacles of nature disappear." He was of the "firm conviction that slavery was a moral wrong and a political evil, and that it must cease, sooner or later. He believed it to be the duty of every good citizen, and especially of every Christian, to labor to hasten that day, or God's judgment would be poured out upon the nation. He educated, as far as he was able, (their education being contrary to the laws of Louisiana,) his own slaves, and adopted a system by which they could work out their freedom. He even purchased slaves to give them this opportunity, and thus aided them in gaining their liberty." To avoid the influence of slavery in his own family he moved North in 1856, and after a short residence in Philadelphia, Pa., and Delanco, New Jersey, he settled in Newark, entering, as was his habit, into every philanthropic work that opened before him. He was an active member of the New Jersey Legislature during the civil war; was appointed collector of the Port of New Orleans by Lincoln, (which he declined); gave material aid to the Government during the war; was appointed aid on Governor Butler's staff (which he also declined); was President of Insurance and Trust Companies; of the State Sunday School Association,

Young Men's Christian Association of Newark, and other public associations. He is now the executive officer of the New York Real Estate and Traders Exchange, New York city, and active as a lay preacher of ability.

1665. EZRA SMITH, born in New Haven, Vt., Apr. 19, 1822, and was drowned in Dover Creek, Aug. 17, 1838, and buried in Middlebury, Vt.

### 851. JOHN LA.

1666. JULIA, born Dec. 9, 1821.
1667. LUMAN FULLER, born Dec. 5, 1822.
1668. THOMAS LAFAYETTE, born April 30, 1824.
1669. JAMES AUGUSTUS, born Sept. 30, 1826.
1670. JANE AUGUSTA, born Sept. 30, 1826.
1671. MARY ELIZABETH, born July 7, 1830.
1672. NANCY, born Aug. 21, 1831.

### 853. DANIEL.

1673. ———.
1674. ———.

### 857. ELISHA. Bridgeport, Conn.

1675. FREDERICK FANNING, born in Norwich, May 20, 1808, and married, Jan. 27, 1831, Adelia, daughter of Timothy and Betsey Risley, of Bridgeport, Conn., who was born in New York city, Mar. 22, 1810. They are living in Bridgeport.

1676. CHARLES HENRY, born in Bridgeport, Conn., May 24, 1810, and married, Oct. 14, 1841, Susan Peck of Stratford. He died March 20, 1877, in Bridgeport.

1677. WILLIAM LEROY, born in Bridgeport, Dec. 9, 1812, and married, in 1835, Lydia Warren of Watertown, Mass., where they reside (1873).

1678. SALLY ANN, born in Bridgeport, Aug. 9, 1815, and is now living unmarried in Bridgeport.

1679. MARY AMELIA, born in Bridgeport, Nov. 18, 1817, and married George Bailey, and settled in St. Louis, Mo. She died Jan. 1, 1864. Children:

   i.    Mary Bailey, died ———.
   ii.   Sarah Bailey, died ———.
   iii.  Charles H. Bailey, married.
   iv.  George W. Bailey, married.
   v.   Missouri Bailey, died ———.
   vi.  David Bailey.
   vii.  Frank Bailey, died 1883.
   viii. Anna Bailey, died ———.
   ix.  Willie Bailey.
   x.   Emma Bailey, married.

1680. ELISHA NELSON, born in Bridgeport, Aug. 28, 1820, and married, Feb. 9, 1860, widow Lydia Ann Mowry. They lived in San Francisco, Cal., where his wife died, July 15, 1883, and then he removed to West Oakland, Cal.

29

1681. GEORGE LEVERETTE, born in Bridgeport, April 27, 1828, and married, Dec. 17, 1848, Esther Downs of Weston, Conn. They live in East Bridgeport, Conn.

1682. LUCY PALMER, born in Bridgeport, Aug. 27, 1826, and married James Clark. They lived in Plainfield, N. J., where she died, Aug. 12, 1855. Two children:

    i.   Frank Lathrop, born Oct. 1, 1851.

    ii.  James Ephraim, born April 24, 1855.

1683. CAROLINE MATILDA, born in Bridgeport, Sept. 29, 1829, and died in 1830.

1684. FRANCES LOUISA, born in Bridgeport, Oct. 8, 1832, and married, Aug. 17, 1857, Walter John Skinner, and lives in East Bridgeport. Children:

    i.   Mary Louisa, born Sept. 2, 1858, m. May 27, 1880, C. E. Lewis.

    ii.  Emily Augusta, born July 8, 1860, m. May 11, 1881, L. H. Salensky.

    iii.  Hattie Elizabeth, born Jan. 9, 1864, died July 31, 1865.

    iv.  Katie Lathrop, born July 28, 1866.

    v.   Walter James, born Feb. 16, 1869.

    vi.  William Henry, born April 28, 1871.

    vii. Alice Lathrop, born Feb. 3, 1873, died July 28, 1873.

    viii. Ella Frances, born July 28, 1875.

## 858.  SIMON.

1685. LYDIA ELINORA, born in Lisbon, Oct. 11, 1814, and married, Nov. 28, 1833, William A. Johnson of Franklin.

1686. ANNA ESTHER, born in Lisbon, Oct. 13, 1816, and married, March 25, 1835, Stephen A. Field.

1687. LEVERETT MINOR, born in Lisbon, May 7, 1819, died ———.

1688. RHODA CORDELIA, born in Lisbon, June 15, 1821, died ———.

## 860.  HENRY.                              Lisbon, Conn.

1689. MARY, born in Lisbon, March 18, 1817, and married, March 23, 1840, Martin Kinney. Children:

    i.   Henry Kinney, born April 5, 1841.

    ii.  Luther Kinney, born Aug. 13, 1843.

## 873.  SEPTIMUS.                          Griswold, Conn.

1690. SAMUEL SALISBURY, born in Providence, R. I., May 8, 1812. He went in the fall of 1834 to Chicago, Ill., and after two years removed to Bristol, Ill., where he married Nancy McClellan. .

1691. HENRY ADAMS, born in Providence, R. I., Oct. 29, 1813, and at two years of age was brought by his parents to Jewett City. He has resided in the neighborhood ever since. He is now a manufacturer of woolen goods at Hope-dale, in Griswold. He married (1), in September, 1842, Eliza A., daughter of Reuben and Sally Barber of Griswold, who died Feb. 10, 1857. He married (2), in December, 1858, Mary Kinsman, daughter of Roswell and Sarah K. Adams of Lisbon.

1692. HIRAM BEMENT, born in Jewett City, March 21, 1816, and married Charlotte Barrett of Saugerties, N. Y., where he settled, and where he died Jan. 28, 1856.

1693. ELIZABETH, born in Jewett City, May 2, 1818, and died there Nov. 1, 1842.

1694. RICHARD SALISBURY, born in Jewett City, Aug. 14, 1820, and married (1), in Providence, R. I., Sept. 26, 1848, Jane Frances, daughter of Festus and Eliza Thompson of Warwick, R. I. She died in Plainfield, Conn., July 7, 1857, in the thirty-fourth year of her age. He married (2), Feb. 7, 1861, Emily Mason, daughter of Jeremiah and Rosalie Fuller of Sterling, Conn., where she was born Aug. 23, 1837. He is now (1873) settled in West Killingly as a reed manufacturer.

1695. GEORGE CADY, born in Jewett City, Oct. 7, 1822, and died in the same place March 15, 1842.

1696. JOSIAH O., born in Jewett City, Jan. 21, 1825. He married, March 23, 1846, Caroline A. Bigelow, who died June 20, 1847. He soon removed to Illinois, and married (2), Ann Pearson of Bristol, in that State. He settled in Mendota, Ill., where he still resides.

### 874. SOLOMON. Lisbon, Conn.

1697. MARY MARIA, born in Lisbon, Sept. 18, 1813.

1698. ELIZABETH.

1699. JANE.

### 875. HENRY B. Albany, N. Y.

[This family were all born in Albany.]

1700. SARAH, born Feb. 17, 1819, married Daniel True. Their children were:

   i.   Charles True, who died.

   ii.  Henry True.

   iii. Bartlett True.

   iv. William True.

   v.   Sarah True.

   vi. Frances True, died Sept. 4, 1859.

1701. HENRY, born March 30, 1821, and died Feb. 17, 1822.

1702. MARIA, born Nov. 29, 1822, and married Samuel Parks. He died in 1852. They had two children:

   i.   Elizabeth Parks, who married in April, 1856, Samuel McCray. He died in April, 1860, leaving two children, who soon died. Mrs. McCray married in 1861, Joel Jaquins. They are now living in Troy, and have four children, Alfred, John, George, and Lottie.

   ii.  Sarah Parks, who married in 1860, Edward Snow. They had one daughter, Eva Lathrop, born in 1862. Mrs. Snow died March 21, 1864.

1703. HENRIETTA, born Sept. 26, 1824, and died in infancy.

1704. JUSTUS, born Sept. 4, 1826, and died July 15, 1827.

1705. GEORGE WASHINGTON, born April 19, 1828. In 1845, he went to California, and married in 1860, a lady from Arkansas. He is now (1873) a farmer in California. They have four children.

1706. CHARLES HENRY, born March 15, 1830, and married, June 13, 1851, Lydia Amanda, daughter of Hazen and Emily Presby, who was born in Eden, Vt., Aug. 15, 1831. They are now (1873) living in Albany, where he is engaged in the express business.

1707. LUCY, born Jan. 12, 1832, and married, May, 1849, Augustus Benjamin. They went to California in 1858. They had one son:

Mortimer A. Benjamin, who was drowned in California, Aug. 6, 1860.

1708. AUGUSTUS BEACH, born Oct. 8, 1833, and married, Oct. 8, 1854, Mary Jane, daughter of Peter and Elizabeth Vallient, who was born in Albany, April 2, 1836. He is engaged as a bank messenger (1873).

1709. MINERVA, born May 21, 1835, and died Dec. 25, 1837.

## 884. GURDON. Charleston, S. C.

1710. MARY, born in Charleston, S. C.

## 885. JAMES. New York, N. Y.

1711. EDWARD, born in Norwich, and married ———. They went to New Orleans, where he died. No children.

1712. JAMES WILLOUGHBY, born in New York.

1713. MARY JANE, born in New York.

## 887. EDWARD. Norwich, Conn.

1714. MARY SOPHIA WETMORE, born July 20, 1819, and married Charles N. Farnham of Boston. She died Sept. 15, 1838.

1715. AMANDA GRISWOLD, born Nov. 9, 1822, and died Oct. 6, 1823.

1716. EUNICE CLARK, born Oct. 12, 1825, and married, May 27, 1844, Edwin H. Loomis of Lebanon, Conn. No children.

1717. EDWARD, born Feb. 3, 1828, and married Nancy Rozilla Harrington of Shrewsbury, Mass. She is a daughter of Adam and Mercy Harrington, and was born Oct. 17, 1831. They are settled in Worcester, Mass. (1873).

1718. JAMES, born in Norwich March 11, 1831, and married, Nov. 20, 1856, Ellen M., daughter of Archibald and Agnes (Mourhead) Leishman of Edinburg, Scotland. She was born in Bergen, N. J., Dec. 20, 1835. During the war of the rebellion he was in the service as inspector of arms. He is settled in Norwich Town (1873).

1719. CHARLES HENRY, born Dec. 7, 1833, and died Sept. 28, 1835.

1720. HARRIET WETMORE, born Oct. 6, 1837, and married, June 6, 1861, William Leishman of New Haven, a brother of Ellen M., wife of James, No. 1718.

1721. JOHN CLARK, born July 13, 1839, and married, Aug. 26, 1862, Alice E. Wright.

## 889. GEORGE H. Lebanon, Conn.

1722. SARAH HYDE, born in Lebanon, May 31, 1852. Now living there.

1723. RALPH GREEN, born in Lebanon, May 10, 1855, and died July 31, 1856.

1724. HARRIET HARDING, born in Lebanon, Feb. 11, 1859.

## 892. JOHN. Norwich, Conn.

### [All born in Norwich.]

1725. JOHN ADGATE, born Sept. 25, 1815, and married, Oct. 23, 1836, Lucy Louisa Cottrell, daughter of Jesse and Mary (Armstrong) Cottrell. He united with the First Congregational Church in 1842.

1726. FREDERICK MOORE, born May 24, 1822, and graduated at Yale in 1843. He pursued the study of law at the Harvard Law School and in the office of the Hon. John A. Rockwell of Norwich, and Judge Marvin Wait of Lyme, and was admitted to the bar in New London County in 1846. He commenced the practice of law in Norwich, his native city, and in 1853 removed to Chicago, Ill., where he devoted himself too closely to his profession until his physical and intellectual powers were exhausted. He died of paralysis at the Retreat for the Insane, in Hartford, Conn., Aug. 22, 1860, aged thirty-seven years and three months. He had never married.

1728. EUNICE ADGATE, born March 31, 1826, and died Aug. 26, 1828.

1729. CHARLES HENRY, born April 28, 1877, and married ———. He went into business in Buffalo. He settled in California, where he died ——— 1870, leaving a widow and one child.

1730. HARRIET EUNICE, born Dec. 3, 1828, and died Jan. 8, 1844.

1731. WILLIAM BACON, born March 1, 1832, and married in Norfolk, Va., Aug. 4, 1859. Lived in Yonkers, N. Y. Seven children. He died in Yonkers June 18, 1873.

1732. FRANKLIN KINNEY, born Jan. 3, 1834. Single; in New York City.

1733. WASHINGTON ADGATE, born June 1, 1836, and married in Buffalo. He died 1870, in New York City. No children.

## 899. ELEAZER L. Norwich, Conn.

1734. ELIZABETH LORD, born in Norwich, Oct. 16, 1821, and married, Oct. 3, 1844, Edward C., son of Samuel Fish and Mary Cleveland Denison of Stonington, where they are settled. Their children are:

    i. Evelina Thatcher, born Dec. 7, 1845.

    ii. Elizabeth Lathrop Denison, born Nov. 28, 1847.

1735. WILLIAM BALDWIN, born in Norwich, March 7, 1824, and married, Oct. 14, 1851, Amelia R., daughter of Pomeroy and Rachel (Ellis) Smith of Norwich. He is now, 1872, living on the homestead of his father in Norwich Town.

1736. MARY LEFFINGWELL, born in Norwich, July 19, 1826, and died in the same place, May 17, 1850, unmarried.

1737. HANNAH LORD, born in Norwich, Dec. 21, 1828, and married in the same place, July 26, 1852, William Bacon Lathrop. She died May 15, 1855, leaving no children.

1738. CORNELIA EVEREST, born in Norwich, Dec. 16, 1830, and died in the same place, Dec. 13, 1854.

1739. CHARLES THOMAS, born in Norwich, Nov. 12, 1832, and died in the same place, Feb. 21, 1864.

1740. BURREL, born in Norwich, Dec. 1, 1835, the first of this family not recorded in Norwich, and died in the same place, Aug. 8, 1837.

1741. JANE ELIZA, born in Norwich, Nov. 27, 1838, and died Oct. 4, 1845.

### 907. JOSEPH EDWARDS.    Middletown, Conn.

1742. JOSEPH BACKUS, born in Middletown, Dec. 22, 1826, and married Nov. 24, 1856, Caroline Maria Gregg, in Galena, Ill. He died in Dunleith, Ill., March 23, 1861. He left no children.

1743. SARAH ELIZABETH TOWNSEND, born in Middletown, Dec. 23, 1830, and died in the same city, Mar. 4, 1839.

1744. HENRY EDWARDS, born in Middletown, Nov. 28, 1832, and married in Waterbury, Conn., May 23, 1859, Harriet Newell, daughter of John Miles and Emily (Newell) Stocking, of Waterbury. He was a silverware manufacturer, and for years before his death was the superintendent of the extensive works of the Gorham Manufacturing Company of Providence, R. I., of which he was also a member. Died at Providence, Jan. 13, 1871.

At a meeting of the employees of the Gorham Manufacturing Company the following preamble and resolution were adopted:

WHEREAS, It has pleased God to remove from the scene of his earthly labor Henry E. Lathrop, with whom many of us have been associated for a number of years,

*Be it Resolved*, That we feel in the death of Henry E. Lathrop, our late Superintendent, we have lost a sincere friend, and the community one of its best and most exemplary members. That during the fifteen years with which he was connected with the company (a part of the time as Superintendent) his intercourse with all was always marked by kindness and consideration. That the fidelity with which he discharged every duty, the unselfish and unwearied care he gave to every interest committed to his charge, the uprightness and honesty of his character as shown in his dealings with all, have always commanded our respect and won our highest esteem.

### 913. REV. DANIEL W.    New Haven, Conn.

1745. GEORGE HOWLAND, born in Elyria, O., March 13, 1825, and married May 21, 1851, Cornelia D. Turner, of Jackson, Mich., where they are settled.

The Bible brought from England by the Puritan Immigrants is now owned by Mr. George H. Lathrop, of Jackson, Mich., having descended to him from his father, the Rev. Daniel W. Lathrop. It was accompanied by the following memorandum:

This copy of the "Bishop's Bible" in the old English text was printed by Robert Barker in the city of London in 1603, in the early part of the reign of James I. It was brought to this country in September, 1634, by the Rev. John Lothropp, or Lathrop, the pastor of the first Independent church in London, shortly after his release from the imprisonment of two years which he suffered for the faith he professed.

Soon after his arrival in this country he became pastor of the first church in Scituate and in 1639 of the church in Barnstable, Mass. This Bible was brought to Norwich, Conn., by his son, Samuel Lathrop, in 1668, eight years after the settlement of the town.

The book passed into the possession of a line of his descendants residing here (Samuel 2d, Nathaniel, and Azariah), to Deacon Charles Lathrop of the sixth generation, father of the writer. During the voyage to this country Mr. Lothropp dropped on one of its pages a spark of fire while reading at his evening devotions. Unaware of the accident he fell asleep with the book partially closed, his fingers between the leaves. At length, awakened by the heat, he found that a hole had been burned through several pages of the sacred Book, the only copy on the ship. Before the voyage was completed the space thus burned was carefully filled, and the missing words on most of the pages supplied from memory with pen and ink in the old English text in which they had been printed. The interest of the Book is therefore enhanced not only by the antiquity of its imprint and other facts of its early history when it was the companion of Mr. Lothropp during his imprisonment, but also by this unique memento of its appreciation by the venerable servant of Christ, from whom descended so many families of different and respected names who for generations have dwelt on the plains and among the hills and vales of this beautiful town, and so many who have gone hence, an honor to various professions and employments in every portion of our country, and who have borne the light of science and the glad tidings of salvation to distant portions of the world.

At the bi-centennial celebration in Norwich (September, 1859,) the scriptures were read from this Book, and the foregoing history was given, being principally from my recollection of the statements made to me by my grandfather, Azariah Lathrop.

DANIEL W. LATHROP.

Norwich, Conn., September, 1859.

1746. MARY WOODHULL, born in Norwich, Ct., Jan. 4, 1827, and died in Elyria, O., June 17, 1843.

1747. CHARLES CHRISTOPHER, born in Elyria, O., June 16, 1829, and died March 18, 1830.

1748. CHARLES CORNELIUS, born in Elyria, O., Nov. 10, 1830, and died in November, 1831.

1749. DANIEL WINSLOW, born Nov. 1, 1832, and died Nov. 13, 1832.

1750. HARRIET WINSLOW, born in Elyria, O., June 23, 1834, and married in New Haven, Ct., May 21, 1863, James H. Dunham, of New York city. She died Nov. 22, 1879. They lived in New York. Children:

    i.   Harriet Lathrop, born April 1, 1864.

    ii.   Lilian Howland, born June 3, 1867.

    iii.  Helen Bliss, born Sept. 19, 1868.

    iv.  Elizabeth Howland, born March 12, 1871, and died Nov. 7, 1871.

    v.   Catherine Skinner, born Mar. 12, 1871 (twin with Elizabeth).

    vi.  Grace Louise, born Feb. 4, 1876.

1751. JOANNA LEFFINGWELL, born in Elyria, O., June 3, 1836, and died at the same place April 20, 1848.

1752. ELIZABETH HOWLAND, born in Elyria, O., Sept. 28, 1838, and died in New Haven, Conn., March 9, 1851.

1753. ABBY HOWLAND, born in Elyria, O., Jan. 28, 1841, and died in Elyria, Aug. 3, 1843.

1754. FRANCES HOWLAND, born in Elyria, O., June 30, 1844, and died Dec. 21, 1844.

### 915.  C. LEFFINGWELL.                Cleveland, Ohio.

1755. SAMUEL HUTCHINS, born July 22, 1834.

1756. ELIZABETH HUTCHINS, born Feb. 8, 1836, and married, 1860, William M., son of Rev. Joseph Merriam, of Randolph, O.  He died of consumption, Nov. 5, 1867, leaving two children.

  i.    William Lathrop Merriam, born 1862.

  ii.   Fanny Hallock Merriam, born 1865.

1757. CHARLES, born June 1, 1839, and died fifteen months old.

1758. CHRISTOPHER LEFFINGWELL, born Feb. 24, 1841, and died the next month.

### 919.  GEORGE AUGUSTUS.                Savannah, Ga.

1759. A SON, who died in infancy.

### 920.  REV. EDWARD, D.D.                Stamford, Conn.

1760. ADELAIDE REBECCA, born in Beaufort, S. C., Feb. 20, 1842, and married, 1864, Edward, son of Hiram Ketchum, Esq., of New York.  Children:

  i.    Georgiana Lathrop Ketchum, born in New York city, Jan. 3, 1865, and died Sept. 27, 1865.

  ii.   Cornelia Ketchum, born in Yonkers, N. Y., Nov. 28, 1866.

  iii.  Edward Lathrop Ketchum, born in Savannah, Ga., Jan. 3, 1870, and died Feb. 23, 1870.

  iv.  Edmund Ketchum, born in Thompson, Ct., July 25, 1872.

1761. GEORGIANA ELIZABETH, born in New York city, Jan. 21, 1845, and died May 11, 1860.

1762. ANNA GRANGER, born in New York city, June 24, 1849, and died March 31, 1850.

### 923.  JOSEPH J.                Augusta, Ga.

1763. LOUISA ADELAIDE, born in Savannah, Dec. 20, 1843, and died Aug. 12, 1846.

1764. FRANCES JOSEPHINE, born in Savannah, Sept. 3, 1845, and died April 14, 1850.

1765. WILLIAM BURRELL, born in Savannah, April 8, 1847.

1766. ALICE GERTRUDE, born in Savannah, Dec. 28, 1848.

1767. GEORGE AUGUSTUS, born in Augusta, Nov. 21, 1850.

1768. WALTER HENRY, born in Augusta, May 2, 1853.

1769. JOSEPH THOMPSON, born in Augusta, May 1, 1855.

1770. EDWARD SIMPSON, born in Augusta, April 30, 1857.

1771. SUSAN ELIZABETH, born in Augusta, Jan. 9, 1862.

### 930. WILLIAM G.

Boonton, N. J.

1772. Maria Jennings, born in New York city, Dec. 11, 1838, and died in Rahway, N. J., Feb. 7, 1841.

1773. William Gerard, Jun., born in Rahway, N. J., Aug. 24, 1841. He graduated at Columbia College, in law at Harvard in 1864, and is a lawyer in Wall Street, N. Y.

1774. Donald McKenzie, born in Rahway, N. J., Aug. 24, 1841.

1775. Anna Margaretta, born in Rahway, Jan. 15, 1843, and died Aug. 8, 1843.

1776. Anna Catherine, born in Rahway, Jan. 15, 1843.

### 933. CHAS. CHRISTOPHER.

Newark, N. J.

1777. Charles Halsted, born June, 1857, died March, 1861.

1778. William Gerard, born October, 1858, died May, 1861.

1779. Theodore Andruss, born April, 1860.

1779-1. Emma Goble, born November, 1862.

### 936. AZARIAH.

Willimantic, Conn.

1780. Mary Augusta, born July 21, 1838, in Willimantic, and died Feb. 24, 1841.

1781. Sarah Jane, born in Norwich, Nov. 5, 1840, and married, Jan. 1, 1863, Henry Lewellyn, son of Horace and Elizabeth Jane (Manning) Hall of Willimantic, where they now live. They have two children: Alice Lathrop Hall, born June 21, 1869; and Harvie Archie Hall, born Oct. 25, 1872. Mr. Hall is editor of the Willimantic *Weekly Journal* (1873).

1782. Edward Whiting, born in Norwich, May 10, 1846, and died Aug. 7, 1846.

1783. Wm. Gale, born in Norwich, Aug. 18, 1847, and died Nov. 3, 1847.

1784. Abby Whiting, born in Norwich, Feb. 7, 1851.

1785. Charles Rockwood, born in Willimantic, April 14, 1855, and died Aug. 9, 1855.

1786. Mary Augusta, born in Willimantic, Oct. 25, 1856.

### 941. JAMES S.

1787. Henry A., born April 1, 1845, enlisted in the late war into the service of the Union from Meriden. He died Sept. 27, 1864.

### 947. ARIEL.

Stark, N. Y.

1788. Daniel, born Aug. 22, 1800, and died Aug. 22, 1802.

1789. Charles, born Oct. 3, 1803, and married Polly, daughter of Dr. Moses Graves. He died Dec. 24, 1830, in California.

1790. Almira, born Aug. 27, 1806, and married, Jan. 3, 1828, John Willsey, who was born in Stark, N. Y., Dec. 5, 1798. They settled in South Columbia, New York, where she died, Aug. 15, 1872, and where he still lives (1873). He has been a carriage manufacturer. He had three children.

30

   i.    Ariel L. Willsey, born May 5, 1820, and died in Stark, June 19, 1832.

   ii.   Mary Jane Willsey, born Dec. 22, 1832, and died in Plainfield, N. Y., Nov. 3, 1846.

   iii.   Uphemia Armena Willsey, born June 17, 1842, and married, Oct. 24, 1858, Dewitt T. Biggs, by whom she has a daughter Nettie.

1791. DANIEL, born March 20, 1809, and married Caroline, daughter of Jedidiah Bennett. He died Aug. 7, 1849, in Richfield Springs, Otsego, N. Y.

1792. ANDERSON, born April 27, 1812, and married, Oct. 8, 1837, Marinda Keller, who was born March 21, 1812.

1793. JAMES, born Aug. 22, 1814, and married (1), Sept. 23, 1838, Mary, daughter of John and Mary Siner, who was born Sept. 24, 1819, and died May 20, 1851. He married (2), Nov. 12, 1851, Maria, daughter of John and Mary Monk, who was born May 20, 1825. They are settled at Van Hornesville, N. Y.

1794. MEHETABLE, born April 4, 1818, married —— Krum, South Columbia, Herkimer County, N. Y.

1795. HARRIET, born Aug. 22, 1820, and died Aug. 27, 1822.

1796. MARIA, born May 7, 1823, married —— Miles of West Galway, N. Y.

## 951.  DYER. Albany, N. Y.

1797. DANIEL SHIELDS, born in Albany, N. Y., April 13, 1825, and married, in the same city, Dec. 18, 1855, Harriet Monteath, daughter of James A. and Jane Monteath Wilson of Albany. They resided in Albany, and lived on a lot which for three generations has belonged to the family.

Mr. Lathrop received his early education at the Albany Academy, and at a boarding school kept by Rev. Mr. Bulkley in Rensselaer County. He early entered into mercantile life, at first with his father, and later in various positions in which he received a thorough and practical business training. While still a young man, in 1850, he was appointed by the Common Council, one of the Aldermen of his native city. But while he always had an intelligent interest in municipal and general politics, he was not to be drawn away by them from his chosen pursuits. He was a commercial man, and as such he was chiefly known and esteemed. In 1855 he became a partner in the well-known house of Thatcher, Lathrop & Co. Mr. Lathrop was not satisfied with the mere routine and drudgery of his calling, but mastered its principles; he was a merchant and not a tradesman. He was possessed of those virtues which ennobled the man as well as the business; of that strict probity and integrity which made his word as good as his bond, wherever he was known. His methods of business were prudent and safe, he followed its legitimate channels and never engaged in those dangerous speculations which so often make commercial wrecks. If crises and panics came, Thatcher, Lathrop & Co. hardly had occasion to change their course or take in sail; they enjoyed the character which wisdom and prudence deserve and gain. He exercised the same care in his personal investments and took all his steps advisedly; if he bought stock in a railway, it was because he had thoroughly studied it, and the system with which it was connected. The wealth which he acquired was the tribute to his judgment and ability, and to that providence and wisdom which fitted him, not only to act for himself, but to be the adviser of others. But while Mr. Lathrop was a business man, that was not all; he took time to cultivate his mind, to study political economy, to understand the history and progress of his country, to visit its remote borders, to indulge in recreation as a relief from business cares. He was particularly interested in the horse, and in many ways he sought its development, and to make it more serviceable to men. Mr. Lathrop was a merchant, and found the rewards of his profession in the accumulation of wealth; but he loved wealth not for itself but for its uses. His heart and his hand were ever open to those who were in want, and no man had more friends among the poor whom he had befriended; when his death came, they felt it as a personal loss. He had been not only their bene-factor but their friend. In a tribute to his memory, to which we are indebted, it is said: "His benevolence did not have its rise in the annoyance which comes from importunity, but from deep and quick sympathy with the unfortunate, and his abiding reverence for the Divine Commandments which encircle duty." He was a man of good appearance, with a strong understanding, fine social qualities, an excellent conversationalist, and when he died, February 13th, 1883, he was mourned not only by his family, but by the community in which all his years had been passed, as a good man and true.

1798. ANNA MARIA, born in Albany, N. Y., Dec. 2, 1826, and died in the same city, Jan. 21, 1830.

1799. JANE ELIZABETH, born in Albany, N. Y., Aug. 25, 1828, and married, Sept. 30, 1850, the Hon. Leland Stanford of California. He is one of the enterprising business men of the age. They have one child: Leland DeWitt Stanford, born in Sacramento City, Cal., May 14, 1868.

1800. ARIEL, born in Albany, N. Y., Dec. 30, 1830, and married in the same city, Oct. 6, 1857, Catherine P. Beardsley. Occupied the position of paying and receiving teller in the Union National Bank of Albany, for some years. He is now living in California.

1801. ANNA MARIA, born in Albany, N. Y., Sept. 23, 1832. In California.

1802. HENRY CLAY, born in Albany, N. Y., May 30, 1844. In California.

1803. CHARLES GARDNER, born in Albany, N. Y., March 11, 1849, and married —— Griswold.

### 957. ZEPHANIAH, JUN. Oriskany Falls, N. Y.

1804. HENRY W., born in Hawley, Mass., Oct. 28, 1819, and married at Hamilton, N. Y., April 14, 1847, Mary, daughter of William and Mary (Sanger) Wilton of Waterbury, Conn. She was born in Madison, N. J., Nov. 19, 1820. He removed from Oriskany Falls in 1847, to Iowa City, Iowa, where he has continued to reside. He has attained an excellent reputation as teacher and as superintendent of the schools of Johnson County. He has also been for years a practicing lawyer, and a practical farmer. His influence has been greatly enlarged as editor and publisher of a local newspaper. The offices to which he has been called, attest the esteem in which he is held. As member of the Common Council, as Mayor of the city in which he lives, as one of the Regents of the University of the State, and Treasurer of the University Fund.

1805. RACHEL W., born in Hawley, Mass., Jan. 11, 1821, and married, at Oriskany Falls, April 26, 1842, Beaumont S. Holmes.

1806. JOSEPH H., born at Oriskany Falls, Dec. 16, 1823, and married in Chicago, Ill., Oct. 13, 1852, Mrs. Olive Miranda Calhoun, who died Jan. 21, 1869. He married (2), at Denver, Colorado Territory, May 16, 1873, Mrs. A. J. Tiffany. At Georgetown, Colorado.

1807. SOLON F., born at Oriskany Falls, Sept. 5, 1827, and married (1), at Augusta, N. Y., Oct. 29, 1851, Sarah A. Durker, who died June 4, 1854. He married (2), in Waterloo, Iowa, Dec. 2, 1857, Emily Moore.

1808. Ro \ IOND OLIVIA, born at Oriskany Falls, Jan. 5, 1830.

1809. TRYPHENA FIELD, born at Oriskany Falls, Oct. 26, 1834, and died in Iowa City, July 21, 1853.

1810. DORCAS A., born at Oriskany Falls, Dec. 15, 1837, and died in the same place, Nov. 20, 1850.

### 958. HON. GEORGE H. LA.     Hawley, Mass.

1811. JAMES MILLER, born in Hawley, June 19, 1824, and married (1), March 16, 1850, Esther W. Cooly, who died March 10, 1858, leaving a single son. He married (2), Dec. 25, 1862, Josephine M. Smith. He is a physician. Is settled in Dover.

1812. THOMAS IRWIN, born May 10, 1837. Married, Aug. 22, 1850, Mary P. Phillips of Blackstone, Mass. Engaged in farming and lumbering, Saginaw City, Mich.

1813. EDWIN, born in Hawley, Mass., March 31, 1831, and married at Shelburne Falls, March 2, 1852, Ann E., daughter of John and Elizabeth Henry. They are settled on a farm in Round Grove, Ill., their post-office address being Dwight, Ill.

1814. FREEMAN, born July 23, 1837. Married, May, 1864, Barbara A. Alvord of Wilmington, Vt. Lawyer and land agent, Saginaw City, Mich.

### 961. MYRON.     Va.

1815. SON.

1816. SON.

1817. DAUGHTER.

### 968. AUSTIN.     Lawrenceville, Pa.

1818. MARGARET, born Sept. 3, 1833, and married in Sept., 1851, Charles Mosell of Ludlamville, Tompkins County, N. Y. They have four children: Fred. L., Augustus B., Mary E., and Helen.

1819. MARTHA, born June 28, 1836, and married, Dec. 3, 1868, John W. Knox, of Knoxville, Tioga County, Pa.

1820. AUSTIN, born in Covington, Pa., April 9, 1839. He began business as an inspector of lumber at the early age of seventeen years, for Sampson & Ball of Williamsport, but after two years removed to Lawrenceville, Pa., where he was in a store until 1869, when he settled at Corning, in the hardware business, as one of the firm of Kulker & Lathrop. He is now largely interested in timber lands and in the manufacture of lumber. He has been the treasurer of the village for two years, and president of the village three years, and has entered on his fifth year as supervisor of the town of Corning (1873).

1821. DELOS, born in Lawrenceville, Oct. 1, 1811, and now (1873) in Florida for his health.

1822. DANIEL, born in Lawrenceville, Dec. 1, 1813, and died Dec. 2, 1869; of consumption. He was a young man of more than ordinary promise.

1823. WILLIAM, born May 21, 1817, and married, May 24, 1869, ———— Bissell of Corning, N. Y., where he is settled in the furniture business.

1824. MAY, born March 18, 1850.

1825. CHARLES K., born in Lawrenceville, Pa., Jan. 27, 1858.

1826. ELLEN, born in Lawrenceville, Jan. 6, 1861.

1827. JOHN COLVIN, born Jan. 24, 1864.

1828. ANNIE, born Aug. 29, 1867.

### 974. OLIVER. Batavia, N. Y.

1829. MARY, born, ————. Married Jeabez Warren. In Bethany, N. Y.

1830. AURELIA, born, ————. Married a Mr. White. Western N. Y.

### 989. SIMEON. Bozrah, Conn.

1831. ANDREW, born Aug. 23, 1815, and died March 7, 1846.

1832. WILLIAM, born in Bozrah, April 17, 1817, and married, June 6, 1839, Lucretia Peckham. He died July 21, 1861, from a wound received in a skirmish near Fairfax Court House. He left no children.

1833. ANDREW, born in Bozrah, March 19, 1822, and married Laura Royce.

1834. LUCY, born in Bozrah, May 22, 1823, and married ———— 1871, John H. Ashcroft of Montville.

1835. JABEZ SMITH, born in Bozrah, May 28, 1824, and married, Dec. 4, 1848, Julia R. Backus. He is a teacher in the Union School in New London, and resides in Norwich (1873).

1836. ALANSON PECKHAM, born in Bozrah, July 21, 1826. He married, Dec. 26, 1859, Josephine Cottrell, and died in Norwich, Sept. 23, 1867. He left no children.

1837. JANE B., born in Bozrah, Oct. 25, 1828, and married, Nov. 21, 1852, Lucian H. Smith. They have had two children: Estella Jane Smith, born Aug. 30, 1856, Lucian Smith, born Oct. 17, 1863, and died Sept. 21, 1864.

1838. DAVID AUSTIN, born in Bozrah, April 23, 1832, and married, Feb. 17, 1856, Amelia A. Smith.

1839. LYDIA ZERVIAH, born in Bozrah, April 23, 1833, and married Jan. 1, 1852, Henry N. Smith. Children:

    i.  Miron Winslow Smith, born March 29, 1853.

    ii.  Horace Irving Smith, born June 4, 1854.

    iii.  David Lathrop Smith, born July 26, 1855.

    iv.  Louis Henry Smith, born Feb. 16, 1857.

  v. Julius Simeon Smith, born Oct. 3, 1859.
  vi. Anna Calista Smith, born Aug. 21, 1863.
  vii. Everett Prentice Smith, born Jan. 17, 1867.
  viii. Bertha Frances Smith, born June 10, 1872.

 1840. ANNA HAZELTINE, born in Bozrah, May 20, 1834, and married Feb. 14, 1867, Albert F. Park. Children:
  i. Emeline Calista Park, born Sept. 7, 1868, and died Aug. 31, 1869.
  ii. Anna Estelle Park, born June 13, 1872.

 1840-1. PHEBE CALISTA, born in Bozrah April 23, 1837, and died May 9, 1863.

### 991. AZARIAH. Vernon, Conn.

 1841. AZARIAH WILLES, born in Franklin, Conn., April 24, 1826, and married Adelaide Augusta, daughter of Albert and Hannah (Fargo) Hyde, of Franklin, where she was born Dec. 30, 1834. They settled in Elmwood, Peoria county, Ill., but removed to Butler Center, Iowa.

 1842. ELISHA HUNTINGTON, born in Franklin, Aug. 27, 1827.

 1843. PHILENA MARIA, born in Franklin, April 26, 1829, and died July 11, 1831.

 1844. ELIZA L., born Nov., 1831.

 1845. NANCY HUNTINGTON, born Oct. 3, 1835.

### 995. JAMES.

 1846. JONATHAN.

 1847. DICE.

### 997. JAMES. Blue Hill, Franklin, Conn.

 1848. LUCY WHITING, born in Franklin, Aug. 27, 1817, and died Sept. 13, 1822.

 1849. DeWITT CLINTON, born June 20, 1819; married Feb. 26, 1849, Charlotte, daughter of Thomas and Lucretia (Webb) Gray, of Windham, Conn. He was surgeon of the 8th Reg. Conn. Vols., and died April 10, 1863, at New Berne, N. C., from his protracted exertions in the care of the wounded soldiers. He was honored for his unselfish faithfulness, and died deeply regretted.

 1850. EDWIN RUTHVIN, born March 28, 1825, and was drowned Nov. 25, 1846.

 1851. JOHN MILTON NEWTON, born in Franklin May 20, 1830, and married (1), Lydia Eliza, daughter of Samuel A. Gager and Wealthy Ann Huntington, Dec. 30, 1852. She died Dec. 15, 1867. He married (2), April 7, 1869, Lucretia Hyde, daughter of Col. Dyer and Lydia A. (Fowler) Hough of Bozrah.

 1851-1. AVERY NELSON, born Sept. 20, 1832, and died July 20, 1841.

### 999. ERASTUS. Hinsdale, N. Y.

 1852. ALICE.

 1853. FANNY.

### 1001. OLIVER. Vermont.

 1854. MARY P., who married a Mr. Cotton, of Middlebury, Vt.

## 1002. HAZEL. Rome, N. Y.

1855. HARRIET, born Aug. 12, 1807, and married in Lisbon, Conn., William Freeman. They soon settled in Agawam, Mass. Children:

    i.    Harriet A. Freeman, born Feb. 18, 1831, and died Jan. 22, 1850.

    ii.    William D. Freeman, born Aug. 29, 1835, and died Sept. 16, 1837.

    iii.    James P. Freeman, born Dec. 28, 1839. He married and is living in Westfield, Mass. (1873).

1856. THOMAS K., born Jan. 5, 1809, and married in Pennsylvania, and went thence to Fort Wayne, Ind.; and, about 1856, removed to Sugar Mound, Kansas, where he died.

1857. ELIZA ANN, born Jan. 1, 1812, and married Frank Baker, in Springfield, Mass. Children:

    i.    Eliza R. Baker, born April 5, 1838, and died Aug. 11, 1840.

    i..    Francis A. Baker, born Sept. 16, 1842.

    iii.    Rodolphus Lathrop Baker, born March 12, 1844. He entered the Union army during the recent war and was killed in battle.

    iv.    Ellen Baker, born Aug. 24, 1847.

    v.    Alice Baker.

1858. RODOLPHUS, born Feb. 12, 1815, and married in Waretown, N. J., where he still lives (1873).

1859. JAMES WOLCOTT, born in Rome, N. Y., Feb. 8, 1818. He graduated at Brown University in 1847, and at the Newton Theological Seminary in 1850. He was ordained to the work of the ministry, and installed as pastor of the North Baptist Church in Dorchester, Mass., in Feb., 1851. He married in Chicopee, Mass., May 18, 1852, Thirsa K. Fish. No children.

## 1003. JARVIS. Norwich, Conn.

1860. HANNAH, born in January, 1810.

1861. DANIEL, born Oct. 15, 1813, and married Oct. 28, 1840, Desire D. Lee, daughter of Brewster and Annis (Downer) Lee of Lebanon. They are living in Cleveland, O. (Brooklyn village).

1862. EZRA, born in Norwich, May 17, 1817, and married Jan. 12, 1845, Abby Willi ns, daughter of Joseph and Lucy (Denison) Kingsley of Franklin, where she was born Oct. 31, 1819. He died July 18, 1854, and she July 11, 1871.

1863. ERASTUS DARIUS, born in Norwich, and married Aug. 3, 1845, Elizabeth H., daughter of Martin Bushnell. They live in Canterbury.

## 1003. ALFRED, ESQ. Carthage, N. Y.

1864. STEPHEN HUBBARD, born in Champion, N. Y., Jan. 21, 1815, and married Dec. 20, 1843, Dorcas Eliza Beardsley, who was born in Richfield, N. Y., Feb. 7, 1819. They reside in Oswego, N. Y., where he is cashier of a Bank (1873).

1865. SAMUEL PARSONS, born in Champion, N. Y., April 12, 1817, and married in Richmond, Va., Jan. 21, 1847, Caroline Currie, daughter of Charles Pickett of Richmond. He is settled in Richmond, Va.

1866. George Alfred, born in Champion, N. Y., Aug. 19, 1819, and married Jan. 13, 1847, Frances Maria, daughter of James and Hannah (Pratt) Smith, who was born May 11, 1826, at Evansville, N. Y. He studied medicine at the New York Medical College, and at Pittsfield, Mass., where he took his medical diploma in 1846. He resided some years in Louisiana, where he practiced medicine. In 1849 he went to the Sandwich Islands, where he was a U. S. hospital surgeon and a consul of the government at Honolulu. Died in 1877.

1867. Eliza Storrs, born in Champion, N. Y., Dec. 30, 1822, and married Sept. 25, 1844, James Willard Smith, who was born Sept. 27, 1819, at Champion. They have lived in Carthage, Oswego, and New York; now in Rochester. Children:

    i.    Mary Elizabeth Smith, born May 26, 1847.
    ii.   Margaret Parsons Smith, b   June 18, 1851.
    iii.  Eliza Lathrop Smith, born Sept. 26, 1854.
    iv.  Julia Frances, born June 14, 1858.
    v.   Willard Pratt Smith, born ———.

1868. Enoch Thomas, born Aug. 1, 1824, and was a merchant of Oswego.

1869. Frederick B., born March 13, 1828, and married June 5, 1850, Mary Elizabeth, daughter of Sylvester and Mary A. (Ward) Mather, of Binghamton, N. Y., where she was born, Dec. 16, 1828. They removed from Binghamton to Oswego, where he is now of the firm of Howlett, Lathrop & Co., millers and commission merchants.

### 1009.  WILLIAM, M.D.

Butternuts, N. Y.

1870. Ann Elizabeth, born Sept. 15, 1825, and married John Henry, son of J. T. Gilbert, of Gilbertville, Otsego Co., N. Y., where they settled. They have six children:

    i.    Helen Lathrop Gilbert, born March 31, 1850.
    ii.   Frances Anna Gilbert, born Nov. 9, 1851.
    iii.  Caroline Lathrop Gilbert, born Aug. 8, 1854.
    iv.  William Lathrop Gilbert, born Nov. 4, 1859, and died in a few weeks.
    v.   Catherine Winter Gilbert, born Nov. 2, 1860.
    vi.  Henry Lathrop Gilbert, born Feb. 26, 1865.

1871. William; never married.

### 1010.  JAMES E.

1872. Eunice, died Aug. 31, 1851.

1873. Ruby Maria; married (1), James E. Foreman; married (2), 1857, Davis Soule, of Richfield, N. Y., and removed to Lyons, Clinton county, Iowa, in 1859.

1874. George; married Amanda Williams.

1875. Orlanda; married John McQueen.

## 1013. FAYETTE. Richmood, Va.

1876. MARY COWLES, born in Richmond, Feb. 1, 1837, and is now a teacher in her native city (1873).

## 1016. WILLIAM. Albany, N. Y.

1877. ALMIRA, born in Broome, N. Y., Feb. 23, 1824, and married in Middleburgh, Schoharie county, N. Y., Oct. 23, 1845, William II. Engle, where they now live.

1878. EUGENIA L., born in Albany, N. Y., May 23, 1830, and married Abel Bennet of Binghamton, where they live.

1879. ANDREW, born in Blenheim, N. Y., April 10, 1834, and married. He died in Pennsylvania March 14, 1870. Two children.

## 1020. REV. CALVIN. Somerville, N. J.

1880. ELLEN SOPHIA HARRIET P., born in Caldwell, Essex county, N. J., May 22, 1826, and married in Belleville, N. J., Dec. 27, 1848, William Henry Emerson. She died Feb. 14, 1870.

1881. CHARLES DANIEL, born in Bloomfield, N. J., Dec. 28, 1830, and married in Newark, N. J., April 25, 1854, Eveline I. Fowler. He is in business in New York city and lives in Newark.

1882. JOHN DODD, born in Bloomfield, N. J., Apr. 3, 1834; unmarried.

## 1021. LATHROP E.

1883. MARY, born in Newark, N. J., Apr. 8, 1836, and married —— Haight. Died in July, 1866.

1884. RICHARD, born in Newark, N. J., May 17, 1839. Married west.

1885. HARRIET, born in Newark, N. J., March 28, 1845, and married Deizendorf. They live in Perth Amboy, N. J.

## 1022. RICHARD D. Ottawa, Kan.

1886. ASA STARKWEATHER, born in Blenheim, N. Y., Jan. 4, 1835.

1887. ANDREW RICHARD, born in New York city Dec. 12, 1846; drowned.

1888. JANE.

## 1027. JOHN B.

1889. RICHARD BACKUS, born July 31, 1825, and married, Nov. 3, 1851, Catherine, daughter of Marvin and Abby (Pitcher) Waters of Norwich. He settled in Lisbon, where he was a farmer. He died Nov. 10, 1859. She is now living in Lisbon.

1890. HARRIET ELIZABETH, born Sept. 5, 1827; married, Apr. 19, 1858, Thomas, son of John Pomeroy and Rachel (Fitch) Smith. They are settled in Norwich. Children:

   i.   Emma Ellis Smith, born Aug. 15, 1851.
   ii.  Adeline Ackley, born Sept. 13, 1856.
   iii. Charles Thomas, born Sept. 17, 1859.

31

iv.   Anna Ellsworth, born Sept. 2, 1865.

v.   Carrie Ellsworth, born Sept. 2, 1865.

1891.  JONATHAN LESTER, born June 10, 1829, and married, July 17, 1853, Harriet E., daughter of Austin Bliss of Lisbon, where they now reside. He is a farmer.

1892.  JANE MEHITABLE, born March 17, 1831, and married, Oct. 30, 1854, Joseph A. Fargo, son of William Dwight and Mary A. (Standish) Fargo. He was born in Bozrah Dec. 31, 1833.  He is settled in Norwich in the dry goods trade.  They have had one son, Joseph Warren Fargo, born in Norwich Apr. 18, 1857, and died May 1, 1865.

1893.  LUCY SOPHIA, born Dec. 13, 1832, and married, Oct. 15, 1857, Nelson Foster, son of Nelson Allen of Illinois.  They are now (1872) living in Nebraska.  No children.

1894.  WILLIAM DARIUS, born June 24, 1837, and married, Feb. 1, 1862, Aurelia R. Hayden of Warren, Ill.  They lived in Illinois.  He entered the service of the United States Government, and died at Paducah from a wound received at the battle of Shiloh, Apr. 22, 1862.  No children.

#### 1046.  JOHN L.                          Bozrah, Conn.

1895.  EDWIN E., born in Bozrah Apr. 29, 1846.

1896.  JANE E., born in Bozrah June 10, 1853.

#### 1047.  JONATHAN GEORGE.                 Norwich, Conn.

1897.  ANNIE ELIZABETH, born in Bozrah Sept. 13, 1858.

#### 1050.  REV. JOHN P.                     Philadelphia, Pa.

1898.  JOSEPH, born ———, and died Sept. 21, 1833, unmarried.

1899.  JULIUS, died single.

1900.  FRANCES ANNA, born ———; married, Nov. 8, 1855, Thos. Lafayette Wakefield, of Dedham, Mass.  They have had four children:

i.   John Lathrop Wakefield, born July 3, 1859.

ii.   Frank Mortimer Wakefield, born July 19, 1862.

iii.   Julius Ross Wakefield, born April 27, 1866.

iv.   Ann Margaretta Wakefield, born June 15, 1870.

1901.  MARIA MARGARETTA, born ———, and married Sept. 1, 1864, Hiram DeWitt Hall of Elyria, O.  Children:

i.   Julius Mortimer Lathrop Hall, born July 23, 1865.

ii.   Joseph DeWitt Hall, born Aug. 14, 1866.

iii.   Anna Edith Livingston Hall, born Aug. 31, 1868.

1902.  JOHN, born Feb. 8, 1835, and graduated at Burlington College, N. J., in 1853, and at the Harvard Law School in 1855.  He was admitted to the Suffolk bar, Massachusetts, in 1856.

1903.  JANE AUGUSTA; married, Nov. 23, 1855, Edward Sprague Rand, Jr., of Dedham.  Their children are:

i.   Edward Sprague Rand.

ii. Harry Lathrop Rand.

iii. Jennie Lathrop Rand.

1904. JULIUS MORTIMER, born in Bordentown, N. J., May 5, 1840.

1905. JOSEPH HENRY, born in Bordentown, N. J., Dec 31, 1842, and married, Oct. 13, 1870, Carrie Edith Olin of Boston. Like his two next older brothers, he enlisted in 1862, in the Forty-third Massachusetts Infantry. In January, 1864, he was commissioned lieutenant in the fourth regiment of Massachusetts cavalry. He was afterwards promoted to the adjutancy of the same regiment, and continued in the service until the close of the war.

### 1058. PORTER. Lansing, Mich.

1906. GEORGE DELOS, born in Lodi, Mich., June 17, 1830, and married at Lansing, Mich., Amelia, daughter of Rev. ——— Wood of Lansing. He was a soldier in the recent war, and died at Lansing, Mich., July 5, 1863, the day after reaching home from his war service. He had been a nurseryman.

1907. MARY ANN, born at Lodi, Mich., ———, and married at Lansing, Rufus Crane. They are settled in Greenville, Michigan.

1908. PORTER M., born in Concord, Mich., Oct. 15, 1838, and married, Oct. 10, 1865, Frances A. Day, daughter of John W. Day of Dryden, Mich. He enlisted in the Seventh Michigan Infantry, from which he was discharged for inability, but re-enlisted in the regular army, and served for three years. They now reside in Sheboygan, where he is a merchant.

1909. JULIUS BLISS, born in Concord, Mich., May 3, 1842, and died at sea, Oct. 31, 1862, on his return homeward from the war service he had been rendering the United States government. He was in the Sixth Michigan Infantry, and had been on service at New Orleans.

1910. EDWIN J., born in Concord, Dec. 27, 1843, and like his brother Julius, died, while on his return from the war, at Cleveland, Ohio. He had been a prisoner, taken at Travellian Station, June 11, 1864. He died in the Soldiers' Home at Cleveland, March 22, 1865.

1911. CLEVELAND THAYER, born in Concord, April 26, 1847, and is now a salesman in Chicago, Illinois.

### 1059. GEORGE C. Mason, Mich.

1912.  
1913. } Three children, names not learned.  
1914.  

### 1062. LUMAN.

1915. HOMER.

1916. FRANKLIN.

### 1063. HOMER. Lansing, Mich.

1917. ROSETTA.

### 1066. SEWELL STEPHEN. Warren, Penn.

1918. SIMON.

1919. ELIZABETH.

1920. HARRIET.
1921. MARY JANE.
1922. STILLMAN.
1923. JANETTE.
1924. ISAAC HENRY.
1925. MARTIAL, who died about two years old.

### 1070.  JOSIAH CLEVELAND.                    Illinois.

1926. WILLIS BRONSON.
1927. A DAUGHTER.
1928. CORNELIA JANE.
1929. GURDON.
1930. OCTAVIA.
1931. STEPHEN.
1932. A SON—twin with Stephen.

### 1073.  GURDON.

1933. MARY SOPHIA.
1934. ANNA MARIA.

### 1078.  JOHN.                    Tolland, Conn.

1935. JUSTIN, born Sept. 18, 1802, and married (1), Mary, daughter of James and Polly (Kingsley) Isham of Tolland, where she was born July 15, 1806, and died May 2, 1838, aged thirty-two, nd (2), Ruth (Kendall) Abby, Jan. 22, 1856. He died April 6, 1874, in Tolland. A farmer.

1936. JOHN, born July 26, 1804, and died at about five years of age.

1937. CHARLES, born in Tolland, Dec. 23, 1806, and married, Oct. 13, 1845, Mary E., daughter of Jesse and Mary (Kinney) Vaughn, of Sterling, Conn. He is settled in Tolland, and has always pursued farming. She died June 10, 1873, aged fifty-seven.

1938. WEALTHY KINNEY, born Sept. 13, 1810.  Married John Calvin Willey. Children:

    i. Sarah Willey, a young lady of great beauty and promise, died at the age of seventeen in New Hampton.

    ii. Louisa.

    iii. John.

    iv. Charles.

    v. Mary.

    vi. James.

    vii. John.

1939. SAMUEL MANNING, born Aug. 11, 1815, and married Eliza A. Bump.

1940. MARY ANGELINE, born April 2, 1818, married A. K. Brown. They are living at Mansfield depot. Mr. Brown has represented Mansfield in the State Legislature. They have no children.

### 1080.  VARANUS LA.                    Cambridge, Vt.

1941. ALICE, born in Lebanon, Conn., Feb. 17, 1798, and married (1), Thomas Ellenwood, after whose death she married a Gardner. Children: Julia, Benjamin T., Marvin, Thomas, Charles, Louisa, and others. Died in Canada West, Sept. 7, 1844.

1942. HORATIO NELSON, born in Lebanon, Conn., April 19, 1800, and married, July, 1823, Sarah Whitney, daughter of Jesse Whitney, born in Wolcott, Vt., March 15, 1803. He lived in Cambridge, Vt., from 1836 to '73. A clothier in Wolcott. Died Feb. 24, 1874, in Bakersfield, Vt.

1943. LUCIUS, born in Lebanon, July 26, 1802, and married Sarah, daughter of Solomon Keyes. Died in Cambridge, Vt., March 23, 1841.

1944. LUCRETIA EDGERTON, born in Hyde Park, Vt., Nov. 26, 1806, and married Burrel S. Miner, M. D. Children: Emerson S., George W., Charles, and Mary. Residence, Cambridge, Vt.

1945. WILLIAM, born in Hyde Park, Vt., Dec. 29, 1809, and married (1), Adaline, daughter of Thomas Perkins; (2), Maria L., daughter of Gershom Newton, M. D. Residence, Manston, Wis.

1946. CHARLES, born in Hyde Park, Vt., June 8, 1812, and died in Johnson, Vt., June 7, 1813.

1947. CHARLES TAINTOR, born in Johnson, Vt., May 18, 1814, and married Matilda B., daughter of Caleb Wilder of Newport, N. H.

1948. URIAH, born in Hyde Park, Vt., Sept. 18, 1818, and married (1), Ann Holmes, and (2), ———. He lived several years in Cambridge, Vt., and removed to Waterville, in the same State, where he died.

1949. ELIAS, born in Cambridge, Vt., Aug. 8, 1820, and married Louisa Wilder, sister to his brother Charles's wife. Lawrence, Mass.

### 1981. WILLIAM. Tolland, Conn.

1950. KELLEY, born in Tolland, Oct. 17, 1803, and married, March 20, 1826, Flora, daughter of Daniel and Elizabeth (Holbrook) Cobb, also of Tolland. He settled in South Coventry, where he died Sept. 4, 1867, his wife having died July 7, 1867.

1951. JULIUS, born in Tolland, March 17, 1805, and married ——— Strickland of Bolton. After several children were born to them, they separated, and he soon joined the Mormons at Nauvoo, Ill. She afterwards married.

1952. MARIA, born in Tolland, March 30, 1807, and died July 23, 1807.

### 1994. AZEL J. Utica, N. Y.

1953. JULIA ETTA, born Oct. 16, 1839.

1954. FRANCES CORNELIA, born July 2, 1841, and married. One daughter.

1955. EMILY ISADORE, born June 18, 1844, and married.

1956. ALCIE ELCOTT, born April 26, 1847, and married.

1957. MARY GERTRUDE, born in June, 1850.

1958. CHARLES HENRY, born Sept. 13, 1852.

1959. HELEN ARTHUR, born Aug. 15, 1854.

1960. NELLY HAMILTON, born Sept. 14, 1858.

## 1101. JOHN W. Springfield, Mass.

1961. JOHN KIBBE, born in Jacksonville, Ill., June 7, 1844.

1962. EDWARD BILLINGS, born in Jacksonville, Ill., March 4, 1844, and was married by Rev. J. P. Gulliver, D.D., in Chicago, Ill., Dec. 4, 1866, to Sarah Lombard, who died Aug. 23, 1868.

1963. CLARA LOUISA, born in Jacksonville, Ill., Jan. 17, 1847, and was married in the same place, June 6, 1867, by Rev. J. G. Roberts, to Henry C. Brunson.

1964. JULIA EMMA, born in Jacksonville, Ill., June 29, 1855.

## 1107. ALBERT. Syracuse, N. Y.

1965. FRANCES.

1966. ALBERT.

1967. ISABELLA.

## 1118. ELIAS, JUN. Chelsea, Vt.

1968. BETSEY, born Nov. 22, 1798, and married, in 1836, B. F. Carlton. They reside in Morristown, Vt., and have two children:

   i.  Alfred Carlton.

   ii.  John Carlton.

1969. ELIAS, born May 18, 1800, and married, in 1838, Nancy Durgin, and settled in Chelsea, where he died March 13, 1863. They had no children.

1970. RUFUS, born March 23, 1802, and married, in 1830, Ruth Shaw. They live in Aroostook County, Me.

1971. CHAUNCEY, born Feb. 11, 1805, and married, in 1834, Sarah Pickering of Chelsea, Vt. They have no children.

1972. OLIVE, born Oct. 8, 1807, and married, in 1838, Peter Bragg. They reside in Strafford, Vt. They have no children now living.

1973. ALFRED, born July 21, 1811, and married, in 1838, Mary Sawyer. He died in Elmer, Vt., in 1866.

1974. HIRAM, born June 24, 1814, and married, in 1843, Harriet W. Richardson. They live in Vershire, Vt.

1975. WARREN, born March 25, 1820, and married, in 1866, Nellie Aldrich. They live in Vershire, Vt.

1976. LOVICY, born Nov. 19, 1824, and married, in 1848, John Long, and is living in Amesbury, Mass.

## 1119. RUFUS. Chelsea, Vt.

1977. PHILURA, born in Chelsea, Dec. 30, 1791, and married, June 30, 1810, John, son of Levi and Elizabeth Bean, a farmer of Chelsea. He was born in Gilmantown, N. H., March 29, 1785. They had a family of seven children, all born and brought up in Chelsea. He died Jan. 30, 1832, and she, Sept. 10, 1864.

   i.  Rufus L. Bean, born Monday, Nov. 23, 1812. He went West in 1836, and was for years e......, ...s a land surveyor for the Government, and located himself on a farm in Dubuque, Ia., where he lived until 1849. He then started for the gold regions of the Pacific coast, and, after much tribulation, with the loss of his cattle, he reached in the early winter the Feather River, where he made his successful beginning in the search for gold. But his search was short. He died Nov. 17, 1850.

ii. Lura Bean, born Wednesday, Nov. 9, 1814, and married, Nov. 16, 1836, Samuel P. Alexander, a farmer, born in Tunbridge, Vt., April 25, 1819. They have lived for the past twelve years in Beloit, Wis., where he is a builder. They have four children: Marcia E., born March 16, 1838, and married in Beloit, Wis., Jan. 28, 1863, Charles A. Danforth, a hardware merchant of Hamburg, Iowa, and has Hattie S., born in Beloit, March 28, 1864; Gertie A., born in Hamburg, Iowa, June 4, 1868; Gracie E., born Aug. 19, 1870, and Charles Clarence, born April 9, 1872. John B., born Feb. 16, 1843, and died in Middlesex, Vt., Sept. 10, 1849. Lura Margaret, born in Middlesex, Vt., Nov. 14, 1847, and married in Beloit, Wis., Ezra J. H. Beard, who was born in Jefferson, N. Y., Feb. 23, 1844, and has one daughter, Lura Vesta, born in Watson, Mo., Nov. 28, 1870. Frank P., born in Dannemora, N. Y., Sept. 14, 1852, and now living in Beloit, Wis.

iii. Almond Bean, born Tuesday, April 11, 1816, and married Laura A., daughter of Wm. Wilson of Chelsea, Vt., Jan. 26, 1843. He was a teacher of music, and died in Chelsea, May 26, 1843.

iv. John Bean, born Oct. 17, 1817, and married in Burlington, Vt., in 1851, Eliza J., daughter of Xury Spear. He is settled in Portage City, Wis., and is in the stock and produce business. He is a man of some earnestness and versatility, and can use both voice and pen in the furtherance of his ends. They have two children living: Jenny, born in New York State, in 1853, and Anna, born in Wisconsin in 1860; a son and daughter, twins, died in infancy.

v. Lovisa Bean, born Tuesday, April 6, 1824, and married, March 26, 1843, Elva, son of Hezekiah and Hannah Bicknell of Rehoboth, Mass. He was born Feb. 22, 1814, and they are settled in Tunbridge, Vt. We are greatly indebted to her for her persistent and successful endeavor to collect the record of the descendants of her grandfather Rufus Lathrop, No. 1119. She has had four children, all born in Tunbridge. Her daughter Hannah L., born Jan. 24, 1844, married Dec. 10, 1872, Daniel S., son of Stoddard and Eliza (Smith) Hunt, who was born Dec. 10, 1826, and now lives in Chelsea, Vt.; Orlana E., born July 6, 1845, and married, Jan. 1, 1866, Walter F., son of Major and Alma (Andrus) Smith of Tunbridge, and has two sons, Charles H., born March 22, 1867, and George W., born Oct. 20, 1868; Almond B., born July 11, 1847, and married in Watson, Mo., Oct. 7, 1872, Clarissa J. Morgan of Watson. In the style of the earlier times, they made their wedding tour a business trip, with all needed appointments, to their new home in Gaylord, Kansas; and Frank Huntington, born July 31, 1852, lives still (1873) in Tunbridge.

vi. Dolly Bean, born Sunday, Sept. 6, 1829, and married in Chelsea, Vt., Jan. 1, 1856, Jabin H., son of Jabin and Abigail Corwin of Chelsea. They have four children: Herbert, born Aug. 28, 1861; Eliza J., born Feb. 12,

1863; Solon C., born June 26, 1864, and Lura A., born June 4, 1868. Mr. Corwin is a farmer and lives in Chelsea.

vii.  Solon H. Bean, born Feb. 25, 1831, and married, March 27, 1856, Amanda M., daughter of Shadrach W. and Asenath B. Folsom of Chelsea. They are settled on a farm in Spillville, Iowa, and had two children: Ida, born in June, 1864, and a son, born in August, 1865, and died in November of the same year.

1978. Lovisa, born in Chelsea, Nov. 22, 1793, and married, Jan. 19, 1811, William Kimball of Chelsea, Vt.  He was a Methodist preacher.  She died in Illinois, April 29, 1868, and he, June 27, 1869, aged ninety-one years.  They had eleven children:

i.  Margaret L. Kimball, born Nov. 1, 1812, and married, April 16, 1837, Jude P. Gary of Thompson, Conn., and had a family of eight children.  She died in Illinois, July 25, 1862.

ii.  Samuel B. Kimball, born Jan. 8, 1814, and married, June 20, 18—, C. A. Lathrop, and had two children.  They live in Wheaton, Ill.

iii.  William H. Kimball, born Oct. 11, 1817, and married, May 13, 1846, Charlotte Leonard, and lives in Aurora, Ill.  They have two children.

iv.  Edson A. Kimball, born July 3, 1820, and married, in 1845, Ellen Willard, in Elgin, Ill.  They have six children.

v.  Mariah L. Kimball, born Sept. 12, 1822, and married, Oct. 23, 1840, G. N. Roundy.  They are settled in Turner, Ill., and have twelve children.

vi.  Frank G. Kimball, born Sept. 9, 1825, married, Sept. 27, 1866, Mary M. Barnes, in Mendota, Ill.  They are settled in Wheaton, Ill.  We are indebted to him for the records of this family.

vii.  George P. Kimball, born May 26, 1827, married, Sept. 1, 1849, Charlotte Wagor, in Wheaton, Ill., and has six children.

viii.  Rufus L. Kimball, born Feb. 19, 1829, married, Jan. 26, 1853, Imogene A. Adams, in Aurora, Ill.  They have two children.

ix.  Wilbur S. Kimball, born April 23, 1833, married, Jan. 20, 1858, Frances M. Rice, in Austin, Minn.

x.  Charles F. Kimball, born March 19, 1831, and married, Nov. 20, 1850, Martha Smith, in Michigan.  Their residence is in Elgin, Ill., and they have one child.

xi.  Jane L. Kimball, born Dec. 30, 1836, and married, Feb. 20, 1862, E. J. Masters, in Wheaton, Ill., and they are living in Oak Park, Ill.  They have five children.

## 1122.  JOSEPH                                    Brookfield, Vt.

1979. Marcia, born in Norwich, Vt., Nov. 26, 1806, and died Nov. 20, 1816.

1980. Lucia, married Willey.

1981. Benjamin Gordon, born 1810, married, Jan. 10, 1841, Clara Jacobs. They have no children, and live in Montpelier, Vt.

1982. Paul Brigham, born Nov. 26, 1811, and married, Feb. 5, 1841, Laura, born Dec. 11, 1813, daughter of Jacob Chase of Derby, Vt.  They settled in Elma, Erie county, N. Y., where she died April 2, 1872.

1983. JOSEPHUS DWIGHT, born in Brookfield, Vt., June, 1814, and married, in 1843, Harriet Houghton Hall. They lived in Montpelier, Vt.

1984. ALBERT G., born Aug. 9, 1818, and died of yellow fever in New Orleans, Sept. 9, 1843.

## 1129. LEBBEUS, JUN. Bozrah, Conn.

1985. MARY, born 1805, married Isaac Herrington. Children: Mary, Isaac, Giles, Jane, and Julia. She lives in Bozrah.

1986. CAROLINE, born Aug. 6, 1807, married Charles Avery. Children:
  i.   George Hill Avery, lives in Salem.
  ii.  Elizabeth Avery, married Nicholas Stebbins, and lives in Waterford.
  iii. Sally Ann Avery, married Austin DeWolf.
  iv.  Charles Willoughby Avery, married Carrie Austin.
  v.   Sherwood Gardner Avery, married Emma Maples.

1987. ELISHA, born October, 1808, married Charlotte Avery, daughter of Charles Avery, who lived and died in Bozrah. According to their Bible records they had thirteen children, and he died Aug. 22, 1855.

1988. HARVEY, born Oct. 23, 1808, in Bozrah, and married, January, 1831, Octavia, daughter of Dea. Oliver Woodworth, who was born in 1812 ?. They lived for thirty-five years in Lebanon, farming, and now live in Waterford, Ct.

1989. HARRIET, born 1814, died in September, 1831, aged seventeen years.

1990. LEONARD, born in Bozrah, July 20, 1814, married, Sept. 12, 1842, Susan, daughter of Peter C. and Alice (Hoxie) Brown, who was born May 19, 1821, and was a Selectman of Andover. They had two children.

1991. HENRY, born in Montville, June 16, 1821, and married Mary A. Brown, April 1, 1841. He kept a livery stable in Norwich.

1992. ERASTUS, born Feb. 20, 1821, and married Prudence M., daughter of Abijah and Lydia Park of Bozrah, Aug. 15, 1843. She died in Lebanon, March 30, 1856, aged thirty years. He died in Lebanon, July 31, 1865, where he owned and improved a farm.

## 1130. ELISHA. Canaan, N. H.

1993. ELISHA.

1994. AZEL, married in Chelsea.

1995. JOHN H., was at one time settled in Aurora, Ill., and had a son Cephas.(?)

1996. CHARLOTTE.

1997. HARRIET.

1998. MARCUS.

## 1131. HARRIS G. Canaan, N. H.

1999. LUCINDA A., born in Canaan, Oct. 2, 1809, and married, Jan. 6, 1833, Elijah R. Colby, who died in 1864. She married (2), Thomas B. Sanborn, a merchant at East Canaan, N. H., where they now live. She has no children.

2000. DAVID C., born in Grafton, N. H., Oct. 29, 1810, and died in Enfield, March 30, 1819.

32

2001. THADDEUS SLUMAN, born in Canaan, April 23, 1812, and married, June 13, 1847, Mrs. Sarah Mussy. He has always resided in Canaan, where he is a stone cutter.

2002. JOSHUA STEVENS, born in Canaan, April 23, 1812, and married, Feb. 25, 1841, Dorothea Hamilton Fales, who died March 18, 1857. He is a farmer and is living in Monticello, Iowa. His wife died March 18, 1857, and he married (2), in Lyme, N. H., Nov. 17, 1858, Lydia C., daughter of Reuben and Nancy Bliss, who died Aug. 3, 1866. He married (3), June 17, 1866, Julia Ann (South) Horton, who died Nov. 13, 1871. He married (4), Aug. 31, 1873, Harriet Maria Waterhouse, daughter of Hiram and Flora Barnes. He removed from Canaan, N. H., to Castle Grove, Jones Co., Iowa, where he is now living.

2003. HARRIS, born in Canaan, Nov. 11, 1813, and died in the same place, May 25, 1825.

2004. ELISHA, born in Canaan, Oct. 1, 1815, and married in Barre, Vt., in November, 1838, Nancy Richardson. They are living at Enfield Center, N. H., where he is a tanner.

2005. SUSAN B., born in Canaan, April 30, 1818, and married, Feb. 25, 1841, Reuben Goss. She died in Canaan, having had five children.

    i.   Isabel Goss.
    ii.   Joshua Harris Goss.
    iii.  Calista Goss.
    iv.  Reuben Wallace Goss.
    v.   Bernice Goss.

2006. JOHN HEAD, born in Canaan, Feb. 14, 1821, and married, July 5, 1846, in Dorchester, Urvilla M. Ross, who was born Aug. 8, 1825, in Hanover, N. H. He is settled in Canaan, and we are indebted to him for the most of the lists of his grandfather's descendants. He is a lumber merchant.

2007. GEORGE HERRIMAN, born in Canaan, April 13, 1826, and married in Manchester, Nov. 27, 1861, Emily Gleason. He is a carpenter. Four children.

## 1132. THOMAS. Canaan, N. H.

2008. JAMES B., born Feb. 22, 1812; married; died in Arkansas in 1851.

2009. BENJAMIN GORDON, born in Canaan, New Hampshire July 6, 1815. He removed, while still a child, with his parents to South Carolina, and there received such advantages of a common school education as that State then afforded. He early inclined to a mercantile life, and in 1832 we find him in Montgomery, Alabama, engaged in general merchandise as a clerk. He was given charge of a trading post well up in the Indian country, and, such was his ability and integrity, that he soon became a partner in the house where he had been a clerk. It was at this time that he had his first experience in the Indian wars. He was a Lieutenant-Colonel and Division Inspector on the staff of Major-General Taliaferro, but, waiving his rank, he entered into active service as a private in the company of Captain Whitmore. The war ended, large bodies of lands became subject o sale, and Mr. Lathrop engaged extensively in the business of buying and selling lands, and at the same time acquired a controlling interest in a bank in Montgomery with a branch in Georgia. The growth of Montgomery was rapid, and upon its organization as a city, Mr. Lathrop was elected one of its first aldermen. But he was naturally a pioneer, and he soon moved from Alabama to the wilds of Arkansas, and for a while entered upon a business career in that State. He did not long remain there, however. In 1849, after the discovery of the gold mines on the Pacific coast, he was taken with what was known as the California fever. He organized a little band of fifteen men, white and black, and with them undertook the dangerous and difficult over-land journey. Beside the ordinary difficulties of the way there were hostile Indians to encounter, but his military experience stood him in good stead, and he brought his little band safely through. He now engaged in mining and in other business pursuits, and as in the east, so in the extreme west, by his energy, industry and integrity he secured the respect of all men. In the days of the Vigilance Committee, his home was in San Francisco county, where lawlessness was resorted to to put down lawlessness, and rogues with a short shrift were made to dangle at the end of a rope. Mr. Lathrop, with firm courage and a wise head, was always found upon the side of justice and right. When San Mateo county was set off from San Francisco county, in 1856, he was chosen County Clerk and Recorder, and filled the position until 1864. He also was chosen to the office of Supervisor and was made Chairman of the Board. Subsequently he engaged again in mining in Shasta county, and in farming in Sonoma county, but, while we write (1884), resides in San Francisco in the enjoyment of the fruits of a well-spent life. Wherever Mr. Lathrop has lived he has been prominent in all affairs, making no enemies except on the part of those whose friendship would have been a disgrace. He has been a progressive man, was an original incorporator of the Southern Pacific Railroad, and he was not the least distinguished of the men of '49, the pioneers of the Golden State. He is a man whose integrity was never impeached, with a deep sense of justice and right, bold to plan, resolute to act, and his life has been alike honorable to himself and to the family of Lathrops of which he is an honored son.

2010. ELIZABETH A., born Aug. 27, 1827, and died in 1883.

2011. THOMAS W., born Jan. 11, 1831, and married ——. He died in 1852.

### 1133. THADDEUS, JUN. Strongville, Ohio.

2012. NANCY.

2013. SUSAN, born 1806, and married Benjamin Tuttle of Strongville. She has two children.

2014. ELIZA; died single.

2015. THOMAS, born in 1811, and died single.

2016. WILLIAM AUSTIN, born Oct. 21, 1813, and married Phebe Christmas, who died.

2017. HAZEN, born Oct. 18, 1815, and married Mary Ann Bean, and settled in Strongville, Ohio. One child.

2018. PERSIS; married Jacob Leney. No children.

## 1137.  JAMES.

[This family were all born in Hartford.]

2019.  JAMES, jun., born Oct. 14, 1792, and married, in 1817, Sarah Holkins, of Warehouse Point.  He was a merchant and settled in Hartford.  He died in New Orleans, Aug. 28, 1824, and his widow married the Hon. Walter Booth of Meriden, who died much honored in 1870.  She still survives.

2020.  AZEL, born Oct. 3, 1794, and married Catherine Miller of Middletown.

2021.  HORACE, born Oct. 3, 1795, and died of the yellow fever in New Orleans, Nov. 29, 1817, unmarried.

2022.  HENRY, born March 18, 1797, and married Juliette ———.  He lived in New Orleans.  He united with the Presbyterian church in 1847, and died in New Orleans Dec. 15, 1854.

2023.  BLISS, born Sept. 25, 1798.  He married and lived south.  He died in Iberville, La., aged about 70.

2024.  NORMAN, born Oct. 12, 1800, and died of yellow fever in New Orleans, July 17, 1821.

2025.  PARTHENIA, born Nov. 25, 1802, and married Ahorn L. Pease. They lived in Waverly, Ill., where she died July 15, 1861.  "From her early youth she was an humble, earnest Christian, and to the end adorned her profession by a life of faith in Christ."

2026.  LYDIA, born Jan. 9, 1806, and married C. C. Tyler, Esq., of Middletown, where she died Dec. 10, 1870.  She was a member of the South Congregational Church in Middletown, and was greatly endeared to her acquaintances for her social and intellectual qualities, and especially for her warm-hearted and fervent piety.

2027.  ELIZABETH, born in Hartford Aug. 23, 1807, and married at Jacksonville, Ill., (Sept. 16) June 31, 1830, Dr. Maro McLean Read, a son of Dr. Elijah Fitch and Hannah (McLean) Read, who was born Oct. 18, 1801.  He graduated at Yale College in 1822, and studied medicine with his father, taking his degree of M. D. in 1826.  After practicing in East Windsor and Hartford, Conn., he removed to Jacksonville, Ill.  Children:

    i.    Harriet Read, born June 31, 1831.
    ii.   Edward Read, born March 6, 1833, and died July 3, 1833, of cholera.
    iii.  Albert Hale Read, born Feb. 12, 1836.
    iv.  Maria Lathrop Read, born Jan. 27, 1839.
    v.   Elijah Fitch Read.  Died young.
    vi.  Sarah Read, born ———
    vii.  Julia Read, born April 20, 1846.
    viii. Henry Read, born Feb. 15, 1848, and died Aug. 17, 1849.
    ix.  Mary Eliza Read, born June 25, 1849.

## 1139.  REV. JOHN.

2028.  JOHN.

## 1140.  URBAN.

2029.  JOHN, who lives in Boston, and has a son Horace.

2030.  HARVEY, of Boston.

2031. Uriel, of Nickerville.

2032. GEORGE, and other children, names not learned.

## 1142. DENISON. Buffalo, N. Y.

2033. HORACE, born in Littleton, N. H., July 20, 1798, and died March 10, 1799.

2034. ELDERKIN, born May 11, 1800, and married (1), Miss Ryan, by whom he had two children, sons, Dan and Albert; and (2), Harriet Austin, by whom he had two children, boy and girl, Charles and Anna.

2035. ALBERT, born April 18, 1802, and died in 1823, in Erie, Pa.

2036. DAN, born Oct. 9, 1802, and died July 8, 1823, unmarried.

2037. ELIZA, born Aug. 31, 1806, and married, Nov. 10, 1831, Benjamin Eldridge of Buffalo, where they now (1873) live. They have no children.

2038. HARRY BAKER, born July 6, 1808, and married, Feb. —, 1830, Sarah M. Deming. He is living in San Francisco, Cal. They had three children, one of whom, Henry B., is married and lives in Aronville, Cal.

2039. HORACE, born March 23, 1810, and died Feb. 2, 1835.

2040. ADALINE, born March 17, 1812. She has never married.

2041. MARY ANN, born May 23, 1813, and died Nov. 20, 1841, unmarried, in Michigan.

2042. RIAL WOODWORTH, born July 8, 1819, and married, May 9, 1843, Charlotte A. Rice, and lives in Buffalo. Children all dead:

    i. Emily.

    ii. Harriet.

    iii. Harriet.

2043. HEMAN FINNEY, born May 1, 1822, and married. Children:

    i. Son, who died.

    ii. Ella, married a Mr. Sykes, and lives in Buffalo.

2044. BELINDA ANN, born Jan. 26, 1824, and died May 25, 1827.

## 1143. ELIJAH. Batavia, N. Y.

[The sons all born in Lebanon, N. H.]

2045. HORACE, born in 1806, and is living (1873) at Ann Arbor, Mich.

2046. ORVILLE, born in 1808, and died in St. Louis, Mo., 1848.

2047. NELSON, born in 1810, and died in Detroit, in 1832.

2048. EDWIN, born in 1812, and died in California, in 1867. No children.

2049. LUCINDA, born in Batavia, N. Y., in 1815, married, and has a daughter living in California.

## 1145. GEORGE.

2050. GEORGE.

2051. CYNTHIA.

2052. ELIZA.

## 1146. FREDERICK.

2053. FREDERICK.

2054. ORLANDO.

2055. James.
2056. Elijah.
2057. Martha.
2058. Elizabeth.

### 1149. GEORGE H.                        Lebanon, N. H.

2059. George White.   .

2060. Solon Huntington, born June 23, 1823. He married, July 23, 1847, in Buffalo, N. Y., Elizabeth Stewart. On the opening of the recent war in 1861, he was commissioned captain, and assigned to the Seventeenth Regiment, United States Infantry. He was appointed, in 1863, assistant inspector-general of volunteers, with rank of lieutenant-colonel, and was at the head of the military staff of Major-General Heintzelman, whose wife's sister he had married.

### 1152. AZARIAH A.                        Sullivan, N. Y.

2061. Allen, born Jan. 29, 1803, and became a preacher. He married Azuba Ackley of Lincoln, N. Y. He died at Wyanett, Illinois.

2062. Nancy, born June 25, 1804, and died in Chenango, N. Y., Oct. 14, 1843.

2063. Philemon, born in Manlius, N. Y., Sept. 1, 1805, and married, Feb. 18, 1835, Sophia Shurtleff, who was born in Oneida County, N. Y., Aug. 2, 1804, and settled in Onondaga County, N. Y.

2064. John Smith, born Oct. 1, 1807, and married in Milford, N. Y., Feb. 25, 1829, Juliet D. Wilber of Malden, Bureau County, Illinois.

2065. Ann, born Nov. 2, 1809, and married, Jan., 1835, Benjamin Stark. She died Nov. 3, 1835.

2066. Lecta, born Nov. 1, 1811, and died Sept. 4, 1812.

2067. Elba Mallory, born June 19, 1813. He was editor and proprietor of a religious paper, the *Protestant Methodist*, at Nauvoo, Ill. Himself, wife, and four children all died within one year.

2068. Levi Beneet, born April 30, 1815, and married, March 26, 1839, in Bureau County, Illinois, Lora Judd. He is a Methodist preacher. He was in California, and laid out the Lathrop addition to San Juan, and his last post-office address reported, was Hollister, California (1873).

2069. Curtiss, Green, born Nov. 29, 1816, and married, Feb. 17, 1840, in Bureau County, Illinois, Phebe Judd. He has also been a Methodist preacher (Methodist Episcopal), and for about thirty years a presiding elder. His residence is in Nebraska.

2070. Semantha Sarah Hannah, born Nov. 25, 1818, and married, in Otselic, N. Y., Jan. 20, 1845, Miles F. Perkins. They settled in California, where he died. She afterwards married a Mr. Warner, and has lived in Una-dilla Forks, N. Y. She has had several children.

2071. Merrit Adams, born Dec. 3, 1820, and married, April 22, 1844, Betsey Goodwin, and is settled in Annawan, Ill. He also has been a Methodist preacher.

2072. Wm. Bradford Adams, born Dec. 27, 1822, and married, in Dayton, N. Y., Dec. 26, 1845, Mary Newitt, who died. He removed to California, where he married (2), ———.

2073. Marian Maria, born Oct. 25, 1824, and died May 16, 1846.

### 1153. ELISHA.

2074. A DAUGHTER.
2075. A DAUGHTER.

### 1154. ELIJAH.

2076. MALVINA, and others.

### 1161. SAMUEL.

2077. ⎫
2078. ⎪
2079. ⎬ FIVE DAUGHTERS, names not learned.
2080. ⎪
2081. ⎭

### 1165-1. JEDIDIAH II.  Washington, D. C.

2081-1. BRYAN, born Aug. 6, 1844, in Alexandria, Va., and at the breaking out of the rebellion he was in the preparatory department of the University of Virginia. Escaping from conscription into the Southern army, he went with his father's family into Pennsylvania, and in 1862, on account of ill-health, he went to Europe. He remained abroad three years, devoting himself to the study of modern languages. On his return, in 1865, he entered into partnership with T. B. Bryan of Chicago, as real estate agents. He remains still in Chicago, in the same business. He married in Washington City, D. C., April 21, 1875, Helen Lynde Aldis of Washington, D. C.

2082. BARBOUR THOMAS, born in Alexandria, Va., Jan. 28, 1846. He completed his classical education in the University of Bonn, Germany. He returned home and graduated at the Harvard Law School, and was for a time in the law office of Wirt Dexter, Esq., of Chicago. A failure of health forced him to give up the profession, and he re embarked on the tour of the world. When last heard from he was in Japan.

2083. CAROLINE HUNTINGTON, born Oct. 16, 1853, and died Nov. 3, 1854.

2084. MINNA BYRD, born May 4, 1857.

2085. FLORENCE WENTWORTH, born Oct. 19, 1858.

### 1186. CHARLES.  York, Ill.

2086. CAROLINE C., born in Lebanon, Conn., Nov. 27, 1811, and married in Norwich, Oct. 8, 1834, Daniel Kennedy. They settled in Virginia, where she died.

2087. LUCY ANN, born in Lebanon Oct. 22, 1813, and married, Jan. 5, 1836, John Chandler Bartlett, son of Cyrus McCall Bartlett and Betsey McCall of Lebanon. He was born Dec. 16, 1803, and died in Hartford Jan. 1, 1865. They settled in Natchez, Miss. Children:

i. Leonora Frances Bartlett, born at Natchez, Miss., Oct. 9, 1837, and married Benjamin F. Parsons.

ii. Charles James Bartlett, born at Port Gibson, Miss., Nov. 10, 1839, and died at Hawkinsville, Ga., Sept. 25, 1869. She died while on a visit to her mother in Colchester, Conn., July 5, 1840.

2088. JAMES WILLIAMS, born in Lebanon, Sept. 6, 1815, and married in Perry, Ga., July 1, 1846, Margaret, a daughter of Eli and Eliza Jane (Love) Warren. He began his business life before he was of age in Hawkinsville, Ga. He settled first in Pulaski county, at Hawkinsville, but afterwards moved to Savannah, as affording more ample scope for the exercise of his large business qualifications. For twenty-five years or more he had been one of the leading merchants of this city, and filled many positions in which his experience, judgment, and business qualifications were fully brought out and exemplified. At the time of his death he was the honored President of the Savannah Cotton Exchange, of which he was one of the founders and its first and only President. He was in the prime of an active life, being about fifty-eight years of age, at the time of his death.

2089. CHARLES TENNANT, born in Vincennes, Ind., June 28, 1817, and married in Pulaski, Ga., Nov. 21, 1854, Margaret Rebecca Mikell. She died in Griffin, Ga., Dec. 3, 1855, leaving no children. President Hawkinsville Bank and Trust Company.

2090. HENRY WILLIAMS, born in York, Crawford county, Ill., Jan. 7, 1820, and married, in Staunton, Va., Oct. 1, 1860, Mary Louisa, daughter of David Fultz, Esq., who died in May, 1862, leaving no children. He married (2), July 27, 1865, in Newbury, S. C., Annie, daughter of P. E. Kinsley, of Charleston, S. C. Retired from business to his farm, "Swansea Park," near Baltimore, Md.

2091. ALMIRA M., born in York, Ill., Jan. 5, 1822, and married in Colchester, Conn., Aug. 18, 1858, Solomon Everest Swift, M.D., who was born in Farmington, Conn., July 27, 1819. He was the son of Dr. Zephaniah and Nelly M. Everett. His first wife was Mary M., daughter of Rev. Isaac Parsons of East Haddam, by whom he had three sons, Theodore Everett, George Parsons, and Edward Hulstead. He is now settled in Colchester. They have three children, all born in Colchester:

   i.   Rebecca Lathrop Swift, born July 25, 1859, and died Aug. 7, 1860.
   ii.  John Trumbull Swift, born April 3, 1861.
   iii. Caroline Louise Swift, born Sept. 21, 1863.

## 1187. ANDREW. Lebanon, Ct.

2092. MARY J., born in Lebanon Nov. 23, 1816, and married, Oct. 22, 1837, William Frank Geer, and settled in Syracuse. N. Y. She died Nov. 26, 1866. They have had six children,—Wm. C., Mary J., Andrew L., Mary, David W., and Charles F.

2093. WILLIAM S., born in Lebanon, April 29, 1820, and married, Jan. 24, 1847, Grace S. Briggs, who died July 16, 1867, aged 41 years. He is now living in Lebanon.

2094. NANCY M., born in Lebanon, Sept., 1825, and married, Sept. 22, 1852, Coddington Smith, and lived in Lebanon, Goshen Society. He died April 27, 1865, aged 59 years.

## 1191. ABIEL, JUN. Berlin, N. Y.

2095. I. R.

### 1193. SYLVESTER R. Ripon, Wis.

2096. ALVIN B., born April 15, 1821, and married, Jan. 2, 1865, Mrs. F. L. Stillwell, now of 239½ Newbury Av., Chicago. No children (1873).

2097. MARY E., born Dec. 1, 1823, and married Rev. John Fridd, a clergyman of the Methodist Episcopal Church, who was born in England. They have seven children: Lizzie, who married Lafayette van Eaton, and has two children; Jenny, who married Aaron Walker; John A., who married Addie Atkins; William; George; Nellie; and Charlie.

2098. LUCY J., born Feb. 8, 1826, and married J. H. Foster. Children:
    i. Florette Foster, who married M. C. Goucher, and has one child.
    ii. Frances Foster.
    iii. Jenny Foster.

2099. MARILLA B., born Sept. 18, 1831, and married N. C. Hoit. Children:
    i. Eugene Lathrop Hoit.
    ii. Isabel J Hoit.
    iii. Frances S. Hoit, Green Lake, Wis.
    iv. Lowell Sylvester Hoit.

2100. AUSTIN C., born Aug. 13, 1835; officer in late war.

### 1197. JOHN. Pittsford, Vt.

2101. MARY, born in Pittsford, Sept. 24, 1822.

2102. WILLIAM, born in Pittsford, April 17, 1825.

2103. ANN, born in Pittsford, March 8, 1828.

2104. WHITMAN, born in Pittsford, June 16, 1830.

2105. JULIA, born in Pittsford, July 6, 1835, and died April 23, 1847.

### 1200. CHARLES. New York, N. Y.

2106. CHARLES ADGATE.

2107. GEORGE N.; Rochester, N. Y.

2108. JAMES A.; in Erie depot.

2109. MARY A.; married B. F. Harris.

2110. JOHN PARKER.

2111. LEWIS ELBRIDGE.

2112. ELBRIDGE.

### 1208. JOHN B. Arlington, Vt.

2113. A DAUGHTER, born in Sunderland in 1828, and lived but two days.

2114. CORNELIA C., born in Arlington in 1831, and married, in 1851, Jesse Burdett, Esq., now Superintendent of the Rutland division of the Central Vermont Railroad (1873). They have one son:
    John Lathrop Burdett, born in November, 1852.

### 1211. AUSTIN H. LA. Racine, Wis.

2115. LUCAS BRADLEY, born Dec. 14, 1836, and married a Mr. Bowman, and lives in Racine; has one child, a daughter.

33

2116. LOUISA ANNETTE, born June 30, 1840, and died Aug. 9, 1861.

2117. WILLIAM RUFUS, born Aug. 1, 1838, and died in Washington, D. C., Sept. 26, 1862, in service.

2118. AUSTIN H., born May 21, 1842, and married in November, 1872, Mary Winslow, in Racine. Residence, Vermillion, Dakota.

2119. LAURA J., born Sept. 28, 1845, and married William Crane of Racine, Wis. Four children, in Racine.

2120. EDMUND KING, born Nov. 9, 1847. Chicago, Ill.

### 1213.  WILLIAM H. LA.                    Racine, Wis.

2121. GENEVE, born April 1, 1843, and died in Racine, Feb. 3, 1845.

2122. FRANK, born June 10, and died Oct. 3, 1847.

### 1214.  HUBBEL LA.                        Sunderland, Vt.

2123. LAURA B., born Aug. 13, 1841, and married Oct. 10, 1865, Fletcher O. Hanaman of Arlington, Vt. Children:

    i.   Willie Hanaman, born Aug. 15, 1868.

    ii.   Azuba Hanaman, born April 4, 1873.

2124. ROLAND, born March 4, 1844, and died Feb. 13, 1846.

2125. CLARA H., born Nov. 12, 1846, and married, May 21, 1871, William B. Anderson of Enosburg, Vt.

2126. FRANK H., born Feb. 18, 1850, and died Dec. 23, 1859.

2127. SARAH P., born May 4, 1852.

2128. WILLIAM H., born June 11, 1855.

### 1215.  ELI B.

2129.  ⎫
2130.  ⎬ Four children, names not learned.
2131.  ⎮
2132.  ⎭

### 1217.  CHAUNCEY A.                       Racine, Wis.

2133. LORIN R.

2134. NELLIE.

2135. JENNIE.

### 1230.  ERASTUS C.                         York, O.

2136. A DAUGHTER, who died July 5, 1840.

### 1231.  WILLIAM C.                         Liberty, O.

2137.  ⎫
2138.  ⎬ Four children, names not learned.
2139.  ⎮
2140.  ⎭

### 1232.  EBENEZER.                          Appleton, Minn.

2141. ALFRED W.

2142. MARY.

### 1234. GRIFFIN C. Felton, N. Y.

2143. EUGENE.

### 1235. REV. ALFRED C. Glenwood, Minn.

2144. JUDITH CORNELIA, born in Williamson, Mayne Co., N. Y., March 8, 1841, and is now living, single, with her father.

2145. STANLEY EDWARD, born in Orville, Onondaga Co., N. Y., May 7, 1843, and married, at Tomah, Wis., Sept. 6, 1870, Elizabeth, daughter of William and Ann Littell, of Tomah. He was educated at Beloit College, Wis., class of 1867, and at the Chicago Theological Seminary, class of 1870.

2146. ALFRED HOUGH, born in Collamer, Onondaga Co., N. Y., Nov. 1, 1849.

2147. LEANDER ERASTUS, born in Pompey Center, Onondaga Co., N. Y., Nov. 6, 1851, and died in the same place March 24, 1852.

2148. IDA ESTELLA, born in New London, Waupaca Co., Wis., Feb. 9, 1855, and is living with her parents.

### 1242. EMORY S. Glenwood, Minn.

2149. ———.

2150. ALMOND.

2151. VINNING.

2152. EMORY CLAIRE, born Feb. 11, 1859.

2153. MARY AGNES, born May 24, 1862.

2154. CHARLOTTE A., born Nov. 2, 1865.

2155. GLENWOOD NEWTON, born in Glenwood, Pope Co,, Minn., Nov. 3, 1867,—the first white child born in the new town.

### 1248. SEPTIMIUS.

2156. ALFRED GRANGER, born at Albany, March 1, 1841; entered the United States navy in 1862; served under Admiral Farragut at New Orleans and capture of forts in Mobile Bay; resigned in 1866; engaged in building Union Pacific Railroad; resided several years in Europe; now (1875) in New York.

2157. CHARLOTTE LOUISE, born at Albany Aug. 15, 1842; married Henry W. Burt, Esq., banker at Buffalo, June 11, 1862.

2158. EUNICE PAULINE, born at Albany April 8, 1843; married, 1864, at New York, Henry W. Cowell, Esq., of England.

2158-1. HARRIET VICTORIA, born at Albany Oct. 16, 1846; married Oct. 21, 1871, John H. Tingley, Esq., at Nyack-on-Hudson.

2158-2. KATHERINE HILTON, born May 21, 1849, at Buffalo. Died April 20, 1850.

2158-3. FLORENCE ADELE, born Aug. 23, 1851, at Buffalo.

2158-4. CHARLES TOWNSEND, born Oct. 8, 1853, at Buffalo; educated at Racine College, Michigan, under Rev. Dr. DeKoven.

### 1250. REV. SAMUEL GURDON. Evanston, Ill.

2159. EDWARD; a physician in Ottumwa.

2160. BEST; a lawyer in Chicago.

2161. ELLA.

2162. MINNIE BELLE.

### 1259. DANIEL, JUN.          New Milford, Conn.

[This family were all born in New Milford.]

2163. HARRY, born March 2, 1813, and is now living, single, in Prospect.

2164. ALVA, born Aug. 7, 1814, and married, September, 1837, in New York city, Eliza Pulis, who was born March 12, 1819. He still lives in New York city.

2165. GEORGE, born Sept. 5, 1816; married Lucy Scott. He is now living in Northville in New Milford.

2166. ASHBEL, born Jan. 27, 1818, and married Viola Morgan, of Kent, and lived and died in New Milford. They had no children.

2167. JOHN MANN, born Jan. 4, 1820, and married Sophia Coverly of New Jersey, and now lives in Oswego, N. Y.; merchant.

2168. DELIA ANN, who died at twelve years of age.

2169. HARRIET, who died when 22 months old.

2170. LAURA, who married (1), Clark Morehouse of New Milford, (2), John Bogardus. She is now living in Danbury.

2171. CHARLES, born Oct. 24, 1826, and married (1), Mary Bingham, and (2), Oct. 4, 1857, Jane Miranda Neal, of Winsted, Ct. He has been for twenty years in the railroad service on the Naugatuck and Housatonic roads, and is now, 1873, a conductor on the latter road. He resides in Bridgeport.

2172. FREDERICK, born June 7; married, in Cornwall, Lorinda Palmer.

### 1260. AMASA.          Roxbury, Conn.

2173. POLLY ANN.

2174. FREDERICK.

2175. HENRY.

2176. JANE.

2177. LYDIA.

2178. MARIA.

2179. FRISBE.

### 1261. HENRY.          New Milford, Conn.

2180. CAROLINE; married Edward Jones.

2181. HARRIET; married.

2182. JANE; married Daniel Maginnis.

2183. NANCY; married ——— Smith.

### 1262. BARNABAS.          New Milford, Conn.

2184. MARIA, who married Beecher Morehouse, and died in New Milford. They had two children born in New Milford.

i. George Walter Morehouse, born Aug. 21, 1828, and died Sept. 15, 1843.

ii. Helen Maria Morehouse, born July 2, 1830.

## 1264. ALANSON. Becket, Mass.

2185.
2186.
2187.
2188.
2189. } Nine children, names not learned.
2190.
2191.
2192.
2193.

## 1265. JOHN. New Milford, Conn.

2194. JEROME, born in New York March 27, 1826, and married Laura Morehouse, sister of Beecher, above; died in New Milford May 27, 1850. No children.

2195. ELIZA ANN, born Jan. 23, 1828; married John Dunlap, Bridgeport. Children: Walter; Carrie; Lizzie.

2196. SOPHIA, born in New Milford, April 8, 1841, and married, April 21, 1860, William Henry Dunlap, and (2), James L. Fleetham.

2197. CHARLOTTE, born Oct. 25, 1842; married in Meriden, July 12, 1864, William H. Stannis.

2198. FRANCES, born Jan. 17, 1844, and died in New Milford July 20, 1844.

2199. FRANCES ADELLE, born July 25, 1845, and married in New Milford, Oct. 29, 1863, Edwin A. Lampson. Children:

   i.   Frank Dunlap Lampson was born May 27, 1862.

   ii.   Luie Lampson was born the 29th of August, 1865.

   iii.   William Th. Stannis Lampson was born in 1866.

   iv.   Fred Fleetham Lampson was born 2d of July, 1870.

   v.   Anna Agnes Lampson was born March 17, 1871.

   vi.   Walter Stannis Lampson was born Jan. 23, 1873.

2200. SARAH JANE, born Oct. 8, 1846; married, Aug. 6, 1864, William Gilbert Lathrop.

2201. MARY AMELIA, born Nov. 10, 1849, and died March 6, 1854.

2202. DELPHENE, born Dec. 17, 1851, and died Feb. 22, 1854.

## 1274. SOLOMON. Oakwood, Mich.

2203. SOPHIA POMEROY, born Jan. 6, 1821, and died March 2, 1821, in East Saginaw, Mich.

2204. GEORGE ABBOTT, born in West Springfield, March 18, 1822, and married (1), Dec. 2, 1858, Carrie E., daughter of John and Rebecca (Punchard) Derby, of Andover, Mass. She was born Dec. 7, 1828, and died in East Saginaw, June 11, 1869. He married (2), Mrs. Helen L. Derby, daughter of Norman and Jane Lyon Little, of East Saginaw. He commenced the study of medicine with Dr. I. D. Whitney of Romeo, Mich., and graduated at the Medical College at Woodstock, Vt., in 1847. He crossed the plains and Rocky Mountains in 1849, and settled in the practice of his profession in Olympia, W. T.

He was one of the local committee which called the first Republican Convention in that territory. In 1855 returned to the States, and settled in East Saginaw, where he still resides.

2205. HENRY KIRKE, born in West Springfield, Feb. 21, 1824, and married in Romeo, Mich., Feb. 11, 1846, Elizabeth Abbott, daughter of William. She was born in Bath, N. H., and died in Oakwood, Mich., March 2, 1861. He is a physician and is now settled in Royal Oak, Mich. He studied medicine with Dr. Whitney, now of San Francisco, and in 1846 was admitted to practice. He was skillful in his profession.

2206. SOPHIA, born July 2, 1826, and died Aug. 10, 1826.

2207. FRANCES MARAH, born in West Springfield, Sept. 2, 1827, and died in Oakwood, April 1, 1853, unmarried.

2208. SOLOMON, born in West Springfield, Dec. 20, 1829, and married in Detroit, Jan. 26, 1852, Cornelia S., daughter of James and Maria Guild. She was born in Williamsburgh, N. Y., July 31, 1832. He is a jeweler, and in business at Gross Valley, Cal., having removed from Detroit, Mich., in 1861, to the Pacific coast.

2209. CATHERINE SOPHIA, born in West Springfield, Feb. 23, 1832, and is living, unmarried, with her brother, Henry H., in Royal Oak, Mich.

2210. JOSEPH, born in West Springfield, June 10, 1834, and married in Detroit, Mich., Sept. 9, 1863, Ada Maria, eldest daughter of Dr. Henry P. Pulling and Johanna I. Bridgeman, who was born at Amsterdam, N. Y., Sept. 10, 1839. He has been located in the dentist's profession in Detroit since 1861. He is a Lathrop of the Lathrops, having shown a very deep interest in this work of collecting and compiling the materials for the Lathrop Memorial.

2211. MARY, born in Armada, Mich., May 25, 1837, and married in East Saginaw, Jan. 1, 1856, George, son of Rev. Elisha and Betsey (Lathrop) Andrews. Mr. Andrews commenced the practice of law in Detroit, where he had studied his profession, and in 1865 removed to Knoxville, Tenn., where he is still engaged.

## 1275. EDWARD.        Armada, Mich.

2212. CHARLES ABBOT, born Oct. 25, 1816, and married, May 22, 1858, Rachel Ann Youngs. He and his brother Seth were early engaged in successful mercantile business in Armada, until they dissolved partnership in 1864. He then associated with him his brother Elisha D., and the firm thus constituted stands high for business integrity and enterprise.

2213. SETH, born July 1, 1818, and married (1), Dec. 25, 1849, Polly Walker, who died July 18, 1854. He married (2), May 5, 1856, Lydia McAlister. On dissolving partnership with his brother Charles A., he removed to Richmond, Mich., and united with his brother Jonathan D. in business, where they are still doing a heavy business.

2214. GEORGE ANDREWS, born in April, 1820, and died in Aug., 1821.

2215. JANE MARY MARIA, born in West Springfield, Mass., March 18, 1822, and was married at Armada, Mich., Dec. 26, 1843, by Rev. S. A. Benton, to Henry O., son of Obadiah and Susan (Norton) Smith, who was born in Hatfield, Mass., Jan. 1, 1817. They are settled in Romeo, Mich., where he is

Cashier of the National Bank and one of the trustees, and an honored business man of the town. Parents and children, except the last two, are members of the Congregational Church. Children:

    i.  Frances Lathrop Smith, born in Romeo Feb. 7, 1845.

    ii.  Henry Augustus Smith, born in Romeo, Sept. 3, 1846.

    iii.  Florence Elizabeth Smith, born in Romeo, Nov. 16, 1849, and married in the same place, Oct. 22, 1868, William A. Swan.

    iv.  Mary Emma Smith, born in Armada, Mich., June 24. 1853.

    v.  Charles Edward Smith, born in Armada, Oct. 10, 1856.

    vi.  Jane Maria Smith, born at Mt. Clemens, Mich., Aug. 18, 1860, and died in same place, Feb. 7, 1861.

    vii.  Edwin Norton Smith, born in Mt. Clemens, Nov. 13, 1861.

    viii.  Carrie Ellen Smith, born in Mt. Clemens, Sept. 30, 1864.

2216. HORACE ANDREWS, born March 6, 1824, and married, Feb. 12, 1851, Elizabeth Mariette, daughter of Franklin and Eliza (Wheeler) Gilbert, who was born in East Bloomfield, N. Y., Oct. 15, 1834. He is settled in Armada, Mich., having been driven out of Missouri, where he was living when the recent war of the rebellion began, because of his adherence to the Union.

2217. JAMES EDWARD, born Oct. 18. 1826, and married, Feb. 27, 1850, Helen M. Dunham. He died June 16, 1856.

2218. SAMUEL, born in West Springfield, Dec. 7, 1828, and married, Nov. 10, 1852, Adeline Tenny. He is a successful physician and surgeon, and has been in the practice of his profession in Clio, Mich., about twenty years. During the recent war he was a volunteer surgeon at Fredericksburg, and rendered good service to the Union cause.

2219. ELIZABETH, born in Pittsford, N. Y., July 29, 1832, and married, Feb. 10, 1868, Jerome Bonaparte Littlefield, who was born May 18, 1869. Children:

    i.  Henry J. Littlefield, born May 18, 1869, and died Sept. 1, 1869.

    ii.  Emma Jane Littlefield, born June 23, 1870.

    iii.  Ella Lorinda Littlefield, born March 30, 187–.

2220. JONATHAN DWIGHT, born in West Bloomfield, N. Y., Aug. 16, 1834, and married, Nov. 9, 1862, Emeline Littlefield.

2221. ANN ABBEY, born in Pittsford, April 27, 1837, and married Durfee Pettibone, March 28, 1860. Children:

    i.  William Ezra Pettibone, born Sept. 13, 1864.

    ii.  Jenny Pettibone, born Dec. 11, 1866, and died Feb. 3, 186–.

    iii.  Edith Pettibone, born June 23, 1868, and died Dec. 11, 1869.

    iv.  Frances Emma Pettibone, born June 4, 1876.

2222. ELISHA DEMING, born in Armada Dec. 25, 1839, and married, April 19, 1864, Mary Jane Kellogg. He is settled in business with his brother Charles in Armada.

## 1276. JOSEPH.

2223. JOSEPH WELLS, born June 15, 1817, and was drowned in the Connecticut River, June 17, 1833.

2224. JOHN LENTNER, born July 4, 1819, and married, Oct. 10, 1850, Ann, daughter of Almon and Betsey (Ashley) Day of South Hadley Falls. She was born June 27, 1825. He has been living in Hannibal, Mo., for several years, and since 1857, has been Secretary and Treasurer of the Hannibal & Saint Joseph Railroad. During the recent war of the rebellion, he was of no little service to the Union cause.

2225. PAOLI, born Dec. 3, 1821. New York City.

2226. ROBERT, born Sept. 5, 1825, and married, Jan. 6, 1852, Rosella, daughter of Walter M. and Sally (Frost) Langdon of Wilbraham, Mass. She was born Sept. 16, 1832.

2227. MARIA LOUISA, born April 17, 1827, and married, Oct. 23, 1845, Ogden Hoffman, son of Abijah and Sarah (Caswell) Osborn of Albany, N. Y. He was born April 10, 1824, and died in Poughkeepsie, N. Y., July 17, 1866. Children:

    i. Kate Jane Osborn, born June 4, 1849. .

    ii. Paoli Lathrop Osborn, born June 12, 1852, and died Dec. 28, 1855.

    iii. Richard Ogden Osborn, born April 7, 1855.

    iv. Anna Louisa Osborn, born Dec. 23, 1859.

### 1278. WELLS. South Hadley, Mass.

2228. ELIZABETH, born in Springfield, April 28, 1821, and married, Aug. 23, 1842, George Bliss, son of Judge Oliver B. and Caroline (Bliss) Morris of Springfield. He was born Nov. 12, 1815, and graduated at Amherst in 1837, and has been a lawyer in Springfield, and Clerk of the County Court. Children:

    i. George Bliss Morris, born Nov. 5, 1843, and graduated at Harvard in 1864.

    ii. Robert Oliver Morris, born Oct. 18, 1846.

    iii. Caroline Morris, born Sept 18, 1848.

2229. JAMES, born in Springfield, Aug. 7, 1823, and married, Aug 24, 1848, Harriet Angeline Day, sister to the wife of John L. Lathrop, No. 2224. She was born Oct. 25, 1827.

2230. CATHERINE BONTICOU, born at South Hadley Falls, Dec. 23, 1826, and married, Oct. 22, 1863, Oliver Ellsworth, son of Judge Joseph and Fanny (Ellsworth) Wood, who was born in Stamford, Conn., April 14, 1812. He was a commission merchant in New York City. They had one child, Winthrop Wood, born Jan. 27, 1865, and died Sept 4, 1871.

2231. DANIEL BONTICOU, born in South Hadley Falls, June 23, 1829, and was drowned in the Connecticut River, Aug. 16, 1858.

2232. WELLS, JUN., born Aug. 13, 1844, and died July 14, 1849.

2233. MARY, born Feb. 15, 1847, and married, July 5, 1871, Mark Temald.

### 1279. HON. PAOLI. South Hadley Falls.

2234. HELEN, born in Ludlow, Mass., March 16, 1832.

2235. FANNY, born at South Hadley Falls, Jan. 15, 1836, and married in Delaware, Ohio, Sept. 2, 1868, Daniel Pierson, M. D., of Augusta, Ill. He was

was born July 1, 1823. They have one child, Paoli Lathrop Pierson, born in Augusta, Ill., Dec. 1, 1869.

2236. Seth, born in South Hadley Falls, May 10, 1838. and married, Aug. 20, 1861, Ellen L., daughter of Warren Asherton and Louisa (Lyman) Read of Northampton, Mass. She was born July 19, 1843. They settled in Chester, Mass.

2237. George Merrick, born in South Hadley Falls, Sept. 28, 1840, and died Sept. 25, 1843.

2238. Emma, born in South Hadley Falls, April 17, 1844, and died in her native town, May 19, 1868.

2239. Abby Merrick, born in South Hadley Falls, Feb. 3, 1847, and died Oct. 20, 1847.

2240. Bessie Champion, born in South Hadley Falls, May 9, 1855.

## 1289. WILLIAM McC. Boston, Mass.

2241. Charlotte Ann, born Aug. 18, 1834, and died in Flushing, L. I., April 12, 1872, unmarried.

2242. William Henry, born March 11, 1840, and married. Graduated at Harvard in 1863; is a physician and professor in Detroit Medical College.

2243. Henrietta Sprague, born Jan. 5, 1859.

2244. Elizabeth Rogers, born March 5, 1866.

## 1290. JOHN. Oxford, N. Y.

2245. Henry Miller, born Sept. 6, 1839, in Jordan, N. Y., and died in New York, Dec. 18, 1868.

2246. Mary Elizabeth, born at Oxford, N. Y., Oct. 6, 1845.

## 1293. JOSEPH. St. Louis, Mo.

2247. Mary Sprague, born Aug. 23, 1839.

2248. Abby Pomeroy, born Aug. 23, 1841.

2249. Elizabeth Dwight, born April 7, 1844, married May 8, 1873, Oscar Livingston Whitelaw, a wholesale druggist in St. Louis.

2250. Joseph, born Oct. 3, 1845, and died Dec. 21, 1846.

2251. Caroline Dewey, born Dec. 16, 1847.

2252. Joseph, born Aug. 8, 1849.

2253. Sarah Grace, born April 7, 1851 or 2.

2254. William Addison Howe, born Feb. 20, 1854.

## 1297. FRANCIS S. Madison, N. J.

2255. Louisa Gibbons, born Aug. 19, 1831, and married, June 19, 1849, Joseph Abbot Dean. Children:

  i    Alice Dean, born Oct. 10, 1850.
  ii   Eleanor Dean, born Feb. 15, 1852.
  iii  Arthur Dean, born July 25, 1858.

34

2256. FRANK, born Dec. 24, 1832, and married, Nov. 12, 1856, Isabel, daughter of William and Abby (Taintor) Gibbons of Madison, N. J., who was born Oct. 31, 1833. He settled as a farmer in Madison, and died in Morristown, N. J., Dec. 12, 1866.

2257. ELLEN, born April 9, 1834, and married, Nov. 13, 1851, Henry Hopkins, a banker of New York city. He died July 10, 1870. Children:

    i.    Frank Lathrop Hopkins, born Jan. 17, 1853.

    ii.   Henry Hopkins, born Feb. 17, 1854, and died May 15, 1854.

    iii.  Ellen Hopkins, born May 30, 1855.

    iv.  Edward Macalester Hopkins, born July 10, 1857.

    v.   Caroline Lathrop Hopkins, born March 2, 1859.

    vi.  Fannie Hopkins, born Jan. 25, 1861.

    vii.  Richard Hopkins, born Sept. 4, 1862.

    viii. Marie Gilmore Hopkins, born April 17, 1864.

### 1298. DWIGHT.

2258. CATHERINE ANN, born March 9, 1832, and died Aug., 1832.

2259. DWIGHT, born at Savannah, Ga., July 27, 1833, and married in Macon, Ga., April 27, 1865, Maria Louisa Brantly, who died Nov. 8, 1865. He died in Savannah, Dec. 20, 1866.

2260. FRANCIS HENRY, born in Savannah, Ga., July 27, 1835, married (1), in New York, April 29, 1869, Frances A. Macdonough; (2), June 5, 1883, Julia Pinkney Dellinger.

2261. EDWARD STEBBINS, twin with Francis, born July 27, 1835, married in Macon, Ga., Sept. 11, 1862, Georgia M. Brantly, sister to his brother Dwight's wife, and lives in Atlanta, Ga.

2262. MARY CLELAND, born Oct. 2, 1839, and married, Sept. 26, 1860, James Renwick Gibson, Jr. Children:

    i.    Robert Renwick Gibson, born in July, 1861.

    ii.   Maud Gibson, born May 27, 1862, and died Aug. 12, 1862.

### 1299. HENRY. Northampton, Mass.

2263. HENRY STEBBINS, born July 28, 1850, and died May 14, 1853.

2264. JOSEPH DWIGHT, born Oct. 11, 1851.

2265. CLARA WELLS, born May 22, 1853.

2266. BESSIE STEBBINS, born Nov. 8, 1854.

2267. CHARLES HENRY, born Jan. 19, 1858, and died May 21, 1859.

2268. LUCIA, born May 7, 1860.

### 1300. JERE STEBBINS. Northampton, Mass.

2269. ELIZABETH S., born July 9, 1841, and married, June 16, 1870, J. Hunt Butler. Children:

    i.    Stephen Lathrop Butler, born April 9, 1871.

    ii.   Marianne Elizabeth Butler, born Oct. 11, 1872.

### 1302. Rev. LEONARD E. Sharon, Conn.

2270. CAROLINE ELIZABETH, born in Wilmington, March 10, 1820, and died in Rochester, Aug. 22, 1858.

2271. HENRY, born in Kinderhook, Aug. 13, 1822, and married, Nov. 22, 1853, Eunice P. Knight.

2272. LEONARD, born in Kinderhook, May 24, 1824. Married and died.

2273. MARIA LUDLOW, born in Salisbury, April 8, 1826, and married, Nov. 27, 1849, Theodore F. Sharpe.

2274. EMMA MALVINA, born in Salisbury, May 9. 1828, and died Jan. 29, 1829.

2275. MARY WHITTLESEY, born in Salisbury, Jan. 19, 1830, and married in Stamford, Conn., at the residence of her sister, Mrs. Dr. Booth, June 2, 1858, Aaron T. Smith. Children:

    i.  Leonard Lathrop Smith, born March 6, 1859.

    ii.  Richard Smith, born July 10, 1861.

2276. EMMA LOUISA, born in Salisbury, March 12, 1832, and married, Oct. 26, 1853, Robert R. Booth, D.D. Children:

    i.  Maria Lathrop Booth, born May 19, 1855, and died April 24, 1862.

    ii.  William Agur Booth, born Sept. 24, 1859, and died May 6, 1862.

2277. WILLIAM EUGENE, born in Salisbury, Sept. 6, 1834, and died Dec. 13, 1835.

2278. JAMES MATHEWS, born in Salisbury, Sept. 1, 1836.

2279. WILLIAM EDWARD, born in Auburn, N. Y., June 29, 1839, and married Nellie Sweet. They reside in Brooklyn, and have no children (1873).

2280. FREDERICK EUGENE, born in Auburn, July 26, 1843, married Camilla Van Auken of New York City, May 12, 1868. He died suddenly at Lake Mahopac, July 15, 1876.

2281. ANNA HALSEY, born in Auburn, Nov. 18, 1844, and died in New York City, Tuesday, April 14, 1874. The funeral was from the residence of her brother-in-law, Rev. Dr. Booth, and the remains were taken to Sharon for interment.

### 1307. BENJAMIN H.

2282. MARIA.

2283. SALLY.

2284. SYBIL.

2285. BETTY.

2286. LORD.

### 1308. SAMUEL B. Hartford, Conn.

2287. THOMAS, born in Windham, June 14, 1805, and married, Feb. 26, 1825, Sarah Orchard, who was born in Boston, Jan. 18, 1805. He was a builder, and lived in Springfield, Mass., where he died July 16, 1860. Children:

    i.  Twins: "Samuel B. and Prudence," died May 30, 1807, aged three days.

    ii.  Freelove, died Aug. 19, 1807, aged two months and twenty-three days.

2288. PRUDENCE, born in Windham, March 27, 1809, and married, May, 1841, M. R. Stevenson, and lived in Boston and Springfield. She died in Springfield, in July, 1867.

## 1310. CHARLES. Springfield, Mass.

2289. DELIA, born in Granby, Conn., Sept. 5, 1805.

2290. EMÉLINE, born in Granby, Jan. 9, 1807, and died May 20, 1813.

2291. BELIA, born in Springfield, Mass., May 2, 1835, and married, Dec. 2, 1835, Lucinda, daughter of Elias Russel of Springfield, where she was born Aug. 15, 1814.

## 1312. HORACE. Cherry Valley, N. Y.

2292. A SON, who became a physician.

## 1314. OLIVER. Windham, Conn.

2293. GEORGE EARL, born in Windham, June 29, 1817, and married Sept. 12, 1862, Sarah Jane, daughter of Rev. Roger and Nancy (Waldo) Bingham of Windham.

2294. ANN DAVENPORT, born March 27, 1818, and married, Dec. 4, 1840, John De Leroche Wheeler of Stonington. He is settled in Willimantic, Conn. Children:

    i.  Charles Edwin Wheeler, born Dec. 14, 1841; married Phebe Wilson, and died June 30, 1870, leaving one child.

    ii.  George Lathrop Wheeler, born 1848, and married Jenny Ladd of Bozrah. They live in Willimantic.

## 1315. WILLIAM A. Windham, Conn.

2295. ABNER, born in Windham, Oct. 6, 1826.

2296. A DAUGHTER.

2297. A DAUGHTER.

## 1321. LEE. Windham, Conn.

2298. JOHN, born in Windham, Sept. 10, 1832, and died April 2, 1835.

2299. ELLEN FRANCES, born in Windham, July 13, 1835, and resides in Willimantic with her mother.

2300. HENRY LEE, born in Windham, Sept. 23, 1837; living in Hartford.

2301. LOUIS DEVOTION, born in Windham, March 7, 1851. Employed as bookkeeper in the Dunham Manufacturing Company's office, and afterwards by the Willimantic Linen Company (1873).

## 1327. LEBBEUS W. New York City.

2302. LAURA LAVINA; died.

2303. HARRIET MARIA.

## 1329. REV. SAMUEL KIRKLAND, D.D. Boston, Mass.

2304. THORNTON KIRKLAND, born in Boston, June 3, 1830, and graduated at Harvard in 1849, and received at the same university the degree LL.B. in 1853. He settled as a lawyer in Boston. He married, April 30, 1866, Annie Maria, daughter of the Hon. Samuel and Anna (Sturgess) Hooper, of Boston,

2305. ELIZA LEE, born April 6, 1832, and married, May 6, 1856, Charles Dudley Homans, a physician of Boston.

2306. JOSEPH STEPHENS BUCKMINSTER, born Dec. 27, 1834, and died March 8, 1838.

2307. MARY ANN, born Nov. 25, 1837; married, Jan. 1, 1859, Oliver W. Peabody, son of Rev. Oliver W. B. Peabody, of Springfield. Was in the war. Child: Amelia White, born Oct. 21, 1864; died in 1867.

2308. OLIVIA BUCKMINSTER, born May 21, 1841; married, March 17, 1868, Lewis William Tappan, and lives in Brookline.

2309. SAMUEL K., JUN., born March 28, 1844; merchant at Yokohama; firm of Walch, Church & Co.

### 1335. HORACE C. Waterbury, Conn.

2309-1. EDWIN.

### 1336. WILLIAM.

2309-2. ELVIRAH, born Nov. 2, 1828.

2309-3. MOSES C., born May 27, 1830.

2309-4. GARDNER, born in 1837, and died the next year.

2309-5. ELLEN M.

2309-6. ELIZABETH.

2309-7. WILLIAM.

2309-8. JOHN.

2309-9. MARY ELLEN born July 27, 1839.

2309-10. LILLIE BELLE, born Sept. 12, 1854.

### 1338. BENJAMIN. Tolland, Conn.

2310. CHARLES GARDNER, born May 20, 1847, and died Jan. 31, 1848.

2311. BENJAMIN FRANKLIN, born June 1, 1849, and died Aug. 16, 1851.

2312. MARY EVA, born July 12, 1852. Settled in Tolland.

2313. FREDERICK BENJAMIN, born May 12, 1854; now in Springfield.

2314. CHARLES ARIEL, born June 15, 1859.

2315. GEORGE ROWLAND, born July 8, 1864, and died Sept. 10, 1866.

2316. BENJAMIN, born July 13, 1871, and died Dec. 25, 1871.

### 1340. ROLLIN.

2316-1. CHAUNCEY ROWLAND, born Sept. 9, 1844.

2316-2. CAROLINE ELIZA, born April 26, 1846.

2316-3. CHARLES GARDNER, born Oct. 26, 1848.

2316-4. WILLIE, born May 16, 1854.

2316-5. JENNIE, born May 26, 1857.

### 1341. THOMAS C. Stafford Springs, Conn.

2316-6. GEORGE C., born July 15, 1852, and died in October, 1852.

2316-7. IDA E., born Sept. 7, 1853, and married in Stafford Springs, May 28, 1873, Edwin L., son of Charles Cummings of Lebanon, Conn. Child:

i. Claudius Lathrop Cummings, born in Lebanon, Feb. 27, 1871.

## 1318. PRESCOTT.                    Wilmington, Vt.

2317. LUTHER H., born July 20, 1832.

2318. LUCY SOPHIA, born Oct. 24, 1835, and died in May, 1842.

2319. MARY JANE, born Nov. 24, 1838, and married, Oct. 28, 1861, Erastus Myers of Brooklyn, N. Y., where she died Aug. 10, 1867. Children:

    i.    A daughter, born Aug. 1862, and died same day.

    ii.    Luther Lathrop Myers, born Nov. 14, 1863.

    iii.    Helen Kellogg Myers, born June 12, 1866, and died Dec. 5, 1867.

2320. A CHILD; died young.

## 1351. HALSEY.                    Pennsylvania.

2321. HALSEY.

2321-1. NANCY.

2321-2. ANNE.

2321-3. SALLY.

2321-4. LUCY.

2321-5. DAVID.

## 1352. JOSEPH.

2322. DAVID, born Sept. 26, 1818, and married, April 2, 1846, Charlotte, daughter of Lewis Taylor. He has always lived in Longmeadow, where he has been a successful farmer. He has been a Selectman, and Assessor, and the Judge of Probate of his district.

2323. LAURANA, born July 4, 1820, and married, Aug. 30, 1843, James, son of Job Hulburt. She died in Somers, Jan. 21, 1854. Children:

    i.    Edward L. Hulburt, born August, 1845.

    ii.    Freddie Hulburt, born in 1847, and died young.

    iii.    Eleanor C. Hulburt, born Jan. 5, 1851, and married, Dec. 30, 1873, Edward Aldrich.

2324. FREDERICK K., born Sept. 24, 1822, and married (1), Jan. 7, 1852, Angeline, daughter of Warren Billings. He married (2), in June, 1860, Luella, daughter of Ebenezer McGregory. He settled in Springfield, Mass., in the livery business. For fourteen years he was deputy sheriff for Hampden county. He died Jan. 3, 1874.

2325. JOSEPH F., born June 27, 1834, and married, Oct. 16, 1855, Harriet, daughter of Warren Billings.

## 1358-1. WILLIAM.                    Longmeadow, Mass.

2326-1. MIRIAM JANE, born in 1832; died unmarried, Sept. 2, 1856.

2326-2. MARY ELIZA, married H. L. Goudy. Child: Willie, who died six months old.

2326-3. JULIA, born January, 1814; died Oct. 8, 1858.

2326-4. CARRIE, born March, 1837; died, Dec. 24, 1855.

2326-5. EDWARD WILLIAM, born in 1834; died, Jan. 1, 1839.

2326-6. ETHAN WHITNEY E., born in 1842; died in 1863.

2326-7. EDWARD WILLIAM, born June 21, 1840, at East Longmeadow;

married, Jan. 18, 1861, Amelia S., daughter of Randolph and Sophia P. (Keyes) Stebbins, of East Longmeadow; live in Springfield.

### 1358-5. LORING, Jun.

2326-8. ALICE, born in Longmeadow, June 14, 1853; married, March 15, 1871, James P., son of Isaac S. Brown of Bangor, Me.; lives in New Haven.
2326-9. FURBER FOSTER, born Sept. 14, 1860, in Springfield.

### 1383. HORACE, M.D.    Columbus, O.

2326-10. EMELINE, born March 17, 1823, and married, June 27, 1843, James Denny Osborn. Children:

    i.    Charles Lathrop Osborn, born Dec. 10, 1844.
    ii.   Frank Stewart Osborn, born June 24, 1847.
    iii.  Jane Lathrop Osborn, born Aug. 13, 1850.
    iv.  Lizzie Baldwin Osborn, born Feb. 15, 1854, and now dead.
    v.   John Osborn, born June 22, 1859, and now dead.
    vi.  Mary Osborn, born Aug. 1, 1860.
    vii.  James Denny Osborn, born April 9, 1862.
    viii. Susan Adams Osborn, born March 2, 1864.

2327. MARTIN DONALSON, born Oct. 14, 1825, and married (1), Charlotte Higgins of Alton, Ohio. He married (2), in June, 1869, Mary Check, in Terre Haute, Ind.

### 1394. ORMAN CARPENTER.    Sullivan, N. Y.

2327-1. LUCRETIA P., born July 26, 1839, in Sullivan.
2327-2. EMMA L., born Feb. 22, 1848, at Ellisburg, Jefferson county; married, March 10, 1870, Mr. O. L. Neisler, residing at Indianapolis, Ind.
2327-3. CHARLES D., born Nov. 11, 1849, at New Bremen, Lewis county; graduated at Syracuse University in 1875, and subsequently occupying editorial positions.
2327-4. ELLA M., born No. 19, 1853, at Evans Mills, Jefferson county; a successful teacher in the public schools.

### 1406. Hon. DWIGHT N.    Wilkesbarre, Penn.

2328. AN INFANT, born in 1839 and died.
2329. WILLIAM W., born in Carbondale, Oct. 9, 1840, and graduated at Kenyon College, O., in 1861, and studied law with his father. After being admitted to the bar in 1863, he graduated in 1864 at the Harvard law school. He settled in the practice of law in Wilkesbarre, Pa., and married in 1870, Mary O., daughter of V. L. Maxwell.
2330. THOMAS R., born in Carbondale, Sept. 9, 1842. Soon after the opening of the late war he went to Harrisburg to offer his services to the Government as a soldier, but was rejected as he had no written consent from his father. During the invasion of the State by the rebels in 1862-3, he served in the State Militia. He is now in the fire insurance business at Carbondale.
2331. DWIGHTY, born 1844, and died about a year of age.

2332. MARY GRANT, born in Carbondale, Feb. 6, 1847, and married in December, 1867, Israel Crane. They are now living in Scranton, Pa. Children:

    i.   Maggie Crane.

    ii.  Dwight Lathrop Crane.

2333. AURELIA NOBLE, born in Carbondale, in June, 1849, and married, in June, 1870. Eugene, son of the Hon. W. B. Scates, ex-Chief Justice of Illinois. They are living in Evanston, Ill. (1873). Children:

    i.   Bessie Lathrop Scates, born in Evanston, Oct. 27, 1871.

    ii.  Walter Brunet Scates, born in Evanston, Feb. 11, 1873.

2334. HARRIET JEANETTE, born at Grove Cottage, near Carbondale, Sept. 30, 1860.

## 1410. CHARLES E.     Carbondale, Penn.

2335. HELEN AUGUSTA, born Dec. 26, 1849.

2336. DWIGHT NOBLE, born March 7, 1854.

2337. EDWARD D., born Feb. 19, 1858.

2338. WILLIAM M., born Dec. 26, 1863.

2339. MARY JEANETTE, born Jan. 7, 1866.

## 1429. REV. HENRY DURANT, D.D.     San Francisco, Cal.

2340. MARIA BURROWES, born Nov. 1, 1856, and died Nov. 27, 1860.

2341. LORIN ANDREWS, born June 11, 1858.

2342. JAMES McELROY, born Aug. 5, 1860.

2343. JOHN MASON, born Aug. 4, 1862.

2344. HENRY BURROWES, born March 22, 1867.

2345. CHARLES NEWTON, born Nov. 16, 1871.

## 1437. GEORGE W. LA.     Algoma, Wis.

2346. MARY C., born in Sherburne, N. Y., Sept. 15, 1855.

2347. HARRIET A., born in Algoma, Wis., June 26, 1860.

2348. CHILD, born in Algoma, Wis., June 5, 1862, and died July 22, 1862.

2349. GEORGE H., born in Algoma, Wis., June 22, 1867.

## 1444. EBENEZER.     Ilion, N. Y.

2350. ELOISE, born Oct. 24, 1858.

## 1456. COL. WILLIAM H.

2351. WILLIAM ADDISON, born Jan. 8, 1864.

## 1457. JOHN CHARLES.

2352. CHARLES ASHLEY, born Feb. 26, 1867.

## 1460. CHARLES HENRY.     Stormont, Canada.

2353. ALVAN, born in Maple Grove, Minn., Oct. 8, 1872.

## 1466. JAMES R. Carbondale, Penn.

2354. CARRIE ROOSEVELT, born in Washington City, D. C., Aug. 19, 1867.
2355. HENRY ALVAN, born in Washington April 30, 1869, and died in the same city, June 7, 1870.

## 1482. THOMAS. Provincetown, Mass.

2356. SALOME COOK, born in Provincetown, Feb. 9, 1828, and married Robert C. Soper of Provincetown, and are now (1873) living in Melrose, Mass.
2357. EBENEZER, born in Provincetown, June 11, 1830, and married, Feb. 13, 1859, Sarah Francis Wharf. He resides in Provincetown.
2358. ADELINE, born in Provincetown, Dec. 16, 1833, and married, Nov. 12, 1856, Amaziah Baker of South Yarmouth, Mass. They are settled in Provincetown.
2359. THOMAS, born in Provincetown, April 16, 1836.
2360. ROSETTA COOK, born in Provincetown, Feb. 5, 1842, and married, Aug. 5, 1864, Joshua R. Atkins of Provincetown. They reside in Boston, Mass.
2361. REBECCA COOK, born in Provincetown, Jan. 23, 1845, and married, Dec. 7, 1865, Warren Fielding of Provincetown, where they still reside. Child:
　Grace Lothrop Fielding, born March 21, 1877.
2362. BENJAMIN LAMBERT, born in Provincetown, Nov. 1, 1848. He is an M. D, and resides in Buffalo.

## 1486. JOHN L. (M. D.) East Somerville, Mass.

2363. STEPHEN NICKERSON.

## 1492. THOMAS W. Belfast, Me.

2364. LOIS WHITTIER, born in Belfast, Me., March 15, 1847.
2365. ANSEL, born in Belfast, Me., Feb. 25, 1849.
2366. MARY BECKETT, born in Belfast, Me., March 21, 1853.
2367. THOMAS W., born in Belfast, Me., Jan. 6, 1860.

## 1495. ANSEL. Portland, Me.

2368. SAMUEL BORLAND, born in Damariscotta, Me., Feb. 22, 1846.
2369. HORATIO J., born in Portland, Me., in 1851, and died in infancy.

## 1496. BENJAMIN W. Rockland, Me.

2370. CARRIE BRADLEY, born in Rockland, Me., in October, 1852, and married Joseph E. Maxwell, now (1873) of Ottawa, Kansas, in the legal profession.

## 1497. SUMNER P. Belfast, Me.

2371. LIZZIE LUDWIG, born in Belfast, Me., Sept. 22, 1851.
2372. SUMNER WILLEY, born in Boston, Mass., Jan. 6, 1858.
2373. ANN PAMELIA, born in Belfast, Me., Nov. 15, 1861.
35

### 1511. JAMES B.     East Cambridge, Mass.

2374. HARRIET MARICE, born July 2, 1830, married Stillman Grant of Walpole. Died ———.

2375. JAMES FRANKLIN, born July 31, 1836. Was killed in the battle of Bull Run, July 21, 1861.

2376. MARY ELIZABETH, born Aug. 28, 1838.

2377. EUNICE ABBY, born Feb. 8, 1842, and married, Jan. 1, 1873, Dr. Samuel Grover of Boston.

### 1512. ANSELM.     Boston, Mass.

2378. ELIZABETH MOORE, born in East Cambridge, Dec. 6, 1830, and married, June 8, 1852, Augustus Bacon, of Roxbury, where they now live. Children:

    i.    Horace, born Dec. 6, 1856.
    ii.   Hattie Wyman, born June 9, 1858, and died 1861.
    iii.  Augustus, born July 10, 1860.
    iv.  William, born, April 25, 1863.
    v.   Anselm L., born Aug. 19, 1866.
    vi.  Elizabeth M., born Nov. 22, 1870.
    vii.  Fannie W., born April 30, 1873.

2379. SARAH JANE, born in East Cambridge, Aug. 22, 1833, and married April 20, 1859, John R. Morse, of Dublin, N. H. They live in Chicago. Children:

    i.    Ruth Jane, born Mar. 4, 1869.
    ii.   Augustus L., born Feb. 12, 1871.
    iii.  Mabel Serena, born Mar. 15, 1873.

2380. WILLIAM ANSELM, born in East Cambridge, Aug. 11, 1835, and died Nov. 11, 1836.

2381. WILLIAM ANSELM, born in East Cambridge, Feb. 10, 1838, and died Oct. 17, 1853, by a fall.

2382. CHARLES LOWELL, born in Boston, Oct. 28, 1840, and died Jan. 28, 1841.

2383. HARRIET SPAULDING, born in Boston, May 7, 1845, and married, July 7, 1873, Edward A. Talbot, of Boston, where they now live.

2384. CHARLES LOWELL, born in Boston, Oct. 11, 1846, and married, Sept. 1, 1869, Mary F. Heustis of Boston.

2385. CLARA MARIA, born in Boston, Apr. 4, 1848.

2386. EMMA FRANCES, born in Boston, Nov. 12, 1849, and married, Apr. 19, 1871, Melzar V. Farnsworth of Shirley, Mass. They have one daughter: Angeline L. Farnsworth, born July 18, 1872.

2387. ANGELINE MOULTON, born in Boston, Feb. 25, 1852, and is now living in Boston. We are indebted to her not a little for the record of her grandfather's descendants.

### 1513. URIAH LINCOLN. East Cambridge, Mass.

2388. JULIETTE, married Joseph D. Wellington. Children:
 i. Charles Lincoln, born Feb. 3, 1850, now in Detroit, Ill.
 ii. Arthur.
 iii. Addie.

2389. ADELINE, born at East Cambridge, and died.

2390. SARAH LINCOLN, married Harry F. Farr of Lowell. One child: Harry (1873).

### 1518. GEORGE BEAL. Cambridgeport, Mass.

2391. RUTH JANE, born at Cambridgeport, Apr. 1, 1843, and married John H. Butler of Boston, Aug. 29, 1867. He is in business in New York City. Children:
 i. Henry Lothrop Butler, born July 22, 1868.
 ii. Rachel Greenleaf Butler, born July 28, 1870.

2392. PRISCILLA LINCOLN, born at Cambridge, Dec. 12, 1845, and died Jan. 22, 1846, at East Boston.

2393. PRISCILLA LINCOLN, born May 20, 1849, at East Boston.

2394. GEORGE BEAL, JR., born Sept. 12, 1851, at Cambridge.

2395. JOHN MURDOCK, born at Cambridge, Dec. 6, 1853.

2396. LUCIUS ROBINSON PAIGE, born at Cambridge, Dec. 14, 1855, and died Mar. 10, 1856.

2397. CUMMINGS LINCOLN, born at Cambridge, Mar. 6, 1861.

### 1520. CUMMINGS LINCOLN. Charlestown, Mass.

2398. ALMIRA ANNA, born June 8, 1851.

2399. EDITH LINCOLN, born May 29, 1866.

### 1522. CALEB. Cohasset, Mass.

2400. PRISCILLA N., born in Cohasset, May 20, 1820, and died unmarried, Aug. 17, 1846.

2401. JOSHUA RICH, born in Cohasset, Oct. 16, 1822, and graduated at Dartmouth College, in 1844, and in medicine at Harvard, in 1852. He married, in Plymouth, Mass., Oct. 13, 1857, Lydia G., daughter of Thomas Hedge of Plymouth.

He received an appointment to the Rainsford Island Hospital, where he made ample proof of his fitness for his professional life. In 1858, he removed to Buffalo, where he entered upon the practice of medicine, and soon won a large place equally in the hearts of the families whose physician he became and in the confidence, and esteem, and hopes of the medical fraternity.

He died in Plymouth, Mass., July 22, 1869. He has an elegant monument erected over his remains in the new cemetery in Plymouth, on which is the simple yet eloquent motto, "THE BELOVED PHYSICIAN." And another inscription, not less expressive, testifies that his life had not been in vain: "Erected by his friends in Buffalo."

He had no children. His widow now lives with her mother in Plymouth.

Few young men in any family have left behind them, at their deaths, more sincere mourners. The abundant testimonials which the occasion called out bear witness both to his marked ability in the profession which he so singularly adorned, and to the loveliness of his private character and life, which was so conspicuous. Dr. Miner, editor of the *Buffalo Medical Journal*, and also president of the Erie County Medical Society, at the meeting of the society called to express their sense of their loss in his death, thus testifies to his character and position among them: "As you know, he has been connected with our public institutions during his entire life among us, and in all the duties of the most responsible positions has shown himself wise and faithful. During the three years' absence in Europe of Prof. Charles A. Lee, Dr. Lothrop occupied the chair of Materia Medica in the Buffalo Medical College, and proved himself a teacher of rare scholarship, of extensive and varied knowledge. As surgeon to the Buffalo General Hospital, he won for himself much professional reputation, and has left a record of faithfulness and worth, worthy the highest ambition. He was president of that society in 1867, and has received many tokens of respect and favor from the profession, who have always delighted to do him honor. He was greatly beloved and admired by the families who received his professional attendance, and those who knew him best loved him most.

"Dr. Lothrop was a man of great mind, an original, independent thinker, a true philosopher. He had canvassed the whole field of human knowledge with great care, and rested his beliefs upon the firmest rocks. He said, on my taking leave of him, 'I am not anxious for the future. I only fear a long invalidism.' He had a true, generous, unselfish nature, and his pure life and character require no eulogy."

Dr. J. P. White, after endorsing fully the testimony thus given in the resolutions which he introduced, and which were passed by the society, thus speaks of Dr. Lothrop, "whom we honored for his professional skill, and loved for his gentleness, modesty, and unvarying kindness, and who, in a comparatively brief period, had established in this city a high professional character, and won the friendship of all his brother practitioners, and whose memory is especially endeared to the younger members of the profession as a judicious counselor and faithful friend."

Others of the society expressed themselves in the warmest terms of admiration of the personal friend whose loss they all so deeply mourned.

Similar testimonials of confidence and esteem are given in the action of the Board of Trustees of the Buffalo General Hospital. They say: "From his earliest association with this institution, his services were rendered with singular assiduity and self-abnegation, and the success which attended his efforts is the best testimony to the skill and attention which he devoted wholly and unweariedly to those entrusted to his care." "He has left a record which is his most fitting memorial, and of which any physician might well be proud."

The following testimonial is from his class-mate and personal friend, Harvey

Jewell of Boston: "I should like to speak of him as an honor to his native town, of his modesty, of his learning in letters, of his thorough mastery of his profession, of his success in reaching the highest reputation, of the depth of attachment felt for him by the friends who surrounded him in his new home, and of the grief which wrung their hearts when the good physician was called away. What treasures has any town like the character and reputation of such a man?"

It is especially grateful to note the deep affection with which his younger brethren in the profession seem to have been drawn to him. The fact speaks more than words can tell of those personal qualities of heart and mind which must have been his best gifts. In a letter of condolence which these confreres addressed to his stricken family, they say: "We all feel that, in his death, we have lost a friend. The universality of this sentiment is the best explanation of the character of his friendship. * * * He has left us a noble example. He was an honest man, a Christian gentleman, a ripe scholar, a good physician. Had he lived, a very eminent career was before him. But he has taught us many things, not the least, that a man may be unassuming, and yet attain appreciation according to his deserts; that he may be just to others, and yet obtain that which is due to himself."

2402. JOHN QUINCY ADAMS, born in Cohasset, Oct. 14, 1824, and married Nov. 30, 1848. Eunice B., daughter of Samuel and Joanna Bates of Cohasset. Mr. Lothrop began life as a merchant with his father, but has been gradually drawn into official service by his town and state, and by the national government. Few of his townsmen have been more in the public service than he, and few have rendered more acceptable service. A recent illustration of the demands made upon him on extra occasions, as well as habitually, occurred at the interesting Centennial Anniversary of his native town, in 1870, of which he was called to be the president. He has been twice the representative of the town in the General Court. He has, since 1862, been the United States Department Collector and Inspector of the port of Cohasset, and, at the same time, selectman and assessor, and one of the overseers of the poor. He is also secretary of the Cohasset Fire Insurance Company. During the recent war, he was actively employed as recruiting officer for the town.

2403. MARY, born in Cohasset, Nov. 8, 1826, and married, Oct. 11, 1848, Joseph B. Thaxter, jun., of Hingham, Mass. He is an optician of Boston, having his residence in Hingham. He has represented his town in the State Legislature, and been one of the inspectors of the State Almshouse in Bridgewater for several years. Mrs. Thaxter died Feb. 27, 1850. They had one son:

Daniel Thaxter, born in Hingham, July 28, 1849, and died Jan. 26, 1850.

2404. ELLEN, born in Cohasset Feb. 1, 1829; unmarried.

2405. JANE S., born in Cohasset, May 25, 1831, and married, July 19, 1853, Caleb F., son of David Nichols of Cohasset. He is a trader, and has been one of the town officers for years. She died July 4, 1864. Their children, all born in Cohasset, were:

    i.    Mary Ellen Nichols, born Dec. 9, 1856.
    ii.   Caleb Nichols, born Sept. 21, 1858.
    iii.  Jane Snow Nichols, born Sept. 23, 1860.

iv.  Elizabeth T. Nichols, born Dec. 13, 1861.

v.  Edward Nichols, born May 13, 1864.

2406. ELIZABETH N., born in Cohasset, April 8, 1836, and married, Jan. 31, 1858, Joseph B. Thaxter, jun., the husband of her deceased sister Mary. They have had also a single son:

Joseph B. Thaxter, 3d, born in Hingham, June 21, 1863.

2407. DRUSILLA SNOW, born in Cohasset, Dec. 18, 1841, and has been a teacher in the High School of Cohasset for years.

## 1530.  LORING.                    Boston, Mass.

2408. ELIZABETH F., born in Boston Aug. 11, 1840; married Gorham Rogers, merchant, born in Roxbury, son of Shubael G. and Susan Rogers.

2409. CLARA A., born in Cambridge Nov. 18, 1842; married Lowell Lincoln, merchant, born in Boston, son of Ezra and Chastine Lincoln.

2410. ISABEL, born in Boston July 6, 1845; died May 8, 1847.

2411. LORING, born in Boston Feb. 29, 1848; married Rosa Marie Roux, daughter of Frederic and Louise Roux, of Paris.

2412. JOSEPHINE, born in Boston Sept. 20, 1851.

2413. CORNELIA W., born in Boston Dec. 18, 1854.

## 1533.  JOHN LO.                    Boston, Mass.

[This family were all born in Boston.]

2414. CORDELIA, born in 1833, and lives in Boston.

2415. NANCY WHITE, born in 1835, and lives in Boston.

2416. SARAH LIBBY, born in 1837, and lives in Boston.

2417. MARY ELIZA, born in 1839, and married, June 30, 1860, Thomas B. Mitchell, of Providence, R. I., where they are now living. They have one child: Edward Lathrop Mitchell, born Oct. 16, 1863.

2418. JOHN, born in 1842, and died Sept. 1, 1844.

2419. MARGARET, twin with John.  Died Oct. 18, 1842.

2420. MARGARET, born in August, and died in October, 1843.

2421. LUCY J., born in 1846; single.

2422. JOHN, born Dec. 4, 1849.  He is now in business as a clothier on Chardon street, Boston, Mass. (1873).

2423. WILLIAM ULMAR, born in 1851, and living single.

2424. ELLA FLORENCE, born in 1853, and died the same year.

## 1534.  EBEN W.                    Boston, Mass.

2425. CORDELIA A., born in Boston in 1834, and married, in 1870, John G. Low of Chelsea.

2426. EMILY A., born in March, 1840, and died in 1857.

2427. EBEN W., jr., born in Chelsea, Mass., in 1852.

## 1536.  CHARLES B. LO.                    Boston, Mass.

2428. LIZZIE, born in Boston in 1845.

2429. ABBY F., born in Boston in 1847.

### 1540. BENJAMIN. Barnstable, Mass.

2430. BENJAMIN, born 1844, and lives in Barnstable; named in his grand-father's will.

2431. ANSEL, born 1840, and lives in Chelsea, Mass., and named in his grand-father's will.

### 1544. CAPT. SYLVESTER B. LO. Hyannis, Mass.

2432. HOWARD BAXTER, born in Hyannis Oct. 29, 1853.

2433. SYLVESTER BAXTER, jun., born in Hyannis Sept. 13, 1862.

### 1545. ASA LO. Charlestown, Mass.

2434. ABBY ANN, born in Hyannis.

2435. FRANKLIN BAXTER, born in Hyannis.

2436. GEORGE, born in Hyannis.

### 1546. JOHN A. B. LO. Boston, Mass.

2437. EMILY, born in Farmington, Me.

2438. MARGARET, born in Farmington, and died.

2439. JOHN A. B., jun., born in Farmington, Me.

2440. ALICE, born in Boston.

2441. ALEXANDER, born in Boston.

### 1547. FRANKLIN BAXTER LO. Galveston, Texas.

2442. LOUISA.

2443. PETER FRANKLIN.

2444. WILLIE CROOKS.

2445. INFANT.

### 1548. HENRY ALLEN LO. Chelsea, Mass.

2446. HENRY ALLEN, born in Yarmouth April 11, 1851.

2447. ATWOOD BAXTER, born in Barnstable Aug. 27, 1852.

### 1558. FREDERICK G. LO. Hyannis, Mass

2448. BETHIA BEARCE, born in Hyannis March 16, 1854.

2449. ISADORE GORHAM, born in Hyannis Nov. 3, 1858.

2450. FREDERICK GORHAM, born in Hyannis Dec. 11, 1862.

### 1559. ALONZO F. LO. Hyannis, Mass.

2451. HENRY BASSETT, born in Hyannis July 7, 1856.

2452. ELLSWORTH FREEMAN, born in Hyannis.

### 1560. JOHN P. K. Washington, D. C.

2453. MARY BASSETT, born May 25, 1869.

### 1561. HARRISON LO.          Charlestown, Mass.

2454. CHARLES HARRISON, born in Boston Feb. 7, 1833, and died Aug. 17, 1854; unmarried, in Charlestown.

2455. JOSEPH FREEMAN, born in Boston Jan. 12, 1837. He enlisted for nine months during the war of the Rebellion into the 45th Massachusetts Infantry, and rendered good service. He was in the Charlestown post-office when taken with his last sickness, and died in Charlestown Feb. 3, 1871.

2456. CANDACE ELIZABETH, born March 4, 1840, and was married, Oct. 20, 1858, to Andrew Jackson Sargent of Boston, son of Hosea. She died Sept. 4, 1870.

2457. EMILY AUGUSTA, born Oct. 24, 1838, and died May 14, 1839.

2458. GEORGE EDWIN, born Oct. 25, 1844, and died Dec. 13, 1859.

### 1566. ANSEL D. LO.          Barnstable, Mass.

2459. EMILY SAUNDERS, born March 6, 1837, and married, Oct. 4, 1860, Russel Matthews, son of Asa and Betsey (Hamblin) Matthews, of Yarmouth. Their children have been:
 i. Franklin Wallace Matthews, born April 14, 1862.
 ii. Charles Lothrop Matthews, born March 16, 1867.
 iii. Emilie Russell Matthews, born Oct. 15, 1872.

2460. JAMES SCUDDER, born Jan. 12, 1839, and lost at sea off the coast of Java, March 15, 1854, on his first foreign voyage.

2461. FREEMAN HINCKLEY, born April 6, 1842, and married, June 6, 1865, Hittie Freeman, daughter of Alvah and Lydia M. (Freeman) Holway, of Greenwich, Mass. He began life as a sailor, and on his return from one of his voyages, during the recent Rebellion, he enlisted into the 45th regiment of Massachusetts Volunteers. After his term of enlistment had expired he was appointed Master's Mate in the U. S. Navy, and, after a year's service, promoted to Acting Ensign, which office he filled to the close of the war. In 1866 he was appointed U. S. Railway Postal Clerk from Boston to Provincetown, which post he resigned in 1872. He is now clerk in the Barnstable Savings Bank (1873).

2462. HITTIE ANNABLE, born Nov. 2, 1843, and married, Sept. 9, 1864, Francis Henry, son of Henry and Francis (Stearns) Brown of Barnstable. Their children have been:
 i. Harry Lothrop Brown, born March 31, 1866.
 ii. Walter Stuart Brown, born in November, 1869, and died in July, 1870.
 iii. Francis Henry Brown, born March 5, 1871.

2463. ANSEL DAVIS, jun., born Sept. 2, 1845, and married Deborah Hamblin, daughter of Gorham and Deborah (Hamblin) Hallet of Barnstable. Since 1860 he has followed the sea excepting five years, which he spent in China. He sails in command of his own vessel.

## 1571. SYLVANUS C. LA. Jersey City, N. J.

2464. CHARLES H., born in Norwich, Conn., June 7, 1833; was a sergeant in the 13th New Jersey Regiment of Volunteers, and was killed at the battle of Chancellorsville, May 3, 1863.

2465. ALLEN C., born in Norwich in 1838, and is now in the corn and feed trade, and is settled in Jersey City. He married Josephine, daughter of Peleg and Jane Barker, who was born in Albion, N. Y., in 1849. I am indebted to him for the record of his father's descendants so far as I have been able to record them.

2466. GEORGE, born at Mystic Bridge, Conn. He also enlisted into the Union service during the recent war, in which he contracted the disease of which he died in Jersey City, Feb. 7, 1867, at twenty-six years of age. He was a carpenter.

2467. SYLVANUS C., Jun., born in Jersey City, N. J., May 21, 1854.

2468. MARY, born in Jersey City Dec. 17, 1856, and married Charles M. Wood, who is now connected with the post-office department in Jersey City.

## 1576. HORATIO J. LO. Boston, Suffield.

2469. JENNIE AUGUSTA, born in Somerville, Mass., Sept. 25, 1855. High School, Charlestown, Mass.

2470. CARRIE MEHITABLE, born in Wasioja, Dodge Co., Minn., Oct. 4, 1858.

## 1580. ISAAC LO. Stockton, Cal.

2471. ISAAC VANCE, born in Stockton, Cal., May 31, 1873, and died Feb. 18, 1874.

36

NINTH GENERATION.

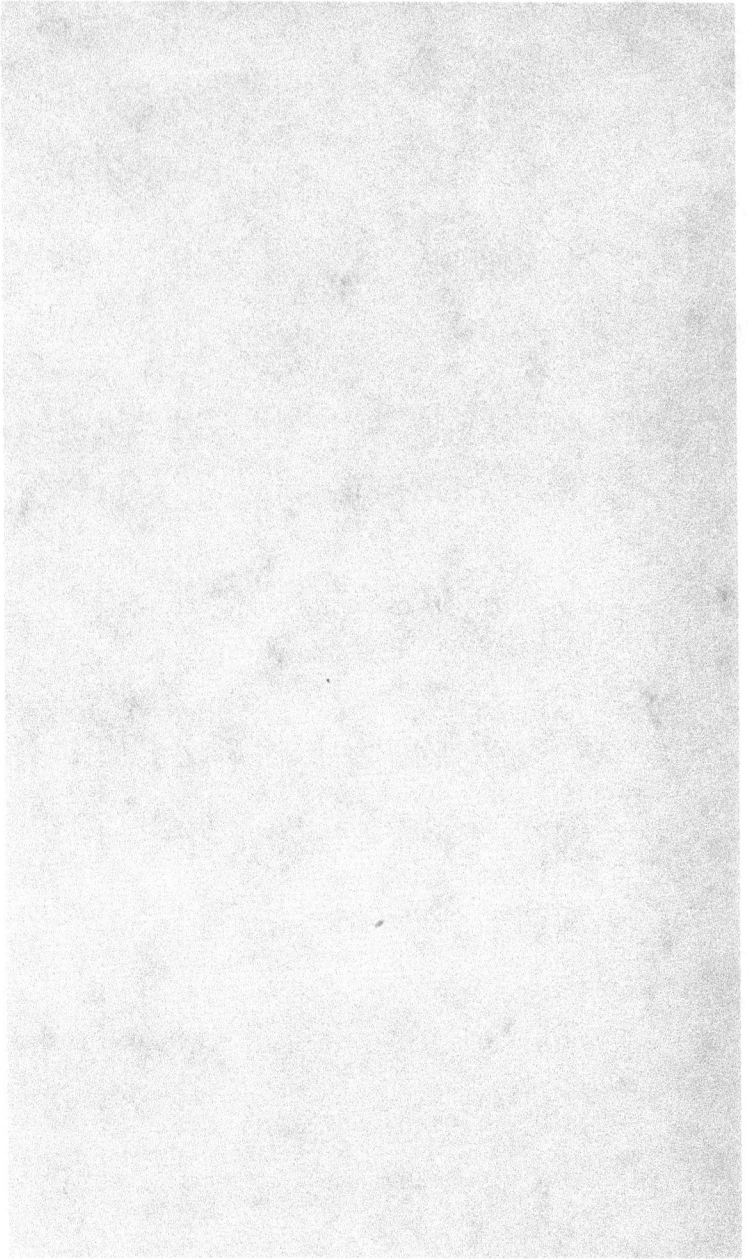

### 1590. CHARLES. Iowa.

2172. MUNRO.
2173. LUCINDA ANN. Married. Three children.
2174. HENRY.

### 1594. OLIVER H.

2175. WELLES.
2176. ELIZA.

### 1599. DANIEL.

2177. OSCAR, born in Bernardston, Vt., Dec. 27, 1856.

### 1611. GEORGE RICHMOND. Bridgeport, Conn.

2178. PAULINE BOWERS, born Sept. 4, 1856.
2179. EMMA AUGUSTA, born in Bridgeport, Aug. 13, 1859.
2180. GEORGE SHERMAN, born in Springfield, Mass., May 20, 1863.

### 1612. ALPHEUS DANIEL.

2181. EDITH ELDERAH, born in Oakville, Conn., Aug. 10, 1858.
2182. MARY ELIZABETH, born July 15, 1861, in Springfield, Mass.

### 1613. CALVIN J. Bridgeport, Conn.

2183. ALBERT RICHARDSON, born in Bridgeport, Jan. 1, 1860.
2184. MARY IRENE, born in Bridgeport, April 30, 1867.

### 1618. JOHN S. Champagne. Ill.

2185. GERTRUDE R., born Aug. 10, 1865.
2186. SON, who died July 15, 1867.
2187. MERTON LEE, born June 3, 1868.
2188. SON, who died Mar. 20, 1870.
2189. RALPH W., born May 19, 1871.
2190. LEWIS G., born Dec. 10, 1873.

### 1629. THOMAS P. New York City.

2191. THOMAS, born in New York, Nov. 1843, and married, in Columbia, S. C., April 25, 1867. Elise Brown, daughter of John P. and Abby (Hinman) Brown, a planter of Sumter, S. C.
2192. THEODORE ALLEN, born in New York, Sept. 11, 1845, and died May 19, 1846.

### 1633. JOSHUA. Astoria, L. I.

[This family were all born in Astoria. L. I.]

2493. JOSEPHINE BLACKWELL, born May 9, 1851.

2494. CHARLES BLACKWELL, born Nov. 30, 1852.

2495. REBECCA P., born Aug. 7, 1854.

2496. JOSHUA, JR., born Aug. 20, 1859.

2497. MARGARET TISDALE, born Nov. 20, 1864.

2498. EMILY BLACKWELL, born Dec. 8, 1867, and died Mar. 22, 1874.

### 1635. JOHN PELATIAH PERIT. New York City.

2499. MARY NOYES, born in Astoria, L. I., May 28, 1863.

2500. JOHN PELATIAH PERIT, born in New York city, Nov. 2, 1866, and died Jan. 25, 1867.

2501. ANNA BARTOW, born in New York city, June 28, 1868.

2502. EMILY BLACKWELL, born in New York city, June 5, 1870.

### 1637. FRANCIS C. Le Roy, N. Y.

2503. RUTH WEBSTER, born in Le Roy, May 23, 1862.

2504. JOHN PELATIAH PERIT, born in Le Roy, Sept. 28, 1870.

### 1641. GEN. WILLIAM E. Rochester, N. Y.

2506. WILLIAM COMANCHE, born in Rochester, Sept. 10, 1840. On the breaking out of the recent war, he enlisted as a volunteer in the service. He died at the Marine Hospital, near Baltimore, Md., Sept. 7, 1862. He rendered good service also as correspondent for the *Rochester Advertiser*, while in the army.

2507. CHARLOTTE HELEN, born in Rochester, Jan. 7, 1842, and has been a teacher in Rochester.

2508. GEORGE THOMAS, born in Rochester, Oct. 28, 1845, and married in New Orleans, La., Nov. 22, 1868. Fanny E. Butler. They are now living in New Orleans, where he is a stationer (1873).

2509. CLARISSA CALDWELL, born in Rochester, Apr. 12, 1847.

2510. ANNIE WIGHT, born in Rochester, Apr. 7, 1860.

### 1642. CHARLES C. New York City.

2511. MARY CALDWELL, born in Rochester, Sept. 14, 1827, and is now living in New York city (1873).

2512. CHARLES GREEN, born in Rochester, Dec. 30, 1830, and now lives in New York city, where he is engaged in a bank.

2513. CORNELIA AMANDA, born in Rochester, Aug. 30, 1835.

2514. GEORGE THOMAS, born in Rochester, N. Y., Apr. 27, 1841, and died July 2, 1841.

2515. SARAH GREEN, born in Rochester, N. Y., May 29, 1842, and is now living in New York city (1873).

2516. HENRY JOHN CALDWELL, born in Rochester, N. Y., Feb. 4, 1844. Married, Mar. 8, 1866, Mary C. Stevens.

## 1652. BENJAMIN C. Syracuse, N. Y.

2517. HARRIET ELIZA, born Nov. 2, 1833, and married Oct. 1, 1865, E. A. Bennett, of Syracuse, N. Y.

2518. GEORGE CHAPMAN, born in 1838, and died Nov. 4, 1842.

2519. EDWARD COLVIN, born in Syracuse, Feb. 15, 1841, and is now one of the firm of Edwin Bennet & Co., manufacturers of boots, shoes, and rubbers, at Syracuse, N. Y. Single (1873).

2520. LEVI CHAPMAN, born Nov. 22, 1845, and married Nov. 5, 1867, Francis Rosella Graves, daughter of Rufus R. and Mary Jane (Arms) Graves, of Brooklyn, where she was born Mar. 8, 1845.

2521. GEORGE NELSON, born Apr. 15, 1847, and died Aug. 23, 1849.

## 1655. SAMUEL M.

2522. GEORGE, born Nov. 15, 1844, and married in Dec. 1870, Sarah Johnson. Lives in Buffalo, N. Y.

2523. ANNIE, born May 1, 1846, and married Apr. 22, 1873, Mead Carpenter, of Syracuse, where they now live.

2524. CHARLES, born Dec. 8, 1848.

## 1656. NEAL M. DUFFIE.

2525. ALBERT NEAL, born in Syracuse, N. Y., Aug. 26, 1841. Entered the army in July, 1861. Was in all the battles before Richmond, Va., up to his death. Killed at Chickahominy Swamp, near Richmond, Va., while on picket duty, June 6, 1862. Sergeant Co. H, 14th N. Y. Vols., 5th Corps. Enlisted company from Syracuse, N. Y. Joined regiment at Utica, N. Y. Mustered at Albany.

2526. JOEL CADY, born in Syracuse, N. Y., Apr. 11, 1843, and married in Washington, D. C., Aug. 2, 1866, Mary L. Bates. Enlisted as a private in the 14th regiment, N. Y. Vols., Col. McQuade of Utica commanding, on the 12th day of Dec., 1861. Remained in active duty in the advance upon and the retreat from Richmond, Va., up to the 1st of Sept, 1862. During said time was engaged in the following battles (in addition to numerous skirmishes, etc.), viz.: Battle of Big Bethel, Va ; siege of Yorktown; battle of Hanover Court-house ; battle of Williamsburg ; Mechanicsville, commencement seven days' battles ; Gaines' Mills ; June 28, 1862, running fight during entire day ; battle of Peach Orchard and Savage Station ; Malvern Hill. Was honorably discharged Dec. 24, 1862, because of protracted exposure while on picket duty in the Chickahominy swamp, increased by the above severe battles and over-exertion ; was also injured in the ankle at Malvern Hill, July 2, 1862.

2527. RACHEL CHARLOTTE, born Nov. 26, 1846, and married Nov. 26, 1870. Died of heart disease, Apr. 1, 1872.

### 1661. Capt. GIDEON. Stockport, N. Y.

2528. Helen Elizabeth, born in Burlington, Vt., Nov. 24, 1837, and married at Stockport, Mar. 31, 1856, Francis H., son of Jonathan Stott, of Stockport, N. Y., where he is a woolen manufacturer. Their children, all born in Stockport, are:

i. Elizabeth Dunlop Stott, born Mar. 16, 1857.
ii. Arthur Curtiss Stott, born Oct. 19, 1858.
iii. Robert Lathrop Stott, born Apr. 14, 1862.
iv. Janet Lathrop Stott, born Feb. 24, 1865.
v. Frank Strong Stott, born Sept. 18, 1866.
vi. Lawrence Bradley Stott, born Aug. 24, 1869.
vii. Dora A. Stott, born Nov. 30, 1870.
viii. Bertha Dunlop Stott, born Nov. 2, 1872.

2529. Robert Dunlop, born in Burlington, Dec. 9, 1840. How amiable and promising he was in his boyhood and youth all who knew him cheerfully testify. How unselfish and patriotic in his early manhood, his military career in the recent war fully shows. On the opening of the war, he promptly offered himself to the government for the ranks and enlisted into the 14th N. Y. State Volunteers. His regiment was assigned to the Army of the Potomac, in which he endured the hardships of the memorable winter of 1861-2. Being sent home as a recruiting officer, Corporal Lathrop was largely instrumental in raising two regiments in his native county. For one of these, the 159th, he was chosen and commissioned adjutant, and the regiment was assigned to the Banks expedition. In this command, he won more than ordinary reputation for his good sense, skill, and valor. It was while leading and cheering on his men, in the battle of Irish Bend, on the Bayou Teche, La., April 14, 1863, that a fatal ball passed through his body, and one more of our brave sons had sealed with his blood his devotion to the Union. By order of Gen. Banks, his body was sent home, and now lies in a patriot's grave in the cemetery at Albany.

2531. Janet Andrews, born in Albany, Aug. 29, 1843.

2532. Archibald Dunlop, born in Albany, May 26, 1847. He went into Arkansas as a merchant, and died in Little Rock, Jan. 9, 1872. His remains were brought home and interred in the cemetery in Albany.

2533. Alexander Dunlop, born at Fort Edward, N. Y., Sept. 30, 1851.

### 1663. STEPHEN PEARL

2534. William Pearl, born in Middlebury, Vt., Jan. 30, 1845. Killed in the "Battle of the Wilderness," May 7 or 8, 1864, aged 19 years. A member of the 8th regiment, Mich. Volunteers, U. S. A.

2535. Charles Linneus, born in Middlebury, Vt., Feb. 27, 1847. Died in Beloit, Wis., Mar. 30, 1850.

2536. Mary Bowditch, born in Beloit, Wis., Oct. 4, 1850. Married William Wheeler, Dec. 4, 1862.

2537. John Clement, born in Beloit, Wis., Feb. 12, 1853.

2538. Helen Hoyt, born in Beloit, Wis., May 31, 1855.

## 1664. CHARLES COAN.

Newark, N. J.

2539. LOUISE ELIZABETH, born in Jackson, La., July 13, 1842, and married in Philadelphia, July 22, 1867, Stacy A., son of Stacy and Mary (Van Cleves) Paxson, of Trenton, N. J. He died in Philadelphia, July 1, 1875. Children:

    i.  Clara Beulah Paxson, born in Philadelphia, Feb. 27, 1871.

    ii.  Stacy Edmund Paxson, born in Newark. N. J., Sept. 17, 1873.

2540. ROBIE ALMA, born in Jackson, La., July 25, 1847, and married at Delanco, N. J., Oct. 15, 1868, William C. Warner, of Titusville, Pa., son of George and Edith (Crim) Warner, of Burlington, N. J. He was born Aug. 3, 1843. She died Sept. 18, 1877. Children:

    i.  George Wm. Warner, born in Titusville, Pa., June 11, 1871.

    ii.  Charles Lathrop Warner, born in Newark, N. J., Jan. 31, 1873.

2541. CHARLES EZRA, born in New Orleans, La., March 7, 1850, and died on the Mississippi River, Nov. 9, 1852, and was interred in New Orleans.

2542. CHARLES CORNING, born in New Orleans, April 9, 1853. Graduated at Princeton College in 1873 and at Bellevue Hospital College, New York city, Feb. 25, 1875; was in charge of the hospital, Jersey City, one year. Now practicing medicine in Denver, Colorado.

2543. STEPHEN PARK, born in New Orleans. La., Jan. 20, 1855, and married, Oct. 17, 1877, Carrie L., daughter of Nathaniel L. and Emma B. Douglass of Newark, N. J. He is in the hardware business in Philadelphia.

2544. CLARA FLORELLA, born in Philadelphia, Pa., July 4, 1857.

2545. DAVID NICHOLS, born in Philadelphia, Pa., Mar. 12, 1861. Now in Philadelphia.

2546. EDMUND DORRANCE, born in Delanco, N. J., Apr. 23, 1864.

## 1675. FREDERICK F.

Bridgeport, Conn.

2547. JOHN WILLIAM, born in Bridgeport, June 28, 1832, and married (1), Dec. 6, 1855, Margaret Osborne Clark, of Westfield, N. J. She died Aug. 2, 1872. Married (2), Feb. 21, 1881, Mary Irene Rockwell, of Bridgeport.

2548. CHARLES AUGUSTUS, born in Bridgeport, July 9, 1834, and married, Oct. 1, 1856, Emma Maria, youngest daughter of Edward Sandland, Esq., of Waterbury, Conn.

2549. JANE MARIA, born in Bridgeport, Nov. 21, 1838, and died in the same place Sept. 16, 1840.

2550. GEORGE FREDERICK, born in Bridgeport, Aug. 4, 1843, and married July 4, 1861, at Quincy, Fla., Mrs. Bettie Titus. He died in Bridgeport, Sept. 17, 1868. His widow is now living in New York City.

2551. WILLIS HENRY, born in Bridgeport, Apr. 7, 1845, and died in the same place, Aug. 27, 1851.

2552. HERBERT NELSON, born in Bridgeport, June 5, 1847, and married, Sept. 19, 1871, Lucy Kingsley, second daughter of William K. and Julia (Bolling) Thurber, of Mobile, Ala.

2553. CAROLINE REBECCA, born in Bridgeport, Oct. 24, 1849, and died Jan. 18, 1852.

2554. JAMES CLARK, born in Bridgeport, July 29, 1852, and married Aug. 13, 1874, Anna Roselle Manning, of Philadelphia.

### 1676. CHARLES H. East Bridgeport, Conn.

2555. SARAH J., born in Bridgeport, Aug. 1, 1842, and married (1), in Stamford, Oct. 14, 1863, James M. Fitzgerald, who was born in Manchester, Conn., in 1840. In marriage record her name is Jennie S. They were divorced March, 1870, and she married (2), Dec. 22, 1873, George W. Clark.

2555-1. IRENE, born in Bridgeport, Sept. 14, 1844. Married Sept. 12, 1872, George E. Botsford. Two children.

2556. CHARLES H., born in Bridgeport, Feb. 16, 1847. Married June 5, 1877, Carrie A. Beecher, of East Bridgeport. They are now living in California.

2557. DELIA, born in Berea, Ohio, Oct. 8, 1849, married June 25, 1873, Benjamin I. Hicks. They are living in Jersey City.

2558. FRANK, born in Berea, Ohio. Sept. 10, 1851, married Oct. 12, 1876, Alice M. Peck. They are living in Brooklyn.

### 1677. WILLIAM L. Watertown, Mass.

2558-1. ANDREW JONES, born March 19, 1836, married, Dec. 5, 1861, Angie Shedd. He graduated at Harvard in 1859, received the degree of M.A. in 1862. For years he was engaged in teaching. Is now practicing law.

2558-2. JANE CORNELIA, born March 31, 1838, died Sept. 4, 1853.

2558-3. ALICE GREY, born Dec. 23, 1839.

2558-4. ALBERT WARD, born Aug. 9, 1841.

2558-5. KATE AUGUSTA, born Dec. 18, 1844, married, Nov. 24, 1870, Wilbur Franklin Learned. They live in Watertown and have two children:

  i. Earnest Freeman Learned, born Nov. 24, 1874.

  ii. Willis Lathrop Learned, born Sept. 17, 1876.

### 1681. GEORGE L. East Bridgeport, Conn.

2559. } Twins born and died in 1850.
2560. }

2561. SARAH ELIZABETH, born April 6, 1853.

2562. NELLY F., born Nov. 25, 1860. Died Dec. 1, 1862.

### 1691. HENRY A. Griswold, Conn.

2563. HELEN GODDARD, born June 25, 1843.

2564. WILLIAM HENRY, born Aug. 20, 1845. Died Jan. 20, 1847.

2565. ELIZA EUDORA, born Aug. 10, 1847.

2566. MARY SALISBURY, born Mar. 22, 1849.

2567. WILLIAM HENRY, born Apr. 9, 1851.

2568. GEORGE OWEN, born Apr. 28, 1853.

*Children by second wife:*

2569. EDWARD ADAMS, born Sept. 25, 1861.
2570. SARAH GREENLEAF, born Nov. 17, 1862.
2571. LYDIA CAMPBELL, born Nov. 10, 1865.

## 1692. HIRAM B.

2572. HARRY BARRELL, born Apr. 9, 1852.

## 1694. RICHARD S. West Killingly, Conn.

2573. MARY ELIZA, born in Griswold, Conn., Oct. 19, 1849. She is now engaged as teacher in Newport, R. I. (1873).
2574. HENRY VAUGHN, born in Norwich, Conn, Apr. 9, 1851. He is engaged as a reed manufacturer in Danielsonville, Conn. (1873).
2575. ANNIE AMANDA, born in Moosup, Killingly, Conn, Nov. 12, 1861.

## 1706. CHARLES H. Albany, N. Y.

2576. CHARLOTTE EVA, born Oct. 16, 1852, and died May 21, 1858.
2577. HENRY, born May 8, 1854, and died June 6, 1858.
2578. ELIZABETH BURNHAM, born Sept. 25, 1857.
2579. AMANDA, born Sept. 9, 1859.
2580. CHARLES HENRY, JR., born May 27, 1862.
2581. MARIA, born May 30, 1866.
2582. VIRGIL, born Dec. 18, 1868.
2583. MARGARET ROBB, born Sept. 27, 1873.

## 1708. AUGUSTUS B.

2584. GEORGE WASHINGTON, born Nov. 5, 1855.
2585. EMMA JANE, born June 15, 1857.
2586. LUCY MINERVA, born Dec. 8, 1859.
2587. ELLA AUGUSTA, born Dec. 5, 1861.
2588. JESSIE VAN ZYLE, born Dec. 23, 1863.
2589. EDWIN AUGUSTUS, born Feb. 24, 1866.

## 1717. EDWARD. Worcester, Mass.

2590. HATTY LOUISE, born in Worcester, Aug. 11, 1852.
2591. JAMES WALTER, born in Worcester, Aug. 3, 1857.

## 1718. JAMES. Norwich, Conn.

2592. FREDERIC HENRY, born in Norwich, July 14, 1858.
2593. AGNESS LEISHMAN, born in Hartford, Jan 31, 1862.
2594. EDWARD BARTLETT, born in Norwich, July 7, 1867, and died Mar. 10, 1868.
2595. NELLIE MAY, born May 1, 1869.

### 1725. JOHN ADGATE. Norwich, Conn.

2596. DANIEL WEBSTER, born Dec. 14, 1837, married, and has no children.
2597. NANCY LOUISA, born June 3, 1843, and died Oct. 5, 1843.
2598. FERDINAND AUGUSTUS, born Oct. 12, 1845. Lives in Buffalo, and is in the coal business.

### 1735. WILLIAM BALDWIN. Norwich, Conn.

2599. CHARLES ELEAZER, born in Cincinnati, O., Dec. 14, 1855.
2600. BURREL WILLIAM, born in Iowa City, Ia., Jan. 12, 1858.
2601. EDWARD DENISON, born in West Liberty, Ia., Apr. 12, 1862, and died Dec. 21, 1862.
2602. MARY CORNELIA, born in Norwich, May 6, 1864.
2603. ELIZABETH DENISON, born in Norwich, Feb. 24, 1866.
2604. ANNA BAKER, born in Norwich, Aug. 17, 1869, and died Oct. 8, 1869.

### 1744. HENRY E. Providence, R. I.

2605. WILLIAM GILBERT, born in Providence, July 27, 1865.
2606. FREDERICK EDWARDS, born in Providence, July 16, 1867, and died Jan. 30, 1869.
2607. HELEN SAUNDERS, born in Providence, Feb. 4, 1870.
2608. LUCY NEWELL, born in Providence, Oct. 1, 1861.

### 1745. GEORGE H. Jackson, Mich.

2609. ARTHUR DOUGLAS, born June 14, 1852.
2610. GEORGE HOWLAND, JR., born March 17, 1854.
2611. EDWARD PRATT, born Apr. 12, 1859, and died Aug. 11, 1862.
2612. WILLIAM WHITING, born Apr. 8, 1862.
2613. ABBY HOWLAND, born July 25, 1868, and died Dec. 16, 1876.
2614. CHARLES TURNER, born June 26, 1872, and died Dec. 16, 1876.

### 1789. CHARLES. California.

2615. SON.
2616. DAUGHTER.

### 1791. DANIEL.

2617. DYER.
2618. ABBOT.
2619. LUCY.

### 1792. ANDERSON. Van Hornesville, N. Y.

2620. CHARLES M., born Dec. 22, 1839.

### 1793. JAMES. Van Hornesville, N.Y.

2621. LEWIS, born Aug. 31, 1842, and married, Jan. 1, 1866, Martha Young.
2622. MAY, born Jan. 13, 1853.

## 1797. DANIEL S. Albany, N. Y.

2623. JENNIE WILSON, born in Albany, N. Y., Sept. 17, 1859.
2624. TIENA DUNN, born in Albany, N. Y., July 4, 1862.
2625. AMY GARDNER, born in Albany, N. Y., Aug. 13, 1865.

## 1804. HON. HENRY W. Iowa City, Iowa.

[All born in Iowa City.]

2626. WILLARD A., born Oct. 23, 1848.
2627. GEORGE FRED, born Dec. 17, 1851.
2628. ZEPHANIAH W., born Apr. 24, 1854, and died Sept. 23, 1854.
2629. MAGGIE A., born Mar. 1, 1857.
2630. EDITH MAY, born Aug. 28, 1861.

## 1811. JAMES M., M.D. Dover, O.

2631. JAMES COOLEY, born Nov. 16, 1856.
2632. FANNY SMITH, born Feb. 27, 1865.
2633. GEORGE, born July 21, 1867.
2634. MARY, born Oct. 13, 1871.

## 1812. THOMAS I. Saginaw City, Mich.

2635. MARY ELMINA, born in Blackstone, Mass., Nov. 13, 1851, and married Jan. 12, 1872, Frank Lawrence, of East Saginaw, Mich., where they reside.
2636. ADDIE PHILLIPS, born in Dwight, Ill., Aug. 22, 1862, and died in three days.
2637. WILLIAM IRWIN, born in Dwight, Ill., Oct. 8, 1863.

## 1813. EDWIN. Dwight, Ill.

2638. ANN E., born Aug. 22, 1856, and died Oct. 15, 1863.
2639. MARY I., born Oct. 17, 1859, and died Oct. 17, 1863.
2640. ELLA E., born Oct. 24, 1864, and died June 11, 1866.
2641. ABBIE E. C., born June 23, 1867.
2642. CHARLES E., born Aug. 11, 1869.

## 1814. FREEMAN. Saginaw City, Mich.

2643. CLARA MAY, born in Gardner, Ill., Oct. 8, 1866.
2644. JESSIE GROVER, born in Gardner, Ill., Jan. 15, 1868.
2645. GEORGE SIDNEY, born in Saginaw, Mich., Dec. 14, 1871.

## 1823. WILLIAM. Corning, N. Y.

2646. WILLIAM, born in Corning, Feb. 26, 1871.
2647. ISABELLE, born in Corning, Aug. 13, 1872.

### 1833. ANDREW.

2648. LAURA A., born in 1845, and died in 1849.

### 1835. JABEZ S.   Norwich Town, Conn.

2649. HELEN MARSHALL, born May 31, 1850.
2650. JOSEPH BACKUS, born Feb. 28, 1853.
2651. JULIA SMITH, born Sept. 3, 1856.
2652. CARRIE BLOOMER, born July 7, 1858, and died July 24, 1858.
2653. ALANSON PECKHAM, born Apr. 13, 1860.
2654. GERTRUDE, born Mar. 13, 1870.

### 1838. DAVID A.

2655. JULIA S., born May 8, 1857.
2656. SIMEON FRANCIS, b. Sept. 18, 1868.

### 1849. DeWITT CLINTON.   Windham, Conn.

2657. JAMES GRAY, born March 1, 1853, married Dec. 19, 1876, Mary Amanda, daughter of Charles and Mary A. (Burnham) Larrabee, of Windham.
2658. WILLIAM WEBB, born April 23, 1857.
2659. HENRY CLINTON, born Feb. 18, 1860.

### 1851. JOHN M. N.   (Blue Hill,) Franklin, Conn.

2660. CHARLES EDWIN, born in Franklin, Dec. 24, 1854.

### 1861. DANIEL.   Norwich, Conn.

2661. HENRY LEE, born in Norwich, 1849.
2662. CAROLINE MARSH, born in Cleveland, O., 1852.

### 1862. EZRA.

2663. JOSEPH OLIVER, born Oct. 8, 1846, and married Sept. 8, 1866, Helen Deborah, daughter of Jedidiah and Deborah Morgan Kilburn (Preston) Baldwin. He enlisted in Company "I," Eighteenth Regiment Connecticut Volunteers Infantry, Aug. 6, 1862, at sixteen years of age, and was mustered into the United States service Aug. 22, 1862, at Norwich. Mustered out of the United States service at Harper's Ferry, Va., and discharged July, 1865, at Hartford, Conn.

### 1863. ERASTUS D.

2664. HANNAH.
2665. DESIRE.
2666. EUNICE.
2667. JAMES BUCHANAN.
2668. CHARLES.

## 1864. STEPHEN H. Oswego, N. Y.

### [All born in Oswego.]

2669. JOSEPH BEARDSLEY, born Oct. 17, 1844, and married, Aug. 26, 1869, Mary Faulkner Herrick.

2670. STEPHEN ALFRED, born Aug. 15, 1848.

2671. MARY TURRILL, born Jan. 20, 1850.

2672. JANE ELIZABETH, born Feb. 3, 1852.

2673. SAMUEL HOLDEN PARSONS, born Oct. 29, 1854.

2674. JAMES WILLIAM, born July 19, 1856, and died Mar. 6, 1857.

## 1865. SAMUEL PARSONS. Richmond, Va.

### [All born in Richmond, Va.]

2675. MARGARET ADAMS, born Mar. 20, 1848, and married, Oct. 30, 1867, James Blythe Moore, son of Rev. S. V. Moore, D.D. They are settled in Va. They have had two children:

    i.  Samuel Lathrop Moore, born Feb. 7, 1870, and died June 23, 1871.

    ii.  Caroline Pickett Moore, born June 22, 1872.

2676. GEORGE ALFRED, born Aug. 19, 1850.

2677. CHARLES PICKETT, born Jan. 11, 1852 or 3.

2678. SARAH CARRINGTON, born Aug. 8, 1857.

2679. CORA, born May 10, 1865.

## 1866. GEORGE A., M.D. Sandwich Islands.

2680. FRANCIS AUGUSTUS, born at sea, June 29, 1849, on the Pacific Ocean, three days out from the Sandwich Islands, latitude 20° 39′ and west longitude 152° 25′.

2681. GEORGE PARSONS, born on the island of Oahu, Hawaiian Islands, Aug. 25, 1851, his father being a physician of large practice there and also United States Consul, which post he retained until his final return to this country in 1858. The son pursued the earliest studies from the last date until 1867, at Oswego, New York, in private schools and under tutors, with an interval in 1862, during which the family traveled in England, France, Germany, and Italy. In 1867 the subject of this sketch went to Dresden, Germany, and at private gymnasia accomplished a partial college course. Returning to the United States in 1870 he entered the law school of Columbia College in New York, and upon finishing his studies found for a short time a place in the office of Evarts, Southmayd & Choate. His health, however, would not permit his making a profession of the law, and he decided to devote himself to literature, not as less laborious, but as affording more frequent opportunities for rest and recreation. He was but seven years old when he first saw a theatrical performance, and in consequence, began to read Shakespeare and undertook to write a play, which unhappily is lost to the world. Though fond of outdoor life, he had from these early days cherished a literary ambition, and had practiced writing in various lines. Reading Virgil in the original first awakened his taste for poetry when he was about sixteen, and he became an occasional contributor to the press. In 1871 he went to London, and Sept. 11, married Rose, the younger daughter of Nathaniel Hawthorne, in St. Peter's Church, Chelsea, where Charles Dickens had been married many years before. After his marriage he settled in Cambridge, Mass., and lived there and in Concord for eleven years, purchasing the "Wayside" in Concord, Hawthorne's former home, in 1879. In 1883 he sold it and removed to the city of New York. In the meantime he had, in 1881, made a short trip to Spain, and he wrote a series of articles upon that country for *Harper's Monthly*, which were afterwards published in book form. Mr. Lathrop has been a widely known contributor to the newspaper and periodical press as a correspondent and poet and in editorial columns. Some of his poetical contributions may be found in Epes Sargent's *Collection of Poets*, and in Bryant's *Household Library of Poetry*, but the greater part of his poems, short stories, reviews and critical essays have not as yet been collected. Of his poems, perhaps the most popular is "Keenan's Charge," founded on an incident of the war. It has been widely copied and used for public recitation. Literature has been indebted to Mr. Lathrop for a study of Hawthorne (1876), a semi-biographical and critical memoir, and also for a new edition of Hawthorne's works, containing a new biographical sketch of that author, and a short story found by Mr. Lathrop in an old annual. In 1878 Mr. Lathrop contributed to and edited a *Masque of Poets*, made up of new poems by English and American authors. In 1883 he published the history of the Union League of Philadelphia, and in 1884 *Newport* appeared, a novel which is at this writing in the hands of the critics, and is receiving favorable comment. Among the magazines and papers to which Mr. Lathrop has chiefly contributed papers may be mentioned *The Atlantic*, *Harper's*, *Appleton's Journal*, *Scribner's*, *The Century*, *The Manhattan*, *The Christian Union*, *The Independent*, and *Boston Courier*. In the summer of 1883 Mr. Lathrop was instrumental in organizing the American Copy-right League, which now embraces six hundred authors and journalists. The object of this is to establish international copy-right between the United States and other countries. As Secretary of the League, Mr. Lathrop has exerted a wide influence upon the subject, and the prospect is that its object will soon be attained. The subject of this sketch is still young, and has before him many years of full promise, and by his native ability and his well-directed industry, will, without doubt, win a name and place in the *Valhalla* of American literature.

### 1869. FREDERICK B. Oswego, N.Y.

2682. FRANCES MATHER, born in Binghamton, Feb. 21, 1851, and died in Oswego, Sept. 11, 1852.

2683. FREDERIC B. SURRILL, born in Oswego, N. Y., Feb. 4, 1853.

2684. HELEN MORGAN, born in Oswego, N. Y., Mar. 5, 1855.

2685. CAROLINE MATHER, born in Oswego, Sept. 30, 1859.

2686. HENRY MATHER, born in Oswego, Oct. 8, 1861, and died Oct. 19, 1861.

2687. GEORGE ALFRED, born in Oswego, Nov. 15, 1864, and died in the same place, Jan. 14, 1870.

2688. LILLY MATHER, born in Oswego, Jan. 2, 1871.

### 1889. RICHARD B. Lisbon, Conn.

2689. CLINTON LESTER, born in Lisbon, Mar. 4, 1854, and died Oct. 8, 1854.
2690. JOHN VIRGIL, born Dec. 5, 1855.

### 1891. JONATHAN L. Lisbon, Conn.

2691. HATTIE LESTER, born in Franklin, Oct. 15, 1854.
2692. FRANK LESLIE, born in Franklin, Sept. 26, 1856.
2693. GEORGE AUSTIN, born in Lisbon, Sept. 21, 1858.

### 1906. GEORGE DELOS. Lansing, Mich.

2694. LOTTIE.
2695. GEORGE.

### 1908. PORTER M. Sheboygan, Mich.

2696. MARY LUCILLA, born Feb. 2, 1868.

### 1935. JUSTIN. Tolland, Conn.

2697. JOHN, born in Coventry, Jan. 31, 1829, and married, Jan. 25, 1860, Annie J. Eppeheimer, of Philadelphia.

2698. DON FERDINAND, born in North Coventry, Conn., Oct. 18, 1832, and married (1), Nov. 2, 1855, Harriet A. Waldo, who died in 1862. He married (2), Dec. 2, 1864, Marietta, daughter of John Fuller, of Stafford. They are now living (1877) in South Coventry, where he is the treasurer of the Millbrook Woollen Co., also the Wilbraham Woollen Co.

2699. JAMES OLIVER, born Sept. 2, 1855. Died of consumption, aged 20.
2700. JAMES ABBOT, born Dec. 25, 1857, in Willington.
2701. PERKINS LORD, born June 11, 1858, in Willington.
2702. MARY ANGELINE, born Nov. 24, 1862, in Willington.

### 1937. CHARLES. Tolland, Conn.

2703. JOSEPH VAUGHN, born in Tolland, Mar. 20, 1846. He is now a book-keeper in Hartford (1873).
2704. MARY JANE, born in Tolland, Aug. 4, 1847.
2705. HARRIET NEWEL, born in Tolland, July 5, 1850, and died Dec. 28, 1857.
2706. JOHN CHARLES, born in Tolland, Mar. 17, 1862.

### 1939. SAMUEL M. Tolland, Conn.

2707. EDWARD.
2708. ANN ELIZA, married John Taylor, an engineer on railroad. One child: Mary Taylor.
2709. JOHN SAMUEL.
2710. DAN.
2711. NELLIE JOSEPHINE.

38

### 1942. HORATIO N.        Bakersville, Vt.

**2711-1.** VERANUS, born Oct. 3, 1824. Died unmarried.

**2711-2.** ELIZA ANN, born in Wolcott, Oct. 19, 1825. Married (1), Hollis Gray ; (2), Earl Boutelle. Lived in Bakersville, Vt. Children:

*(By first husband.)*

   **i.**   Daniel Gray. Married Henrietta Randall.

   **ii.**  Horatio Nelson Gray, of Bakersville.

  **iii.**  John Gray.

*(By second husband.)*

  **iv.**  Carrie Boutelle. Died 1863.

   **v.**  Florette Boutelle.

  **vi.**  George Boutelle. Died.

**2711-3.** MARVIN, born in Wolcott, Oct. 21, 1828. Married (1), Bridget Rafferty ; (2), Harriet Leach, of Grand Rapids, Mich., and lived in Forest, Richland Co., Wis., in 1874.

**2711-4.** JESSE WHITNEY, born Jan. 1831. Died Mar. 27, 1832.

**2711-5.** CHARLES, born Oct. 9, 1835. Married (1), Caroline Page ; (2),——— Dustin. Lived in Hillsboro, Wis.

**2711-6.** JOHN, born in Cambridge, Vt., Sept. 3, 1837. Married, Delia Leach. Lived in Forest, Wis., in 1874. Children:

   **i.**   Nellie, born 1859.

   **ii.**  Charles, born in 1868 or '69.

**2711-7.** NAPOLEON BONAPARTE, born in Cambridge, May 28, 1840. Married Nancy Jane Aldrich, and lived in Cambridge with his father. Children:

   **i.**   Harvey, born Apr. 29, 1868, in Danville, Vt.

   **ii.**  Henrietta, born in Fletcher, Vt., March, 1870.

  **iii.**  Horace, born in Fletcher, Vt.

**2711-8.** LUCY ANN, born in Cambridge, July 27, 1842, and married Sept. 30, 1863, Luther Dickinson, a farmer, born in Underhill, July 15, 1836, son of Ira and Martha (Story) Dickinson. Settled in Underhill. Children:

   **i.**   Carrie Dickinson, born Aug. 9, 1864.

   **ii.**  Fannie Dickinson, born Apr. 15, 1866.

  **iii.**  Francis Dickinson, born Mar. 31, 1870.

### 1943. LUCIUS.        Cambridge, Vt.

**2712.** DANFORTH KEYES.

**2713.** HOMER E.

**2714.** HENRY.

**2715.** ELIZABETH.

**2716.** LUCRETIA.

### 1945. WILLIAM.        Mankato, Minn.

**2717.** AUGUSTA.

**2718.** DARWIN.

**2719.** HARRISON.

**2720.** ELLEN.

**2721.** NORMAN.

**2722.** ANDREW.

**2723.** ELIZABETH.

## 1947. CHARLES T.

2724. ADDISON BARBOUR, born Apr. 13, 1838, and married Lucie A. King.

2725. WILLIAM LOCKE, born June 22, 1840, and married Adeline Emerson.

2726. LUCIUS, born Apr. 22, 1842.

2727. ADELIA JANE, born Jan. 1, 1844.

2728. ALONZO WETHERBEE, born June 18, 1847. Died Nov. 12, 1850.

2729. CHARLES WILDER, born Apr. 6, 1850.

2730. FRED DANIEL, born Oct. 18, 1852, and married Jennie G. Munyan, of Worcester, Mass.

2731. ADAH LOUISE, born, Apr. 15, 1855. Died July 2, 1863.

### 1948. URIAH.                                      Waterville, Vt.

2732. ALFRED.

2733. JULIA.

2734. ALICE.

### 1949. ELIAS.                                       Lawrence, Mass.

2735. MARY L., born Jan. 1858, and married Edward W. Emerson, of Boston, Mass.

### 1950. KELSEY.                                  South Coventry, Conn.

2736. AURELIA, born Jan. 31, 1827, and married, Sept. 13, 1852, Gilbert, son of William and Mary Barto, of Panton, Vt., who died Dec. 26, 1863. She died Feb. 9, 1886. They had three children: Ida Janette, born Apr. 21, 1856, and died Mar. 13, 1860; Edgar Fayette, born Mar. 27, 1858; and Franklin Murray, born Apr. 5, 1862.

2737. WILLIAM, born in Tolland, Dec. 15, 1828, and married, Mar. 19, 1857, Mary, daughter of Augustus and Clara Clark, of South Coventry, where he is living on a farm.

2738. WAIT COBB, born Jan. 30, 1831, and died Aug. 25, 1832.

2739. GEORGE FAYETTE, born in Tolland, June 13, 1833, and married, Sept. 3, 1854, Ellen, daughter of Josiah and Rebecca Beers, of Norwich, Conn. They settled in South Coventry, but removed to a farm in South Windsor in 1872.

2740. DANIEL ZEBULON, born in South Coventry, Apr. 9, 1836, and married Nov. 26, 1854, Lucy, daughter of James and Sophia Pierce, of Colchester, Conn. They settled in Winnebago City, Faribault Co., Minnesota, and are living there now.

2741. CAROLINE JANE, born in South Coventry, July 20, 1840, and married in New York City, Nov. 25, 1868, Calvin, son of Captain Elijah and Kezia Whiton of Tolland, who was born Feb. 18, 1818. He is an architect and builder, and a deacon in the Congregational church in Tolland, Conn. They have one child: Flora Daisy Whiton, born Feb. 25, 1874.

2742. WALTER HOLBROOK, born in South Coventry, Nov. 30, 1844, and married, Nov. 17, 1869, Cora Kirtland, daughter of Calvin and Mary (Redfield) Hayden, of Westbrook, Conn. He is in the grocery business in Hartford, Conn.

2743. CORA ELIZABETH, born in South Coventry, Apr. 3, 1847.

### 1970. RUFUS.        Aroostook Co., Me.

2748.  
2749. ⟩ Two daughters and one son.  Names not learned.  
2750.  

### 1973. ALFRED.        Elmer, Vt.

2751. A DAUGHTER.

### 1974. HIRAM.        Vershire, Vt.

2752.  
2753. ⟩ Two daughters and one son.  Names not learned.  
2754.  

### 1975. WARREN.        Vershire, Vt.

2755.  
2756. ⟩ One son and a daughter.  Names not learned.

### 1982. PAUL B.        Elma, N. Y.

2757. ALBERT, born July 8, 1843, and died July 22, 1843.

2758. EMMA, born Aug. 9, 1844, and died Mar. 29, 1848.

2759. GRACE, born Feb. 15, 1847, and married Sept. 29, 1869, Jireh Kinney, Jr., of Mettapoisett, Mass.

2760. PAUL, born Nov. 16, 1848.

2761. CHASE, born Dec. 26, 1849, and married in October, 1870, Louisa Stillman, of Aurora, N. Y.

2762. DON J., born June 25, 1851, and graduated at the Buffalo Medical College, and is in Iowa.

2763. HERBERT, born Nov. 3, 1852.

### 1983. JOSEPHUS DWIGHT.        Montpelier, Vt.

2764. MARY E., born Dec. 29, 1843.

2765. CHARLES DWIGHT, born Nov. 3, 1845. He was in the Northern service during the recent war, in Co. D, 17th regiment of the U. S. army. He died May 4, 1865.

2766. GEORGE ALBERT, born Mar. 10, 1848.

2767. JAMES WILLIE, born June 4, 1850.

2768. HELEN BAYLEE, born Dec. 17, 1853.

2769. BENNIE FRANKLIN, born Nov. 30, 1856.

### 1987. ELISHA.        Bozrah, Conn.

#### [All born in Bozrah.]

2770. CHARLES NELSON, born Sept. 30, 1834, and married Delia ———, of Westerly, R. I., where he settled. He died there Dec. 1, 1863, having had but one child, who died in infancy.

2771. JOHN AVERY, born Mar. 17, 1836, and married (1), Varian Abell; (2), Sarah Thomas. He lives in Preston, near Norwich, where he is farming. Two children.

2772. HARRIET PARTHENA, born Apr. 20, 1838, and married Jeremiah Saunders. They live in Uncasville, and have three children.

2773. JANET RUHAMAH, born Dec. 15, 1839, and married Samuel Chappel. They live in Uncasville, and have had no children.

2774. ABBY ANN, born Mar. 10, 1841, and married Alvah Farnum. They are living in Canterbury, and have one child.

2775. ELIJAH, born Jan. 24, 1842, and is now (1873) living, unmarried, in Salem, Conn.

2776. ELISHA, born Jan. 24, 1842, and married Emily Miner, and lives in Montville.

2777. HANNAH MARIA, born Feb. 14, 1844, and married William Paine, of Meriden, where they now live. No children.

2778. HENRY, born Jan. 22, 1846, and married Julia Rose, of Westerly, R. I., where they live.

2779. MARY ELLEN, born Apr. 19, 1848, and married Orrin Spencer, of Montville. She died soon after her marriage, Dec. 23, 1866.

2780. LEBBEUS, born Jan. 9, 1850.

2781. FRANCIS, born Dec. 9, 1853.

2782. WALTER CHARLES, born Nov. 14, 1855.

### 1988. HARVEY.      Waterford, Conn.

2783. ALBERT HENRY, born in Lebanon, Nov. 24, 1831, and married Jane Hale of Glastonbury. They are now living in Lisbon, Ct.

2784. CHARLES WOODWORTH, born in Greeneville, Dec. 31, 1833, and married Harriet Bliss, of Burnside, where they are living.

2785. HARRIET LUCRETIA, born in Lebanon, Apr. 10, 1836, and married, Jan. 19, 1858, Richard, son of Hiram and Eunice Palmer, of Colchester, where he was born in 1832, and died in 1865. His widow is now (1872) with her father, in Waterford. Children:

    i.    Harriet Lathrop, born Jan. 23, 1859, in Colchester.

    ii.    Minnie Lincoln, born Sept. 20, 1860, in Colchester.

2786. HENRIETTA CAREY, born in Lebanon, June 23, 1838, and married Charles Browning, and now lives in Greeneville, Conn. Children:

    i.    Frank Woodworth Browning, born in Greeneville.

    ii.    Etta Perkins Browning, died.

    iii.    Charles Lathrop Browning.

    iv.    Henry Prentice Browning.

2787. EDWIN HARVEY, born in Lebanon, Feb. 20, 1840, and married Lydia Houston, of Greeneville, where they live.

2788. OLIVER WOODWORTH, born in Lebanon, Sept. 26, 1841. He enlisted in the 8th Connecticut regiment, and was in the service. Was wounded Thursday, at the battle of Antietam, and lived until Monday.

2789. FANNY MARIA, born Dec. 28, 1843, and married, June 26, 1869, William S., son of Thomas and Sally (Sterry) Standish, of Lebanon, where they now live, in Goshen Society.

2790. ARTHUR DOUGLAS, born in Lebanon, Feb. 25, 1846, and married Belle

Bolles, daughter of John and Nancy (Chapman) Bolles, of Waterford. They live in Montville.

2791. JOHN BALDWIN, born in Lebanon, Mar. 24, 1840.

2792. FREDERICK WILLIAM, born in Lebanon, Aug. 16, 1850.

### 1990. LEONARD.        Andover, Conn.

2793. JANE L., born in Lebanon, Conn., May 3, 1845, and married, Dec. 25, 1865, William E. Smith, of Odin, Marion County, Ill. She died at Odin, July 17, 1870, leaving one daughter, Carrie May Smith, born Feb. 25, 1868.

2794. LIZZIE S., born in Lebanon, Conn., Dec. 1, 1850, and married Nov. 19, 1872, W. B. Sprague, of Manchester, Conn. He is now agent for a commercial house in New York City (1873).

### 1992. ERASTUS.        Lebanon, Conn.

2795. ASAHEL P., born in Lebanon, Apr. 12, 1846, and married, Jan. 7, 1867, Ellen C. Blackman, of Andover, Conn.

2796. JAMES K., born in Lebanon, Aug. 2, 1848, and married, Dec. 1, 1869, Fannie A. Cleveland, of Andover. He died in Sprague, Conn., Sept. 6, 1872.

2797. JOSEPHINE E., born in Lebanon, May 12, 1851, and died in the same place, Aug. 8, 1865.

2798. GEORGE LEBBEUS, born in Lebanon, May 1, 1854, and died Aug. 5, 1855. (In the town record this name is given as Albert.)

### 2001. THADDEUS SLUMAN LA.        Canaan, N. H.

2799. HENRY SLUMAN, born Jan. 8, 1848.

2800. MARY ELLA, born June 26, 1852.

### 2002. JOSHUA STEVENS LA.        Monticello, Ia.

2801. ANN AUGUSTA, born July 28, 1843, and married, May 28, 1864, Laban Pierce, born June 5, 1835. They have a daughter.

2802. HORACE WILLIS MILLER, born May 16, 1848, and married, Dec. 31, 1870, Elizabeth Aggola, who was daughter of Kasper and Catherine Aggola, from Switzerland, and was born July 8, 1851.

2803. LUCINDA ALICE, born Jan. 30, 1852, and married, in Iowa, May 20, 1872, Henry, son of Kasper and Ursula Gadmer, who was born Nov. 28, 1846. They have one child: Dorothy Ursula Gadmer, born June 4, 1873.

### 2004. ELISHA LA.        Enfield Center, N. H.

2804. CAROLINE MALVINA, born June 27, 1839.

2805. GEORGE ELISHA, born Nov. 10, 1853.

### 2006. JOHN H.        Canaan, N. H.

2806. ELLEN E., born in Dorchester, Sept. 6, 1850, and died in Canaan, July 17, 1852.

2807. FRANK R., born in Canaan, July 4, 1853, and died Sept. 10, 1871.

2808. DELLA C., born Aug. 26, 1856.

2809. HATTIE ALMA, born in Canaan, Aug. 26, 1860, and died Nov. 19, 1867.

2810. CHARLIE LANGDON, born in Canaan, Dec. 17, 1864.

### 2007. GEORGE H. LA.

2811. CLARA ESTELLE, born Dec. 4, 1853.

2812. ISABELL LUCINDA, born Mar. 15, 1857.

2813. EMMA LAURA, born May 10, 1859.

2814. EDWIN GEORGE, born July 22, 1864.

### 2008. JAMES B.       Arkansas.

2815. ELIZABETH A.

### 2009. BENJAMIN G.     San Francisco, Cal.

2816. JANE. Deceased.

2817. VIRGINIA A.

2818. WILLIAM N. Deceased.

2819. FANNIE R.

2820. BENJAMIN GIRAULT.

### 2011. THOMAS W.

2821. ALFRED. Deceased.

2822. MARIAN.

2823. EDWARD B.

2824. ISABEL L.

### 2016. WILLIAM A.     Cleveland, O.

2825. WILLIAM, born in Muskingum County, O., Feb. 21, 1848, and married Mary Taylor, of Cleveland, where they are now settled (1872).

### 2019. JAMES, JUN.     New Orleans, La.

2826. MARIA, born in St. Clarville, New Orleans, Sept. 7, 1817, and died in Jacksonville, Ill., Sept. 10, 1840.

2827. JAMES, born in Warehouse Point, Conn., July 4, 1821, and died in New Haven, Conn., Jan. 1, 1842, while a member of the junior class in Yale College.

### 2020. AZEL.

2828.
2829.
2830. } FOUR DAUGHTERS, of whom one is Mrs. Julia Eaton, of Middletown.
2831.

### **2022.** HENRY.　　　　　New Orleans, La.

2832. JAMES.
2833. HORACE.
2834. TOCLAIR.
2835. JOHN.
2836. NESIDA.
2837. LYDIA.

### **2023.** BLISS.　　　　　Iberville, La.

2838. JOSEPHINE.
2839. EDOAR.

### **2034.** ELDERKIN.

2840.
2841.
2842.
2843. } SEVEN CHILDREN, names not learned.
2844.
2845.
2846.

### **2038.** HARRY B.　　　　　San Francisco, Cal.

2847.
2848. } THREE CHILDREN. One, Henry B., of Oroville, Cal.
2849.

### **2042.** RIAL W.　　　　　Buffalo, N. Y.

2850. EMILY.
2851. HARRIET.
2852. HARRIET.

### **2043.** HEMAN F.　　　　　Buffalo, N. Y.

2853. A SON.
2854. ELLA.

### **2045.** HORACE.　　　　　Ann Arbor, Mich.

2855. ALBERT.
2856. ORLANDO.
2857. FREDERICK.
2858. WALTER.
2859. PORTER.

### **2046.** ORVILLE.　　　　　St. Louis, Mo.

2860. EDGAR, born in Kalamazoo, Mich.
2861. JULIA KENING, born in Chicago.

### **2063.** PHILEMON.　　　　　Onondaga Co., N. Y.

2862. DELIA ASENATH, born in Onondaga County, N. Y., Oct. 23, 1830.
2863. MERCELIA SOPHIA, born Aug. 15, 1838, and died Aug. 24, 1842.
2864. ARVILLA PARMELIA, born Oct. 21, 1840, and died Aug. 15, 1842.
2865. ALBERT PHILEMON, born Dec. 16, 1842.　To be married Dec. 1873.
2866. CHARLES DEVILLO, born Aug. 6, 1847.

### 2068. LEVI B. Hollister, Cal.

2867. MARTIN A. In Lowell, Mass.

### 2069. REV. CURTISS GREEN. Nebraska.

2868. A SON, living in Enterprise, Nebraska.

### 2071. MERRITT ADAMS. Annawan, Ill.

2869. ⎫
2870. ⎬ THREE SONS, one a preacher.
2871. ⎭

### 2088. JAMES W. Savannah, Ga.

2872. JAMES WARREN, born in Hawkinsville, Pulaski Co., Ga., Mar. 7, 1849.

2873. LUCY, born in Hawkinsville, July 18, 1851.

2874. CHARLES HERVEY, born in Pulaski Co., Mar. 7, 1853, and died in Savannah, in 1876.

### 2090. HERVEY W. Baltimore, Md.

2875. KATE PARKER, born in Savannah, Ga., Jan. 21, 1867.

2876. MARY LUCY, born in Savannah, Ga., Mar. 22, 1868.

2877. LEONORA CHARLESSA, born in Baltimore, Md., Dec. 30, 1869.

2878. ANNIE HERVEY, born in Baltimore, Md., Sept. 2, 1871.

### 2093. WILLIAM S. Lebanon, Conn.

2879. WILLIAM R.

2880. CHARLES C.

2881. PHILIPS A.

### 2145. REV. STANLEY E. Macon, Ga.

2882. JOHN LITTELL, born Dec. 10, 1871, and died Dec. 16, 1871.

2883. PAUL WILFRED, born Dec. 18, 1872, and died Sept. 19, 1878.

2884. STANLEY HOUGH, born Nov. 25, 1874, and died Sept. 16, 1878.

2885. SUSIE, born Oct. 1, 1876.

2886. BESSIE, born Oct. 6, 1878.

2887. THEODORE, born Nov. 19, 1881.

2888. ALFRED WILLIAM, born Nov. 19, 1883.

### 2164. ALVA. New York City.

2889. A DAUGHTER.

2890. ALVA.

2891. ALBERT.

2892. MARY.

2893. ALONZO WHEELOCK, born Jan. 17, 1842. Married.

2894. SARAH FRANCES, born Oct. 20, 1842, and married Thomas Martin.

2895. ENOS MITCHELL, born Oct. 21, 1845.

2896. EVA ISIDORE, born Aug. 6, 1857.

39

### 2165. GEORGE.          Northville, Conn.

2897. ORIN FOWLER, married Charlotte Packard, in Birmingham.

2898. WILLIAM GILBERT, born Feb. 11, 1844, and married, Aug. 6, 1864, Sarah Jane, daughter of John Lathrop, and now lives in New Milford.

2899. HEMAN STARR, married Alice Tucker, of Birmingham, Conn.

2900. SHERMAN WALLACE, Birmingham.

2901. ROWLAND LEE, died in New Milford.

2902. ALFRED ALDORUS.

2903. ELDRIDGE SOLOMON.

2904. ABBY SCOTT, born Apr. 23, 1857.

2905. EDWARD T.

2906. SAMUEL CLARK.

2907. JOHN, died Mar., 1871.

### 2171. CHARLES.          Bridgeport, Conn.

2908. EGBERT, born in New York City, and died young, in Brookfield, Conn.

2909. EUGENE, born in Bridgeport, Mar., 1851. Now living in Indianapolis.

2910. CARLTON SHERMAN, born in Winsted, in 1853. Now in Waterbury.

2911. WILLIE, born in Bridgeport, and died at the age of twelve years.

2912. LENA JANE, born in Winsted, Conn., Mar. 17, 1866.

### 2204. GEORGE A., M.D.          East Saginaw, Mich.

2913. GEORGE DERBY, born Oct. 28, 1859.

2914. FRANK POMEROY, born Dec. 10, 1863, and died July 18, 1864.

2915. CARRIE DERBY, born June 11, 1869.

### 2205. HENRY K., M.D.          Royal Oak, Mich.

2916. HENRY KIRKE, JUN., born in Orion, Mich., Dec. 27, 1847, and married, June 1, 1871, at Detroit, Mich., Mary Woodward, daughter of R. W. Gillet, of Detroit She was born in Torringford, Conn., Feb. 19, 1849. He is a dentist, having received his diploma in the Ohio College of Dental Surgery, in Cincinnati, in 1870, and is now in the practice of his profession in Detroit.

2917. GEORGE KOSSUTH, born in Oakwood, Mich., May 12, 1850, and died at Royal Oak, Mich., Sept. 3, 1866, of heart disease.

2918. FRANCES MARIA, born in Oakwood, Mich., July 23, 1852.

2919. LIZZIE, born in Oakwood, Mich., Mar. 6, 1858, and died at Royal Oak, Mich., Nov. 22, 1871.

### 2208. SOLOMON.

2920. FRANK HENRY, born in Flint, Mich., May 20, 1854, and is a photographer in Oakland, Cal.

2921. EUGENE HAROLD, born in East Saginaw, Mich., Apr. 7, 1856. He studied dental surgery with his uncle Joseph, in Detroit.

2922. GUILD, born in East Saginaw, July 9, 1858, and died Oct. 23, 1858.
2923. CORNELIA MARIA, born at North San Juan, Cal., Oct. 23, 1864, and died at Grass Valley, Cal., June 29, 1865.
2924. MARY LOUISE, born at Grass Valley, Cal., Dec. 7, 1868.

### 2210. JOSEPH; D.D.S. Detroit, Mich.

2925. CLARA MARIA, born in Detroit, June 5, 1864.
2926. HENRY PULLING, born in Detroit, Dec. 10, 1869.
2927. JOSEPH, JR., born in Detroit, Dec. 27, 1871.

### 2212. CHARLES A. Armada, Mich.

2928. CHARLES EDWARD, born June 17, 1859.
2929. LILLIE ANNA, born Oct. 1, 1860.

### 2213. SETH. Richmond, Mich.

2930. ALICE EVELYN, born Mar. 27, 1859.
2931. SETH DWIGHT, born Feb. 3, 1861.
2932. JENNY.
2933. CLARENCE, died in Mar., 1873.

### 2216. HORACE A. Armada, Mich.

2934. GEORGE PAOLI, born Oct. 26, 1851, and married Sept. 27, 187-, Emma Van Houghton. He is a dentist, and lives in Wales, Mich.
2935. MARY LEE MALVINA, born Sept. 15, 1856, and died Sept. 3, 1866.
2936. EDWARD FRANKLIN, born July 7, 1859.

### 2217. JAMES E.

2937. EMMA, born Mar. 10, 1852, and married, Jan. 1, 1872, Lovell Lock.
2938. ANNIE, born Apr. 16, 1856.

### 2218. SAMUEL, M.D. Clio, Mich.

2939. CHARLES ARTHUR, born Dec. 25, 1856, and died May 6, 1858.
2940. MARY ADELINE, born Dec. 13, 1858.
2941. EDITH JOANNA, born Oct. 28, 1860.
2942. EDWARD, born Sept. 13, 1863.

### 2220. JONATHAN D. Richmond, Mich.

2943. ELIZABETH MAY, born Aug. 2, 1863.
2944. GEORGE LEWIS, born Dec. 27, 1864.
2945. CARRIE, died Mar. 9, 1871.

### 2222. ELISHA D. Armada, Mich.

2946. FRANK ELISHA, born Feb. 7, 1865.

## 2224. JOHN LENTNER. Hannibal, Mo.

2947. JOHN LENTNER, born Dec. 11, 1850.
2948. LIZZIE JANE, born Sept. 3, 1852.
2949. JOSEPH, born July 12, 1855.
2950. MARY ASHLEY, born Aug. 7, 1860.
2951. GEORGE BARTLETT, born Sept. 21, 1866.

## 2226. ROBERT.

2952. JOSEPHINE ROSA, born Aug. 16, 1857, and died May 23, 1859.
2953. MARY JANE, born June 2, 1860.

## 2229. JAMES. South Hadley Falls, Mass.

2954. JAMES BONTICOU, born July 4, 1854, and died Feb. 5, 1870.
2955. EDWARD FLINT, born Sept. 16, 1859? (Strong, 780.)

## 2236. SETH. Chester, Mass.

2956. ABBY LOUISE, born Jan. 16, 1866.
2957. LYMAN REED, born Apr. 28, 1869.

## 2256. FRANK. Morristown, N. J.

2958. WILLIAM GIBBONS, born Feb. 19, 1859.
2959. FRANK, born Dec. 28, 1860.
2960. LOUISA GIBBONS, born Apr. 4, 1863.

## 2260. FRANCIS H. Savannah, Ga.

2961. HENRY STEBBINS.

## 2261. EDWARD STEBBINS. Atlanta, Ga.

2962. EDWARD ADAMS, born in Macon, June 21, 1863, and died July 25, 1866.
2963. DWIGHT, born in Macon, Mar. 12, 1866.
2964. GEORGE, born in Savannah, Feb. 12, 1868.
2965. LOUISE, born in Savannah, Nov. 19, 1870.
2966. FRANK, born in Savannah, Jan. 29, 1873.

## 2271. HENRY. New York City.

2967. LESTER OTIS, born Aug. 3, 1855.
2968. JESSIE B., born Feb. 6, 1858.

## 2287. THOMAS. Springfield, Mass.

2969. THOMAS SIMS, born in Springfield, Dec. 12, 1825, and married Mary A., daughter of Alvan Baldwin, who was born in Union, Conn., Aug. 11, 1827. He has been for years in Hartford.

2970. SAMUEL B., born in Springfield, July 5, 1829, and married Louisa Fox.

2971. SARAH JANE, born Apr. 17, 1831. Married in Cleveland, O., Jan. 29, 1859, Joshua D. Tyler of Elkhart, Ind. No children.

2972. MARY A., born in Springfield, Mar. 8, 1833, and married in Springfield, Jan. 29, 1859, George Henry Dupee of New Haven, where they now live. Children:

. i. Benjamin Tyler Dupee, born Oct. 17, 1865.

ii. Charles A. Dupee, born Aug. 8, 1868.

iii. Frank Dupee, born July 13, 1871.

2973. BENJAMIN LEE, born in Springfield, Mar. 27, 1836, and married in Springfield, Aug. 2, 1860, Kate Benton Thayer, daughter of Geo. W., of Montpelier, Vt. She was born in Springfield, Nov. 23, 1840 Master Mechanic Winchester Repeating Arms Co.

2974. SUSAN SIMONDS, born in Springfield, Jan. 28, 1841, and died Nov. 22, 1842.

### 2291. BELIA. West Springfield, Mass.

2975. EDWARD H., born in Springfield, Dec. 2, 1837, and married, Nov. 26, 1867, Susan T., daughter of Benjamin Little of Huntington, Mass.

2976. CHARLES TRUMAN, born in Hartford, Conn., May 19, 1841, and died Jan. 21, 1842.

2977. ·SARAH BARTLETT, born in Hartford, Aug. 27, 1843, and married at West Springfield, Mass., Apr. 27, Lucien H. Brooks of Hamilton, Canada. No children.

### 2304. THORNTON, K., LL.B. Boston, Mass.

2978. MARY BUCKMINSTER HOOPER, born in Boston, July 15, 1867.

2979. AMY PEABODY, born Mar. 28, 1869.

2979-1. WILLIAM STURGIS HOOPER, born June 19, 1870.

### 2322. DAVID. Longmeadow, Mass.

2980. ABBIE FOLSOM, born Jan. 1, 1851. Married, Nov. 4, 1874, Benjamin Wallace Hunn, son of Erastus and Caroline Foster Hunn.

2981. NANCIE JANE, born Dec. 16, 1852. A teacher.

### 2324. FREDERICK K. Springfield, Mass.

2982. FREDERICK W., born Mar. 4, 1855.

### 2326-7. EDWARD W. Springfield, Mass.

2983. FRANK WHITNEY, born in Hartford, July 27, 1865.

2984. MIRIAM LOUISA, born in E. Longmeadow, Feb. 28, 1869.

### 2327. MARTIN D. Chicago, Ill.

2985. EUNICE JANE.

2986. FRANK.

2987. MAUDE.

## 2330. THOMAS R.                    Carbondale, Pa.

2988. DWIGHT NOBLE, born Sept. 25, 1881.
2989. REXFORD GILLESPIE, born March 31, 1882.

## 2357. EBENEZER.                    Provincetown, Mass.

2990. LETTIE FRANCES, born in Provincetown, Nov. 29, 1859.
2991. SUSAN ADELINE, born in Provincetown, Mar. 13, 1867.

## 2384. CHARLES L.                    Boston, Mass.

2992. CHARLES ORLANDO, born Sept. 3, 1870, and died Oct. 25, 1870.
2993. HATTIE MABEL, born Nov. 12, 1871.
2994. ETHEL, born Apr. 16, 1873.

## 2402. JOHN QUINCY ADAMS.          Cohasset, Mass.

[All born in Cohasset.]

2995. CALEB, born Sept. 7, 1849, and is a clerk.
2996. MARY THAXTER, born Jan. 17, 1851.
2997. JOSEPH THAXTER, born June 1, 1853, and died Oct. 16, 1853.
2998. QUINCY ADAMS, born Nov. 3, 1856.
2999. ELLEN, born Mar. 30, 1860, and died Sept. 4, 1860.
3000. MINNIE JACOB, born June 29, 1862.

## 2461. FREEMAN H. LO.              Barnstable, Mass.

3001. WILLIAM FREEMAN, born in Barnstable, Sept. 23, 1866.
3002. RUTH HINCKLEY, born in Barnstable, July 17, 1868.
3003. JOSEPH HENRY, born in Barnstable, June 17, 1870.

## 2463. ANSEL D. JUN. LO.           Barnstable, Mass.

3004. JAMES FREEMAN, born Aug. 22, 1872.

## 2465. ALLEN C. LA.                Jersey City, N. J.

3005. GEORGE ALLEN, born in Jersey City, Aug. 14, 1867, and died of diphtheria, Sept. 3, 1874.
3006. JAMES FRANCIS, born in Jersey City, Feb. 15, 1872.
3007. CLARENCE GAYLORD, born in Jersey City, Oct. 21, 1873.

TENTH GENERATION.

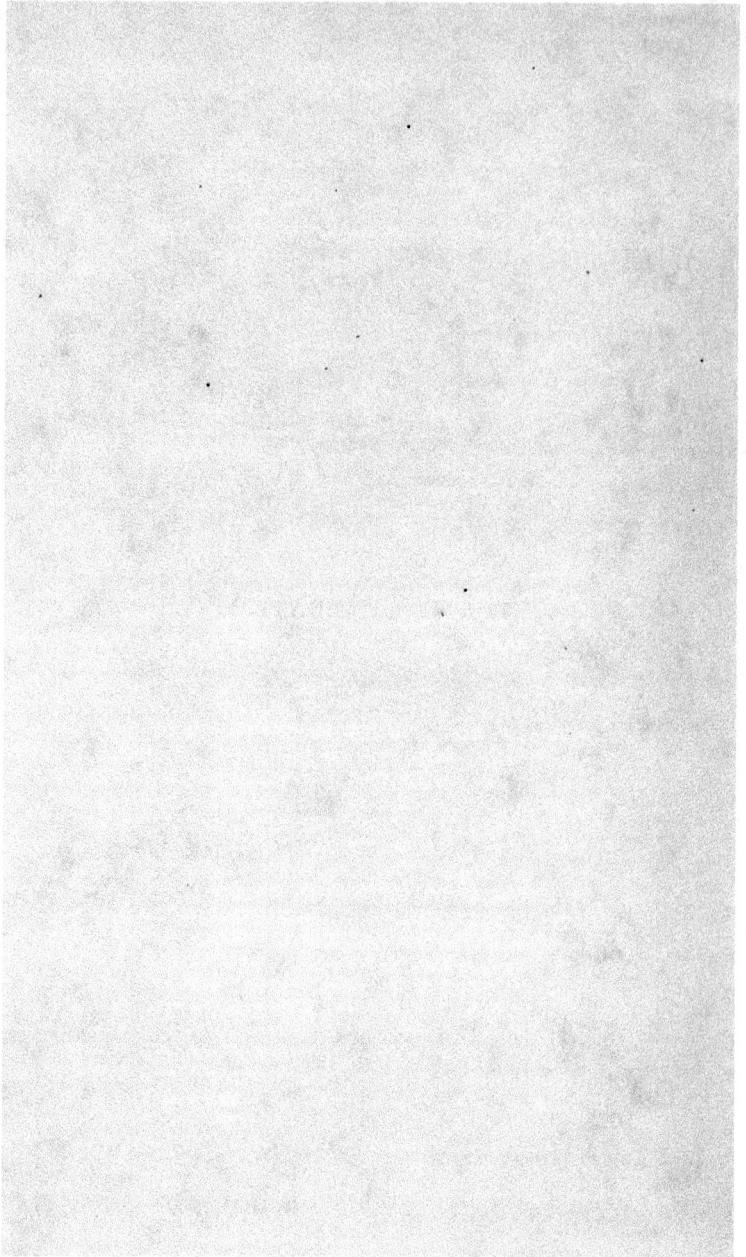

### 2491. THOMAS. New York City.

3008. ELIZA, born in Sumpter, S. C., Aug. 28, 1868.
3009. HELEN, born in New York City, Feb. 21, 1873.

### 2508. GEORGE THOMAS. New Orleans, La.

3010. WILLIAM EDWARD, born in New Orleans, La., Sept. 17, 1869.
3011. GEORGE ALBERT, born in New Orleans, La., Oct. 21, 1871.

### 2520. LEVI C. Brooklyn, N. Y.

3012. ARTHUR GRAVES, born Aug. 16, 1868.
3013. CLARENCE GRAVES, born Mar. 22, 1870.
3014. FLORENCE GRAVES, born Oct. 26, 1871.

### 2522. GEORGE. Buffalo, N. Y.

3015. MARY, born Sept. 4, 1871.
3016. GEORGE, born Oct. 13, 1872.

### 2526. JOEL C. Washington, D. C.

3017. ELLA VIRGINIA, born in Washington, D. C., Apr. 28, 1867.
3018. LOTTIE MAY, born in Washington, D. C., Mar. 16, 1873.

### 2543. STEPHEN PARK. Philadelphia, Penn.

3018-1. EMMA LOUISE, born in Newark, N. J., Sept. 26, 1878.
3018-2. WALTER DOUGLASS, born in Newark, N. J., Oct. 28, 1879.
3018-3. ROMIE MAY, born in Newark, N. J., July 27, 1883.

### 2547. JOHN W. Bridgeport, Conn.

*(Children by first wife:)*
3019. ANNA LOUISE, born in Bridgeport, Oct. 14, 1856. Died Dec. 12, 1875.
3020. CYRUS CLARK, born in Bridgeport, Feb. 21, 1862.
3021. GERTRUDE, born in Brooklyn, N. Y., July 15, 1865.
*(By second wife:)*
3022. HELEN ROCKWELL, born in Bridgeport, Nov. 15, 1883.

### 2548. CHARLES AUGUSTUS. New York City.

3023. EDWARD SANDLAND, born Aug. 6, 1858.
3024. FREDERICK MANDEVILLE, born June 20, 1860.

3025. GEORGE KETCHUM, born Oct. 23, 1861. Died June 9, 1862, at Montgomery, Ala.

3026. MARY ADELE, born Sept. 10, 1863.

3027. CHARLES AUGUSTUS, born Sept. 3, 1865.

3028. ROSA LEE, born Aug. 24, 1868. Died Dec. 15, 1874, at Mobile, Ala.

3029. WILLIAM FAULKNER, born Aug. 11, 1871.

3030. FANNIE TOMPKINS, born July 21. 1874.

3031. HAROLD LEE, born Dec. 2, 1875.

3032. SADIE STERLING, born Jan. 17, 1878.

3033. EMMA LOUISE, born Dec. 17, 1878. Died July 6, 1879, at Brooklyn, N. Y.

3034. MURRAY DEFORREST, born Oct. 24, 1881. Died July 16, 1882, at Brooklyn, N. Y.

## 2550. GEORGE FRED. New Jersey.

3035. GEORGE FRED, born in Bridgeport, Sept. 23, 1865.

3036. CARRIE BELLE, born in Bridgeport, Aug. 4, 1867.

## 2552. HERBERT N. New York City.

3037. WILLIAM THURBER, born Jan. 6, 1873, in New York City, and died same day.

3038. HERBERT NELSON, JUN., born April 9, 1875, in Orange, N. J.

3039. JULIA BOLLING, born Jan. 11, 1878, in Mobile, Ala.

## 2554. JAMES CLARK. Bridgeport, Conn.

3040. SUSIE ADELE, born May 21, 1875.

3041. JAMES CLARK, JUN., born Oct. 23, 1876.

3042. ELLA ROSELLE, born Dec. 24, 1877.

3043. MARIETTA KNAPP, born June 11, 1881.

## 2663. JOSEPH O.

3044. HATTIE BELL, born Jan. 10, 1868.

## 2697. JOHN. Philadelphia, Pa.

3045. MARY FLORENCE, born in Philadelphia, Dec. 10, 1860.

## 2698. DON F. South Coventry, Conn.

3046. WILLIE WALDO, born in Bridgeport, Apr. 7, 1862.

3047. MARY FULLER, born in Coventry, May 13, 1873.

## 2721. ADDISON B. Lawrence, Mass.

3048. WILLOUGHBY WILDER, born Oct. 29, 1866.

3049. CHARLES TAINTOR, born Sept. 30, 1870. Died Jan. 26, 1873.

## 2725. WILLIAM L.                    Cambridgeport, Mass.

3050. CARRIE ADELIA, born Sept. 23, 1865.
3051. ARTHUR WILLIAM, born Aug. 28, 1871.
3052. ALICE E., born July. 31, 1873.

## 2730. FRED D.

3053. MYRA, born July 20, 1883.

## 2737. WILLIAM.                    South Coventry, Conn.

3054. ALICE MARY, born Nov. 25, 1858.
3055. FANNIE ESTELLA, born Apr. 28, 1861.
3056. EVERETT WILLIAM, born June 3, 1863.
3057. ARTHUR ELLIOT, born Jan. 22, 1868.

## 2739. GEORGE F.                    South Coventry, Conn.

3058. CHARLES EUGENE, born in Faribault, Minn., April 2, 1856.
3059. FREDERICK H., born in South Coventry, Sept. 23, 1860, and died in Brooklyn, N. Y., Oct. 19, 1867.
3060. GEORGE K., born in South Coventry, Jan. 11, 1870.

## 2740. DANIEL Z.                    Minnesota.

3061. ALIDA, born Aug. 27, 1857.
3062. ALMA, born Nov. 15, 1858.
3063. ARTHUR, born March 23, 1860.
3064. FREDERICK, born May 10, 1863.

## 2742. WALTER HOLBROOK.                    Hartford, Conn.

3065. HERBERT WALTER, born in Hartford, April 17, 1871.
3066. HAYDEN REDFIELD, born in Hartford, June 28, 1872.

## 2783. ALBERT H.                    Lisbon, Conn.

3067. LOUISA, born in Danbury.
3068. FANNY, born in Danbury.

## 2784. CHARLES W.                    Burnside, Conn.

3069. JULIA BLISS, born in Burnside.
3070. LELIA BANKS.

## 2787. EDWIN H.                    Greeneville, Conn.

3071. JAMES HOUSTON, born in Greeneville, Nov., 1869.

### 2790. ARTHUR D.    Montville, Conn.

3072. ARTHUR DOUGLAS, born in Montville, Sept. 13, 1871.

### 2795. ASAHEL P.    Andover, Conn.

3073. CHARLES A., born in Andover, May 27, 1871.

### 2796. JAMES K.    Sprague, Conn.

3074. GEORGE E., born Sept. 15, 1870.
3075. JAMES K., born Nov. 21, 1872.

### 2802. HORACE W. M.    Canaan, N. H.

3076. FRANK, born June 17, 1872.
3077. KASPER, born Sept. 8, 1873.

### 2825. WILLIAM.    Cleveland, O.

3078. ABIGAIL.

### 2898. WILLIAM G.    New Milford, Conn.

3079. ERNEST, born in New Milford, March 17, 1866.
3080. WALLACE, born in New Milford, June 14, 1867.
3081. ADELLE, born in New Milford, Feb. 27, 1873.

### 2916. HENRY K., JUN., (D.D.S.)    Detroit, Mich.

3082. RUFUS GILLETT, born in Detroit, Mich., April 7, 1872.
3083. KIRKE, born in Detroit, Mich., Sept. 12, 1873.
3084. CHARLES GILLETT, born in Detroit, Mich., April 5, 1880.

### 2969. THOMAS S.    Hartford, Conn.

3085. EMMA W.
3086. ELLA W.
3087. IDA B. M.
3088. JENNY TYLER.

### 2973. BENJAMIN L.    New Haven, Conn.

3089. KATE BESSIE, born in New Haven, Sept. 2, 1871.

### 2975. EDWARD H.    Springfield, Mass.

3090. MAUD, born in West Springfield, July 7, 1869, and died Aug. 7, 1869.

MARK—THE PIONEER.

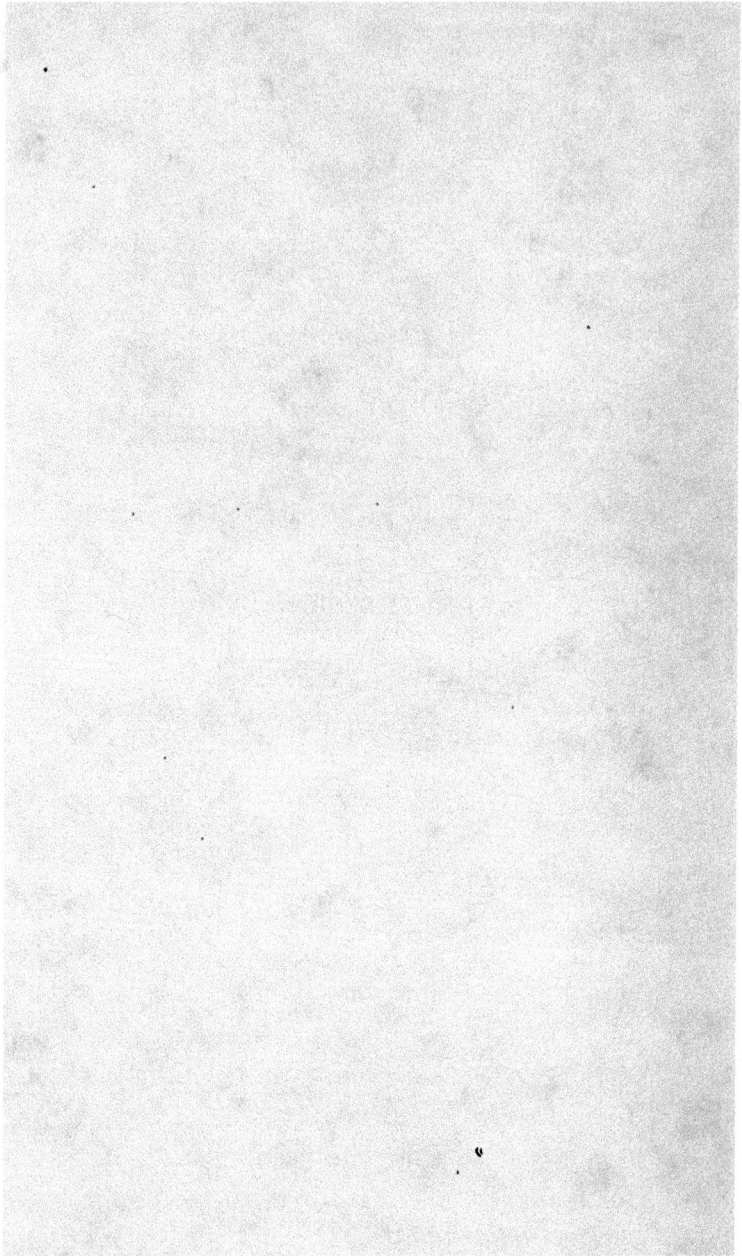

## MARK LOTHROP—PIONEER.

MARK LOTHROP may be considered the second pioneer of the Lothrop-Lathrop family in this country.

The following items relating to him are found on the town records of Salem, Mass. :

"At a meeting of the 7 men on the 11th day of the 10th month 1643, Marke Lothrop is receeved an inhabitant, and hath a request for some ground neer to his kinsman, Thos. Lothrop."

"At a meeting of the selectmen, the 17th 3rd mo. 1652, granted to Hugh Woodberrie, Marke Lothrop and Thomas Priton a spot of medoe, lying between Benjamin Felton's medoe and the Great Swamp, near Wenham, to be equally divided between them."

As his name does not appear on any town records previous to 1643, it is probable that he settled in Salem immediately after his arrival in this country. It is uncertain how long he remained there. In 1656, we find him living in Bridgewater, Mass., and one of the proprietors of the town. In 1657, he took the "Oath of Fidelitie," and in 1658 was elected constable, and for about twenty-five years held a prominent place in town affairs. He was often elected one of the jury for trials, a grand juror, and surveyor of highways, and was one of the committee appointed "to lay out all the waies requisett in the township of Bridgewater."

The records also indicate that he took an active part in the affairs of the church.

He died Oct. 25, 1685. His son Samuel was appointed administrator on his estate March 2, 1686.

The following is a copy of the inventory of his property:

AN INVENTORY OF THE ESTATE OF MARK LATHROP, OF THE TOWN OF BRIDGEWATER, DECEASED THE 25TH OF OCTOBER, 1685, WHICH IS AS FOLLOWETH:—

*Imprimis*, one & fourty pound & seven shillings in money, 8 shilling upon bill.

| | | | |
|---|---|---|---|
| Ir.—Linen cloth 11s., remnants of cloth ten shillings, | | 01 | 01 | 00 |
| Ir.—To powder, bullets & lead, 8s.—Three guns, 30s., | | 01 | 18 | 00 |
| Ir.—To a bed and bolster & rug & blanket, | | 03 | 00 | 00 |
| Ir.—To two pair of sheets, a pair of drawers, a shirt, | | 01 | 04 | 00 |
| Ir.—To a coverlid & blanket & shirt, pillow & pillow-beer, | | 01 | 05 | 00 |
| Ir.—To wearing cloths, shoes, stockings & hat, | | 03 | 10 | 00 |
| Ir.—To woolen cloth and linen cloth, | | 03 | 05 | 00 |
| Ir.—To leather, flax and woolen yarn, | | 01 | 12 | 00 |
| Ir.—To hemp & iron, six and twenty shillings, | | 01 | 06 | 00 |

| | | | |
|---|---|---|---|
| IT.—To a cart & wheels, plows, chains, axes, scythes, reaping hooks & wedges, pot hangers, hoes & yokes & tongs, table & chaires, chests and spinning-wheels, | 07 | 00 | 00 |
| IT.—To brass & iron & tin & pewter, | 02 | 10 | 00 |
| IT.—To six trays, three butter tubs, 11s., 2 barrels cider, | 01 | 06 | 00 |
| IT.—To tubs and other wooden lumber, | 00 | 10 | 00 |
| IT.—To rye & Indian corn & peas and bags, | 04 | 00 | 00 |
| IT.—To a winnowing sheet, grindstone & butter, | 04 | 18 | 00 |
| IT.—To fodder four pound, | 01 | 00 | 00 |
| IT.—To sheep, £2 3s., hogs, £3, which in all is | 05 | 06 | 00 |
| IT.—To mare and halfe & horse colt, | 02 | 00 | 00 |
| IT.—To neat cattle, | 17 | 00 | 00 |
| IT.—To ye dwelling-house & barns & all ye land adjoining thereunto, | 60 | 00 | 00 |
| IT.—To a twenty acre lot & lot of meadow at ye brook called Flag Meadow Brook, | 15 | 00 | 00 |
| IT.—To a fifty acre lot at ye bay path, | 10 | 00 | 00 |
| IT.—To a twenty acre lot & lot of meadow at Poor Meadow, | 05 | 00 | 00 |
| IT.—To a fifty acre lot not far from Goodman Washburns, | 05 | 00 | 00 |
| IT.—To a lot of meadow at Great Meadow, | 01 | 00 | 00 |
| IT.—To a lot in ye cedar swamp, | 01 | 10 | 00 |
| IT.—To the undivided land within the four mile, | 85 | 00 | 00 |
| IT.—To a right at Titicut, | 01 | 10 | 00 |
| IT.—To a right beyond the four mile, | 02 | 10 | 00 |
| The sum total, if no mistake in casting up is, | 255 | 1 | 0 |

A fair prisal of the estate of Mark Lathrop, according to our best judgment. Taken by us the twenty-seventh of October, one thousand six hundred eighty and five, as witness our hands.

| | |
|---|---|
| JOHN HAYWARD, | SAMUEL LATHROP. |
| JOHN FIELD, | SAMUEL SHIVERICK. |
| JOHN HAWARD, | MARK LATHROP. |
| THOMAS SNELL, | SAMUEL PACKER. |

Samuel Lathrop appeared before the court & gave oath that the above-written is a true inventory of the estate of his father, Mark Lathrop, deceased, so far as he knows, & when more comes to his knowledge to bring it to this inventory, by virtue of this oath.

Sworn in court,          Attest:          NATH'L CLARK, Sec'y.

1685-6          Court Orders, Vol. 6, Part 2, Page 47.

March 2.    Administration is granted by this Court to Samuel Lathropp of Bridgewater in ye Colony of New Plymouth on ye estate of Mark Lathrop of Bridgewater afores'd deceased giving bonds for his administration according to law.

His children were: Elizabeth, Samuel, Mark, and Edward. The dates of their births are not known, but from the Bridgewater records it appears that his three sons were twenty-one years of age, or more, and were freemen in Bridgewater in 1682.

SECOND GENERATION.

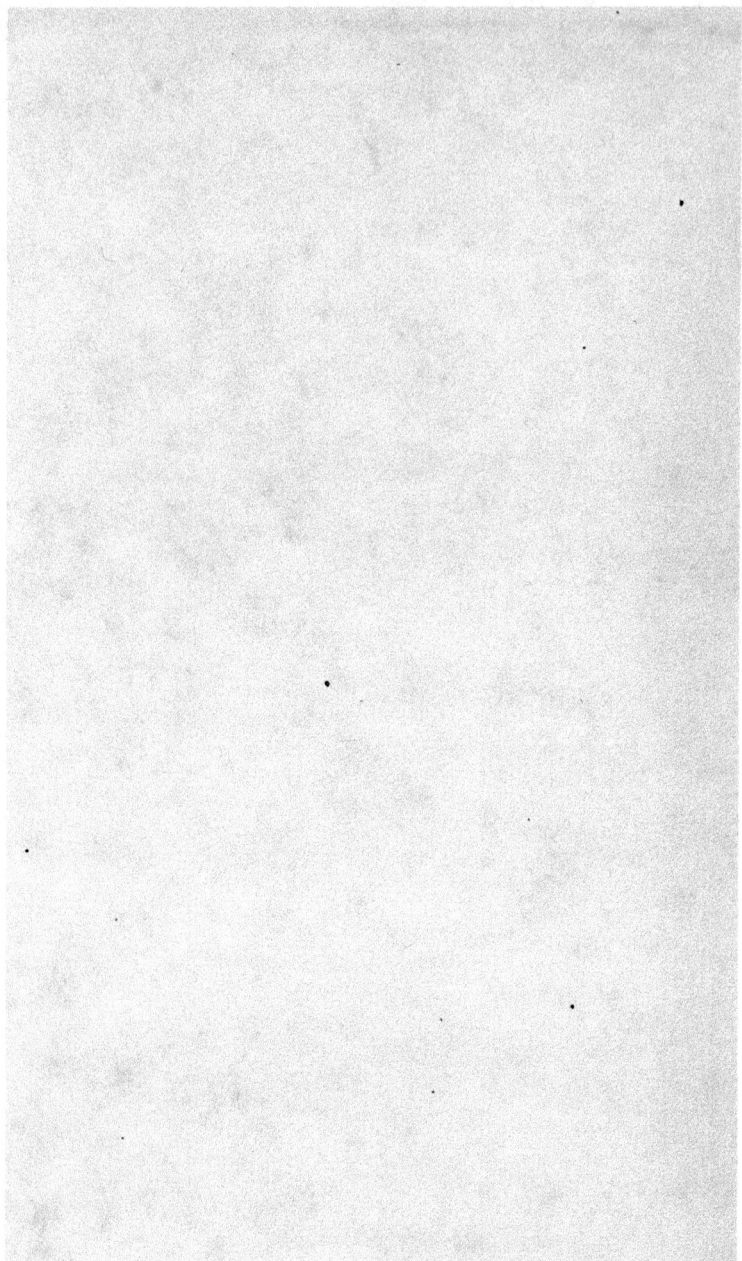

# 1. MARK. Salem and Bridgewater, Mass.

2. ELIZABETH, married Samuel Packard, Jr., son of Samuel and Elizabeth Packard, who had come from Wymondham Co., Norfolk, in England. Their children were: Samuel, Daniel, Joseph, Elizabeth, Mary, and Susannah.

3. SAMUEL, born before 1660, married Sarah Downer. He is reported, in 1682, as then of age and among the proprietors of Bridgewater. His will, dated Bridgewater, Apr. 11, 1724, he "being old," names as legatees daughter Mary Keith, Josiah's wife, sons Samuel, John, Mark, and Joseph, to each of whom he had given lands before, and to his son Edward, who is also made executor, the rest of the estate.

March 10, 1675, the constables of Bridgewater were fined £2 "for pressing Samuell Laythorpe illegally, and hee a man unfit to goe forth on the service."

### THE WILL OF SAMUEL LOTHROP.

In y[e] name of God, Amen. April y[e] 11th, 1724. I Samuel Lothrop of Bridgewater in y[e] County of Plymouth in New England being old & full of days & under much bodily weakness tho' of a sound mind & memory expecting speedily to put off my earthly tabernacle, do therefore give & recommend my soul unto God that gave it, and I commit my body to y[e] earth to a decent burial at y[e] discretion of my Executor, & touching such worldly goods as I have not already disposed of I dispose of them in manner following.

First, I give unto my daughter Mary Keith, Josiah Keith's wife, y[e] sum of Thirty & Two Pounds to be paid to her by my Executor at my decease.

Secondly, I give unto my son Samuel Lothrop four Pounds and no more having conveyed him land already by deed.

Thirdly, I give unto my son John Lothrop Two Pounds & no more having conveyed him lands by deed already.

Fourthly, I give unto my son Mark Lothrop Thirty & Two Shillings and no more having made conveyance of lands to him already.

Fifthly, I give unto my son Joseph Lothrop Two Pounds & no more having conveyed to him likewise his portion by deed.

Sixthly, I appoint my son Edward Lothrop sole Executor of this my last Will and Testament & accordingly order and empower him hereby to pay out all y[e] several sums that I have given above unto my children, & I do by these presents then give unto him my s[d] son Edward all y[e] residue and remainder of my estate that shall remain after y[e] sums above mentioned shall be paid; & further I do by these presents utterly revoke & disannul all other & former wills, declaring this & no other to be my last Will and Testament.

4. MARK, born before 1660, died in the Phips expedition against the

Indians, in Canada, in 1690, having no children. He and his two brothers were voted shares, in 1682, in the "easterly end of the six miles on the west side of the land to be layed out, as they were 21 years." Will dated July 14, 1690, in Bridgewater. His name in the probate record is Lathrope.

### WILL OF MARK LOTHROP.

Know all men before whom these presents shall come that I Mark Lothrop of Bridgewater in the County of Plymouth in New England being designed into the wars against the French enemy, and knowing my life and breath to be in the hands of God of whom I first had my being, and from whom I have hopes of mercy in the merits of Jesus Christ, and knowing that if it be his holy will that I should go as aforesaid, that he can take me away either by the sword or other ways. Therefore to prevent any difference that may arise among my relations concerning my estate, I dispose of my s⁴ estate as followeth.

Item, I give unto my consin Samuel Lothrop of said Bridgewater and to his heirs and assigns forever all my whole right and title to and of lands within the limits of the said Bridgewater.

Item, I give unto my loving brother Samuel Lothrop all my apparel and my sheep except one serge coat which was my father's which said coat I give to my brother Edward Lothrop.

Item, I give unto my said brother Saml. Lothrop one cow and all my tools and one yearling heifer.

Item, I give unto my sister Elizabeth Packard of the said Bridgewater one cow and one yearling heifer. And to confirm the truth hereof I do hereunto set my hand and seal it being July y⁴ 14th, 1690.

The following declaration was made in court by two of the witnesses to the will, at the time of probate:

The above s⁴ Mark Lothrop did also declare at the time abovesaid that it was his will that his above s⁴ brother Samuel Lothrop should have all the remainder of his estate, but being in great haste it was forgotten till the s⁴ Mark Lothrop was gone.

Administration was granted by s⁴ Court unto Samuel Lothrop of Bridgewater to administer upon the estate of his brother Mark Lothrop deceased.

5. EDWARD, died single. He was also reported, with his brothers Samuel and Mark as of age in 1682. He died in 1696. Letters of administration were granted to his brother, Samuel Laythrop, on his estate, May 23, 1696. He is designated as "Edward Laythrop, late of Bridgewater, deceased."

THIRD GENERATION.

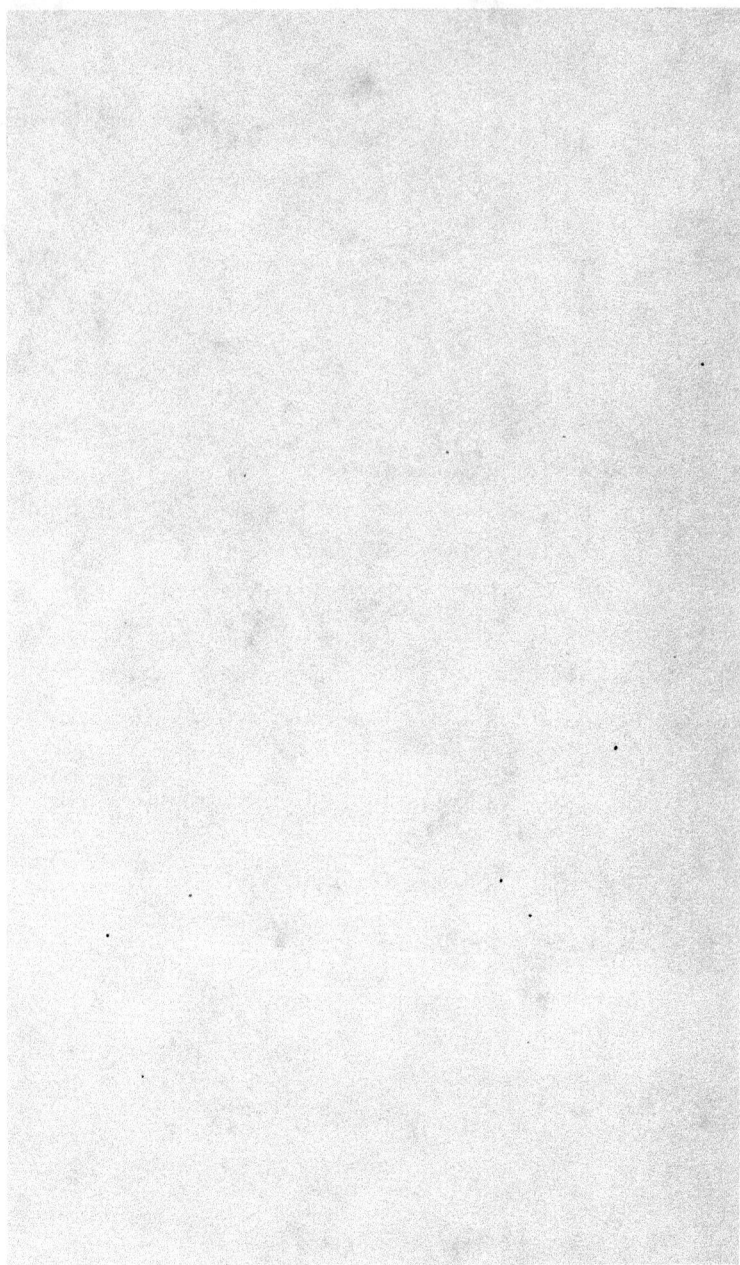

### 3. SAMUEL. West Bridgewater, Mass.

6. MARY, born Oct. 28, 1683, and married, Jan. 6, 1703, Josiah. son of Rev. James and Susanna (Edson) Keith. He had come from Aberdeen, Scotland, in 1662, when 18 years of age, and was the first minister ordained in Bridgewater, having been ordained in 1664.

7. SAMUEL, JUN., born May 17, 1685, and married (1), Nov. 14, 1710, Abial, daughter of Isaac Lassell. She was born June 25, 1688, and died Nov. 3, 1749. Married (2), in 1751, Lydia Hayden. He died Jan. 13, 1772.

8. JOHN, born Oct. 15, 1687, and married, May 23, 1716, Mary, daughter of Joseph Edson, and granddaughter of Deacon Samuel and Susannah (Orcutt) Edson.

9. MARK, born in Bridgewater, Sept. 9, 1689, and married, Mar. 29, 1722, Hannah Alden, born Feb. 1, 1696. She was daughter of Dea. Joseph Alden of Bridgewater, and great-granddaughter of Hon. John Alden of Duxbury. He settled in Easton, on land conveyed to him by his father; was one of the proprietors at the time the town was incorporated, and took an active part in establishing and maintaining the first church in Easton. He was also prominent in town affairs, and was one of the selectmen four years. The records state that in 1743 he was again elected, but declined to serve. The date of his death is not recorded. She died in 1777.

10. SARAH, born June 5, 1693, and married, Nov. 16, 1715, Solomon, son of Zaccheus and Sarah (Howard) Packard, who was born Mar. 20, 1689. She lived but a short time after her marriage, probably leaving no child.

11. JOSEPH, born June 5, 1696 (twin), and married, Jan. 17, 1718, Mary, daughter of Joseph and Hopestill Snow, and died without children.

12. EDWARD, born July 7, 1697, and married Hannah, daughter of Thomas and Elizabeth (Curtis) Wade, of Bridgewater.

# FOURTH GENERATION.

### 7. SAMUEL, Jun. West Bridgewater, Mass.

13. SAMUEL, born Sept. 23, 1711, and married Apr. 3, 1735, Elizabeth, daughter of Joseph Keith. He died, Nov. 9, 1776. His will, dated Oct. 17, 1776, he being a yeoman of Bridgewater, names as legatees his wife Elizabeth, son Jonathan, son Mark, and his "trusty maid Mary Tomson to encourage her in serving my family. Son Mark exr."* He also mentions son Samuel who was then deceased.

14. ISAAC, born Dec. 21, 1714, and married Bethiah, daughter of Maj. Edward Howard. After her death he married (2), Apr. 13, 1742, Patience, daughter of Joseph Alger. He died Nov. 25, 1774, and his wife Aug. 16, 1779.

15. SARAH, born Sept. 15, 1717, and married, Nov. 17, 1737, Aliezer Edson.

16. DANIEL, born May 2, 1721, and married, in 1744, Rhoda, daughter of Thomas Willis. He was a Major of Militia in Col. Crafts regiment at Dorchester Heights when Washington took command of the army. Died at Leeds, Me., Mar. 18, 1818.

17. ABIEL, born Dec. 7, 1729, and married, in Bridgewater, May 28, 1747, Israel Alger, jun. He died May 3, 1755, leaving all his property to his "beloved wife Abial."

### 8. JOHN. West Bridgewater, Mass.

18. MARY, born Oct. 21, 1720, and died unmarried.

19. SARAH, born Jan. 26, 1723-4, married, Oct. 16, 1755, Alexander Kingman.

20. SUSANNA, born Oct. 12, 1726, and married, Dec. 14, 1747, Theophilus Haward.

### 9. MARK. Easton, Mass.

21. JONATHAN, born Mar. 11, 1722-3, married, Apr. 13, 1746, Susannah, daughter of Solomon and Susannah (Edson) Johnson of Bridgewater. She was born in 1723. He was a deacon of the church, and a prominent man in the town. He died in 1771, and his estate was divided in 1781 among his four children then living. His widow Susannah was appointed administratrix on his estate, Sept. 9, 1771.

22. JOSEPH, born Mar. 23, 1725, married, Oct. 24, 1746, Content, daughter of John and Margaret (Packard) Washburn of Bridgewater. She was born in 1724, and died Mar. 26, 1807. He died May 10, 1809.

23. SETH, born July 7, 1729, and married (1), Sept. 11, 1755, Martha, daughter of Thomas Conant. She was born in 1735. Married (2), May 30, 1762, Martha, daughter of Benjamin and Priscilla Kinsley. She was born March 21, 1737. Settled in Easton, Mass. Married (3), Hannah Smith, who

---

* Witnesses, Philip Bryant, Zephaniah Lothrop, and Shepherd Fisk.

died in 1805. He died Nov. 10, 1815, at Enfield, aged 86 years, 4 months, and 3 days. He is reported by his granddaughter, Mrs. Cook, who distinctly remembers him, as a venerable man. He was a prominent man in Easton for many years, having held the offices of Constable, Surveyor of highways, Tything-man, and Selectman. In 1772 he was an Ensign in Capt. Abial Mitchell's Company, and his name occurs frequently on the old proprietor records.

## 12. EDWARD.                    Bridgewater, Mass.

24. SETH, born Aug. 3, 1722, and married, Mar. 26, 1752, Lydia, daughter of George Packard. She died Sept. 23, 1756. After her death he married (2), June 9, 1757, Mehitable Daily of Easton, who died in 1770. He died Mar. 1, 1804. His will, dated Bridgewater, Apr. 19, 1800, had as witnesses John Snow, Josiah Lothrop, and Daniel Snow. Its legatees were: "Daughter Susanna, wife of Calvin Kingsley; son Seth; grandchildren, Seth and Mehetable Fobes, children of my daughter Mehetable; grandchildren Barzillai, Cyrus, and Bette Lothrop, children of my son Seth, jun.; daughter-in-law Abigail Lothrop, wife of Seth, for her kind and tender usage; and nephew to take shares of his two grandsons if they die; and his granddaughter Bette when 20 years old."

25. EDWARD, born Nov. 1, 1724, died young.

26. JOSIAH, born Feb. 14, 1726, and married, June 21, 1749, Sarah Church of Scituate. He died May 15, 1808, and she, Aug. 28, 1815.

27. EDWARD, JUN., born Aug. 14, 1728, and married, Oct. 19, 1752, Abigail, daughter of Ephraim Howard.

28. HANNAH, born Jan. 28, 1731, and died Jan. 27, 1739.

29. SUSANNAH, born Oct. 15, 1733, and died July 5, 1734.

30. DAVID, born Sept. 11, 1735, and married, Dec. 2, 1762, Mary, daughter of Ephraim Howard, and died without children, Oct. 14, 1807. In his will, dated Bridgewater, Sept. 29, 1807, he is styled yeoman, his wife Mary, executrix; he leaves his property to his wife, to be divided at her death between his niece Mary Lothrop Perkins, and his nephew Foster Perkins.

31. MARK, born Sept. 15, 1738, and died Feb. 21, 1740.

FIFTH GENERATION.

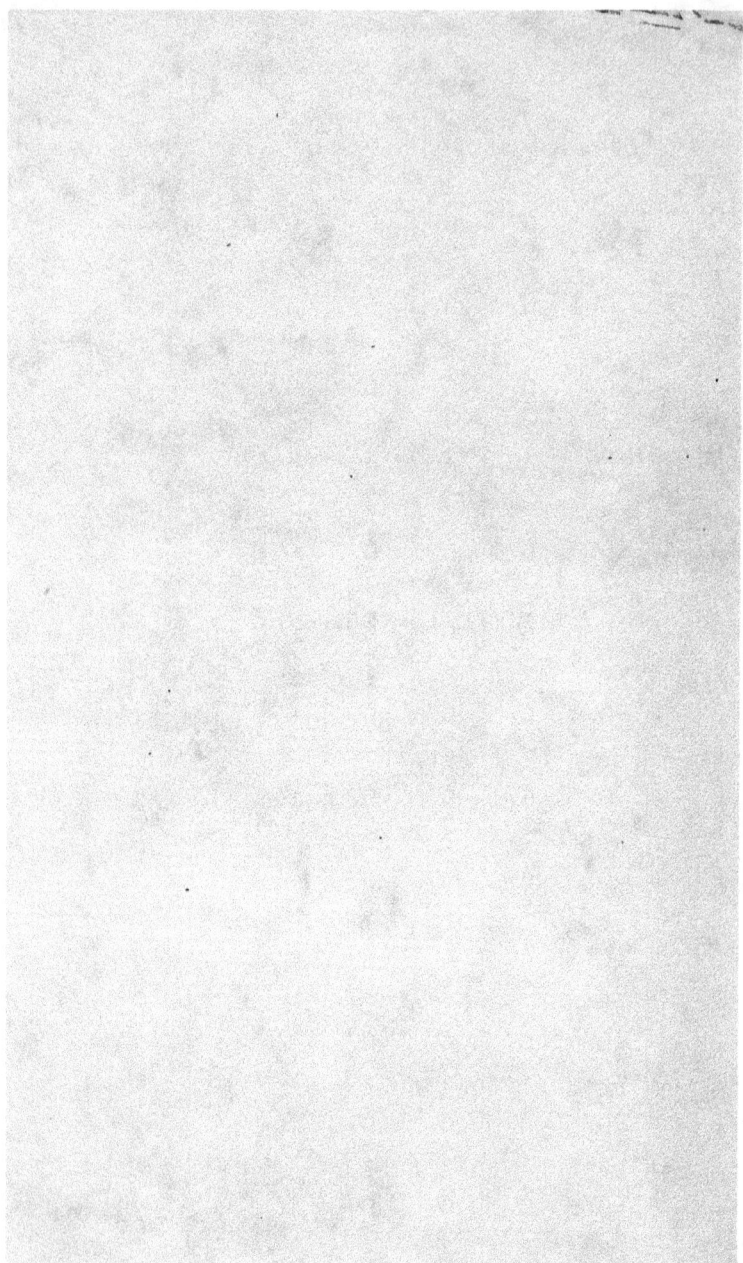

### 13. SAMUEL. West Bridgewater, Mass.

32. NATHAN, born Sept. 13, 1735; died Mar. 12, 1739.

33. JONATHAN, born July 10, 1738, and married, in 1765, Chloe Dickerman. His will was dated Bridgewater, Apr. 27, 1815, and proved Feb. 1, 1819. He is styled yeoman, and names as legatees, sons Lemuel and Libbens; daughters Sarah, wife of David Alger, and Chloe, wife of Jacob Fisher; and his wife Chloe, who also is made executrix.

34. SARA, born Aug. 5, 1742, and died Jan. 3, 1759.

35. MARK, born Feb. 21, 1745-6, and married, Nov. 20. 1777, Elizabeth Dickerman, who was born Apr. 9, 1753.

36. SAMUEL, born Jan. 8, 1750; died Oct. 7, 1776.

### 14. ISAAC. West Bridgewater, Mass.

37. BETHIA, born Mar. 20, 1743-4, and married, Sept. 3, 1767, Samuel Willis.

38. EDMUND "of Easton," born Feb. 15, 1745-6, and married, Sept. 29, 1774, Bettie, daughter of George Howard, born in 1751, and died Apr. 3, 1831; he settled in Easton, and died Mar. 26, 1815. Will, May 23, 1811, and probated Apr. 7, 1815. Howard, his son, sole executor. [Taunton Rec., B. 50, p. 223.]

39. ISAAC, born June 10, 1748, and married, Aug. 31, 1775, Sarah, daughter of Adams Bailey of Bridgewater, and settled in Easton. He died May 11, 1815. She died Nov. 6, 1844.

40. ZEPHANIAH, born Mar. 30, 1750, and married, Sept. 2, 1779, Sarah, daughter of Capt. Nathan and Lydia (Jackson) Packard, who was born Sept. 14, 1759, and died Feb. 14, 1790. He married (2), Mar. 17, 1791, Sylvia Manly, who was born Dec. 14, 1762, and died June 10, 1838.

41. ABIHAIL, born Oct. 14, 1752, and married, Nov. 24, 1768, Lemuel Keith of Easton.

42. NATHAN, born June 10, 1755, and married (1), Charity ———, and (2), widow Phebe Beach, daughter of Seth Johnson, of Hardwick, Mass. She was born Sept. 29, 1764, and died in Worcester, Mass., Apr. 1, 1861.

43. JOHN, born Oct. 12, 1757, and married, Dec. 7, 1780, Sarah Cook. They both joined the Congregational Church of Easton in 1792, and had, at the same time, seven of their children baptized. After they were seventy years of age they both were immersed and joined the Baptist Church.

44. SARAH, born Apr. 30, 1763, and married, in 1790, John Cook.

45. KEZIAH, born Sept. 23, 1767, and married, Aug. 11, 1785, Simeon Lathrop. (No. 91.)

### 16. COL. DANIEL.     W. Bridgewater; Leeds, Me.

46. DANIEL, JUN., born Dec. 10, 1745, and married, Aug. 23, 1764, Hannah, daughter of George Howard, who died after the birth of her fourth child, and he married (2), Sept. 5, 1775, Lydia, daughter of Samuel Willis. After her death he married (3), Sept. 1, 1785, Mary, daughter of George Turner. He died in Wilton, Me., in 1837.

47. RHODA, born Apr. 9, 1747, and married, in 1763, Daniel Williams, Jun., of Easton.

48. MOLLY, born Aug. 2, 1755, and married, June 20, 1771, Thomas Johnson.

49. ABIHAIL, born Feb. 4, 1758, and married, Feb. 1, 1775, Isaac Hartwell of West Bridgewater.

### 21. JONATHAN.     Easton, Mass.

50. SUSANNAH, born Oct. 3, 1748, and died Dec. 17, 1748.

51. SUSANNAH, born Aug. 26, 1750, and died Aug. 23, 1753.

52. MARY, born May 8, 1753, and died unmarried.

53. JONATHAN, born July 13, 1755, and married, in Feb., 1774, Elizabeth, daughter of Solomon and Susannah Hewet of Easton. She was born Aug. 18, 1753. He served in the War of the Revolution, and removed to New York State.

54. SARAH, born Jan. 29, 1758. She was unmarried at the time of the distribution of her father's estate in 1781.

55. SOLOMON, born Feb. 9, 1761, and married Mehitable, daughter of Cornelius White of Taunton, and settled in Easton, and afterward removed to Norton, where he died Oct. 19, 1843. She died Sept. 14, 1832, aged 73.

56. SUSANNAH, born Nov. 2, 1766, and married, Jan. 12, 1786, Abiel Lapham of Bridgewater, and moved to Maine.

### 22. JOSEPH.     Easton, Mass.

57. HANNAH, baptized Nov. 22, 1747, married, Feb. 10, 1773, Alexander, son of Daniel and Johanna Keith of Easton. He was born Feb. 7, 1745.

58. JOHN, baptized Oct. 30, 1748, married, Nov. 19, 1778, Rebecca Cocks of Pembroke. He served in the War of the Revolution, and became a pensioner. He died in March, 1840. She died in 1843.

59. CONTENT, baptized Feb. 17, 1750, died unmarried in Jay, Me.

60. MEHITABLE, baptized Aug. 23, 1752, married Daniel Howard. They lived in Winthrop, Me.

61. JOSEPH, born in 1755, and married, Dec. 26, 1781, Martha Packard of Easton; was a Revolutionary pensioner; removed to Maine about 1800, and died there.

62. REBECCA, baptized June 5, 1759. Married, Mar. 19, 1786, as his second wife, Matthew Hayward, Esq., of Easton. They removed to Maine.

63. JACOB, born about 1762, and married Sarah Snow, of West Bridgewater, in 1787. Removed to Jay, Me.

64. CALEB, baptized Oct. 26, 1766.

65. ZENAS, baptized Oct. 26, 1766, and married Sally Tower in 1788.

## 23. SETH. Easton and Enfield. Mass.

66. ALDEN, born Apr. 27, 1763, married Mary Stevenson, of Greenwich, Mass., Oct. 15, 1792, and lived in Enfield. He died in Pottsford, N. Y. ; she in Adrian, Mich.

67. ANNA, born Mar. 19, 1765, and married, Mar. 6, 1791, Oliver Williams, of Easton, Mass.

68. THOMAS, born in Easton, Oct. 4, 1766, and married, Feb. 20, 1792, Deborah Pope, who was born Feb. 10, 1767. He died in Leyden, Mass., June 4, 1820, and she in Newfane, Vt., Mar. 2, 1844. Mr. Lothrop was a public-spirited and active Christian man, and his death, as the local papers show, was regarded as a great public loss. They thus testify to his worth: "The strict morality of his life, his zeal in rebuilding the waste places of Zion, the pleasure he seemed to take in the sanctuary, at the domestic altar, and, in short, wherever the God of Jacob was worshiped, the integrity and benevolence of his heart, the beneficence of his hand, and his undeviating affection as husband and father, altogether furnish his friends the consolation that their loss is his gain."

69. HANNAH BRADFORD, baptised June 26, 1774, married —— Belcher.

70. MARTHA, married —— Williams.

71. SYBIL, married —— Thompson.

72. DARIUS, married, and lived in Sharon, Mass.

73. LAVINIA, who married (1), Joseph Ruggles ; and (2), —— Messenger, of Esperance, N. Y.

74. POLLY, born Sept. 26, 1768, married Mr. Lane, of Greenwich.

75. ZEBADIAH, born Nov. 19, 1770, married, Oct. 1, 1795, Sarah Adams, and settled in Providence. He died Sept. 4, 1818. She died Sept. 11, 1861.

76. GILBERT, born 1780, married Mrs. Hetty Gillet, of Boston.

## 24. SETH. West Bridgewater, Mass.

### (First Wife's Children.)

77. SUSANNA, born June 3, 1754, and married, in 1773, Calvin Kingsly of Easton.

78. LYDIA, born Sept. 5, 1756, and died Oct. 8, 1756.

### (Second Wife's Children.)

79. LYDIA, born Sept. 8, 1758, and died June 1, 1770.

80. MEHITABLE, born Jan. 4, 1761, and married Apr. 5, 1781, Alpheus Fobes. As appears from her father's will, in 1800, they had at least two children:

   i. Seth Fobes.

   ii. Mehitable Fobes.

81. SETH, born Feb. 26, 1765, and married, Nov. 25, 1784, Abigail, daughter of Joseph Bassett. His three children are provided for in his father's will.

43

### 26. JOSIAH. West Bridgewater, Mass.

82. HANNAH, born Aug. 6, 1753, and married, June 6, 1776, Joseph Bassett, Esq.

83. SARAH, born Nov. 6, 1755, and married, Dec. 3, 1772, Edward Williams of Easton. .

84. GAMALIEL, born July 30, 1758, and died Sept. 17, 1758.

85. JOSIAH, born Oct. 15, 1759, and married, Dec. 15, 1785, Susannah, daughter of Theophilus and Susannah (Lothrop) Howard. He settled in Canada.

86. HULDAH, born May 22, 1764, and married, Dec. 28, 1786, Edmund Alger.

87. CHARLES, born May 2, 1767, and married, in 1788, Rowena, daughter of Capt. Jonathan Howard. He settled in Canada.

### 27. EDWARD, JR. West Bridgewater, Mass.

88. EDWARD, born June 4, 1753.

89. ABIGAIL, born Oct. 26, 1755.

90. BARNABAS, born Feb. 25, 1757, and married Nov. 27, 1777, Sarah Bosworth, who was born Apr. 16, 1761. She died Feb. 2, 1813, and he married (2), Rachel, daughter of Samuel Bartlett, of Bridgewater, who died Mar. 13, 1862.

91. SIMEON, born May 4, 1760, and married, Aug. 11, 1785, Keziah (No. 45), daughter of Isaac Lathrop. Married (2), Margaret Nevens. He died (so the records say) Feb. 3, 1808, his will having been made Jan. 20, 1808. Names wife Margaret and daughters Hannah (Miller) and Keziah. His widow, Margaret, and Josiah Lothrop, Jr., of Bridgewater, executors.

92. HANNAH, born Nov. 27, 1762.

93. JANE, born Mar. 4, 1764. Married, July 4, 1782, Capt. Daniel Briggs, of Milton.

94. AMBROSE, born Oct. 2, 1768. He lived and died in Cohasset.

95. MOLLEY, born Oct. 22, 1770.

96. VINEE, born "June y⁵ Auo Dom." 1773, married, in 1793, Dr. John H. Perkins.

SIXTH GENERATION.

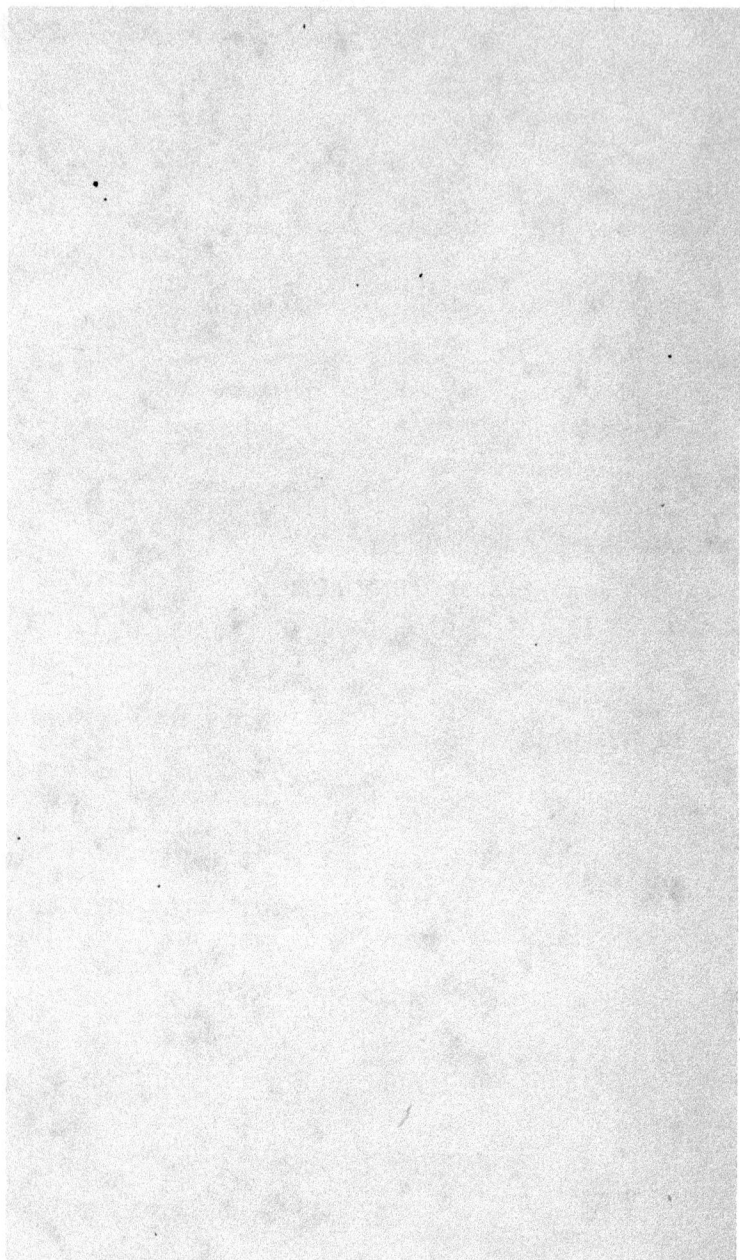

### 33. JONATHAN. West Bridgewater, Mass.

97. LEMUEL, born Apr. 22, 1766, and married, Apr. 18, 1794, Sarah, daughter of Abijah and Sarah (Bates) Reed, of Easton, who was born Apr. 25, 1770.

98. LIBBEUS, born Oct. 16, 1769, and married, in 1803, Charity Wharton, and settled in Easton, where he died Oct. 27, 1819.

99. SARAH, born Feb. 21, 1772, and married, in 1790, David Alger. Removed to Winchendon, Mass., where she died Feb. 1, 1858. He died March 20, 1843. ·Children:

    i.   Chloe Alger, born Jan. 7, 1793, married Benjamin Adams.

    ii.  Jonathan Alger, born Sept. 20, 1795, married Huldah Marcy.

    iii. David Alger, born Oct. 3, 1798, died Oct. 22, 1810.

    iv. Joseph Alger, born Jan. 13, 1804, married Eunice Wyman.

    v.  Benjamin Alger, born Jan. 13, 1804, married Rebecca Leath.

    vi. Susanna Alger, born Dec. 30, 1806, married Raymond Lathrop (No. 131).

    vii. Sarah Alger, born Sept. 12, 1814, married Samuel Beal.

100. CHLOE, married, in 1797, Jacob Fisher.

### 35. MARK. West Bridgewater, Mass.

101. SAMUEL, born Sept. 25, 1778.

102. ELIJAH, born Dec. 3, 1780, in West Bridgewater, and married, Jan. 8, 1818, Lavina, daughter of Barnabas Dunbar, of the same place. He settled as farmer in Stoughton, Mass., where he died Mar. 24, 1857, and his widow in North Bridgewater, Mar. 31, 1863.

103. MARK, born Nov. 6, 1783, married, in 1805, Katy, daughter of Capt. Amasa Howard, and settled in Millbury, Mass.

104. SPENCER, born Sept. 29, 1786, married, in 1812, Bathsheba, daughter of Thaddeus Howard. She died in 1813, and he married (2), in 1817, Eleanor White, of Littleton, Mass. He lived in West Bridgewater, on the old homestead, where he died July 29, 1850. She died Oct. 2, 1853.

105. BETSEY, born June 24, 1789, married, in 1811, Samuel Dunbar.

106. SILVEY, born Feb. 9, 1794, married, in 1810, Thaddeus Howard, Jr.

### 38. EDMUND. Easton, Mass.

107. ISAAC, born Feb. 4, 1775, and married Celia Keith, of Bridgewater, who was born Apr. 10, 1777. He died Oct. 21, 1857. His will, dated July 10, 1849, and probated Mar. 2, 1858, names his wife Celia; children: Welcome, Celia Harlow, Mary A., Isaac, Martin K., and Edmund. Edmund Lothrop, executor.

**108.** HOWARD, born in Easton, Dec. 17, 1776, and married, in 1805, Sally, daughter of Edward Williams, of Easton, who was born May 9, 1787, and died May 15, 1864. He early invested in the Keith furnace, in Pittsford, Vt., and in time became sole owner, and for twelve years he superintended the works, but sold in 1809. His father's health failing, he returned to Easton, where he remained for the rest of his life on the old homestead. He died, Aug. 23, 1857, and his widow in 1864. Mr. Lothrop was a gentleman of the old New England type, and a splendid specimen of what the common school can make of a youth with good strong common sense. He had a large local influence, and was for many years a representative of the town in the State legislature, and of his district in the State senate, and also in the executive council. He was also once presidential elector, and as such voted for Daniel Webster.

**109.** EDMUND, born 1780, and settled in Norton. He married, Mar. 30, 1802, Rhoda Bishop. He died, and a guardian was appointed for his children in 1821.

**110.** CYRUS, born in Easton, Mass., in 1789, and graduated at Brown University in 1810, and from the Litchfield Law School. He married, about the year 1814, Abby W., daughter of Dea. John Seabury of Taunton, Mass. She was born May 22, 1795, and died in her native town, Nov. 22, 1851—a lady of great personal excellence and worth. Mr. Lothrop was for many years an honored member of the Bristol County bar, earning a good reputation in his profession, and for his financial and business thrift. He died in Taunton, May 21, 1854.

### 39. ISAAC.      Easton, Mass.

**111.** SARAH, born in Bridgewater, Aug. 6, 1776, married, May 23, 1797, Jonas Pratt of Easton.

**112.** CATHERINE, born March 7, 1778, married Oct. 23, 1800, Abijah, son of Abijah and Sarah (Bates) Read of Easton, where he was born Jan. 5, 1777. Children:

    i.    Abijah Read, who died young.

    ii.    Lydia Read, born Feb. 3, 1800, married Edmond Curtiss, and had a family. She died July 1, 1859.

    iii.    Mary Read, born March 23, 1801, and married Benjamin Buck.

    iv.    Sarah Read, born Dec. 7, 1804, and married Edward W. Dean, and died July 23, 1829.

    v.    Abijah Read, born Mar. 14, 1813, and died in Boston, Sept. 14, 1835.

**113.** RUTH, born Feb. 10, 1780, died Mar. 23, 1796.

**114.** WASHINGTON, born Mar. 26, 1782, died young.

**115.** POLLY, born Feb. 8, 1784, and married, Aug. 8, 1811, Jotham Ames, of Easton.

**116.** ISAAC, born Mar. 1, 1786.

**117.** BETSEY, born July 23, 1788.

**118.** CHARITY, born Aug. 14, 1790, married Jan. 4, 1807, Sever Pratt of Easton.

**119.** ABIGAIL, born March 15, 1792, married Oct., 1818, Giles Randall, of Easton.

120. ANNIS, born Nov. 22, 1794.

121. JARVIS, born June 5, 1798, married Esther Newcomb of Quincy.

### 40. ZAPHANIAH. West Bridgewater, Mass.

122. SYLVIA, born Dec. 8, 1779, and died Apr. 18, 1792.

123. OLIVER, born Oct. 21, 1773. Married (1), Jan. 12, 1804, Hannah, daughter of Major Curtis of Stoughton, Mass. She was born Nov. 19, 1775, and died May 1, 1829. He married (2), Betsey Tisdale of Easton. He lived in Stoughton, where he died July 24, 1834.

124. AZEL, born July 12, 1783, and married, in 1805, Anna Eaton. His will, dated West Bridgewater, Jan. 4, 1832, was approved Apr. 3, 1832, his wife Anna being executrix. Sons, John and Azel; and daughters, Philine, Sarah, Sylvia, Anna, and Vesta. He died Mar. 13, 1832.

125. ZEPHANIAH, born Sept. 17, 1785, and died Feb. 9, 1787.

126. ZEPHANIAH, born Aug. 1, 1787, and married, in 1812, Lydia Ripley of Plympton, daughter of Ezekiel and Priscilla Ripley. She was born Aug. 27, 1789, and died June 29, 1833, and he Feb. 16, 1850. He was married three times, but had no children by last two wives.

127. AVERY, born Feb. 10, 1792, and married (1), Mar. 23, 1819, Hannah, daughter of Jacob and Hannah (Hayward) Dunbar, and (2), in 1821, Joanna, daughter of John Bacon of Bridgewater. He died Mar. 27, 1871. He had been a farmer in Bridgewater.

128. SALLY, born Feb. 11, 1794, and married, in 1814, George Alger, jun., of Easton. They settled in Winchendon, Mass. Children:

    i.   Sally Lothrop Alger, born Oct. 3, 1814, married Moses Hancock.

    ii.  George Warren Alger, born Oct. 22, 1815, married Susan E. Saunders, and died Aug. 23, 1849.

    iii.  Franklin Alger, born June 13, 1817, and died single Feb. 9, 1873.

    iv.  Shepherd Alger, born May 6, 1819, married Nancy Morse.

    v.  Sidney Alger, born Mar. 14, 1821, and died Sept. 4, 1823.

    vi.  Leonidas Alger, born Jan. 14, 1824, married Lavina Drury.

    vii.  Angeline Alger, born Dec. 15, 1825, married John L. Reed.

    viii.  Israel Francis Alger, born Jan. 8, 1828, married Martha S. Wood.

    ix.  Roland Alger, born Apr. 15, 1830, and died Oct. 15, 1836.

    x.  Cyrus Alger, born June 6, 1832, married Katharine M. Hale.

    xi.  Olivia Alger, born July 11, 1834, married (1) Joseph K. Reed, and (2) Norman L. Jefts.

    xii.  Milton Alger, born Jan. 19, 1839, and died Oct. 9, 1850.

129. BEZAR, born Feb. 7, 1796, and married, in 1820, Vesta Cobb of Mansfield, and died Sept. 30, 1820, leaving no children.

130. PEREZ, born Aug. 13, 1797, and married, in 1807, Eliza, daughter of Hartwell Keith. They settled in Newton, Mass., and afterward removed to Mt. Vernon, Ohio, about 1840. Died Oct. 18, 1856.

131. RAYMOND, born Aug. 24, 1799; married Susannah, daughter of David and Sarah (Lothrop) Alger of Winchendon, and settled in Newton and Winchendon, where he now lives.

132. RHODA, born Nov. 14, 1801, and married, Feb. 27, 1823, Leonard, son of Willis Alger of West Bridgewater, and died Oct. 26, 1835.

133. OLIVE, born Oct. 25, 1803, and married Nahum Williams of West Bridgewater, and moved to Mt. Vernon, Ohio.

134. MANLEY, born Dec. 11, 1807, and married Martha Williams of West Bridgewater. He died Feb. 2, 1859.

## 42. NATHAN. Easton, Mass.

### (First Wife's Children.)

135. ABIJAH, born May 21, 1778.

136. NATHAN, born July 31, 1780, and married, and died in Essex, Dec. 28, 1846, leaving no children.

137. CALEB, born Oct. 6, 1782, and married ——— Pinney.

138. OLIVE, born June 15, 1786, and married ——— Beach.

139. CHARITY, born Aug. 16, 1789, and married ——— Bisbee.

### (Second Wife's Children.)

140. KEZIA, born July 2, 1791, and married Fisher Mann. Children:
i. Geo. W. Mann.
ii. Benj. Franklin Mann.
iii. Asa Mann.
iv. Mary E. Mann.
v. Louisa Mann.
vi. Sophia Mann.

141. CHARLES, born May 21, 1793, and died Aug. 11, 1818.

142. OTIS, born Mar. 25, 1795, and married Mary Darling. daughter of Rev. ——— Darling of Keene, N. H. He died at sea.

143. PALACE, born Apr. 30, 1797, and died Dec. 2, 1822.

144. SOPHILA, born June 5, 1799, and married Asa Farnsworth of Alstead, N. H. She died Apr. 2, 1868. She had two children:
i. Phebe Olivia Farnsworth.
ii. John B. Farnsworth.

145. ORVILLE, born in Pittsford, May 21, 1801, and married (1), Sarah Fitch of Leominster, who died soon after her marriage, Aug. 30, 1823, æt. 23. He married (2), Jan. 20, 1825, Lucy Johnson of Hardwick. They live in Worcester, Mass.

146. CHAUNCEY, born July 16, 1804, and married Relief Ann Johnson. He died in Ware, Mass.

## 43. JOHN. Easton, Mass.; Cornish, N. H.

147. CALVIN, born in Bridgewater, Sept. 24, 1781, and married, 1805, Betsey Clapp, daughter of David and Hannah (King) Clapp of Norton. He was a carpenter, and spent the most of his business life in Boston or its vicinity, and died there in 1855. She died Sept. 7, 1871, æt. 90 years, in Medford, at the residence of her son, David W.

148. FRANCIS, born Sept. 18, 1783, and married twice.

149. ANSEL, born Aug. 3, 1785, lived in Boston; was a chair-maker; died in Malden, Mass.

150. NABBY, born Oct. 13, 1787, and married, Sept. 30. 1804, Isaac Goward of Easton; died in Cornish. N. H. Children:

    i.    Isaac Goward, died in New York.
    ii.   Francis Goward.
    iii.  Reuel Goward.
    iv.  Watson Goward.
    v.   Jason Goward.
    vi.  Sally Goward.
    vii.  Fidelia Goward.
    viii. Betsey Ann Goward.

151. REUEL, born July 7, 1789, and married, Nov. 6, 1821, Sally, daughter of Jesse and Hannah (Clark) Spalding, who was born Apr. 22, 1800. He was a Baptist preacher. After the death of his wife he married again, but I have been unable to learn his second wife's name.

152. CHARLES, born in Easton, Oct. 26, 1791, and married, in Cornish, N. H., Apr. 11, 1816, Mary Johnson, who was born in Portsmouth, N. H., Apr. 30, 1782. They lived in Milford, Mass. She died in Milford, May 10, 1857. He served in the War of 1812, and drew a pension till his death, Sept. 12, 1858, in Cornish, N. H.

153. JASON, born May 16, 1794, and became a Baptist preacher. In a letter to his nephew David, dated Feb. 15, 1865, he gives us a very pleasant account in rhyme of his father and mother. Of the father he says:

> When, at sixteen, though youngest of them all,
> He left his brothers at his country's call,
> In that first conflict he, with little pay,
> Spent his first youth for what we fight to-day.

To the mother of these brothers he pays this filial tribute:

> They had a mother, with the best of skill,
> Who taught and trained them . . .
>
> . . . . . . . . . . . .
> Not one of these, while living, can forget
> That tender watch-care.

He has written much of a local interest, both in prose and rhyme. Three or four editions of his "Juvenile Philosophy" were published in Utica, N. Y., and at least five editions of his "Poetical Precepts."

154. RHODA, born May 29, 1797, and married ——— Kingsbury.

155. WILLIAM, born July 1, 1799.

### 46. DANIEL, JUN. Wilton, Me.

156. GEORGE, born June 13, 1765, and married, in 1783, Polly, daughter of Jeremiah Thayer, and settled in Leeds, where he died, Mar. 4, 1839.

157. DANIEL, born Mar. 28, 1767, and married, in 1787, Sally Whiting of Attleboro. After her death he married Lucy Gilbert. He removed to Maine, and died in Lee, Me. He was a member of the Massachusetts Legislature.

158. THOMAS, born in 1768, and died in infancy, in Bridgewater.

44

159. THOMAS, 2d, married Cynthia Pratt. Removed to Leeds, Me.

160. HANNAH, born in 1771, and married, in 1789, Joshua Gilmore of Easton. They had six children.

161. SAMUEL, born in 1777, and married, in 1799, Bethiah, daughter of Joseph Johnson. He settled in Maine, and died in Leeds, in 1871. Twelve children, names not learned.

162. SULLIVAN, born in 1778, and married (1), —— Haynes; (2), —— Jennings. Twelve children, only one name learned. (See No. 383.)

163. LYDIA, married Stillman Howard, and had seven children.

164. POLLY, married Luther Carey, and had seven children.

165. RHODA, married Nathan Richmond, and had one child.

166. ALSON, married Huldah Richmond; had nine children.

## 53. JONATHAN. Pomfret, Conn.

167. APOLLOS, born Sept. 25, 1779, and married Adah ——, who was born Oct. 18, 1783, in Canaan, Mass., and who died in Malone, N. Y., June 21, 1823. He was reported in 1808 as constable at Malone, having gone into Franklin County in 1805.

168. MARTIN.

169. RHODA.

170. PARNEL.

171. ELIZA.

172. SALLY.

173. LAURA.

## 55. SOLOMON. Easton and Norton, Mass.

174. CELIA, born Aug. 30, 1784, and married, in 1806, Samuel Short of Pawtucket, R. I., and died childless.

175. HOWELL, born in Easton, Apr. 16, 1787, and married (1), Sally, daughter of Capt. Timothy White of Taunton. She was born Sept. 2, 1784, and died Sept. 2, 1822. He married (2), Widow Nancy C. Phillips, who was daughter of Ambrose Lincoln of Raynham. She was born June 9, 1799, and died Nov. 10, 1842, and he married (3), Widow Mary Wilbur, Nov. 25, 1845. He was a farmer, and at one time was engaged in the manufacture of straw braid. He died in Taunton, Mass., June 9, 1857.

176. JAMES, born June 29, 1789, and married (1), Sept. 1, 1814, Hannah, daughter of Abijah and Sarah (Bates) Reed of Easton, where they settled, on the old homestead. She was born March 16, 1790, and died Jan. 15, 1837. He married (2), Dec. 2, 1838, Ruth, daughter of Caleb and Anity Carr of Easton. She was born June 1, 1802, and died Nov. 1, 1872. He died Oct. 2, 1844.

177. SOLOMON, born June 17, 1791, and married Fanny Chase. They lived in Norton, where he died in Jan., 1861. She died Nov. 26, 1868.

178. MEHETABLE, born June 23, 1793, and married Samuel Short of Pawtucket, R. I., husband of her sister Celia. Children:

  i. Celia Short.

  ii. Mehetable Short.

iii. Barton Short.

iv. Augustus Short.

v. Mary Jane Short.

179. Susan, born May 22, 1795, and married Kingman Cook of West Bridge-water, as his second wife. No children.

180. Darius, born Apr. 4, 1797, and married, Dec. 18, 1826, Philura S. Avery of Connecticut. He lived in Easton when he died, after which his family removed to Foxboro. He was a large landholder in Easton.

181. Daniel, born in Easton, Mass., Jan. 9, 1801, and married, Oct. 16, 1825, Sophia, daughter of Dea. Jeremiah Horne of Rochester, Vt. She died Sept. 23, 1848, and he married (2), Sept. 24, 1849, Mary E. Chamberlin. He settled in Rochester, N. H., and was one of the public men of the town. Of the strictest integrity, and possessing sterling qualities of mind and heart, Mr. Lothrop was chosen to fill important offices of public trust in his town and State; and he repeatedly represented his town in the Legislature, where his sound, practical sense and clear wisdom were of much service, particularly in the formation of the Free Soil party, in which he was a bold defender of the rights of liberty to all men. He died May 31, 1870.

## 58. JOHN. Easton, Mass.

182. Caleb, born Aug. 11, 1779 and married, in 1806, Hannah W. Ellis of Middleboro. She was born June 11, 1784, and died Aug. 27, 1866. He died Dec. 7, 1863.

183. Joshua, born Apr. 30, 1782 and married, in 1808, Martha Skinner of Mansfield. She was born Sept. 7, 1790, and died Dec. 24, 1882. He died Nov. 7, 1865.

184. Sebra, born in 1784, and married, Jan. 16, 1806, Charles Skinner of Mansfield. She died Sept. 4, 1842. Children:

i. John Skinner, died in infancy.

ii. John Skinner.

iii. Julia Skinner.

iv. Henry Skinner.

v. William Skinner.

185. Rebecca, married, Aug. 11, 1811, John Snow, Jr., of West Bridge-water. Children:

i. Edward James Snow.

ii. George M. Snow, died young.

186. Mehitable, married, July 3, 1817, Alfred Pratt of Easton; removed to Raynham. He died Nov. 15, 1844. She died March 3, 1851. Children:

i. Rebecca Pratt, died April 9, 1841, aged 21.

ii. Zenas L. Pratt, died Aug. 24, 1841, aged 20.

iii. Orinda Pratt.

iv. Joseph, } twins.

v. John, }

**61.** JOSEPH.    Easton, Mass., and Buckfield, Me.

186-1. ABRAHAM, born July 9, 1783, and married, in 1803, Hannah Pierce of Pembroke, Mass., who was born Oct. 19, 1783. Removed to Maine.

186-2. ABIGAIL, married Timothy Record of Buckfield, Me.

186-3. MARTHA, married Joel Foster of Buckfield, Me.

186-4. STEPHEN, married Mary White of Houghton, British Provinces.

186-5. EDWARD, born Jan. 17, 1790, and married Rebecca Whitman of Buckfield, Me.    She was born Mar. 1, 1792.

186-6. MARGARET, married Elias Taylor of Buckfield, Me.

### 63. JACOB.    Jay, Me.

186-7. BENJAMIN.

186-8. MILCAH, married ——— Packard.

### 66. ALDEN.    Enfield, Mass.

187. SYLVANUS, born at Enfield, Mass., Feb. 5, 1794.  His great-grandmother Hannah Alden was the great-granddaughter of John and Priscilla Alden, of the "Mayflower."  He was a natural-born, civil engineer and architect, and his first contract was on the Erie Canal, embanking the Irondequoit valley and stream, one mile east of Pittsford, N. Y.  He also had a contract at Akron, O.  In 1828, he became engaged in the iron business at Pittsburgh, Pa., and built the third rolling-mill there.  (See History of Monroe Co., N. Y.)  He married (1), at Pittsford, N. Y., in 1822, Caroline Clayus.  She died in 1829 childless.  Married (2), at Allegheny, Pa., in 1831, Eliza Alden Stockton, and died there in 1861, leaving six children.  The following extract from the *St. Louis Republican* of July 5, 1874, pays a just tribute to Mr. Lothrop:

"In the year 1836, a writer, over the signature of 'Progress,' contributed to the newspapers several articles on the subject of bridging the Mississippi river.  This was the first attempt made to discuss the feasibility of bridging the mighty stream at St. Louis.  Little attention seems to have been given to the project of 'Progress,' and, in the light of the present, we cannot say that his ideas were very deserving of consideration.

"A few years later, Sylvanus Lothrop, of Pittsburgh, Pa., an engineer of national, if not world-wide reputation, noted for the originality of his conceptions and the boldness of his plans, came here and made a thorough examination of the locality, and a scientific calculation of the work.  He pronounced the project entirely feasible, and drew plans for the execution of the work.  But the conception was too great, and the undertaking of too stupendous a nature, to lay hold upon the people.  The vast sum of money required to carry out Mr. Lothrop's plans was not at all attainable at that time, and so the whole matter was remanded to silence.  Mr. Lothrop went away, and the problem remained unsolved.  But the documents Sylvanus Lothrop had prepared, the facts he first made accessible, served as a basis for discussion of the project for many years.  The starting-point of practical discussion of the subject of the St. Louis bridge, opened to the public July 4, 1874, dates from Mr. Lothrop's examinations."

188. MARY, born Dec. 24, 1796, and married Capt. Joseph Hull of Enfield, Mass., where she died. Children:

    i.    Joseph Hull.

    ii.   Alden Hull.

189. SAMUEL, born Apr. 1, 1806, and married Moriah Harwood; died in Adrian, Mich., 1871.

190. MARTHA, born Feb. 26, 1798, and married Elijah Linnell, of Adrian.

    i.    Martha Linnell.

    ii.   Caroline Linnell.

    iii.  James Linnell.

    iv.  Lothrop Linnell.

191. SALLY, born in Enfield, Jan. 3, 1801, and married Erastus Gaylord of Mansfield, Conn. Children:

    i.    Mary Lothrop Gaylord, born in Esperance, N. Y., Mar. 5, 1836, and married, Dec. 14, 1853, Reuben L., son of Reuben Anderson of Delaware. They had three children: Lawrence Gaylord, Alfred Reuben, and Charles Tracy. He was a banker of St. Louis, Mo., where he died in 1866, and where she still lives.

    ii.   Samuel Augustus Gaylord, who lives in St. Louis, and married Frances A. Otis of Batavia, N. Y.

    iii.  Josiah Alden Gaylord, married Elizabeth Malloy of Newbury, who is dead. He lives in New York City.

192. ANN, born March 22, 1804, and married Ira Buck. Children:

    i.    George Buck, died at Pittsford.

    ii.   Marvin Buck, died at Adrian.

193. ALDEN, born June 25, 1812. Went, when about 27 years old, to Mobile.

## 68. THOMAS. Stratton, Vt.

194. ELIZABETH, born in Northbridge, Mass., Mar. 14, 1793, and married, Jan. 24, 1828, Rev. Caleb Burge, who died Aug. 31,1838. She married (2), in Oct., 1846, Ira Pond of Camden, N. Y., who died in February, 1848.

195. MARIA, born in Northbridge, Oct. 31, 1794, and married, Aug. 31, 1820, Enoch Briggs of Leyden, who was born Apr. 19, 1795. Their children have been:

    i.    Thomas Lathrop Briggs, born Oct. 19, 1821, and died in Geneva, Wis., Nov. 25, 1867.

    ii.   Henry Briggs, born Sept. 27, 1823, and married and settled in Greenfield, Mass.

    iii.  Elizabeth Briggs, born Apr. 6, 1825, and married, June 6, 1860, Dexter Childs. They have one child, Arthur S., born Dec. 22, 1862.

    iv.  Frances Adams Briggs, born July 29, 1827, and married, Apr. 26, 1853, Mortimer L. Brown, then Superintendent of Public Instruction in Syracuse, N. Y. He afterwards removed to Auburn, N. Y., and established the Auburn Young Ladies' Institute, which is still in successful operation. Their children are: Edward Mortimer, born Oct. 19, 1858; Lathrop Curtiss, born Oct. 23, 1861; Frances Amelia, born June 10, 1864; and Mortimer Lauren, born Feb. 10, and died Mar. 8, 1866.

v. Enoch Pope Briggs, born Mar. 18, 1828, and died in hospital, in Vicksburg, Miss., Sept. 26, 1863.

vi. Sarah Maria Briggs, born Sept. 24, 1832, and died in Deerfield, Mass., Feb. 1, 1861.

vii. William Arthur Briggs, born Nov. 2, 1835. He died in Denver, Col., Apr. 8, 1871, and his family are now in Kansas City.

viii. Jane A. Briggs, born Aug. 28, 1837, and lives in Deerfield, Mass.

ix. Alden Bradford Briggs, born July 2, 1839, and now lives in South Deerfield.

196. DANIEL B., born in Northbridge, Dec. 6, 1796, and died in Utica, N. Y., in 1832.

197. ZEBADIAH, born at Stratton, Vt., Sept. 27, 1798, and was brought up at his uncle Zebadiah's. He married, in Providence, R. I., Feb. 1, 1825, Elizabeth Terry, daughter of Caleb and Amy Earle, who was born in Providence, Sept. 8, 1799. He afterwards removed to Philadelphia.

198. TIMOTHY, born in Stratton, Vt., Jan. 23, 1801, and married Catherine, daughter of Col. Eliel Gilbert, of Greenfield, Mass. He died in Rochester, May, 1839.

199. HANNAH POPE, born in Stratton, Vt., Dec. 28, 1802, and married Oct. 24, 1844, Lyman Cook of Rochester. They now live in Syracuse. They have had one son:

i. Henry Lothrop Cook, born Aug. 21, 1845, and died in Rochester, N. Y., Jan. 18, 1846.

200. MERCY, born in Stratton, Vt., Apr. 9, 1805, and married, May 10, 1827, Orrin Smith of Greenfield, Mass. She died April 2, 1859. Children:

i. Catherine Gilbert Smith, born June 18, 1828, and died Mar. 2, 1844.

ii. Elijah Worthington Smith, born Aug. 16, 1830, and married, Mar. 15, 1859, Malinda Plumb of Halifax, Vt. Their children were: Charles Lathrop, born Aug. 23, 1860; Mary Louise, born Nov. 15, 1862; Ellen Olivia and Alice Maria, twins, born Jan. 19, 1867; a daughter, born June 21, 1873.

iii. Mary Maria Smith, born Dec. 8, 1833.

iv. Thomas Lathrop Smith, born Feb. 4, 1836, and married Hattie C. Holton, of Gill, Mass., June 1, 1864. Children: Hattie Mary, born June 30, 1869; Edward Lathrop, born Nov. 1, 1870.

v. Hannah Lathrop Smith, born Feb. 3, 1840; died Mar. 11, 1862.

201. JERUSHA, born in Newfane, Vt., Apr. 28, 1807, and died in 1809.

202. THOMAS, born in Newfane, Vt., Jan. 28, 1809, and died in August, 1814.

203. NYE ADAMS, born in Newfane, Vt., Jan. 6, 1812, and died in Utica, N. Y., in 1845.

## 72. DARIUS. Sharon, Mass.

204. DARIUS R., born Mar. 2, 1806, and married, July 29, 1841, Fanny H. Belden, daughter of Aaron Belden of Whately, Mass. She was born July 19, 1815. He died in Taunton, Mass., May 5, 1875.

205. LUKE, married, and lived in Norton, Mass.

206. DANIEL, died unmarried about 1866.

207. SARAH, married, and lived in Dedham, where she died, leaving no children.

208. ELIZABETH, died unmarried about 1850.

209. LUCRETIA, married Tisdale Drake of Boston. . She died in 1852, leaving one son, Alden Drake.

210. MARY, married Alonzo Curtis of Westminster, Mass. Had four children, two of whom died unmarried.

211. CLARA, married Charles Brown of Boston. Has a daughter, Florence Brown.

212. HANNAH, married Alonzo Leonard of West Roxbury, Mass.

## 75. ZEBADIAH. Providence, R. I.

### (Children all born in Providence.)

213. ADAMS, born Feb. 27, 1796; died Aug. 2, 1796.

214. SARAH, born Aug. 13, 1797; died Dec. 21, 1800.

215. SETH KINSLEY, born Sept. 9, 1800; died Feb. 22, 1802.

216. HENRY WOOD, born Jan. 5, 1802, and married, Aug. 9, 1827, Louisa Thornton.

217. HARRIET KINSLEY, born Apr. 27, 1803; died May 16, 1807.

218. MARIAH, born Aug. 2, 1805.

219. SOPHIA ANN, born Feb. 6, 1807; died Sept. 12, 1808.

220. ZEBADIAH KINSLEY, born Mar. 28, 1809; died June 17, 1827.

221. CHRISTOPHER, born Dec. 20, 1811, and was drowned in Seekonk river, July 18, 1830.

222. WARREN ADAMS, born Jan. 25, 1814; died Jan. 14, 1816.

223. CYRUS, born May 28, 1816; died June 16, 1819.

## 76. GILBERT.

224. GEORGE, a civil engineer, died unmarried.

224-1. SARAH.

224-2. ABBY.

224-3. ELLEN.

## 81. SETH. Bridgewater, Mass.

225. BARZILLAI, born in ———, and died at sea, after his grandfather's will was made in 1800.

226. CYRUS, born ———, and married, in 1801, Mary, daughter of Daniel Willis, and settled in Livermore, Me., but removed to Randolph.

227. BETSEY, born in ———, and married, in 1813, Warren French, and settled in Maine.

## 85. JOSIAH. Canada.

228. VESTA, born Oct. 2, 1795, and married, June 3, ——, —— Webster. Died in Bridgewater, childless.

229. SUSANNA, born Aug. 4, 1798.

230. JOSIAH, born Sept. 1, 1802.

231. HOWARD, born Oct. 10, 1804, married. Was a Second Advent preacher; had a daughter, who married a Howard, and lived in West Bridgewater.

232. EDWIN, born June. 7, 1807.

233. MARGARET NEVENS, born Sept. 26, 1809.

## 87. CHARLES. Canada.

234. PHEBE AMES, born May 3, 1789, and married David Farnsworth of Bridgewater, whose nephew is General John Farnsworth.

235. GALEN, born Feb. 12, 1791, and married Lucy Loomis, and had a large family born in Dudswell, C. E. Children:

    i.    Galen Loomis.
    ii.   Charles Loomis.
    iii.  Franklin Loomis.
    iv.   Francis Loomis.
    v.    Allen Loomis.
    vi.   Hiram Loomis.
    vii.  Amanda Loomis.
    viii. Atilda Loomis.

236. CHARLES, born Apr. 26, 1793, and died young.

237. EDWARD, born Jan. 29, 1795, and married Thankful, daughter of Jonas and Franceina (Pond) Osgood, and settled in Dudswell, C. E. She died Mar. 28, 1872.

238. ROWENA, born Dec. 7, 1796, and married Joseph Rolfe of Dudswell, C. E. She died, leaving children:

    i.    Joseph Rolfe, who is dead.
    ii.   Gershom Rolfe.
    iii.  Rowena Rolfe.
    iv.   Noble Rolfe.
    v.    Nelson Rolfe.

239. RANNY, married Seaver Willard of Dudswell. Children:

    i.    Mary Ann Willard.
    ii.   Sophronia Willard.
    iii.  Cynthia Willard.
    iv.   Galen Willard.
    v.    Solomon Willard.
    vi.   Phebe Willard.
    vii.  Agnes Willard.
    viii. Florence Willard.

240. SALLY, married Holloway Philip Osgood, brother of Edward's wife. Children:

i. 'Nabby Ann Osgood.
ii. Martha Osgood.
iii. Amanda Osgood.
iv. Jonas Osgood.
v. Franceina Osgood.
vi. Rowena Osgood.
vii. Church Osgood.
viii. Mary Osgood.

241. Cyrus, born ——, and married, in New Haven, Conn., 1826, Mercy, daughter of Neus and Cynthia (Read) Andrews. He was a farmer, and is now living in Stoke, C. E. She died in Dudswell, Aug. 10, 1854.

242. Sophronia, married Elijah Westman of Dudswell, who died. Children:

i. Aylmer Westman.
ii. Cyrus Westman.
iii. Eliza Ann Westman.
iv. John Westman.
v. Amos Westman.
vi. Maria Westman.

## 90. BARNABAS. Bridgewater, Mass.

[All of this family were born in Bridgewater, Mass.]

243. Clarrissa, born Feb. 19, 1778.

244. Stillman, born Feb. 11, 1780, and married, Feb. 25, 1808, Elizabeth Berry. He resided in Boston, where he was for years a deacon in Dr. Sharp's (Baptist) church. He and his wife were active members of the church. As deacon of the church, he was ever faithful to his convictions of duty, and was emphatically a good man, united to a woman of rare excellence, greatly beloved and respected. For over thirty years he was a prominent merchant in Boston, strictly just in all his dealings, liberal to the extent of his ability, and given to hospitality. He early espoused the cause of the oppressed slave, and in later years suffered much persecution from his adherence to his principles. At his death he bequeathed, after the decease of his son Stillman, a large portion of the income of his estate to the American Baptist Free Mission Society, to be devoted to the education of the free colored people, which they enjoyed many years. His wife was born in Andover, Mass., and died in Cambridgeport, Aug. 29, 1849, aged 69 years. He died in Cambridgeport, May 13, 1853.

244-1. Sarah, born Mar. 26, 1782, and married, in 1807, John Hersey of Bridgewater, who was born Jan. 24, 1782. They had six children, two of whom are living: i. John Hersey; ii. Stillman W. Hersey.

244-2. Barnabas, born in Bridgewater, Mass., Mar. 18, 1784, and married, in Braintree, Mass., Apr. 21, 1810, Clara, daughter of Col. John Holbrook of Braintree, Mass., who was born Dec. 23, 1790. They settled in Randolph, Mass., where all of their children were born.

244-3. Edward, born in Bridgewater, Mass., June 8, 1786, and married,

May 10, 1812, Elizabeth Crane, who was born in Salem, Mass., June 2, 1787. They were settled in Boston, where he was engaged in the manufacture of looking-glasses. They were members of the Baptist Church. He died Jan. 12, 1836, and she Mar. 6, 1854.

244-4. ELIZABETH, born Nov. 24, 1788, and married, in 1810, Bernard Alger of Easton, Mass. She died June 22, 1833, and he Nov. 30, 1872.

    i.  Cyrus Alger, born May 4, 1811, married Asenith Howard, Dec., 1832.

    ii.  Bernard H. Alger, born Jan. 5, 1813, married Martha F. Howard.

    iii.  Catherine L. Alger, married Thomas J. Johnson.

    iv.  Rachel H. Alger, died Nov. 6, 1838, unmarried.

244-5. TISDALE, born Feb. 15, 1791, and died unmarried, in Boston.

244-6. MARY, born Apr. 15, 1794, and died young.

### 91. SIMEON. Bridgewater, Mass.

244-7. HANNAH, who, at the date of her father's will, was the wife of William Miller.

244-8. KEZIAH, married, in 1808, Ezekiel Wilson of Methuen.

SEVENTH GENERATION.

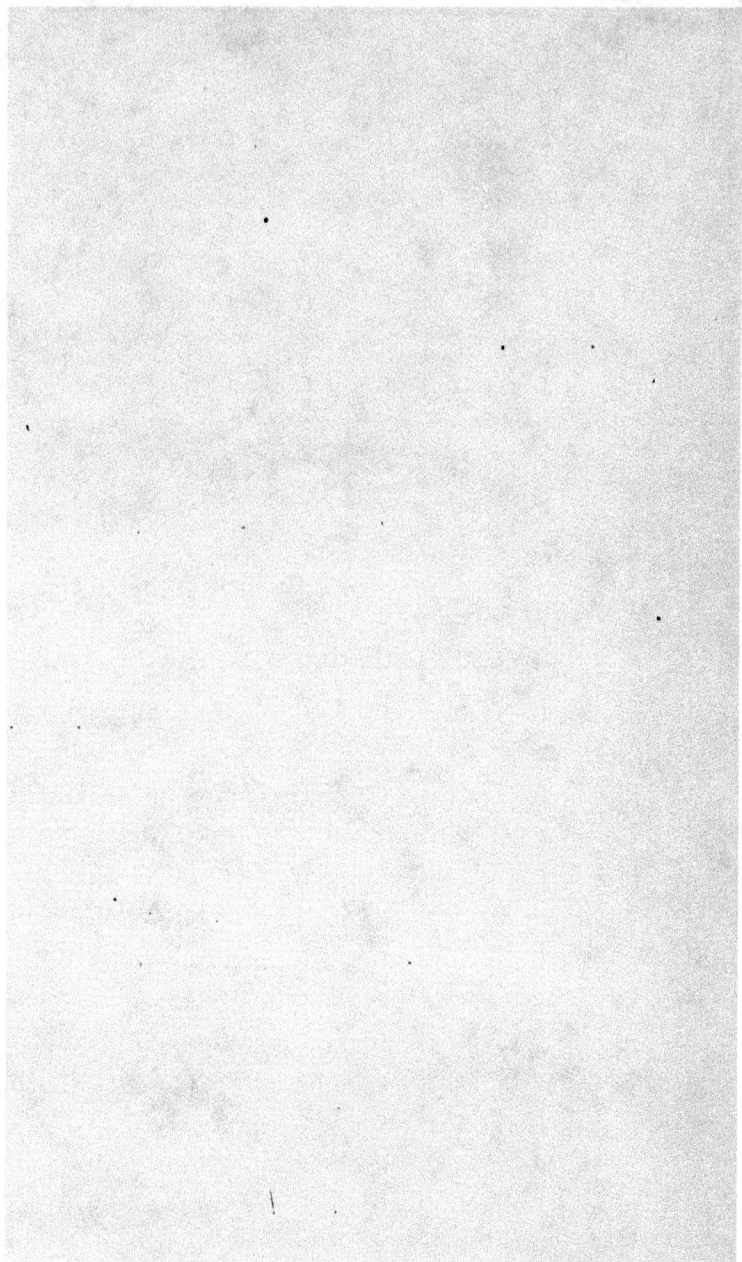

## 97. LEMUEL. Bridgewater, Mass.

**246.** HANNAH R., born July 22, 1796, and married, April 26, 1821, Leonard Alger. She died Oct. 13, 1821, leaving one child: Leonard Warren, who married Ruth Chase.

**247.** GEORGE WATSON, born Oct. 22, 1805, in Bridgewater. Married, in 1811, Rhoda Alger.

## 98. LIBBEUS. Easton, Mass.

**248.** ELIZA H., married, as his second wife, in 1852, William J., son of Samuel Morgan, and lived in Providence, R. I. Children:

   **i.** Edward Franklin Morgan, born Sept. 11, 1853.

   **ii.** Helena Judson Morgan, born Oct. 10, 1854.

## 102. ELIJAH. Stoughton, Mass.

**249.** MARK, born in Stoughton, Dec. 9, 1819, and married (1), Miss Dickerman; and (2), in June, 1860, Elizabeth Landy, and lives in Stoughton, where he is a farmer.

**250.** ELIZABETH, born in Stoughton, Mar. 29, 1824, and married, July 8, 1847, Edmund, son of Galen and Mary (Horton) Packard of North Bridgewater, where they are now settled. They have had one son, Edward Lothrop Packard, born Apr. 17, 1849, and died Apr. 26, 1849.

## 103. MARK. Millbury, Mass.

**251.** SAMUEL, born in Bridgewater, Feb. 23, 1806.

**252.** CATHERINE, born in Bridgewater, May 21, 1808.

**253.** ALMER, born Aug. 18, 1810, and went to Millbury.

## 104. SPENCER. West Bridgewater, Mass.

**254.** BATHSHEBA HOWARD, born Dec. 31, 1812, and married, Feb. 13, 1832, William Alger. They are now living in West Bridgewater.

**255.** SERAPHINA W., born Aug. 29, 1818, and married, Nov. 4, 1839, Benjamin Keith. They lived in Brockton, where he died in April, 1853. She died in Quincy, Mass., Dec. 30, 1883.

**256.** ELMIRA N., born Feb. 10, 1820, and married, in West Bridgewater, Nov. 2, 1842, the Rev. James L. Stone. He died Aug. 11, 1873, in Taunton, where they then lived.

**257.** THOMAS S., born in West Bridgewater, March 1, 1822. After graduating at the State Normal school at Bridgewater, he entered the Theological school at Meadville, Pa., from which he also graduated. He is a Universalist preacher, and is now settled in North Salem, N. Y. He married, April 1,

1861, Eliza Ann (Munroe), widow of Rev. Henry Bacon, and has been a very acceptable contributor to Universalist papers and periodicals (1873).

258. ALINDA W., born Sept. 15, 1824, and died June 12, 1840, unmarried.

259. NANCY J., born Dec. 3, 1825, and married Oct. 25, 1843, Charles F. Howard of West Bridgewater.

260. SAMUEL PIERCE, born Feb. 4, 1828, and married, July 26, 1864, Elizabeth Springer of Attleboro, Mass., where they now reside.

261. ELIZABETH E., born Oct. 5, 1829.

262. JOHN MARK, born July 9, 1832, and married Olive J. Alger of West Bridgewater, where he died, Feb. 10, 1868.

### 107. ISAAC.  Easton, Mass.

263. WELCOME, born in Easton, Dec. 30, 1798, and married, May 23, 1825, Caroline, born Oct. 8, 1801, daughter of Marlborough and Susannah Williams of South Bridgewater. He lived in Easton and Groton. His wife lives with her son.

264. BETSEY, born May 13, 1800, and died June 26, 1827, in Easton.

265. CELIA, born Dec. 9, 1802, married Jan. 29, 1828, Tisdale Harlow. She died in Easton, Jan. 16, 1852. Their children were:

 i. Elizabeth L. Harlow, born Feb. 18, 1829, and married, in 1846, Joel H. Smith of Boston, Mass. Her children are: Henry R., born Sept. 27, 1847, and died Mar. 22, 1873; Maria E., born May 26, 1850; and Frank H., born Sept. 20, 1852.

 ii. Maria Louisa Harlow, born Feb. 27, 1832, and died Nov. 18, 1851.

 iii. Tisdale Harlow, born Apr. 12, 1836.

266. MARY ANN, born Oct. 18, 1804, and still lives in Easton.

267. ISAAC, born Feb. 9, 1807, and married, in 1834, in Cincinnati, O., Ellen M. Gilbert. He died Nov. 15, 1872.

268. MARTIN KEITH, born Dec. 24, 1809, and married, in 1844, Lydia Morris of Brownsville, Pa. He lives in New Richmond, O.

269. EDMUND, born Nov. 10, 1815, and lives on the old homestead in Easton. He is unmarried.

270. HARRIET NEWELL, born Aug. 6, 1819, and died May 11, 1821.

### 108. HON. HOWARD.  Easton, Mass.

(This family were all born in Easton, Mass.)

271. EDWIN HOWARD, born Mar. 22, 1806, and graduated at Amherst College, 1828. In 1830, he went into the territory of Michigan, and purchased a tract of wild land, on which he settled. He married, Dec. 22, 1831, Hannah R., daughter of Rev. Benjamin and Mary Taylor, who was a native of Swansey, Mass. He removed from his farm to Three Rivers, Mich., in 1855, where he has since then resided. He has been considerably employed in public life, and has represented his town in the legislature, in which, in 1844, he was Speaker of the House of Representatives. He has been, also, president of the State Board of Internal Improvement. He died Feb. 17, 1874, and the following tributes, taken from the local papers, testify to his worth:

"The funeral of the late Hon. E. H. Lothrop took place at Three Rivers, February 20th, and in its character seemed a most eloquent tribute to the virtues of the deceased. Several prominent citizens of Kalamazoo were present, and the burial service was performed by Rev. J. F. Conover of this place. Arrived at Three Rivers, it was found that all business had been suspended, and the people gave themselves up to the duty of paying their last respects to the dead. It was the intention to hold the services in Trinity Episcopal Church, of which the deceased had been a member, but it was found entirely inadequate. The Presbyterians very kindly offered the use of their house of worship. Rev. Mr. McCord accompanied Rev. Mr. Conover and the cortege to the church, and sat in the pulpit. The beautiful and impressive burial service of the Episcopal church was read, and the choir of Trinity church sang a part of the 33d psalm, concluding with the verses of 'I would not live always.' The house was filled, and hundreds were unable to get in. The coffin was an elegant one, and resting upon the cover was a large and magnificent floral cross. The pall-bearers were as follows: Judge Dyckman, E. L. Brown, Jonas Allen, Dr. N. M. Thomas, of Schoolcraft; Hon. E. S. Moore, Hon. A. C. Prutzman, Mr. Millard, and Mr. McComber, of Three Rivers. A large number of those within the church were old pioneers, people from Kalamazoo, Schoolcraft, Three Rivers, Mendon, Centreville, Constantine, and many other places. Mr. Conover, though wholly unprepared for any such service, officiated in a most impressive manner. He gave a brief sketch of the deceased, and showed how useful his life had been. He was one of the State Commissioners at an early day. He had been Speaker of the House in 1844, and had served in various legislative positions. He was always esteemed for his integrity, for his love of peace, and for his generosity to those in trouble. This demonstration was the best of eulogies. After the services, which began at half-past one and lasted for about an hour and a half, were over, a special train took the remains and funeral party to Schoolcraft. Here an immense number of people were gathered, business was suspended, and the remains were followed by a great concourse of people to the cemetery, where the last of earth of this old pioneer and useful citizen was deposited in its last earthly resting-place. Hon. G. V. N. Lothrop and family were present from Detroit."

"*Special dispatch to the Detroit Tribune.*

"SCHOOLCRAFT, Feb. 20.—Hon. E. H. Lothrop was buried here to-day. A special train brought the remains from Three Rivers, together with the relatives and a large number of friends of the deceased. Business was entirely suspended here during the ceremonies. The citizens turned out *en masse*, and followed the remains to the grave. It is closely estimated that 1,500 persons were in the procession. Rev. J. F. Conover, of St. Luke's church, Kalamazoo, officiated. Mrs. Lothrop was too ill to attend the remains here."

272. EDWARD WILLIAMS, born Mar. 9, 1808, and died June 26, 1812.

273. THOMAS CHURCH, born July 16, 1810, and married, in New Bedford, Mass., Ann Avery, born Feb. 25, 1817, daughter of John A. Parker. He settled as a merchant in New Bedford, and was drowned, April 3, 1838, in Wareham, Mass.

**274.** SARAH, born Sept. 23, 1812, and married, June 11, 1833, Hon. Oliver Ames, JR., of North Easton, Mass., where they resided. He was born Nov. 5, 1807. He was an eminent manufacturer, and one of the builders of the Union Pacific railroad, of which he was at one time the president. He died Mar. 9, 1877. His widow still survives him, esteemed and beloved in her hospitable and beautiful home at North Easton. Children:

    i.  Frederick Lothrop Ames, born June 8, 1835, and married, June 7, 1860, Rebekah C. Blair, who was born Dec. 30, 1839, and had: Henry S., born Mar. 20, 1861, and died Oct. 18, 1861; Helen Angier, born July 28, 1862; Oliver, born Oct. 21, 1864; and Mary Shreve, born Feb. 1, 1867.

    ii.  Helen Angier Ames, born Nov. 11, 1836, and died Dec. 13, 1882.

**275.** EDWARD WILLIAMS, born Apr. 8, 1815, and died at Schoolcraft, Mich., Sept. 22, 1838, unmarried.

**276.** GEORGE VAN NESS, born Aug. 8, 1817. He graduated at Brown University in 1838, and afterwards studied at the Cambridge Law School, and received the degree of LL.D. from Brown University in 1863. He located himself in his profession in Detroit, Mich., in 1843. He there married, May 13, 1847, Almira, eldest daughter of the late Gen. Oliver Strong and his wife, Anna Colton Chapin. She was born in Rochester, N. Y., Oct. 1, 1823. Mr. Lothrop has attained a high rank in his profession, and has filled acceptably the several places of public honor and trust to which he has been called. From 1848 to 1851, he was attorney-general for the State of Michigan. In 1852, he was recorder of Detroit. In 1867, he was a member of the Constitutional Convention of the State, and is now (1884) one of the commissioners of the Public Library of Detroit.

**277.** HENRY FRANKLIN, born Mar. 1, 1820. He settled, in 1844, in Pittsford, Vt. He married, Oct. 5, 1848, Eleanor B., daughter of Dea. Sturges and Laura Penfield, who was born Jan. 6, 1821. He is a man of great business energy and of public spirit. He makes the interest of the community his own, and is never wanting when the public call for aid. He served several terms in the State legislature, and has been president of the Rutland County Agricultural Society. They have no children.

**278.** CYRUS, born Oct. 13, 1822. Received a good academic education. About 1849, he visited California, viâ Cape Horn, in a sailing ship, and returning by the Isthmus. After his return, he was for some years engaged in iron manufacturing business in Sharon and in Canton, Mass. He was afterwards an iron merchant in Boston, but has lately retired from active business. He was never married. He is a gentleman of pleasant manners, and of the highest character for integrity.

**279.** DEWITT CLINTON, born Feb. 21, 1825, and married, Oct. 3, 1847, Elizabeth Harris, daughter of the honorable Elijah and Nancy Harris (John son) Howard of Easton, where she was born Apr. 9, 1829. They lived on the homestead in Easton, where he died, Aug. 25, 1851. His wife is now dead.

**280.** HORACE AUGUSTUS, born Apr. 3, 1828, and married (1), in 1850, Susan J., born Feb. 22, 1832, daughter of Albert A. Roach of Easton. She died May 5, 1860. He married (2), Apr. 13, 1864, Sarah G., daughter of William

C. Swain of Nantucket, Mass. As soon as he attained manhood, he engaged in the manufacturing business in Sharon, Mass., which he carried on with enterprise and success until about 1883, when he sold his works.

## 109. EDMUND. Norton, Mass.

281. Louisa, born 1803, and married Rev. Horace Seaven. She died June 26, 1864. They had one daughter:

i. Louisa Seaven, who married Edgar Blanden, and is now living in Taunton, Mass.

282. Rhoda, born 1805, and married, 1836, Williams Keith, who is now living (1873) in his 84th year. She died June 27, 1847. Their children were:

i. Louisa F. Keith, born May 21, 1837.

ii. Amelia L. Keith, born Oct. 9, 1838.

iii. Theodore W. Keith, born Aug. 15, 1843, and died while in the service of the government in the recent war.

iv. Otis L. Keith, born May 28, 1847.

283. Edmund, born 1807, and died in 1872 or '73.

## 110. CYRUS. Taunton, Mass.

284. Abby Maria, born in Easton, Mar. 10, 1816, and was educated at Warren Seminary—an excellent scholar, and valedictorian of her class. She was a young woman of promise, devotedly Christian, and died, a felt loss to those who knew her, in August, 1838.

285. Eliza, born in Easton, in 1817, and died Jan. 26, 1819.

286. Emeline, born in Easton, Dec. 21, 1823. She graduated at the Charlestown Seminary, and was every way a superior scholar. Her life was mainly spent in teaching, in which profession she stood well. She died in Taunton, Mar. 8, 1870.

287. Cyrus Howard, born in Easton, Sept. 4, 1826, and married (2), May D., daughter of Charles Godfrey of Taunton. He began business life with his father, having Taunton as his home, and his business relations in Newport and Boston. He is now living in Taunton.

288. Charles Dexter, born in Taunton, Apr. 16, 1828, and graduated with honor at Amherst College, in 1849. He entered on the study of theology, and, in 1853, graduated at the Theological Seminary at Andover. In 1854, he accepted a call to the Congregational church in Attleborough, Mass., where he was ordained and installed. Since that date, he has pursued the work of the ministry with acceptance. He is an active advocate of the temperance cause, and is now (1874) the district agent of the National Temperance Association. He married Aug. 11, 1854, Anna Chase Gilman of Lowell, Mass., daughter of Chase and Eliza (Lawrence) Gilman of Epping, N. H. She was the valedictorian of her class in 1849, and became a teacher in her alma mater. She was afterwards teacher and associate principal in the Norton Female Seminary. This gifted woman, after a life of singular devotion to the duties of pupil, teacher, wife, and mother, died in joyful hope, at Amherst, Oct. 30, 1864. Mr. Lothrop married (2), Aug. 1, 1865, Mrs. Mary G., daughter of

46

Israel and Hannah Ward of Salem, and widow of the Rev. J. W. Underhill. She was born in Salem, June 15, 1830.

### 121. JARVIS. Easton, Mass.

289. CATHERINE, born in Easton, and married Noble, son of Apollos and Olive (Cary) Howard. Children:

    i.   Harriet Howard, married Francis Sanderson.

    ii.  Sarah Nettie Howard, married Adams Lathrop.

290. ADAMS BAILEY.

291. ELIZA DOYLE, married Capt. W. W. Smith.

292. JARVIS, born in Easton, Aug. 30; 1834, and married in Boston, June 16, 1861. In business at 38 Central Wharf, Boston.

293. MARY ANN, married Edward Patterson of Brighton.

### 123. OLIVER. Sharon, Mass.

#### (Children by First Wife.)

294. OLIVER PACKARD, born Feb. 20, 1806, and married, Apr. 19, 1835, Lois P. Towne of Stoughton. She was born Oct. 15, 1815. He died Dec. 16, 1837.

295. FRANCIS, born Jan. 2, 1808, and died Feb. 23, 1828, unmarried.

296. WILLIAM, born Feb. 12, 1811, and died unmarried, March 13, 1838.

297. HANNAH, born July 3, 1813, and died June 27, 1823.

298. SARAH H., born July 13, 1815, and married May 27, 1835, Franklin A. White of Mansfield. She died Dec. 15, 1843. Children:

    i.   Sarah J. White, born Aug. 13, 1836.

    ii.  William F. White, born Mar. 20, 1838.

    iii.  Willard L. White, born Apr. 2, 1840.

299. SUSAN T., born Dec. 7, 1817, and died unmarried, Dec. 8, 1854.

300. ABIEZER C., born May 12, 1821, and died unmarried May 23, 1839.

301. THOMAS Z., born Oct. 21, 1823, and died, unmarried, Mar. 12, 1858.

#### (Children by Second Wife.)

302. FRANCIS, residence not learned.

### 124. AZEL. West Bridgewater, Mass.

303. PHILENE C., born Mar. 6, 1806, and died Dec. 6, 1852.

304. SARAH P., born May 24, 1807, and died Feb. 3, 1851.

305. SYLVIA, born June 19, 1809, and married John Eaton of North Bridgewater, where they now live.

306. JOHN EATON, born Feb. 18, 1812, and married Lucinda S. ———. He died Oct. 4, 1861.

307. AZEL, born Sept. 8, 1817, and married Ann, daughter of John Eaton of Middleborough, Mass. He died Nov. 9, 1845.

308. ANN E., born Apr. 11, 1820, and is now living.

309. VESTA C., ' 1 Sept. 2, 1823, and died in Sept., 1863.

## 126. ZEPHANIAH. West Bridgewater, Mass.

310. ALMON, born Oct. 13, 1815, and married, July 2, 1840, Hannah Ellis Lothrop (No. 427), of Easton. Died May 15, 1857.

311. ELON, born Sept. 2, 1817, and married, June 25, 1840, Salome Drake of Easton. He was a shoe manufacturer of Easton, where he died Feb. 25, 1850.

312. DIANA, born Apr. 8, 1822, and married, Sept. 24, Thomas S. Ripley, a farmer of Plympton. She died Dec. 31, 1870.

313. ADELIA, born Mar. 20, 1824, and married ——— Goble of California.

## 127. AVERY. Bridgewater, Mass.

314. JOHN A., born in Bridgewater, Apr. 16, 1827. He is unmarried. His correspondence has been invaluable in supplying quite a list of this branch of the family.

## 130. PEREZ. Mt. Vernon, O.

315. AMASA, born in Bridgewater, Mass., Sept 22, 1819, and married in St. Mary's Town, La., July 11, 1857, Mary K. Knight. He is a lawyer, and is located in New York City.

316. CORNELIA, born in Brookline, Mass., May 5, 1821, and married in Mt. Vernon, Ohio, May 5, 1845, John Gwin. He is a farmer, and is settled in in Santa Barbara, Cal. They have five children:

i. Amasa Gwin, born in Bellefontaine, Ohio, Apr. 10, 1846, and died in the same place, Oct. 9, 1847.

ii. Alonzo Warren Gwin, born, as above, Aug. 28, 1848, and died Aug. 18, 1849.

iii. Sylvester Gwin, born, as above, Jan. 6, 1851, and died Mar. 7, 1851.

iv. Sylvanus Gwin, twin wi'h Sylvester, died Aug. 17, 1851.

v. Marion Bruce Gwin, born in Spring Green, Wis., Jan. 22, 1858, and died at same place, Mar. 23, 1858.

317. EDWIN, born in Newton, Mass., May 2, 1824, and died in Mt. Vernon, O., June, 1882.

318. JONAS KEITH, born in Newton, Mass., June 24, 1827, and died in Harrisonburg, La., Oct. 27, 1857.

319. SARRAY WILBER, born in Newton, Mass., June 25, 1829, and married, in Mt. Vernon, O., Oct. 19, 1847, Henry R. Gilmore, a farmer of Fox Lake, Wis. They have three children, all born in Mt. Vernon, O.:

i. Lois Amanda Gilmore, born July 13, 1849, and married in Waupun, Wis., Jan. 11, 1870, George W. Kimble, a miner of Deadwood, Dakotah.

ii. George Milton Gilmore, born Aug. 18, 1852, and is a farmer in Fox Lake, Wis.

iii. Jonas Chauncey Gilmore, born Apr. 17, 1854, and lives in Fox Lake, Wis., where he is a farmer.

320. ELIZA JANE, born in Newton, Mass., Mar. 4, 1832, and married in Mt. Vernon, O., Oct. 17, 1852, John Gilmore. She died in Mackford, Wis., Aug. 14, 1856, leaving one child. Her husband is a farmer, and is living in Fox

Lake, Wis. Child: Eliza Jane Gilmore, born in Fox Lake, Wis., July 12, 1856, and died Sept. 9, 1856.

321. JOSEPH GRAFTON, born in Newton, Mass., Mar. 22, 1836, and married in Greensburg, La., in November, 1867, Florida Watson. He died, Jan. 16, 1868, in Arcola, La.

322. SYLVIA MARIA, born in Mt. Vernon, O., Oct. 18, 1839, and married, in the same place, June 26, 1866, Richard Blackmare Marsh. He is living in Mt. Vernon, O., where he is Superintendent of Public Schools for the city. They have four children, of whom the last three were born in Mt. Vernon, O.:

    i.    Sylvia Lothrop Marsh, born in Gambier, O., July 6, 1867.
    ii.   Hattie Keith Marsh, born July 31, 1870.
    iii.  Richard Blackmare Marsh, born Nov. 15, 1872, and died Dec. 4, 1873.
    iv.  Henry Frederick Marsh, born Nov. 12, 1874.

323. WILBUR CLAY, born in Mt. Vernon, O., Sept. 25, 1845, and married, in his native town, Oct. 14, 1868, Hattie E. Culver. In 1861, he graduated in preparatory course in the public high school in Mt. Vernon, O.; in 1861, entered Kenyon College, Gambier, O.; in 1865, removed from Mt. Vernon, O., to Denver, Colorado; in 1869, was elected Superintendent of Schools of Arapahoe County, Colorado; no opposition; both Republicans and Democrats united in his election. In 1870, the governor of Colorado appointed him Territorial Superintendent of Public Instruction. In 1871, he prepared a bill for the revision and improvement of the school laws of Colorado, which bill was passed without amendment by the legislature, and became a law in 1872; was reappointed in 1872 to the office of Territorial Superintendent of Public Instruction, and, in the summer of 1873, resigned the office on account of private business requiring his attention. The following is a copy of the governor's letter accepting his resignation:

"TERRITORY OF COLORADO,

"EXECUTIVE DEPARTMENT, DENVER, July 11, 1873.

"SIR:—Your letter, tendering your resignation as Territorial Superintendent of Public Institutions, is received.

"I regret that you have felt it necessary to resign an office which you have so long filled so acceptably to our people. I take pleasure in expressing to you my high appreciation of your services in the organization of our public schools and your fidelity and efficiency as a public officer.

"I have the honor to be your obedient servant,

"S. H. ELBERT, *Governor of Colorado.*

"To Hon. W. C. Lothrop, Denver, Col."

In 1874 he was elected a member of the Board of Education of Denver, being Treasurer of the Board, and Chairman of the Committee on Teachers and Text-books. In 1875, he was elected County Clerk of Arapahoe County, Colorado; was three times re-elected, serving as such officer until Jan. 7, 1884. The following resolutions were passed by the Board of County Commissioners of Arapahoe County, at the expiration of his term of office:

"WHEREAS, Mr. W. C. Lothrop, having filled the office of County Clerk of our county for four successive terms, being thrice re-elected to that important position, and during all the eight years of his official service having been ex-officio clerk of this Board, and having witnessed the good and devotion which he has at all times manifested in the public service, and deeming it appropriate to make record of our high appreciation of his long, faithful service, do

"*Resolve,* That we have noted with pride and satisfaction the watchful care which he has always bestowed upon the records of the county, the accuracy with which the same have been kept under his supervision, and the urbanity which he has shown to all having business to do with his office, deserves, as it commands, the gratitude of all; that, as the Clerk of this Board, he has been at all times faithful and efficient in the discharge of the arduous task which the position imposed upon him, wise in season, honest in all things, faithful in the smallest, and courteous and kind to the humblest, we have always found him, as he has proved himself, a model public officer; that as an upright, honest, and obliging citizen, we commend him as a faithful and firm friend, as we know him, and going from us amid universal good-will, he takes from us and each of us, as we know he does from all, a high appreciation of his great public services and esteem as a friend, and best wishes for his success.

## 131. RAYMOND. Winchendon, Mass.

323–1. MARCELLUS A., born Feb. 24, 1825, and married, Oct. 19, 1870, J. Augusta Keith.

323–2. CHASTINA, born Feb. 25, 1827, and died March 24, 1828.

• 323–3. CHASTINA, born July 19, 1831, and died Feb. 6, 1832.

323–4. MERRILL G., born July 9, 1836, and married, Oct. 9, 1866, Jane E. Redmond.

323–5. MELINDA S., born Sept. 11, 1847, and died Sept. 19, 1863.

## 134. MANLEY. West Bridgewater, Mass.

324. MARTHA, died young.

325. CYRUS M., married, and lives in Winchendon. No children.

326. MARY W., married, and now dead.

## 142. OTIS.

327. PALACE, married a Mr. Wheeler, of Providence.

328. JULIETTE PATTERSON.

## 145. ORVILLE. Worcester, Mass.

329. PHILIP, born in Shrewsbury, Mass., Oct. 23, 1825, and married, Jan. 1, 1850, Susan Elizabeth, daughter of Joseph and Sally Whitney of Westminster. He is living in Leominster, Mass., where he is a carriage manufacturer.

## 147. CALVIN. Boston, Mass.

330. MARIA CLAPP, born May 28, 1808, and married, in 1827, Joseph Douglas. They had no children.

331. ELIZA BALDWIN, born May 19, 1810, and married (1), John McAllister,

by whom she had two daughters, both of whom died of consumption. She married (2), Charles Snell, from Maine, and had one daughter, who is still living. She died in Woburn in 1853.

332. JASON, born in Boston, Mass., Jan. 15, 1814, and married, in Boston, June 1, 1836, Cynthia, daughter of John and Almira Cutler of Lexington, Mass. They removed to Wisconsin in 1836, and he is now living there in Lancaster. He has been a farmer and carpenter, having learned the latter trade in Boston.

333. DAVID WAYLAND, born in Boston, July 27, 1816, and married, in 1841, Caroline, daughter of Robert and Mary (Savery) Mendon of Portsmouth, N. H. He has always been a printer in Boston. He is a man of intense physical and mental activity. His residence is in West Medford, Mass., where he purchased and built.

334. RACHEL GODFREY, born Apr. 29, 1819, and married, Feb. 7, 1840, Lorenzo, son of John and Abigail (Rogers) Chase. They settled next her brother David, in West Medford. Their children have been:

    i.   Juliana Chase, born Mar. 6, 1841.

    ii.  Rosetta Chase, born July 3, 1847, and died Sept. 13, 1847.

    iii. Ella Augusta Chase, born June 28, 1850.

    iv.  Josephine Chase, born June 28, 1854.

335. CHARLES, born Dec. 15, 1821, and died at five years of age.

### 148. FRANCIS.                      Cornish. N. H.

336. WILLARD, married —— Drake, and died in Easton.

337. JOSEPH, married Keyes, Roxbury.

338. EDWIN, died young, single.

### 149. ANSEL.                      Malden, Mass.

339. MARY ANN.

340. SARAH.

341. GEORGE, of Claremont, N. H., married —— Dymond.

### 151. REV. REUEL.

342. REUEL.

343. SARAH.

344. MARY.

345. JAMES WINCHEL, born in Dec., 1823, and died June 9, 1849.

### 152. CHARLES.                      Milford, Mass.

346. CHARLES DARWIN, born Apr. 5, 1817, and married (1), Sept. 1, 1839, Mary Elizabeth, daughter of Allen Richardson of Acton; (2), Mary Ann Gallup, widow of Wesley R. Gallup of Claremont, N. Y., and daughter of Peter Rifinburgh. He is in the chair business in New York City.

247. MARY E., born at Cornish, N. H., May 19, 1818, and married at Cornish, May 11, 1843, to David Cummings, who died soon after. Married again, at Acton, Mass., for her second husband, Albert Haynes, and settled at Cherokee, Iowa.

348. HARRIET E., born at Cornish, N. H., July 2, 1819, and married at

Acton, Mass., Oct. 26, 1846, to Francis Huntoon, who was killed by the falling of a railroad bridge in Athol, Mass., in 1847. Married again, at Acton, to Lafayette Huntoon, for her second husband.

349. WILLIAM REED, born at Cornish, N. H., Sept. 30, 1820, and married at Acton, Mass., Sept. 11, 1845, to Mary E. Weston, who died June 25, 1848. Married again, at Acton, Sept. 14, 1849, to Susan Putnam of Acton. He died Feb. 22, 1853.

350. JOHN JOHNSON, born at Cornish, N. H., June 17, 1822, and married at Acton, in Jan., 1845, to Nancy Hildreth, who died in 1850. Married again at Acton for his second wife Mary M. Mead, of Foxborough, Mass., in 1850. Settled at San Francisco, Cal.

351. HENRY O., born at Cornish, N. H., Sept. 16, 1823, and married at Acton, Mass., Nov. 22, 1846, to Rebecca W. Wood of Acton, who died Aug. 23, 1854. Married again, for his second wife, Mar. 6, 1856, at Acton, to Susan P. Lothrop, widow of William R. Lothrop. After his first marriage, he settled at Milford, where he held several town offices, and represented the town in the legislatures of 1861, 1862, and 1863. He is now living at Boston.

352. ALMIRA M., born at Cornish, N. H., Feb. 13, 1825, and married at Acton, June 19, 1845, to Cyrus Noyes, and settled at Milford, Mass.

### 156. GEORGE. Leeds, Me.

353. ALSON, born in 1785, and died in Bridgewater, 1790.

354. DANIEL, born in 1787, and died in Bridgewater, 1790.

355. SOLOMON, born in Bridgewater, Feb. 26, 1788, and married, in Leeds, Me., July 15, 1810, Sarah W. (No. 365), daughter of Daniel Lothrop, Jr. He settled in Leeds, Me., where he was the first postmaster, which office he held twenty-five years with great acceptance to the people. He was selectman of Leeds for seven years, and represented the town in the State legislature twice. He was a merchant at Leeds Center, and became quite wealthy. He died Aug. 12, 1873, in Leeds.

356. RHODA, died in 1790, at Bridgewater.

357. LEAVITT, born in Vassalborough, Me., May 19, 1793, and married Betsey Lane. Settled in Leeds, Me.

358. ABSOLOM, died young in Vassalborough.

359. JEREMIAH, born in 1798, and died in 1801.

360. HANNAH, born Mar. 19, 1800, and married, in 1828, George Gould. They settled in Leeds, Me. Their children were:
    i. Mary Gould, born in 1830, and died the next year.
    ii. George O. Gould, born in Jan., 1832, and died in California in 1867.

361. JEREMIAH, born Oct. 29, 1802. He was an examiner in the U. S. office in New York City. He died Sept. 25, 1874, at No. 78 Madison Avenue.

362. POLLY, born Dec. 17, 1805, and married Reuel Foss of Auburn, Me. Children:
    i. Orinthia Foss, married Dana Goff. They have had two children: Hobart, who died at five years of age; and Ralph, now nine years old (1874).
    ii. Rodney F. Foss, a merchant of Auburn, Me. Unmarried.
    iii. Flora Foss, married Benjamin Hill of Auburn, S. C.

## 157. DANIEL. Leeds, Me.

363. IRA, born in Bridgewater, and married Sarah Leach.

364. MATILDA, married Warren Drake, and died in China.

365. SARAH WHITING, married, July 15, 1810, Solomon Lothrop (No. 355).

366. HANNAH, married Henry Jennings, and died in Leeds.

367. ALICE, married Thomas Francis, son of Rev. Thomas Francis. Now living at Leeds.

368. DANIEL, killed in the woods at New Brunswick.

369. ABIGAIL, married Benjamin Berry of Leeds, and died at Chesterville, Me.

370. EATON, born in 1800, and married (1), Sarah Richmond; (2), Mrs. Holmes, and lives in Lewiston, Me.

371. GEORGE, born in 1802, married, and died in Pittsburgh, Pa.

372. WILLARD, born in 1804, and married, Feb. 13, 1831, Eveline A. Russel, at North Easton.

373. LUCY, married ———— Brown in Lee, Me.

374. DULCINEA, married Calvin Lane, in Lee.

375. AUGUSTUS, married ———— ————, North Easton, Mass.

376. WILLIAM, married ———— ————, Lowell.

377. JANE, married Frank Reed.

378. EMILY.

379. ORMOND.

380. DANIEL.

381. MARY.

## 159. THOMAS. Leeds, Me.

382. RUFUS DANIEL, born in Leeds, July 28, 1817, and married Hannah, daughter of Isaac and Polly (Clifford) Elliot. He went to Groveland in 1856, to superintend the town farm.

## 162. SULLIVAN. Leeds, Me.

383. Sullivan, born Oct. 15, 1802, and living at St. Albans, Vt. State Senator. Has a family.

## 166. ALSON. Wilton, Me.

384. ALSON, born in Wilton, and married Orissa, daughter of Solomon Lothrop, and settled in Jay, Me.

Eight other children, names unknown.

## 167. APOLLOS. Malone, N. Y.

385. LUCY E., born in Weybridge, Vt., Nov. 16, 1804.

386. MARTIN L., born in Moira, N. Y., Oct. 2, 1808, and died Nov. 11, 1823.

387. LOYAL C., born in Malone, N. Y., Aug. 31, 1810, and married, in Fort Covington, N. Y., Jan. 24, 1837, Irena D. Spencer, who was born in Moira, N. Y., Sept. 3, 1818. He was reported in 1851 as sheriff of Franklin County, N. Y.

388. MARY C., born in Malone, N. Y., May 2, 1813, and died Mar. 24, 1829, in the same town.

389. ELIZA ANN, born in Moira, N. Y., May 2, 1815.

390. GEORGE D., born in Malone, Aug. 29, 1819, and married, May 18, 1843, Sarah C. Peck. She was born Sept. 18, 1821, and died in Malone, July 4, 1841. He married (2), Feb. 24, 1847, Caroline Wilcox, in Bangor, N. Y. She was born in Watertown, N. Y., Oct. 24, 1828.

391. ADAH S., born in Malone, N. Y., June 9, 1823.

### 175. HOWELL. Taunton, Mass.

[All born in Taunton.]

392. SALLY MARIA WHITE, born Jan. 9, 1810, and died single, in Taunton, Oct. 27, 1829.

393. CORNELIUS WHITE, born Mar. 28, 1812, and married, as her second husband, Eleanor Lincoln, daughter of James Smith of Taunton, where they settled. He was early engaged in the manufacture of straw braid, and investing his funds in land, he became a farmer. He came to an accidental death in Raynham, Mass., Dec. 8, 1847, in a saw and shingle mill which he and his brother-in-law, Lloyd Wilbur, were then operating. His widow died in Taunton, Nov. 25, 1872.

394. MELINDA M., born Aug. 5, 1814, and died Feb. 19, 1815.

395. LAURA ELIZABETH, born June 17, 1816, and married, Mar. 5, 1846, Joseph S., son of Ephraim Paull of Berkeley, where they lived for awhile, and where he was engaged as a farmer. He removed to Taunton in June, 1870, where he died January 5, 1875. Children:

    i. Cornelius H. Paull, born in Berkeley, Oct. 22, 1848. Married, Nov. 24, 1869, Mary Leonard Wilbur, and is living in Chicago. Children: Mildred Mary Paull, born Feb. 20, 1876, died Aug. 5, 1876; Arthur Victor Paull, born Dec. 9, 1878.

    ii. Caroline L. Paull, born in Berkeley, June 6, 1853. Unmarried, and living with her mother in Taunton.

396. LUCY, born Dec. 5, 1818, and married, in Mar., 1847, Alden B., son of Solomon Woodward of Taunton. They settled in Newcastle, Pa., afterward removing to Wheatland. She died Jan. 7, 1878. He was an iron founder. Children:

    i. Lucy Maria Woodward, born in Taunton, Mass., Feb. 20, 1840, married, Jan. 2, 1856, Isaac Reno, and resides in Sharon. Their children are: (1) Newton Woodward Reno, born July 26, 1858; (2) Earl Reno, born Aug. 6, 1863; (3) Lucy May Reno, born Aug. 5, 1865; (4) Charles Madison Reno, born Dec. 11, 1867.

    ii. Josephine Elizabeth Woodward, born Aug. 2, 1844, married, Jan 1, 1863, Albert Shilling. They reside in Wheatland, Pa. Children: (1) Virgie May Shilling, born Nov. 7, 1866; (2) Mary Belle Shilling, born Oct. 9, 1871.

    iii. Mary Alice Woodward, born Dec. 22, 1850, married, May 11, 1871, A. S. Rebout. Children: (1) Charles Rebout, born Feb. 13, 1872; (2) Frank Rebout, born Mar. 26, 1874; (3) Cora Rebout, born May 10, 1876.

47

397. SUSAN, born Dec. 5, 1818, and married, Nov. 12, 1817, William, son of Apollos Eddy of Taunton. They settled in Taunton, where he was a farmer. He died Nov. 18, 1872. Children, all born in Taunton:

. i. Willard H. Eddy, born Aug. 2, 1848, married, Mar. 28, 1872, Susan, daughter of John H. Eddy of Taunton. They have three children living in Taunton.

ii. Susan Maria Eddy, born July 22, 1850, married (1), Nov. 14, 1872, Frank A. Gushee of Raynham. He died Mar. 30, 1873, leaving no children. (2), May 12, 1881, Alanson Pratt of Taunton. They have no children.

iii. Helen J. Eddy, born Sept. 25, 1853, married, Jan. 9, 1870, William I. Reed. They live in Taunton. Children: Frank I. Reed, born Oct. 10, 1870; Bertha J. Reed, born Dec. 28, 1873.

iv. Cora L. Eddy, born Jan. 17, 1856, married Frank R. Kirby of Westport. They reside in Westport, and have no children.

398. MARY, born in Aug., 1822, and died Nov. 13, 1822.

399. MARY L., born June 18, 1826, and married, Jan. 18, 1843, Lloyd, son of Enoch Wilbur of Raynham, Mass., where she died Dec. 27, 1862. He was a farmer and a trader, having had a store in Bridgewater. He died in 1859. Children, all born in Raynham, were:

i. Gustavus L. Wilbur, born Mar. 8, 1843, married, Feb. 23, 1861, Jane Lincoln of Taunton, Mass.

ii. Nancy I. Wilbur, born Apr. 22, 1846, married Chas. A. Knapp of Raynham.

iii. Daniel E. Wilbur, born Apr. 6, 1849, married and living in Taunton.

iv. Enoch P. Wilbur, born Dec. 12, 1851, married and living in West Bridgewater.

v. Sarah I. Wilbur, born June 12, 1855, married Charles Franklin Dean of Taunton, Mass.

400. WARREN HOWELL, born Dec. 10, 1829, and married, Apr. 25, 1848, Ann E., daughter of Jabez Rounds of Taunton, where they settled. Having inherited a large part of his father's farm, he became a farmer. Died, Nov. 16, 1872.

401. SARAH C., born Aug. 9, 1834, and married, Sept. 24, 1850, John, son of Ichabod Bassett of Taunton. They settled in Foxboro', Mass., where they still reside. He is engaged in the manufacture of straw hats. Children:

i. Alice E. Bassett, born in Taunton, Sept. 18, 1862, married Forrest Bassett of Taunton. They now reside in Foxboro', Mass.

ii. Lillie S. Bassett, born Dec. 20, 1856, in Foxboro'.

iii. Charles E. Bassett, born in Foxboro', Mass., July 6, 1863.

### 176. JAMES. Easton, Mass.

#### (Children by First Wife.)

402. HANNAH REED, baptised June 28, 1816, and married, Nov. 6, 1834, John Vose, Jr., of Boston. They have had one son and three daughters.

403. J. FRANKLIN, moved to Boston.

*(Children by Second Wife.)*

404. EUGENE TERRY, born March 22, 1840, and married Sarah Southworth of Easton. They live in Brockton, Mass.

405. WILLIAM HENRY, born Dec. 25, 1841, and married, Oct. 11, 1874, Elizabeth, daughter of John A. and Lieuphemia E. Hall of Raynham, Mass. She was born Nov. 5, 1850. They live in Easton, on the old homestead.

### 177. SOLOMON. Norton, Mass.

406. ELIZA REED, born Feb. 18, 1818, and married Franklin, son of Enoch and Phebe Haskins of Lakeville, where they live. Children:

   i. Irving Haskins, born in 1842.
   ii. Harriet Haskins, born in 1847.
   iii. Bowers Haskins, born in 1852.

407. MELVIN OTIS, born Jan. 24, 1820, and married, in Oct. 1850, Mary Ann, daughter of Dr. Elijah Hayward of Raynham. They lived in Norton, where she died in 1857.

408. CORNELIA WHITE, born Mar. 14, 1822, and married (1), May 4, 1844, Alvin D. Wilbur of Raynham. He died in 1872. Married (2), in 1877, Lorenzo LeBaron of Easton, who died in 1881.

*(Children by First Husband.)*

   i. Harrison Dean Wilbur, born Jan., 1846, and married, in 1877, Hattie Davis of Taunton. They live in Brockton, Mass.

   ii. Ella Cornelia Wilbur, born Feb., 1852, and married, in 1872, Henry Wilbur of Raynham. They live in Brockton.

409. ANDREW JACKSON, born July 28, 1824, and married, Dec. 14, 1850, Eliza A., daughter of Joseph E. and Abby M. Dean. They live in Norton, and have no children living.

410. JAMES, born Mar. 7, 1827, and married Sophia D., daughter of John and Sally Dean of Berkley, Mass. They live in Raynham, Mass.

411. CELIA, born Sept. 29, 1829, and died Sept. 27, 1850.

411-1. MEHITABLE, born May 12, 1831, and died May 25, 1832.

411-2. NATHAN CHAPMAN, born June 19, 1850, and married Sarah J. Lovejoy of Laconia, and are living in Deerfield, N. H. He is a Baptist minister. They have three children.

### 180. DARIUS. Easton, Mass.

412. HENRY D., born in 1829, and died Aug. 19, 1858, unmarried.

413. HELEN MAR, born Dec. 1831, and died Oct. 10, 1832.

414. WILLIAM A., born 1834, and died in Andersonville prison, Sept. 15, 1864, unmarried. He was a member of Company C, 58th Regiment, Mass. Volunteers.

415. WALCOTT SHEPARD, born Dec., 1835, and died Oct. 2, 1836.

416. PHILURA S., born in 1838, and died Feb. 28, 1865, unmarried.

417. HELEN, died unmarried in Foxborough.

417-1. CARMELIA M. D., born 1845, and died Nov. 10, 1865, unmarried.

417-2. LUTHER, unmarried, and living in Foxborough.

417-3. CHAUNCY BUSHNELL, born May, 1850, and died Oct., 1850.

## 181. DANIEL.                                    Rochester, N. H.

**418.** JAMES ELBRIDGE, born Nov. 30, 1826, and married, Sept. 29, 1852, Mary E. Morrill, daughter of Joseph and Nancy Morrill of Dover, N. H. He graduated at Jefferson Medical College, Philadelphia. He superintends a very extensive mercantile business in Dover, N. H.; has represented his city in the legislature; fills many offices of trust in Dover, as President or Director of corporations; is President of Cocheco Bank, and Mayor of Dover. No children.

**419.** JOHN COLBY, born Sept. 12, 1828, and married (1), Dec. 11, 1848, Lydia B. Hanson. She died July 8, 1868. Married (2), Jan. 26, 1870, Judith A. Mills. Carries on an extensive and successful mercantile business in Great Falls, N. H., where he is prominent in church and Sabbath-school work, and influential in all matters of public interest.

**420.** DANIEL, born Aug. 11, 1831, and married (1), July 25, 1860, Ellen J., daughter of Joseph and Nancy Morrill of Dover, N. H. She died Mar. 22, 1880. Married (2), Oct. 4, 1881, Harriett Mulford, daughter of Sidney M. and Harriett Mulford Stone of New Haven, Conn. He founded the publishing house of D. Lothrop & Co., one of the largest and most widely-known in America. Inheriting, in large measure, the marked characteristics of his Puritan ancestry, he originated the business at a time when great difficulties blocked the way, and the extremest caution and sagacity were needful for its development. A wise discrimination in the selection of manuscripts, and a resolute purpose to issue only publication · helpful and educational in the best sense, have secured for this house its solid reputation of to-day. Mr. Lothrop is, as from the first, its sole manager.

In 1848, the three brothers, James E., John C., and Daniel, formed the partnership which has continued, without interruption, for thirty-six years. Although each brother is engaged in a different business in the city in which he resides, their interests are one, and the unanimity of feeling perfect.

**421.** MATTHEW HENRY, born Jan. 1, 1851, and married, Dec. 15, 1875, Olive S., daughter of Albert H. and Sarah Locke Littlefield.

**422.** MARY SOPHIA, born Aug. 15, 1853, and married, Dec. 19, 1871, Charles W. Fisher. Children:

    i.   Mary Viletta Fisher, born Feb. 1, 1877.

    ii.  Charlotte Eleanor Fisher, born Aug. 22, 1879.

## 182. CALEB.

**423.** HANNAH, born Nov. 11, 1806, and died May 1, 1807.

**424.** ALBERT, born Sept. 7, 1808, and married, Feb. 10, 1853, Elmira Simpson of Hamden, Maine. She was born May 30, 1822, and is now living in Easton (1883).

**425.** JOSEPH BRADFORD, born Nov. 15, 1809, and married, July 6, 1831, Mary D. Stetson, daughter of Lot Stetson of Pembroke. She was born Nov. 11, 1817. They are now living in Easton (1883).

**426.** OLIVE, born July 13, 1811, and died unmarried, May 27, 1867.

**427.** HANNAH ELLIS, born Aug. 23, 1814, and married, July 2, 1840, Almon

(No. 310), son of Zephaniah Lothrop of West Bridgewater. He was born Oct. 13, 1815, and died May 15, 1857.

428. CALEB STRONG, born May 27, 1817, and married, Nov. 26, 1852; Laura Holbrook of Stoughton, Mass. She was born Dec. 5, 1820.

429. HARRIET NUEL, born Nov. 25, 1818, and died Feb. 22, 1829.

430. JOHN BROOKS, born May 27, 1821. Unmarried, and lives in Easton.

431. DEBORAH MARIA, born June 7, 1823. Unmarried, and lives in Easton.

432. SHEPHEARD, born Jan. 16, 1826, and died Apr. 30, 1837.

433. CHARLES FOX, born June 19, 1828, and married, Nov. 19, 1868, Annie A. Blanchard of West Bridgewater. She was born Nov., 1840.

## 183. JOSHUA.

434. PRESCOTT, born May 11, 1809, and married (i), Betsey Tubbs; (2), Lucinda Keeler.

435. ELIZA, born Mar. 29, 1811, and married, June 5, 1831. Joseph Towne. Children:

    i.    Joseph Hiram Towne, married May Boardman of Amesbury, Mass., where they live.

    ii.    John Towne, died young.

    iii.    Martha Towne, married P. Tileston of Randolph, Mass.

    iv.    John Davis Towne, died young.

    v.    Enoch Henry Towne, married Sarah Gale of Amesbury. They live in Worcester, Mass.

    vi.    Mary Elizabeth Towne, married John Simmons of Stoughton.

436. DAVIS, born June 21, 1812. Unmarried. He died at sea.

437. MARDA, born Aug. 1, 1815, and married (1), Thomas Braman of Norton, Mass; (2), William Woodward of Taunton, Mass. Children:

    i.    Cordelia Braman, married William Smith. Lives in New Hampshire.

    ii.    Jane Woodward.

    iii.    Alice Woodward.

    iv.    William Woodward.

    v.    Ida Woodward.

438. MARY, born Oct. 20, 1817, and married Levi Briggs of Randolph.

    i.    Luther Briggs, died unmarried.

    ii.    Eddy Briggs, died unmarried.

    iii.    Herbert Briggs, married, and living in Randolph.

439. SARAH S., born Dec. 22, 1819, and married, May 29, 1842, Addison C., son of Thomas Wetherell, of Taunton. He was born Aug. 15, 1819. Children:

    i.    Edwin Wetherell, born June 21, 1843, and died Aug. 26, 1843.

    ii.    Sarah Adelaide Wetherell, born Aug. 21, 1844, and married Charles Wetherell of Taunton.

    iii.    Clarence E. Wetherell, born May 27, 1853, and married Elizabeth Pinkerton of Taunton.

**440.** Joshua, born Sept. 8, 1822, and married (I), Adelaide Bacon of Charlton, Mass.; (2), Emily Bacon. Lives in Pawtucket, R. I. (1883).

**441.** Ruth S., born Oct. 24, 1824, and died Dec. 3, 1845, unmarried.

**442.** Vesta, born Dec. 22, 1826, and married Ezekiel Briggs of Randolph. No children.

**443.** Edwin R., born Jan. 4, 1829, and married Lydia Graham of Pawtucket, R. I.

**444.** Harriet N., born Aug. 9, 1831, and died Nov. 17, 1850, unmarried.

### 186-1. ABRAHAM. Buckfield, Me.

**445.** Hannah, born Aug., 1804, married Morris Dodge of Hallowell, Me. Children:

   i.  Charles Morris Dodge.

   ii.  Hannah Elizabeth Dodge.

   iii.  Adelbert Green Dodge.

**446.** Content, born Sept. 19, 1811, married (1), Harrison Davee of Hebron, Me.; (2), John True of Livermore, Me.

#### (Children by First Husband.)

   i.  William Gerrish Davee.

   ii.  Christiana Dacey Davee.

   iii.  Hannah Francis Davee.

   iv.  Houaton Davee.

   v.  Orinton Davee.

   vi.  Pauline Evelyn Davee.

   vii.  Ann Sarah Davee.

   viii.  Joseph Eliot Davee.

   ix.  Almira Ellen Davee.

   x.  Susan Davee.

All living in Hebron, March, 1884.

No children by second husband.

**447.** Emeline, born Sept., 1815, married Leander Hodgdon of Buckfield, Me. No children.

**448.** Delphina Paris, born Oct. 25, 1817, married, Apr. 27, 1843, her cousin, Edward Wilkinson Lothrop. (See No. 460.)

**449.** Elmira Cummings, born Sept. 12, 1820, married, in 1844, George Murdock of Hebron, Me. One child: Harmon Murdock, living in Auburn, Me.

**450.** Joseph Packard, born Mar. 21, 1822, married, Feb. 14, 1844, Margery Ann Bryant of Scarborough, Me. He died in the late war. She died in 1878.

**451.** Matilda, born Oct. 28, 1825, married William Morrill of Buckfield, Me. Children:

   i.  Walter Morrill, died unmarried.

   ii.  Emma Morrill.

   iii.  Flora Morrill.

   iv.  Agnes Morrill.

   v.  Roderick Morrill.

   vi.  Addie Morrill.

   vii.  George Morrill.

452. ELIAS TAYLOR, born May 12, 1829, married (1), Juliette Oliver, who was born Apr., 1838, and died Aug. 16, 1860; (2), Elvira A. Oliver, sister of his first wife. She died in 1870. He died May 20, 1874. They lived in Stoughton, Mass. He served in the late war.

## 186-5. EDWARD. Maine.

453. JACOB, married Elizabeth Wallace of Stoughton, Mass. They live in Sumner, Me.

454. JANE, married Mr. Cooper. No children.

455. BETHUEL, living in Buckfield, Me. Unmarried.

456. Louisa, living in Buckfield, Me. Unmarried.

457. Abigail, married Mr. Farr. She is now dead.

458. BETHIA, married Granville Chaflin. They live in Norway, Me.

459. REBECCA, died unmarried.

460. EDWARD WILKINSON, born Jan. 16, 1813, married, Apr. 27, 1843, Delphina Paris Lothrop. (See No. 448.) He died in Stoughton, Mass., in 1870.

## 187. SYLVANUS. Allegheny City, Pa.

461. HETTIE STOCKTON, Allegheny City.

462. MARY STEVENSON, married Byron H. Painter of Pittsburgh, Pa. He died in 1870, leaving two children:

   i.   George Edward Painter.

   ii.  Charles Albert Painter.

463. ANNE BUCK. married Frederic R. Fowler of New York City. She died, leaving one child, Sylvanus Lothrop Fowler.

464. MARTHA STOCKTON, married William P. Weyman. He died in 1877. Children:

   i.   Annie Lothrop Weyman.

   ii.  Helen Eliza Alden Weyman.

465. JOSEPH ALDEN, married Helen Bidwell. They live in Pittsburgh, Pa.

466. CLARA STOCKTON, married George G. McMurtry of Pittsburgh, Pa. Children:

   i.   Charles W. McMurtry.

   ii.  George McMurtry.

   iii.  Alden Lothrop McMurtry.

   iv.  Edward Painter McMurtry.

## 189. SAMUEL. Adrian, Mich.

467. RUFUS, died.

468. A SON, died.

## 197. ZEBADIAH. Philadelphia, Pa.

469. SARAH ELIZA, born in Philadelphia, Jan. 8, 1826, and married, Jan. 31, 1851, Richard Henry Lee, who was also born in Philadelphia, May 13, 1826. They have lived in Philadelphia, where they have had five children, all born in Philadelphia:

   i.    Eliza Lothrop Lee, born Nov. 18, 1854.
   ii.   Edward Clinton Lee, born Dec. 5, 1857.
   iii.  Emile Duval Lee, born Mar. 24, 1863.
   iv.  William Jenks Lee, born June 5, 1865.
   v.   Helen Randolph Lee, born Feb. 10, 1869, and died July 21, 1869.

470. HELEN EARLE, born in Philadelphia, Aug. 5, 1839, and married Edmund D. Randolph, who was born in Philadelphia, Aug. 26, 1839. They have had six children, all born in Philadelphia:

   i.    Margaret Randolph.
   ii.   Edmund Randolph.
   iii.  Helen Randolph.
   iv.  Charles Randolph.
   v.   Mary Randolph.
   vi.  Cornelia Randolph.

471. CHARLES BROWN, born in Philadelphia, Aug. 25, 1841, and married, Feb. 7, 1866, Deborah Kuhl Kelly, who was born in Philadelphia, Dec. 24, 1840. He is in the wholesale dry goods business in New York City, at 100 Worth street.

## 198. TIMOTHY.            Rochester, N. Y.

472. JANE SAXTON, married George H. Roberts of Syracuse.

473. ELIEL GILBERT, married in Syracuse.

## 204. DARIUS R.            Sharon, Mass.

474. HOWARD BELDEN, born Oct. 16, 1842, and married, Nov. 26, 1868, widow Anna Louisa Waldron, daughter of Thomas and Anne Andrews of Smithfield, R. I. She was born Nov. 20, 1836. They live in Taunton.

475. JOHN FITCH, born Dec. 17, 1847, and married, Oct. 16, 1872, Mary L. Tucker of Hardwick, Mass. They live in Newton, Mass.

## 216. HENRY WOOD.            Providence, R. I.

476. HENRY GREENE, born July 3, 1828; died Aug. 24, 1830.

477. CHRISTOPHER, born Aug. 22, 1831; died Feb. 3, 1833.

478. ZEBADIAH, born Dec. 3, 1833; died Sept. 29, 1840.

479. HENRY WOOD, JR., born Jan. 27, 1841.

## 237. EDWARD.            Dudswell, C. E.

480. WILLIAM HENRY, born in Eaton, C. E., and married Martha Louisa, daughter of Tyler and Nancy Parker.

481. MARY ANN, married Daniel Harrison Winslow, son of Samuel and Abby Winslow of Canada. Children:

   i.    Edward Augustus Winslow.
   ii.   Phebe Genet Winslow.
   iii.  Cynthia Adaline Winslow.
   iv.  Darwin Halsey Winslow.
   v.   Zerah Evans Winslow.

    vi.   Jonas Osgood Winslow.

    vii.  Persis Annette Winslow.

    482. PERSIS, married Zerah Evans, a native of Lyndon, Vt. She is dead. Children:

    ·i.   Charles Holloway Evans.

    ii.  William Henry Evans.

    iii.  Albert Hart Evans.

    iv.  George Calhoun Evans.

    v.   Jonas Herbert Evans.

    vi.  Frederick Alanson Evans.

    482. WELLINGTON, married Mary Hurd, daughter of Elisha and Sarah (Willard) Todd. She died in Stoke, C. E.

    483. ANNETE, married Zerah Evans. They have no children.

    484. PHEBE AMES, deceased.

    485. HORACE, married Ruby Ann Forbes, daughter of David and Rachel (Spaulding) Forbes.

    486. THOMAS, died in Dudswell, unmarried.

    487. ADALINE, born in Dudswell, Apr. 11, 1843, and is now living with her eldest brother.

## 241. CYRUS.        Stoke, C. E.

    488. CYRUS STUART, married Harriet, daughter of Lewis S. and Julia (Alexander) Arnold. Have two children.

    489. ERASTUS REED, married, and has four children. Resides in Dudswell.

    490. EDWARD HOWARD, died young.

    491. ALFRED TRUMAN, married, and has four children. Resides in Dudswell.

    492. CYNTHIA ROWENA, married ——— Bishop, and has five children. Resides in Dudswell.

    493. FREEMAN HOWARD, unmarried, and resides in Stoke.

    494. SIMEON COLBURN, unmarried, and resides in Stoke.

## 241. STILLMAN.        Boston, Mass.

    495. A CHILD, born and died May 3, 1809.

    496. STILLMAN LUTHER, born in Boston, June 27, 1811. He married, Dec. 23, 1839, Abigail Robbins of Lexington, Mass. He was educated for the ministry. His wife was the daughter of Eli and Hannah Simonds of Lexington, and was born there Dec. 5, 1814. He died of yellow fever, Nov. 22, 1859, at St. Croix, West Indies, whither he had gone for his health. He was the only son of the late Dea. Stillman Lothrop, and was a person of delicate health. He was educated at Brown University, Rhode Island, and studied for the ministry at Newton Theological Institution, Mass. He was a man of culture and refinement, great originality of thought, and remarkable conversational powers. He fully sympathised with his father in the cause of freedom and humanity. He was frequently obliged to travel for his health, and contemplated writing a history of his travels in California and Oregon, when he

48

was compelled, from the severity of our climate and failing health, to seek a milder clime. Soon after his arrival at the West Indies, he was prostrated by the yellow fever, and died at the age of 49.

497. ELIZA ANN, born in Boston, Apr. 27, 1816, and died in Watertown, Dec. 7, 1835; and of her it is recorded: "Her life was free from guile, her trust was in Christ."

### 244-2. BARNABAS. Randolph, Mass.

498. CALEB HOLBROOK, born in Randolph, Mass, Nov. 6, 1810, and married in Randolph, Oct. 13, 1836, Ann Maria, daughter of Captain Jonathan Cobb, who died May 14, 1839. He then married (2), in Oct., 1840, Sarah Cobb, her sister, who died Jan. 1, 1843; and he married (3), Sally, daughter of Nathan Perkins, Nov. 18, 1844. She died June 2, 1858, aged 61. He is a leather cutter, and lives in North Bridewater, Mass.

499. BARNABAS, born Oct. 12, 1813.

500. HENRY TISDALE, born May 22, 1817, and died young.

501. MARY ANN, born in Randolph, June 15, 1821, and married George Bradford Dubois, of Braintree, Vt., who died Mar. 15, 1847. They had but one child, that died in infancy.

502. HENRY TISDALE, born in Randolph, Mar. 6, 1823, and graduated at Amherst College in 1844, and in Theology at the East Windsor Institute, in 1847. He married, in Auburn, N. Y., May 13, 1851, Jane, daughter of Uriah and Sally (North) Benedict, Ledyard, N. Y. Ordained Home Missionary at Palmyra, Wis., Sept. 11, 1850.

503. ELEANOR, born Feb. 26, 1827, and married Warren Edwards Wilkins of Salem, Mass. They settled in Brattleboro, Vt., and have had three children:

    i.    Eddie Wilkins, who died young.

    ii.    Mary Ella Wilkins.

    iii.    Anna Holbrook Wilkins.

504. EDWARD EVERETT, born May 17, 1833, and married Myra S. Lyon.

### 244-3. EDWARD. Boston, Mass.

505. EDWARD AUGUSTUS, born in Boston, Sept. 11, 1813, graduated at Brown in 1835, and studied law with Richard Fletcher, Esq., of Boston, but died before entering on his profession.

506. GEORGE WHITFIELD, died young.

507. ELIZABETH, born June 8, 1817, and died Dec. 20, 1820.

508. SARAH HILL, born Dec. 19, 1819, and married, Oct. 7, 1844, as his second wife, Lewis Tappan, son of Solomon and Sarah (Tappan) Stoddard of Northampton, who was born Feb. 8, 1807, and who died July 6, 1865. They resided in Boston, Mass. She died Dec. 17, 1863. Children:

    i.    Edward Lathrop Stoddard, born July 11, 1845, and is now (1873) assistant pastor of Dr. Bancroft, of Christ church, Brooklyn, N. Y.

    ii.    John Lawson Stoddard, born Apr. 24, 1850, and now (1873) a student of theology in the New Haven Theological Seminary.

iii. Frederick Tappan Stoddard, born Sept. 24, 1854, and died May 21, 1855.

iv. David Tappan Stoddard, born Aug. 4, 1858, and died Sept. 2, 1858.

509. EMMA LINCOLN, born in Boston, Nov. 8, 1822, and married, in San Joaquin, Cal., Nov. 9, 1854, Timothy, son of Nehemiah and Martha R. Hoyt, who was born in Cato, N. Y., Oct. 5, 1826. He is a real estate broker, and now lives in New York. Children:

i. Martha Elizabeth Hoyt, born on Ship Ringleader, south latitude, 7°, 48′, west longitude, 34° 30′, in sight of Pernambuco, S. A., Dec. 7, 1857.

ii. Edward Nehemiah Hoyt, born in Cayuga Co., N. Y., May 30, 1859.

511. MARY, born in Boston, Dec. 14, 1824. In the autumn of 1829, she was seized with a lingering sickness, from which she was never fully to recover. The following spring, a spinal disease set in, and her rest and relief from suffering were not reached until Friday morning, Mar. 18, 1831.

512. JOHN LAWSON, born Apr. 5, 1827, and died Jan. 2, 1849. Though so young, he showed with great distinctness some of the most delightful of the Christian graces.

513. CHARLOTTE ELIZABETH, born Mar. 17, 1829, and died Mar. 26, 1851.

514. ELIAS CORNELIUS, born Mar. 31, 1831, and died in Marysville, Cal., May 12, 1865.

EIGHTH GENERATION.

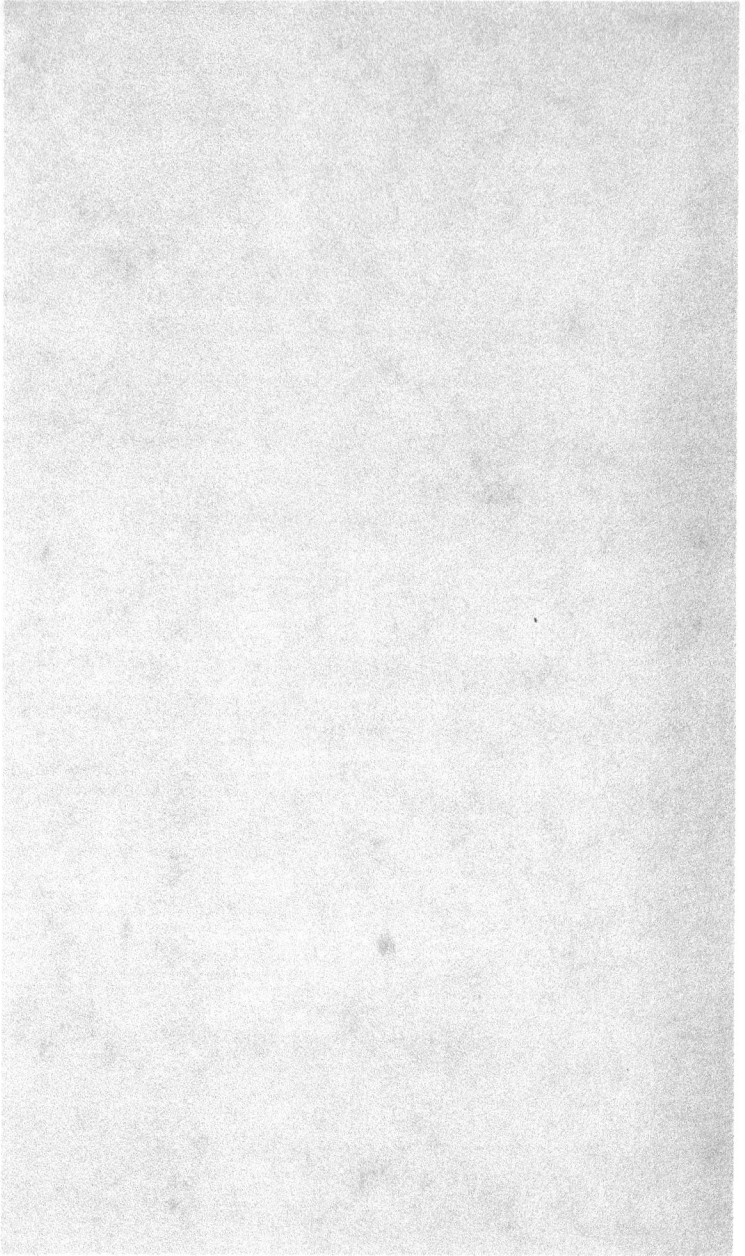

## 287. CYRUS H. Taunton, Mass.

556. FREDERICK G., born Sept. 4, 1854, and died June 16, 1856.
557. MINNIE A., born Aug. 16, 1856, and died Sept. 10, 1864.
558. CHARLES GODFREY, born July 29, 1859, and died Dec. 15, 1867.
559. FRANK H., born June 16, 1867.

## 288. REV. CHARLES D. Amherst, Mass.

560. ANNA MARIA, born in Attleboro, June 3, 1856.
561. MARY SEABURY, born Mar 31, 1858.
562. EMMA HOWARD, born at Norton, June 16, 1860.
563. CHARLES FREDERICK, born Jan. 17, 1862.

## 294. ALMON.

564. LYDIA A., born March 10, 1841. Now living in Easton.

## 306. JOHN E. West Bridgewater, Mass.

565. AZEL.
566. ELIZABETH.
567. FRANCIS.
568. WALDO.
568. HERBERT.
570. JULIA A.

## 315. AMASA. New York City.

571. MICHAEL MILTON, born in 1858, in St. Mary's Town, La., and is now (1875) living in Houma, Terre Bonne parish, La.

## 323. WILBUR C. Denver, Col.

572. ROLLIN CULVER, born in Denver, Col., Aug. 27, 1869.
573. BESSIE PAULINE, born Sept. 28, 1875.
574. ROLLIN CLARENCE WILBUR, twin with Bessie, born Sept. 28, 1875.

## 329. PHILIP. Leominster, Mass.

575. FRANK ORVILLE, born Jan. 1, 1851, and married, Oct. 29, 1873, Susie Emily Damon of Cohoes, N. Y.
576. ELLA JULIETTE, born Feb. 4, 1857, and married, June 6, 1878, Charles Henry Graves of Ludlow, Vt. One child:
    i. Louis Whitney Graves, born July 21, 1880.
577. FREDERICK JOSEPH, born Feb. 19, 1859, and married, Dec. 13, 1882, Nellie Louisa Pierce of Westminster.

## 332. JASON. Lancaster, Wis.

578. EMELINE H., born in Lexington, Mass., May 16, 1837, and died in Jamestown, Wis., Oct. 27, 1848.

49

579. GEORGE C., born in Jamestown, Wis., Feb. 13, 1840. He married in Jamestown, Mar. 25, 1866, Caroline, daughter of Isaac and James Richards. He is a farmer, and is now living in Howard County, Nebraska. He was a soldier in the recent war, serving in the same corps with his brother Alonzo.

580. ALONZO H., born in Jamestown, Wis., Dec. 19, 1841. He is a physician, and is practicing in Howard County, Nebraska. He enlisted in 1862 in the Union Army, Co. I, 25th regiment, Wisconsin Volunteers. He was at the fall of Vicksburg, and afterwards accompanied Sherman's march to the sea. He served later in North Carolina, and at the close of the war was honorably discharged.

581. FRANK B., born in Jamestown, Wis., July 3, 1844, and married in the same town, Jan. 1, 1869, Katie M. McCallum, daughter of Archie and Margaret McCallum. He is a carpenter, and is settled in Dubuque, Ia. He was also a volunteer with his brother Alonzo in the recent war.

582. AGNES M., born in Lancaster, June 28, 1848, and married in Cassville, Wis., Oct. 5, 1871, a Lawrence, son of William and Jemima Lawrence, who is a carpenter, and in business in St. Louis, Missouri.

583. ADELAIDE, born in Jamestown, Wis., Feb. 13, 1852, and died Feb. 23, 1868.

584. ELLA F., born in Jamestown, Wis., Jan. 9, 1854.

### 333. DAVID W. West Medway, Mass.

585. PHILIP CLAPP, born in Boston, Oct., 1848, and died at eighteen months of age.

586. ERSKINE, born in West Medford, Dec. 30, 1854, and now engaged in the freight department of the railroad.

### 346. CHARLES D. New York City.

587. CAROLINE, born Sept. 14, 1841, and married William Stearns of Acton, where they live. No children.

588. EMORY DARWIN, born in 1844, and married in Milford, where he lives.

589. ALVIN MASON, born in 1846, and is clerk in the dry goods business in Boston.

590. FRANKLIN BYRON.

### 349. WILLIAM R. Acton, Mass.

591. CLARA J., born at Acton, Aug. 22, 1850, and married, at Boston, Nov. 5, 1873, James E. Walker of Milford, Mass.

### 350. JOHN J. Acton, Mass.

592. ALBERT H., born at Acton, Apr. 24, 1846. Now living at San Francisco, Cal.

### 351. HENRY O. Boston, Mass.

593. WILLIAM H., born at Milford, Sept. 8, 1851. Now living at Boston.

594. GEORGE J., born at Milford, Jan. 26, 1853. Now living at Boston.

Three other children of Henry O. and Rebecca W. Lothrop died a short time after birth.

## 355. SOLOMON. Leeds, Me.

595. GEORGE DANIEL, born in Leeds, Aug. 24, 1811, and married, at same place, April, 1835, Huldah, daughter of Col. John Gilmore of Leeds. He remained in Leeds until 1864, when he went West, and is now supposed to be dead. His wife died Nov. 30, 1862.

596. BETSEY, born in Leeds, Dec. 13, 1813, and married, in Sept, 1833, Joshua S., son of Lewis Turner of Leeds, where they settled. Their three children, born in Leeds, were:

    i.  Ermina Jane Turner, born Aug. 6, 1834, and married E. D. Hamleton of Augusta, Me.

    ii.  Emma Clark Turner, born Jan. 13, 1837, and married James Norris of Augusta, Me. They have had one child, born and died in Jan., 1869.

    iii.  Francis Armon Turner, born Apr. 16, 1839, and married Nancy Wells of Augusta, Me.

597. SOLOMON LEAVITT, born in Leeds, June 10, 1817, and married, Apr. 20, 1840, Hannah, daughter of George Turner, Esq., of Leeds. He is now living at Leeds.

598. ORISSA, born in Leeds, Dec. 30, 1819, and married, June 20, 1842, Alson Lothrop, Jun., son of Alson of Jay, where they settled. They have had eight children, all born in Jay.

599. WILLARD, born in Leeds, June 18, 1828, and married in Jan., 1860, Emeline, daughter of Rev. Samuel Boothby of Lewiston, Me.

## 357. LEAVITT. Leeds, Me.

600. ELIAS, married Jane Morse, who died in California. Married, and left two children, Dan and Mary. He graduated at Bowdoin college, studied law, and resides in New Orleans.

601. DAVIS FRANCIS, married. Has been a member of the Maine Legislature from Leeds. Has four or five children.

602. CAROLINE LANE, married —— Foss.

603. WARREN LANE, died single in Florida, in 1866. Was colonel of 1st Missouri Artillery in the Mexican War, and Chief of Artillery on Sherman's staff, and on Pope's staff.

604. MARY JANE, married Charles Lane. Has one child.

## 382. RUFUS D.

605. CHARLES L., born in Rowley, Mass., Feb. 2, 1814.

606. NAHUM MORREL, born in Georgetown, Mar. 2, 1817.

## 383. SULLIVAN.

607. DANIEL O. Now living in New York State, near Malone.

### 384. ALSON. Jay, Me.

[This family were all born in Jay.]

608. EDWIN H., born Mar. 11, 1843, and married, in 1868, Addie Baldwin of Canada. They have two children.

609. EMERY R., born Sept. 14, 1844, and married a daughter of John Dailey of Canton. They have one child.

610. SARAH E., born Aug. 23, 1847.

611. FREDERICK T., born May 29, 1850.

612. GEORGE H., born Nov. 6, 1853.

613. HULDAH T., born Jan. 13, 1856.

614. SOLOMON W., born July 15, 1858.

615. LEWIS L., born Sept. 17, 1860.

### 387. LOYAL C. Malone, N. Y.

616. MARY L., born in Malone, Jan. 31, 1838, and married, May 1, 1861, Charles W. Allen.

617. WARREN, born in Malone, Sept. 16, 1841, and died in the same place Feb. 27, 1864.

### 390. GEORGE D. Chicago, Ill.

618. SARAH C., born June 26, 1844, and married, Feb. 28, 1865, Sylvester S. Willard of Waterbury, N. Y.

619. GEORGE W., born in Malone, Nov. 15, 1847.

620. LESLIE L., born in Malone, Feb. 28, 1851, and married, Aug. 12, 1873, Hattie G. Barnes, who was born in Boston, Mass., in Feb. 1847.

621. CARRIE A., born in Malone, July 1, 1862.

### 393. CORNELIUS W. Taunton, Mass.

622. CHARLES HENRY, born Sept. 3, 1831, married (1) Sept. 1, 1856, Sarah E., daughter of Charles Loring of Ellsworth, Me., and (2) May 6, 1873, Sarah V., daughter of Rev. John Naille of Elizabethtown, Pa. She was born Dec. 26, 1840. He commenced teaching school when sixteen years of age, and taught several years in Taunton and vicinity. He was educated at Brown University, Providence, R. I., and graduated at the New York Medical College, in 1858. He then located himself in Lyons, Iowa, where he soon attained a good rank in his profession. When the war of the rebellion opened he volunteered his services, and for the four years of the struggle did excellent service as assistant surgeon, and surgeon of the First Regiment of Cavalry of the Iowa Veteran Volunteers. He was present in not less than fifty-two engagements. He is a member of the Iowa and Illinois Central Medical Association, the Iowa State Medical Society, and the American Medical Association. He has also been an efficient president of the Clinton County Medical Society, a member of the examining committee of the Medical Department Iowa State University, and since 1868 an examining surgeon for pensions. He is author of the Medical and Surgical Directory of Iowa, and has written several medical essays, some of which have been published in the Boston Medical and Surgical Journal.

623. THOMAS JACKSON, born Mar. 2, 1834, and married, Aug. 24, 1858, Catherine Prescott, daughter of Prof. John W. and Harriet Hickling Webster of Cambridge, Mass. He attended country schools until about thirteen years of age, fitted for college at Bristol Academy, in Taunton, and entered Harvard in July, 1850. While in college, he taught school in Taunton three winters. He graduated in 1854, and immediately sailed from Boston for Fayal, where he remained nearly three years as private tutor in the family of Frederick Dabney, American Vice-Consul for the Azores. He returned to Taunton in May, 1857, studied law and was admitted to the bar in September, 1858. In May, 1859, he formed a law partnership with Hon. John Daggett of Attleboro', who was then Register of Probate and Insolvency for Bristol County. In the autumn of 1861, he joined the " Taunton Light Guard," one of the companies of the 4th Mass. regiment. Sept. 2, 1862, was appointed quartermaster of the regiment, and soon afterwards post quartermaster for Camp " Joe Hooker," Lakeville, Mass. In December, 1862, he was re-appointed quartermaster, and left camp with the regiment above named, which formed a part of the " Banks Expedition " to Louisiana. While in Louisiana, he was detailed for a time to act as port commissary at Brashear City. He returned to Massachusetts with the regiment in August, 1863. In November, 1863, he was elected a representative from Taunton to the Legislature of Massachusetts, and in November, 1864, was elected treasurer of Bristol County, and held the office nine years. He was for several years treasurer of the Old Colony Historical Society, and for eighteen years a member of the School Committee of Taunton, having been elected first in 1859. In June, 1867, he was chosen treasurer of the Taunton Tack Company, and in June, 1868, was made agent, as well as treasurer, and since that time has had the general management of the company. He is a commissioner to qualify civil officers, a trustee of the Bristol County Savings Bank, and a director and one of the managing committee of the Central Manufacturing Company of Boston. He has also been an active member of the Massachusetts and New England Woman Suffrage Associations, and was one of the originators of the Prohibitory party of Massachusetts.

623-1. S. ELLEN, born Mar. 24, 1840, and married, Mar. 18, 1862, Theodore G., son of Theodore L. Lincoln of Taunton, where they still reside. Children:

    i.    Frederick Theodore Lincoln, born in Taunton, Apr. 26, 1863.
    ii.    Louis Lothrop Lincoln, born in Taunton, Nov. 1, 1870.
    iii.    Alfred Newland Lincoln, born in Taunton, Dec. 15, 1871.
    iv.    Frank Oscar Lincoln, born in Taunton, Jan. 21, 1874.
    v.    Helen Beatrice Lincoln, born in Taunton, July 18, 1876.

### 400.  WARREN H.                Taunton, Mass.

[All born in Taunton.]

624. FRANCIS W., born Sept. 29, 1849, and married, Feb. 23, 1872, Martha E., daughter of George Rounds of Rehoboth, Mass. They live in Taunton.

625. EDNA A., born Apr. 28, 1851, and married, Jan. 14, 1873, Henry F., son of Theodore L. Lincoln of Taunton, where they are settled.

626. HARRIET F., born Dec. 1, 1857, and married, June 5, 1883, William Hartshorn of Walpole, Mass.

627. MAY, born Mar. 10, 1865, and died Apr. 17, 1865.

### 404. EUGENE TERRY.        Brockton, Mass.

628. LAWRENCE E.
629. BRADFORD V.
630. SARAH M.
631. DANIEL J.
632. RUTH C.
633. LENA W.

### 405. WILLIAM HENRY.        Easton, Mass.

634. HARRY AVERY, born March 19, 1876.
635. ELLEN AUGUSTA, born April 17, 1881.

### 407. MELVIN OTIS.        Norton, Mass.

636. EVERETT M., born Feb. 9, 1852, married Feb. 5, 1875, Mary Ann Clifford.

### 407-1. EVERETT M.

637. FANNY ELIZABETH, born Feb. 26, 1877.

### 410. JAMES.        Raynham, Mass.

638. CLARENCE, born in 1853, married in 1880, Elizabeth, daughter of Seth D. Hall of Raynham. They live in Brockton, Mass.
639. HERBERT, born in 1861. Not married.

### 411-2. NATHAN CHAPMAN.        Deerfield, N. H.

640. ORMSBY ADDISON, born in 1867.
641. FANNY BELLE, born in 1870.

### 419. JOHN C.        Great Falls, N. H.

642. FRANCIS TIMOTHY, born Oct. 21, 1849.
643. ALPHONZO, born May 20, 1856, and died Sept. 4, 1875.
644. MYRA, born July 8, 1858.
645. BERTHA, born July 20, 1864.
646. JOHN C., born July, 1868, and died Feb., 1869.
647. LYDIA MAY, died in infancy.
648. DANIEL J., born July 1, 1876.

### 420. DANIEL.        Boston, Mass.

649. WINIFRED HERBERT, born June 1, 1861, and died Aug. 4, 1861.

### 421. MATTHEW HENRY.

650. THOMAS WILFRED, born Dec. 19, 1876.
651. HAROLD L., born Aug. 7, 1881.

### 424. ALBERT.        Easton, Mass.

652. WILLIAM HERBERT, born Dec. 6, 1853, and married, Nov. 18, 1875. Eugenia Morton of Easton. She was born in Nov. 1858. No children.

653. LEONORA NANCY, born Aug. 17, 1855, and married, March 5, 1878, Warren D. Jones of Brockton. He was born Nov. 15, 1852. Children:

    i.  Bertha Warren Jones, born Nov. 14, 1879, and died May 11, 1882.

    ii.  Florence, born Nov. 18, 1881.

### 425. JOSEPH BRADFORD.      Easton, Mass.

654. HARRIET ANNA, born Mar. 29, 1836, and married, in 1872, George R. Marshall of Newport, R. I. Child:

    i.  George B. Marshall, born Aug. 7, 1874.

655. MARY WINSLOW, born May 1, 1838, and died Nov. 15, 1838.

656. ALBERT S. B., born June 27, 1852, and married, June 5, 1882, Ella L. Caswell of Fitchburg, Mass. They live in Easton.

### 428. CALEB STRONG.      Easton, Mass.

657. WILLIAM BROOKS, born June 1, 1855.

658. LAURA L., born Jan. 12, 1858, and married, July 3, 1877, Thomas W. Howard of Easton. Child:

    i.  Earl T. Howard, born May, 1880.

659. GEORGE HECTOR, born June 27, 1860.

### 433. CHARLES FOX.      Easton, Mass.

660. EMILY E., born Jan. 19, 1871.

661. CHARLES C., born Apr. 5, 1875.

### 434. PRESCOTT.

*(First Wife's Children.)*

662. ALICE, died young.

663. CORDELIA, died young.

664. ELBRIDGE, married Jane Edson of West Bridgewater, and lives in Weymouth, Mass.

665. OZIN, married, and died in 1884 in Rockland, Mass.

666. IRVING, died in the late war, unmarried.

*(Second Wife's Children.)*

667. ALICE, died young.

668. ALZEDA, marrried Josiah Loud of Weymouth.

### 440. JOSHUA.      Pawtucket, R. I.

*(First Wife's Children.)*

669. FRANK, died young.

670. ADELBERT, lives in Pawtucket, R. I.

671. HENRY, died unmarried.

### 413. EDWIN R.

672. LILLIE MAY, born in Apr., 1865, and married Frank Cook of Taunton, Mass.

### 450. JOSEPH PACKARD. Scarborough, Me.

673. MELISSA ANNA.

674. ELIAS ATWOOD.

675. NANCY.

676. JOSEPH ARETAS.

677. ELLSWORTH.

678. EDWARD.

679. HANNAH.

### 452. ELIAS TAYLOR. Stoughton, Mass.

*(First Wife's Children.)*

680. FRED PIERCE, born Mar. 26, 1854, and married widow Anna Crane. They live in South Braintree, Mass., and have no children.

681. WALDO FREMONT, born June 23, 1856, and died unmarried.

682. CHARLES MELVIN, born in 1858, and married, in 1883, Alice Crocker of Holbrook, Mass.

*(Second Wife's Children.)*

683. ELIAS BLAISDELL, born Feb. 24, 1862, and married, in 1883, Ida Peck of Holbrook, Mass.

### 460. EDWARD WILKINSON. Stoughton, Mass.

684. GEORGE WILKINSON, born Oct. 19, 1845, and married, Mar. 6, 1879, Nancy Ann McKenzie of Abington, Mass. They live in Stoughton.

685. ELLIS AMES, born Oct. 15, 1846, and married, Mar. 30, 1878, Emily Wales Hackett of Stoughton, Mass. She was born Apr. 20, 1856. They live in Stoughton, and have no children.

686. HARRIET ALMY, born Jan. 29, 1850, and married, May 6, 1876, Elisha S. Hawes of Stoughton. Children:

    i. George Malcolm Hawes, born Aug. 18, 1877.

    ii. Annie Mildred Hawes, born May 27, 1881.

687. DELPHINA ADELAIDE, born Sept. 14, 1851, and died Sept. 24, 1851.

688. MYRON WILSON, born Sept. 15, 1853, and married July 19, 1879, Annie E. Pierce.

689. HENRY WALLACE, born Jan. 16, 1856, and married Lelia Florence Barden. No children.

690. EDWARD ALBION, born Mar. 15, 1858, and died Sept. 17, 1858.

### 465. JOSEPH ALDEN. Pittsburgh, Pa.

691. MARY PAINTER.

692. ALICE BIDWELL.

### 471. CHARLES B. New York City.

693. CHARLES, born in New York City, Feb. 23, 1867.

694. WELLING, born in New York City, July 25, 1868, and died Feb. 14, 1870.

695. MARGARET KUHL, born in New York City, Aug. 11, 1872.

### 475. JOHN FITCH.

696. WILLIAM HOWARD, born Sept. 1, 1873.

697. STANLEY BELDEN, born July 6, 1881.

### 480. WILLIAM HENRY. Dudswell, Wolfe Co., C. E.

698. EDWARD.

699. JANE.

700. WILLIAM HENRY.

701. CYRUS.

702. THOMAS.

### 482. WELLINGTON. Dudswell, Wolfe Co., C. E.

703. PHEBE AMES, married Stephen Brazel of Eaton, C. E. They have one child:

   i. Wellington Stephen Brazel.

### 485. HORACE. Dudswell, Wolfe Co., C. E.

704. MARY LOUISA ALBERTA.

705. BERTHINA THANKFUL RACHEL.

### 488. CYRUS STUART.

706. AN INFANT, born in Fall River, Dec. 8, 1858, and died.

707. JULIA STUART, born in Fall River, Apr. 16, 1860.

708. HARRIET ARNOLD, born in Fall River, Sept. 2, 1867, and died May 27, 1870.

709. HOWARD, born in Cambridge, July 24, 1872.

### 489. ERASTUS R. Dudswell, Wolfe Co., C. E.

710. ⎫
711. ⎬ Four children, names not learned.
712. ⎪
713. ⎭

### 491. ALFRED T. Dudswell, Wolfe Co., C. E.

714. ⎫
715. ⎬ Four children, names not learned.
716. ⎪
717. ⎭

### 496. STILLMAN L. Boston and California.

718. STILLMAN FOLLEN, born in Lexington, Mass., May 1, 1841, and married, in Winchester, Mass., Nov. 18, 1867, Sarah Jane, daughter of Edward

50

and Frances Louisa (Doane) Holbrook, who was born in Boston, Jan. 24, 1844. He is a merchant of Boston, where he was one of the sufferers by the calamitous fire of 1873.

719. GEORGE LANGDON, born in Lexington, Mass, Jan. 27, 1846, and was educated at the Norwich University, Vt. He is a merchant, and in business in Portland, Me., of the firm of Lothrop, Devens & Co., importers and dealers in window shades, etc., 61 Exchange and 48 Market streets. He is unmarried.

### 498. CALEB H. North Bridgewater, Mass.

720. ANN MARIA, born July 17, 1841, and married, Nov. 5, 1865, Andrew Jackson of North Bridgewater. They have two children:

    i.   Lizzie Northrop Jackson, born Apr. 24, 1868.

    ii.  Nettie Maude Jackson, born Jan. 10, 1871.

721. GEORGE, born May 23, 1843, and died July 29, 1843.

722. NAHUM PERKINS, born Sept. 11, 1845, and married, Oct. 6, 1869, Maria S. Parker. He died Dec. 19, 1869.

723. LIZZIE PERKINS, born Sept 18, 1847, and died Apr. 26, 1867.

### 502. REV. HENRY T. Palmyra, Wis.

724. EDWARD EVERETT, born May 9, 1852.

725. IRVING TISDALE, born Jan. 25, 1857.

726. AILIE NORTH, born July 26, 1859.

727. CLARA HOLBROOK, born July 18, 1861.

### 504. EDWARD E.

728. HATTIE PHILLIPS.

NINTH GENERATION.

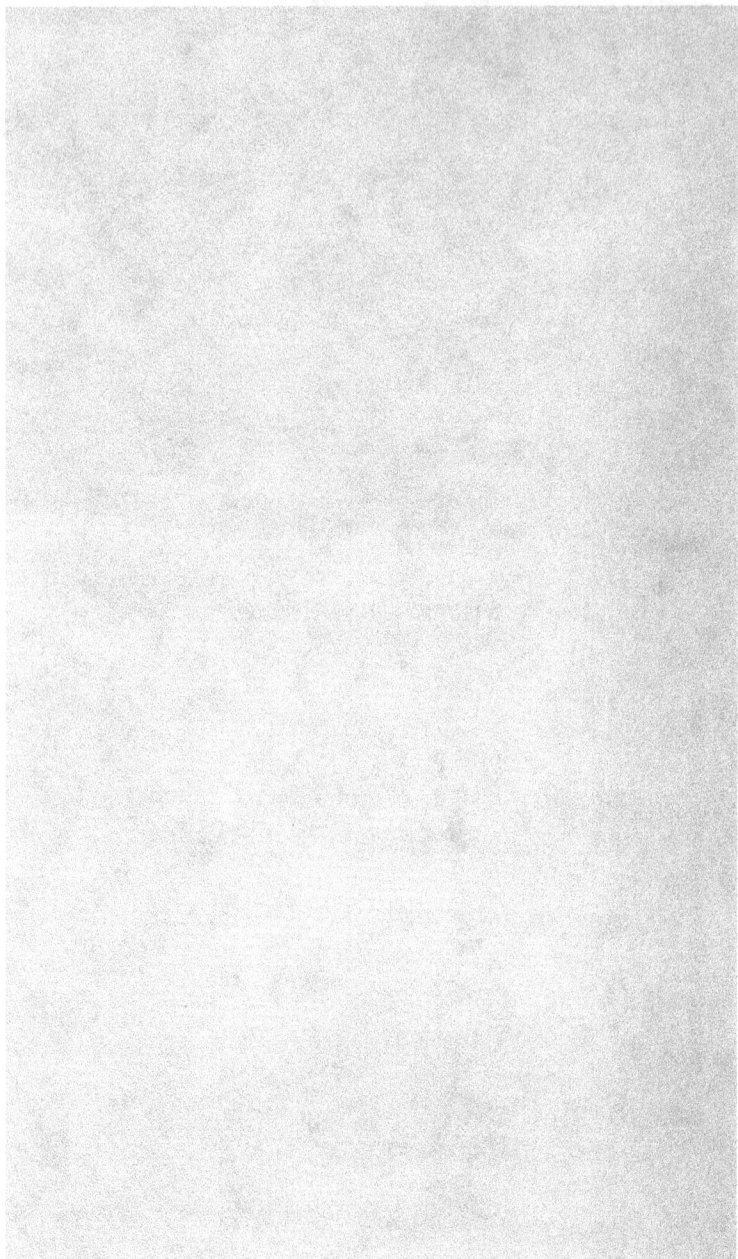

### 524. WELCOME, JUN. Boston, Mass.

729. FREDERICK WELCOME, born in Boston, Oct. 4, 1854.
730. ALFRED EVERETT, born Jan. 6, 1860, and died in 1865.

### 525. ISAAC N. East Boston, Mass.

731. SARAH FRANCES, born May 1, 1851.
732. EDWARD NEWTON, born Jan. 31, 1853.
733. JENNIE CAROLINE, born May 7, 1868.

### 538. THOMAS C.

734. MABEL, born Jan. 31, 1872.

### 547. WILLIAM H.

735. HELEN G., born Oct. 30, 1872.

### 575. FRANK ORVILLE.

736. WILLIAM ELBRIDGE, born Oct. 15, 1873.

### 595. GEORGE D. Leeds, Me.

737. MARY FRANCIS, born in Leeds, Dec. 3, 1837, and is still living there, unmarried.
738. HELEN AUGUSTA, born in Leeds, July 15, 1841, and married W. W. Noyes of East Livermore.

### 597. SOLOMON L. Leeds, Me.

739. WILLIAM HENRY, born in Leeds, May 17, 1842, and married, Dec. 12, 1866, Georgia F., daughter of W. S. Noyes of Boston.
740. LYDIA ALBINA, born in Leeds, Aug. 3, 1844, and married, Jan. 26, 1864, Cyrus B., son of Giddens Lane of Leeds. They have one daughter:
   i. Cassie Benson Lane, born in Leeds, Oct. 16, 1865.

### 599. WILLARD. Leeds, Me.

741. SUSAN, born in Leeds, Jan. 11, 1861.
742. FRANK B., born in Leeds, in July, 1862.

### 622. CHARLES H., M.D. Lyons, Iowa.

743. CHARLES, born Oct. 1867, and died in August, 1869.

### 623. THOMAS J.          Taunton, Mass.

[All born in Taunton.]

744. HARRIET ELEANOR, born June 11, 1859. A medical student in the University of Zurich, Switzerland.

745. ARTHUR PRESCOTT, born Sept. 10, 1860. Graduated at Harvard College in 1882, and now in the Harvard Law School.

746. OLIVIA DABNEY, born July 17, 1865. A student in the Art Museum, Boston.

747. CORNELIUS REDFORD, born Apr. 24, 1869.

748. THOMAS MARK, born June 10, 1873.

### 624. FRANCIS W.          Taunton, Mass.

749. GEORGE FRANCIS, born Oct. 25, 1874.

### 656. ALBERT S. B.          Easton, Mass.

750. MAUDE EVELYN, born Aug. 16, 1883.

### 664. ELBRIDGE.          Weymouth, Mass.

751. EDWIN, married Eliza Houghton of Braintree. Have one son.

752. MARIA.

753. MINERVA, married Wm. Burrell of Weymouth. Have one son.

754. ALLEN.

### 665. OZIN.          Rockland, Mass.

755. ALICE.

756. WILLIAM.

### 684. GEORGE W.          Stoughton, Mass.

757. HATTIE ETHELYN, born Oct. 27, 1879.

758. CORA L., born July 24, 1881.

### 688. MYRON W.          Stoughton, Mass.

759. ADELAIDE MAY, born Mar. 26, 1882, and died Sept. 20, 1883.

# APPENDIX.

## UNCONNECTED IMMIGRANTS.

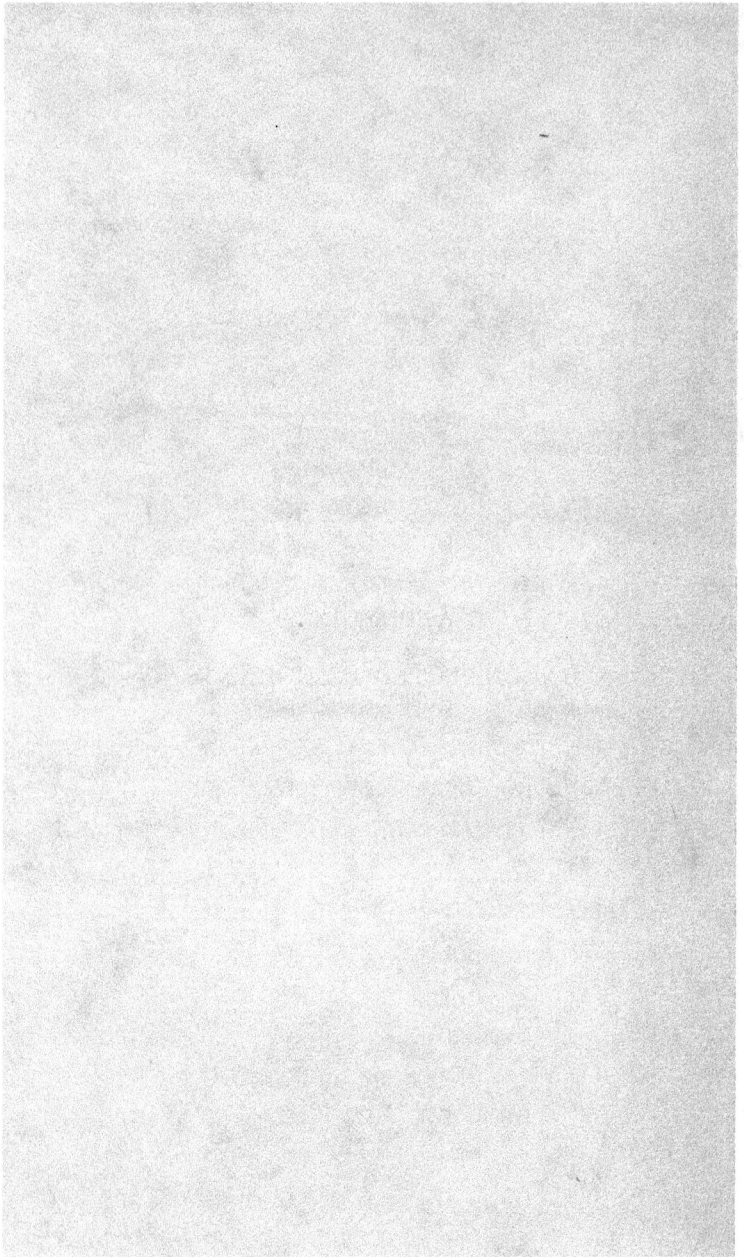

# I.

## Capt. THOMAS LOTHROP.

Of the parentage of this famous pioneer in early Massachusetts history, we have not been able to learn. He probably was a near kinsman of Rev. John of Barnstable, and had preceded him, by some months certainly, to his American home. The first record of his presence here yet found is that which reports him in Salem, Mass., when he was admitted freeman, May 14, 1634. That he was prominent among the citizens of Salem, and later at Beverly, which was set off from Salem in 1664, is evident from his public services rendered. In military and in civil life he seems to have been equally prominent. Of his age we have no record. He married in Salem, Bethia Rea, or Ray, daughter of Daniel and Bethia Ray of Salem. As this Daniel Ray was admitted freeman at the same date with Mr. Lothrop, it is not unlikely that they had come together, settling first in Plymouth, where Mr. Ray is reported in 1631.

Of the character and life of Mr. Lothrop we have a very pleasant account in that elaborate sketch of "Salem Village," with which Upham has introduced his "History of Witchcraft":

"Thomas Lothrop originally lived in the town between Collins Cove and North River. He became a member of the First church in Salem, and was admitted a freeman in 1634. He soon removed to the Farms, and his name appears among the rate-payers at the formation of the village parish. For many years he was deputy from Salem to the General Court; and after Beverly was set off, as his residence was at the time on that side of the line, he was always in the General Court as deputy from the new town, when his other public employments permitted. No man was ever more identified with the history of Salem Farms. He contributed to form the structure of its society and the character of its population by all that a wise and good man could do. During his whole life in America he was more or less engaged in the military service, in arduous, difficult, and dangerous positions and operations, acting sometimes against Indians, and sometimes against the French, or, as was usually the case, against both combined. He was occasionally sent to distant posts, commanding expeditions to the eastward as far as Acadia. He was at one time in charge of a force at Port Royal, Nova Scotia."

But the hazardous enterprise in which he last engaged, and which proved fatal to himself and to so many of the "flower of Essex," who were in his command, we shall allow the old historians of the events to narrate. Under date of Sept. 18, 1675, we find in Baylie's "Memoir of Plymouth Colonies" the following account of the disaster:

"At Deerfield there were about 3,000 bushels of corn in stacks. It was thought expedient to bring it away. On this service, Captain Lothrop volunteered to go with eighty men to guard the teams. On the 18th of September, while on an easy march, not apprehending the least danger, he was suddenly assailed by a numerous body of Indians, and, after maintaining an unequal contest for several hours, was totally defeated and slain. Ninety men, including the drivers, fell in this disastrous fight, and only seven or eight escaped. Lothrop was a young man of great promise, of intrepid courage, and of competent skill in the art of war, but a theorist. He had adopted an opinion that the Indians could be the most effectually encountered in their own mode, and that during a fight every soldier should gain the shelter of a tree. . . . Lothrop's company comprised the flower of the youth of the county of Essex, all having been selected for their courage, strength, activity, and enterprise."— *Baylie's Memoir, Part III, p. 69.*

In Hubbard's "Indian Wars" we have this version of the disaster:

"It came to Capt. Lothrop's turn, or rather it was his choice, with about eighty men to guard several carts laden with corn and other goods. . . .

"But, upon September 18th, that most fatal day, the saddest that ever befell New England, as the company were marching along with the carts, it may be, too securely, never apprehending danger so near, they were suddenly set upon, and almost all cut off, not above seven or eight escaping, which great defeat came to pass by the unadvised proceeding of the captain, who was himself slain in the first assault, although he wanted neither courage nor skill to lead his soldiers."

In Drake's old "Indian Chronicle," we find this apology for the captain:

"Yet, let not the world censure too much Capt. Lothrop. He, in the Pequot wars, had done exploits; nor in this would he have been behindhand, if the narrow passage or causes, when his unexpected enemies set on him, would have given him leave to have drawn up his men."—p. 318.

From Mr. Upham's "Salem Village," we give this sketch of the "Bloody Brook" engagement, which completes our account of the military career of one of the worthiest of the New England pioneers:

"When the last decisive struggle with King Philip was approaching, and aid was needed from the eastern part of the colony to rescue the settlements on the Connecticut river from utter destruction, the 'flower of Essex' was summoned to the field. It was a choice body of efficient men, 'all called out of the towns belonging to this county,' numbering about one hundred men. Lothrop, of course, was their captain. In August, 1675, they were on the ground at Hadley, the place of rendezvous. On the 26th of that month, Capt. Lothrop with his company, and Capt. Beers of Watertown, with his, after a vigorous pursuit, attacked the Indians in a swamp about ten miles from Hatfield, at the foot of 'Sugar Loaf Hill.' Ten were killed on the side of the English, and twenty-six on the side of the Indians, who were driven from the swamp, and scattered in their flight, to fall, as was their custom, upon detached settlements, and continue to waste and destroy, by fire and sword, with hatchet, scalping-knife, torch, and gun. On the 18th of September, Lothrop, with his company, started from Deerfield, to convoy a train of eighteen wagons, loaded with grain and furniture of the inhabitants seeking refuge from danger, with teamsters and others. Mosely, with his men, remained behind, to scout the woods and give notice of the approach of Indians; but the stealthy savages succeeded in effecting a complete surprise, and fell upon Lothrop as his wagons were crossing a stream. They poured in a destructive fire from the woods in all directions. They were seven to one. A perfect carnage ensued. Lothrop fell early in the unequal fight, and only seven or eight of his whole party were left to tell the story of the fatal scene. The locality of this disastrous and sanguinary tragedy has ever since been known as 'Bloody Brook.' In the list of those who perished by bullet, tomahawk, or arrow on that fearful morning, we read the names of many village neighbors of the *brave and lamented commander*," or, as Mr. Mather has eulogized him, "*the godly and courageous commander.*"

Of the personal character of the home life of Capt. Lothrop we are happy to report this sketch by Mr. Upham:

"Capt. Lothrop was as remarkable for the benevolence of his spirit and the tenderness of his nature as for his wisdom in council, energy in command, or gallantry in battle. Indeed, his character in private life was so beautiful and lovable that I cannot refrain from leading you into the recesses of his domestic circle. It presents a picture of rare attractions. He had no children. His wife was a kind and amiable person. They longed for objects upon which to gratify the yearning of their affectionate hearts. He had a large estate. If there were an occurrence calling for commiseration anywhere in the vicinity, it was managed to bring it to his notice. Orphan children were received into his household, and brought up with parental care and tenderness. Many were in this way the objects of his charity and affections. . . . I know not where to find a more perfect union of the hero and the Christian, of all that is manly and chivalrous with all that is tender, benevolent, and devout."

Owing to the important place Thomas Lothrop occupies in the early history of New England, we append to this sketch a liberal extract from the Rev. Mr. Thayer's bi-centennial address:

"Of his leading associate in their establishment (Lothrop) I could not, in view of his sincere, upright, and honorable character, and restrained, no less than moved by that, speak in terms of extravagant eulogy. Brave and gentle, generous and just, confiding, yet cautious and wise, of large estate for the time, bountifully and skillfully administered, never sparing of his own exertions, but always ready for every good word or work, he had a rare and remarkable hold on the confidence and affection of the community in which he lived. Not sustaining in strictness the parental relation, he bore the best attributes, sympathies, and adornments of the parental heart, thus resembling him who, having discharged in private the duties of a loving and faithful parent to children not his own, came at length to be universally acknowledged the father of his country. He was a father of the fatherless, the widow's friend and support, and the helper of any who had none else to abet or plead their cause.

"As a military man, he had what seems, amid the hardships, perils, servitudes, and fierce conflicts of war, an unnatural combination of qualities, which, if seldom, are sometimes seen—of gentleness and bravery, of stern, inflexible purpose, with kindness and generosity, of unwavering determination with tenderest sympathy, of mild forbearance with exalted courage, of persevering, unfaltering energy, with true magnanimity. Says one who, from thorough investigation, could be relied on, 'He was the friend of all. I know not where to find a more perfect union of the hero and the Christian, of all that is manly and chivalrous with all that is tender, benevolent, and devout.'

"His house was not only the abode of a liberal hospitality, but an asylum for the orphan and the distressed. As objects of his bounty arose and multiplied, his dwelling, as his heart, seemed to expand, and he, who otherwise had been solitary, was, in the exercise of his kindly spirit, surrounded by a numerous family. Among those who shared his fostering care was a younger sister, Ellen, whom he brought with him on his return from a visit to England, who fulfilled his fondest wishes, and to whom he was ever afterward as both father and elder brother. . . . Lothrop, having in early manhood emigrated from England, settled in what is now the city of Salem; but, a few years after, he received a grant of land on this shore, near the Cove, where is a continuation of the most populous part of the town, and there fixed his residence for the remainder of his life. There he lived for about forty years, a model of fidelity to all his public and private relations. Nothing of the kind can exceed the charming picture of his domestic life which has been handed down to us, and been of late most skillfully and appreciatively drawn. To his ever-ready sympathy as a man, a neighbor, counsellor, friend, there is abundant witness. Various, almost innumerable, were the calls made on him for advice, for con- solation, for attesting, drafting, and executing wills, for appraisal of estates, as trustee and guardian. For several years he was deputy to the General Court, first from Salem, then from this town, and a selectman of it all the time after its incorporation till his death. This last office was sometimes dignified with the title of ' townsman'; and comprehending, as it then did, the powers and duties of overseer of the poor, assessor of taxes, surveyor of highways, and police judge, without specifying others, we may conclude that it was no sinecure, and that its incumbent might have been entitled also the 'man-of- all-work.'

"His interest and activity in ecclesiastical were no less than in secular affairs. Soon after his arrival, when quite a young man, he became a member of the Salem church, with which he continued for a long time to worship and commune. When, in consequence of the increased population on this side, and the inconveniences of distance and crossing the intervening ferry, it was felt that new accommodations must be provided for the worshippers resident here, he took an active part in all the measures which resulted first in tempo- rary arrangements for religious services, and ultimately—though not till about twenty years after their inception—in the complete organization of this soci- ety. Toward its establishment and primitive prosperity, his character, so high, pure, trusted, efficient, and altogether worthy, greatly contributed, especially connected, as it was in the general esteem, with that of Conant, his elder companion in the undertaking. The characters of the two, taken together, constituted a tower of strength and an indubitable pledge for the suc- cess, the stability, and spiritual growth of the embryo parish. That when absent on distant expeditions, and even amidst the din and stress of war, he was not unmindful of his parochial relations, and of the ties, religious as well as social, which bound him to his home, is evinced by the fact, that on his return from the attack of St. Johns and Port Royal, where he held an important command, and the capture of which he materially aided, he brought from the latter place, now Annapolis, and presented to the parish, a bell which had been in use on a friary there. . . . .

"But the end of all this life of activity, energy, and usefulness was drawing on. A fearful tragedy was at hand, in which he was to act the most conspicuous part, to suffer, and fall a sacrifice. King Philip, foremost of Indian chiefs in this quarter, subtle as powerful, had roused his own and neighboring tribes to the determination of desperate warfare—of nothing less than a life or death struggle between them and the colonists. . . . Meantime, Lothrop— who had raised a company of a hundred men in his county, that, from their being of the young and most promising, might well be styled its 'flower,' and who, from his varied experience and tried courage and valor, was, of course, to take the command—pressed on, and joined the forces under Willard at Hadley. Being charged by the latter with the transport of supplies of provisions from Deerfield, he. with his company, was on the route thence, and feeling no apprehension of immediate danger, they had laid aside their arms, and paused to regale themselves from the clusters of grapes which hung by the wayside, when the coveted fruit turned to ashes in their grasp, and its sweetness was changed to the gall and bitterness of death. Volleys from hundreds of savages in ambush were poured upon them, like lightning from a clear sky. Their gallant and beloved commander fell at the outset. They fought bravely, as best they could, with the pall of death over them. But few survived to tell the tale, which, from that time, gave to the little stream they were crossing, which proved to so many 'the narrow stream of death,' the sad name of 'Bloody Brook.'

"This catastrophe sent a thrill of terror and dismay through all the New England colonies. Especially did the news of it come with appalling force to this county, from which its choicest flowers, 'all culled out of its towns,' and blooming so lately in manly strength and beauty, had been thus suddenly cut down and withered, as by an untimely, killing frost. Throughout its length and breadth, scarcely was there a village or hamlet left unscathed by this great calamity,

> 'No flock, however watched and tended,
> But one dead lamb was there.'

More particularly, and with stunning effect, did the blow fall here, where, beside several that were deeply lamented, the fallen chief was best known, and for that reason most respected, trusted, and loved. Writers at or near the time do but express the feeling generally prevalent, whether in wider or more restricted circles, while they accumulate, almost without limit, the phrases descriptive of sorrow, agony, and horror, such as, 'a dismal and fatal blow,' 'a sadder rebuke of Providence than anything that had hitherto been,' 'a black and fatal day,' 'the saddest that ever befell New England.'

"Edward Everett, the Cicero of our country and age, said, in conclusion of his eloquent address at the laying of the corner-stone of the Bloody Brook monument, with his own peculiar felicity, 'The flower of Essex shall bloom in undying remembrance, as the lapse of time shall continually develop, in richer abundance, the fruits of what was done and suffered by our fathers.'"

We also give some court proceedings in reference to the estate of Thomas Lothrop, which we find printed in connection with Mr. Hassam's excellent monograph upon Ezekiel Cheever. It will throw some light upon the family relations of Mr. Lothrop:

"At a court held at Salem, 22d, 10, 1675, administration on the estate of Capt. Thomas Lathrop of Beverly, 'who latelye dyed in the warrs betwixt the English and the heathen,' was granted to his widow, Bethiah Lathrop, who offered for probate a nuncupative will, in favor of herself and her relatives, and Sarah Gott, an adopted daughter. This decree occasioned the following petition: 'To the Honoured County Court, now sitting at Salem. The humble peticōn of Ezekiel Cheever, Schoolmaster, sheweth, that whereas Capt. Thomas Lowthrop, who lately lost his life in ye service & cause of God & his countrey, being his wives own, dear, naturall brother, dying intestate & without issue, he humbly conceives himself on ye behalf of his wife to be ye true, naturall, proper heir of his estate left, & therefore his duty to make his humble address to this Honored Court, that he may declare & legally plead ye same— To which end he came & attended ye Court neer a weeks space. But ye Court by publick occasions of ye Countrey being necessarily adjourned, he was forced to return home, and resolved (God willing) to attend ye Court, ye time appointed. But by ye providence of God, ye season being extraordinarily stormy & himself under bodily infirmity, he could not possibly come without apparent hazard of life, limb, or health. Yet had cautiously left order, & instructions for his son to appear for him in such an exigence. Which accordingly he did, though not in season, being by the same providence hindered. So that the Honored Court (no heir appearing) granted Administration to his sister Lowthrop, according to what then appeared. But seeing ye estate was not then setled, nor ye case fully issued, many things alledged being dark and dubious, & nothing legally proved, he hath much to say, to invalidate yt very writing given in, & ye seeming force of it. He humbly requests this Honoured Court, that being a party so neerly concerned and interested, he may have ye liberty of making, & pleading his claime, & title according to law. And for ye better securing of what shall be judged his right, he may be joyned together with his sister Lathrop in administration of ye said'estate. And he shall as in duty bound, pray, &c.'"

From one of the papers on file in this case, the following extract is made:

"6. The matter which they testify is so unjust and unreasonable, that none that knew my brothers goodness and love, will believe, that my brother would be so unnaturall as to preferr strangers before his owne naturall Sister and her children, whom he so dearly loved, as many that knew them both can abundantly testify. 7. My Brother, when he brought his sister from England with him from all her friends and relations very loth to part with her, used this as a great argument with her Mother to perswade her, viz.: that he had no children of his own, nor was likely to have any: otherwise he must give what he had to strangers. And her mother told this to friends in her hearing, that that was a great motive that induced her to be willing to part with her; and commited her to the love and care of her brother as a Father, with great confidence and assurance of his tenderness toward her. 8. His sister by coming over, lost the value of twenty-five pound, beside what her mother would have given her at her decease." "These are to signify that Capt. Lathrop & myself being well acquainted, I being frequently at his house did at severall times observe that he did bring up divers children that were neither his owne nor the children of his sister Cheever, I asked him why he did not rather bring up some of his sister Cheever's children, they having many & their condition but low, his answer was at several times to this effect that he intended in time to doe more for her & her children than for any other, telling me the story (how when he was in England having land of some value he disposed of it for the benefit of his brother or sister there), & having brought over his sister Cheever hither he intended in time to doe something that should be for the benefit of her children. These things in general I doe well remember but for particular words or expressions I cannot say. John Higginson Sen." The decree of the Court, 27: 4: 1676, in favor of the widow, concludes as follows: "This division & ppconing of the said estate wee iudge equall & iust according to the mynde of the deceased. Web wee submitt to the honor'd general Court further appbacon and confirmaeon." The decision of the court was confirmed at a General Court held at Boston, Oct. 15, 1679.

## II.

### ELLEN LOTHROP.

ELLEN, a sister of the Captain Lothrop reported above, came to this country about the year 1650. The captain had in that year visited his English home, and prevailed on his mother, to let this daughter, then just grown to early womanhood, return with him. In due time she became the second wife of Ezekiel Cheever, the most famous of our early New England teachers. They were married Nov. 18, 1652, and she became the mother of six children. Her death occurred Sept. 10, 1706.

    i.   Abigail Cheever, born Oct. 20, 1653, and died Jan. 24, 1705.

    ii.   Ezekiel Cheever, born July 1, 1655, and married, June 17, 1680, Abigail Lippingwell.

    iii.   Nathaniel Cheever, born June 23, 1657, and died the next month.

    iv.   Thomas Cheever, born Aug. 23, 1658, graduated at Harvard College in 1677, and settled in the ministry, a Congregationalist, first in Malden, and second in Chelsea, Mass., where he died, in 1749.

    v.   Susanna Cheever, married, June 5, 1693, Joseph Russell.

    vi.   William Cheever, born Jan. 23, baptised Jan. 29, and died Feb. 5, 1664-5.

## III.

### LATHROPE.

1. WILLIAM LATHROPE is reported by his grandson William, now (1874) living in Warsaw, Ind., as living in Ottery, St. Mary, Devonshire. His father is supposed to have been of a German family.

### 1. WILLIAM.                    Ottery, Devonshire.

2. WILLIAM, born in Ottery, Devonshire, about 1767, lived in Ottery, where he married Elizabeth Benday, or Bendin. He was buried in Leicester, England, in 1861, and his widow, at the age of 89 years, in 1868.

3. ROBERT was a silk dyer of Honiton, Devonshire.

4. JOHN, who is reported as having come to America about the year 1812.

### 2. WILLIAM.                    Leicester, Eng.

5. WILLIAM, who was born in 1800, and came from his home in Leicester, Eng., in August, 1865. He settled at Warsaw, Ind., where he is now living.

6. ROBERT, who came from Deep Carr, Eng., to America, and settled in Salt Lake City, in 1868.

7. JOHN, removed from Bradford, Yorkshire, Eng., to Delphi, Ind., in 1849, and died there in August, 1870.

8. SARAH, who died in Leicester, Eng., in 1863.

9. JANE, who is now (1873) living in Salt Lake City, Utah.

### 5. WILLIAM.                    Warsaw, Ind.

10. JOHN, who lives in Delphi, Ind.

11. ROBERT, who lives in Warsaw, Ind.

12. HENRY, who lives in Warsaw, Ind.

13. ELIZABETH, living in Leicester, Eng.

14. SARAH, living in Leicester.

15. MARY ANN, living in Leicester.

## IV.

### LOWTHORP.

1. FRANCIS, presumably the oldest of three brothers, born in England before 1750. He married —— ——, in England. In the latter part of the eighteenth century, he removed to Newberne, North Carolina, where he is supposed to have died some time after 1806, leaving two sons, and perhaps other children.

2. John, perhaps the second brother—though of this there is no certainty—born in England, and there married —— ——. He died in England, in 1801, leaving two sons, and perhaps other children.

3. Thomas, another brother, lived in London, England, and in July, 1806, lived at 1st George's Fields, Surrey, London. He married Elizabeth Cowlyn, sister of Francis Cowlyn. He died some time after 1806, leaving a son and a daughter.

## 1. FRANCIS.

4. John, perhaps the eldest son of Francis. Of him nothing is known.

5. Francis, probably born in Newberne, N. C. He married —— ——, an English woman. He was a prominent citizen of Newberne, and a well-known Free-Mason; and for him the present theater and masonic building in Newberne was named Lowthorp Hall. He died quite young, between 1820 and 1825, leaving a widow and one daughter. His widow died in 1854, at Newberne.

## 2. JOHN.

6. John.

7. William.

## 3. THOMAS.

8. Thomas, born in London, about 1782. Came to America in 1798, and settled in Albany, N. Y. He subsequently removed to New York City, where he was employed in the store of Elias Kane, at that time one of the leading importers of New York. In 18—, he married Mary Ann Lilly, daughter of the Rev. Samuel Lilly of Albany, N. Y. In 1810, he removed to Geneva, N. Y., and entered the wholesale and retail trade in general merchandise. With him were associated Elias Kane of New York, and William Lilly, under the firm style of Thomas Lowthorp & Co. He continued in business until 1818, about which time he lost his sight. He was one of the pioneers of that part of the country, which was then largely peopled by the Indians, the Six Nations holding their annual powwows at the old castle, within two miles of Geneva. He was a man of energy and good judgment. As appears by a *Geneva Gazette* of 1813, he was one of a number who applied for a charter of the Seneca Lock Navigation Company, their purpose being to open navigation between Seneca and Cayuga lakes. He was one of the trustees of the Geneva Academy. Although an Englishman, he was so well esteemed by his adopted countrymen that he was elected an honorary member of the Society of the Cincinnati of New York. He had eight children, of whom two died in childhood. He died in 1859, in the 78th year of his age. His widow died in 1865, in the 84th year of her age.

9. Lucretia, born in London, after 1781, and married —— Whittemore, an artist. Died in London 18—.

52

### 5. FRANCIS.

10. SARAH C., born in Newberne, N. C., early in the present century. Died unmarried, at Newberne, in 1877.

### 8. THOMAS.

11. ANN DEBORAH, born in New York City, and married Alexander Coryell, at Lambertville, N. J. Died at Lambertville.

12. ELIZABETH, born in New York City, and married George Angell, at Geneva, N. Y. Living at Geneva.

13. FRANCIS C., born in New York City Feb. 8. 1810, and married (1). Anna B. Chambers, daughter of Clark Chambers, at Beaver Meadow, Pa., in 1841: (2), Anna M. Bailey, at Trenton, N. J., in 1868. By his first wife, he has had a daughter and a son. He is a civil engineer and a Fellow of the American Society of Civil Engineers. He lives at Trenton, N. J.

14. MARY, born at Geneva. Died there in childhood.

15. SAMUEL, born at Geneva, and married Susan Mullen, at Geneva. By her he has had one daughter. Is living at Geneva.

16. CHARLES HENRY, born at Geneva, and died there in childhood.

17. CATHARINE, born at Geneva, and married Edward Kingsland, at Geneva. Died at Geneva, in 1877.

18. JANET, born at Geneva, N. Y., and lives there.

### 13. FRANCIS C.

19. MARY E., born at Beaver Meadow, Pa., and married Josias J. Henderson, at Trenton, N. J., in 1868. Living at Plainfield, N. J.

20. FRANCIS C., born at Trenton, N. J. Is a lawyer, and living at Trenton.

### 15. SAMUEL.

21. ELIZA W., born at Geneva, N. Y., and lives there.